Stefanie Leimeister

IT Outsourcing Governance

GABLER RESEARCH

Informationsmanagement und Computer Aided Team

Herausgegeben von Professor Dr. Helmut Krcmar

Die Schriftenreihe präsentiert Ergebnisse der betriebswirtschaftlichen Forschung im Themenfeld der Wirtschaftsinformatik. Das Zusammenwirken von Informations- und Kommunikationstechnologien mit Wettbewerb, Organisation und Menschen wird von umfassenden Änderungen gekennzeichnet. Die Schriftenreihe greift diese Fragen auf und stellt neue Erkenntnisse aus Theorie und Praxis sowie anwendungsorientierte Konzepte und Modelle zur Diskussion.

Stefanie Leimeister

IT Outsourcing Governance

Client Types and
Their Management Strategies

With a foreword by Prof. Dr. Helmut Krcmar

GABLER

RESEARCH

Bibliographic information published by the Deutsche Nationalbibliothek
The Deutsche Nationalbibliothek lists this publication in the Deutsche Nationalbibliografie;
detailed bibliographic data are available in the Internet at http://dnb.d-nb.de.

Dissertation Technische Universität München, 2009

1st Edition 2010

Editorial Office: Ute Wrasmann | Anita Wilke

Gabler Verlag is a brand of Springer Fachmedien.
Springer Fachmedien is part of Springer Science+Business Media.
www.gabler.de

Coverdesign: KünkelLopka Medienentwicklung, Heidelberg
Printed on acid-free paper
Printed in Germany

ISBN 978-3-8349-2275-5

Stefanie Leimeister

IT Outsourcing Governance

Client Types and
Their Management Strategies

With a foreword by Prof. Dr. Helmut Krcmar

GABLER

RESEARCH

Bibliographic information published by the Deutsche Nationalbibliothek
The Deutsche Nationalbibliothek lists this publication in the Deutsche Nationalbibliografie;
detailed bibliographic data are available in the Internet at http://dnb.d-nb.de.

Dissertation Technische Universität München, 2009

1st Edition 2010

Editorial Office: Ute Wrasmann | Anita Wilke

Gabler Verlag is a brand of Springer Fachmedien.
Springer Fachmedien is part of Springer Science+Business Media.
www.gabler.de

Coverdesign: KünkelLopka Medienentwicklung, Heidelberg
Printed on acid-free paper
Printed in Germany

ISBN 978-3-8349-2275-5

Foreword

Information systems (IS) outsourcing is a key driver as well as an outcome of the professionalization, industrialization, and service orientation in the IT services industry. It has become an established business practice and a popular research issue. Along with this popularity, outsourcing has changed tremendously over the past decades and so have its scope, complexity, and the variety of outsourcing options. Surprisingly, still many outsourcing arrangements are not successful. Divergent expectations of both parties towards the venture along with an insufficient governance can cause the outsourcing relationship to turn sour. Current research shows that a one-size-fits-all governance approach for outsourcing projects is not appropriate and a differentiation of outsourcing clients is necessary.

Encouraged by the current challenges of the outsourcing market, this work presents a differentiated approach to investigate various types of IS outsourcing relationships and their characteristics depending on the underlying expectations of the outsourcing clients. Grounded on the current body of knowledge of the outsourcing research literature and a variety of current theories in the fields of information systems, business administration, and social theories, it develops a framework for classifying outsourcing projects and clients. This framework builds the foundation to empirically examine different outsourcing projects, their constitutive elements, and management approaches among German IT executives and CIOs. Based on these insights, the work proposes appropriate governance mechanisms for the management of each outsourcing client type.

Stefanie Leimeister's work shows that outsourcing endeavors should be linked to the needs and expectations of their stakeholders, both on the client and on the vendor side. She clearly depicts that outsourcing governance goes beyond contractual issues. It has to consider various management aspects in order to shape a successful long-term outsourcing venture.

This work is an important contribution to the research field of managing information systems. In a methodological way it gives valuable impulses for combining different theories and research methods depending on the actual context of an outsourcing arrangement. The work appeals by its broad scope of theory, multimethodological background and approaches, and its comprehensive argumentation by which literature and empirical findings are presented. Researchers of information systems will gain new insights on which research methods and theories are applicable given the motivation of the stakeholders to engage in an outsourcing endeavor. For practitioners, it provides recommendations for orchestrating the development of a healthy outsourcing relationship and for effectively and efficiently allocating resources.

I recommend this book as a valuable reading and resource. It provides new and promising insights into an established research field and inspires different kinds of readers to adopt a new perspective on make-or-buy decisions in information systems.

I hope this work will find the broad dissemination and attention it deserves.

Prof. Dr. Helmut Krcmar

Acknowledgements

From the beginning of my academic career to the final version of this book more than five years have passed. Those who have completed this journey understand that there are so many people to thank for contributing to this work and supporting me. I would like to express my gratitude to everyone involved – I appreciated and enjoyed every minute of their time.

Thank you

to my doctoral advisor *Prof. Dr. Helmut Krcmar* for his continuous support, his trust and the freedom he gave me to unfold my ideas and personality, and his transition from an instructor to a mentor

to *Prof. Dr. Florian von Wangenheim* for accepting to be my second doctoral advisor and providing me with valuable input for the methodological and statistical part of this work

to *Prof. Dr. Phillip Yetton* and *Joan Spiller* for their interest in my work and me and their unobtrusive stimulation towards academic brilliance

to *Prof. Dr. Marilyn Tremaine* and *Prof. Dr. Scott Tremaine* who inspired me to think outside the box, to modestly question established things, who shared their joy for Canada with me – and became good friends

to *Prof. Dr. Tilo Böhmann* who ignited the initial thoughts towards the final thesis topic, for supporting and accompanying me in my academic career from being his graduate assistant to the doctor's degree

to *Dr. Holger Hoffmann, Uta Knebel, Dr. Michael Schermann*, and *Cathleen Stephan* for sharing the joy and burden of our work life, inspiring my thoughts, and their transition from colleagues to good friends

to *Dr. Holger Jehle* for broadening my horizons, inspiring my curiosity, and for his time

to *Stefanie Hammer* and *Tina Kopf* for being my best friends and believing in me

to *Martin* for being my big brother and soul mate

to *Marco* for his love

The deepest appreciation and gratitude goes to my parents who instilled in me a love of reading, writing, and learning. They encouraged and supported my ideas and believed in what I did even if it was not their way of thinking. Thank you for your unquestioned love, trust, and patience.

Stefanie Leimeister

Abstract

Problem Situation and Motivation: The outsourcing of information systems has been a wide-spread management practice for several decades and has been a popular research issue since then. Surprisingly, despite the experience with IS outsourcing, numerous outsourcing arrangements are renegotiated or even terminated. Likely reasons for such failures can be ascribed to divergent expectations of both parties towards the venture and an insufficient governance of the outsourcing relationship. Current research shows that a one-size-fits-all governance approach for all outsourcing projects regardless of the underlying outsourcing motivation is not appropriate. A differentiation of outsourcing clients and the configuration of their venture is needed.

Purpose: The objective of this thesis is to explore and understand different types of IS outsourcing relationships and their configuration depending on the underlying expectations of the outsourcing clients. Furthermore, appropriate governance mechanisms for the successful management of IS outsourcing relationships are to be identified for each client type. The thesis will answer the following three research questions: 1) What are the constitutive elements of a client-vendor relationship in IS outsourcing? 2) Which different configurations of outsourcing relationships can be identified empirically? 3) What are appropriate governance approaches and mechanisms for the successful management of different outsourcing relationships?

Research Design and Methodology: This work applies a multi-method approach and triangulates results from various qualitative and quantitative methods. Preceding the main study, an extensive qualitative pre-study is conducted with 18 expert interviews from both the client and vendor side. For the main study, an empirical-quantitative, but exploratory approach is chosen. Data is collected from the client perspective, i.e., IT managers and Chief Information Officers, through an online survey, resulting in 268 data points. The data is analyzed with cluster analysis to identify homogeneous groups of outsourcing clients. Group differences are examined with analyses of variance (ANOVA). Then a governance model is developed to examine different governance approaches (determinants) and their effects on outsourcing performance for each client group. This model is tested with Partial Least Square (PLS) structural equation modeling and multi-group comparisons (t-tests).

Findings: Four predominant outsourcing motives are identified: Cost-focused, business-oriented, strategy-focused, and IT-related motives. A cluster analysis along these outsourcing motives reveal four client groups with different and very focused expectations: 1) business-efficiency clients, 2) cost-conscious smart shoppers, 3) strategists and innovation seekers, and 3) IT excellence and reliability-oriented clients. Three client groups have very straightforward expectations focused on only one category of outsourcing motives (e.g., cost focus), while clients in group 4 have heterogeneous motives, expecting both business and IT motives. In terms of governance approaches, the business-efficiency clients manage their outsourcing venture via management processes and relational governance; cost-focused clients govern via the contract and staff experience; the strategy-oriented group uses the contract and relationship management as primary governance modes. Surprisingly, for the heterogeneous last group none of the established and tested governance modes works appropriately. Rather, vendor flexibility seems to be a promising management approach for this group. Each group establishes different governance approaches that lead to a successful overall outsourcing performance.

Contributions to Theory: In contrast to prior research, this thesis adopts a more differentiated perspective on outsourcing by examining unique outsourcing client types and linking clients' outsourcing expectations with appropriate governance approaches. It *applies and confirms* common theories such as transaction cost economics and social exchange theories by clarifying key outsourcing motives and by deriving a framework with characteristics of outsourcing relationships. It also *extends* these theories by applying them depending on the context (i.e., underlying motive structure) of the venture and stating which theories on governance approaches are most appropriate to *explain* outsourcing performance depending on the underlying expectations. Based on the results, governance determinants of outsourcing success can be better *predicted* depending on the context of client expectations.

Contributions to Practice: The results of this work help IT decision makers to get a clear understanding about the primary underlying motivations of clients to engage into an outsourcing venture. Building upon an informed decision, characteristics of other outsourcing ventures with similar expectations can be benchmarked against the characteristics of their own venture. A specialized governance concept for each of the identified groups is required for a successful management of the different configurations of outsourcing relationships. This will provide IT decision makers with workable strategies for successfully governing different outsourcing projects. It eventually helps to effectively and efficiently allocate the appropriate economic and human resources for the outsourcing venture.

Research Limitations / Further Research: Methodological constraints of the work comprise some known weaknesses of the multivariate method of cluster analysis. Especially, group sizes suggested by the chosen cluster algorithm do not necessarily reflect the client population in reality. Also, only single-source data is used that is collected at one point in time. This might increase a potential common method bias (CMB), although the analysis shows that CMB does not impact the results. Concerning the object of inquiry, a consideration of the vendor perspective could provide fruitful insights and contrast mutual expectations towards an outsourcing relationship.

Keywords: IS outsourcing, governance, relationship management, formal contract, factor analysis, cluster analysis, structural equation modeling, partial least squares, SEM, PLS.

Table of Contents

List of Figures

List of Tables

List of Abbreviations

ASP	Application Service Provider
AMOS	Analysis of Moment Structures
ANOVA	Analysis of Variance
AVE	Average Variance Extracted
B2B	Business to Business
BPO	Business Process Outsourcing
CA	Cluster Analysis
CAGR	Compound Annual Growth Rate
CFA	Confirmatory Factor Analysis
CFO	Chief Financial Officer
CIO	Chief Information Officer
CMB	Common Method Bias
CMV	Common Method Variance
CR	Composite Reliability
EFA	Exploratory Factor Analysis
et seq.	et sequentes; and following (pages)
FA	Factor Analysis, often used synonymously to PAF or PFA
ff.	and following pages
IS	Information Systems
ISR	Information Systems Research
ITO	IT Outsourcing
KMO	Kaiser-Meyer-Olkin Measure of Sampling Adequacy
LISREL	Linear Structural Relations
MAR	Missing at Random

MCAR	Missing Completely at Random
MDA	Multivariate Discriminant Analysis
MLE	Maximum Likelihood Estimation
MSA	Measure of Sampling Adequacy
PCA	Principal Component Analysis
PAF	Principal Axis Factoring, also known as Principal Factor Analysis or Common Factor Analysis
PFA	Principal Factor Analysis, also known as Principal Axis Factoring or Common Factor Analysis, sometimes only abbreviated as FA
PLS	Partial Least Squares
RET	Relational Exchange Theory
SAHN	Sequential, Agglomerative, Hierarchical and Non-overlapping
SD	Standard Deviation
SET	Social Exchange Theory
SEM	Structural Equation Model
SLA	Service Level Agreement
S-N-K	Student-Newman-Keuls Test (non-parametric post-hoc test)
SPSS	Statistical Package for the Social Sciences
StD	Standard Deviation
TCE	Transaction Cost Economics
VAF	Variance Accounted For
VIF	Variance Inflation Factor

1   Introduction

1.1   Problem Statement and Motivation for this Research

Outsourcing of information systems (IS) has seen unprecedented growth in the past few years and continues to be an important issue on the agenda of corporate IT executives (Luftman/ Kempaiah/Nash 2006; Pütter 2007). A recent market study by the German Association for Information Technology, Telecommunications and New Media (BITKOM) found that outsourcing is one of the top three IT issues of the year 2009 (BITKOM 2009a). With a 2007 worldwide market growth rate of 10.2%, both IT outsourcing (ITO) and business process outsourcing still hold a huge potential in the global IT market and are forecast to reach US $563.3 billion[1] by 2011 (Potter 2007). According to the European Information Technology Observatory (EITO), the growth rate of outsourcing in Germany is estimated to be 7.2% for 2009 with a market volume of 14.6 billion Euro (BITKOM 2009b).

Outsourcing has been established as a common business practice and has evolved beyond providers merely taking over a function and performing higher quality work at lower cost (Apte 1990; Child 1987). Since its early days more than three decades ago, the IS outsourcing market has changed tremendously. Diversified approaches of outsourcing practices have emerged ranging from short-term selective outsourcing deals to long-term strategic alliances and transformational outsourcing (Dibbern et al. 2004; Lee et al. 2003). Outsourcing arrangements have become more sophisticated not only with regard to the service itself, but also with regard to the seemingly boundless global delivery of IT components (Rottman/ Lacity 2004). In this context risk-sharing models and collaborative service development of innovative IT services have begun to shape customers' expectations towards the IT service provider (Jahner/Böhmann/Krcmar 2006b).

Surprisingly, despite the myriad of approaches to outsourcing, many ventures fail to live up to their expectations and have to be interrupted, renegotiated, or even prematurely terminated (Hild 2008; Kern/Willcocks 2002; Lacity/Willcocks 2003). It seems that the variety of outsourcing approaches has contributed to increased complexity and a Babylonian confusion of sourcing practices, rather than to successful outsourcing arrangements with satisfied clients and vendors. Many organizations still need to develop a mature and reflective understanding of outsourcing. In a current study of outsourcing projects (Robinson 2008), 39% of the respondents reported that they had terminated at least one outsourcing contract and transferred it to a different vendor in their careers. Another study on outsourcing projects (Butters 2005) found that more than half of the ventures (58%) were considered problematic or failed. In most of these deals (80%) the problems could be clearly ascribed to divergent and incongruous expectations of both parties towards the venture and a lack of understanding of the need for continuous governance of the outsourcing relationship (Hild 2008; Cohen/Young 2006). In line with this, Lacity and Willcocks found in their outsourcing cases that "conflict-

---

[1] Outsourcing Forecast 2011: Infrastructure Outsourcing - US $247 billion; Application Outsourcing - US $81.1 billion; Business Process Outsourcing - US $235.2 billion (Scardino/Young/Anderson 2007; Singh et al. 2007; Tramacere/Matlus 2007)

ing stakeholders' expectations place IS managers in the precarious position of providing a Rolls Royce service at a Chevrolet price" (Lacity/Hirschheim 1995b, 158).

Strikingly, a Gartner study reported that less than 30 percent of organizations had formal sourcing strategies and appropriate governance in place (Overby 2007; Cohen/Young 2006) although outsourcing consultants emphasize that governance is the most important factor in determining the success of an IS outsourcing arrangement (Overby 2007; Pütter 2007). In fact, it has become obvious that a detailed and properly structured contractual agreement is necessary for a continuous successful relationship, but it is often not a sufficient governance mechanism for outsourcing success (Klepper 1995, 1998; Goles/Chin 2005). Governing beyond traditional contractual clauses towards a closer relationship-focused management that operates 'within the spirit of the contract' becomes necessary (Kern/Willcocks 2000b). As Dwyer et al. point out, an outsourcing venture cannot be regarded as a discrete event or a one-time transaction, but rather as an ongoing buyer-seller relationship (Dwyer/Schurr/Oh 1987). In line with this, Cohen and Young (2006) argue that successful outsourcing is built on "a network of relationships not transactions". Taking the huge economic size of the IS outsourcing market into account, fostering a healthy outsourcing relationship becomes not only vital for the interpersonal relations between client and vendor. It also helps to save money for both parties. In other words, neglecting a holistic governance approach to outsourcing can impose substantial costs for an organization. Researchers have thus increasingly turned their attention to managing the relationship between client and vendor in IS outsourcing arrangements (Goles/Chin 2005; Kern/Willcocks 2000b; Kern/Willcocks/van Heck 2002; Kim/Chung 2003; Klepper/Jones 1998; Lee/Kim 1999; Lee et al. 2003; McFarlan/Nolan 1995; Sargent 2006).

Although literally all commentators allude to the critical importance of the relationship dimension (Kern/Willcocks 2001; Kern 1997; Lee/Kim 1999), to date, little research has been directed towards a thorough examination and analysis of outsourcing relationships compared to other IS outsourcing research streams (Dibbern et al. 2004; Gonzalez/Gasco/Llopis 2006). Most studies that have evaluated the relationship dimension in IS outsourcing (cf. Lee/Kim 1999; Goles 2001; Goles/Chin 2005) have solely focused on elaborating general relationship factors thereby not capturing the complexity of an outsourcing venture. There has been little rigorous analysis of what makes for successful and less successful relationships and the effect this can have on the long-term viability of contractual agreements (Willcocks/Lacity 1998a, 12). Even more, prior research on relationship factors in IS outsourcing has failed to explain how expectations of both parties towards an outsourcing venture result in different outsourcing configurations which should be managed accordingly to make the outsourcing successful.

The role, relevance, and characteristics of certain relationship factors might indeed vary in different outsourcing settings and according to different expectations of clients and vendors towards an outsourcing venture. Some clients might expect their IT service providers to leverage IT innovations and thus expect some sort of strategic partnership with shared risks and rewards. In this case, a specific governance mode is necessary to facilitate the expected innovative IT services. Relationship factors such as commitment and trust towards the outsourcing partner might play a more important role than other outsourcing relationship factors. On the other hand, some vendors might focus on cost efficiency with low risk involvement and a quick return on investment from their outsourcing client. Here, governance mechanisms different from the example above must be set in place which consider the efficiency and cost focus of the relationship. Trust and mutual risk reward sharing structures might not play a major role, but the reliance on clearly assigned and communicated service level agreements (SLA) does. A mismatch of mutual expectations can then cause the outsourcing relationship to turn sour as it does not allow for an appropriate and mutually successful management of the relationship. In line with this, DiRomualdo and Gurbaxani (1998) found that the relationship of client and vendor must be aligned with the intents and expectations underlying the outsourcing initiative.

Obviously, given the ambiguous outcomes and many reported failures of outsourcing undertakings, outsourcing projects cannot be managed all the same way, but certain factors such as expectations of both parties, relationship factors such as trust, and governance mechanisms such as the contract seem to differ and have to be set in place differently according to the underlying core of the outsourcing venture. Extant research distinguishes between different outsourcing *modes* and *functions* (e.g., data center/infrastructure outsourcing, application hosting, business process outsourcing etc.), but does not consider the appropriate configurations of outsourcing relationships and the different governance mechanisms that result from both client and vendor expectations towards these outsourcing arrangements. To be able to manage outsourcing ventures successfully one needs to distinguish between different outsourcing relationship configurations, identify the elements each configuration is composed of and the mechanisms for managing and governing each relationship accordingly with relevant management strategies.

1.2   Research Objective and Research Questions

This thesis aims to answer the following overall research question: How (with which governance mechanisms) can different outsourcing ventures / relationships be successfully governed? The objective of this thesis is to explore and understand different types of outsourcing relationships and their configuration. Based on these findings, appropriate governance mechanisms and organizational structures for the successful management of IS outsourcing relationships are proposed. The development of a classification of various outsourcing relationships – the core contribution of the thesis – is needed as a prerequisite to be able to suggest a specialized governance concept for a successful management of the identified configurations of outsourcing relationships and thus provide IT decision makers with workable strategies for successfully governing different outsourcing projects.

Three research questions frame this thesis. As little is known about the relationship aspects in IS outsourcing arrangements, the first research question is:

1. What are the constitutive elements of a client-vendor relationship in IS outsourcing?

The following subsequent issues to be addressed stem from the first research question:

- What are related theories in various disciplines that explain the dyadic interchange and different expectations in an outsourcing venture?

- What are the structural, governance, and social factors to be considered in an outsourcing arrangement?

- What differentiates IS outsourcing relationships from other buyer-seller relationships?

The first research question is addressed by a comprehensive review of the existent body of literature on IS outsourcing relationship issues in various disciplines (e.g., information systems, psychology, business administration, and marketing). Although new in the context of IS, relationship management has been extensively researched in other academic disciplines. Examining different approaches to the characteristics of buyer-seller relationships in other disciplines highlights the interdisciplinary character of IS outsourcing relationships. The appropriateness of applying existing approaches in the context of IS outsourcing needs to be further evaluated. Literature on relationship factors has not sufficiently explored the issues of expectations and reciprocity. Because of this gap in existing knowledge, a thorough examination of related theories such as, e.g., social (relational) exchange theory and expectation confirmation theory is conducted.

Methodological foundations for classifying data are introduced which are blended into the conceptual design of the framework of outsourcing relationship configurations.

From the theoretical findings on outsourcing relationship as well as from methodological knowledge about how to conceptually design a classification, a detailed framework of different aspects to be considered when describing and governing an outsourcing relationship is developed. The primary research result from addressing the first research question will be the development of a framework with key categories along which the relationship configurations can be structured and described. The content of the framework (i.e., the characteristics of the different outsourcing relationship configurations) will then be used in an empirical study which is addressed in research question 2, the core question of this thesis:

> 2. Which different configurations of outsourcing relationships can be identified empirically?

The following three issues will be addressed in relation to this research question:

- How many different configurations of outsourcing relationships can be found in practice?

- In what respect do these outsourcing relationships differ in practice (e.g., strategic intent, governance mechanisms, architecture, or interactions)?

- Are there differences between client and vendor expectations that result in different outsourcing relationship configurations?

The second research question will be approached by a multi-method approach combining qualitative and quantitative research methods.

Little is known about what relationships in the IS outsourcing context look like in practice, how they evolve over time, and what determinants for their success or failure can be found. As domain knowledge on the research subject is essential for identifying sensible configurations and for interpreting the empirical results (Duda/Hart/Stork 2001; Hotho 2004), first empirical evidence needs to be gathered through qualitative case studies consisting of exploratory expert interviews before conducting a broad quantitative analysis. These interviews provide domain knowledge and a deeper understanding of the research subject (Yin 2002; Eisenhardt 1989).

A survey among top IT decision makers (CIOs) on the client side of IS outsourcing services is carried out to identify configurations of outsourcing relationships on a broad empirical basis. Different expectations, structures, governance mechanisms, and interaction schemes of an outsourcing relationship will be assessed. This part of the thesis uses the developed framework of IS outsourcing relationships for exploring different configurations of outsourcing relationships in practice. A multivariate cluster analysis will be applied to group the results into different configurations of outsourcing relationships. The objective of this approach is to classify a sample of entities (individuals or objects) into a small number of mutually exclusive groups based on the similarities among the entities. The data generated from answering question 2 will provide an empirical classification of different outsourcing relationships which can then be characterized along the key categories of the developed framework.

This classification will serve as a necessary basis for the design of a detailed governance investigation which will characterize successful management strategies for different outsourcing relationship profiles. Hence, research question 3 is:

> 3. What are appropriate governance approaches and mechanisms for the successful management of different outsourcing relationships?

This research question addresses the following subsequent issues:

- What governance approaches, organizational structures, and management measures are appropriate for each of the identified relationship configurations?

- How is each governance approach related to the success of the outsourcing venture?

Based on the identified types of outsourcing relationships, this part of the thesis will look at the governance mechanisms and organizational structures that are suitable and promising for a successful management of each of the outsourcing relationship configurations. Appropriate measures for determining the success of an outsourcing relationship such as client satisfaction or quality of the partnership will be introduced (Kim/Chung 2003; Lee/Kim 1999). From a methodological point of view, this research question is addressed by structural equation modeling (SEM), i.e., Partial Least Squares (PLS). With a PLS model, the impact of each governance approach on the success of outsourcing is investigated for each configuration of outsourcing relationships.

Overall, this approach provides recommendations on the effective and efficient scheduling of resources and appropriate management measures for a successful realization of an outsourcing project.

1.3   Outline and Structure of the Thesis

This thesis is organized in seven chapters. While chapters 2 to 4 focus on theoretical and methodological foundations underlying this work, chapters 5 and 6 provide empirical insights on
the different client types and their governance approaches.

Chapter 2 lays out the epistemological foundation and research methodology of this work. It
introduces different philosophical perspectives on research in general, comprising positivist,
interpretive, and critical research. It then contrasts quantitative vs. qualitative research methods. This chapter serves as a general underlying basis to understand the research paradigm
applied in this thesis.

Chapter 3 is dedicated to the foundations of outsourcing research and according theories in
this research field. It covers a broad range of topics, starting from defining outsourcing in
general and elaborating on outsourcing information systems and their peculiarities particularly. Then, theories relevant to the realm of outsourcing research are presented that help to understand outsourcing phenomena and the aspect of interorganizational relationships in general. Having laid out a theoretical foundation, variations of outsourcing phenomena and different expectations towards outsourcing are described to emphasize the complexity and multidimensionality of an outsourcing relationship. Prior research on IS outsourcing relationships
and constituent characteristics are discussed in order to elaborate on the shortcomings of current outsourcing research. As the predominant and fundamental result of this chapter, a
framework for classifying different outsourcing relationships is developed. The elaboration of
constituent characteristics of an outsourcing relationship that are incorporated as integrative
pillars of the framework answers research question 1.

Chapter 4 introduces the basis for classifying data. It defines classifications in general and
contrasts typologies vs. taxonomies. After then, it lays out the fundamental grouping techniques, such as cluster analysis or factor analysis. These techniques are necessary to deal with
the empirical data collected in the next chapter.

Chapter 5 focuses on answering research question 2. Here, empirical evidence on the existence of different outsourcing relationship types is collected and presented. First, a qualitative
pre-study serves the purpose to get a first glimpse of how a taxonomy of different relationships could look like, based on qualitative expert interviews. Then, the actual large quantitative study is carried out and different client types of outsourcing relationships are portrayed
and interpreted. A consolidated description of the types completes this chapter.

Chapter 6 uses the client types that were identified in the previous chapter and investigates
how these types are best, i.e., successfully governed. It therefore tests a structural equation
model with the PLS algorithm, using various governance mechanisms as determinants for
outsourcing performance. It then describes which mechanisms work best for each group. Determining the appropriate governance mechanisms for reach outsourcing relationship type is
the overall goal of research question 3.

Chapter 7 concludes this thesis. It summarizes the findings and discusses contributions for both theory and practice. It furthermore gives an outlook on open issues and suggests future research directions.

The structure of the thesis and the organization of the chapters are illustrated in Figure 1-1. This figure does not strictly represent an overview of the main and subchapters of this work. It rather follows the approach of an *analytical index* as introduced in the work of (Feyerabend 1975). Such an analytical index is a sketch of the main argument of each chapter. It depicts the main results and learnings of each chapter. Consequently, the following figure names the chapter with the according title and lists the main results of each chapter in white boxes. Furthermore, the research questions (RQ) are located in the relevant chapters to show which chapter answers the according research question.

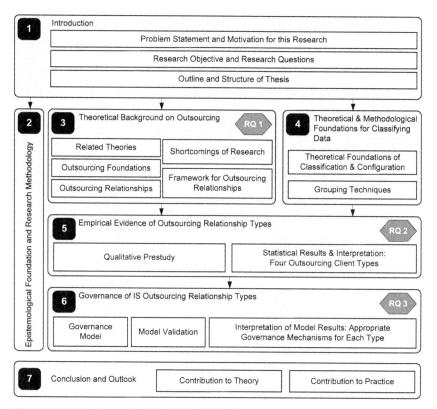

Figure 1-1. Work structure and analytical index of the thesis

2 Epistemological Foundation and Research Methodology

This chapter lays out the epistemological basis for the research in this thesis as to research methodology chosen for this work and philosophical perspectives underlying this approach.

2.1 Philosophical Perspectives and Research Epistemology

Every research endeavor is based on general underlying assumptions about what constitutes "valid" and "good" research and which research methods are appropriate. Those philosophical assumptions are related to the underlying epistemology that guides the research. In general, epistemology refers to the assumptions about knowledge and how it can be obtained (Hirschheim 1992). Several authors have come up with various distinctions of epistemological paradigms. Tschamler (1996), for example, suggests six philosophical research streams: the phenomenological-hermeneutic approach, the empirical-analytical approach, constructivism, critical rationalism, radical constructivism, and critical theory. In contrast, Guba and Lincoln (1994) mention four epistemological approaches especially applicable in a qualitative research context: positivism, post-positivism, critical theory, and constructivism. Orlikowski and Baroudi (1991), on the other hand, suggest three research epistemology streams: positivist, interpretive and critical.

While a detailed analysis and examination of various epistemological approaches is beyond the focus of this thesis, the three-fold classification of Orlikowski and Baroudi (1991) is adopted here as it is one of the most appropriate overviews of the underlying epistemological perspectives and assumptions in IS research (Myers 1997). Nevertheless it has to be mentioned that, although these three research epistemologies are regarded as philosophically distinct types (Myers 1997), in social research these distinctions are not always so clear cut (see, e.g., Lee 1989). It is still unclear and an unsolved issue of discussion as to whether these epistemological paradigms are necessarily opposed or can be pursued within one research undertaking (Myers 1997).

Another caveat to be put forward is the synonymous use of qualitative and interpretive or quantitative and positivist. While both pairs might often go together in practice and especially in the case of quantitative research only the positivist paradigm is meaningful (Straub/Gefen/Boudreau 2004), the underlying philosophical position does not necessarily determine the choice of a specific research method (qualitative vs. quantitative) (Myers 1997). For example, there is well-cited qualitative work that has an underlying positivist research approach (cf. the case study research by Yin 2002).

2.1.1 Positivist Research

Positivism takes its origin from the scientific epistemology of logical positivism that was developed by the Vienna Circle of Positivists around Karl Popper who is considered to be one of the most prominent promoters of the positivist perspective. At the heart of the positivist mind set is the understanding of scientific exploration as a search for the ultimate truth. The underlying view of the positivist understanding is that the world has an objective reality that can be captured by measurable properties which are independent of the observer and his instruments. This single-focused view of the positivist perspective has been attenuated and replaced in recent years with the recognition that eventually all measurement is based on theory and therefore capturing a truly objective truth is impossible.

Positivist scholars generally aim to translate this objective reality into testable hypotheses (typically in the form of statistical or other numerical analyses). In this way they attempt to increase the predictive understanding of phenomena and thus produce knowledge (Myers 1997; Straub/Gefen/Boudreau 2004). Orlikowski and Baroudi examined quite a number of IS studies and classified the research as positivist if it met one or more of the following criteria: a. evidence of formal propositions, b. quantifiable measures of variables, c. hypothesis testing, or d. the drawing of inferences about a phenomenon from the sample to a stated population (Orlikowski/Baroudi 1991, 5).

One of the core assumptions of positivism is the concept of deduction in contrast to induction (Straub/Gefen/Boudreau 2004). In general, deduction draws conclusions from the general to the particular, i.e., the particular is inferred from the general. Deduction provides arguments whose premises are claimed to provide conclusive evidence for the truth of its conclusion. Four cornerstones mark the concept of deduction (see also Straub/Gefen/Boudreau 2004):

1. Test of internal consistency, i.e., verifying that there are no internal contradictions. This also implies the postulate of *Wertfreiheit*, i.e., no normative judgments.

2. Distinction between the logical fundamentals of the theory and its empirical, testable hypotheses.

3. Comparison with existing theory, demonstrating that the new (not yet falsified) theory expands extant knowledge and thus has superior empirical substance.

4. Verifiability of the theory through empirical testing aimed at falsifying a theory with data. If the data does not contradict the hypothesized predictions of the theory, it is temporarily corroborate. The objective of this test is to *falsify*, not to verify, the predictions of the theory. Only if a hypothesized prediction is falsifiable at all, does it qualify as a (possible) theory.

While being the predominant paradigm in IS research until the 1990s, the positivist approach met with criticism for producing results that are mostly irrelevant in practice, despite applying highly rigid methods. In the Anglo-American scene this discussion has been labeled as the "rigor versus relevance" debate (for a detailed discussion see, e.g., Benbasat/Zmud 1999; Davenport/Markus 1999; Kock et al. 2002; Lee 1999). Furthermore, the descriptive and mostly retrospective-oriented manner of research is criticized for not generating new, but rather delayed results of established practice. Another issue for criticism is the often narrow and exclusive focus on the rigidity and consistency of the research methods while neglecting the actual research object (Frank 2003).

Finally, Habermas (1995, 162) proposed that understanding reality cannot happen objectively and independently, but is always closely related to the researcher. This perception is also the underlying credo of the interpretive paradigm that has increasingly found its way into the An-glo-American centric IS research since the 1990s (Orlikowski/Baroudi 1991) along with non-quantitative oriented research methods (Myers 1997) (see also the following chapters).

2.1.2 Interpretive Research

In contrast to positivism, the basic assumption of an interpretive researcher is that access to reality (either given or socially constructed) is only possible through social constructions such as language, consciousness, or shared actions and meanings (Bernstein 1983). The philosoph-ical foundation of interpretive research is hermeneutics and phenomenology (Boland 1985). In line with this, interpretive studies aim at understanding phenomena through the meanings that people give to them and their context. In an interpretive research attempt thus, one does not find hypothesized predictions or predefined exogenous (independent) and endogenous (dependent) variables as this does not fully capture the complexity of human sense making in emerging situations (Kaplan/Maxwell 1994).

In the IS field, several researchers such as Walsham (1993) elaborated on the use of the inter-pretive perspective on IS phenomena. While the interpretive paradigm has a long tradition in the German IS discipline, positivist research was the predominant and almost exclusive re-search stream with a strong focus on quantitative methods in the Anglo-American scene as the study of Orlikoswki and Baroudi (1991) shows.

2.1.3 Critical Research

Critical research builds upon the assumption that reality is socially and historically constituted and that it is produced and reproduced by individuals (Held 1980). In the critical view, the behavior of individuals is constrained by their economic, social, cultural, and political con-text. The major claim of critical scholars is the social criticism of the "restrictive and alienat-ing conditions of the status quo" in the contemporary society (Myers 1997). In a normative attempt, critical research addresses the oppositions, conflicts and contradictions of today's society and seeks to eliminate the causes of alienation and domination. A popular promoter of the critical theory is Jürgen Habermas, a member of the *Frankfurter Schule* together with oth-er leading philosophers of the 20th century such as Adorno and Horkheimer. In IS research, several researchers applied a critical perspective in their work (cf. Hirschheim/Klein 1994).

2.2 Research Design and Methods: Quantitative vs. Qualitative Research

Just as there are various philosophical and epistemological perspectives which can inform research, so there are various research methods. A research method is a strategy of examina-tion that moves from the underlying philosophical assumption to the research design and col-lection of data (Myers 1997). The choice of research method thus highly impacts the way the researcher collects data. Research methods can be classified in different ways. One of the most widespread distinctions, however, is between quantitative and qualitative research me-thods (Myers 1997).

Quantitative research methods were originally developed in the natural sciences to examine natural phenomena. By now quantitative methods are well established in the social sciences and examples include survey methods (applying all sorts of descriptive and multivariate analysis), laboratory experiments, formal and numerical methods such as mathematical modeling. While qualitative research has several basic epistemological positions to choose from, in the case of quantitative research only the positivist position is meaningful (Straub/Gefen/ Boudreau 2004). Quantitative research methods rely on quantitative data, i.e., numbers represent values and levels of theoretical constructs and concepts. The interpretation of the numbers is viewed as strong scientific evidence of how a phenomenon works. The presence of quantities is so predominant that statistical tools and packages are an essential element in the researcher's toolkit, e.g., SPSS (Statistical Package for the Social Sciences) (Straub/Gefen/Boudreau 2004). The source of data is of less concern for a quantitative approach than the fact that empirically derived numbers lie at the core of the scientific evidence assembled. Quantitative data can be archival data, data gathered through structured interviews or through a survey. In all cases, the researcher is motivated by the numerical outputs and how to derive meaning from them (Straub/Gefen/Boudreau 2004).

On the contrary, *qualitative research methods* were developed in the social sciences to enable researchers to study complex social and cultural phenomena. Qualitative research methods intend to help researchers understand individuals and the social and cultural context in which they live. Examples of qualitative methods especially in the IS context are action research (cf. Rapoport 1970; Baskerville/Wood-Harper 1996; Baskerville/Myers 2004), case study research (cf. Yin 2002; Benbasat/Goldstein/Mead 1987; Walsham 1995), ethnography (cf. Myers 1999; Orlikowski 1991), and grounded theory (cf. Glaser/Strauss 1967; Strauss/Corbin 1994; Glaser 1992; Orlikowski 1993). Qualitative data sources include observation and participant observation (fieldwork), interviews and (narrative) questionnaires, documents and texts, as well as the researcher's impressions and reactions.

The motivation for doing qualitative research, in contrast to quantitative research, comes from the observation that "if there is one thing which distinguishes humans from the natural world, it is our ability to talk" (Myers 1997). The particular attempt of understanding people and their point of view in a certain social context is, however, mostly lost when textual data is being quantified (Kaplan/Maxwell 1994). As Myers points out (Myers 1997), there is one caveat when it comes to qualitative research: The word "qualitative" is not a synonym for "interpretive". Qualitative research can rely on an interpretive, positivist, or critical position depending upon the underlying philosophical assumptions of the researcher (Myers 1997). Therefore, the choice of a specific qualitative research method is independent from the underlying philosophical position adopted. A good example of an IS research method applied in different epistemological contexts is action research given by Myers (Myers 1997): Action research can be positivist (Clark 1972), interpretive (Elden/Chisholm 1993), or critical (Carr/Kemmis 1986).

Traditionally most researchers conduct either quantitative or qualitative research. For some years, however, there have been efforts to combine one or more research techniques and viewpoints of positivist and non-positivist research in one study in order to triangulate on phenomena (cf. Kaplan/Duchon 1988; Gable 1994; Lee 1991; Mingers 2001). Regarding triangulation issues, Lacity and Janson come to the conclusion that both qualitative and quantitative research approaches can be viable and valid for their contexts (Lacity/Janson 1994). In line with this, Krcmar (1998) argues that the choice of the appropriate research method is highly dependent on the knowledge about the research object and the research object itself. In other words, Krcmar postulates that *research methods follow research questions*.

2.3 Summary of Epistemological Foundations of this Thesis

Chapter 2 intended to provide an overview of different epistemological positions and to lay out the research methodology and basic beliefs that underlie this thesis.

Some of the philosophical positions and epistemological claims describe contrary and opponent assumptions and thus are incommensurable. Each philosophical position applies a number of research methods, e.g., quantitative research methods go along with positivist research. However, the most important caveat and learning from comprising the epistemological foundations in this chapter is that philosophical assumptions, epistemological positions, and research methods do not have a clear "if-then" relation and cannot necessarily be derived from each other. For example, while quantitative research methods are tied to positivist research and the interpretive and critical positions are not meaningful, the positivist epistemology on the contrary relies on a host of scientific methods that produce numerical and alphanumeric data. Accordingly, epistemological assumptions for both quantitative and qualitative research are meaningful. Even more, qualitative research can rely on an interpretive, positivist, or critical position depending upon the underlying philosophical assumptions of the researcher (Myers 1997).

Caution is thus advised when allocating different research approaches. In the context of this thesis, it became obvious that although IS outsourcing seems to be a mature and widely explored research area, there are still gaps in the analysis and understanding of IS outsourcing phenomena. Thus, considering the recent approaches of combining various research methods for a rich understanding of IS phenomena, this thesis adopts a positivist epistemological position and will apply both quantitative and qualitative research methods depending on the research question addressed.

3 Theoretical Background on Outsourcing

3.1 Definition and Background of Information Systems Outsourcing

The generic notion of outsourcing refers to a decision of an organization whether to *make or buy* certain products, services or parts thereof (Loh/Venkatraman 1992a, 9, 1992b, 336). The business practice of making arrangements with an external entity for the provision of goods or services to supplement or replace internal efforts has been around for centuries (Dibbern et al. 2004). In the course of establishing a trend towards "lean production" (Womack/Jones/Roos 1991), organizations more and more focused on their core competencies in order to leverage the organization's unique potential and comparative advantages over their competitors (Wintergerst/Welker 2007). Consequently, companies assigned commodity or non-specific assets (i.e., processes, products, or services) to external entities. By reducing the level of in-house production and the degree of the company's vertical integration, companies also shifted those components away from a "hierarchical" mode toward a "market" mode of governance (Loh/Venkatraman 1992a, 8; Malone/Yates/Benjamin 1987; Wintergerst/Welker 2007, 938pp.).

A large body of research examines the outsourcing of various business functions such as human resources, payroll, logistics, or facility management. In its generic form it has been studied in several settings and industries such as "the manufacturing of parts in the automotive industry, the sales function in the electronic industry, the procurement of components or services in the naval shipbuilding industry, and the distribution of equipment, components, and supplies across a broad set of industrial firms" (Loh/Venkatraman 1992a, 9, 1992b, 336).

In the field of information systems, the outsourcing of information technology began to evolve in 1963 when *Electronic Data Systems (EDS)* as a service provider signed a contract with *Blue Cross of Pennsylvania* for the management of its data processing services. This was the first time that a large business had turned over its entire data processing department to an external vendor. The arrangement was also different from other EDS service providing contracts since EDS also took over the responsibility for Blue Cross's IS people (Dibbern et al. 2004). Despite the pioneering role of this outsourcing case, information systems outsourcing experienced a real boost not until 1989, when Eastman Kodak announced its well-publicized decision that it was outsourcing its information technology function to IBM, DEC and Businessland (Wilder 1989, 1990). Never before had such a large and well-known organization, where IS was considered to be a strategic asset, turned its IT over to external service providers (Applegate/Montealegre 1991). Kodak's US $1 billion outsourcing deal led to a widespread interest in outsourcing and legitimized for both large and small companies to transfer their IT assets, processes, and staff to outsourcing service providers (Arnett/Jones 1994), leading to what some authors have labeled "the Kodak effect" (Loh/Venkatraman 1992b; Caldwell 1994).

Trying to replicate the success of the Kodak deal, other large US companies promptly followed, e.g., Delta Airlines, Continental Bank, Xerox, Chevron, Dupont, JP Morgan, and Bell South (Dibbern et al. 2004). But the trend is not an exclusive US phenomenon. Deals by Lufthansa, Commerzbank, Deutsche Bank, and Bundeswehr (Herkules) in *Germany*, Inland Revenue, BP, British Aerospace, and BBC in the *United Kingdom* (Lacity/Willcocks 2000b; Kumar 2006), the South Australia government, Telestra, LendLease, and the Commonwealth Bank of Australia in *Australia* (Beaumont/Costa 2003), Swiss Bank, Credit Suisse in *Switzerland*, and Telecom Italia, Banca di Roma in *Italy* document the rise of the outsourcing phenomenon worldwide (Dibbern et al. 2004, 8).

The growth of the worldwide IS outsourcing market can be attributed to two primary phenomena (Lacity/Willcocks 2001). First, the increased interest in IS outsourcing is mainly a consequence of a shift in business strategy. As elaborated on in the introductory section on outsourcing above many companies have abandoned their diversification strategies to focus on core competencies that the organization does better than its competitors. As a result of this focus strategy, information systems came under scrutiny. Company executives often consider the IS function as a non-core activity with the underlying belief that IT providers have economies of scale and technical expertise to provide IS services more efficiently than internal IS departments. Second, the increase in outsourcing is a consequence of the lack of clarity around the value delivered by IS. In many companies, IS is regarded as an overhead and (essential) cost factor. Thus, the *refocus to core competencies* and the *perception of IS as a cost burden* prompt many companies to engage in a variety of outsourcing arrangements (Dibbern et al. 2004).

3.1.1 Specific Characteristics of Information Systems Outsourcing

Even though the term outsourcing is not specific to information systems (Nagengast 1997), in this thesis the term outsourcing is solely focused on the IS domain. Senior executives often argue that information systems outsourcing does not warrant attention, since it is no different from the outsourcing of other non-core business functions, such as legal, administrative, or custodial services of a firm (Lacity/Hirschheim 1995b, 217). What renews interest in IS outsourcing and deserves attention especially with regard to information systems is the dramatic change in scope (Lacity/Hirschheim 1993a, 3). Some authors even call IS outsourcing an "administrative innovation", i.e., "significant changes in the routines (or behavioral repertoires) used by the organization to deal with its tasks of internal arrangements and external alignments" (Venkatraman/Loh/Koh 1992), because of three distinct features (Loh/Venkatraman 1992b, 337).

First, it represents a significant shift in the mode of governance from the traditional locus of control and coordination within the hierarchy (combined with relatively standardized market transactions with vendors) towards newer modes that could be characterized as hybrids or partnerships. Second, it leads to significant changes in the internal processes of the user organization. And third, it constitutes a significant change in the organizational routines used to deal with the external environment. This includes specifically a shift away from an arms-length approach for dealing with the "IT marketplace" towards a mutual relationship mode (with longer-term alliances involving a few selected partners) where increased mutual understanding, enhanced goal compatibility and recognition of complementary skills and requirements is required (Loh/Venkatraman 1992b, 337pp.).

In many respects, information systems outsourcing is different from other forms of (business) outsourcing (Apte 1990; Lacity/Hirschheim 1995b; Lacity/Willcocks 2001; Dibbern et al. 2004). Lacity et al. (1994; 1994) identified six distinctive features which characterize information systems as being different from other outsourcing candidates:

1. **Information technology and IT capabilities evolve at a dizzying pace** (Lacity/Willcocks 2001, 184). Thus, predicting IT needs in every detail and clearly specifying systems requirements past a three-year horizon is inherently fraught with uncertainty and practically not possible (Lacity/Willcocks 2003, 121; Apte 1990, 292).

2. **The underlying economics of information technology (IT) changes rapidly.** IS is complex in nature and a permanent object to change due to the dynamic nature of a company's IS needs and technology leaps (Apte 1990, 292). In line with the projection of Intel co-founder Gordon Moore, the cost of computing resources rapidly fall every year, while the computing (processing) power increases double every two years (this phenomenon is also known as Moore's law (Hutcheson 2005)). Consequently, it is difficult to gauge the economics of IS activity.

3. **The penetration of IS to all business functions is ubiquitous**: Although not necessarily strategic or a differentiating asset from competitors, information technology is business-critical and pervasive throughout the organization (Dibbern et al. 2004, 9). It is a rather heterogeneous function that comprises a wide variety of IT activities and is interrelated with practically all organizational activities (Willcocks/Fitzgerald/Lacity 1996). Thus, it cannot easily be isolated from other organizational functions, but penetrates every business function in the value chain as well as support activities (Porter/Millar 1985).

4. **The switching costs to alternative IT and IS suppliers are high**. In contrast to other business functions large switching costs are associated with IS sourcing decisions, especially when large portions of IT are outsourced (Lacity/Willcocks 2001, 185). The threat of vendor opportunism due to the lock-in effect of the customer is extremely likely because the effort and switching costs to another vendor or to an in-house IT function are expensive.

5. **Customers' inexperience with IS outsourcing**: Many customers lack experience with managing an outsourcing project and do not understand the imperative need of a continuous and ongoing governance of an IS outsourcing relationship (Cohen/Young 2006). Moreover, while IT service providers sign large contracts quite often, outsourcing clients often do not have experience with negotiating outsourcing contracts. This information asymmetry often leads to a favorable position for the outsourcing vendor.

6. **IS management practices rather than economies of scale lead to economic efficiency**. Many medium-sized and most large-sized companies can achieve similar economies of scale in some aspects of their IT. Economic efficiency in IS outsourcing then is a consequence of a better IS management practice rather than inherent economies of scale.

The characteristics above demonstrate that because IS is distinctive, one should treat IS sourcing decisions differently (Lacity/Hirschheim 1995b, 222). Hence, management approaches or governance strategies from other academic disciplines may not be applicable for the context of IS outsourcing relationships in this thesis. New approaches have to be developed that consider the specific features inherent to information systems.

3.1.2 IS Outsourcing Definitions

Definitions of information systems outsourcing abound, with little consistency or agreement in sight (Willcocks/Lacity/Cullen 2007). Precise definitions of IS outsourcing differ in the IS literature (Glass 1996). The label outsourcing has been applied to "everything from use of contract programmers to third party facilities management" (Dibbern et al. 2004). Understanding how each study defines outsourcing is important since minor variants in terminology can result in the study of a slightly different phenomenon. Thus, Table 3-1 lists a variety of definitions of IS outsourcing in the literature.

Definition of IS Outsourcing	Outsourcing Perspective / Focus	Author
"... selectively turning over certain functions of information systems and processing services to a subcontractor"	movement from in-house to external sourcing	(Apte 1990, 288)
"... selectively turning over to a vendor some or all of the IS functions, ranging from simple data entry to software development and maintenance, data centre operations and full system integration"	Selective process, variety of outsourcing objects	(Apte et al. 1997, 289)
"... request of services of an outside party to fulfill a function or functions that involve computer systems."	External / Third-party provision	(Buck-Lew 1992, 3)
"...the contracting of various systems sub functions [...] by user firms to outside information systems vendors"	External / Third-party provision	(Chaudhury/Nam/Rao 1995, 132), taken from (Apte/Winniford 1991)
"...the organizational decision to turn over part or all of an organization's IS functions to external service provider(s) in order for an organization to be able to achieve its goals"	movement from in-house to external sourcing	(Cheon/Grover/Teng 1995, 209)
"... the commissioning of a third party (or a number of third parties) to manage a client organization's IT assets, people and/or activities (or part thereof) to required results"	External / Third-party provision, variety of outsourcing objects	(Fitzgerald/Willcocks 1994, 92)
"... contracting with one or more third party vendors for the provision of some or all of an organization's IS functions, where "functions" include one or more IT activities, processes, or services to be provided over time"	Focus on service dimension of outsourcing	(Goles/Chin 2005, 49)
"... the practice of turning over part or all of an organization's IS functions to external service provider(s)"	movement from in-house to external sourcing	(Grover/Cheon/Teng 1994b, 34)

Definition of IS Outsourcing	Outsourcing Perspective / Focus	Author
"…involving a significant use of resources – either technological and/or human resources – external to the organizational hierarchy in the management of information technology"	External / Third-party provision	(Grover/Cheon/Teng 1996, 90) taken from (Loh/Venkatraman 1992a)
"… using external agencies to process, manage, or maintain internal data and provide information-related services"	External / Third-party provision, variety of outsourcing objects	(Gupta/Gupta 1992, 44)
"…the third party provision of IT products and services"	External / Third-party provision	(Hancox/Hackney 1999, 1)
"…the practice of transferring IT assets, leases, staff, and management responsibility for delivery of services from internal IT functions to third-party vendors"	movement from in-house to external sourcing, variety of outsourcing objects	(Hirschheim/Lacity 2000, 99), also used by Gottschalk (2006a)
"…business practice in which a company contracts all or part of its information systems operations to one or more outside information service suppliers"	External / Third-party provision	(Hu/Saunders/Gebelt 1997, 288)
"… a decision taken by an organization to contract-out or sell the organization's IT assets, people, and/or activities to a third party vendor, who in exchange provides and manages assets and services for monetary returns over an agreed time period"	External / Third-party provision, variety of outsourcing objects, long-term focus	(Kern 1997, 37), see also (Willcocks/Kern 1998, 29)
"… a process whereby an organization decides to contract-out or sell the firm's IT assets, people, and/or activities to a third-party supplier, who in exchange provides and manages these assets and services for an agreed fee over and agreed time period"	Long-term interaction, process-oriented	(Kern/Willcocks 2002, 3)
"…the purchase of a good or service that was previously provided internally"	movement from in-house to external sourcing	(Lacity/Hirschheim 1993b, 74)
"… the use of a third party vendor to provide information products and services that were previously provided internally"	movement from in-house to external sourcing	(Lacity/Hirschheim 1995b, 1)
"… the use of external agents to perform one or more organizational activities"	External / Third-party provision	(Lacity/Hirschheim 1993a, 2)
"… to dismantle internal IT departments by transferring IT employees, facilities, hardware leases, and software licenses to third-party vendors"	External / Third-party provision	(Lacity/Willcocks/Feeny 1996, 13)
"… a phenomenon in which a user organization (client) transfers property or decision rights over information technology infrastructure to an external (vendor) organization	Focus on infrastructure, financial and managerial benefits	(Levina/Ross 2003, 332)
"…the significant contribution by external vendors of the physical and/or human resources associated with the entire or specific components of the IT infrastructure in the user organization"	External / Third-party provision, focus on IT infrastructure	(Loh/Venkatraman 1992a, 9, 1992b, 336)

Definition of IS Outsourcing	Outsourcing Perspective / Focus	Author
"… the off-loading of previously internal processes to outside suppliers"	movement from in-house to external sourcing	(Tapscott/Caston 1993, 8)
"… a multiyear or annuity-based contractual arrangement whereby an organization provisions services on an ongoing basis at a specified level of competency. Outsourcing involves some degree of transfer of management responsibility for the ongoing delivery of IT services to an external provider, with performance tied to service levels or outcomes."	Definition in practice (Gartner), focus on external provider, ongoing basis	(Tramacere/Matlus 2007, 2)
"…the handing over to third party management, for required result, some or all or an organization's IT information systems and related services"	External / Third-party provision, agreed results	(Willcocks/Lacity/Fitzgerald 1995, 334)
"… the handing over to a third party management of IT/IS assets, resources, and/or activities for required results"	External / Third-party provision, agreed results	(Willcocks/Lacity 1998b, 3)
" … decision taken by an organization to contract-out or sell the organization's IT assets, people and/or activities to a third party vendor, who in return provides the services for a certain time period and monetary fee"	External / Third-party provision	(Willcocks/Kern 1998, 29)

Table 3-1. Definitions of information systems outsourcing
(Source: extended from Dibbern et al. 2004; Gottschalk/Solli-Sæther 2006a; Hancox/Hackney 1999)

The definitions above reveal that there is a general agreement that outsourcing is understood as the carrying out of IT functions by third parties (Kettler/Walstrom 1993). However, it also shows that some authors have been more specific about their definition by pointing out certain aspects. Cheon et al. (1995), Lacity and Hirschheim (1993b; 1995b), Apte (1990) as well as Tapscott and Caston (1993) mention the movement from in-house to external provision (Hancox/Hackney 1999), thereby limiting the definition of outsourcing to only those services or functions previously conducted in-house. Other authors (see, e.g., Buck-Lew 1992; Gupta/Gupta 1992; Loh/Venkatraman 1992a; Lacity/Hirschheim 1993a) do not implicate that the activities were necessarily provided internally previously. In the media and among business managers in practice, outsourcing is largely understood as involving the transfer of assets and staff. This is a common, but not essential part of outsourcing (Willcocks/ Lacity/Fitzgerald 1993) (see also chapter 3.3.2, p. 33ff.). Some authors also tried to define outsourcing by contrasting it with insourcing. But since definitions of insourcing vary, these approaches of exclusion have only limited use in clarifying outsourcing (Hancox/Hackney 1999).

Taken the manifold definitions of IS outsourcing into account and acknowledging that some sources mentioned above have different interpretations and notions, this thesis defines IS outsourcing as

"handing over to one or more third party vendors (i.e., legally independent) the provision of some or all of an organization's IS functions such as, e.g., IT assets, activities,

people, processes, or services for a contractually agreed monetary fee and period of time".

This definition points out clearly that outsourcing is a form of interorganizational relationship that involves at least two separate and distinct firms – the customer and the vendor – in a contractual arrangement characterized by a series of interrelated and ongoing exchanges and responsibilities. Various theories in different disciplines have dedicated efforts to describe and explain these interorganizational relationships. They can help to understand the outsourcing phenomenon in greater detail and will be part of the next chapter.

3.2 Theoretical Foundation: Related Theories

Quite a number of theories have been applied to understand, describe, and explain IS outsourcing in general. Expanding the work of Cheon et al. (1995), Lee et al. (2003) grouped these theories into three categories: strategic management, economic, and social theories.

Economic theories stress efficiency, cost, and benefits of outsourcing. They examine the coordination and governance of economic agents in their transactions and thereby aim at explaining the characteristics of governance or the contract (Hallén/Johanson/Seyed-Mohamed 1991; Meyer 1994). Economic theories that have been found relevant for analyzing IS outsourcing phenomena mainly include transaction cost economics (TCE), economic efficiency, as well as agency cost and principal agent theory.

Strategic management theories (involving, e.g., resource-dependency, resource-based / core competencies, and coordination theories) consider outsourcing as a means to improve a firm's competitive advantage. They are concerned with how enterprises develop and implement strategies in order to accomplish a certain performance goal (Schendel/Hofer 1979).

Social theories (involving, e.g., political, social contract, social exchange, and relational exchange theories) focus on the interaction and exchange between the customer and the vendor of outsourcing in order to understand the structure, ongoing interaction, and dissolution of the interorganizational relationship. Social theories assume that relational processes dynamically evolve over time as participants mutually demonstrate their trustworthiness in each other.

While a detailed description of theories applied in outsourcing is beyond the focus of this thesis, only the theories that are most relevant for this research will be explained in more detail. First, transaction cost economics will be introduced as one of the fundamental and most widespread theories appropriate to explain outsourcing phenomena. Then, social theories will be laid out as the characteristics of outsourcing relationships are best understood applying the category of social theories on outsourcing. For a better overview and additional readings on outsourcing theories, Lee (2003) provides a comprehensive collection of references on theories applied in outsourcing[2].

---

[2] For an overview of outsourcing theories, see also Lee's online source: http://www.is.cityu.edu.hk/staff/-isjnlee/out_theory_ref.htm.

3.2.1   Transaction Cost Economics

Traditionally, theoretical considerations of IS outsourcing research have heavily focused on economic theories, esp. transaction cost economics (TCE) / transaction cost theory that was initially introduced by Coase (1937) and further developed by Williamson (1975, 1979; 1985). In many ways, TCE seems to be the ideal theoretical foundation for IS outsourcing because it specifically addresses make-or-buy decisions based on the generic attributes of assets and describes appropriate ways to govern customer-supplier relationships from an economic point of view (Cheon/Grover/Teng 1995; Lacity/Willcocks 2003). Transaction cost theory explains the advantages of performing an economic activity within the firm (using the governance structure of intra-organizational hierarchy) or through market exchange mechanisms (using the external market-based governance structure). It examines the conditions under which market governance (i.e., using an outsourcing vendor) is more cost efficient than governance within the boundaries of a firm (i.e., providing in-house services through organizational hierarchy) (Apte 1990). "The main hypothesis out of which transaction cost economics works is this: [Firms seek to] *align transactions, which differ in their attributes, with governance structures, which differ in their costs and competencies, in a discriminating (mainly transaction costs economizing) way*" (Williamson 1991b, 79), italics in original.

Transaction cost economics relies on the general assumption that economic exchange of goods and services is associated with costs. These costs are comprised not only of production costs, but mainly of transaction costs (often labeled as coordination costs) for searching, initiating, negotiating, monitoring, adapting, and ending an exchange agreement (Wintergerst/Welker 2007, 940). In comparing the "make" versus the "buy" decision, both *production* and *transaction costs* of the alternatives have to be compared (Lacity/Hirschheim 1993a, 25) and the one with the lower overall cost is the alternative to be preferred as the predominant (i.e., the most cost efficient) governance structure (Apte 1990). Regarding the *production costs*, i.e., the costs of capital, labor, and materials for delivering information systems functions, the market option tends to lead to lower production costs because of the economies of scale a vendor can leverage (Malone/Yates/Benjamin 1987). These economies of scale can primarily be seen in data center and communication operations or system development where volume discounts and shared expertise of IT specialists among various customers and projects lead to better cost efficiency.

The main focus of TCE is on minimizing transaction costs (Dibbern/Winkler/Heinzl 2008). *Transaction costs* are defined as all costs in terms of time, effort and money spent, that arise for "[negotiating, enforcing,] planning, adapting, and monitoring task completion under alternative governance structures (Williamson 1981, 552pp.). These costs tend to be higher in outsourcing arrangements since the client needs to explain his information needs to the vendor. The effort of explaining and the possibility of failure or undesired outcome due to miscommunication is a significant part of transaction costs. In addition, negotiation and monitoring an outsourcing contract also leads to high transaction costs. In this case, hierarchies are more efficient due to internal control mechanisms that prevent opportunism (Lacity/Hirschheim 1993a, 37).

The existence of these costs is based on two key behavioral assumptions: *Bounded rationality* and *opportunism* of the actors. According to the assumption of bounded rationality (based on Simon 1957), the actors tend to act rationally, but face the limitations of imperfect markets and information asymmetry. Consequently, contracts can only be designed incompletely since "it is impossible to deal with complexity in all contractually relevant aspects" (Williamson 1981, 554). This incompleteness of the contract would not matter if the involved actors were completely trustworthy (Williamson 1975, 26). This, however, is ruled out by the second assumption of opportunism. Actors tend to take advantage of opportunities to "self-interest seeking with *guile*" at the expense of other actors (Williamson 1975). Because it is difficult to anticipate the other person's attitude and behavior towards opportunisms, actors even more tend to opportunistic behavior (Williamson 1985, 64). Costs for setting up contractual agreements and control costs for monitoring the exchange partner arise.

Transaction costs depend on three contingencies that drive the make or buy decision (Apte 1990):

1. *Asset specificity* that evolves in transaction-specific investments or facilities (site, physical, or human asset specificity)

2. *Uncertainty* of outcome due to difficulties in specifying system requirements

3. *Frequency* of transactions associated with multiple and numerous vendor arrangements

Overall, the outsourcing option tends to have lower production costs and higher transaction costs compared to the in-house option (Apte 1990). But the ultimate decision on which option to choose depends on the level of total costs. Wintergerst and Welker (2007, 942) also put forth that outsourcing can rarely be regarded as a "spontaneous acquisition of goods on a market", but rather as a hybrid form between market governance and hierarchy.

The sole recognition of TCE for explaining the exchange between actors in an outsourcing arrangement has come under scrutiny more recently (Dibbern/Winkler/Heinzl 2008). As a core proposition, TCE suggests governing the market-based outsourcing option via an appropriate contractual arrangement with the vendor. However, while an outsourcing arrangement highly depends on the governance of the contractual relation part, an exclusively economic view falls far short of a comprehensive understanding of an outsourcing relationship because it views the actor (i.e., the person or the company) as not interacting with another actor but rather directly with the market and thus does not include the perspective of exchanges between individual actors (Kern/Willcocks 2000b). Moreover, the exclusively economic view treats each sourcing arrangement as a discrete and independent event regardless of possible prior sourcing relationships that might affect the ongoing relationship and behaviors of the actors (Walker/Weber 1984; Richmond/Seidmann 1993). But this treatment may be inappropriate when organizations frequently engage in multiple interorganizational relationships. Lee and Kim point out that adopting a purely economic perspective is unjustifiable because "interorganizational relationships form from the social learning experiences based on specific sequential interactions" (Lee/Kim 1999, 32).

Many more economic theories could be described and applied in this context, such as agency theory (Jensen/Meckling 1976), game theory (Kreps et al. 1982), or strategic management theories (Chandler 1962; Miles/Snow 1978; Porter 1985). But as this thesis focuses on the interorganizational relationship aspects of an outsourcing venture and the interchanges between the actors on both the client and the vendor side, social theories are primarily regarded as adequate theoretical approaches to understand the phenomenon of IS outsourcing relationships.

3.2.2 Exchange Theories: Social Exchange and Relational Exchange Theory

Interorganizational relationships have been researched from various academic perspectives. Among them are, e.g., law (Macneil 1978; Macneil 1980), marketing (Dwyer/Schurr/Oh 1987) as well as predominantly psychology and sociology (Homans 1958; Emerson 1962). Many theories have focused on the *exchange* aspect as it is one of the inherent and fundamental elements of an interorganizational relationship. As pointed out above, a purely economic exchange perspective does not necessarily reflect realities. Thus, two social theories evolved that explain governance modes that fall between pure market exchanges and hierarchies, as set forth in Transaction Cost Economics. Social Exchange Theory and Relational Exchange Theory both consider – although grown from different disciplines – social relations and relational norms between commercial entities.

3.2.2.1 *Social Exchange Theory*

Social exchange theory is one of the most prominent and appropriate theories to explain interorganizational behavior. Evolving from the junction of economics, sociology, and psychology, social exchange theory was originally introduced by Homans (1958) and advanced by Blau (1964), Cook (1977), Emerson, (1962), Levine/White (1961), and Thibaut/ Kelly (1959) to understand the social behavior of humans in an economic context. It can be traced to one of the oldest theories of social behavior – any interaction between individuals is an exchange of resources. The theory focuses on dyadic interpersonal exchange relations involving the transfer of resources for the mutual benefit of the actors. The need for social exchange is created by the scarcity of resources, prompting actors to engage one another to obtain valuable inputs (Gottschalk/Solli-Sæther 2006a). Hereby, social exchange is understood as a reciprocal process in which voluntary actions of individuals are contingent on rewarding actions from others.

The key tenet of the theory is best captured in Homans's original words (Homans 1958, 606): "Social behavior is an exchange of goods, material goods but also non-material ones, such as the symbols of approval or prestige. Persons that give much to others try to get much from them, and persons that get much from others are under pressure to give much to them. This process of influence tends to work out at equilibrium to a balance in the exchanges. For a person engaged in exchange, what he gives may be a cost to him, just as what he gets may be a reward, and his behavior changes less as profit, that is, reward less cost, tends to a maximum." In other words, social behavior is the result of an exchange process. The purpose of this exchange is to maximize benefits and minimize costs. According to the theory, people weigh the potential benefits and risks of social relationships. When the risks outweigh the rewards, people will terminate or abandon that relationship. Thereby, the theory builds on essential social norms' constructs such as trust, communication, commitment, collaboration, risk-reward share etc.

The theory has evolved from a *dyadic model* that accentuates interactions, interdependencies, and reciprocities between two actors (Johnson/Bonoma 1977) to a *network focus* with market orientation (Cook 1977; Cook/Emerson 1978). Over time, it has been enriched by different facets, varying from a technical economic analysis (Blau 1964) to the psychology of instrumental behavior (Homans 1958). While its origins are at the individual level, social exchange theory has been extended to organizational and interorganizational levels (Das/Teng 2002).

In the context of IS outsourcing research, social exchange theory has served as an underlying theoretical model for explaining outsourcing relationships (see, e.g., Kern/Willcocks 2000b; Lee/Kim 1999; Goles 2001; Goles/Chin 2002).

3.2.2.2 Relational Exchange Theory

Also based on the fundamental idea of exchange between commercial entities, relational exchange theory grew out of the intersection of marketing (Anderson/Narus 1984; Dwyer/Schurr/Oh 1987) and law (Macneil 1974, 1978; 1980). It acknowledges the fact that traditional institutional (mostly contractual focused) governance such as market transactions vs. complete vertical integration (hierarchies) as set forth in Transaction Cost Economics (Williamson 1975, 1979) does not appropriately cover all governance mechanisms in reality. For example, hybrid forms such as joint ventures, strategic alliances, networks and other sorts of partnerships (Dwyer/Schurr/Oh 1987; Heide/John 1990; Alter/Hage 1993; Ring/Van de Ven 1994) are neither clear forms of hierarchy governance nor governance through the market. They rather fall somewhere on a continuum between these polar extremes of governance options (Williamson 1985, 1991a).

As these new types of governance forms have emerged and spread throughout the organizational landscape, they have motivated theorists to adapt extant frameworks or develop new ones to account for these phenomena. In this context, relational exchange theory (RET) was brought up (Joshi/Stump 1999).

The theory is based on the notion that exchanging parties are in mutual agreement that the resulting outcomes of the social exchange are greater than those that could be attained through other forms of exchange (Goles/Chin 2002). For that reason the exchange partners consider the exchange relationship valuable to devote resources towards its maintenance and development (Anderson/Narus 1984; Dwyer/Schurr/Oh 1987). The theory builds upon relational norms as a unique class of governance mechanism in between markets and hierarchy that "prescribes (commitment) and proscribes (opportunism) certain behaviors in exchange relationships" ((Morgan/Hunt 1994; Macneil 1980) in (Joshi/Stump 1999)). Key concepts of relational exchange theory involve relational norms such as flexibility, shared expectations / information exchange, dependence, as well as solidarity (Kern/Blois 2002).

Macneil (1974, 1978; 1980)set the stage for developing relational exchange theory further by introducing a social contract perspective. He argued that the traditional view of contract did not adequately address the empirical realities of relational norms (Goles 2001) and therefore proposed revamping classical contract theory so that it caters for prior and future actions of individuals participating in exchange relations (Macneil 1980). Macneil's conclusion also considers the fact that it is hardly possible to design complete contracts because not all possible events during an outsourcing venture can be anticipated and included upfront in contract clauses – which is the core assumption of incomplete contract theory[3] (Beulen/ Ribbers 2003; Gietzmann 1996; Hart 1998).

Despite the relevance generally ascribed to the idea of exchange (cf. Frazier 1983), a lot of research has largely neglected the ongoing relationship aspect of a buyer-seller behavior while tending to study the relationship as a single transaction and discrete event (Dwyer/Schurr/Oh 1987). Macneil introduced a differentiation of discrete transactions (short-term agreements with a largely economic focus) from relational contracts / exchange (open-ended, long-term arrangements combining economic and socio-emotional exchanges) as polar archetypes of exchange on a continuum along several key dimensions (Macneil 1978; 1980). Accordingly, relational exchange theory views exchange as a continuum, ranging from discrete to relational. In this understanding, an outsourcing relationship can be classified in the corner of relational exchange rather than a discrete event (Dwyer/Schurr/Oh 1987) and thus be termed a contractual-based ongoing exchange relation (Kern/Willcocks 2000b).

In IS outsourcing research, relational exchange theory was the underlying theoretical basis of the work of, e.g., Goles (2001; 2002) as well as Kern et al. (2002).

3.2.3 Psychological Contract Theory

Although not predominantly focused on the idea of exchange, psychological contract theory shares the basic thoughts of social and relational exchange theory. It also acknowledges the fact that an exclusively economic view or focus on a legal contract alone is insufficient for capturing an (inter- or intra-)organizational relationship. Evolving from the discipline of organizational studies, the key tenet of psychological contract theory is a reciprocal exchange agreement that contains mutual obligations, typically between employee and employer (Rousseau 1989). A psychological contract refers to people's mental beliefs and expectations about their mutual obligations in a contractual relation between that person and another party such as an employer (either a firm or another person) (Rousseau 1995). This belief is predicated on the perception that a promise has been made and a consideration offered in exchange for it, binding the parties to some set of reciprocal obligations. This conceptualization of psychological contracts relies upon certain assumptions.

First, by definition, a psychological contract is an *individual* perception. Consequently, these beliefs may diverge from what is in writing and from interpretations by other principals or third parties (Rousseau/Tijoriwala 1998). Reviews of research on this topic mention that the

---

[3]   Incomplete contract theory is beyond the scope of the thesis and this theoretical section. Nevertheless, it is closely related to the work of Macneil and the idea of social exchange and thus had to be mentioned in this context. For detailed description of the theory see, e.g., (Beulen/Ribbers 2003; Gietzmann 1996; Hart 1998).

focus of psychological contracts upon individual cognitions is a major defining factor (Pearce 1998; Roehling 1997).

Second, the main focus of the theory lies on the *intra-organizational* perspective between an employee and an employer. To date, little research exists regarding other parties to the contract aside from individual employees (Rousseau/Tijoriwala 1998). As Rousseau (1998) points out a related issue arising in response to changes in contemporary firms are the 'new partners' to the psychological contract such as outsourced relations or guest workers from other firms performing functions within a host organization. In early research, Levinson et al. (Levinson et al. 1962, 38) recognized that in addition to the psychological contract between individual and organization there are also psychological contracts between people and groups and outside organizations.

Concluding, psychological contract theory has a strong focus on the individual perceptions and an intra-organizational perspective which is not originally in the focus of an interorganizational outsourcing relationship. However, as Rousseau (1998, 693) stressed efforts should be made to expand and apply the general ideas of psychological contract theory to other contexts such as outsourcing relationships. Therefore, outsourcing relationships could also be examined in the light of psychological contracts.

3.2.4 Expectation Confirmation Theory

The interactions between several actors (individuals, companies etc.) described in the theories above result in various contingencies, in which the actors modify their resources to each other's expectations. Considering and aligning mutual expectations is especially important in interorganizational relationships such as IS outsourcing arrangements. Lacity and Hirschheim (1995b, 157p.) mention that "conflicting stakeholders' expectations place IS managers in the precarious position of providing a Rolls Royce service at a Chevrolet price."

Expectation Confirmation Theory (ECT) addresses such mutual expectations towards the exchange relation. The theory originated from the marketing and consumer behavior area. It applies four major concepts: expectations, perceived performance, disconfirmation, and satisfaction. The underlying key tenet of ECT is that expectations together with the following perceived performance lead to post-purchase satisfaction (Oliver 1977; Oliver 1980). Disconfirmation – either positive or negative – stems from the interaction of expectations with performance and is regarded as a mediating variable in between expectations, performance, and satisfaction. Outperforming expectations cause positive disconfirmation, lower performing expectations lead to negative disconfirmation. Expectations are hereby understood as the anticipated or estimated behavior and precede the perceived outcome or performance of a relationship (Churchill/Suprenant 1982).

In contrast to individual consumer behavior situations where the focus lies clearly on the customer, in outsourcing exchange relationships expectations of both parties, i.e., client and vendor, have to be considered. Because perceived performance and overall success or satisfaction are highly dependent on the individual expectations of each participant, these expectations have to be congruent in order to achieve mutual benefits and perceived success of an outsourcing relationship. The expectations of both parties towards the venture thus strongly determine the relationship and the overall perceived satisfaction of the outsourcing relationship.

Expectations, performance, and satisfaction are the main concepts that are used in the IS outsourcing literature to determine and document the resulting experiences of the outsourcing decision. According to Dibbern et al. (2004, 69), outsourcing outcome or success can be viewed either as satisfaction, expectations of objectives and their realization, or the performance of the processes/operations outsourced. All three approaches depend on individual factors that drive satisfaction, objective realization, or performance. Looking through the governance lens of an outsourcing venture, the acknowledgement and consideration of different expectations of client and vendor is crucial for designing and applying appropriate governance structures and instruments that eventually lead to satisfaction and outsourcing success.

A prominent example of the application of Expectation Confirmation Theory and these concepts to determine the success of an outsourcing venture is the work of Susarla et al. (2003). They found that expectations about application service provisioning (ASP) services have a significant influence on the performance evaluation and thus satisfaction with ASPs. Lacity and Willcocks (1995b) also mention the importance of similar goals and expectations in a very illustrative way. According to their outsourcing cases, "conflicting stakeholders' expectations place IS managers in the precarious position of providing a Rolls Royce service at a Chevrolet price" (Lacity/Hirschheim 1995b, 158).

3.2.5   Theories of Power: Power-Political, Power Dependence, Power Conflict

Besides social exchange and mutual expectations, another concept has to be introduced to comprehensively describe the theoretical pillars of IS outsourcing relationships between organizations: political power and dependency. In the words of Emerson exchange relations are "by definition reciprocal, and if this reciprocity is broken the relationship will extinguish over time. Within the attribute of reciprocal reinforcement, the concept of an exchange relation contains an 'exchange ratio' [balance-imbalance]. This variable sets the stage for introducing dependence, power, and cohesion" (Emerson 1969, 387pp.).

Even though the importance of *power* for a social exchange relation is widely recognized, in the early days the large body of research on power and related concepts could not achieve the integrated character desired (Emerson 1962, 31). Instead of a systematic treatment of social power with the outcome of a theory, it produced a variety of typologies and approaches on, e.g., power-dependency, power-politics, or power-conflict relations. Two theories – both similar, but originated in a different time and focus on slightly different, but interrelated constructs – have become very prominent in this context: In the 1960s, Emerson introduced an integrated *theory of power-dependence relations* (Emerson 1962). In the 1980s, Pfeffer adopted Emerson's ideas that power comes from offering something of value that few other sources can provide and thus causes dependencies (Pfeffer 1981; Pfeffer 1992). Pfeffer focused on the political perspective, using the main theoretical constructs of *power and politics*:

General power theory can offer valuable insights to understanding the behavior between organizations (Blau 1964; Emerson 1962). Power is hereby broadly understood as "the ability to evoke a change in another's behavior, i.e., the ability to cause someone to do something he/she would not have done otherwise" (Gaski 1984; Pfeffer 1981; Pfeffer 1992). In the simple words of Tushman (1977), power is the "potential of an actor to influence the behavior of another actors on a particular issue". According to Emerson, power is the property of a relation and not the attribute of an actor itself, because it "resides implicitly in the other's dependency" (Emerson 1962, 32). Consequently, power is determined by the relative dependence between two actors in an exchange relationship and this concept is only meaningful when compared with another organization (Bacharach/Lawler 1981; Pfeffer 1981).

Politics as the second main construct in Pfeffer's power-political approach is defined as "the structure and process of the use of authority and power to effect definitions of goals, directions, and other major parameters of the organization" (Tushman 1977, 207). Pfeffer consequently derives a delineate of power and politics: "If power is a force, a store of potential influence through which events can be affected, politics involves those activities or behaviors through which power is developed and used in organizational settings. Power is a property of a system at rest; politics is the study of power in action" (Pfeffer 1981, 7).

The notion of reciprocity and dependency in power relations raises the question of equality or inequality of power between the involved actors (Emerson 1962). Although in theory interorganizational relations could be balanced and equal in power, differences in, e.g., expectations, resources, or dependencies lead to an imbalance of power in practice. Easton states that asymmetries in power relations result from mutual dependencies (Easton 1992). Simon even incorporates the inherent imbalance of power in a social relation in the definition of power which he defines as "an *asymmetrical* relation between the behavior of two persons" (Simon 1953). Such asymmetries become critical if the impact of one party is dominant and leads, e.g., to the danger of opportunistic behavior.

Applied to the context of IS outsourcing relationships, several consequences arise for the understanding of the power dependencies between client and vendor. For example, in long-term, stable outsourcing relationships, where large parts of the information technology have been outsourced to a service provider, the vendor most often dominates the outsourcing relationship due to lock-in effects. In selective outsourcing arrangements in contrast, a client can distribute the risk and alleviate power imbalances by giving small portions of IT to various vendors and thus minimize the overall risk (Kern 1997; Currie/Willcocks 1998; Willcocks/Lacity 1999; Willcocks/Lacity/Kern 1999). Lacity and Willcocks (2003) emphasize that well-balanced power structures play a major role when common goals and expectations are pursued. Lacity and Willcocks state that customer and supplier relationships will sometimes be adversarial, but "the important lesson here is that each side must have equal power so that they can achieve equitable outcomes" (Lacity/Willcocks 2003, 123). While an outsourcing contract can be a means to manage or control such imbalances between the involved actors, relationship structures and behaviors can be another to balance inequalities between client and vendor – depending on the context and type of outsourcing relationship.

3.2.6   Summary of Theories for IS Outsourcing Relationships

Although IS outsourcing arrangements are different in a variety of ways, all outsourcing relationships share constitutive elements at their most basic level: the idea of *exchange* between interacting participants with different *expectations* on the basis of an *ongoing social relationship*, while the participants are *mutually dependent* on each other to a certain extent which results in different *power* allocations. The perspectives of the theories described above, namely social, relational exchange theory, expectation confirmation theory and power-dependence theory, cover these basic commonalities of outsourcing relationships quite well and may function as the lens through which to examine the phenomenon of IS outsourcing relationships may yield further insights.

Consequently, the relevant concepts incorporated in these theories (such as, e.g., trust, communication, commitment, risk benefit share, conflict, coordination, mutual dependency, power imbalance etc.) will be applied to this research. The concepts will be integrated as building blocks for the development of a conceptual framework for assessing and understanding different IS outsourcing relationship types.

The following Table 3-2 gives a summarizing overview of the theories incorporated and applied in this thesis.

Theoretical foundation	Level of analysis	Basic assumptions	Main variables / main focus	Key authors
Transaction Cost Theory / Transaction Cost Economics	individual, organizational (transactions between actors)	Bounded rationality, opportunism	Transaction costs, production costs	(Coase 1937; Williamson 1975, 1979, 1981; 1985)
Social Exchange Theory	Individual, organizational	Participation in exchange occurs with the assumption of rewards and obligation to return rewards	Exchange of activities, benefits/costs, reciprocity, balance, cohesion, and power in exchanges	(Blau 1964; Emerson 1972; Homans 1961)
Relational Exchange Theory	Organizational	Parties in the relationship assume that the outcome of a relationship is greater than achieved by individual parties separately	Cooperation, interactions, reciprocal social and economic exchanges	(Klepper 1995; Kern 1997; Anderson/Narus 1984; Dwyer/Schurr/Oh 1987; Macneil 1974, 1978; 1980)
Psychological Contract Theory	Organizational, individual	People's beliefs and expectations about their mutual obligations in a contractual relation between that person and another party	Reciprocal exchange agreement, binding mutual obligations	(Rousseau 1989; Rousseau 1995; Rousseau et al. 1998)
Expectation Confirmation Theory	Individual, organizational	Expectations together with the following perceived performance lead to post-purchase satisfaction	Mutual expectations towards the exchange relation, confirmation, disconfirmation	(Oliver 1977; Oliver 1980)

Theoretical foundation	Level of analysis	Basic assumptions	Main variables / main focus	Key authors
Power and Politics Theories	Individual, organizational	Power, idiosyncratic interests, and politics play major roles in organizational decision-making, dependency on other organization	Different degrees of power, organizational politics, dependency	(Pfeffer 1981, 1982; Pfeffer 1992; Markus 1983; Emerson 1962)

Table 3-2. Overview of theoretical foundations applied in this thesis

3.3 The Multi-Dimensionality of Outsourcing IS Functions

3.3.1 Outsourcing Functions and the IT Service Lifecycle

The definitions above capture the term outsourcing at a very general level. While practice (cf. PAC SITSI categorization Termenière 2007, 10pp.) often classes IT services into *Project/Professional Services* (including, e.g., IT Consulting, Fixed-Price Development and Systems Integration, Contract Staff, IT Training), *Hardware Maintenance*, and *Outsourcing* (including, e.g., BPO, Application Management, Processing, Infrastructure-related Outsourcing, Application-related Outsourcing, Complete Outsourcing), literature suggests a broad use of the term outsourcing and its functions, assuming that basically all IT services can be outsourced for provision by a third party vendor (Apte 1990). Following Apte (1990, 289), Grover et al. (1994b, 35), as well as Loh and Venkatraman (1992a, 9) today's outsourcing – once tracing its roots back to the traditional timesharing and professional services of the 1960s – is an umbrella term which covers many information services, such as:

1. *Information processing* services include routine and well defined tasks such as data entry, transaction processing, or back-office clerical tasks

2. *Contract programming* comprises software development and maintenance activities such as systems analysis, programming, and testing

3. *Facilities management* agreement addresses operation and support of a system or data center functions, including hardware, software, networks, and staff; The service provider has a significant role in operating the technological resources of the service receiver

4. *System integration* includes the development of a fully integrated system from design to implementation; a systems integrator is contracted to manage the installation and operation of the integrated systems and assumes the overall responsibility for the quality and performance of a multi-vendor environment

5. *Support operations* (sometimes covered under facilities management) involve activities for maintenance and disaster recovery, as well as training, education, help desk etc.

The examples above demonstrate that the term outsourcing covers the entire spectrum of information services – ranging "from leasing a whole IS department, to just having a programmer or two to develop a simple application" (Apte 1990, 289).

In a more general and systematic way, outsourcing functions can be classified and allocated onto three levels considering the outsourcing object that is addressed (Scardino/ Young/Anderson 2007; Singh et al. 2007; Tramacere/Matlus 2007):

1. *Infrastructure-related outsourcing* includes any combination of, or all of, the product support and professional services as they specifically relate to the ongoing management of IT infrastructure. (e.g., data center operations, desktop management, network)

2. *Application-related outsourcing* includes the purchase of ongoing application services for managing, enhancing and maintaining custom or packaged software in server/host or desktop/client platforms (e.g., application development, web-hosting, ASP)

3. *Processes* involve the delegation of one or more IT-intensive business processes to an external provider that manages the selected process(es) (e.g., help desk, processing services such as payroll, card or transaction processing)

Applying a lifecycle perspective, information systems functions can be outsourced in several stages of the general lifecycle of information technology systems and services (cf. Silver/Markus/Beath 1995). The general IT service lifecycle of contains three major phases, i.e., a *planning* stage, a *design/build* phase, and a *run/operation* phase (Zarnekow/Brenner 2004; Moll 1994). However, especially in the context of outsourcing information systems, a fourth stage becomes relevant, i.e., the *support/maintenance* stage: "Because the IS manager continues to be responsible for the legacy systems that currently support the business, there is significant contention for management attention, knowledgeable resources, and project manager focus. Outsourcing of applications maintenance is a potential solution to this dilemma" (Judenberg 1994). Following (de Looff 1998, 253), IS activities in the IT services lifecycle thus comprise the *planning, design/development/implementation, operation,* and *maintenance* of the IS function.

Although the lion's share of outsourced IS functions still lies in the *operation/run stage* of infrastructure hosting (e.g., data center, desktop, network) (Tramacere/Matlus 2007), information systems functions could be outsourced in any of the four IT services lifecycle stages.

Figure 3-1 shows the different levels of outsourcing functions within the IT service lifecycle.

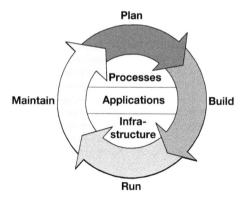

Figure 3-1. Outsourcing functions and the IT service lifecycle

3.3.2 Forms of Outsourcing Arrangements

Although outsourcing is often portrayed as an all or nothing decision, in actuality, a variety of outsourcing arrangements and options exists (Lacity/Hirschheim 1995b, 4). Since its early days more than three decades ago, outsourcing has evolved beyond providers merely taking over a function and performing higher quality work at lower cost (Apte 1990; Child 1987). Diversified outsourcing practices have emerged superseding the simple one vendor – one client arrangement where the vendor provides seemingly all IS services. Sophisticated approaches have been set in place ranging from short-term selective outsourcing deals involving multiple vendors and multiple clients to long-term strategic alliances and transformational outsourcing (Linder 2004; Lee et al. 2003).

Even more, client and vendor often share risk and reward or engage in collaborative service development of innovative IT services to generate added value (Jahner/Böhmann/Krcmar 2006b; Willcocks/Lacity 1998b). The motivation for outsourcing deals has moved beyond simple cost-savings to include value-based outsourcing, equity based outsourcing, eBusiness outsourcing, and business process outsourcing (Willcocks et al. 2004; Dibbern et al. 2004). In addition, the boost of Indian service providers such as Tata Consulting Services or Wipro has made offshoring a popular and often low-cost outsourcing practice (Apte 1990; Rottman/Lacity 2004).

A variety of classifications and typologies of sourcing decision options and also sourcing objects exists in the outsourcing literature. Not all of these classifications are very consistent, but rather mix up different categories. For the purpose of this thesis, only a selection of classifications and forms of outsourcing arrangements will be shortly depicted, considering the works of (Lacity/Hirschheim 1993a), (Millar 1994), (Wibbelsman/Maiero 1994), (Lacity/Hirschheim 1995b), (Willcocks/Lacity 1998b), (Lacity/Willcocks 2001), (Lee/Kim 1999), and (de Looff 1998).

Lacity and Hirschheim (1993a, 2pp.) proposed a taxonomy of three outsourcing options distinguished by the vendor involvement and scope of outsourcing:

1. *Body Shop* – client uses outsourcing as an option to meet short-term demand. The most common type of body shop outsourcing is the use of contract programmers/consultants which are managed by client employees. In this scenario, no assets, staff or other resources are transferred to the vendor.

2. *Project Management* – similar to the body shop scenario, outsourcing is used for a specific project or portion of IS work. Examples of project management outsourcing include the use of vendors to develop a new system, support an existing application, handle disaster recovery, provide training, or manage a network. In these cases, the vendor is responsible for managing and completing the work.

3. *Total outsourcing* – the vendor is in total charge of a significant piece of IS work. The most common type is entire outsourcing of the hardware (e.g., data center, desktops and/or telecommunications) operations or software to an outside vendor. This outsourcing strategy has become very common in the late 1980s and throughout the 1990s. Typically, the vendor charges a fixed fee for a pre-specified amount of services. Some have euphemistically termed this type of outsourcing "turning over the keys to the kingdom" (Lacity/Hirschheim 1993a, 3).

Millar (1994) suggests four common types to capture the variety of outsourcing arrangements distinguished – sometimes inconsistently – by the outsourcing degree as well as strategic aspects:

1. *General outsourcing* encompasses three alternatives:

    i. selective outsourcing – one specific portion of IS activity is chosen to be turned over to a third party, such as data center operations or desktop management;

    ii. value-added outsourcing – some IS activity is turned over to a third party vendor who is sought to provide a service which adds value to the activity that could not be cost-effectively provided by the internal IS of the client;

    iii. cooperative outsourcing – some IS activity is jointly performed by a third party provider and the internal IS department of the client.

2. *Transitional outsourcing* involves the migration from one technological (legacy) platform to another (new technology/system). This outsourcing form consists of three phases of which any one or all of these stages could be turned over to an external provider: management of the current legacy systems, transition to the new technology/system, and stabilization and maintenance of the new platform (including hardware, software, and data).

3. *Business process outsourcing* is a relatively recent outsourcing arrangement. It refers to an outsourcing relationship where a third party provider is engaged for performing an entire business function for the client organization (Willcocks et al. 2004). A number of

industries perform business processing outsourcing, in particular government, financial services (banks and insurance companies) (Wüllenweber 2007a), health care, transportation, and logistics.

4. *Business benefit or performance contracting* is also a relatively new outsourcing phenomenon. It refers to a "contractual agreement that defines the vendor's contribution to the client in terms of specific benefits to the business and defines the payment the customer will make based upon the vendor's ability to deliver those benefits. The goal is to match actual costs with actual benefits and to share the risks" (Millar 1994). Given the risks associated with traditional outsourcing (Gewald/Wüllenweber/Weitzel 2006; Wüllenweber 2007b), there is considerable interest in this form of outsourcing. However, this type of outsourcing arrangement is pursued relatively seldom in practice due to difficulties of measuring the duties of both parties and also the actual benefits. Only if the outsourced service can be easily specified and controlled by, e.g., service level agreements (SLA), measuring the benefits of the outsourcing venture can be assessed.

With a focus on the amount of outsourced services, the scope of the possible IS activities to be outsourced, as well as the involvement of external supply, Wibbelsman and Maiero (1994) discuss several variants of outsourcing. They understand the sourcing question as a "multisourcing" issue of multiple sourcing of IS services. In their point of view, the various outsourcing options can be allocated on a continuum ranging from insourcing through cosourcing to outsourcing.

On the endpoint of "insourcing" two strategies can be followed: 1) "ok as is" refers to the belief that the status quo, i.e., all IS activities are provided in-house, is the most favorable sourcing strategy. 2) "fix and keep in-house" relates to the assumption that insourcing is the preferred alternative, but the internal IS department needs to become more efficient and effective.

In a "co-sourcing" arrangement, the IS organization is re-organized by the help of a third party and then kept in-house. Another variant of the "co-sourcing" option is the "transition assistance" strategy where a third party takes on certain IS activities while the internal IS group transitions itself to a new set of skills. A last co-sourcing option is called "capability development" where a third party takes on either permanently or temporarily IS activities while the IS organization develops new capabilities. This allows the IS organization to focus on certain core capabilities (Wibbelsman/Maiero 1994).

At the other extreme point of the continuum, "outsourcing" can be pursued with an "option to reverse". Thereby IS is outsourced to a third party, but there is a specific plan which could allow the function to return in-house without excessive suffering at a later time. Lastly, there is the "divest completely" strategy where the IS function is outsourced permanently. In such cases, IS is perceived to be a non-core business function best handled by an outsourcer (Dibbern et al. 2004).

In a later work, Lacity and Hirschheim (1995b, 4pp.) offer a taxonomy of another three sourcing decision options distinguished by the degree of external supply:

1. *Total outsourcing* – the decision to transfer IS assets, leases, staff, and management responsibility for delivery of IS products and services from an internal IS function to a
   single third party vendor which represents more than 80% of the IS budget.

2. *Total insourcing* – the decision to retain the management and provision of more than
   80% of the IS budget internally after evaluating the IS services market.

3. *Selective sourcing* – the decision to source selected IS functions from external provid-
   er(s) while still providing between 20% and 80% of the IS budget internally. This strategy may include single or multiple vendors. The use of percentages of IS budget as differentiating total from selective decisions is consistent with the studies done by Willcocks and Fitzgerald (1994) which show that selective sourcing usually takes up between 25 to 40% of the formal IS budget.

Willcocks and Lacity (Willcocks/Lacity 1998b, 26pp.; Lacity/Willcocks 2001, 18pp.) distinguish between eight (resp. six) types of what they call "emerging sourcing practices":

1. *Value-added outsourcing* – the strengths of both outsourcing parties are combined to
   market new products and services (new service development) or develop mutually beneficial internal business improvements

2. *Equity holdings* – customer and vendor taking ownership in each other's companies
   (equity position)

3. *Multi-sourcing* – there is one outsourcing contract but multiple suppliers of services

4. *Offshore outsourcing* – leveraging price advantages, and skill and performance resources, abroad

5. *Co-sourcing* – the outsourcing vendors' revenue is tied to performance of the company
   that the services are provided to (performance-based contracting)

6. *Business process outsourcing* – outsourcing as process and its IT, identified as "non-
   core" that a third party can do at least as well, at competitive price

7. *Spin-offs* – the internal IS department (or selected successful IS functions) is spun off to
   become a new independent entity selling its services to the market

8. *Creative "smarter" contracting* – tougher shoppers attempt to improve on the limitations of traditional contracts; this form encompasses specialist clauses to satisfy particular customer needs

Lee (1999, 31) mentions a differentiation of outsourcing options that is not necessarily discussed extensively in the literature or in theory, but is quite common in practice. According to
Lee (1999), IS outsourcing can be classified into two categories according to the ownership of
the resources or the transfer of assets:

1. *Asset outsourcing*, which involves transfer of assets such as hardware, software, and people to service providers

2. *Service outsourcing*, which involves system integration and system management services without asset transfer

Accordingly, in practice many companies distinguish between "outtasking" (Lingnau/Stauber 2005), thereby meaning a temporary selective outsourcing of IS activities without asset transfer, and "outsourcing", meaning a long-term handing over of IS activities to a third party vendor including the transfer of assets.

A first approach to capture the multi-dimensionality of outsourcing forms and arrangements is given by de Looff (1998). Instead of simply listing some variations of outsourcing arrangements without criteria for systematically describing them, he suggests a matrix with three dimensions along which the IS function can be illustrated and allocated. Following Brussard (1988) who described information systems (as can all dynamic open systems) in analytical, functional and temporal terms, de Looff (1998, 253) suggested to apply the same trichotomy for an IS function and distinguish between the *functional information systems*, the *analytical components*, and the *temporal IS activities*. With regard to the functional dimension, information systems can be distinguished by the (business) process they support or control, i.e., the order scheduling IS, the financial IS, the IS for processing insurance claims, project planning and so on. In terms of components, an IS function can comprise hardware, software, personnel, the procedures, as well as the data. Lastly, IS activities can involve the planning, development, implementation, maintenance, and operation of information systems.

These exemplary approaches to classify different outsourcing arrangements demonstrate on the one hand the manifoldness of the outsourcing field and the varieties to carry out an outsourcing venture. On the other hand, it clearly shows the difficulties of systematically depicting different options along standardized categories or criteria. Most authors only focus on one or two specific aspects, if at all. Also, many authors do not build their classification in a systematic and consistent way and mix up different categories. While Lacity and Hirschheim (1993a) differentiate outsourcing arrangements by the *vendor involvement* and *scope of outsourcing*, Millar (1994) focused on the *outsourcing degree* as well as *strategic aspects*. Wibbelsman and Maiero (1994) instead point out the multidimensionality and describe a continuum of outsourcing options with regard to the *involvement of external supply*. Lacity and Hirschheim (1995b) offer in a later approach sourcing decision options distinguished by the *degree of external supply*. Willcocks and Lacity (Willcocks/Lacity 1998b; Lacity/Willcocks 2001) do not introduce categories, but rather describe current "trends of sourcing practices". Another quite practice-oriented distinction is put forward by Lee (1999) addressing the *ownership of the resources* or the *transfer of assets*. At last, de Looff (1998) attempts to systematically depict IS functions along their *functional, analytical,* and *temporal* character.

What even adds to the jumble of categorization efforts is the fact that the use of certain outsourcing options is not clearly specified and outsourcing researchers have not standardized on definition of outsourcing arrangements. Willcocks and Lacity (Willcocks/Lacity 1998b; Lacity/Willcocks 2001), for example, define the option "value-added outsourcing" as combining the strengths of both outsourcing parties in order to market new products and services. In

contrast, Klepper and Jones (1998) regard this type of outsourcing as an "intermediate" relationship characterized by complex work and substantial benefits. Under the same term "value-
added outsourcing" Millar (1994) understands "some IS activity that is turned over to a third
party vendor who is sought to provide a service which adds value to the activity that could not
be cost-effectively provided by the internal IS of the client". Instead, Millar (1994) defines
"cooperative outsourcing" (i.e., "some IS activity is jointly performed by a third party provider and the internal IS department of the client") in Willcocks's and Lacity's understanding of
value-added outsourcing.

To systematize the different outsourcing options mentioned in the literature, this thesis builds
upon and extends the work of von Jouanne-Diedrich et al. (2004; 2005; 2007) by integrating
the different notions of outsourcing arrangements found in the literature. Figure 3-2 summarizes the categorization attempts mentioned above and characterizes outsourcing arrangements
along nine dimensions.

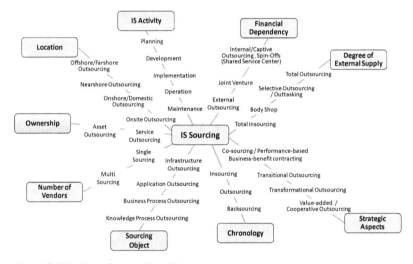

Figure 3-2. Dimensions of outsourcing options
(Source: extended from von Jouanne-Diedrich 2004; 2005; 2007)

This categorization of different outsourcing options is the result of a digest of the literature
and aims at shedding light into the jumble of inconsistent categorization approaches found in
the extant literature. Such a literature digest is an essential feature of any academic project.
"An effective review creates a firm foundation for advancing knowledge. It facilitates theory
development, closes areas where a plethora of research exists, and uncovers areas where research is needed" (Webster/Watson 2002, xiii). This categorization allows describing and
classing any outsourcing phenomenon along various dimensions.

3.4   Outsourcing Determinants and Expectations: Advantages and Disadvantages

The decision of an organization to outsource information systems to a third party provider is based on a variety of different reasons and motivations. Even if two companies decide to outsource the same IT function, this choice could be induced by a completely different rationale of each organization. Early outsourcing research thus centered its focus on examining the motivation, potential advantages and disadvantages, i.e., the benefits and risks associated with the outsourcing decision (Chalos 1995; Earl 1996; Grover/Cheon/Teng 1994a; Martinsons 1993; Palvia 1995). In this area, one of the seminal papers that investigate the determinants of outsourcing is an early work by Loh and Venkatraman (1992b).

Literature provides an abundance of determinants that examine why companies choose the outsourcing option. Some researchers argue that outsourcing results in significant cost reductions with increased management control, effective use of human resource, capacity on demand, and better access to advanced technologies (Apte 1990; Child 1987). In contrast, the opponents of outsourcing describe that it involves critical risks with potential loss of control, flexibility, qualified personnel, and competitive advantage in information management (Benko 1992; Gupta/Gupta 1992).

Dibbern et al. (2004, 25pp.) categorized the variety of motives in three areas: 1) Determinants external to the firm at the society and industry level (e.g., institutional pressures and diffusion drivers such as Kodak event); 2) Firm level determinants outside of the IS function (e.g., costs/financial situation, strategic orientation); and 3) Determinants at the IS level (e.g., characteristics of the firm's IS asset, general firm's attitude towards the IS function). Other authors differentiate between financial / economic, technological, strategic / risk / business, and political benefits as to major intents and objectives for outsourcing IT (Lacity/Hirschheim 1995b; Grover/Cheon/Teng 1994b; Grover/Cheon/Teng 1996; Cheon/Grover/Teng 1995; Smith/Mitra/Narasimhan 1998; Lee et al. 2003). And some authors even reduce the variety of outsourcing determinants to four specific motives of outsourcing: cost issues, focus on core competencies, performance enhancement, and risk dissemination (Matiaske/Mellewigt 2002).

To narrow the scope of this thesis, the categorization efforts of (Dibbern et al. 2004), (Bongard 1994), and (Grover/Cheon/Teng 1994b; Grover/Cheon/Teng 1996) will be combined and three key areas of outsourcing objectives on the level of firm determinants (excluding determinants external to the firm) will be highlighted. Determinants external to the firm will be neglected since they can hardly be shaped by the outsourcing client firm and are thus outside the scope of the strategy and governance considerations and recommendations of this thesis.

Although outsourcing is pursued for a range of objectives, the primary and most common benefits sought are *economic, i.e., financial and cost-oriented reasons* (Smith/Mitra/ Narasimhan 1998; DiRomualdo/Gurbaxani 1998). They refer to a firm's ability to utilize outsourcing to better manage its cost structure (Apte 1990; Huff 1991; Loh/Venkatraman 1992a, 1992b). Reasons include cost reduction and efficiency, improving cost control and transparency, rendering fix costs as variable costs, as well as cost degression by leveraging economies of scale, scope, and skill (Loh/Venkatraman 1992a, 12pp.; Kern/Blois 2002; Willcocks/Fitzgerald/Lacity 1996, 143; Matiaske/Mellewigt 2002). The often-cited rationale behind this motivation is that the vendor typically has better economies of scale, tighter control over fringe benefits, better access to lower-cost labor pools, and more focused expertise in managing IS. It must be noted, however, that cost reduction through IS outsourcing is controversial, especially because the provider often maintains the identical infrastructure in terms of equipment and staff and still has to make a profit through the arrangement (Lacity/Hirschheim 1993b).

Strategic objectives refer to the ability of an organization to focus on a strategic use of IS, enhance IT competence and leverage vendor's capabilities to achieve strategic advantages (Lacity/Willcocks 2001; Willcocks et al. 2004). In this case, outsourcing allows management to focus the available IS talent on IS activities, promoting competitiveness, rather than "spending time on routine activities of systems maintenance or operations" (Apte 1990). Put in simple words, the underlying motto of strategic allocation of outsourcing resources is "do what you do best, outsource the rest" (Matiaske/Mellewigt 2002).

But strategic focus in IS outsourcing can also go even further than focus on core competencies and a reallocation of resources: In between strategic intents aiming at business advantages and technological intents aiming at improved IT services, *IT-enabled innovations* have recently become an emerging customer demand for competitive success (Jahner/ Böhmann/Krcmar 2006a). While IS outsourcing is only recently and in a few cases seen as a contributor to innovation in practice, firms could draw on external resources for many activities in the innovation process in theory (Quinn 2000). Outsourcing can offer a unique knowledge potential, flexibility, and support for innovation (Willcocks et al. 2004). Especially the design, implementation and operation of IT-enabled business innovation requires a complex web of technical and business knowledge that often only a network of specialist providers can offer (Mahnke/Özcan/Overby 2006). If the client firm does not have all necessary competences in-house to generate IT-enabled innovation or internal development is slow and cost-intense, outsourcing the innovation potential by acquiring external capabilities across firm boundaries is a legitimate means to continuously fuel the organizational innovation pipe (Barney/Lee 2000). But only a few companies use the innovation capabilities of their vendor. A prominent example of IT-enabled innovations for business advantage through outsourcing is the case of the British Broadcasting Corporation (BBC) which contracted their outsourcing provider for continuous innovation in a 10-year deal (Kumar 2006).

Technological motives comprise an organization's attempt to gain access to leading-edge IT, technological expertise, improved and innovative services, i.e., the bank's ability to exploit modern IT technologies and achieve IT continuity (Lacity/Willcocks 2001). This also comprises efforts to "avoid the risk of technological obsolescence that results from dynamic changes in IT" (Grover/Cheon/Teng 1996, 93). Access to leading-edge technology and know-how also enables the competitiveness of product offerings of the company's general portfolio through the use of state-of-the-art technology that may not be easily available in-house (Apte 1990).

These categories, described above, are not exhaustive, but identify the major drivers of IS outsourcing. For a more comprehensive and detailed understanding of motivation factors that inspire the outsourcing decision, Table 3-3 integrates categorization attempts of various authors and gives an extended overview of different motives of outsourcing beyond the specific description of the three key motives described above. Thereby it has to be noted that the motives as well as the categories cannot fully be mutually exclusive, as they are multidimensional by nature. For example, the general strategic motive of achieving business flexibility will probably come along with rendering IT as a variable cost or meeting short-term demand of highly qualified IT personnel.

Level of analysis	Category / Focus Motive	Specific motive	Exemplary references for investigated motive
Determinants external to the firm at the society and industry level / Environment	Institutional pressures	Influence from peer organizations	(Ang/Cummings 1997)
		Influence from federal regulators, government etc.	(Ang/Cummings 1997)
	Communication channels as diffusion drivers	Internal (individuals from other organizations)	(Loh/Venkatraman 1992b), (Hu/Saunders/Gebelt 1997)
		External (e.g., media)	(Loh/Venkatraman 1992b), (Hu/Saunders/Gebelt 1997)
		Specific influence of Kodak outsourcing event: imitating behavior	(Loh/Venkatraman 1992b), (Hu/Saunders/Gebelt 1997), (Willcocks/Lacity 1998b)
	Technological and human dynamics	Dynamics of (IS) skills market	(Slaugther/Ang 1996)
	Environmental uncertainty	Reduce technological risk and uncertainty	(Kim/Chung 2003), (McLellan/Marcolin/Beamish 1995)
Firm level determinants outside of the IS function	Costs / Financial situation	Cost reduction / containment (through economies of scale, scope and skill)	(Alpar/Saharia 1995), (Arnett/Jones 1994), (Lacity/Hirschheim 1994), (McFarlan/Nolan 1995), (Palvia 1995), (Jurison 1998), (Sobol/Apte 1998), (Lacity/Hirschheim 1995b), (Lacity/Hirschheim 1993a), (Lacity/Willcocks 2001)
		Variabilization of fixed costs / restructure IS budget	(Bongard 1994), (Lacity/Hirschheim 1995b), (Lacity/Willcocks 2001)
		Cost control	(Lacity/Hirschheim 1995b)
		Cost transparency and predictability	(Bongard 1994), (Apte 1990), (Grover/Cheon/Teng 1994b)
		Cost awareness	(Bongard 1994)
		Business cost structure	(Loh/Venkatraman 1992a)
		Business financial performance	(Loh/Venkatraman 1992a)
		Financial leverage	(Loh/Venkatraman 1992a)
		Generating cash / Cash infusion	(Smith/Mitra/Narasimhan 1998), (Lacity/Hirschheim 1994), (McFarlan/Nolan 1995), (Jurison 1998)
		Financial impact: Business benefits of outsourcing (focus, financial, savings)	(Loh/Venkatraman 1995)
	Strategy / Business	Focus on core competencies, core business (and thus strategic IS use)	(Apte 1990), (Smith/Mitra/Narasimhan 1998), (Slaugther/Ang 1996), (Sobol/Apte 1998), (Lacity/Willcocks 2001), (Grover/Cheon/Teng 1994b)
		Dissemination of risks induced by technological dynamics	(Bongard 1994)

Level of analysis	Category / Focus Motive	Specific motive	Exemplary references for investigated motive
		Contractually agreed shifting of risks to the vendor	(Bongard 1994)
		Flexibility of business action	(Kim/Chung 2003), (Jahner/Böhmann/Krcmar 2006a), (Slaugther/Ang 1996), (Jurison 1998)
		Combine IT excellence of client and vendor to generate new products or services / business or IT innovation (value-added outsourcing) → see section 'Strategy'	(Willcocks/Lacity 1998b; Lacity/Willcocks 2001)
		New market activities: Facilitate mergers and acquisitions, or carve outs (demergers), provide IS for start-up company, joint ventures, spin-offs, equity-holding deals	(Lacity/Hirschheim 1995b), (Lacity/Willcocks 2001)
	Political	Reaction to the efficiency imperative	(Lacity/Hirschheim 1993a), (Lacity/Hirschheim 1995b)
		Need to acquire or justify new resources	(Lacity/Hirschheim 1993a), (Lacity/Hirschheim 1995b)
		Reaction to the 'bandwagon' of outsourcing (i.e., positive media reports)	(Lacity/Hirschheim 1993a), (Lacity/Hirschheim 1995b)
		Vehicle for organizational change (e.g., elimination of a troublesome function) / business transition	(McLellan/Marcolin/Beamish 1995), (Jurison 1998), (Lacity/Hirschheim 1993a), (Lacity/Hirschheim 1995b), (Lacity/Willcocks 2001)
		Enhance personal or departmental credibility	(Lacity/Hirschheim 1993a), (Lacity/Hirschheim 1995b)
	Personnel / Access to Resources	Access to highly qualified IT personnel	(Bongard 1994), (Sobol/Apte 1998), (Lacity/Willcocks 2001), (Grover/Cheon/Teng 1994b)
		Load removal of internal IT	(Bongard 1994)
		Independence from staff shortages / Meet short-term volatile demands	(Bongard 1994), (Lacity/Willcocks 2001), (Grover/Cheon/Teng 1994b)
		Independence from individual internal IT knowledge	(Bongard 1994), (Apte 1990)
		Downsizing of staff, reduce head count	(Bongard 1994)
Determinants at the IS level	Technology / Know-How	Access to leading-edge technology (systems)	(Apte 1990), (Bongard 1994), (Jurison 1998), (Sobol/Apte 1998), (Lacity/Hirschheim 1995b)
		Faster applications or systems development	(Jurison 1998)
		Improved quality of IS and service	(Smith/Mitra/Narasimhan 1998), (Lacity/Hirschheim 1995b)
		Access to highly qualified IT personnel, technical expertise → see also section 'Personnel'	(Apte 1990), (Bongard 1994), (Sobol/Apte 1998), (Lacity/Hirschheim 1995b), (Lacity/Willcocks 2001), (Grover/Cheon/Teng 1994b)
		Focus the internal IS staff on core technical activities	(Lacity/Hirschheim 1995b), (Grover/Cheon/Teng 1994b)
		Avoidance of obsolescence risk	(Grover/Cheon/Teng 1994b)

Level of analysis	Category / Focus Motive	Specific motive	Exemplary references for investigated motive
		Combine IT excellence of client and vendor to generate new products or services / IT innovations (value-added outsourcing) → see section 'Strategy'	(Willcocks/Lacity 1998b; Lacity/Willcocks 2001)
		Increased data security (through back-up data)	(Bongard 1994)

Table 3-3. Compilation of outsourcing motives
(Source: adapted and extended from Dibbern et al. 2004; Bongard 1994; Grover/Cheon/Teng 1994b;
Grover/Cheon/Teng 1996)

Although outsourcing motives might be multi-dimensional and should be considered cumulative, rather than mutually exclusive, several studies indicate that there is a trade-off between achieving efficiency (cost and quality related) and strategic advantages (outlining strategic and transactional style) (Weill/Broadbent 1998; Kogut/Zander 1992; DiRomualdo/Gurbaxani 1998; McLellan/Marcolin/Beamish 1995; Moran/Ghoshal 1999; Miranda/Kavan 2005). As outlined by Miranda and Kavan (2005) efficiency objectives are closely related to value capture (allocative efficiency) and strategic objectives are related to value creation (adaptive efficiency). However, there is a trade-off between value creation and capture: achieving value capture makes organizational environment more secure and efficient, but hinders innovative, knowledge creation processes. For example, vendors that are contracted to minimize costs will hardly suggest innovative systems or processes as this will not be rewarded by the client (DiRomualdo/Gurbaxani 1998).

The risks and costs of outsourcing are sometimes lost amid the rhetoric about outsourcing's benefits (Meyer 1994). Thus, the motives and benefits mentioned above need to be weighed against a number of risks and potential disadvantages associated with outsourcing. Grover (1994b, 38pp.) distinguishes three categories of potential disadvantages and pitfalls in IS outsourcing:

The first category addresses *managerial factors*. Within this category, *loss of flexibility or control* could be identified as one potential threat: From the point of view of IS executives, outsourcing reduces real or perceived control over both the quality of software and the timetable of a project since the work is now being carried out by people not under direct supervision (Foxman 1994) which might eventually lead to a loss of strategic alignment (Walker 1985). Also the outsourcing client can lose touch with the advances in information technology and thereby may lose the ability to plan and implement strategic application of IT (Sobol/Apte 1998). Paradoxically, the issue of flexibility, here a potential hindering factor, is also often mentioned as an expected benefit of outsourcing (Kim/Chung 2003). A second problem of managerial disadvantages deals with the *threat to long-term career prospects*. With outsourcing, the service client often finds that many IS professionals do not find suitable jobs or promising career paths in other areas of the corporation. In fact, addressing the personnel displacement caused by outsourcing discourages many IS executives from evaluating the option objectively. IS personnel is often little motivated to do the remaining internal IS once the internal IS department is downsized (Bongard 1994). A third problem might arise due to *technology and know-how dependencies*. For an organization, it is also difficult to retain the key

IS people and know-how. If the outsourcing venture fails or does not want to continued, insourcing or backsourcing is a difficult to pursue. Not only might the client be obligated to a long-term contract in some cases, but even more can this option only be conducted with high costs. The service client is "locked-in" and dependent on the technology, processes and knowledge of the service provider (Bongard 1994).

The second category of disadvantages concerns *cost related issues*. Two sub-factors affect cost-induced problems. First, *increased coordination or transactional costs* might pose a problem. Outsourcing may require increasing time to communicate and coordinate with the service provider, typically, in formalized settings. The costs of negotiating and monitoring the outsourcing contract are potentially wide ranging, exhaustive, and substantial. Second, *hidden or potential costs* that may not be calculated upfront may arise. Additional costs may be sustained, e.g., in switching costs to establish an outsourcing client-vendor mode, releasing or transferring employees, license transfer by software vendors, maintenance costs for legacy systems, and re-negotiating contracts (Due 1992). Due to the dynamics of the field of information technologies, price calculations are difficult to pursue upfront (Bongard 1994).

A last category of potential outsourcing barriers deals with *conflicting interest factors between stakeholders*. Here, general problems between principal and agent as theorized in agency theory might arise. One dilemma is caused by a *profit-motivated service provider*. In some cases, the profit motive of the service provider might not be in the best interests of the service receiver. As Lacity and Willcocks (2003, 122) state there is an inherent adversarial nature in outsourcing contracts "in that a dollar out of the customer's pocket is a dollar in the supplier's pocket". Some service providers are in the business of maximizing their profit at any cost; but this could run counter to a service receiver's interest. Second, *systems and data confidentiality* is a critical issue in outsourcing. Since the service provider may offer a customized, but standardized system to several customers, with some direct competitors, concern arises over data security.

The abundant variety of advantages and disadvantages associated with IS outsourcing reveals that outsourcing might not necessarily be a 'panacea' for all organizations. Moreover, benefits and risks have to be evaluated carefully against each other and more important, against the vendor's expectations. All too many organizations contract and manage tightly for cost efficiency, but then also expect the sort of risk sharing and business transformation that can only be obtained from a strategic alliance partnership – a clear mismatch of mutual expectations between client and vendor (Kern/Willcocks/van Heck 2002) caused by mixed and incongruent outsourcing motives which will eventually lead to unsuccessful outsourcing.

Finally, a detailed description of the manifold expectations towards outsourcing is also crucial to develop an understanding that this diversity of expectations results in the necessity to apply different mechanisms to successfully manage and govern an outsourcing relationship. So far, outsourcing research has missed to link outsourcing expectations with appropriate governance patterns by differentiating several groups of outsourcing clients. It is yet unclear under which circumstances certain governance modes such as contractual governance or relational governance are appropriate. Many aspects of outsourcing ventures have been investigated, but contingency factors and the context in which outsourcing arrangements are best governed have not been addressed comprehensively in the literature. This challenge is addressed in this thesis and will be empirically analyzed in chapter 5 (p. 111ff.) and 6 (p. 215ff.). The foundation of outsourcing relationships as one of the current research streams in IS outsourcing as well as governance aspects of IS outsourcing ventures are laid out in the subsequent chapters.

3.5 Prior Research on IS Outsourcing Relationships: State of the Art

3.5.1 Evolution of IS Outsourcing Research towards a Relationship Focus

Information systems outsourcing has been one of the core research issues of the management of information systems for quite a few years (Krcmar 2005; Willcocks/Lacity 1998b). But outsourcing research[4] and its perspectives have changed a lot in the last three decades.

Early outsourcing research had centered on acquisition with a focus on the *make-or-buy* decision between in-house and external acquisition of information technology (Buchowicz 1991). But with Kodak's 1989 outsourcing decision, outsourcing emerged as a key method of managing information systems (Loh/Venkatraman 1992b) (see also chapter 3.1, p. 15ff.) and a pivotal issue concerned the *motivation* why to outsource. Debates then shifted from whether or not to outsource to *how much* to outsource (scope) with various options such as e.g., selective or total outsourcing (Lacity/Hirschheim 1993a). A difficult research issue pertained to, determining the effective outsourcing performance (Loh/Venkatraman 1995). Due to the largely unsolved *performance* issue, research experienced a backlash of the outsourcing euphoria resulting in a discussion about *insourcing* and *backsourcing options* of information technology. But despite its critics, outsourcing was by then already entangled into most organizations' strategic plans and the *contract* specifying the relation between outsourcing providers and their clients emerged as a centerpiece issue (Saunders/Gebelt/Hu 1997). Although outsourcing contracts were often designed in a complex fashion to cover unexpected contingencies or opportunistic service provider behavior, it was impossible to account for every possible scenario in a contract, and client-vendor interactions often went beyond rules and contractual agreements. Instead they additionally relied on soft factors such as trust, commitment, and mutual interest. A closer relationship between clients and their service providers emerged, recognized as *partner-based* or *relationship* outsourcing (Kern 1997; Willcocks/Kern 1998; Lee/Kim 1999; Goles 2001). Many organizations engaged in this sort of partnership with their outsourcing vendors after experiencing the limitations of legal contracts (Koh/Ang/Straub 2004; Kern/Willcocks 2000a). As a result, an effective relationship rather than the actual service or outsourcing function itself became known as a key predictor of outsourcing success (Lee/Kim 1999; Goles 2001).

Lee et al. (2003) graphically illustrate the evolution of outsourcing research issues from the plain "make-or-buy" decision towards the role of relationship issues and the emergence of a partnership-based view in IS outsourcing (see Figure 3-3). The authors distinguished between two stages of IS outsourcing evolution, the first being characterized as "driven by client's self

---

[4] A remarkably comprehensive digest of literature on the topics and evolution of IS outsourcing is given by (Hui/Beath 2002; Dibbern et al. 2004; Gonzalez/Gasco/Llopis 2006; Lee et al. 2003; Sargent 2006).

interest, shaped by a hierarchical relationship and dictated by a win-lose strategy" (Lee et al. 2003, 87). The second stage of IT outsourcing in contrast marked the beginning of a mutual exchange relationship orientation where the outsourcing vendor is regarded as a partner. The vendor is provided with management responsibility and risk sharing competence, eventually joining the client as an equal stakeholder in the process.

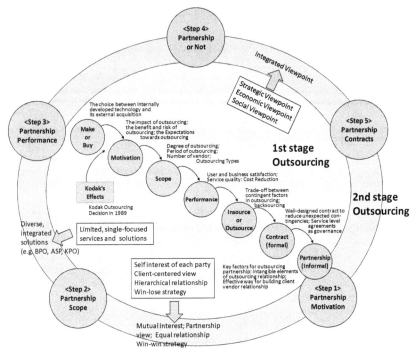

Figure 3-3. Evolution of outsourcing research issues
(Source: adapted from Lee et al. 2003)

3.5.2 The Relationship Perspective in IS Outsourcing

In line with this relationship-focused development and new understanding of outsourcing, outsourcing can be termed a contractual-based exchange relation (Kern/Willcocks 2000b) and a form of strategic information partnership which offers both parties mutual access to information, resources, and customers (Konsynski/McFarlan 1990). Interorganizational or business-to-business (B2B) relationships are neither new to the information systems literature, nor to other fields of research. They have been studied from various perspectives and in several academic disciplines, among them are general management (Ring/Van de Ven 1994; Oliver

1990), marketing (Anderson/Narus 1990; Dwyer/Schurr/Oh 1987), psychology (Smith 1998), and IS[5] (Henderson 1990; Konsynski/McFarlan 1990; Lasher/Ives/Jarvenpaa 1991).

Recalling the general definitions of IS outsourcing compiled in chapter 3.1.2 (p. 18ff.) and combining them with a broad understanding of interorganizational relationships[6] as relatively enduring transactions and linkages that make the relationship participants interdependent, and thus require coordinated action and cooperation to achieve mutual benefits (Oliver 1990, 241; Anderson/Narus 1990, 42), leads to a specific definition of an outsourcing relationship. This definition is adopted from Goles and Chin (2005, 49) - who extensively explored the relationship perspective in IS outsourcing - and will be used as a working definition of an IS outsourcing relationship throughout this research:

An IS outsourcing relationship is *"an ongoing [...] linkage between an outsourcing vendor and customer arising from a contractual agreement to provide one or more comprehensive IT activities, processes, or services with the understanding that the benefits attained by each firm are at least in part dependent on the other."* (Goles/Chin 2005, 49)

Despite a shared understanding of interorganizational relationships between various disciplines (IS being among them), one has to acknowledge that relationship management in information systems outsourcing is fundamentally different from other interorganizational relationships. As elaborated on in chapter 3.1.1 (p. 16ff.), this difference arises from the nature and inherent characteristics of information systems as being interrelated and pervasive through basically all organizational activities, heterogeneous and difficult to anticipate and specify upfront (Lacity/Willcocks 2001; Dibbern et al. 2004; Willcocks/Fitzgerald/Lacity 1996; Lacity/Willcocks 2003). Hence, general relationship management approaches or classifications from other academic disciplines as, e.g., developed in marketing business-to-business relationships, strategic management or other contractual literature are not necessarily applicable for IS outsourcing. New approaches have to be developed that consider the specific features inherent to IS.

IS outsourcing relationships are a multi-faceted and complex phenomenon. Literature thus provides various relationship factors that determine an outsourcing relationship (Alborz/Seddon/Scheepers 2004; Goles 2001; Goles/Chin 2005; Kern 1997; Kern/Willcocks 2000b). To gain a systematic overview of this vast variety of elements several authors have grouped such relationship factors in two distinct categories: inherent, sustainable characteristics that underlie a relationship and on-going, operational factors that affect the daily routines of the relationship (Henderson 1990; Goles/Chin 2005; Lambe/Spekman/Hunt 2000). Henderson (1990), for example, differentiates between Partnership in Context (PIC), focusing on embedded factors of the relationship, and Partnership in Action (PIA), i.e., ongoing everyday actions. For the purpose of this research a similar distinction provided by Goles and Chin (2005) will be adopted. They present a detailed and systematic conceptualization of those factors, distinguishing between attributes of an outsourcing relationship and processes. In this context, *attributes* can be described as the inherent characteristics or key properties that estab-

---

[5] Kern and Willcocks (2000b) provide a comprehensive overview of IS literature on relationships.
[6] Klepper summarizes studies of partnering from the management literature (Klepper 1998).

lish the relationship and contribute to its sustainability and functionality, while *processes* are understood as ongoing actions that affect the operational performance of the partnership and also form the attributes. Processes focus on the operational aspects of an outsourcing relationship can thus be regarded as the "key factors that create the day-to-day working relationship" (Henderson 1990, 9).

Chapter 3.6.4 will describe the relationship factors in more detail. Table 3-4 (to be found in chapter 3.6.4, p. 65ff.) illustrates the myriad of relationship factors that can be found in the management literature. This digest was based on an extensive literature review of papers related to relationships in various disciplines (mainly marketing, behavioral science, psychology, sociology, economics, administrative science, and IS). Astonishingly, despite the exorbitant number of relationship factors, extant research has missed to accordingly consider and integrate these factors depending on the outsourcing context and configuration.

3.5.3   Approaches for Classifying IS Outsourcing Relationships

Literature shows that first approaches of a systematization of IS outsourcing relationships exist (Kern/Willcocks/van Heck 2002; Kishore et al. 2003; Nam et al. 1996). Nam et al. (1996) propose a two-dimensional framework for describing outsourcing relationships along the dimensions "extent of ownership substitution by outsourcing vendors" and "strategic impact of the outsourced IS." Ownership substitution focuses on the aspect most important in an outsourcing relationship—the degree to which ownership or control of various IS assets have been transferred to a third party provider. "Strategic impact of the outsourced IS" captures the influence the outsourced ITS portfolio has on a firm's competitive positioning and its long-term strategy. If the outsourced ITS portfolio adds value to a firm's competitive advantage (e.g., by improving key business processes, or by enhancing its relationships with its customers or suppliers) the strategic impact of the outsourced portfolio is deemed to be high. The framework classifies outsourcing relationships into four types (a framework called FORT – four outsourcing relationship types): support, alignment, reliance, and alliance. According to Kishore et al. (2003) the framework can be used to depict both static and dynamic aspects of client-provider relationships and then utilized to examine the movement of organizations' changing IS outsourcing relationships over time within or across the four relationship cells. As outsourcing relationships are not static, but rather likely to change and evolve over time due to changes in the external and internal environment, Kishore et al. (2003) proposed an evolution of outsourcing relationships in terms of possible movements of client firms across and within the four identified types of the framework. The empirical basis for the framework is grounded on a number of exploratory case studies.

Based on the notion that a strong relationship exists between a client's organization's strategic intent, the kind of technical capability, and the type of relationship needed to match strategy to supplier capability, Kern et al. (2002) classified four main types of IS outsourcing relationships along two other dimensions: "strategic intent" and "technical capability." Strategic intent, in terms of expectations from outsourcing, is divided here into whether the focus is on achieving business value or on achieving IT efficiencies. The other dimension, i.e., technical capability, refers to choosing an external source to gain a distinctive technical leadership or to gain access merely to technical resources from a resource pool (Kern/Willcocks/van Heck

2002, 65). The matrix sets up four possible relationships: Technical Supply Relationship, Business Service, Business Alliance, and Technology Partnering. The framework of Kern et al. (2002) is based on conceptual thinking rather than an empirical basis.

These classification approaches contribute to a more systematic understanding of outsourcing relationship arrangements. They categorize different types of outsourcing relationships along important dimensions such as strategic intent or technical capability. However, the approaches are rather one-sided, as they include only two selected, rather than an exhaustive set of dimensions to describe a type of outsourcing relationship. It remains unclear why certain dimensions such as "strategic intent" and "technical capability" are chosen as the main and constitutive dimensions to distinguish different outsourcing relationships. As the field of IS outsourcing has become more complex and diversified, it becomes necessary to include various factors into the analysis of relationship types to provide a comprehensive typology of different relationships. Furthermore, existing classifications are often grounded on weak empirical assumptions and rely on anecdotal evidence or conceptual thinking. Representative recommendations can hardly be derived from such classifications.

As seen above, different approaches use different categories to classify outsourcing ventures. But it is yet unclear which dimensions should be drawn on to comprehensively describe an IS outsourcing relationship. The elements of an IS outsourcing relationship will thus be described in the next chapter.

3.6 Constitutive Factors of an IS Outsourcing Relationship

When browsing the literature on outsourcing relationships, a vast variety of relationship factors can be identified. Before showing this variety of relationship factors (see Table 3-4), a general picture of the pillars of an IS outsourcing relationship has to be given. To gain an overall perception of an IS outsourcing relationship, these factors have to be expanded with general factors that need to be considered in an outsourcing arrangement (e.g., motivation for outsourcing, outsourcing object, etc.).

The most important and constitutive factors of an outsourcing relationship can be grouped into four categories. These categories build upon and expand the relationship properties suggested by Kern and Willcocks (2000b). The categories and their subsequent factors were the basis for the development of the framework for describing and differentiating outsourcing relationships (see chapter 3.8, p. 71ff.).

3.6.1 Strategic Intent and Contextual Factors

Strategic intent focuses on what Kern and Willcocks (2000b) call the contextual dimension of an outsourcing relationship. It encapsulates the objectives and expectations of the client towards the outsourcing engagement and also defines the role of the vendor. Derived from Expectation Confirmation Theory and also elaborated in chapter 3.4 (p. 39ff.), the client's decision to outsource IS is based on a number of expectations associated with outsourcing. Usually, these expectations comprise some combination of financial / economic, technological, strategic / risk / business, and political benefits (Lacity/Hirschheim 1995b; Grover/Cheon/Teng 1994b; Grover/Cheon/Teng 1996; Cheon/Grover/Teng 1995; Smith/Mitra/Narasimhan 1998; Lee et al. 2003). Such expectations and objectives in turn are determined by the internal and external environment and challenges of both client and vendor (Lacity/Hirschheim 1994).

External factors such as the industry of the outsourcing client shape the outsourcing environment as well as internal characterizing factors. Those internal factors comprise on the one hand company characteristics such as firm size (in annual sales or number of employees), but also IT-specific determinants such as the company's dedicated IT budget or the general role of IT for the company on the other hand. It can be assumed that depending on the essence of the outsourcing deal, those factors might vary. For example, in cost- or efficiency-focused outsourcing arrangements – as opposed to strategic alliance arrangements – the strategic impact of IT for the company is regarded differently. Also the involvement of the service provider in proactive planning and developing of new IS in the client firm might play a different (e.g., minor) role compared to, e.g., strategic alliance arrangements (Kishore et al. 2003). Those assumptions have to be validated by empirical data (as laid out in chapter 5, p. 111ff.).

3.6.2 Relationship Architecture

By relationship architecture the structure and conditions of an outsourcing arrangement are comprised. Concerning relational architectures Sambamurthy and Zmud (2000) distinguish between (1) strategic architectures that reflect relatively stable relationships with a limited number of partners; (2) extended networks that arise for providing external commodity IT, and (3) virtual networks which are loose arrangements with a large number of potential partners as needed. But within these different setups, the relational architecture, i.e., the setup of the outsourcing arrangement, can be characterized in greater detail along a number of criteria. For example, the architecture of the outsourcing, mutual dependency, or relationship duration comprises factors that determine the arrangement and experience a wide variety in different outsourcing settings. Many of the factors that constitute the relational architecture of an outsourcing arrangement have been introduced in the previous chapters and will thus be only briefly described on the surface.

For example, the degree of mutual dependency between the outsourcing parties as derived from power politics theory (see chapter 3.2.5, p. 28ff.) strongly shapes the relationship between the outsourcing partners. In this context the power relation between client and vendor has to be considered. Asymmetries in the power relations result from mutual dependencies (Easton 1992). They become critical if the impact of one party is dominant and leads, e.g., to the danger of opportunistic behavior. In long-term, stable outsourcing relationships, where large parts of the information technology has been outsourced to a vendor, the vendor most often dominates the outsourcing relationship due to lock-in effects. In selective outsourcing arrangements a client can distribute the risk and dependencies to various vendors and thus minimizes the overall risk (Kern 1997). Lacity and Willcocks (2003) emphasize that well-balanced power structures play a major role when common goals and benefit expectations are pursued, but also identified three other common types of customer-supplier interactions besides adversarial: tentative, cooperative, and collaborative.

Another important factor that has a strong impact on the outsourcing deal is the company's experience with outsourcing. The issue of managers' prior experience with outsourcing has been scrutinized in some studies (Benamati/Rajkumar 2002). Some authors have empirically researched the influence of outsourcing experience on the outsourcing decision (see, e.g., Lacity/Willcocks 2003; Grover/Cheon/Teng 1996; Lee et al. 2000). Others have investigated the aspect of partnership experience (Lee/Kim 1999). Featherman and Pavlou (2003) and also Aubert et al. (2002) investigated the relation between outsourcing experience and perceived risk. In his work, Dibbern considered experience as a driving factor for the composition of the outsourcing arrangement (Dibbern 2004).

Further constitutive elements of the relational architecture of the outsourcing venture comprise the actual outsourcing object/function, the number of involved vendors, the degree of outsourcing, the duration / length of outsourcing contract, the dominating pricing model, the outsourcing alliance model, as well as the dependency on the service provider (degree of switching costs) and the goal alignment between the outsourcing parties. Most of these aspects have been elaborated in the previous chapters and will thus be only mentioned shortly here (see chapter 3.3, p. 31ff.). An overview of the elements of each category is given in chapter 3.8 (p. 71ff.) where the framework is presented.

3.6.3 Governance and Monitoring Mechanisms

Given the sometimes inconsistent reports on outsourcing successes and failures (Lacity/Willcocks 1998), various researchers have attributed an important role to a thoughtful and thorough *management and governance* of the outsourcing venture as an important design element of an outsourcing relationship (Clark/Zmud/McCray 1995; Davis 1996; Klepper 1995; McFarlan/Nolan 1995; Willcocks/Choi 1995). Clark et al. noted that "the truly critical success factors associated with successful outsourcing are those associated with vendor governance" (Clark/Zmud/McCray 1995, 234). From a managerial perspective IT decision-makers design instruments to measure and monitor performance and take appropriate actions to achieve the necessary balance of risk and return that makes the outsourcing venture successful. In general, the OECD's Principles of Corporate Governance (2004) states that governance provides the structure through which the objectives for an organization are set, attained, and monitored. Governance frameworks should also offer a means for providing an incentive for the management to achieve the objectives. Governance designates the decision rights related to objective-setting, monitoring, and evaluation in organizations, while the management function makes and implements decisions that are consistent with the governance frameworks (George/Hirschheim/Murungi 2007).

Within the research community, IT governance has begun to be recognized as an important component of IT strategy in conceptual frameworks (Henderson/Venkatram 1992). In general, IT governance is the organizational capability exercised by the board, executive management and IT management to control the formulation and implementation of IT strategy and in this way ensuring the fusion of business and IT (van Grembergen 2006). The governance of IT in a broad sense has been introduced and extended in academia by Weill and Ross who are among the most prominent researchers in this research stream. They defined IT governance as "specifying the decision rights and accountability framework to encourage desirable behavior in the use of IT" (Weill/Ross 2004). In contrast, the IT Governance Institute expands the definition to include underpinning mechanisms: "... the leadership and organisational structures and processes that ensure that the organisation's IT sustains and extends the organisation's strategies and objectives" (ITGI 2003). To some extent, IT governance is similar to the governance of other management areas, such as the financial management. In general, firms encourage particular desirable behavior that exploit and reinforce human resources, systems, and intangible assets that comprise their core competency in order to achieve their goals (Weill 2002). Four critical domains with key decisions for IT can be identified in the IT governance domain (Weill 2002):

1. *IT principles*: they are high-level statements about how IT is used in a company. These principles capture the essence of a firm's future direction and which role IT plays in this context (Broadbent/Weill 1997; Davenport/Hammer/Metsisto 1989)

2. *IT infrastructure strategies*: they relate to shared and standard IT services including the network, help desk, customer data, and applications (Weill 2002)

3. *IT architecture*: the architecture is a set of policies and rules that govern the use of IT and includes standards and guidelines for technology, use of data, design of application as well as IT-related processes (Weill 2002)

4. *IT investment and prioritization*: these issues cover the whole decision process of where IT investments should be focused

While this understanding of IT governance is very much focused on the internal management of the IT resources, other authors expand the perspective of governance to an interorganizational context and stress the management aspect. Then, governance can be understood as the "means by which order is accomplished in a relation in which potential conflict threatens to undo or upset opportunities for mutual gains" (Williamson 1998, 76). In the context of IS outsourcing, governance encompasses the management techniques employed to establish and maintain a cooperative relationship between the client and the vendor organization (Behrens 2006). Most research on governance in IS outsourcing (e.g., Miranda/Kavan 2005) also uses Weill and Ross' definition as a starting point.

Miranda and Kavan see outsourcing governance as a more dynamic concept, comprising not only of pre-specified frameworks, but also including the structural frameworks that arise from the interaction between client and vendor. Outsourcing governance encompasses a complex set of issues including performance measurement and management, staffing and talent management, and relationship building and development (George/Hirschheim/Murungi 2007).

Beulen (2004) developed a descriptive framework that depicts governance factors for three dimensions of the IS outsourcing relationship. While the framework identifies the structural factors associated with the outsourcing relationship, it does not provide a categorization of key decisions or responsibilities(George/Hirschheim/Murungi 2007). Miranda and Kavan (2005) identify "two moments of governance" revolving around two types of contracts that they identify occur during an outsourcing contract: the legal promissory contract and the relationship-based psychological contract (this will be described in more detail later).

Gewald and Helbig (2006) present a best-practice governance model deployed by a large out-sourcing service provider. The organizational structures for communication, joint processes, and relationship management of ITO and the facilitation of the management of the outsourc-ing arrangement through these structures are described. When reviewing different governance frameworks in IS outsourcing, George et al. (2007) conclude that published reports of such comprehensive frameworks are hard to find; and substantiates the need for further research in this area.

Vendor governance can be viewed as a range of alternatives from a very tight, lengthy, and properly structured contract (arm's length governance) to no contract with a true partnership alliance build on mutual trust (embedded governance) (Clark/Zmud/McCray 1995). Many researchers stress the importance of both contractual and relational governance (Klepper 1995; Goles/Chin 2005). Therefore, outsourcing is often labeled a contractual-based exchange relation (Kern/Willcocks 2000b). However, the importance and design of the contract and the relationship change during outsourcing phases (Miranda/Kavan 2005). As shown by Miranda and Kavan (2005) the development of these instruments differ with respect to value capture (achieving desired efficiency) and value creation (achieving desired innovations), but become more relational than transactional. In other words, the adequate governance approach (rela-tional vs. formal) depends on the intent and the expected and achieved benefits (strategic vs. non-strategic) of the outsourcing venture.

The organization and management literature has also identified a number of different control and coordination mechanisms besides contractual and relational governance (for classi-fications see, e.g., Jaworski 1988; Martinez/Jarillo 1989). Other mechanisms set in place to manage an outsourcing venture comprise, e.g., governance via structures and roles, gover-nance via certain processes or governance via experience and risk-reward-sharing incentives.

A commonly used distinction of governance mechanisms is between formal and informal me-chanisms (Behrens 2006).

Formal governance mechanisms are focused on structured results and use explicit policies to monitor and reward desirable behavior (Das/Teng 2001). According to Ouchi and Maguire (1975), two main types of formal mechanisms can be distinguished: Outcome-based mechan-isms rely on the measurement of end results, whereas behavior-based mechanisms are grounded on observing behaviors directly and rewarding compliance with mandated proce-dures. Behavior-based approaches can be personal or impersonal depending on whether the bonds and relationships between individual actors are in the focus or not.

Informal approaches focus on social ties and inter-personal contact between the involved ac-tors to monitor and encourage desirable behavior. In contrast to formal mechanisms, rules and expectations are not necessarily explicitly defined and codified and most often they can hard-ly be observed directly.

In the context of IS outsourcing, Behrens (2006) suggested four important governance me-chanisms: *contracts* (formal, outcome-based), *processes* (formal, behavior-based, imperson-al), *structural liaison devices / roles* (formal, behavior-based, personal), and *relational norms* (informal). In addition to these four mechanisms, two other approaches also gained attention as governance means, i.e., the role of *risk-reward sharing incentives* (Lacity/Willcocks 1998) as special case and element of contracts and also the role of *staff experience with outsourcing* as a means to govern the daily working relationship (Lee/Kim 1999).

Figure 3-4 gives a systematic overview of different approaches for outsourcing governance. The four main approaches and also the additional approaches of risk-reward sharing incentives and staff experience will be described in the following chapters.

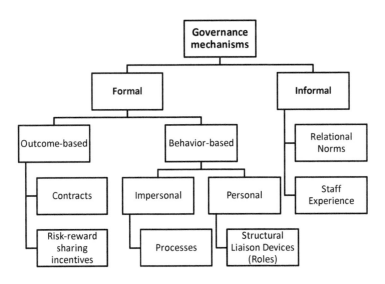

Figure 3-4. Classification scheme of IS outsourcing governance approaches
(Source: extended from Behrens 2006)

3.6.3.1   Formal Contractual Governance

Contracts as formal mutual agreements engaged by both parties have traditionally been an essential part of every outsourcing arrangement and the primary vehicle of governing outsourcing relationships (Saunders/Gebelt/Hu 1997; Clark/Zmud/McCray 1995). Formal contracts represent promises or obligations to perform particular actions in the future (Macneil 1978). From a theoretical perspective, literature on TCE suggests that managers design governance approaches by responding to exchange hazards (risks) (Williamson 1985; 1991b). According to the logic of transaction cost economics, the manager's task is to build governance arrangements with minimal cost that ensure the delivery of the desired quantity, price, and quality of the vendor's services. The manager, therefore, crafts governance arrangements to match the exchange conditions that accompany various services. As exchange hazards rise so must contractual safeguards, which act to minimize the costs and performance losses arising from such hazards. But crafting a complex contract is costly, and thus parties undertake such a cost only when the consequences of a contractual break are substantial. Transaction cost economics scholars commonly point to three categories of exchange hazards that necessitate contractual safeguards (or vertical integration): asset specificity, measurement difficulty, and uncertainty (Poppo/Zenger 2002). If asset specificity, difficulty in performance measurement or uncertainty increases, managers extend contractual clauses to protect against those risks and thus create more complex contracts. If these investments in contract negotiations and re-designing exceed a certain threshold, managers choose to vertically integrate, i.e., hierarchical governance. Formal contracts are written to prevent from opportunistic behavior (Jensen/Meckling 1976). As the client transfers decision rights to the vendor, the client must assure that the vendor behaves in the client's best interest. By developing penalty-reward-systems and introducing change clauses (e.g., early termination clause) financial and quality related issues resulting from opportunistic behavior as well as (business or technological related) uncertainty can effectively be countered (Kern 1997; Willcocks/Lacity 1998b; Jurison 1995; Fitzgerald/Willcocks 1994). In particular, Gellings and Wüllenweber (2006) showed that contractual means function as a moderator and effect the impact of risk causes (e.g., uncertainty or opportunistic behavior) on risk consequences (e.g., quality debasement or cost escalation). By setting tight service level objectives and negotiating fix prices the client can even try to contractually ensure to achieve desired quality levels and cost savings. Contracts can even help to achieve quality improvements or to set an appropriate environment to stipulate innovations (DiRomualdo/Gurbaxani 1998; Miranda/Kavan 2005). In particular, annual renegotiation of service levels, requested volume of service and a bonus system can make the contract flexible enough to improve operations (DiRomualdo/Gurbaxani 1998). The contract can even incorporate clauses on agreed service objectives including innovation chapters (DiRomualdo/Gurbaxani 1998).

3.6.3.2 Informal Relational Governance

Despite the importance and value of a written formal contract, outsourcing research has acknowledged that reliance on a legal contract alone is insufficient, given the complexities of real-life outsourcing arrangements and the rapid changes in technology and organizational environments (Koh/Ang/Straub 2004; Jahner/Böhmann/Krcmar 2006a). Specifying long-term exchange relations such as outsourcing arrangements is complex as they have to cover various unspecified obligations and thus are inherently incomplete. Rendering contracts is expensive, often inflexible and adaptation is costly. Moreover, contracts are often the root of misunderstanding, when clients are not aware of the technical terminology of the service provider used in the contract. "Contracts, however, are not panaceas" (Clark/Zmud/McCray 1995). Thus, depending on the type of relationship contracts might not be an appropriate governance mechanism. It has become obvious that in such a continuous relationship a detailed and properly structured contractual agreement is a necessary, but often not a sufficient governance mechanism for outsourcing success (Goles/Chin 2005; Klepper 1995; Klepper/Jones 1998). Governing beyond traditional contractual clauses towards a closer relationship-focused management that operates 'within the spirit of the contract' becomes necessary (Kern/Willcocks 2000b) and are to be set in place alternatively or complementary to contracts (e.g., Dyer/Singh 1998; Uzzi 1997; Poppo/Zenger 2002; Koh/Ang/Straub 2004). Several studies have shown that a well-established client-vendor relationship leads to outsourcing success (e.g., Lee/ Miranda/Kim 2004; Poppo/Zenger 2002; Kern/Willcocks 2000b). To be successful, outsourcing ventures must incorporate a cooperative environment shaped by trust, flexibility, commitment, communication and other relational attributes. Through these relation attributes and processes client and vendor get a better understanding as to what type of agreement is being entered into (scope) and what are the specific expectations of both parties towards that agreement (Sargent 2006). The duration and ongoing character of the relationship creates personal bonds and ties between the parties and might also foster mutual commitment towards sharing risk and rewards. This can even manifest itself in a psychological contract where individuals develop a belief of mutual obligations to be fulfilled in collaborative tasks (Rousseau/Tijoriwala 1998; Robinson/Kraatz/Rousseau 1994). The development of such mutual obligations has also been shown to have a significant influence on outsourcing success (Koh/Ang/Straub 2004). As outlined by Willcocks and Kern (1998) communication and trust between the parties contribute to avoiding conflicts, facilitating solutions to problems, reducing uncertainty, and managing expectations. Another benefit of communication is the development of mutual goals and objectives, which influences the commitment (willingness to invest resources) to the relationship by both the client and the vendor. Relational norms can help mitigate quality risks emerging from (business or technological) uncertainty and opportunism (van der Meer-Kooistra/Vosselman 2000; Uzzi 1997; Fitzgerald/Willcocks 1994). Especially in embedded governance forms relationships are long term oriented and shaped with strong mutual commitments and personal ties (Dwyer/Schurr/Oh 1987; Jarillo 1988). Partners undertake joint efforts to react on uncertainty and solve problems (Uzzi 1997). Lee and Kim (1999) showed that the relationship quality has a strong influence on outsourcing success and especially on reducing the risk of technological obsolescence.

3.6.3.3   The Interplay of Formal Contractual and Informal Relational Governance

Many scholars have investigated the interplay between contractual and relational governance. The academic discussion has come up with two alternative views of the interplay of those governance mechanisms: the two approaches can be considered as complements or substitutes (Poppo/Zenger 2002; Dyer/Singh 1998).

Within the 'substitutive view', the presence of one governance device obviates the need for the other (Macaulay 1963; Dyer/Singh 1998). For example, trust can reduce transaction costs by "replacing contracts with handshakes" (Adler 2001). Gulati (1995, 93) is very explicit about the substitutive roles of contracts and relational norms, specifically trust when he argues: "...trust avoids contracting costs, lowers the need for monitoring, and facilitates contractual adaptation. [...] Trust counteracts fears of opportunistic behavior and as a result, is likely to limit the transaction costs associated with an exchange [...] In other words, trust can substitute for hierarchical contracts in many exchanges..." In this view, relational norms are seen as a less expensive alternative of contracts. But it can also be argued that formal contracts undermine the formation of relational governance and can even be interpreted as a sign of mistrust causing instead of protecting from opportunistic behavior (Ghoshal/Moran 1996; Lyons/Mehta 1997). Overall, Poppo and Zenger (2002, 711p.) conclude that the net effects of formal contracts and relational governance on the outsourcing performance in the substitutive view are rather ambiguous. While both might have positive effects on performance when functioning as replacements for one another, the net effect on performance is, at a minimum, reduced and might also be negative.

Although the substitutive relationship between contracts and relational governance has been very widespread among scholars and also holds compelling arguments, the logic for viewing the two approaches as complements seems to be equally compelling (Poppo/Zenger 2002, 712). The complementary relation suggests an additive relation. In settings where hazards are severe, the combination of both contractual and relational governance might deliver greater performance that either mechanisms alone. In particular, the contract is an instrument to build trust by limiting the scope and severity of risks and by providing a track record of performance (Poppo/Zenger 2002; Das/Teng 1998). Rather than replacing or hindering relational governance, contracts actually foster long-term, cooperative, and trustful social relations by discussing service objectives and related contractual terms. Moreover, well-specified contracts narrow the severity of risk to which an exchange relation is exposed and thus encourage trust and commitment (Miranda/Kavan 2005). The complementary view also addresses the inability to design complete contracts: incomplete contract theory suggests that not all possible events during an outsourcing venture can be predicted and included upfront in contract clauses (Beulen/Ribbers 2003; Gietzmann 1996; Richmond/Seidmann/Whinston 1992; Hart 1998).

3.6.3.4 Governance via Management Processes

Besides contractual and relational governance as the two most prominent and best researched governance devices, the classification scheme of governance mechanisms as introduced by Behrens (2006) suggests additional mechanisms to govern the outsourcing relationship, i.e., management processes. A process can be very roughly understood as a systematic series of actions that lead to a specific result. As to IS outsourcing, formally agreed processes explicitly define roles, structures, and expected behaviors of the involved participants with regard to particular activities (Behrens 2006). Process definitions are often complemented by detailed manuals, standard forms or guidelines for decision making.

When processes are formally defined and agreed upon by the involved partners, both parties can better agree on how to work together and ensure compliance (Mahoney/McNally 2004, 21). Laying out and codifying business rules and procedures makes valuable business knowledge explicit and allows for more effective knowledge transfer between client and service provider. This is even more important when the key account manager or other staff is replaced or changes throughout the project. By codifying and making the knowledge explicit, the knowledge transfer can be assured even beyond and independent from specific persons and staff. Decision making is sped up since decision points are known in advance and can be anticipated (Gulati/Singh 1998, 785p.). Furthermore, processes provide both parties with a shared understanding, context, and vocabulary, which enables more effective collaboration (Nahapiet/Ghoshal 1998). Standardization of interactions and routines through processes also leads to increased "embeddedness" (Uzzi 1997), which on the other hand promotes closer bonds and the realization of mutual gains from outsourcing (Kern/Willcocks 2002, 17).

Management processes in outsourcing have been introduced and promoted from different roots, both from academia and practice. In academia, the outsourcing literature has identified several processes that are particularly relevant in managing IS outsourcing relationships, such as, e.g., monitoring, performance management / measurement (Alborz/Seddon/Scheepers

2003), contract management (Kern/Willcocks 2002; Gellings 2007), planning service demand and delivery, i.e., service management (Kaufmann/Schlitt 2004), strategic management processes (Mahnke/Overby/Vang 2005), and also benchmarking (Reilly/Rouse/Seddon 2001; Lacity/Hirschheim 1995a).

As to process orientation and initiatives in practice, the IT Infrastructure Library (ITIL) has become a "de facto" standard in service management throughout many organizations in the world. ITIL defines the organizational structure and skill requirements of an information technology organization and a set of standard operational management procedures and practices to allow the organization to manage an IT operation and associated infrastructure. Starting as a guide for the UK Government, the framework has proved to be useful to organizations in all sectors through its adoption by many service management companies as the basis for consulting, education and software tools support. It documents industry best practice guidance (van Bon 2002). Within ITIL, a number of different IT-related processes have been developed and defined that can be incorporated within IT organizations. These processes position themselves in 5 different areas of the ITIL framework: Service strategy, service design, service transition, service operation, and continual service improvement. While the ITIL processes are well established throughout different organizations, they are rather *practice-oriented* instead of theoretically grounded on the one hand and on the other hand primarily focused on providing and structuring *internal* IT services. Although the processes could also be applied in an outsourcing setting with a third-party provider that is committed and contracted to deliver the outsourced services according to the ITIL best practice standard and at a certified ITIL level, for the purpose of this thesis, the focus will be on four academically researched management processes for governing an IT outsourcing venture: SLA and contract management, performance and service management, strategic processes, benchmarking processes (Alborz/Seddon/Scheepers 2003; Kern/Willcocks 2002; Gellings 2007; Kaufmann/ Schlitt 2004; Mahnke/Overby/Vang 2005; Reilly/Rouse/Seddon 2001; Lacity/Hirschheim 1995a).

3.6.3.5   Governance via Organizational Structures

Besides classical means of contractual and relational governance or governance via established processes, outsourcing coordination and control can also be enhanced through defined roles and staff structures. Liaison roles, task forces, and management committees are among the well-documented examples of such established structures (Mintzberg 1979, 1980). Behrens (2007) defined the governance practice of organizational structures as "the degree to which the client organization's management relies on structural liaison devices – i.e., joint committees / boards, regular management meetings, or liaison personnel – to manage the outsourcing relationship" (p. 109). Such structural mechanisms can facilitate problem-solving and also enhance the buy-in for decisions between both parties (Behrens 2006).

In IS outsourcing ventures, structural liaison devices are often established as boundary-spanning interorganizational management structures between the outsourcing parties for managing the outsourcing relationship. Thereby, it is important to notice that those staff structures should be established on both sides. Kern and Willcocks (2002, 16) point out that "the supplier needs to formalize an account team that mirrors the customer's management group". For example, a steering committee with representation from both vendor and client can provide an oversight for all management aspects of the outsourcing venture (Alborz/Seddon/Scheepers 2004, 3353). In addition, McFarlan and Nolan (1995) recommend specific relationship or key account managers that take care of the tactical and operational activities of the daily working relationship and balance the alignment of goals (McFarlan/Nolan 1995, 22). Gewald and Helbig (2006) described a best-practice governance model with three interaction modes between the client and the vendor organization on a strategic, functional, and operational level: 1) joint strategic committee involving senior executives, 2) a joint functional management committee entailing the head of the retained organization and the head of delivery, and 3) joint operational meetings between the staff of the retained organization and the delivery teams. Establishing such interactions on different levels of the organization also promotes the formation of strong personal bonds and social "embeddedness" of the relationship (Uzzi 1997).

Overall, a well-designed management structure with defined roles and tasks can support the outsourcing parties to coordinate their operational activities as well as to control the performance of the provided services (Alborz/Seddon/Scheepers 2003). Practitioners as well as researchers thus consider the implementation of such a management structure as a pivotal element of a successful outsourcing relationship (Kern/Blois 2002; Kern/Willcocks 2002). Kern et al. specifically argued that establishing "an appropriately skilled management structure prior to outsourcing that [the client] can implement during the post-contract stage" is critical to the success of the outsourcing relationship (Kern/Willcocks 2002, 16).

Behrens (2007, 108p.) summarized different structural liaison devices and elaborated on three main structural devices applicable to IS outsourcing relationships:

1. Joint steering committees / management boards for decisions regarding strategy and general policy at an upper senior executive level (Gewald/Helbig 2006; McFarlan/ Nolan 1995; Willcocks/Choi 1995)

2. Regular operational management meetings that deal with daily functional and operational issues (Beulen/Ribbers 2003; Gewald/Helbig 2006; Sparrow 2003)

3. Dedicated roles and liaison personnel, i.e., account, contract, or relationship managers that function as key contact persons for the other party and within the organization (Beulen/Ribbers 2003; Sparrow 2003)

3.6.3.6   *Governance via Experience and Risk-Reward Incentive Mechanisms*

While many authors have elaborated on the four classic governance devices above, namely contractual and relational governance as well as governance via processes and structural liaison devices, literature has acknowledged two mechanisms that have recently gained attention as a management practice among outsourcing clients.

Since outsourcing has been around as an established business practice for several decades now, outsourcing clients have gained some experience with managing outsourcing ventures. In many cases, experience solely focuses the vendor's experience and capabilities with outsourced IT services (Kishore et al. 2003). But, for establishing and managing a long-term interaction the experience of the customer – the experience of the organization as a whole and the IT manager or CIO likewise – is a vital success factor. The relevance of customer experience, however, varies according to the complexity and focus of the outsourcing venture. The role of experience of the client company has been stressed as an important element of the relational architecture (see chapter 3.6.2, p. 50ff.). However, the client company's experience is not only a constitutive element of an outsourcing relationship. In fact, many clients use the experience of their staff to *govern* their outsourcing relationship. This governance device is rather implicit than explicit and can hardly be formalized. Instead, informal rules and individual behavior of the staff that is involved in the daily working relationship with their counterparts on the vendor side, coin this governance style. The issue of managers' prior experience with outsourcing and its impact on the outsourcing management has been elaborated in some studies (Benamati/Rajkumar 2002). Lacity and Willcocks (2003, 123), e.g., found that clients that slowly and incrementally developed experience with outsourcing can feed back this experience into further outsourcing and thus govern the current outsourcing venture based on the experience collected from past experience with outsourcing. Featherman and Pavlou (2003) and also Aubert et al. (2002) could show that governing via experience in outsourcing is strongly related to the risk perception towards the overall outsourcing venture.

A second governance mechanism that has been quite recently introduced as an outsourcing governance practice is the implementation of risk-reward incentive mechanisms. These mechanisms belong to the group of formal governance mechanisms and are – if set in place – part of the outsourcing contract and the pricing model agreed upon by the outsourcing parties. The basic idea of sharing risks and rewards is that "in the contract, the partners agree to furnish a part of the capital and labor for a business enterprise, and each shares in profits and losses" (Lacity/Willcocks 1998, 379). Those risk-reward structures are most often part of strategic partnerships and alliances where both parties engage in long-term ventures and dedicated special resources to such a relationship. Linder (2004) coined the term "transformational outsourcing" to emphasize the character of radical and fundamental change of those partnerships to "facilitate rapid organizational change, launch new strategies or reshape company boundaries" (p. 52).

Clients most often associate three major motives with engaging in such risk-reward sharing structures with their vendor: first, in traditional outsourcing arrangements, the vendor is a mere supplier of external goods and services while all management issues and risks remain on the side of the client. By sharing risks and rewards, the client is able to transfer the risk at least to a certain amount to the vendor side. Thus, the client spreads and mitigates the risks that used to be in his responsibility solely. Second, sharing not only risks, but also the rewards associated with the outsourcing venture helps to motivate the outsourcing vendor and works as an incentive mechanism. Providing the outsourced services is not an externally assigned task anymore, but can be defined and enhanced by the actual behavior and engagement of the outsourcing vendor. The vendor thus becomes part of the outsourcing venture. The third argument combines both previous aspects, focusing on partnership and equality. Setting risk-reward-mechanisms in place endorses the aspect of mutual, shared, and equal engagement and responsibility of both outsourcing parties that should equally devote resources to the outsourcing venture. Consequently, such mechanisms are most often found in strategic partnerships and alliances.

3.6.4 Relational and Behavioral Interactions of the Outsourcing Parties

This chapter links with and extends the general chapter on the relationship perspective in IS outsourcing (chapter 3.5, p. 45ff.), the chapter on the management practice of informal relational outsourcing governance (chapter 3.6.3.2, p. 55ff.), as well as the general chapter on social exchange theories (chapter 3.2.2, p. 24ff.). On the basis of a general understanding of the relationship perspective in IS outsourcing, the elements of interorganizational relationships as described in social exchange theory will be elaborated and set in context with relational outsourcing governance.

Derived from social exchange theory, interaction-related factors emphasize behavioral mechanisms and interactions between the parties. In their work, Kern and Willcocks (2000b) distinguish between interactions and behavioral dimensions. In their understanding, interactions focus on the exchange of the outsourcing partners and "vary in their nature of either contractual or embeddedness" (p. 329). Interactions are pervaded by factors that affect both the working climate and the behavior of the individuals and largely depend on the atmosphere that surrounds the overall outsourcing deal, i.e., the behavioral aspects of the involved actors. However, since Kern and Willcocks could not point out a clear distinction between interactions and behavioral dimensions and both aspects are rather intertwined, this thesis understands both aspects under the umbrella of "relational and behavioral interactions between the outsourcing parties".

Behavioral interactions can be characterized by such dimensions as communication, commitment, transfer of skills, information sharing, trust, and the role of cultural similarity between client and vendor (Kern/Willcocks 2000b). As elaborated in previous chapters, those behavioral factors are of critical importance given the insufficiency of an outsourcing contract. Recognizing the critical role of these factors in relational exchange, researchers have attempted to catalog them (Goles/Chin 2005). However, these efforts have been hampered by the complex nature of relational exchange as well as the according exchange theories. The "often-messy reality of relational exchange" (Goles/Chin 2005, 50) as well as the "definitional ambiguity of the associated norms and constructs" (Spriggs 1996, 158pp.) cause complications in compiling and describing relationships factors. Furthermore, prior studies have been inconsistent in their selection, definition, and treatment of the relationship factors utilized to explore relational exchange (Fontenot/Wilson 1997; Goles/Chin 2005). For example, one of the most popular relational constructs, i.e., communication, has been used inconsistently in various studies (see, e.g., Klepper 1995; Grover/Cheon/Teng 1996; Kern 1997; Willcocks/ Kern 1998; Lee/Kim 1999). In these studies, the construct is variously treated as an element of contract structuring and relationship building, as a determinant of relationship quality, and as an attribute of relationship quality. This example highlights that not only does a myriad of different relational norms and constructs exist, but also do the definitions of these constructs differ significantly among the authors (Goles/Chin 2005).

In order to shed light on the "current untidy domain of relational exchange constructs" (Goles/Chin 2005, 51), previous research was reviewed to identify factors that played a significant role in relationships. The papers were selected on their relevance to the study of long-term relationships in general and their theoretical relevance for this thesis. By extracting the factors as playing a significant role for exchange relationships, papers of various disciplines were examined, among them are psychology, marketing, business administration, as well as IS. This produced a compilation of different relationship factors as shown in Table 3-4. The table describes the 27 most important factors found in the literature and also the references that used the according construct. As a guidance, the idea for this table was taken from a work by Goles and Chin (2005).

References \ Relationship Factors	Age of Relationship	Attitudes	Attraction	Commitment	Communication	Conflict Resolution	Consensus	Cooperation	Coordination	Cultural Similarity	Flexibility	Influence	Information Sharing	Integration	Inter-dependence	Joint Action	Joint Expectations	Participation	Norm Development	Personal Bonds	Power	Reputation	Shared Knowledge	Shared Vision	Service Quality	Management Support	Trust
(Aalders 2002)	X							X	X			X			X	X								X			
(Amason 1996)						X	X																				
(Anderson/Narus 1984)					X	X		X													X						
(Anderson/Lodish/Weitz 1987)																					X						X
(Anderson/Weitz 1989)	X			X						X	X				X			X	X	X					X		X
(Anderson/Narus 1990)					X	X		X							X						X						X
(Anderson/Weitz 1992)				X	X	X															X						
(Assael 1969)						X															X						
(Bailey/Pearson 1983)					X																						
(Bensaou/Venkatraman 1995)				X		X									X	X											
(Bourgeois 1980)							X																				
(Brown/Frazier 1978)																					X						
(Cook/Emerson 1978)			X																		X						
(Dahl 1957)												X									X						
(DeSanctis/Jackson 1994)									X																		
(Deshpande/Webster 1989)										X																	
(Dess/Origer 1987; Dess 1987)							X																				
(Dwyer 1980)		X	X	X											X												X
(Dwyer/Schurr/Oh 1987)		X	X	X											X		X		X								X
(El-Ansary/Stern 1972; 1975)															X						X						
(Emerson 1962)															X						X						
(Etgar 1976a, 1976b, 1977; 1978)																					X						
(Etgar 1979)					X																X						

References \ Relationship Factors	Age of Relationship	Attitudes	Attraction	Commitment	Communication	Conflict Resolution	Consensus	Cooperation	Coordination	Cultural Similarity	Flexibility	Influence	Information Sharing	Integration	Inter-dependence	Joint Action	Joint Expectations	Participation	Norm Development	Personal Bonds	Power	Reputation	Shared Knowledge	Shared Vision	Service Quality	Management Support	Trust
(Fitzgerald/Willcocks 1994)				X						X	X																
(Fontenot/Wilson 1997)				X	X	X		X							X					X				X			X
(Ganesan 1994)															X												X
(Gaski 1984)				X																	X						
(Goles 2001)				X	X	X	X	X	X	X	X			X	X												X
(Goles/Chin 2005)				X	X	X	X	X	X	X	X									X							X
(Grover/Cheon/Teng 1996)				X				X									X								X		X
(Guiltinan/Rejab/Rodgers 1980)							X	X				X			X					X							
(Gulati 1995)	X																										X
(Gundlach/Cadotte 1994)					X							X			X												X
(Gupta/Iyer 2003)	X							X						X		X									X		
(Guth/MacMillan 1986)																											
(Heide/John 1990)															X	X	X										
(Heide/John 1992)				X	X			X																			
(Heide 1994)								X							X	X											
(Henderson 1990)			X	X										X	X					X		X					X
(Hunger/Stern 1976)					X	X		X												X							
(Hunt/Nevin 1974)																				X							
(John 1984)								X				X								X					X		
(Kanter 1994)				X	X	X	X	X						X	X		X										X
(Kern 1997)				X	X			X		X									X					X			X
(Klepper 1994)								X						X			X	X									X
(Klepper 1995)					X			X											X	X							X
(Konsynski/McFarlan 1990)							X	X				X													X		
(Korsgaard/Schweiger/Sapienza 1995)				X			X	X																			X
(Lacity/Hirschheim 1993a)												X															
(Lacity/Hirschheim 1995b)					X																						
(Lacity/Willcocks 2003)					X															X							

References \ Relationship Factors	Age of Relationship	Attitudes	Attraction	Commitment	Communication	Conflict Resolution	Consensus	Cooperation	Coordination	Cultural Similarity	Flexibility	Influence	Information Sharing	Integration	Inter-dependence	Joint Action	Joint Expectations	Participation	Norm Development	Personal Bonds	Power	Reputation	Shared Knowledge	Shared Vision	Service Quality	Management Support	Trust
(Lasher/Ives/Jarvenpaa 1991)				X		X		X				X		X						X			X				X
(Lee/Kim 1999)	X			X	X	X		X	X				X		X	X		X							X		X
(Lewis 1990)				X		X							X	X	X			X							X		X
(Lusch 1976a, 1976b, 1977)					X									X							X						
(Lusch/Brown 1982)										X											X						
(Macaulay 1963)					X																						
(Malone/Crowston 1990)					X			X	X					X													
(Malone/Crowston 1994)					X			X						X													
(Mejias et al. 1996)							X			X																	
(Michie 1978)																					X						
(Mintzberg/Raisinghani/Theoret 1976)							X																				
(Mohr/Spekman 1994)				X	X	X		X						X													X
(Monczka et al. 1998)				X	X	X		X					X		X												X
(Moorman/Deshpandé/Zaltman 1993)																											X
(Morgan/Hunt 1994)				X																							X
(Narus/Anderson 1987)				X				X	X																		
(Pearson 1973)							X		X																		
(Pfeffer/Salancik 1978)								X							X						X						
(Phillips 1981)															X						X						
(Porter 1974)																					X						
(Pruitt 1981)								X													X						
(Rai/Borah/Ramaprasad 1996)					X	X				X							X								X		
(Ring/Van de Ven 1994)				X	X	X					X				X			X		X	X						X
(Robey et al. 1989)				X						X								X									
(Robicheaux/El-Ansary 1976)				X	X		X				X										X						
(Roering 1977)	X														X												
(Rosenberg/Stern 1971)					X																						
(Rousseau et al. 1998)																											X

References \ Relationship Factors	Age of Relationship	Attitudes	Attraction	Commitment	Communication	Conflict Resolution	Consensus	Cooperation	Coordination	Cultural Similarity	Flexibility	Influence	Information Sharing	Integration	Inter-dependence	Joint Action	Joint Expectations	Participation	Norm Development	Personal Bonds	Power	Reputation	Shared Knowledge	Shared Vision	Service Quality	Management Support	Trust
(Scanzoni 1983)	X			X	X																						
(Sethuraman/Anderson/Narus 1988)															X						X						
(Simpson/Mayo 1997)				X								X															X
(Spekman/Salmond/Lambe 1997)								X							X			X									
(Stern/Sternthal/Craig 1973; 1982)					X															X							
(Thompson 1967)								X							X					X							
(Van de Ven/Delbecg/Koenig 1976)								X																			
(Walker 1972)					X															X							
(Wilkinson 1974)																				X							
(Wilkinson/Kipnis 1978)	X											X								X							
(Wilkinson 1979)												X								X							
(Wilkinson 1981)					X															X							
(Willcocks/Choi 1995)					X			X							X												X
(Willcocks/Kern 1998)				X	X			X	X						X												X
(Willcocks/Lacity 1998b)															X												
(Wooldridge/Floyd 1989, 1990)					X		X																		X		
(Yoshino/Rangan 1995)					X			X							X											X	X
(Zaheer/McEvily/Perrone 1998)	X				X																						X

Table 3-4. Compilation of relationship factors in the literature[7]

Apart from the striking and merely endless myriad of relationship factors and their references in the literature, further contemplation of the table led to four insights and conclusions. First, the entire set of constructs – 27 in all – was too unwieldy to be of much use in an empirical study. This finding is in accordance with the work of Goles and Chin (2005) who attempted a similar endeavor to compile relationship factors from the literature. Second, there is some conceptual overlap between many of these constructs. For example, the constructs "communication" and "information sharing" have similar notions among different authors. Lastly, the identified constructs are based on and largely depict a set of norms advanced by Macneil

---

[7] The theoretical and/or empirical basis of the occurrence of these relationship factors is described in the appendix for each author and study.

(1980) who set forth nine common norms that characterize the broad spectrum of relational exchanges. Fourth, there are factors such as trust or commitment that are mentioned by nearly all authors and can thus be regarded as the core components of an outsourcing relationship. In accordance with Macneil (1980) and Goles and Chin (2005) who chose a fairly similar approach and in line with the goal of this thesis, the myriad of relationship factors in the table above was to be distilled to a core set that has a solid theoretical grounding in relational exchange norms. The actual factors that were used in the empirical study of this thesis are described in details in chapter 5.5.5 (p. 188ff.).

One last aspect and caveat has to be mentioned regarding the behavioral interactions of an outsourcing relationship. Many authors claim that focusing on mutual and shared goals is crucial for a successful outsourcing relationship and close relationships are likely to be enduring if they arise from genuine common interests (Elitzur/Wensley 1998). However, an outsourcing client has to be careful not to put too much faith in the natural effectiveness of close relationships in causing the outsourcing vendor to act in the best interest of the client. The interests of outsourcing client and vendor do not naturally coincide (Elitzur/Wensley 1998, 122). Lacity and Willcocks even go one step further and claim that there is an inherent adversarial nature in the contracts "in that a dollar out of the customer's pocket is a dollar in the supplier's pocket"(Lacity/Willcocks 2003, 122). Lacity and Willcocks (2003, 123) thus emphasize the need to embrace the dynamics and development potential as the primary success factor of an outsourcing relationship. They suggest three interaction forms for outsourcing relationships: tentative, cooperative, and collaborative. "Tentative interactions occur when goal alignments are unknown, such as during the bidding process. At such times, each side tends to exaggerate their strengths and hide their weaknesses. Cooperative interactions occur when goals are complementary, such as the customer wants the service, the supplier wants the payment. Collaborative interactions occur when both sides have shared goals, such as educating the user community on what they can expect from the contract" (Lacity/Willcocks 2003, 123). The important message here is that each side must have equal power so that they can achieve fair outcomes.

3.6.5 Success of IS Outsourcing

Once the outsourcing decision is realized and the outsourcing venture is being carried out, the resulting experiences are to be documented and understood (Dibbern et al. 2004, 69pp.). Customers face the need to evaluate the outsourcing outcomes and whether the outsourcing decision employed met the anticipated expectations. Much of the outsourcing literature focuses on such outcomes. In general, outcomes deal with the wider implications of different types of outsourcing decisions (Dibbern et al. 2004, 16p.). One paper that addresses such outcomes is Aubert et al. (1998) who examine potential undesirable outcomes associated with outsourcing (e.g., service debasement), and the risk factors that could lead to these outcomes. The term 'outcome', however, is value-laden and sometimes elusive, as the wider IS evaluation literature shows (Smithson/Hirschheim 1998). By outsourcing outcome, most researchers mean the success of the outsourcing venture. But almost as hard as to guarantee the success of an outsourcing venture (Lacity/Hirschheim 1993a), is to define what success in the context of outsourcing means and comprises (Willcocks/Lacity/Cullen 2007).

Many researchers use success, outcome, benefits, and performance interchangeably in their studies. For example, Grover et al. (1996) identified three categories of outcomes: economic, technological, and strategic benefits, which were further broken down into eight attributes. Domberger et al. (2000) focused on one single attribute, i.e., "desired performance". Lacity and Willcocks (2001) analyzed the factors "objectives against results", "cost reductions", and "satisfaction". Lee et al. (2004) used the dimensions "strategic competence", "cost efficiency", and "technology catalyst". In other cases, contract renewals or expansions of the venture were taken as indicators of outsourcing success (Beulen/Ribbers 2002). "Not surprisingly, different perceptions of what constitutes successful outsourcing have yielded conflicting advice on the degree to which outsourcing practices have been successful" (Willcocks/ Lacity/Cullen 2007). Other outcome factors include, e.g., employee behavior (Ang/Slaughter 1998), continuation of contracts (Fitzgerald/Willcocks 1994), client satisfaction (Grover/ Cheon/Teng 1996; Lee/Kim 1999; Saunders/Gebelt/Hu 1997), vendor satisfaction (Heckman/ King/Beachboard 1994), financial outcomes (Lacity/Willcocks/Feeny 1996) and perceptions of outsourcing from different stakeholders (Hirschheim/Lacity 1998). Table 3-5 lists an extract of various definitions of outsourcing outcomes and success.

Reference	Definition of IS outsourcing outcome and success
(Alborz/Seddon/Scheepers 2005, 1119)	"... a value judgment made by some stakeholder about the net benefits the stakeholder's organization receives from a given ITO arrangement"
(Grover/Cheon/Teng 1996, 95)	"... the satisfaction with benefits from outsourcing gained by an organization as a result of deploying an outsourcing strategy"
(Ives/Olson 1984, 593)	"... [satisfaction as outcome is] the extent to which users believe their information systems meet their information requirement"
(Lacity/Willcocks 2001, 151)	"... [when] the outcome of IT sourcing decisions met expectations"
(Lee/Kim 1999, 39)	"... the level of fitness between the customer's requirements and the outsourcing outcomes"
(Lee 2001, 328)	"... the overall organizational advantage obtained from IS outsourcing"
(Oliver 1996, 144)	"... [satisfaction is] an experiential judgment of outcomes compared to a set of goals or standards resulting in a sense of fulfillment, including over- or under-fulfillment"
(Wang 2002, 161)	"... costs and benefits attained by the software outsourced"

Table 3-5. Exemplary definitions of IS outsourcing outcomes and success
(Source: adapted from Behrens 2007, 9)

These examples show the variety of understandings and approaches when it comes to analyzing the results of an outsourcing venture. While the perceptions of researchers and also the level of detail and granularity of the investigated success dimensions varies a lot, Dibbern et al. (2004) have shed light into the vagueness of outcome dimensions. According to Dibbern et al. (2004, 69pp.), in general, three types of outcome or success can be distinguished. These are 1) satisfaction, 2) expectations and their realization, and 3) performance.

Satisfaction has been a quite prominent and widely used factor for describing and measuring outsourcing success with the concept originating from marketing research on buyer-seller relationships (Anderson/Narus 1990). Satisfaction can be broadly defined as "the extent to which users believe their information systems meet their information requirements" (Ives/Olson 1984, 593). DeLone and McLean (1992) and Ives and Olson (1984) state that user satisfaction is one of the most important and most common measures of information systems success. Consequently, the concept of satisfaction has been widely used in IS outsourcing research to evaluate the outcomes and results associated with the outsourcing decision. Several IS outsourcing studies have measured success using a purely satisfaction-based scale (e.g., Alborz/Seddon/Scheepers 2005; Goles 2003; Poppo/Zenger 1998, 2002; Seddon/Cullen/ Willcocks 2002). Poppo and Zenger (1998), e.g., studied satisfaction with market and also firm performance and found that various factors – each being related to different IS functions – have a different impact on satisfaction with market and firm performance. Grover et al. (1996) investigated the interplay of extent of outsourcing, satisfaction, and the influence of service quality to derive results on outsourcing success. Susarla et al. (2003) draw upon the consumer satisfaction paradigm to analyze post-usage satisfaction with outsourcing ASP services.

Overall, Dibbern et al. (2004, 74) conclude that "satisfaction is a reasonable surrogate for a successful outcome because it allows the subjects to respond based on the criteria most relevant to them".

In contrast, the second type, i.e., "expectations and their realization" is more closely tied to specific criteria and their actual realization. Very often, cost savings are used as a criterion to measure the outcome of an outsourcing venture. Lacity and Willcocks, for example, used "expected cost savings" (Lacity/Willcocks 1998) as a single indicator for outsourcing success. Aubert et al. (1999) investigate undesirable outcomes such as unexpected transition and management costs, costly contractual amendments, and services debasements. Grover et al. (1996) identified economic, technological, and strategic benefits as the most prevailing success measures and combined them with an overall satisfaction measure. Following in the footsteps of Grover et al. (1996), Saunders et al. (1997) also defined outsourcing in terms of benefits attained. In their studies, success was measured along four dimensions: economic benefits, technological benefits, strategic benefits, and overall satisfaction. As the paper points out, "it is important to consider these multiple dimensions in order to form a complete picture" (p. 71).

However, although measuring expectations and their realization promises a more precise understanding of specific outcomes, the focus on only selected expectation criteria can cause a bias, especially since many studies focus on cost aspects exclusively. As documented in this thesis, cost is a powerful and dominant outsourcing expectation, but by far not the only one and a lot of customers do not necessarily aim for cost savings, but rather for innovation or IT excellence. When Lacity and Willcocks (1998) used cost savings as the primary motive behind the decision to outsource, they state that although "reduced IT costs" was the expectation most often cited by the respondents, "caution is still prudent in interpreting the results" (p. 386).

Another important point to notice is the fact that most studies measure success by the realization of benefits (Lacity/Willcocks 1998; Lee/Kim 1999; Loh/Venkatraman 1991; Loh/ Venkatraman 1992a, 1992b; McFarlan/Nolan 1995; Rouse/Corbitt/Aubert 2001; Saunders/

Gebelt/Hu 1997), but do not compare or balance these benefits to originally intended objectives. The arguable assumption within these studies is that the benefits realized are the same as the expected benefits before outsourcing and that the importance of each benefit does not alter during outsourcing stages. However, the business value of the outsourcing cannot be determined if only one side – either expected or achieved benefits – is taken into account. Business value can thus be shown by comparing both intention and outcome of the venture.

While both satisfaction and expectation / realization focus on the actual final outcome of the venture and a consequence of organizational behavior, the last category of outcomes looks at the actual organizational behavior even more precisely – *performance*. Ang and Slaughter (1998) investigated performance with regard to the fulfillment of responsibilities and quality of the workers. Sabherwal (1999) researched performance in outsourced IS development projects from both the client and the vendor perspective. He could show that a balance between trust and structure improves performance in an outsourced IS development context, which he roughly defined as project success.

Another aspect of performance measurement in outsourcing ventures is the (perceived) service quality of the outsourcing provider. Service quality is on the one hand an aspect or instance of performance (which itself is one category of outcomes). On the other hand, service quality is largely seen as a strong determinant of outsourcing success (Grover/Cheon/Teng 1996). Parasuraman et al. (1988; 1985) have researched this area extensively. They identified determinants of service quality and introduced the SERVQUAL instrument, a multiple-item scale to measure customer's service quality. Many studies have also investigated the interplay of service quality and satisfaction (e.g., Susarla/Barua/Whinston 2003). Service quality can therefore be regarded as an outcome measure, but also as a determinant of outsourcing success / outcome (Dibbern et al. 2004).

To summarize the literature review presented above, IS outsourcing outcomes are often elusive and used in various contexts and understandings by different authors. The variety of outcome and success measures can be distinguished into three categories: satisfaction, expectations and their realization, and performance. Satisfaction is a very popular and widely accepted measure of outsourcing success because it allows the subjects to respond based on the criteria most relevant to them. Similarly, expectations and their realization have become a widespread measure to evaluate outsourcing success. This measure is more closely tied to specific criteria and their actual realization, but often the focus lies only on selected expectation criteria which can cause a bias, especially since many studies focus on cost aspects exclusively. Results based solely on an assessment of selected benefits attained may present an incomplete picture of outsourcing success. Lastly, performance as a third category of outcome measures looks at the actual organizational behavior even more precisely. Within this category, the perceived service quality of the outsourcing venture has become a widely used performance measure. Consequently, in order to get a comprehensive picture of outsourcing outcomes and success, one should rather combine different outcome measures instead of basing the results solely on an assessment of single aspects of outsourcing results.

3.7   Shortcomings of the Current Research / Research Gap on Outsourcing Relationships and their Governance

The literature review presented in the chapters above brought to light several particularly interesting findings and features of the existing body of outsourcing research. Before using these insights for building a framework of constituent characteristics of outsourcing relationships, a helicopter perspective on the previous chapters is useful for identifying research gaps in prior research. These shortcomings in prior research on outsourcing and outsourcing relationships in particular will be summarized in the following statements.

1. Lack of empirical data on the client-vendor relationship aspects in IS outsourcing

Although heavily promoted as an important area of research (e.g., by Kern 1997; McFarlan/Nolan 1995; Willcocks/Lacity 1998b; Goles 2001; Goles/Chin 2005), there is still a significant lack of empirical work directed towards an examination and analysis of that relationship.

2. Lack of coherence and integrated approach to understand outsourcing relationships

Research on relationship management in interorganizational relationships has simply enumerated the exorbitant number of relationship factors in a descriptive way, but has missed to integrate these factors in an overall outsourcing context. The previous issues and outsourcing questions have mostly been studied in isolation and have not been consolidated into a coherent framework.

3. Lack of considering the outsourcing context and distinction between different outsourcing customer (expectation) profiles

Despite the vast variety of relationship factors, not all relationship factors and governance mechanisms seem to be appropriate for every outsourcing customer. Instead of a "one-size-fits-all" concept it is necessary to elaborate the role of certain relationship factors depending on the context of and expectations towards an outsourcing arrangement. For managing outsourcing ventures successfully, one has to acknowledge the fact that outsourcing relationships have different underlying expectations and motivations of the involved parties and cannot all be managed the same.

4. Lack of appropriate classification of different outsourcing relationship customers

Classifications from other B2B relationship management approaches are hardly applicable for IS outsourcing relationships due to the specific nature and role of information systems in an organization. Classifications for relationships in information systems outsourcing are often one-sided and do not provide an exhaustive set of dimensions for describing an outsourcing relationship type. A taxonomy of different outsourcing relationships is thus needed based on thorough empirical evidence. Based on an extensive literature review and a derived theoretically-motivated framework, such a taxonomy can deliver a distinct insight into various types of outsourcing clients and describe their constitutive characteristics.

5. Lack of design recommendations and practical implications on the governance of different outsourcing ventures

Actionable advice for IT decision makers on both client and vendor side on how to successfully govern different outsourcing projects is still rare in practice. An empirically derived taxonomy of different outsourcing clients and their underlying outsourcing motives and constitutive characteristics can be the precursor to derive design recommendations on governance strategies that address specific outsourcing ventures. So far, outsourcing research has missed to link clients' outsourcing expectations to appropriate governance approaches to successfully carry out an outsourcing venture.

Overall, the outsourcing literature as well as current outsourcing practices show that one reason for the inconsistent reports on success and failure of outsourcing ventures seems to be that the governance mechanisms that are set in place for managing the outsourcing venture (if set in place at all) are not appropriate and adequate for the underlying motivation and expectation structure of the specific client. Distinguishing different types of outsourcing relationships is necessary. Those types can then be characterized along a set of different constitutive criteria (instead of only two dimensions) and appropriate and specific governance mechanisms for each of these types can be provided. This thesis is geared towards helping to fill these gaps in the research stream through the research approach discussed in the next chapters. As a first step towards a systematic characterization of outsourcing relationships, a coherent and integrative framework is to be conceptualized. The next chapter will thus lay out the methodological foundation for building such a framework. The subsequent chapter 3.8 will then present the actual framework blended from the methodological basics (chapter 3.8.1, p. 72ff.) and the constitutive elements of outsourcing relationships (chapter 3.6, p. 49ff.).

3.8   Framework for Classifying Outsourcing Relationships

In order to develop a conceptual framework as a basis for a taxonomy of empirical outsourcing client types methodological foundations have to be laid out on the one hand and constitutive elements that build the content of the framework have to be introduced on the other hand. Chapter 3.8.1 will introduce the methodological foundations of building a framework. In chapter 3.6 (p. 49ff.) the constitutive elements of outsourcing relationships and their governance were introduced in a descriptive way. Compiling both parts, this chapter will blend the insights from prior literature on outsourcing relationships (chapter 3.6, p. 49ff.) and different classification approaches into an integrative conceptualization of outsourcing relationships. To avoid confusion for the reader, it has to be emphasized that this chapter – although providing a pivotal milestone for deriving outsourcing client types empirically – is mostly a compilation of previous chapters. It combines the methodological steps for building a framework (next subchapter) with the description of constitutive elements of outsourcing relationships (chapter 3.6, p. 49ff.) and describes how the framework was built. Table 3-6 as the main result of this chapter provides the basis for the empirical investigation of outsourcing relationships carried out in chapter 5 (p. 111ff.).

3.8.1   Methodological Approach to the Conceptualization of a Framework on Outsourcing Relationships

Although the taxonomy to be built in this thesis is a classification schema that is empirically derived from multivariate analyses and although the classification is derived only *after* having analyzed some specific set of data, one still needs a conceptual structure of which data to analyze and consider for building the taxonomy. This chapter is thus dedicated to laying out the steps and points of consideration of how to develop and build a framework that serves as a conceptual frame and basis for an empirically grounded taxonomy of different outsourcing relationships.

The first step in developing the framework is the selection of the building blocks for the framework. One has to dedicate great care to the selection of the constructs and input variables used in the framework (Homburg/Workman/Jensen 2002, 43). In Bailey's words (1994, 2), "one basic secret to successful classification [...] is the ability to ascertain the key or fundamental characteristics on which the classification is to be based." While literature provides a number of – sometimes contradictory – guidelines for the selection of input variables to a classification (for a review see Rich 1992), there is one consensus: the input variables should be derived from theory and should be meaningful for the subject under study. Consequently, given the integrative claim of this research, theory-based constructs from the literature that are comparable across a range of industries have to be included for the framework.

While there is consensus on the postulation of a theory foundation of the variables, more discussion is dedicated to the tolerable degree of interdependencies among the cluster variables (Homburg/Workman/Jensen 2002, 43). Some authors suggest excluding variables that are logically or empirically correlated and considering only semantically distinct constructs (e.g., Sneath/Sokal 1973). Other researchers, however, argue that "it is difficult to imagine empirical data arising in the behavioral sciences that would have all columns independent" (Arabie/Hubert 1994, 166). Mutually exclusive and independent constitutive factors for describing outsourcing relationships thus seem to be rather unrealistic and artificial when observing real-world phenomena. Even more, from a methodological point of view, there is no assumption or prerequisite of uncorrelated variables in most cluster methods (see previous chapters and also Milligan 1996, 347). For the purpose of exhaustively describing different outsourcing relationships some conceptual overlap and correlation among the constructs will be accepted for this research (for a similar approach see the work of Homburg/Workman/ Jensen 2002).

Finally, a third debate is focused on the balance between completeness and parsimony of the input variables. One stream of researchers recommends to "define as many organizational attributes as possible" (see e.g., McKelvey 1975, 514). But other researchers argue that there is little use in including more dimensions than necessary to build a profound taxonomy. Especially from a methodological point of view, the presence of spurious dimensions (i.e., dimensions that to not differentiate among the identified clusters) has been shown to have a detrimental effect on the performance of clustering methods (see previous chapters on cluster analysis and also Homburg/Workman/Jensen 2002, 43). Using the "shotgun approach"

(Punj/Stewart 1983, 134) where everything known about the observations is included in the cluster analysis seldom leads to distinct and meaningful groups of data. Consequently, this research follows an approach suggested and applied by Homburg et al. (2002, 43pp.) who distinguished two types of variables. First, parsimonious and constitutive sets of theory-based key constructs are identified that serve as "active" input variables for the clustering algorithm. Then, these variables are complemented with several "passive", sometimes non-theoretical and descriptive variables that will characterize the identified cluster groups in further detail.

3.8.2 Categories of the Framework

The first step of how to develop a conceptual frame for classifying outsourcing relationships involves deriving theoretically-grounded variables that are meaningful for the subject of the study and that are comparable across a range of industries. For this purpose, the overall structure of the framework was based on and expands the relationship properties suggested by Kern and Willcocks (2000b). Five categories which include subsequent factors in more detail were included as pillars to describe an outsourcing relationship. These categories are:

1. Strategic intent / expectation / motivation

2. Context factors

3. Relational architecture

4. Governance mechanisms

5. Interactions (relationship factors)

Each of these categories contains more detailed, descriptive factors that characterize an outsourcing venture. For example, the category "governance mechanisms" includes factors such as formal governance, informal governance, or governance via structures and processes in order to depict the variety of possibilities and approaches of managing an outsourcing venture. The categories as well as the factors and single variables included in the categories were derived from prior literature and existing theories in the research realm of IS outsourcing. Chapter 3.6 (p. 49ff.) has already elaborated on the categories and the included factors in more detail and also depicted the theories that these factors rely upon and were derived from. Thus, the aim of this chapter is only to summarize the building blocks introduced in the previous chapters and blend them into the framework depicted in Table 3-6.

3.8.3 Completeness vs. Parsimony of the Building Blocks

As the literature review has shown in chapter 3.5.3 (p. 48ff.), first approaches of systematizing IS outsourcing relationships exist (Kern/Willcocks/van Heck 2002; Kishore et al. 2003; Nam et al. 1996). However, these approaches are overall too one-sided, as they include only two selected, not collectively exhaustive dimensions for describing an outsourcing relationship type. As the field of IS outsourcing has become more complex and diversified over the years, it becomes necessary to include various factors into the analysis of relationship types to provide a more comprehensive taxonomy of different relationships. In other words, more than two dimensions are necessary to provide a holistic and integrated picture of an IS outsourcing relationship.

In this context, one of the three steps of building a taxonomy framework suggested in chapter 3.8.1 (p. 72ff.) debates the balance between completeness and parsimony of the input variables, i.e., should as less variables as possible be included in the cluster analysis and therefore only the most characterizing and core ones? Or should the taxonomy framework contain a great number and variety of input variables to describe a rich and comprehensive picture of an outsourcing relationship? Following the approach of (Homburg/Workman/Jensen 2002, 43pp.), this research accounted for both arguments and distinguished two types of variables. First, parsimonious and constitutive sets of theory-based key constructs were identified that serve as "active" input variables for the clustering algorithm. Only a small number of variables were chosen as core input variables. Then, these variables were complemented with several "passive", sometimes non-theoretical and descriptive variables that will characterize the identified cluster groups in further detail. For the purpose of this research outsourcing expectations and motivations were chosen as active and constitutive variables to be included in the cluster analysis (see chapter 5.4, p. 126ff.). These factors are contained in the first category of the framework, i.e., "strategic intents". Clients' expectations and motivation issues for the IS outsourcing decision were chosen as the core dimensions to be included in the cluster analysis because the basic and underlying assumption of this research is that outsourcing clients differ in their behavior and in their appropriate governance schemes according to the expectations they utter towards their outsourcing decision. Clients thus should be classified along their underlying outsourcing motives. Consequently, the outsourcing motives that are elaborated in chapter 3.4 (p. 39ff.) and chapter 3.6.1 (p. 49ff.) and structured with a factor analysis in chapter 5.4.2 (p. 132ff.) are most appropriate to serve as active input variables for the cluster analysis. However, the framework in Table 3-6 contains all variables and shows which ones are active and which ones are passive, descriptive variables.

3.8.4 Interdependencies among the Variables

When having decided, which variables serve as the main input variables and which ones are passive, descriptive variables to enrich the picture of the different outsourcing client types, there is still one open issue, i.e., the tolerable degree of interdependencies among the cluster variables (Homburg/Workman/Jensen 2002, 43). Following the argument of (among others) (Arabie/Hubert 1994, 166), it is difficult to imagine empirical data arising in the behavioral sciences that would have all dimensions independent. Usually, from a methodological point of view, there is no strong assumption or prerequisite of uncorrelated variables in most cluster methods. However, as discussed in chapter 4.2.1 (p. 86ff.), there is a caveat when using correlated variables for a cluster analysis since they can possibly cause a bias in terms of over- or underrepresentation of certain aspects. This research will thus choose a two-step approach. The motivation variables that are used as input items for the cluster analysis will be comprised to the most distinct and independent motivation factors to eliminate possible biases. However, as to the complementary, descriptive, and passive variables, no methodological caveat in terms of interdependencies can be argued. Thus, this research will accept some conceptual overlap and correlation among the constructs for the purpose of exhaustively describing different outsourcing relationships. For example, in the "context" section factors such as "annual sales", "number of employees", and "IT budget" are likely to be correlated. Also regarding the interaction factors, items such as "trust", "communication", or "conflict resolution" can hardly be regarded as independent factors. Many researchers state that especially in terms of interaction and relationship factors, many items are closely related and rather facets of each other than completely different aspects (see e.g., Goles/Chin 2005). Accepting at least some conceptual overlap allows the researcher to view one phenomenon through different, but similar lenses and thus gain a comprehensive picture of this phenomenon.

3.8.5 Conceptual Framework for Types in IS Outsourcing Relationships

Having discussed the methodological caveats of how to build the framework and having elaborated on the appropriate outsourcing relationship categories derived from theory and literature now allows compiling the variables into one coherent and comprehensive framework for describing outsourcing relationships along a variety of relationship dimensions. The framework in Figure 3-5 illustrates the five main categories to describe an IS outsourcing relationship. Table 3-6 depicts the details of the framework, i.e., the appropriate items for each category extracted from literature, the type of variable, and the level of measurement (important for the section "statistical results", see also chapter 5.3 (p. 124ff.) and exemplary references.

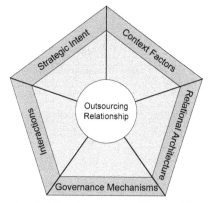

Figure 3-5. Overview of conceptual framework for IS outsourcing relationship types

Category / Dimension	Type of variable (active, parsimonious vs. passive, descriptive)	Level of measurement (scale)	References for variable (selected examples)
Strategic intent / expectation / motivation			
Cost reduction	active, parsimonious	metric, 7pt Likert scale	(Alpar/Saharia 1995; Arnett/Jones 1994; Lacity/Hirschheim 1994; McFarlan/Nolan 1995; Palvia 1995; Jurison 1998; Sobol/Apte 1998; Lacity/Hirschheim 1995b; Lacity/Hirschheim 1993a; Lacity/Willcocks 2001; Smith/Mitra/Narasimhan 1998; DiRomualdo/Gurbaxani 1998; Apte 1990; Huff 1991; Loh/Venkatraman 1992a, 1992b; Kern/Blois 2002; Willcocks/Fitzgerald/Lacity 1996; Matiaske/Mellewigt 2002; Kishore et al. 2003)
Flexibility of costs / cost transparency (rendering IT as a variable cost)	active, parsimonious	metric, 7pt Likert scale	(Bongard 1994; Lacity/Hirschheim 1995b; Lacity/Willcocks 2001; Smith/Mitra/Narasimhan 1998; DiRomualdo/Gurbaxani 1998; Apte 1990; Huff 1991; Loh/Venkatraman 1992a, 1992b; Kern/Blois 2002; Willcocks/Fitzgerald/Lacity 1996, 143; Matiaske/Mellewigt 2002)
Quality improvements (lower error rate / shorter processing time)	active, parsimonious	metric, 7pt Likert scale	(Apte 1990; Huff 1991; Loh/Venkatraman 1992a, 1992b)
Long-term use of systems, applications and data (stability, reliability, retention of status quo)	active, parsimonious	metric, 7pt Likert scale	(Lacity/Willcocks 2001; Grover/Cheon/Teng 1996, 93; Apte 1990)
Improved service orientation	active, parsimonious	metric, 7pt Likert scale	(Apte 1990; Huff 1991; Loh/Venkatraman 1992a, 1992b)
Increased flexibility	active, parsimonious	metric, 7pt Likert scale	(Kim/Chung 2003; Jahner/Böhmann/Krcmar 2006a; Slaugther/Ang 1996; Jurison 1998; Apte 1990; Huff 1991; Loh/Venkatraman 1992a, 1992b)
Shift risk to service provider	active, parsimonious	metric, 7pt Likert scale	(Bongard 1994; Apte 1990; Huff 1991; Loh/Venkatraman 1992a, 1992b)
Modernization of IT / replace legacy systems	active, parsimonious	metric, 7pt Likert scale	(Lacity/Willcocks 2001; Grover/Cheon/Teng 1996, 93; Apte 1990)
Focus on core competencies	active, parsimonious	metric, 7pt Likert scale	(Smith/Mitra/Narasimhan 1998; Slaugther/Ang 1996; Sobol/Apte 1998; Lacity/Willcocks 2001; Grover/Cheon/Teng 1994b; Apte 1990; Huff 1991; Loh/Venkatraman 1992a, 1992b)
Enable and facilitate strategic competitive advantages	active, parsimonious	metric, 7pt Likert scale	(Lacity/Willcocks 2001; Willcocks et al. 2004; Apte 1990)
Access to highly skilled people	active, parsimonious	metric, 7pt Likert scale	(Apte 1990; Bongard 1994; Sobol/Apte 1998; Lacity/Hirschheim 1995b; Lacity/Willcocks 2001; Grover/Cheon/Teng 1994b; Huff 1991; Loh/Venkatraman 1992a, 1992b)
Access to better IT systems and new technology	active, parsimonious	metric, 7pt Likert scale	(Apte 1990; Bongard 1994; Jurison 1998; Sobol/Apte 1998; Lacity/Hirschheim 1995b; Lacity/Willcocks 2001; Grover/Cheon/Teng 1996; Kishore et al. 2003)

Category / Dimension	Type of variable (active, parsimonious vs. passive, descriptive)	Level of measurement (scale)	References for variable (selected examples)
Knowledge acquisition from service provider	active, parsimonious	metric, 7pt Likert scale	(Apte 1990; Huff 1991; Loh/Venkatraman 1992a, 1992b)
Suggestions for new IT based products and services by your service provider (innovation, idea creation)	active, parsimonious	metric, 7pt Likert scale	(Jahner/Böhmann/Krcmar 2006a; Quinn 2000; Willcocks et al. 2004; Mahnke/Özcan/Overby 2006)
Shared development of IT based products and services together with your service provider (joint product and service development)	active, parsimonious	metric, 7pt Likert scale	(Jahner/Böhmann/Krcmar 2006a; Quinn 2000; Willcocks et al. 2004; Mahnke/Özcan/Overby 2006)
Business transformation	active, parsimonious	metric, 7pt Likert scale	(Lacity/Willcocks 2001; Willcocks et al. 2004; Apte 1990)
Context factors			
Dominant industries	passive, descriptive	nominal	(Cullen/Seddon/Willcocks 2005; Willcocks/Lacity/Cullen 2007)
Firm size: annual sales	passive, descriptive	metric, ratio scale	(Cullen/Seddon/Willcocks 2005; Willcocks/Lacity/Cullen 2007)
Firm size: number of employees	passive, descriptive	metric, ratio scale	(Cullen/Seddon/Willcocks 2005; Willcocks/Lacity/Cullen 2007)
IT budget	passive, descriptive	metric, ratio scale	(Cullen/Seddon/Willcocks 2005; Willcocks/Lacity/Cullen 2007)
Role of IT for company	passive, descriptive	ordinal, 5pt Likert	(Kishore et al. 2003)
Relational architecture			
Company experience with outsourcing	passive, descriptive	ordinal	(Lacity/Willcocks 1998; Beimborn/Franke/Weitzel 2005)
Outsourcing objects: IT-supported business processes (degree)	passive, descriptive	ordinal	(Cullen/Seddon/Willcocks 2005; Lacity/Willcocks 2001; Apte 1990)
Outsourcing objects: IT applications (degree)	passive, descriptive	ordinal	(Cullen/Seddon/Willcocks 2005; Lacity/Willcocks 2001; Apte 1990)
Outsourcing objects: IT infrastructure (degree)	passive, descriptive	ordinal	(Cullen/Seddon/Willcocks 2005; Lacity/Willcocks 2001; Apte 1990)
Number of involved vendors	passive, descriptive	ordinal	(Cullen/Seddon/Willcocks 2005; Lacity/Willcocks 2001; Willcocks/Lacity/Cullen 2007)
Degree of outsourcing	passive, descriptive	ordinal	(Cullen/Seddon/Willcocks 2005; Lacity/Willcocks/Feeny 1996; Willcocks/Lacity/Cullen 2007)
Duration / length of outsourcing contract	passive, descriptive	ordinal	(Cullen/Seddon/Willcocks 2005; Lacity/Willcocks 1998; Kishore et al. 2003; Willcocks/Lacity/Cullen 2007)
Dominating pricing model	passive, descriptive	nominal	(Cullen/Seddon/Willcocks 2005; Lacity/Willcocks 1998)

Category / Dimension	Type of variable (active, parsimonious vs. passive, descriptive)	Level of measurement (scale)	References for variable (selected examples)
Outsourcing alliance model	passive, descriptive	nominal	(Cullen/Seddon/Willcocks 2005; Lacity/Willcocks 1998)
Dependency on service provider (degree of switching costs)	passive, descriptive	metric, 7pt Likert scale	(Cullen/Seddon/Willcocks 2005; Kishore et al. 2003)
Goal alignment between outsourcing parties	passive, descriptive	metric, 7pt Likert scale	(Cullen/Seddon/Willcocks 2005; Lacity/Willcocks 2003)
Governance mechanisms			
Role of contract	passive, descriptive	metric, 7pt Likert scale	(Sabherwal 1999; Woolthuis/Hillebrand/ Nooteboom 2005; Ang/Beath 1993; Poppo/Zenger 2002; Mani/Barua/Whinston 2006)
Role of processes: Established SLA and contract management processes	passive, descriptive	metric, 7pt Likert scale	(Beaumont 2006; Goo/Kishore/Rao 2004a; Muller 1999; Goo/Kishore/Rao 2004b; Goo et al. 2003)
Role of processes: Established performance and service management	passive, descriptive	metric, 7pt Likert scale	(Behrens/Schmitz 2005; Wooldridge/Floyd 1990)
Role of processes: Established strategy processes	passive, descriptive	metric, 7pt Likert scale	(Behrens/Schmitz 2005; Wooldridge/Floyd 1990)
Role of processes: Established benchmarking processes	passive, descriptive	metric, 7pt Likert scale	(Feeny/Lacity/Willcocks 2005; Lacity/Hirschheim 1995a; Behrens/Schmitz 2005; Reilly/Rouse/Seddon 2001)
Role of structures: Establishment of management board / steering committee	passive, descriptive	metric, 7pt Likert scale	(Behrens/Schmitz 2005; Venkatesan 1992)
Role of structures: Establishment of relationship manager	passive, descriptive	metric, 7pt Likert scale	(Behrens/Schmitz 2005; Goles 2001)
Role of structures: Establishment of external consultant	passive, descriptive	metric, 7pt Likert scale	(Behrens/Schmitz 2005; Peled 2001)
Role of informal relationship	passive, descriptive	metric, 7pt Likert scale	(Behrens/Schmitz 2005; Goles 2001; Goles/Chin 2005; Kern 1997; Kern/Willcocks 2000b; Kern/Willcocks 2002)
Role of staff experience	passive, descriptive	metric, 7pt Likert scale	(Beimborn/Franke/Weitzel 2005; Feeny/Lacity/Willcocks 2005; Gottschalk/Solli-Sæther 2006b)
Role of know-how to control vendor	passive, descriptive	metric, 7pt Likert scale	(Beimborn/Franke/Weitzel 2005; Lowell 1992; Michell/Fitzgerald 1997)
Role of attributed degrees of freedom to vendor / Extent of vendor's managerial control	passive, descriptive	metric, 7pt Likert scale	(Kishore et al. 2003; Willcocks/Choi 1995)
Role / establishment of risk sharing models	passive, descriptive	metric, 7pt Likert scale	(Lee/Kim 1999; Willcocks/Lacity 1998b; Lacity/Willcocks 1998; Lyons/Krachenberg/Henke 1990; Conklin 2005)

Category / Dimension	Type of variable (active, parsimonious vs. passive, descriptive)	Level of measurement (scale)	References for variable (selected examples)
Interactions (relationship factors)[8]			
Communication	passive, descriptive	metric, 7pt Likert scale	(Anderson/Narus 1990; Anderson/Narus 1984; Goles 2001; Goles/Chin 2005; Lee/Kim 1999)
Conflict resolution / consensus	passive, descriptive	metric, 7pt Likert scale	(Robey et al. 1989; Mejias et al. 1996; Anderson/Narus 1990; Goles 2001; Goles/Chin 2005; Lee/Kim 1999)
Cooperation / coordination	passive, descriptive	metric, 7pt Likert scale	(Malone/Crowston 1990, 1994; Ring/Van de Ven 1994; Anderson/Narus 1990; Goles 2001; Goles/Chin 2005; Lee/Kim 1999)
Commitment / loyalty	passive, descriptive	metric, 7pt Likert scale	(Fontenot/Wilson 1997; Morgan/Hunt 1994; Korsgaard/Schweiger/Sapienza 1995; Goles 2001; Goles/Chin 2005; Lee/Kim 1999)
Cultural similarity / understanding	passive, descriptive	metric, 7pt Likert scale	(Morgan/Hunt 1994; Goles 2001; Goles/Chin 2005; Lee/Kim 1999; Fitzgerald/Willcocks 1994)
Importance of trust	passive, descriptive	metric, 7pt Likert scale	(Zaheer/McEvily/Perrone 1998; Sabherwal 1999; Morgan/Hunt 1994; Korsgaard/Schweiger/Sapienza 1995; Goles 2001; Goles/Chin 2005; Lee/Kim 1999)
Degree of trust	passive, descriptive	metric, 7pt Likert scale	(Zaheer/McEvily/Perrone 1998; Sabherwal 1999; Morgan/Hunt 1994; Goles 2001; Goles/Chin 2005; Lee/Kim 1999)
Vendor flexibility	passive, descriptive	metric, 7pt Likert scale	(Heide/John 1992; Goles 2001; Goles/Chin 2005; Lee/Kim 1999)
Vendor proactivity	passive, descriptive	metric, 7pt Likert scale	(Kern/Willcocks 2001; Goles 2001; Goles/Chin 2005; Lee/Kim 1999)

Table 3-6. Categories of conceptual framework for IS outsourcing relationship types

3.9   Summary of Outsourcing Foundations

This chapter intended to provide a thorough representation and a broad overview of the current research topics in the wide research field of information systems outsourcing. The various topics covered in this chapter show the diversity and complexity of the research area: ranging from definitional aspects of IS outsourcing and theories that help to explain dyadic exchange relationships between actors to the conceptualization of a framework on how to characterize an IS outsourcing relationship in a holistic way. The definition of IS outsourcing and its history show that contracting out services to a third party provider has a long tradition in many industries and research domains and can be understood in many different ways. Consequently, no standard definition of "outsourcing" could be established to date, but most definitions share a common core of understanding what comprises outsourcing in general and especially the outsourcing of information systems. When choosing and examining the theories that help to understand outsourcing phenomena, it became evident that three streams of theo-

---

[8] This section only lists a few exemplary references for each relationship factor. For a more detailed and comprehensive digest of relationship factors see Table 3-4.

ries can be applied to explain outsourcing: strategic management, economic, and social theories. Each of these theories throws a different light on outsourcing relationships and with the focus of this thesis on the *relationship* aspects of outsourcing, it could be concluded that social theories seem to be most appropriate to explain the area of interest in this work. With the emphasis on the relationship aspect, this chapter then illustrated the evolution of outsourcing research towards the current partnership / relationship focus. Accordingly, the characterizing features of IS outsourcing relationships were laid out. These features can be structured in four constitutive categories, i.e., strategic intents / context, relational architecture, governance mechanisms, and behavioral interactions. In order to evaluate these aspects, a separate chapter was dedicated to discussing outcome elements of outsourcing relationships and different measures to evaluate the success of an outsourcing venture.

Depicting the research foundation of outsourcing in the literature quarried a number of shortcomings and research gaps that have not been addressed in the current research stream and will be addressed in this work. One of the most prevailing issues is the suboptimal and unsuccessful management of outsourcing ventures due to inappropriate governance approaches. So far, contingency factors and different client expectations have not been considered in the current outsourcing literature for governing an outsourcing venture. Distinguishing different types of outsourcing relationships and characterizing them along a set of different constitutive criteria is a promising approach to provide appropriate and specific governance mechanisms for each of these types. A main result of this chapter thus dedicated efforts to building a conceptual framework that helps to systematically characterize outsourcing relationships along a set of criteria.

Overall, by depicting constitutive characteristics of outsourcing relationships based on appropriate theoretical approaches and arranging them in a conceptual framework, this chapter answered research question 1: "What are the constitutive elements of a client-vendor relationship in IS outsourcing?"

Before applying the conceptual framework in practice to empirically identify different outsourcing types in chapter 5 (p. 111ff.), the next chapter will lay out the methodological foundations of how to group empirical data.

4 Theoretical and Methodological Foundations for Classifying Data

. After having introduced a conceptual framework of IS outsourcing characteristics to identify and classify different types or configurations of outsourcing relationships, a clear understanding of the variety of terms around "classification", "types", and "configuration" is still missing. Also some methodological knowledge and foundations on the empirical assessment of different configurations of outsourcing relationships have to be laid.

4.1 Theoretical Foundations of Classification and Configuration

Social science is grounded on the assumption that social life is orderly (Meyer/Tsui/Hinings 1993, 1179). Discovering and invoking configurational patterns, types, and categories is therefore essential to social theory and research (Hair et al. 2006, 553). Classificational schemata "play fundamental roles in the development of a discipline since they are the primary means for organizing phenomena into classes or groups that are amenable to systematic investigation and theory development" (Hunt 1991, 176). Configurations allow people to order and make sense out of their reality by sorting things into discrete and somewhat homogeneous groups (Kluge 1999, 13, 43pp.). They are an approach of synthesis and order to reduce complexity or achieve parsimony (Bailey 1994, 12; Miller 1981, 2, 9). Furthermore, in a heuristic attempt, classifications cannot only provide information density to reduce real world's complexity, but also help to understand, reconstruct, and predict context, behavior and structure of, e.g., organizations (Kluge 1999, 45). For academia, classifications can serve as a basis and anticipation of theory building and specification of hypotheses (Friedrichs 1990; Bailey 1994, 14).

Accordingly, configurational approaches have gained increasing attention in organizational research (Meyer/Tsui/Hinings 1993). Although evolving from contingency theory, the configurational approach makes a clean break from the contingency mainstream, within which researchers have been preoccupied with abstracting a limited set of structural concepts and measuring their relationships with a limited set of abstracted situational concepts (Meyer/Tsui/ Hinings 1993, 1176). As one of the most prevailing steps in advancing contingency research, configurational inquiry represents a holistic attitude by assuming that the parts of a social entity take their meaning from the whole and cannot be understood in isolation. The basic premise of the configurational perspective is that "Organizational structures and management systems are best understood in terms of overall patterns rather than in terms of analyses of narrowly drawn sets of organizational properties" (Meyer/Tsui/Hinings 1993, 1181). Thereby, the configurational approach seeks to look simultaneously at a large number of variables that collectively define a meaningful and coherent slice of organizational reality.

4.1.1 Definition of Classification Terms: Classification, Configuration, Type

In essence, classification is merely defined as the "general process and ordering of entities into groups or classes on the basis of their similarity" (Bailey 1994, 1, 4). A configuration or type is the output that results from (empirically or conceptually) building a classification (scheme) that groups objects together. Although "configuration" has emerged as the predominant term in the context of classification schemes, many researchers use the terms "configuration", "pattern", "gestalt", "archetype", and "type" synonymously, sometimes with only a slightly different notion (Miller/Friesen 1984). They can broadly be defined as "commonly occurring clusters of attributes or relationships that are internally cohesive, such as the presence of some attributes suggest the reliable occurrence of others" (Miller/Friesen 1984, 12). These configurations are expected to have tightly interdependent parts, the significance of which can be best understood by making reference to the whole. When such configurations represent very commonly occurring and therefore *predictively useful* adaptive patterns or scenarios, they are called "gestalts" (Miller 1981, 3). While Miller emphasizes the aspect of predictive usefulness as determining, Venkatraman broadly defines 'gestalts' as "feasible sets of internally consistent configurations (Venkatraman 1989, 432). Kluge (1999, 27, 34pp.) understands "type" as a combination of specific characteristic features that describe and constitute a specific configuration. By virtue of its similarity to one configuration, each object or element can be assigned to a specific type or configuration by comparing its individual features with the characteristic features of the type. Although some authors characterize types as both exhaustive and mutually exclusive (Bailey 1994, 3), types or configurations are not necessarily mutually exclusive and sometimes objects could be assigned to more than one type (Kluge 1999, 42; Miller 1996, 506; Miller/Friesen 1984). Also, many configurations are not intended to be fully exhaustive, but rather illustrate a certain aspect of organizational reality (Miller 1996, 505). Due to their comprehensibility and popularity in the literature around classification approaches, this thesis will stick to the terms "configuration", "type", or "cluster" to describe the empirically derived groups of outsourcing relationships.

4.1.2   Characteristics of Configurations or Types

Configurations take a myriad of forms. For example, they may be represented in typologies developed conceptually or captured in taxonomies derived empirically. They can also be situated at multiple levels of analysis, depicting patterns common across individuals, groups, departments, organizations, or networks of organizations. Because of this variety, the thesis will shortly depict the constituting key features of configurations that were summarized by Miller and Friesen (1984, 4pp.):

1. **Configurations are multidimensional.** Configurations are complex clusters of elements or variables that comprise a large number of significant characteristics. They represent different constellations of conceptually distinct variables or elements that commonly cluster together to collectively characterize many aspects of organizational states and processes.

2. **Configurations may be derived empirically or conceptually.** Conceptual configurations are defined in advance on the basis of a theoretical framework or a synthesis of the literature. Empirical configurations are the product of statistical analyses of multivariate data on large samples of organizations.

3. **There are two main types of configurations: elemental and relational.** Elemental configurations comprise consistent, i.e., thematically related constellations of elements. The number of such configurations will depend upon how finely one wishes to discri-

minate among them. Relational configurations are defined not in terms of elements per se, but rather by the nature of the alignment among them.

4. **Configurations should have predictive importance.** Classifying an organization into a configuration should have predictive implications such as inferring things about the structure of an organization when classified on the basis of their technology.

5. **Establishing the boundaries of configurations may be a problem.** Conceptually derived configurations generally stipulate clear boundaries as their membership is determined by whether or not they satisfy pre-established criteria. Empirically derived configurations are defined statistically around the densest clusters of data and therefore do not have obvious "natural" boundaries.

6. **There is no "one best set" of variables that should be used to describe all sets of configurations.** Although some authors (cf. Hall 1972) suggest that a thorough characterization of organizational configurations includes a certain determined set of variables, it would be counterproductive to suggest that only one set of variables is studied, since it depends on the scope of the research.

7. **Configurations may describe departments, divisions, organizations, or even networks of organizations.** The level of analysis for configuration is not limited to a specific scope of research. While Miller and Friesen (1984) focus on configurations describing entire organizations, in some cases it might be impossible to develop meaningful configurations that pertain to entire organizations.

These key features and recommendations were already considered when building the conceptual framework presented in chapter 3.8 (p. 71ff.). However, they are of even higher importance for the empirical investigation of outsourcing relationship types carried out in chapter 5 (p. 111ff.).

4.1.3 Typologies vs. Taxonomies

Underlying most classification schemes or sets of configurations is the attempt to understand organizational diversity through typologies and taxonomies. In Miller and Friesen's words, the ultimate aim is to "generate typologies or taxonomies, i.e., sets of different configurations that collectively exhaust a large fraction of the target population of organizations or situations under consideration" (Miller/Friesen 1984, 12). It is desirable to find a small number of common configurations that encompass a large proportion of the population. This allows many organizations to be classified using only a few distinctive characteristics, and then permits the prediction of many other organizational features or relationships simply by making reference to the configuration.

As implied in the previous paragraph and chapter, two approaches have been used to discover configurations: *typologies* and *taxonomies* (Miller 1981, 15pp.; Miller/Friesen 1984, 31, 32, 64; Miller 1996, 506pp.; Bailey 1994, 4pp.). Many authors do not distinguish between these two terms and instead often use typology as another term for classification, thereby ignoring the term taxonomy (see, e.g., Kluge 1999). Although as an end result, a taxonomy is similar to a typology and in fact, "many people use the two terms interchangeably" (Bailey 1994, 6), there are several constitutive distinctive features between a typology and a taxonomy.

A *typology* refers to a conceptual, multidimensional classification scheme or set of configurations that have been derived without a formally collected and quantitatively analyzed data set. It identifies configurations or types exclusively on the basis of conceptual or theoretical distinctions. The resultant typologies are of an a priori nature; they are generated "mentally and verbally", not by any replicable empirical basis (Miller/Friesen 1984, 31; Bailey 1994, 6). Typologies are exclusively the products of the concepts and intuitions of theoreticians. Although they are often based on empirical evidence or experience, typologies are generated subjectively. They are not replicable in a strict sense. Among the more prominent typologies are those of (Burns/Stalker 1961), (Miles/Snow 1978), and (Mintzberg 1979). These researchers differentiated among types of strategies, organizations, or decision-making styles, thereby making conceptual distinctions that advanced theory by combining elements from different theories and thus providing a more comprehensive picture of the research object (Miller 1996, 506). Other researchers have termed such typologies based on a priori conceptual distinctions "conceptual classification", "deductive classification", "qualitative classification", "a priori classification", or "classification from above" (Hunt 1991, 177; Bailey 1994, 5). Thereby, they emphasize that for a typology, the classification schema is always developed *before* the researcher analyzes any specific set of data (if at all, as typologies are grounded on conceptual models). Typologies are often based on "logical partitioning" procedures in contrast to grouping procedures (Hunt 1991, 178).

The logic of *taxonomy*, the alternate configurational approach, lies in an empirical classification based on statistical analysis of multiple dimensions. A taxonomy is a multidimensional classification schema or set of configurations that is empirically derived from multivariate analyses of replicable, empirical data on organizations. Typically, organizations or aspects of their structure, strategies, or processes are described by numerical scores along a number of variables. Then, natural clusters are identified in the data, and these clusters, rather than any a priori conceptions, serve as the basis for the configurations (Miller/Friesen 1984, 32, 64). Compared to typologies, taxonomies tend to be more firmly based on quantitative data (Miller 1996, 507). The merit of a taxonomy approach is then the result of reliable and conceptually significant clusterings of attributes. In contrast to typologies, taxonomies by virtue of relying on grouping procedures (Hunt 1991, 181) do not generate empty classes since classes can only be formed from existing observations. Some authors have labeled this empirical taxonomic approach "inductive classification", "ex post classification", "classification from below", "numerical taxonomy", "empirical classification", or "quantitative classification" (Hunt 1991, 177; Bailey 1994, 7). Thereby, it is implied that for a taxonomy, the researcher generates his schema only *after* he analyzed some specific set of data and thus "lets the data suggest the system" (Hunt 1991, 178). Empirically derived classifications rely on grouping procedures that share the common characteristic that they determine by an analysis of a specific set of data. The most commonly used grouping techniques will be described in chapter 4.2 (p. 86ff.).

Overall one cannot say that taxonomies are necessarily more objective or more scientifically useful than typologies. Taxonomies are influenced by many subjective decisions concerning the selection and operationalization of variables, the choice of samples and classificatory criteria, and the selection of statistical procedures. The major difference between typologies and taxonomies is simply that only the latter are replicable by other researchers, as they rely on empirical data (Miller/Friesen 1984, 65). Typologies and taxonomies can both identify predictively useful configurations. The former, however, have been by far the more common (Miller/Friesen 1984, 32) and taxonomies are still less frequently developed than conceptual models (Homburg/Workman/Jensen 2002, 39). Regarding the historical background, the terms are also somehow related to the research discipline. The term *taxonomy* is more generally used in the biological sciences, while *typology* is used in the social sciences (Bailey 1994, 6).

Giving the overall goal of the thesis to empirically identify different configurations of IS outsourcing relationships in order to suggest appropriate and tailored governance approaches for the successful management of outsourcing, this work will adopt a taxonomic approach.

Both typologies as well as taxonomies developed in theory resp. in practice have a number of shortcomings in the way they were carried out by researchers. Many typologies are not mutually exclusive and exhaustive (Bailey 1994, 34). According to Miller and Friesen (1984, 33), most typologies have been too narrowly focused. They have isolated extremely suggestive configurations based on arbitrary and ad hoc criteria (Bailey 1994, 34), but often the configurations are not sufficiently encompassing to serve as a basis for reliable prediction or prescription. Most conceptually based typologies are descriptive instead of explanatory and do not attempt to find the most predictive clustering among the variables (Bailey 1994, 15, 34). Instead they start with theoretically rather than empirically based types using only a small and insufficient number of not comprehensive criterion variables (Miller 1981, 16).

On the other hand, taxonomies also show a number of deficiencies (Miller/Friesen 1984, 35; Miller 1996, 507). Many taxonomies have been criticized for their lack of theoretical significance, their arbitrary and narrow selection of variables and grouping methods, and their unreliable or unstable results. Furthermore, much of the effort for generating a taxonomy has had a predominantly methodological focus. More emphasis is given to discussing methods than to describing and interpreting the findings themselves. In the absence of rich, anecdotal, "soft" evidence such as qualitative interviews, it is hard to discover the meaning of the types and the essence of their configurations, and to elicit their themes (Miller/Friesen 1984, 36).

Many taxonomies fall short regarding these aspects. A too narrow range of variables, the failure to closely examine and interpret the configurations and their predictive power, as well as the lack of using anecdotal material to help understand the configurations limit the utility of prior classifications (Miller/Friesen 1984, 36). A detailed description of shortcomings of prior taxonomies helps to identify pitfalls and can demonstrate how these challenges were addressed in the generation of the taxonomy in this thesis. The taxonomy of outsourcing relationships that will be presented in chapter 5 (p. 111ff.) was designed to overcome some of these limitations by, e.g., employing a broader selection of variables, conducting a qualitative pre-study to collect anecdotal evidence that provides valuable detail on different outsourcing relationships, and by seeking out the most densely populated clusters so that as few types as possible encompass the largest number of outsourcing relationships.

As grouping techniques are inherent and closely related to taxonomical classifications (Hunt 1991, 177, 181), the next chapter will introduce at a very general level a selection of grouping procedures that were used to explore the data in the empirical section of this work.

4.2   Grouping Techniques

Configurations, types, or patterns may be indicated by clusters or homogeneity in the data. There are quite a few standard multivariate grouping techniques that can assist researchers to explore the data to empirically find configurations. Among the most commonly used methods are multivariate cluster analysis, (inverse) factor analysis, multiple discriminant analysis, and multidimensional scaling (Miller/Friesen 1984; Bailey 1994). E.g., multidimensional scaling (MDS) is a method of discovering the fewest fundamental or underlying dimensions that can be used to describe a set of objects, or mathematical algorithms, for defining homogeneous groups that minimizes within-group variance (Miller/Friesen 1984, 43, 49, 50). However, for the purpose of this thesis only cluster analysis and factor analysis are described in detail as these two methods are most appropriate in the context of identifying empirically based outsourcing relationship configurations. A common approach that is also followed in this work is to start off the empirical data analysis with a factor analysis as a pre-technique in order to eliminate potential multicollinearity issues when choosing the input variables for the actual cluster analysis. Since cluster analysis is an exploratory, not confirmatory approach, discriminant analysis is often applied in order to test the validity of the identified clusters. These three techniques, i.e., cluster analysis, discriminant analysis, and factor analysis will be described in the next chapters, as they are the fundamental methodological pillars upon which the empirical part of the thesis is built. A schematic depiction of the interplay of these methods as applied in this thesis is given in Figure 5-3 on page 124.

4.2.1   Cluster Analysis

4.2.1.1   Definition of Cluster Analysis

Cluster analysis is a quantitative method of classification and analytical technique for grouping objects based on the characteristics they possess and thereby developing meaningful subgroups of individuals or objects (Hair et al. 2006, 559). It originated in psychology in the 1930s (Tryon 1939; Zubin 1938), where the related term of *pattern analysis* is also used (Bailey 1994, 6). By virtue of its manifold usage in such diverse disciplines as psychology, biology, sociology, economics, engineering, and business, it has been referred to as Q analysis, typology construction, classification analysis, and numerical taxonomy (Hair et al. 2006, 559). Although clustering techniques predate computerization, most are now computer-based (Bailey 1994; Kuckartz 1990, 1996). The term cluster analysis covers a broad variety of grouping techniques. Generally spoken, "cluster analysis is the general logic, formulated as a procedure, by which we objectively group together entities on the basis of their similarities and differences" (Tryon/Bailey 1970, 1). Cluster analysis techniques are concerned with exploring data sets to assess whether or not they can be summarized meaningfully in terms of a relatively small number of mutually exclusive groups or clusters of objects which resemble each other and which are different in some respects from the objects in other clusters (Everitt/Landau/Leese 2001, 10). The attempt is to maximize the *homogeneity of objects within the clusters* while also maximizing the *heterogeneity between the clusters* (Hair et al. 2006, 555).

There is a noteworthy difference between clustering (*unsupervised* classification) and discriminant analysis (*supervised* classification). In supervised classification, researchers are provided with a collection of pre-classified groups or labeled patterns; the problem is to label a newly encountered, but yet unlabeled pattern (Jain/Murty/Flynn 1999, 265). In cluster analysis, unlike discriminant analysis, the groups are not predefined. Instead, the technique is used to identify the groups (Hair et al. 2006, 20) and to group a given collection of unlabeled patterns into meaningful clusters obtained solely from the data (Jain/Murty/Flynn 1999, 265). By virtue of this characteristic, cluster analysis belongs to the group of interdependence techniques of statistical analysis which solely focus on the definition of structure, assessing interdependence without any associated dependence relationships (Hair et al. 2006, 553).

4.2.1.2   General Procedure of Cluster Analysis

The general procedure of cluster analysis is rather simple (following Bailey 1994, 35pp.). One begins with a basic score matrix (S) that shows a set of scores for each N object (cases) on each of M variables (see Table 4-1). The idea is to group the most similar entities (cases) in the data matrix together (Bailey 1994, 35). To group the cases by similarity one could either compute measures of similarity (e.g., a correlation coefficient) or measures of dissimilarity (e.g., distance measures). Objects are then grouped together based on their internal similarity (low distance, high correlation) and based on their dissimilarity from other groups (Bailey 1994, 36).

Variable / Object	1	2	3	...	M
Tim	$Score_{11}$	$Score_{12}$	$Score_{13}$		$Score_{1M}$
Tina	$Score_{21}$	$Score_{22}$	$Score_{23}$		$Score_{2M}$
Marco	$Score_{31}$	$Score_{32}$	$Score_{33}$		$Score_{3M}$
...					
N	$Score_{N1}$	$Score_{N2}$	$Score_{N3}$		$Score_{NM}$

Table 4-1. Basis of cluster analysis: score (S) matrix of objects and variables
(Source: adapted from Bailey 1994, 35)

In addition to determining the similarity algorithm, a general decision is to be made whether objects / cases (such as individuals or organizations) or variables should be clustered. Regarding the score matrix example, one could either correlate pairs of objects (rows) or pairs of variables (column). This distinction is referred to as R vs. Q analysis or approach to taxonomy (Miller/Friesen 1984, 37). The standard practice in social science is to correlate vertically (to correlate variables) because models and hypotheses generally refer to relationships between pairs of variables. This is called *R*-analysis (Bailey 1994, 38). The alternate approach is to correlate horizontally (correlate objects or cases), which is called *Q*-analysis. Although *R*-

analysis is the standard approach when it comes to model or hypothesis testing (i.e., identifying relationships between variables), for cluster analysis, the researcher is interested in grouping objects such as individuals or organizations. Then, constructing clusters of objects on the
basis of their similarity on the variables is the preferred choice. This requires correlations
among objects, or *Q*-correlation (Bailey 1994, 38). But overall, the internal data is the same
for both approaches, it is only a question of direction whether to correlate horizontally or vertically.

4.2.1.3   Different Clustering Techniques and Algorithms

Jain et al. (1999) as well as Bailey (1994, 40pp.) identified an extensive number of criteria
along which different clustering methods or techniques can be distinguished. In order to focus
the scope of this thesis, Figure 4-1 gives an overview of different approaches and algorithms
to clustering data, thereby addressing the most common approaches in literature. For a more
detailed analysis of different clustering techniques, the work of (Jain/Murty/Flynn 1999) and
(Berkhin 2002) is recommended who provide a comprehensive overview of clustering techniques.

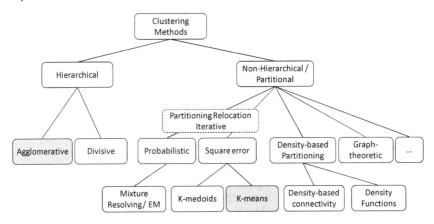

Figure 4-1. Different clustering technique approaches
(Source: adapted from Berkhin 2002; Jain/Murty/Flynn 1999)

At the most general level, clustering techniques can be distinguished as either *hierarchical* or
non-hierarchical, i.e., partitional or single-level clustering algorithms (Bailey 1994; Ketchen/
Shook 1996; Hair et al. 2006; Jain/Murty/Flynn 1999; Berkhin 2002).

Hierarchical clustering received its name by virtue of its characteristics of proceeding in a
sequence for grouping the data (Hotho 2004, 67) and thereby presenting the data in the form
of a hierarchy or treelike structure over the entity set. Hierarchical clustering proceeds successively through a series of steps that build a tree-like structure by either merging smaller clusters into larger ones, or by splitting larger clusters resulting in a nested series of partitions.
The clustering methods differ in the rule by which it is decided which two small clusters are
merged or which large cluster is split. The end result of the algorithm is a tree of clusters

called a *dendrogram*, i.e., a graphical representation (tree graph) of the results in which each object is arrayed on one axis, while the other axis portrays the steps in the hierarchical procedure (Hair et al. 2006, 556). By cutting the dendrogram at a desired level a clustering of the data items into disjoint groups is obtained.

Hierarchical clustering methods can be further categorized into *agglomerative* ("bottom-up") vs. *divisive* ("top-down") methods (Bailey 1994, 40pp.; Berkhin 2002, 7). This aspect relates to algorithmic structure and operation. Agglomerative clustering builds a hierarchy in a bottom-up fashion by starting from smaller clusters and sequentially merging two nearest clusters at each step into "parental" nodes. An agglomerative approach begins with each object in a distinct, one-entity (singleton) cluster, and successively merges two clusters at time until all entities are part of a universal cluster (containing the entire data set) (Mirkin 2005, 112p.).

Divisive clustering builds a hierarchy top-to-bottom by splitting greater clusters into smaller ones starting from the universal cluster containing all entities (i.e., the entire data set) until each is a single-entity cluster (Mirkin 2005, 112p.; Hair et al. 2006, 625). While using agglomerative clustering is very popular and widespread among researchers (Eckstein 2004, 325), the use of divisive methods in the social sciences has been quite scarce (Hotho 2004, 67) and as a result divisive methods are not well known in strategic management nor information systems (Ketchen/Shook 1996, 445). As hierarchical agglomerative procedures have become popular among researchers of various disciplines, Sneath and Sokal (1973) referred to this class of methods as SAHN: sequential, agglomerative, hierarchical and non-overlapping.

Non-hierarchical or partitional clustering, on the other hand, attempts to directly decompose the data set into a set of disjoint clusters at the same level (thus, single-level clustering). The criterion function that the clustering algorithm tries to minimize may emphasize the local structure of the data, as by assigning clusters to peaks in the probability density function, or the global structure. Typically the global criteria involve minimizing some measure of dissimilarity in the samples within each cluster, while maximizing the dissimilarity of different clusters. Specific non-hierarchical methods vary slightly, but function in essentially the same manner (Hair et al. 2006; Ketchen/Shook 1996, 445).

The *k-means algorithm* is by far the most popular non-hierarchical, partitional clustering method used in scientific applications (Berkhin 2002, 15). The name comes from representing each of k clusters by the mean (or weighted average) of its points, the so-called centroid (Berkhin 2002, 15). The overall objective of the k-means algorithm is to minimize the total intra-cluster variance or squared error sum. Several variants of the k-means algorithm exist in the literature, among them Forgy's and Lloyd's algorithm is the most popular and widespread (Forgy 1965; Lloyd 1957, 1982). It consists of two-step major iterations that 1) reassign all objects to their nearest centroids, and 2) recompute centroids of newly assembled groups (Berkhin 2002, 16; Bacher 1996, 309). In detail, first, k cluster centers (centroids) are chosen by the researcher, either randomly or using some heuristic data, e.g., based on a prior result gathered from hierarchical cluster analysis. After these initial cluster centroids are selected, each object is assigned to the group with the closest cluster center, i.e., the nearest centroid (Jain/Murty/Flynn 1999, 279). The data points are thus partitioned into k clusters. As each new object is allocated, the cluster centroids are recomputed using the current memberships or assignments (i.e., centroids are moved to the center of their respective clusters). Multiple successive iterations are made through a data set to allow observations to change cluster membership based on their distance from the recomputed centroids. To arrive at an optimal solution, iteration through a data set continues until a stopping criterion is achieved, e.g., until no observations change clusters (i.e., no reassignments, minimal total intra-cluster variance or squared error) (Ketchen/Shook 1996, 446). The wide popularity of the k-means algorithm is well deserved since it is simple, straightforward and based on the firm foundation of analysis of variances (Berkhin 2002, 17). However, one caveat has to be considered, that is, the k-means algorithm is sensitive to the initial partition and strongly depends on the initial guess of centroids (or assignments) (Jain/Murty/Flynn 1999, 279).

Non-hierarchical methods have two potential advantages over hierarchical methods (Ketchen/Shook 1996, 446). While hierarchical clustering methods facilitate a comprehensive evaluation of a wide range of cluster solutions, they lack flexibility in such that once clusters are joined, they cannot be revisited after being constructed and never be separated in the clustering process (Berkhin 2002, 12). By allowing observations to switch cluster membership, non-hierarchical methods are less impacted by outlier elements. Although outliers can initially distort clusters, this is often corrected in subsequent passes as the observations switch cluster membership (Aldenderfer/Blashfield 1984; Hair et al. 2006).

Second, by making several loops through the data, the final solution optimizes within-cluster homogeneity and between-cluster heterogeneity (Ketchen/Shook 1996, 446). Non-hierarchical clustering procedures are thus often used to develop an optimal cluster solution and improve the results from the hierarchical procedures. Obtaining this improvement, however, requires that the number of clusters be specified a priori. This is problematic because cluster analyses are often exploratory.

A solution proposed by many researchers is to use a combination of hierarchical and non-hierarchical clustering procedures in a two-stage procedure where a hierarchical algorithm is used to define the number of clusters and cluster centroids; these results then serve as the starting points for subsequent non-hierarchical clustering (Hair et al. 2006, 591; Milligan/Cooper 1985; Eckey/Kosfeld/Rengers 2002, 204). Research has shown that this procedure increases validity of solutions (Milligan/Cooper 1985). Ketchen and Shook (1996, 446) mention that "the only cost is the extra time and effort required on the researchers' part; a cost we contend is worth bearing."

4.2.1.4   Clustering Steps

Cluster analysis usually follows a general process of how to conduct the analysis and assessment of clusters (Bülow 1996, 25; Hair et al. 2006, 567pp.; Kluge 1999, 248p.; Bacher 1996, 151; Jain/Dubes 1988). The following steps are distilled and adapted from a variety of authors and summarized in the following 6-stage process:

1. Objective of Cluster Analysis: Specifying the Research Question and Selection of Cluster Variables

Before carrying out a multivariate cluster analysis, the researcher has to define the underlying purpose of the research as well as the appropriateness of the research method. If the research purpose is in accordance with the primary goal of cluster analysis, i.e., to partition a set of empirically gathered objects into two or more (natural) groups based on the similarity of these objects, the researcher can narrow the research focus and consider the content (more specifically the input variables) of the cluster analysis.

As Hair et al. (2006) note "the objectives of cluster analysis cannot be separated from the selection of variables used to characterize the objects being clustered" (Hair et al. 2006, 569). Selecting the appropriate input variables for the cluster analysis is one of the fundamental issues for a successful cluster analysis and meaningful results (Ketchen/Shook 1996, 443). In Bailey's words it is crucial "to ascertain the key or fundamental characteristics on which the classification is to be based" (Bailey 1994, 2). There is a consensus in literature that the input variables should be derived from theory and should be meaningful for the subject under study (Rich 1992). The degree of acceptable interdependencies among cluster variables is more debated. While Arabie and Hubert (1994, 166) argue that it is difficult to imagine empirical data arising in the behavioral sciences where all dimensions are mutually exclusive, Sneath and Sokal (1973) recommend to exclude variables that are logically or empirically correlated because they may overweight underlying constructs and thus cause biases in the results (Ketchen/Shook 1996, 444).

It is not sensible or recommendable to include all variables into the clustering procedure, as this dilutes the results and no meaningful groups can be identified (Bacher 1996, 409).The selection of cluster variables thus has to be carried out with due diligence, as the clusters to be derived reflect the inherent structure of the data and are only defined on the basis of these variables. Selecting the variables has to be done with regard to theoretical, conceptual, as well as practical considerations (Hair et al. 2006, 569). Although authors such as (Eckstein 2004, 324), (Deichsel/Trampisch 1985, 11), or (Backhaus et al. 2006, 549) recommend to include variables that are relevant to the researched object, there is no standard and objective selection procedure. It is in the subjective "eye of the beholder" which variables to include and which to treat as descriptive variables that are only considered in the stage of interpreting the resulting groups (Bäumer 1997, 156).

2. Research Design in Cluster Analysis: Data Preparation

The next step comprises the organizational issues of preparing the data, especially with respect to sample size, data cleansing, scale conversions (if any), and standardization of data. Berkhin emphasizes that a sound data preparation is essential because 'sloppy' data "make[s] chances of a successful clustering futile" (Berkhin 2002, 40).

The issue of *sample size* in cluster analysis does not relate to any statistical inference issues (statistical power). Rather, the sample size must be large enough to provide sufficient representation of small groups within the observed population. In determining the sample size, the researcher should specify the group sizes necessary and relevant for the research question being asked (Hair et al. 2006, 571).

Another issue to be considered for preparing the data is *scale conversion* and *standardization of the data*. Most clustering techniques require metric or continuous data as the level of measurement. However, there is also the possibility of using nominally measured data, i.e., categorical variables. The level of measurement of the data primarily influences the choice of proximity measures that can be applied to measuring distance or similarity of the objects (see step 3: selection of proximity measure). What is important to notice is that all clustering variables should have the same level of measurement (either metric or categorical) (Backhaus et al. 2006, 505, 508). Although there are cluster techniques that allow for clustering different types of data (e.g., the two-step cluster procedure in SPSS producing a simple clustering, not a hierarchical one) (Jain/Murty/Flynn 1999, 272), in practical applications, there are problems with mixing continuous, ordinal and nominal data (Hair et al. 2006, 577).

For considering whether the data should be standardized or not before calculating similarities, the researcher has to take into consideration that most cluster analyses using distance measures are quite sensitive to differing scales or magnitudes among the variables (Hair et al. 2006, 577). Variables with larger dispersion, i.e., larger standard deviation, tend to have a higher impact on the final similarity value. Hair thus concludes that "clustering variables should be standardized whenever possible to avoid problems resulting from the use of different scale values among clustering variables" (Hair et al. 2006, 579, 581). Some critics put forward the removal of valuable natural relationships in the data by conducting a standardization or state that standardization may not even have a noticeable effect (Milligan 1980). But using standardized variables eliminates the effects due to scale differences, but for the same variable as well. The most common form of standardization is the conversion of each variable to standard scores, so called z scores, by subtracting the mean and dividing by the standard deviation for each variable. There are also distance measures which already incorporate a standardization procedure, e.g., the Mahalanobis distance.

In the case of response-style effects, i.e., response patterns specific to certain individuals, a standardization through z scores is not appropriate if groups according to their response style are to be identified (Hair et al. 2006, 580). In this case, standardizing by respondent not to the sample's average, but to the respondent's average score is most appropriate. This so-called within-case or row-centering standardization can be quite useful in removing response-style effects and is especially appropriate for attitudinal data (Schaninger/Bass 1986).

These issues of standardization, however, are mostly important in the case of different scales of measurement of the variables to be included in the cluster analysis. The need for standardization is minimized when all of the variables are measured on the same response scale, e.g., a series of attitudinal questions (Hair et al. 2006, 579).

3. Selection of Proximity Measure

The concept of proximity or similarity is fundamental to cluster analysis. Inter-object similarity can be measured in several ways, with *correlation measures*, *distance measures*, and *association measures* being the most popular ones. Both correlation and distance measures require metric data, whereas association measures are designed for nominal or ordinal data (Hair et al. 2006, 573).

A *correlation measure* of similarity (e.g., the *Q* correlation coefficient) does not look at the magnitude, but rather at the patterns of the values (Eckey/Kosfeld/Rengers 2002, 214; Backhaus et al. 2006, 505; Hair et al. 2006, 573). Correlations represent patterns across the variables and indicate similarity between the profiles of the two objects. Correlation measures are thus primarily used if similarity in the profiles of the objects rather than the magnitude of the values is of interest (Backhaus et al. 2006, 507). While correlation measures are widely used in other multivariate techniques such as factor analysis, they are rarely used in cluster analysis, where distance measures are very common (Jain/Murty/Flynn 1999, 271; Bacher 1996, 199). The following description will thus focus primarily on distance measures and also shortly depict association measures.

Although the principal idea of cluster analysis is to measure similarity between the objects, mostly *distance measures* are set in place to measure the proximity of the objects (Bacher 1996, 199). But as Eckey et al. (2002, 205) mention, distance and similarity are two sides of the same coin and can be transferred in each other. Research provides a variety of distance measures (Backhaus et al. 2006, 494pp.; Bacher 1996, 198pp.; Brosius 2006). Most distance measures are some sort of derivate of the general Minkowski metric[9]. Table 4-2 depicts the most popular distance measures.

Distance Measure	Explanation	Application / Appropriateness
Euclidean distance (L2-norm)	The mostly recognized measure of distance (Jain/Murty/Flynn 1999, 271), often referred to as straight-line distance. The Euclidean distance between two points is the length of the hypotenuse of a right triangle.	Euclidean distance is by far the most popular choice used in k-means algorithms (Berkhin 2002, 41). Works well when a data set has "compact" or "isolated" clusters (Jain/Murty/Flynn 1999, 272). Very robust measure.
Squared (or absolute) Euclidean distance (L2-norm)	Similar to Euclidean distance, but the sum of the squared differences without taking the root. The advantage of not having to take the square root speeds up computation.	Recommended for centroid and Ward's method of clustering. Very robust measure.
City-block (Manhattan, Taxi Driver/Taxicab) distance (L1-norm)	This measure is not based on Euclidean distance. It measures distance by the sum of the absolute differences of the variables (i.e., the two sides of a right triangle rather than the hypotenuse, thus the name city-block or Manhattan).	Very simple procedure, but may lead to invalid clusters if cluster variables are highly correlated.

---

[9] Minkowski metric: $d_{k,l} = \left[\sum_{j=1}^{J} \left|x_{kj} - x_{lj}\right|^r\right]^{\frac{1}{r}}$ with $d_{k,l}$ Distance of objects k and l, x_{kj}, x_{lj}: Value of variable j for object k, l (j=1, 2, ... J), r >= 1: Minkowski Constant (Backhaus et al. 2006, 503)

Distance Measure	Explanation	Application / Appropriateness
Chebyshev (or Tche-bychev) distance	A metric defined on a vector space where the distance between two vectors is the greatest of their differences along any coordinate dimension or across all of the clustering variables. Also known as the chessboard distance.	Particularly susceptible to differences in scales across the variables.
Mahalanobis distance	Generalized distance measure that accounts for the correlations among variables by weighing each variable equally. Relies on standardized variables. It corrects data for different scales and correlations in the variables.	Quite appropriate measure, but not available as proximity measure in many statistical programs (e.g., SAS, SPSS). Requires strong prerequisites to the data (e.g., similar means of variables in all groups). Often used to detect outliers.

Table 4-2. Distance measures in cluster analysis
(Source: adapted from Hair et al. 2006, 575)

Association measures are used to compare objects whose characteristics are measured only in non-metric terms, i.e., categorical data (nominal or ordinal) (Hair et al. 2006, 576). In general, association measures count the match among pairs of objects regarding the existence of characteristics in both objects. Several association measures have been developed for measuring dichotomous data, e.g., the Tanimoto (Jaccard) Coefficient, the Simple-Matching-Coefficient (SMC), the Russel and Rao Coefficient (RR), or the Dice Coefficient (for an overview see Bacher 1996, 200; Backhaus et al. 2006, 494pp.; Eckey/Kosfeld/Rengers 2002, 218pp.). Although association measures are less preferable when continuous variables can be used for the cluster analysis, sometimes association measures are set in place when the level of measurement is adjusted and "downsized" from a metric to a non-metric level in order to get equally scaled data (Backhaus et al. 2006, 508).

4. Selection of Cluster Algorithm (fusion algorithm for merging objects)

After measuring the distance or similarity between the objects, the researcher has to select the cluster algorithm, i.e., the fusion or partitioning procedure used for forming the clusters. The partitioning procedure sets the rules most appropriate to place similar objects into one group or cluster. It determines how similarity is defined between multi-object clusters in the clustering process (Hair et al. 2006, 584, 586). Among numerous approaches, the five most popular (hierarchical agglomerative) algorithms are single linkage, complete linkage, average linkage, centroid method, and Ward's method (Backhaus et al. 2006, 517pp.; Bacher 1996, 144; Hair et al. 2006, 586, 625). The differences among them lie in the mathematical procedures used to calculate the distance between clusters. Each has different systematic tendencies (or biases) in the way it groups observations (Ketchen/Shook 1996, 445). Table 4-3 gives an overview of different algorithms.

Cluster Algorithm	Explanation	Application / Appropriateness
Single Linkage (nearest-neighbor)	Defines similarity between clusters as the shortest distance from any object in one cluster to any object in the other.	Most versatile algorithm, can define a wide range of clustering patterns. Tends to find outliers. Tends to produce many small, less large groups. Problematic when clusters are little delineated. Can then produce long, snakelike chains. Often used as pre-analysis for identifying outliers. Can be used with any data level.
Complete Linkage (farthest neighbor, diameter)	Comparable to single linkage, but cluster similarity is based on maximum distance between objects in each cluster. Called complete linkage because all objects in a cluster are linked to each other at some maximum distance. Within group similarity equals group diameter.	Assumes strict homogeneity and thus tends to produce many small and very homogeneous clusters. Rather does not find outliers. Eliminates chain problem of single linkage. Many researchers find it the most appropriate. Can be used with any data level.
Average Linkage	Similarity of any two clusters is the average similarity of all objects in one cluster with all individuals in the other. Does not depend on extreme values.	Compromise between single and complete linkage. Less affected by outliers. Tends to generate clusters with small within-cluster variation. Can be used with any data level.
Centroid	Similarity is measured as the distance between cluster centroids, i.e., the mean values of the objects on the variables in the cluster variate (cluster means). Every time, individuals are grouped, a new centroid is computed.	Less affected by outliers. Bias toward producing irregularly shaped clusters. Can only be used with metric data.
Ward	In contrast to the other procedures, similarity is not a single measure of similarity, but the sum of squares within the clusters summed over all variables. Selection of which clusters to combine is based on which combination minimizes within-cluster sum of squares.	Tends to produce clusters with roughly the same number of objects. Tends to be distorted by outliers. Difficult to identify clusters representing small proportions of sample. Can only be used with metric data.

Table 4-3. Common cluster algorithms for defining multi-member cluster similarity
(Source: based on Backhaus et al. 2006, 517pp.; Hair et al. 2006, 584pp.; Eckey/Kosfeld/Rengers 2002, 230pp.)

Given the different notions and foci of the cluster algorithms described above, the chosen algorithm should be matched with the underlying structure of the examined data (e.g., sample size, distribution of observations, and level of measurement of variables) (Ketchen/Shook 1996, 445). Thus, for example, the centroid method should only be used when data are measured with metric scales and clusters are expected to be very dissimilar from each other. Likewise, Ward's method is best suited for studies where the number of objects in each cluster is expected to be approximately equal and there are no outliers. The combination of Euclidean distance as a distance measure and the Ward method is very common and is in practice often combined with a following non-hierarchical procedure using the k-means algorithm (Backhaus et al. 2006, 523). There are also non-hierarchical cluster algorithms which will not be elaborated in this thesis. For an overview, see chapter 4.2.1.3 (p. 88ff.) and for a detailed description (see, e.g., Hair et al. 2006, 589pp.).

5. Determining the Number of Clusters: Analysis and Interpretation of Clusters

After applying the cluster algorithm, a major challenge of cluster analysis is to evaluate the output of a cluster algorithm and to determine what characterizes a 'good' clustering result and a 'poor' one. Problematically, all clustering algorithms will – when presented with data – produce clusters regardless of whether the data contains natural clusters or not (Jain/Murty/ Flynn 1999, 267). But virtually all clustering procedures provide little if any information as to the number of clusters presented in the data. Assessing the appropriate number of clusters is thus a largely unsolved issue in practice (Hair et al. 2006, 592; Hotho 2004, 52; Milligan/Cooper 1985, 159). Although there is a number of procedures in order to mathematically or statistically determine (Kaufman/Roussseeuw 1990; Milligan/Cooper 1985) the number, quality and goodness of the cluster solution (for an overview see Berkhin 2002, 38pp.), no standard objective selection procedure exists (Hair et al. 2006, 592, 626). The ultimate decision how many clusters to consider lies with the subjective decision of the researcher. But nevertheless, Backhaus et al. suggest to use statistical criteria instead of practical logic to determine the number of clusters (Backhaus et al. 2006, 534). Often these procedures are referred to as so-called stopping rules (Milligan/Cooper 1985, 159; Hair et al. 2006, 592)[10]. When using hierarchical methods, the most basic procedure is to visually inspect the dendogram, the graphical representation of the order that objects join clusters and the similarity of these objects (Backhaus et al. 2006, 534). Natural clusters of the data are indicated by relatively dense 'branches'. This method, however, relies on interpretation and thus should be used cautiously (Aldenderfer/Blashfield 1984).

Ketchen and Shook mention two other techniques for identifying the appropriate number of clusters, both relying on the agglomeration coefficient or heterogeneity measure (a numerical value which measures heterogeneity as the distance at which clusters are formed) (Ketchen/Shook 1996, 446; Hair et al. 2006, 594): The first technique is called the *elbow criterion* and involves graphing the coefficient (y-axis) against the number of clusters (on an x-axis). The curve of the graph shows the development of heterogeneity. A marked flattening of the graph suggests that the clusters being combined are very dissimilar, thus the appropriate number of clusters is found at the angle of the graph, the so called 'elbow' of the graph. This elbow identifies a leap in the development of the heterogeneity measure. Interpreting a graph, however, may be difficult and the elbow cannot always be unambiguously identified. For example, sometimes there might be more than one elbow in a graph (Aldenderfer/Blashfield 1984). In fact, the two cluster solution always shows the highest leap of heterogeneity change when going from one to two clusters and should thus be dismissed in most cases (Hair et al. 2006, 592; Backhaus et al. 2006, 536). A similar procedure involves examining the incremental changes in the coefficient by numbers, not visually. The percentage increase in the agglomeration coefficient can be calculated for each cluster solution and the solution should be chosen when the percentage increase is markedly larger than occurring at other steps. A large increase implies that dissimilar clusters have been merged and have caused the jump in heterogeneity. Thus, the number of clusters prior to the merger is most appropriate (Hair et al. 2006, 593). Again as for the elbow criterion, a major limitation of this approach is that there

---

[10] For an overview and evaluation of different procedures to determine the number of clusters see the work of Milligan and Cooper (1985).

may be either no large leaps in the coefficient, indicating that there may not be any natural groups in the data. Or in some cases, there may be several ones, indicating more than one natural set of clusters (Ketchen/Shook 1996). Nevertheless, this type of stopping rule has been shown to provide quite reliable decisions in empirical studies (Milligan/Cooper 1985).

6. Interpreting, Validating and Profiling the Clusters

The final step of cluster analysis is to interpret, validate, and profile the clustered objects to determine their composition. Interpreting the cluster results often requires to go back to the raw scores of the variables and develop profile diagrams using this data, especially when the variables used for the cluster analysis, were standardized (Hair et al. 2006, 595). In assessing either correspondence or practical significance, the researcher compares the empirically derived clusters to a preconceived conceptual typology. Beyond more or less reliable stopping rules, such a preconceived framework can help to interpret the cluster results.

Validation of the cluster results involves assuring that the cluster solution has external validity (i.e., is representative of the general population of interest and is stable over time) and criterion-related validity (i.e., is useful for the prediction of important outcomes) (Hair et al. 2006, 596; Ketchen/Shook 1996, 447).

Reliability (i.e., consistency) is a necessary but not sufficient condition of validity. Reliability might be tested either by performing a cluster analysis multiple times, changing algorithms and methods for addressing multicollinearity (cross-validation). The degree of consistency in solutions then indicates reliability (Ketchen/Shook 1996, 447) or researchers may split a sample and analyze the two halves independently (Hair et al. 2006, 596p.). *External validity* may be tested by analyzing both the sample of interest and a another similar sample and then assessing the similarity of the results (Hair et al. 2006, 596). In many studies, however, a 'holdout' sample is not available (Ketchen/Shook 1996, 447). *Criterion-related or predictive validity* can be evaluated through significance tests with selected variables that were not used to form the clusters, but known to vary across the clusters (Aldenderfer/Blashfield 1984). Those variables should have strong theoretical or practical support to serve as predicting criterion-validity (Hair et al. 2006, 597). In summarizing the discussion of reliability and validity measures, Ketchen and Shook state that "the value of these techniques is limited because they use cluster analysis and thus are subject to its inherent problems, most notably the reliance on researcher judgment" (Ketchen/Shook 1996, 447). Instead, they recommend using significance tests with external variables to establish criterion-related validity.

Lastly, *profiling* the clusters consists of describing the characteristics of each cluster to demonstrate its inherent features and differences to the other groups. Thereby, the researcher also draws on other variables that were not included in the actual clustering procedure. Many times this profiling may be accomplished by applying discriminant analysis to the groups identified by the cluster analysis. Using discriminant analysis, the researcher compares average score profiles for the clusters (Hair et al. 2006, 597). The categorical (dependent) variable is the previously identified cluster, and the independent variables are the "external" variables to describe the cluster profile.

4.2.1.5   Strengths and Pitfalls of Cluster Analysis

Cluster analysis has several important strengths as a tool for organizational researchers. One of the main advantages of computer-based approaches such as multivariate cluster analysis is a systematized creation and analysis of identified groups which eventually enhances the traceability, transparency and thus the repeatability and reliability of the generated results (Kuckartz 1990, 501). It provides better classifications than non-quantitative, more subjective, conventional taxonomic methods because it provides greater discrimination of taxonomic differences. It is a very flexible approach to grouping because a number of different clustering rules and procedures are available. A third and obvious advantage of the technique is the ability to deal with a substantial number of variables and data points. It is far more convenient and simpler to use than a mathematical algorithm. Also, clustering encourages more effort to tailor the technique to the nature of the research problem than do many of the factor analysis programs (Miller/Friesen 1984, 46). Finally, the exploratory – instead of a confirmatory, theory-testing – character of cluster analysis allows revealing new insights and exploring unknown research phenomena. It thus combines the advantages of qualitative expert interviews, i.e., exploring new and interesting in-depth insights, with the advantages of quantitative studies, i.e., gathering data on a large, profound, and reliable empirical basis.

On the other hand, clustering methods involve a number of inconveniences and weaknesses: Cluster analysis is descriptive, atheoretical, and non-inferential (Hair et al. 2006, 560p.). Many applications of cluster analysis in strategy have lacked an underlying theoretical rationale (Ketchen/Shook 1996, 442). Without a theoretical foundation, however, the clusters that are identified may not reflect any real conditions but instead may simply be statistical artifacts that capitalize on random numerical variation across organizations. As to inference, cluster analysis has no statistical basis upon which to draw inferences from a sample to a population. Furthermore, cluster analysis will always create a solution regardless of the actual existence of any structure in the data. The cluster solution is then not generalizable because it is totally dependent upon the variables used as the basis for the similarity measure. This criterion can be made against any statistical technique (Hair et al. 2006, 561), but cluster analysis is generally considered more dependent on the measures used to characterize the object of inquiry. There are no absolute rules to determine how many clusters should be formed and mostly there is a lack of a unique clustering solution (Bailey 1994, 65; Ketchen/Shook 1996). Each researcher must decide which sets of groups give the most adequate information (Miller/Friesen 1984, 46). If variables are measured in different units or data levels, it becomes difficult to grasp the concept of similarity. Criteria for establishing the boundaries or membership criteria of clusters are subjective. Trial and error must be applied to find the most homogeneous groups that encompass the largest number of firms. (Miller/Friesen 1984, 46). Also the selection of cluster criteria is critical. High correlation among clustering variables can be problematic because it may overweight or underestimate certain aspects. Such a multi-collinearity can be addressed through subjecting variables to factor analysis and using the resultant uncorrelated factor scores for each observation as a basis for clustering (Ketchen/Shook 1996, 444). Only a few irrelevant variables that are included in the cluster analysis can cause severely biased results (Bacher 1996, 163). Thoroughly choosing the "relevant" cluster variables is thus a necessary and elaborate prerequisite. For an overview and more details on criticism of the method see prior efforts of (Ketchen/Shook 1996;

Punj/Stewart 1983; Aldenderfer/Blashfield 1984, 14, 33pp.; Hair et al. 2006; Everitt/Landau/ Leese 2001).

Thus, in any use of this method, the researcher must take particular care in ensuring that strong conceptual support predates the application of the technique. Only with strong conceptual support and a validation the cluster solutions are potentially meaningful and relevant (Hair et al. 2006). In the context of this thesis, potential pitfalls and weaknesses of cluster analysis were eliminated or at least mitigated by developing a conceptual framework derived from literature on the one hand, and by introducing a qualitative pre-study in order to get a feeling for the appropriateness of a cluster analysis in this research realm. Furthermore, the advantages of this quantitative, but exploratory technique and its appropriateness in answering the research questions posed in this thesis, outweigh the potential weaknesses that have been taken care of.

4.2.2 Discriminant Analysis

Discriminant analysis is a multivariate method to analyze group differences and also to predict group affiliation of new elements (classification) (Backhaus et al. 2006, 156). Discriminant analysis is closely related to other multivariate methods such as regression or variance analysis with regard to analyzing dependencies in data and thus belongs to the group of *structure-validating* methods (Backhaus et al. 2006, 156; Berekoven/Eckert/Ellenrieder 2006, 216). One of the major differences is to be found in the requirements towards the level of measurement.

Table 4-4 illustrates these requirements.

Method	Level of measurement	
	Independent variable	Dependent variable
Regression analysis	metric / continuous	metric / continuous
Analysis of Variance (ANOVA)	nominal / categorical	metric / continuous
Discriminant analysis	metric / continuous	nominal / categorical

Table 4-4. Requirements for the level of measurement of different methods of dependency measures
(Source: Berekoven/Eckert/Ellenrieder 2006, 216)

Analysis of variance examines if affiliation to a certain group has an effect on some dependent variables. It examines whether group membership is associated with reliable mean differences on a combination of dependent variables. In contrast, discriminant analysis examines which independent variables best explain the affiliation to a certain group (Kuß 2007, 244).

Discriminant analysis is also somehow related to cluster analysis, although not with regard to the research question they aim to answer, but rather as subsequent and complementing methods (Backhaus et al. 2006, 157). While cluster analysis aims at *identifying* groups in data, discriminant analysis aims at distinguishing these (pre-defined) groups along a set of variables (Berekoven/Eckert/Ellenrieder 2006, 221). Thus discriminant is often applied after having conducted a cluster analysis. Discriminant analysis treats these a priori defined groups as the dependent variable, often labeled as the grouping variable, and aims at analyzing differences between these a priori defined groups of data (as defined by the dependent grouping variable) with regard to some independent variables.

Discriminant analysis is suitable for answering the following research questions (Hair et al. 2006):

- How can two or more groups of data points be distinguished along certain variables?

- Which variables distinguish these groups best?

- Which contribution does each independent variable deliver to distinguish the groups?

- How can new elements, i.e., data points, be attributed to the defined groups?

Discriminant analysis involves several steps: First, an F test (Wilks' lambda) is used to test if the discriminant model as a whole is significant, and if the F test shows significance, then the individual independent variables are assessed to see which differ significantly in mean by group and these are used to classify the dependent variable. Then, the discriminant functions are estimated. Estimating discriminant functions is somehow similar to estimating regression functions. The number of functions is the lesser of (g - 1), where g is the number of categories in the grouping variable (Garson 2008b). Each discriminant function is orthogonal to the others. The first function usually maximizes the differences between the values of the dependent variable and is regarded as the most powerful differentiating dimension, but later functions may also represent additional significant dimensions of differentiation.

In order to evaluate the goodness of a discriminant analysis, usually the following measures are used (Hair et al. 2006; Tabachnick/Fidell 2001; Brosius 2006):

- The *eigenvalue*, also called the characteristic root of each discriminant function, reflects the ratio of importance of the dimensions which classify cases of the dependent variable. There is one eigenvalue for each discriminant function. The higher the eigenvalue is, the better the dimension discriminates between the variables.

- The *canonical correlation* is a measure of the association between the groups formed by the dependent and the given discriminant function. When the canonical correlation is large (close to 1), there is a high correlation between the discriminant functions and the groups.

- *Wilks' lambda* is used to test the significance of the discriminant function as a whole. The canonical correlation and Wilks' lambda are associated. A significant lambda means one can reject the null hypothesis that the two groups have the same mean discriminant function scores and conclude the model is discriminating (Garson 2008b). The smaller the value for Wilks' lambda the better the groups can be distinguished because the within-group variance is low compared to the between-group or overall variance (Brosius 2006, 752).

- The *classification of objects* assesses the group membership prediction accuracy, i.e., how well the discriminant function works, and if it works equally well for each group of the dependent variable. The classification ratio describes how much observations were classified in the correct (i.e., actual vs. predicted) group (Hair et al. 2006, 296).

For the purpose of the thesis, discriminant analysis will not be explained in more detail since its primary purpose is the validation of the cluster solution. For details on discriminant analysis and further readings see, e.g., (Tabachnick/Fidell 2001; Hair et al. 2006).

4.2.3 Factor Analysis

Factor analysis just like cluster analysis belongs to the group of interdependence techniques which focus on the definition of structure rather than assessing relationships between variables. Its primary purpose is to explore the underlying structure among the variables in an analysis (Hair et al. 2006, 104). Factor analysis can help to manage the myriad of – sometimes overlapping – variables by grouping highly correlated variables together into a smaller set of underlying factors and thereby reducing complexity. Because of this complexity-reducing structure-analyzing characteristics factor analysis can play a unique role in the application of other multivariate techniques and is thus often used as a preceding technique to eliminate multicollinearity (Hair et al. 2006, 582; Berekoven/Eckert/Ellenrieder 2006, 221).

4.2.3.1 General Considerations and Distinctions in Factor Analysis: Exploratory vs. Confirmatory, R vs. Q Analysis

An important distinction has to be made between conducting a factor analysis from an *exploratory* or from a *confirmatory* perspective (EFA vs. CFA) (Hair et al. 2006, 105). The most common approach of factor analysis is exploratory, useful in searching for structure among variables or as a data reduction technique. The researcher's a priori assumption is that any indicator may be associated with any factor. There is no prior theory and one uses factor loadings to intuit the factor structure of the data. However, if knowledge about the structure of the data exists – gathered through theory or prior research – factor analysis might more appropriately take a confirmatory approach, i.e., assessing to which extent the data meets the expected structure. As such, confirmatory factor analysis is integrated in structural equation modeling (SEM), helping confirm the latent variables modeled by SEM.

As EFA is the most common form of factor analysis, the following chapter will primarily view factor analytic techniques from an exploratory, non-confirmatory point of view.

With the decision made whether the factor analysis is to be applied from an exploratory or confirmatory perspective, another distinction has to be considered regarding the unit of analysis. While most researchers use factor analysis for identifying structure among a set of variables, it can be applied in a more general context to identify the structure of relationships either among variables or among cases. The most common type of factor analysis aims at analyzing relationships among variables to identify groups of variables forming latent dimensions (factors) and is referred to as *R factor analysis*. *Q factor analysis* (also called inverse factor analysis) as an alternative involves factoring the subjects vis-à-vis the variables and forms groups of respondents or cases (objects) based on their similarity on a set of characteristics (variables). The result is a "clustering" of the subjects into independent groups based upon factors extracted from the data. This application is not used much today because of computational difficulties and also because of the fact that a variety of clustering techniques has been developed that are designed specifically for the purpose of grouping multiple subjects into independent groups, such as cluster analysis (Hair et al. 2006). Although *Q factor analysis* is comparable to cluster analysis in its objective of assessing structure and grouping objects, it differs with respect to the grouping technique. Factor analysis generates the groupings based on patterns of variation in the data, i.e., correlation, whereas cluster analysis gathers groupings based on distance or similarity (proximity) (Hair et al. 2006, 559).

In this thesis, *R factor analysis* will be applied as a preceding technique to summarize and reduce data and identify structures among variables and cluster analysis will be used (as described before) to identify structures and similarities among respondents (cases).

4.2.3.2   Design and Process of a Factor Analysis

The design and procedure of conduction a factor analysis involves 4 basic steps:

1. Selection of variables and calculation of the input data (correlation matrix)
2. Extraction of factors (commonalities and eigenvalue)
3. Factor rotation and interpretation of factors
4. Factor values

Selection of variables and calculation of the input data (correlation matrix)

Before starting with the actual factor analysis, the variables to be included in the analysis (data level and sample size) have to be chosen and evaluated for their appropriateness.

The primary requirement in terms of data levels is that a correlation value can be calculated among all variables. While metric data is best suited and also the "most prudent approach is to avoid non-metric data" (Hair et al. 2006, 112), non-metric (nominal and ordinal) variables can also be used for a factor analysis, but need a specialized method, such as, e.g., latent class analysis (Hair et al. 2006, 112).

With regard to basic statistical assumptions and requirements towards the distribution of the variables, factor analysis does not strongly require a normal distribution (Tabachnick/Fidell 2001, 588). However, data with a reasonably normal distribution will enhance the solution.

Regarding the sample size, no scientific answer to this question exists and methodologists differ. Alternative arbitrary and not mutually exclusive "rules of thumb" in descending order of popularity, include the one depicted in Table 4-5. In general, the sample must have more observations than variables and there is near universal agreement that factor analysis is inappropriate when sample size is below 50 (Hair et al. 2006, 112).

Name of "Rule of Thumb"	Description	Reference
Rule of 10 (10:1 ratio)	There should be at least 10 cases for each item in the instrument being used.	(Hair et al. 2006)
STV ratio	The subjects-to-variables ratio should be no lower than 5.	(Bryant/Yarnold 1995)
Rule of 100	The number of subjects should be the larger of 5 times the number of variables, or 100. Even more subjects are needed when communalities are low and/or few variables load on each factor.	(Hatcher 1994)
Rule of 150	At least 150 - 300 cases are recommended, more toward the 150 end when there are a few highly correlated variables, as would be the case when collapsing highly multicollinear variables.	(Hutcheson/Sofroniou 1999)
Rule of 200	There should be at least 200 cases, regardless of STV.	(Gorsuch 1983)
Rule of 300	There should be at least 300 cases.	(Norušis 2005)
Significance rule	There should be 51 more cases than the number of variables, to support chi-square testing.	(Lawley/Maxwell 1971)

Table 4-5. Rules of thumb for assessing the appropriate sample size for factor analysis

The first step of conducting a factor analysis includes calculating the input data and assessing the appropriateness of the data to be used for the analysis. To assess such appropriateness, the correlation between the variables is analyzed through a correlation matrix. When visually inspecting the correlation matrix a substantial number of correlations should be greater than 0.30 (Hair et al. 2006, 114). The correlation between variables is also analyzed through the anti-image or partial correlations, i.e., the correlation that is unexplained when the effects of other variables are taken into account (Hair et al. 2006, 114). If two variables share a common factor, their correlation and the degree of variance explained by the other variable will be high. The part of variance that is not explained by the other variable is called *anti-image* (Brosius 2006, 770). As the association of multiple variables is regarded, the partial correlation, i.e., the correlation between two variables with the effect of the other variables removed needs to be considered. The anti-image correlation matrix contains the negatives of the partial correlation coefficients, and the anti-image covariance matrix contains the negatives of the partial covariances. Most of the off-diagonal elements should be small in a good factor model (Brosius 2006, 770), indicating the unique variance the variable pairs share. A small anti-image value thus calls for a high correlation between two variables.

Further analyses of determining the appropriateness of factor analysis examine the entire correlation matrix. *Bartlett's test of sphericity* is a statistical test for the presence of correlations among the variables, and gives one overall output measure. It tests the null hypothesis that the intercorrelation matrix comes from a population in which the variables are non-collinear (i.e., an identity matrix) and that the non-zero correlations in the sample matrix are due to sampling error. Bartlett's test should show a high chi-square value and a highly significant correlation.

Lastly, the *Kaiser-Meyer-Olkin Measure of Sampling Adequacy (KMO)* quantifies the degree of intercorrelation by measuring whether the partial correlations among items are small and thus allows to evaluate if the items are appropriate for a factor analysis. The KMO index ranges from 0 to 1 and can be interpreted along Kaiser's (1974) own thresholds for good values (see Table 4-6).

KMO Value	Degree of Common Variance
0.90 to 1.00	Marvelous
0.80 to 0.89	Meritorious
0.70 to 0.79	Middling
0.60 to 0.69	Mediocre
0.50 to 0.59	Miserable
0.00 to 0.49	Don't Factor

Table 4-6. Evaluation thresholds of KMO values
(Source: Kaiser 1974)

While the KMO gives an overall measure for the adequacy of a factor analysis, the measure of sampling adequacy (MSA) values can also be calculated for each variable. They are similar to the KMO measure (overall MSA), but correspond to single variables. They can be found in the anti-image-correlation matrix and should not fall below 0.50.

Selecting the factor extraction method (commonalities and eigenvalue): initial and extracted solution

At this stage in the analysis, the researcher must extract factors from the variables and then determine the number of meaningful factors. The main challenge hereby is to determine how much the data can be reduced, i.e., how many factors should be extracted that will explain the variance of all variables. So there is a trade-off between a small number of factors to be extracted and a large degree of variance explained by these factors.

Before presenting and discussing various alternatives of extraction methods, some basic understanding for the composition of the variables and their variance has to be laid out as the extraction methods primarily differ with respect to their use of variance.

Factor analysis by definition only uses standardized values (z-values) and thus automatically transforms the variables into standardized ones (Brosius 2006, 773; Bühl 2006, 485). In the initial solution of factor extraction, each variable is standardized to have a mean of 0 and a standard deviation (and variance) of 1.Thus, the total variance to be explained equals the number of variables. Since a single variable can account for 1 unit of variance, a useful factor should account for more than one unit of variance (i.e., have an *eigenvalue* of 1), otherwise the factor extracted explains no more variance than a single variable. Two key concepts regarding the degree of explained variance are important to consider: the *communality* of a variable is the extent to which an item correlates with all other items and describes the total amount of variance of the original variable that is explained by all extracted factors. *Eigenvalue* represents the amount of all the variance in the data that is explained by the factor with which it is associated. The *factor loading* expresses the correlation of the item with the factor. The square of this factor loading indicates the proportion of variance shared by the item with the factor (i.e., the *communality* of the variable if summarized over all factors or the *eigenvalue* of the factor if summarized over all variables). The sum of the square of the factor loadings for each variable with one factor equals the *eigenvalue* of the respective factor (column sum of the squared factor loadings).

With the basic understanding of how variance can be partitioned and expressed via *commu-nality* or *eigenvalue*, the researcher can now address the differences between the two most commonly used extraction methods: principal component analysis (PCA) and principal axis factoring, also known as common factor analysis (PAF, FA). PCA and PAF do not differ with respect to their computation technique, but with respect to their underlying theoretical assumptions.

PCA is used when the objective is to summarize most of the original information in a minimum number of factors for prediction purposes. It asks "how can the variables that load on a factor be combined to one 'collective term' or component?" It does not look for any causal relationship. Common factor analysis in contrast is used primarily to identify underlying factors or dimensions that reflect what the variables share in common. It searches for the cause behind the strong loadings of a variable on a factor. Therefore, common factor analysis is most applicable in structural equation modeling (SEM) when confirmatory factor analysis is conducted as the type of factoring because this method allows the researcher to examine factor loadings of indicator variables to determine if they load on latent variables (factors) as predicted by the researcher's model. This can provide a more detailed insight into the measurement model than can the use of single-coefficient goodness of fit measures used in the SEM approach.

As mentioned, from a computing point of view, PCA and PAF do not differ when it comes to calculating. However, the most obvious difference from a mathematical point of view is their use of explained versus unexplained variance (Tabachnick/Fidell 2001, 585). PCA considers the total variance and derives factors that contain small proportions of unique variance while PAF only analyzes the shared variance. Thus, in PCA the initial communalities are set to 1 due to the use of the correlation matrix and the 1 on the diagonal. Therefore, all of the variance of each item is accounted for in the analysis. Of course some of the variability is explained and some is unexplained. So in the principal component analysis with these initial communalities set to 1, one tries to find both the common factor variance and the unique or error variance. Compared to PAF the extracted communalities will be higher using PCA due to the inclusion of the uniqueness of each item. As an extraction method, principle component analysis is one of the most commonly used methods (Brosius 2006, 772). Some researchers yet suggest using principal axis method (also known as common factor analysis) instead as the more preferable method since it considers only the common or shared variance thereby removing the uniqueness or unexplained variability from the model. Thus, when reviewing communalities, as the values of the communalities decrease, then the more unexplained variability or uniqueness exists within that item. As a result, lower communalities indicate that the item does not add to the proposed factor structure.

The decision for applying either PCA or PAF is led by theoretical or logical, rather than computational considerations (Backhaus et al. 2006, 293). Furthermore, although PCA is generally preferred for purposes of data reduction (translating variable space into optimal factor space), while common factor analysis is generally preferred when the research purpose is detecting data structure or causal modeling, as Wilkinson et al. note, for most datasets, PCA and common factor analysis will lead to similar substantive conclusions (Wilkinson/Blank/Gruber 1996). Especially when commonalities are similar when using common factor analysis and

PCA, then similar results will follow. In fact, both PCA and PAF "arrive at essentially identical results if the number of variables exceeds 30 or the communalities exceed 0.60 for most variables" (Hair et al. 2006, 119).

After having decided on the extraction method, the next step is to extract the unrotated factors and to determine the number of meaningful factors. Determining the number of factors is not a straightforward task, because the decision is ultimately subjective (Backhaus et al. 2006, 295; Brosius 2006, 775). In fact, the researcher should combine conceptual foundation with some empirical evidence (Hair et al. 2006, 119). Several criteria do exist for determining the number of factors, but most of these are just empirical guidelines. One of the most commonly applied techniques is the *Eigen One rule*, also known as the *Kaiser-Guttman rule* or the *latent root criterion*. The rationale behind this rule is that any factor should account for the variance of at least a single variable. As each variable is standardized and has a variance of 1, only those factors whose *eigenvalues* are greater than 1 should be kept while the rest should be discarded. Using the eigenvalue for establishing a cutoff is most reliable when the number of variables is between 20 and 50. If less, the tendency for this method is to extract a conservative number of factors, i.e., too few (Hair et al. 2006, 120).

Another criterion aims at establishing a cutoff based on achieving a specified cumulative percentage of total variance. For this *percentage of variance criterion* no absolute threshold has been set for all applications. While in the natural sciences, the factoring procedure is usually not stopped until the factors account for a cumulative variance of approx. 95 percent, in the social sciences, where information is often less precise, it is not uncommon to consider a solution that accounts for around 60 percent of the total variance as satisfactory(Hair et al. 2006, 120).

The *scree test criterion* can be used to visually determine the number of useful factors to be extracted. The scree test is used to identify the optimum number of factors that can be extracted before the amount of unique variance begins to dominate the common variance structure (Cattell 1966). A scree plot is derived by plotting the *eigenvalues* against the number of factors in their order of extraction. A scree plot should form the intersection of two lines. One line should be an initial steep line of useful factors and the second line should be a gradual trailing line of factors that should be eliminated. The point at which the curve first begins to straighten out, also called the "elbow", is considered to indicate the maximum number of factors to extract.

A last technique recently gained popularity, particularly in the social science literature (Pallant 2005), i.e., *parallel analysis* which was originally developed by Horn (1965). It compares the size of the *eigenvalues* with those obtained from a randomly generated data set of the same size. Only those *eigenvalues* that exceed the corresponding value from the random data set are retained (Pallant 2005, 175). Parallel analysis has been shown to deliver very accurate results, while Kaiser's criterion and Cattell's scree test sometimes tend to overestimate the number of factors (Pallant 2005, 175).

In practice, most researchers seldom use a single criterion in determining how many factors to extract. Instead, initially a criterion such as the eigenvalue is used as a guideline and then the practicality of the factors is assessed (Hair et al. 2006, 121). Moreover, factor analysis is used as a data exploration technique and thus relies on the interpretation and judgment of the researcher rather than on hard and fast statistical rules (Pallant 2005, 183).

Factor rotation and interpretation of factors

Most researchers agree that most unrotated solutions are not sufficient and that rotation will improve the interpretation by reducing some of the ambiguities that often accompany the preliminary analysis (Hair et al. 2006, 126). The ultimate goal and effect of factor rotation is thus to achieve simpler, theoretically more meaningful factor patterns. Methods to rotate factor for a better interpretation can be divided into two groups: *orthogonal* and *oblique* factor rotation. Orthogonal factor rotation maintains the axes at 90 degrees and thus keeps the prerequisite of mathematically independent (uncorrelated) factors. Methods of orthogonal factor rotation include, e.g., QUARTIMAX, VARIMAX, or EQUAMAX, with VARIMAX being the most widespread technique (Hair et al. 2006, 126pp.). Oblique rotation methods rotate the axes with not retaining the 90-degree angle between the reference axes and thus allow correlated factors. Examples of oblique rotation methods are OBLIMIN or PROMAX. Although the principal idea of factor analysis is to reduce data to a small number of independent factors which is in conflict to oblique factor rotation, "realistically, few constructs in the real world are uncorrelated [...] [and thus] no compelling analytical reason suggests favoring one rotational method over another" (Hair et al. 2006, 127).

In interpreting factors, a decision must be made regarding the factor loadings worth attention and further consideration. As the squared factor loading indicates the variable's total variance explained, the absolute size of the factor loading should be as high as possible. In general, when the emphasis is on practical, not strictly statistical significance, factor loadings in the range between 0.30 and 0.40 are considered to meet the minimal level for interpretation of structure (Hair et al. 2006, 128). Loadings of 0.50 or higher are considered practically significant and loadings exceeding 0.70 are indicative of a well-defined structure, but loadings beyond 0.80 are not typical according to Hair et al. (2006, 128). These guidelines are applicable when the sample size is 100 or larger (Hair et al. 2006, 128). According to Thurstone's rules (Coughlin/Knight 2007) items should be selected that relate strongly to the proposed factor (i.e., factor loadings of .40 or above). Items should be deleted or dropped if they have crossloadings and are double loaded (i.e., .40 or above on more than one factor) and items that are unique or do not load on any factor (i.e., all factor loadings are below .40). Regarding the item – factor ratio, for exploratory factory analysis, Thurstone recommends at least three variables per factor (Kim/Mueller 1978, 77).

After analyzing the factor matrix of loadings, the significant loadings for each variable have to be identified according to the practical rules of thumb given above. Also the communalities of the variables should be viewed to assess whether the variables meet acceptable levels of explanation by the newly extracted factors.

With all the significant loadings identified and the communalities examined, the last step is to respecify the factors by options such as excluding variables from the factor analysis, changing rotation methods, or increasing or decreasing the number of factors (Hair et al. 2006, 133).

After having identified the number of factors, many researchers follow up with a reliability analysis to test the internal consistency of the newly constructed scale, i.e., the factor with condensed variables. One measure is the reliability coefficient, Cronbach's alpha (Hair et al. 2006; Brosius 2006).

When the primary purpose of conducting a factor analysis was to reduce data, a very last step of the factor analysis is to compute factor scores[11]. Conceptually, the factor score represents the degree to which each individual scores high on the group of items with high loadings on a factor. The factor score is computed based on the factor loadings of all variables on the factor.

4.3 Summary of the Methodological Foundations for Classifying Outsourcing Clients

This chapter laid out the methodological foundations and statistical techniques that are required and best suited to meet the research aim to empirically identify homogeneous groups of outsourcing clients that are similar in their outsourcing motives. One of the objectives of this chapter was to set a common language and get a clear definitional understanding of different terms in the context of classifications and categorizations of data. It became clear that the conceptual framework that introduced important categories to consider when comprehensively describing outsourcing relationships, can be termed a "typology" since it is a conceptual classification derived from literature. In contrast, deriving outsourcing client types on an empirical basis, as it will be conducted in the next chapter, is termed a "taxonomy".

The chapter also introduced the set of statistical tools and techniques to empirically distinguish groups of data. Hereby, the most prominent methods are cluster analysis, factor analysis, analysis of variance, and discriminant analysis. A common approach to combine methods is the following: In order to avoid multicollinearity in the data and thus an overweight or underestimation of certain aspects, many studies apply a factor analysis as a pre-analysis method in order to derive clear and uncorrelated factors to be used for the further analysis. Factor analysis aims at identifying a common "factor" behind a number of variables that share a common aspect. With these uncorrelated factors, the actual cluster analysis is carried out with the goal to identify internally homogeneous and externally heterogeneous groups in the data. Often, more than one cluster approach is combined. For example, a popular process is to start off with a hierarchical cluster analysis algorithm to identify the appropriate number of cluster and then validate and optimize the cluster solution with a non-hierarchical, partitional (e.g., k-means) algorithm. In order to validate the whole cluster analysis solution, a discriminant analysis is often applied that belongs to the group of *structure-validating* methods and analyzes group differences and also predicts group affiliation of new elements (classification). The identified and validated groups are then often further analyzed with an analysis of variance (ANOVA) in order to identify significant group differences among the clusters.

Such a combination of methods is required and recommended by many authors (Ketchen/ Shook 1996) in order to overcome the shortcomings of the single approaches. The sensitivity

---

[11] Other methods include using single representative, surrogate variables or summated scales. For more details see (Hair et al. 2006, 138pp.).

of cluster analysis in terms of correlated cluster variables is eliminated through factor analysis. The unsteady results of cluster analysis are mitigated and strengthened by combing hierarchical and non-hierarchical cluster algorithms and validating the solution with discriminant analysis. Lastly, the actual interpretation and further analysis of the results is supported and enabled by applying different analyses of variance (ANOVA). A schematic depiction of the interplay of these methods is given in chapter 5.2 (p. 122ff.).

After having described the fundamental issues of grouping techniques, the specific methods will be applied in the next chapter where outsourcing relationship types are empirically identified.

5   Empirical Evidence of Outsourcing Relationship Types

Quantitative research in the social and behavioral sciences follows an established research process (Atteslander 2008). In general, one can distinguish three phases of research:

1. The *context of discovering the object of inquiry*, where the context of the research and the motivation and causes for conducting the research are laid out

2. The *context of exploration and justification*, where the methods of the study are discussed and the actual data is assessed and analyzed, and

3. The *context of interpretation and dissemination*, where the conclusions and contributions of the study are discussed and learnings for theory and practice are elaborated

According to these phases, empirical research has distinguished five phases for conducting empirical studies with only little variation among different researchers (Atteslander 2008; Diekmann 2008; Friedrichs 1990). The following figure depicts these phases.

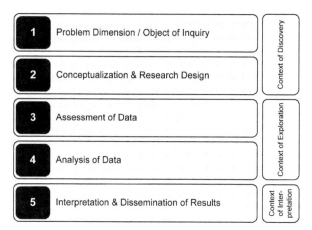

Figure 5-1. Phases of the quantitative research process
(Source: adapted from Atteslander 2008; Diekmann 2008; Friedrichs 1990)

In phase 1, the object of inquiry is determined and the research problem and relevance both in practice as well as in theory is defined. Literature is analyzed and in many cases, first (sometimes anecdotal) empirical evidence (e.g., through qualitative expert interviews) is gathered to get an idea about the problem dimension and the need for research in this area. Such a triangulation with qualitative and quantitative data is also very useful to enhance the reliability of the data and to avoid common method bias in the design of the study. Furthermore, in this phase appropriate theoretical approaches that help to explain the object of investigation are chosen. The problem definition is addressed in the very first chapter of this thesis, i.e., to get an idea of constitutive elements of an outsourcing relationship and examine different outsourcing relationship types, their characteristics, and appropriate governance mechanisms. Besides a theory-grounded and literature-based analysis of the problem realm (see also chapter 3, p. 15ff.), a qualitative pre-study was conducted to collect anecdotal evidence on the research object and to get an idea whether the assumed idea of different client types is supported in practice (see the following chapter 5.1, p. 113ff.).

The research object is specified and operationalized in phase 2. Here, the research design is planned and the method of investigation is determined, e.g., the object of interest is approached with, e.g., qualitative expert interviews, a quantitative survey, or with an action research approach. Additional steps involve choosing the unit of analysis, i.e., who is investigated, developing the questionnaire with the items scales, and defining constructs, variables, and indicators. The research design of the study in this thesis is described in chapter 5.2 (p. 122ff.). It involves describing the design of the questionnaire, the items used in the questionnaire, and also the appropriate item scales.

Phase 3 involves the actual assessment of the data and also the logistics of gathering the data such as sending out a mailing with the questionnaire or organizing an online survey. This is described in chapter 5.3 (p. 124ff.), where also additional information on the context of the study (sent-out dates, return rate, etc.) is given.

The data is consolidated and analyzed in phase 4. This phase involves several sub-steps according to Atteslander (2008, 661): coding the data set and transferring the answers to a standardized scheme and variables; controlling for errors and missing values; recoding of variables or scales; statistical analysis of the data (uni-, bi-, or multivariate analyses). Although the problem definition and the design of the study require much care and thoughtful preparation, the analysis of the data is often regarded as the core of the research process as it involves very intense and laborious efforts and also requires thoughtful attention (Atteslander 2008). Chapter 5.4 of this thesis (p. 126ff.) is dedicated to conducting a comprehensive analysis of the data collected in this study. It examines the data with different multivariate methods such as factor and cluster analysis and then analyzes differences between the identified groups via an analysis of variance (ANOVA). Based on the identified cluster groups, the data is further analyzed in chapter 6 with a different method, i.e., structural equation modeling. As this is a separate analysis (although based on the same data set), the research process with the research design etc. is again presented in chapter 6 (p. 215ff.) specifically for the SEM analysis.

While much focus is laid on the analysis of the data, the last phase, i.e., the interpretation and dissemination of the data (phase 5) is often neglected. However, it should be regarded as equally important as the other phases. Here, the results are prepared for different target groups, involving academics as well as practitioners. The interpretation of the results for this study is found in chapters 5.5 (p. 148ff.), 5.6 (p. 205 ff.), 6.5 (p. 236 ff.), and 7 (p. 243 ff.). Besides contributions to theory and practice, open issues for future research and unsolved challenges and limitations of the current study are discussed here.

Following the research process described above, the remainder of this chapter is as follows: In order to get a rich understanding of the object of inquiry and an accurate problem definition, a qualitative pre-study on the existence of different IS outsourcing relationships is carried out in the next chapter. This pre-study is part of the triangular research design chosen for this work.

By combining different research methods and data such as qualitative and quantitative information, the reliability and mightiness of the data is enhanced (Harvey/MacDonald 1996) and the risk of a common method bias in the design of the study is mitigated. After the research problem is understood and the applicability and sensibility of a grouping approach is scrutinized, the research design of the quantitative study is presented. Here, the methods to be applied for the data analysis are determined as well as the design of the study, i.e., online survey, target group, etc. The data collection and first empirical results on the demographics of the respondents are given in the next chapter 5.3 (p. 124ff.). The data analysis with bi- and multivariate statistical techniques is carried out in chapter 5.4 (p. 126ff.) where factor analysis, cluster analysis, discriminant analysis and ANOVAs are applied to derive meaningful groups of outsourcing clients distinguished along their prevailing outsourcing motivations. Chapter 5.5 (p. 148ff.) will then interpret the results and describe the clusters in further detail, drawing on the passive descriptive cluster variables presented in the framework. The last chapter 5.6 (p. 205ff.) entails a summary and consolidated description of the results in the subchapters before and describes the identified client groups in a condensed way.

5.1 Qualitative Pre-Study: First Evidence of Different IS Outsourcing Relationships

Most researchers do not gather anecdotal material as "soft" evidence to get a prior understanding of the field and help understand the meaning of the types and the essence of their configurations before conducting a large quantitative study in order to develop taxonomies (Miller/Friesen 1984, 36). To overcome these shortcomings and to explore the appropriateness, necessity, and applicability of a classification of outsourcing relationships, this thesis applied a multi-method approach, combining qualitative and quantitative data to get a rich and comprehensive understanding of the research field. Thus, before carrying out a large quantitative survey, a series of exploratory expert interviews was conducted to collect first evidence for the practical importance of the outsourcing relationship types.

5.1.1 Data Collection

Based on findings in the literature on relationship factors and the developed framework for classifying the relationship types, first empirical evidence for different outsourcing types was gathered through 18 exploratory, semi-structured expert interviews with Chief Information Officers and IT managers of outsourcing clients (10) as well as sales and account managers of IT service providers (8). The interviews were conducted between May 2005 and May 2006. They were tape-recorded and transcribed.

Although not accounting for a large sample size, these interviews served as a first exploratory empirical evidence to support the conceptual idea of distinguishing between various outsourcing relationship types. The interview topics covered antecedent conditions of the outsourcing decision, expectations towards the outsourcing relationship, and parameters of the current outsourcing venture. Across the interviews the expectations towards the capabilities and conditions of an outsourcing arrangement and also the characteristics and importance of relationship factors differed significantly. Table 5-1 gives an (anonymized) overview of the conducted expert interviews.

Interview partner (position)	Industry	Contract duration	Experience of expert with IS outsourcing	Areas of out-sourced IT / outsourcing portfolio	Expectations towards outsourcing partner / Success factors of relationship	Identified or assigned type of relationship
Customer A Chief Information Officer (CIO)	Telecommunication	Current contract: since 2004, before that: different vendor since 1998, contract duration: 5 years	>15 years Experience both as client and vendor	Infrastructure (Desktop, laptop, WAN, LAN, messaging, telephone, server and storage)	• Expert know-how / best of breed for technology and processes • Cost reduction: scale effects, synergies • Customized solution • Proactive suggestions for improvement • IT support for new products	Technology Excellence (Partner for Excellence)
Customer B Chief Information Officer (CIO)	Media / Television	Current contract: since 2005, contract duration 4 years, before: 3-year contracts since 1996	>4 years	Infrastructure (network, WAN, SAP, data bases), call center, application hosting	• Flexible adaptation towards changed customer demand / adaptability / quick availability (business critical for live TV) • Specified competencies, responsibilities • Peak demand orientation because of dynamic end consumer demands • Industry know-how of provider	Mixed motives, rather Commodity Supplier (supportive role)
Customer C Head of IT	Banking / Finance	Since 2001, then back-sourced IT, current contract since 2004, contract duration 3 years	>5 years	Current: SAP, desktop services, onsite support, help desk Before also: networks, data center	• Cost reduction • Professional expertise: Expert know-how, state-of-the-art know-how of technology and processes • Fit of delivery model of client and vendor • Flexible adaptation of customer's business development: internationalization, M&A	Commodity Supplier (supportive role)
Customer D Head IT-Management	Manufacturing / Chemistry	Since 1996, contract duration 7 years, current contract since 2003, duration 5 years	>4 years	Network, SAP, special applications	• Industry know-how of provider • Transparent, specified contract with special service level agreements (SLA) • Fit of delivery model of client and vendor	Commodity Supplier (supportive role)
Customer E Chief Information Officer (CIO)	Aerospace	Since 1999, contract duration 3 years (twice), current contract duration 5 years	>4 years	Networks (WAN, LAN), data center, applications, desktop	• Proactive suggestions for efficiency and improvement • No bureaucratic, but rather slim processes • Quick response and flexible adaptation to customer needs	Mixed motives: Reliance Partner (Long-term Stability Partner), Technology Excellence
Customer F Associate Partner strategic IT Management	Consulting	Since 2000, contract duration revolving (rollover, extendable)	>5 years	Total outsourcing to single vendor: infrastructure (server, desktops), application outsourcing, BPO (help desk, call center)	• Focus on core competencies • Technological innovation explicitly not expected • Stability with long-term partnership → ongoing, stable delivery of operations • Cost reduction	Reliance Partner (Long-term Stability Partner)

Interview partner (position)	Industry	Contract duration	Experience of expert with IS outsourcing	Areas of outsourced IT / outsourcing portfolio	Expectations towards outsourcing partner / Success factors of relationship	Identified or assigned type of relationship
Customer G Project Leader Cost Management	Banking	n/a, short-term period (on project-basis)	n/a	Selective outsourcing, only application development	• Cost reduction • Buy in of external know-how • No important drivers: benefit-risk share, knowledge transfer, innovation potential	Commodity Supplier (supportive role)
Customer H Head of IT operations	Insurance	Since 2002, contract duration revolving (rollover, extendable)	>4 years	Infrastructure, help desk, printing services	• Cost reduction • „learning" → knowledge transfer	Commodity Supplier (supportive role)
Customer I CIO	Insurance	n/a, contract duration revolving (rollover, extendable)	>7 years	Infrastructure (network, WAN, SAP, data center), applications	• Cost efficiency, transparency • Flexibility due to volatile business • Technical innovation explicitly expected	Mixed motives: Technology Excellence (Partner for Excellence), Commodity Supplier
Customer J Head of IT / Project Management, CIO	Transport / Logistics	Since 2001 (mother company since 1998)	n/a	Infrastructure (hosts, SAP, desktop services), applications	• Focus on core competencies • Innovation (understood as cost reduction) • No important drivers: knowledge transfer	Commodity Supplier (supportive role)
Vendor A Account Manager	IT Services (Full Service Provider) Current customer in Banking / Finance	Current contract: since 2004, contract duration 10 years	n/a	IT systems, special banking applications	• Transfer of risks to vendor (dynamic end consumer demands in transaction business of banks) • Flexibility of monetary model: pay-on-production • Innovative delivery and market model	Mixed motives: Joint Service Development Partner / Strategic Alliance Partner
Vendor B Account Manager	IT Services (Full Service Provider) Current customer in health care / medicine	Current contract duration between 1 and 3 years	n/a	Infrastructure, applications (ASP)	• Industry know-how of provider • Transfer of risks to vendor: risk-benefit sharing • Collaborative service development of innovative service in ASP medical area	Joint Service Development Partner
Vendor C EMEA Program Manager and Competency Leader, Relationship Alignment Solutions	IT Services (Full Service Provider)	Contract duration approx. 5 years (customer tendency shorter)	>6 years	Full service provision: infrastructure, applications, business processes	• Exchange of values • Information sharing, open communication • Explicit consideration of mutual interests • Adaption of cultures and processes of the partner	Strategic Alliance Partner
Vendor D Managing Consultant Strategy and Change	IT Services (Full Service Provider) Same company as Vendor C	Contract duration approx. 5 years (customer tendency shorter)	n/a	Full service provision: infrastructure, applications, business processes	• Relevance and type of relationship management depends on desired relationship form • Success factors: SLA compliance, customer satisfaction • Quality of service delivery • Day-to-day working relationship	Mixed motives, no dominant type identified

Interview partner (position)	Industry	Contract duration	Experience of expert with IS outsourcing	Areas of outsourced IT / outsourcing portfolio	Expectations towards outsourcing partner / Success factors of relationship	Identified or assigned type of relationship
Vendor E Leader Resource management and Reporting, Service Manager	IT Services (Full Service Provider)	Contract duration approx. 3-5 years	n/a	Full service provision: infrastructure, applications, business processes	▪ Vendor must be proactive, demonstrate up-to-date technology capabilities ▪ Reputation of service provider, industry knowledge ▪ Fit of delivery model of client and vendor ▪ Information and knowledge exchange and transfer ▪ Financial issues: cost reduction	Mixed motives, no dominant type identified
Vendor F Sales Manager	IT Services (Full Service Provider) Same company as Vendor E Current customers in Aeronautic and Defense, Industrial Manufact.	Contract duration application hosting and man.: approx. 3 years Full outsourcing: 5 years	n/a	Full service provision: infrastructure, applications, business processes Current customer focus: enterprise services	▪ High security policy required (due to industry requirements) ▪ Cost reduction not expected, on the contrary: customer expects higher costs due to special security compliance ▪ Trust extremely important, social and personal bonds	Strategic Alliance Partner
Vendor G Sales Director Outtasking and Outsourcing Solutions	IT Services (Full Service Provider)	Contract duration approx. 3-5 years (4 years ago: 4-7 years)	n/a	Full service provision: infrastructure, applications, business processes	▪ Fit of delivery model: vendor looks for large scale enterprise customers ▪ Demonstration of vendor capabilities: vendor must show experience ▪ Customer expectation: cost reduction ▪ Customer expectation: native language of call center agents	Commodity Supplier (supportive role)
Vendor H Client Manager	IT Services (Full Service Provider) Current customers in the public sector	Contract duration approx. 4-7 years	n/a	Full service provision: infrastructure, applications, business processes	▪ Fit of delivery model ▪ Continuous benchmarking ▪ Stable partnership required for long-term business value → stability, not necessarily strategic advantages expected	Reliance Partner (Long-term Stability Partner)

Table 5-1. Overview of expert interviews

5.1.2 Results

Throughout the interviews all interview partners stressed the importance of organizational relationship aspects for the outsourcing arrangement. The expectations towards the outsourcing partner and the overall outsourcing venture, however, varied significantly in the interviews. The perceived differences become most obvious in the different characteristics and relevance of the relationship categories.

5.1.2.1   Strategic Intent, Expectations, and Context

Regarding current business challenges all interviewees emphasized the dynamics of the business environment and the resulting need for flexibility and efficient business processes. From this situation, the interview partners derived different motivations and expectations towards their outsourcing partner. Three of the interview partners focused on cost reduction and IT efficiency as their overall goal for the outsourcing relationship. Two other interview partners in turn highlighted the desire for proactive suggestions for improvement of processes, costs, and the development of competitive advantages.

"For me, it is especially important that the vendor does not approach me in an 'acquisition mode', but rather in an 'improvement mode'. The vendor is too reactive and not proactive. Making things better means a hassle for the vendor, but my vendor is only successful if I am successful. I am successful if my processes are efficient and ahead of competition. So I expect improvement potential of my vendor." (CIO, customer A)

One customer even strives for more expectations: Vendor G mentioned that his client explicitly expects a shared development of innovative ASP services in the medical sector for his end consumer, coupled with a shared benefit-risk model.

5.1.2.2   Relationship Architecture

As a consequence of the evolution of various forms and models of outsourcing arrangements, the interviews reflect the trend towards a multisourcing strategy. Almost all of the interview partners contracted more than one IT service provider. Regarding the contract duration a drift towards short outsourcing ventures can be stated. This, however, seems to be connected with the experience of the clients. The higher the experience with outsourcing in general and with the specific vendor becomes, the more customers dare to engage in long-term arrangements. One major issue in this context is also the industry knowledge of the vendor as client B states:

"A clear distribution of responsibilities and a shared understanding of my business problems is crucial to the relationship. The vendor has to understand the challenges and constraints of my business and my industry." (CIO, customer B)

5.1.2.3   Governance and Monitoring

In coherence with the literature the distinction between formal, outcome-based and informal, behavior-based governance mechanisms could be found in practice. While all interview partners emphasized the importance of a formal contractual agreement as a fundament for the outsourcing relationship, two interview partners explicitly governed their relationship through informal, behavior-based mechanisms. In their view, a contract exclusively is not sufficient for a successful relationship, but rather a cooperative management beyond contractual clauses. These two interview partners regard their IT service provider not as a commodity supplier, but rather as a strategic partner.

"The contract is essential. However, once I have to get out the contract and refer to the specific clauses, it is too late. The relationship is damaged." (CIO, customer E)

5.1.2.4   Interaction

Regarding the reciprocal interaction between the parties the interview partners stressed two aspects: First, the power dependency relation between client and vendor and second the delivery model of the vendor. In both aspects the balance and fit between the expectations of both parties play a major role. Negotiating at eye level was mentioned as a vital success factor.

"We couldn't match the delivery model of the vendor. The vendor was the 'big boss' and imposed his processes and resources on us. We are a small business and the methods and instruments of the vendor were in no relation to our needs and monetary power. In the end, the deal was not profitable for our vendor and he let us feel it." (Head of IT, customer C)

5.1.3   Types of IS Outsourcing Relationships

In order to develop a taxonomy of different outsourcing relationship types, the expectations, experiences, descriptions, and also behavior gathered in the expert interviews were allocated in the framework that was developed in chapter 3.9 (p. 79ff.) and that also guided through the interviews (but without rigidly forcing answers to one category).

An in-depth qualitative content analysis (Mayring 2000; Krippendorff 1980) was conducted by searching for structures and patterned regularities in the different expert interviews (in-depth text analysis). For example, when asking the interviewees for the main motivation to engage in outsourcing, keywords and phrases were collected that formed a common category such as, e.g., "costs". Key phrases in this category comprised, e.g., "reduce costs", "save money", "spend money elsewhere". Another example addresses the different governance modes. It was analyzed which descriptions formed, e.g., a formal, arm's length governance style. Phrases like "we have everything written down clearly" or "we totally rely on SLAs" could be assigned to this governance category.

The main motivation for conducting such a qualitative text analysis was not to count frequencies of statements, but rather to understand commonalities and possible links between the statements. Thus, it was, e.g., analyzed whether a certain category of motives might be loosely coupled with a certain behavior in terms of chosen governance modes. Furthermore, while the framework was a good starting point for considering the important aspects and categories of an outsourcing relationship, some of the categories were refined or extended during the process of allocating the analyzed interviews and interview partners in the framework. Mayring (2000) describes this procedure as an iterative process where in an inductive way, initial categories are subsumed, changed, or extended during the text analysis. An example of a refinement of categories was the outsourcing motive of "innovation through outsourcing". Here, a specific expectation of "jointly developing new products and services together with the vendor / customer" was uttered by several interview partners. This statement formed a refined category of "innovation".

While mixed and sometimes incongruent motives and characteristics could be found in some expert interviews, overall five different relationship types were derived that followed a certain underlying motive and represent constitutive patterns of expectations: Commodity Supplier,

Technology Excellence, Reliance Partner, Joint Service Development Partner and Strategic Alliance Partner.

The most common type – also found to be dominant in the selection of expert interviews that were conducted – is the *Commodity Supply Relationship*. Here the objective is to achieve IT efficiencies by hiring external resources. In such relationships, the focus is on cost reduction or rendering IT as a variable cost. The vendor is regarded as a utility provider offering services from a resource pool on a short-term, often as-needed basis. Ties of the relationship in terms of trust, commitment and informal exchange are quite loose. An appropriate governance mechanism is the formal, outcome-based control via contracts. Strategic elements and long-term competitive advantages cannot be expected in this type.

Another relationship is *Technology Excellence*, where the vendor is chosen for "best-in-class" capability, "future-proofing" on the technological front, and pro-active innovation in technological applications (Kern/Willcocks/van Heck 2002). This relationship is often established for a project-based short-term duration, where the vendor is regarded as a partner for excellence. This relationship also mostly requires outcome-based governance mechanisms.

A third type is the *Reliance Partner*. This relationship requires more commitment, trust and informal exchange, since significant portions of the client's IT operations are transferred to the external vendor for a long period. Also the coordination costs and barriers for changing the partner are higher compared to the first two relationship types. It is important to notice that long-term and large-scale outsourcing arrangements are not necessarily strategic alliances (Kishore et al. 2003). A long-term, stable vendor can provide non-core, commodity IT capabilities without a strategic or transformational component.

Joint Service Development is a highly innovative relationship type, just beginning to evolve in practice. This relationship is neither a short-term commodity outsourcing type nor a fully-strategic type. The focus is on collaborative service engineering, where both partners engage in working together and developing selected outsourcing services together on a risk-reward-basis for a medium period of time. Governance in this relationship type is best achieved through behavior-based forms. The extent of mutual dependency is high and this type also involves strategic elements such as gaining competitive advantage through joint knowledge from both partners. The specification for outsourced services is difficult to define completely a priori as the outcomes are ambiguous and dynamic. This type is the answer to clients' requests for innovation in IS outsourcing. While not being a long-term reliance partner or a long-term strategic alliance partner, a joint service development partnership focuses on the question how an outsourcer can contribute to innovation and deliver value to the client. An example of this type was found in practice: a client in the medical sector explicitly requested the development of a new business model / product of an innovative medical ASP service of his IT service provider that the client could in turn offer to his clients, i.e., hospitals. The development of such services was intended to be a mutual and joint project where both parties dedicate their resources and take risks and rewards alike.

Finally, *Strategic Alliance Partnership* – often labeled as transformational outsourcing – involves working together and sharing the risks and rewards. Coordination is – similar to joint service development – much more complex and monitoring is best achieved through behavioral-based mechanisms and relational norms. This type involves a long-term engagement with high commitment of both partners and experience with outsourcing is required for a successful undertaking.

Based on the review of relationship factors in literature and the exploratory empirical results, the types can be described more comprehensively. Moreover, the existing literature could be extended by not only being able to describe the types in more detail, but also by identifying a new type of outsourcing relationship, i.e., joint service development. The following figure depicts the types in more detail and characterizes them along the proposed categories.

It is important to notice that these types were derived on the basis of very few expert interviews. The results cannot be regarded as representative and it is unclear whether a large study will quarry the same results. Rather, these results serve as a first anecdotal basis to demonstrate that the idea of differentiating outsourcing clients along their expectations is fruitful and applicable in practice. The pre-study revealed interesting insights and raised further questions to be answered in a larger study. For example, it is of immense interest to investigate the identified groups in greater detail. How are the groups best governed, what is their prevailing underlying outsourcing motivation, how do they differentiate from each other and what do the client groups have in common? These questions can only be sufficiently answered in a larger, more detailed, quantitative survey, as carried out in the next sections.

Dimension / Type	Commodity Supplier (Supportive Role)	Technology Excellence (Partner for Excellence)	Reliance Partner (Long-term stability Partner)	Joint Service Development Partner	Strategic Alliance Partner	Supporting References for Dimension (Examples)
Strategic Intent / Expectations / Context						
Strategic Intent and Motivation for Outsourcing	IT Efficiency, Cost Reduction	IT Efficiency, Cost Reduction, Access to world-class technological expertise	Business Value, Performance, Stability, focus on core competencies	Business value, Innovation, collaborative Service Engineering / know-how fusion	Business Transformation, Strategic alliance partner	(Kern/Willcocks /van Heck 2002), (Kishore et al. 2003), (Alborz/Seddon/ Scheepers 2004)
Strategic impact on client's IS components	⊍	∩	⊃	⊃	∩	(Nam et al. 1996), (Kishore et al. 2003)
Expectation / role of service provider	Utility provider, access to commodities	Solution provider "best in class"	Stable solution provider	Joint service development partner		(McFarlan/Nolan 1995)
Motivation of technical capability	Gain access to technical resources from a resource pool	Gain leading-edge technology, "future-proofing"	Gain access to technical resources from a resource pool	Distinctive technical leadership	Distinctive technical leadership	(Kern/Willcocks /van Heck 2002)
Involvement of service provider in proactive planning and development of new IS in the client firm	hardly	extremely important	important	extremely important / crucial	extremely important	(Kishore et al. 2003)
Extent of competitive advantage, business value leveraged and positioning through outsourcing	⊍	⊃/∩	⊍/⊃	∩	∩	(Kishore et al. 2003)
Extent of future development of interorganizational relationship (evolution)	⊍	⊍/⊃	∩	∩	∩	(Kishore et al. 2003)
Influence on long-term strategy	⊍	⊍	⊃	⊃	∩	(Kishore et al. 2003)

Dimension \ Type	Commodity Supplier (Supportive Role)	Technology Excellence (Partner for Excellence)	Reliance Partner (Long-term stability Partner)	Joint Service Development Partner	Strategic Alliance Partner	Supporting References for Dimension (Examples)
Relational Architecture						
Barriers / switching costs to change / mutual dependency	↓	↓/→	↑	↑	↑	(Nam et al. 1996), (Lee/Kim 1999), (Goles/Chin 2005), (McFarlan/Nolan 1995)
Shared goals	↓	→	→/↑	↑	↑	(Easton 1992), (Lacity/Willcocks 2003)
Duration of relationship / contract period	short-term	short-term	long-term	mid-term	long-term	(McFarlan/Nolan 1995), (Fitzgerald/Willcocks 1994), (Lee/Kim 1999)
Time horizon of relationship	Project-based, (ongoing)	Project-based	ongoing	Ongoing / (project-based)	ongoing	(Kishore et al. 2003)
Relational architecture (strategic, extended, virtual)	virtual/ extended	virtual/ extended	extended/ (strategic)	extended/ (strategic)	strategic	(Sambamurthy/ Zmud 2000)
Object Focus of relationship	specific to project / service	specific to service / technology	specific to service	joint service development	strategic alliance	(Kishore et al. 2003)
Outcomes of IS relationship	well defined	well defined	well defined, but dynamic	ambiguous / dynamic	ambiguous / dynamic	(Kishore et al. 2003)
Specification of outsourced information services	well defined	well defined	well defined	difficult to specify a priori	difficult to specify a priori	(Kishore et al. 2003)
Extent of substitution by vendors (amount of outsourced services)	↓	↓	↑	→	↑	(Nam et al. 1996)
Role of experience with outsourcing	↓	↓ / →	→	→	↑	(Lee/Kim 1999)
Governance Mechanisms						
Governance or Control Mechanism (formal/ informal, outcome-based, behavior-based, relational norms)	formal, outcome-based	formal, outcome-based	formal, outcome-based	formal, behavior-based, also informal based on rel. norms	formal, behavior-based, also informal based on rel. norms	(Behrens 2006; Kishore et al. 2003)
Role / Level of contractual control	↑	→ / ↑	↑	↓	↓	(Kishore et al. 2003), (Klepper/Jones 1998)
Extent of outcome fixed in contractual agreement	↑	↑	→/↑	↓	↓	(Behrens 2006)
Interactions						
Importance of informal information channels	↓	→	→	↑	↑	(Kishore et al. 2003)
Transfer and sharing of information	↓	↑	→	↑	↑	(Lee/Kim 1999)
Need for Profit / Risk sharing incentives	↓	↑	→/↑	↑	↑	(Kishore et al. 2003), (Lee/Kim 1999)
Transfer of skills	↓	→	→	↑	↑	(Kishore et al. 2003)
Extent of vendor's managerial control and decision making authority	↓	→	↑	↑	↑	(Kishore et al. 2003)
Coordination costs and intensity	↓	→	↑	↑	↑	(Kishore et al. 2003)
Commitment of client and vendor	↓	→	↑	↑	↑	(Lee/Kim 1999), (Goles/Chin 2005)

Dimension \ Type	Commodity Supplier (Supportive Role)	Technology Excellence (Partner for Excellence)	Reliance Partner (Long-term stability Partner)	Joint Service Development Partner	Strategic Alliance Partner	Supporting References for Dimension (Examples)
Role of trust between parties	☺ low	☺ low	➲ medium	∩ high	∩ high	(Henderson 1990; Kern 1997; Lee/Kim 1999), (Goles/Chin 2005)
Need for cultural similarity	☺ low	➲ medium	∩ high	∩ high	∩ high	(McFarlan/Nolan 1995), (Klepper/Jones 1998), (Lee/Kim 1999)

Legend: ∩= high, ➲= medium, ☺= low

Figure 5-2. Anecdotal types of different IS outsourcing relationships

5.2   Research Design of the Quantitative Study

With the research problem defined and the assurance of the practicability of the research idea through a qualitative pre-study gained, the researcher has to choose the appropriate research design for the actual main study that aims to answer research question 2: "Which different configurations of outsourcing relationships can be identified empirically?" Assessing different client types of outsourcing relationships on a reliable and solid basis is conducted best with a large empirical quantitative study. According to Atteslander (2008), a quantitative survey is appropriate if the area of interest is already well established and thoroughly researched as it is the case for the research topic of IS outsourcing. In the context of IS outsourcing a lot of knowledge and insights could be collected over the past decades and it is also to be expected that the potential respondents already have some experience with outsourcing. But although being heavily researched, there are still some white spots on the outsourcing research agenda. Consequently, a quantitative, but exploratory research technique is most suitable for the purpose of this research.

Cluster analysis as a quantitative, exploratory interdependence technique is chosen as the primary research method. This thesis follows the suggestion of (Hair et al. 2006; Ketchen/Shook 1996; Milligan/Cooper 1985) to use hierarchical and non-hierarchical methods in tandem. It will first apply a hierarchical agglomerative clustering procedure, as this procedure is very common among researchers (Bailey 1994, 42; Hair et al. 2006; Eckstein 2004, 325) in order to assess the number of clusters (and also to derive researcher-specified centroids as starting points for the non-hierarchical solution). It will then apply k-means as a non-hierarchical iterative clustering procedure to optimize and verify the cluster solution found by hierarchical procedures as the k-means algorithm is by far the most popular clustering method used in scientific applications due to its reliable results (Berkhin 2002, 15). Additionally, factor analysis as a pre-method is applied to reduce complexity and avoid methodological issues such as multicollinearity. After cluster groups have been identified, they will be analyzed in greater detail by applying an analysis of variance (ANOVA) that tests for group differences. The criticism of some researchers who contend that cluster analysis is only a descriptive, atheoretical, and exploratory technique is met by a thorough conceptual development (i.e., the literature-based framework) as suggested by Atteslander (2008). Moreover, a confirmatory, theory-testing approach does not fit the research question underlying this thesis. Only an exploratory approach can reveal yet unknown insights on combining outsourcing expectations with according governance mechanisms.

With regard to the steps and combination of methods to be applied in the following, some words of explanation need to be mentioned on combining the two multivariate methods of factor and cluster analysis.

Using the „factor-cluster approach" by combining factor analysis to reduce variables to a set of factors which are then used as clustering variables has been a quite usual approach for market segmentation in tourism research (Sheppard 1996) and also in some marketing areas (Punj/Stewart 1983). In several studies this procedure has been found to be "superior due to its effectiveness in reducing sometimes large number of [...] statements to a smaller set of more understandable factors or components" (Frochot/Morrison 2000, 32). But this approach has also received some criticism (Ketchen/Shook 1996) because "cluster analysis on raw item scores, as opposed to factor scores, may produce more accurate or detailed segmentation as it preserves a greater degree of the original data" (Sheppard 1996, 57). This might be especially problematic when all factors with low *eigenvalues* are dropped which might represent unique, important information. Ketchen and Shook thus conclude that "any remedy to multicollineari-ty has a cost" (Ketchen/Shook 1996, 444). As an ideal approach they suggest to "perform a cluster analysis multiple times changing [...] the method of addressing multicollinearity" (Ketchen/Shook 1996, 444).

In order to address the controversial discussion in the literature on potential problems asso-ciated with applying a "factor-cluster" approach and also in order to balance the benefits of using straightforward uncorrelated factors vs. the limitations, the advice of Ketchen and Shook was followed. Multiple cluster analyses were carried out. Specifically, the same proce-dure of cluster analysis that was carried out for the final solution, was performed on the 16 (resp. 15, leaving out q1409[12]) original and raw outsourcing expectation variables leaving out the pre-processing step of condensing the variables in a factor analysis. As a result, it was found that also with the raw and original variables, the 4-cluster solution is the predominant, stable, and preferred solution, but the clusters themselves were very difficult to interpret and also did not differ obviously from a logical point of view, but formed rather similar profiles (on different levels). Therefore, in the following, the factor-cluster-analysis approach was followed due to its straightforward, clear, and well-interpretable results.

Figure 5-3 schematically depicts the combination of methods and the purpose of each method for this work.

---

[12] The variable q1409 (addressing the outsourcing motive "focus on core competencies") showed some irregu-larities concerning normal distribution (see page 120 in chapter 5.4.1.2) and also the initial factor analysis (see page 123 in chapter 5.4.2.1). Consequently, multiple cluster analyses were conducted with and without this variable and for the final version, the variable was excluded from the final solution.

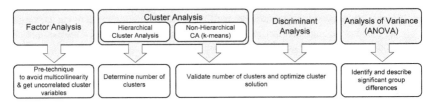

Figure 5-3. Combination of methods applied in this thesis

Atteslander (2008) suggests a number of methods as assessment and data collection techniques. For this thesis, an online survey based on a fully-structured and standardized questionnaire is chosen as the respondents are best reached by this method and the results are best comparable and analyzed. The areas of interest were based on a thorough literature review (see chapter 3.6, p. 49ff.) and transferred into questionnaire items. These questionnaire items are based on the framework that was developed in chapter 3.8 (p. 71ff.). Most constructs were represented by a set of indicators that were measured on a fully anchored 7-point Likert scale expressing attitudes ranging from "strongly disagree" (1) to "strongly agree" (7). Whenever possible, the measures and item scales were derived from other studies and from existing scales and adapted to the specific research domain. The resulting draft questionnaire was discussed with academics from the field and pre-tested independently with several IT managers that were excluded from the final sample (see chapter 5.1.1, p. 113ff.). Based on the insights acquired in these pre-tests, the questionnaire was modified to be precise and understandable for the target audience before being sent out. The original German version as well as the translated English version are found in appendices A 1 and A 2.

A last point to be mentioned in the context of the research design of this study is the challenge of a potential common method bias (CMB) that might occur when the instruments the researcher employs enter into or affect the scores or measures that are being gathered. This is also known as a methodological artifact (Podsakoff et al. 2003). Problems of and techniques for controlling a potential common method bias are addressed in chapter 6.4 (p. 233ff.) where a structural equation model is introduced and laid out.

5.3   Data Collection and Demographic Results

Data for this study was gathered via an online questionnaire survey. The invitation for participating in the survey was sent to highest ranking IS executives of organizations in Germany. The addresses were obtained from a service provider that offers addresses and contacts of company executives depending on industries, sectors, and positions. Top IT decision makers from approx. 5400 German companies in various industries were chosen as the study population and unit of analysis. Among them were all 658 members of a German non-profit CIO networking organization, the "CIO Circle". This CIO networking organization is a self-organized online community that brings together highest ranking IT executives ("IT-Leiter", "CIO", "CTO" etc.)[13].

From June to October 2007, the IT executives were invited to participate in an online survey by a personal letter containing a personal unique access code for the survey website. Overall, 268 usable questionnaires were returned which equals an overall response rate of approx. 5 percent and approx. 15 percent in the CIO network.

The respondents were categorized according to the experience with IT or business process outsourcing in their company. As 11.2% had no outsourcing in place and another 15.7% had only begun to outsource their IT, the participants with low experience in IT outsourcing were excluded from the analysis. Finally, 196 data points remained.

The respondents basically covered all industries with banking and finance (12.24%), diverse manufacturing (12.24%), and automotive (9.18%) being most prominently represented in the sample (see Figure 5-4).

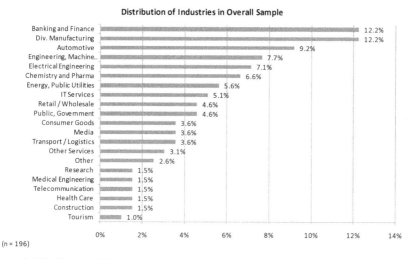

Figure 5-4. Distribution of industries in the overall sample

In terms of annual sales volume, the majority of the respondents had an annual turnover between 1 and 5 billion Euro (19.39%) (see Figure 5-5).

---

[13] The chair for information systems is a co-founder and administrator of the CIO Circle platform (www.cio-circle.org) and could provide the access to the 658 IT executives.

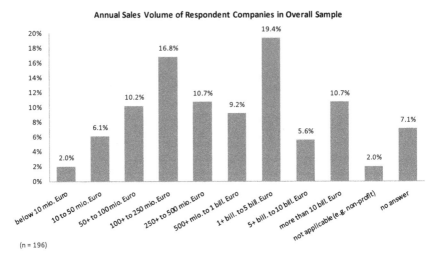

(n = 196)

Figure 5-5. Distribution of the annual sales volume of respondent companies in the overall sample

5.4   Statistical Results: Data Analysis

This chapter lays out the methodological and statistical procedures that were performed on the data set in order to derive meaningful cluster configurations that describe groups of outsourcing clients with similar expectations towards the outsourcing venture.

First, the data (i.e., the relevant variables for outsourcing expectations) was pre-analyzed for missing values treatment and distribution issues. Then, a pre-processing of the variables was conducted with factor analysis (PCA) to account for the problem of multicollinearity and to derive straightforward, well-interpretable expectation factors.

Third, the actual cluster analysis was carried out with the condensed factors as clustering variables. The cluster analysis was conducted in two-steps, involving hierarchical clustering to identify outliers and the number of clusters (with a single linkage algorithm and the Ward algorithm) followed by the iterative, partitioning approach of k-means to find an optimal cluster solution. The solution was then validated with discriminant analysis.

5.4.1   Diagnostic Pre-Analysis of Results: Missing Values and Distribution of Data

This chapter will discuss the diagnostic actions that were taken to ensure the integrity and appropriateness of the data. Missing data patterns and the steps taken to impute missing data will be examined. In addition, descriptive statistics are utilized to present various sample characteristics from the investigated variables, especially with regard to normal distribution etc.

Once the previously described diagnostic and pre-analytic steps have been completed, the data is subjected to bivariate and multivariate statistical procedures, including factor analysis as a pre-analysis to eliminate multicollinearity and cluster analysis to identify patterns of outsourcing customers with regard to their outsourcing expectations to provide answers to the three research questions posed.

5.4.1.1 Diagnostics: Analyzing the Extent and Impact of Missing Values

Missing data, i.e., where valid values on one or more variables are not available for analysis, is one of the most pervasive problems in data analysis (Little/Rubin 2002, 3pp.; Tabachnick/Fidell 2001, 58) and at the same time it is a fact of life and hardly avoidable in multivariate analysis (Hair et al. 2006, 49). Even in the best designed and monitored studies, observations can be missing due to various reasons (Hill 1997). Many classical statistical analyses, however, require complete data sets in order to calculate analyses such as, e.g., factor or cluster analysis. The seriousness of the missing value problem depends on the *extent* of missing data, the *pattern or structure* of missing data, and the *cause* for missing data (Hill 1997). The challenge thereby is to address these issues in order to identify if the generalizability of the results is affected and in order to ensure validity of the results.

Hair et al. (2006, 52) suggest a four-step process for identifying and analyzing missing data and applying remedies, which is also followed in this work:

1. Determine the type and cause of missing data

First, one has to identify the "roots" of the missing data, i.e., whether the missing data is part of the research design and thus under the control of the researcher, or whether the causes and impacts are truly unknown. If missing data is expected and an inherent part of the research design (such as in sample methods where only a sample of a population is selected instead of gathering data from the entire population), the missing data can be regarded as ignorable missing data. In most instances, however, the researcher faces missing data that cannot be classified as ignorable and has to be further analyzed. The most prominent examples of non-ignorable missing data is the refusal to respond to certain questions that are of a sensitive nature, or if the respondent does not have an opinion or insufficient knowledge (Hair et al. 2006). To account for the appearance of these problems, Hair et al. (2006, 54) suggest to anticipate the problem by offering alternatives for the respondents to answer the question instead of leaving it blank.

In the survey used in the thesis, all questions offered an alternative answer option labeled "I don't know". This answer option was later converted to a "99" value and treated as a missing value. All missing values in the data set could thus be traced back to this answer option instead of having to interpret an empty field. Nevertheless, for this data set one cannot easily assume that the missing data is ignorable so further analyses have to be undertaken to understand the structure and impact of the missing data.

2. Determine the extent of missing data

A first look at patterns of incompleteness serves to answer the questions: where are the missing values located and how extensive are they? If a value is missing for one variable, does it
tend to be missing for one or more variables, i.e., is there a pattern of missing values among
the cases? The primary issue in this step is thus to assess whether the amount of missing data
is low enough to not affect the results. If it is sufficiently low and only a few data points are
missing (Tabachnick/Fidell 2001), the problems are less serious and any of the approaches for
remedying missing data may be applied and yields similar results (Hair et al. 2006, 54;
Tabachnick/Fidell 2001, 59). For assessing the extent of missing data, three approaches are
among the prominent analysis: tabulating 1) the percentage of variables with missing data for
each case, 2) the number of cases with missing data for each variable, 3) the number of overall missing data entries in the respective data selection (Hair et al. 2006, 55).

First, the variables are regarded that are used for the further analysis. 16 variables that reflect
the various outsourcing motivations of the clients are analyzed. Table 5-2 gives an overview
of the expectation variables used in this study. Regarding the variables, 6 out of 16 variables
do not have any missing values, another 4 show only one single missing value, while another
3 show only 2 missing values each. Two variables (q1404 and q1416) have a missing value
percentage above 1% (3.6% resp. 4.6%), but both are still way below the threshold of 10%
(Hair et al. 2006, 55). Overall, the range of missing values is from 0% to 4.6% with 13 out of
16 variables having a percentage of missing values of 1% or below.

Second, regarding the cases/observations, 11.2% of all cases (22 out of 196 cases in total)
have missing values with regard to the 16 variables. All of these cases except for one have 2
or less data points missing.

Third, in total 29 data entries with regard to all cases and the 16 included variables are missing. Overall, this accounts for less than 1% of all data entries[14]. These results can also be obtained from the table in appendix A 3.

Regarding the number of missing values, the extent and amount of missing data is very low.
Even though (Hair et al. 2006; Tabachnick/Fidell 2001) mention that there are no firm guidelines for how much missing data can be tolerated for a sample of a given size, the application
of rules of thumb as suggested by Hair et al. (2006, 55) allows the first conclusion that missing data does not have a bias impact on the further analysis and results. Moreover, Schnell et
al. (2005) state that missing values up to approximately 10% (measured as data points with
missing values in relation to all data points) can be regarded as normal. Consequently, one
can assume that missing data did not impact or nurture a common method bias in this study.

---

[14]   Calculated on the basis of the number of overall data entries for this analysis (16 variables x 196 observations
       = 3136 data entries) and the number of missing data entries (29 in total over all observations and the 16 va-
       riables).

3. Diagnose the randomness of the missing data

The previous analysis of the extent of missing data has shown that the amount is not substantial enough to warrant action, but still the data is further analyzed to gain more confidence on this assumption.

A first diagnostic approach to test for patterns in missing data is suggested by Tabachnick and Fidell (2001) and Hair et al. (2006). They recommend to construct a dummy variable with two groups, i.e., cases with missing and non-missing values on a number of variables. With these groups, a test of mean differences between the groups is conducted to see whether any consistent pattern emerges. If there are no significant differences, "decisions on how to handle missing data are not so critical" (Tabachnick/Fidell 2001, 59). Thus, the data set was divided in two groups, one containing the 22 cases with missing values and the other containing 174 complete cases. The two groups were tested for significant mean differences (ANOVA) on a variety of other constitutive variables. Those variables included context factors such as 1) *company characteristics* such as company's outsourcing experience, firm size, IT budget, 2) *characteristics of the outsourcing project* such as type and extent of outsourcing, number of vendors, outsourced objects, as well as 3) *characteristics of the respondent* such as age, experience with outsourcing, working experience in this company. Appendices A 4 and A 5 show that none of these variables had any significant differences among the two groups and no pattern of missing data could be identified.

More sophisticated measures to determine the randomness of the missing data include testing if data is missing at random (MAR) or even missing completely at random (MCAR). MAR assumes that the missing observation may depend on the observed values, but not on the missing values, i.e., the missing value is unrelated to the value of this variable, but might be related to other variables in the data set (Little/Rubin 1987). The higher level of randomness is termed missing completely at random (MCAR). In these cases, the probability of having a missing value is unrelated to the value of this variable or to any other variables in the data set. In other words, the cases with missing data are indistinguishable from cases with complete data and thus truly random (Hair et al. 2006, 57).

The MCAR assumption is testable by Little's and Rubin's (1987) chi-square test[15]. The test analyzes the pattern of missing data on all variables and compares it with the pattern expected for a random missing data process. If the p-value for Little's MCAR test is *not* highly significant ($p < 0.05$), then the data may be assumed to be MCAR, which is the desired result to allow for the widest range of potential remedies (Hair et al. 2006, 57). Little's MCAR test obtained for this thesis' data resulted in a chi-square = 169.830 (df = 143; $p < 0.062$), which indicates that the data is indeed missing at random (i.e., no identifiable pattern exists for the missing data). Thus, the missing data mechanism is ignorable (Allison 2002), which was assumed in the beginning, but had to be tested to gain confidence on this assumption.

---

[15] Little's MCAR test was conducted with SPSS Missing Values Analysis (MVA).

4. Handling missing values / select the imputation method

The last step involves selecting an approach for accommodating missing data in the analysis. Methods of treating missing data include, among others, imputation-based methods (where missing values are filled in and the resultant completed data is analyzed by standard methods) and model-based procedures (where a model for the observed data is defined and parameters are estimated by, e.g., maximum likelihood based on inferences on the likelihood or posterior distribution underlying the model) (Little/Rubin 2002, 20). One popular procedure for handling missing values is to simply drop them by listwise or pairwise deletion of cases or variables with missing values. If missing values are concentrated in a few variables or cases, they can easily be dropped without too much loss of information (Tabachnick/Fidell 2001, 59). But if missing values are scattered throughout cases and variables, deletion of cases or variables can mean a substantial loss of data and valuable information. Thus, imputation methods have become very common and widespread as they allow estimating the missing values instead of deleting valuable cases. Literature provides a large set of methods on imputing missing values, which will not be described in detail here (Little/Rubin 1987; Hair et al. 2006; Tabachnick/Fidell 2001; Decker/Wagner/Temme 2000; Allison 2002; Göthlich 2007).

One of the most widely used methods to impute missing data is the use of mean substitution by which the missing value is replaced by the mean value of that variable calculated from all valid responses. Part of the attraction of this method is that it is conservative. The mean of the distribution as a whole does not change and in most cases the mean is the best guess about the value of the variable (Tabachnick/Fidell 2001, 62). But this approach also involves some disadvantages and has recently gained some criticism due to the fact that it reduces the variance of the variable, distorts the actual distribution and also depresses the observed correlation (Garson 2008a; Hair et al. 2006).

Maximum likelihood estimation (MLE) (such as implemented by the EM algorithm in the SPSS Missing Values Analysis 7.5) is now regarded as the most common method of imputation (Tabachnick/Fidell 2001; Garson 2008a; Allison 2002). In many cases maximum likelihood or multiple imputation leads to more accurate and reliable results. MLE is applied to the task of imputing missing data values without recourse to the simulation involved in multiple imputation methods. "Each iteration consists of an E(stimation) step and an M(aximum likelihood) step. The E step finds the conditional expectation of the missing data, given the observed values and current estimates of the parameters. These expectations are then substituted for the missing data. In the M step, maximum likelihood estimates of the parameters are computed as though the missing data had been filled in" (Hill 1997, 42). MLE makes fewer demands on the data in terms of statistical assumptions, but assumes that missing values are at least MAR.

As mentioned above, in the case of only a few missing values, any of the approaches for remedying missing data may be applied and yields similar results (Hair et al. 2006, 54; Tabachnick/Fidell 2001, 59). Especially if very low levels of missing data exist, mean substitution is still a preferred method because it is easily implemented instead of complex model specifications (Hair et al. 2006, 63). To test for differences in the results, missing values were imputed with both mean values and (afterwards) with the values generated by the EM algorithm in the SPSS Missing Values Analysis for the subsequent multivariate analyses (factor and cluster analysis) of outsourcing expectations. Neither did the results significantly differ with regard to the factor analysis, nor did it differ in the subsequent cluster analysis.

Thus, in conclusion, missing values for the analysis of the data in this thesis were imputed by the means of the respective variable because

- very few missing values exist in the data set
- mean substitution is easy to implement, and
- the alternative EM algorithm did not show different or superior results of mean substitution

5.4.1.2   Normal Distribution of the Data

Underlying most statistical tests and some multivariate procedures is the assumption of univariate or multivariate normality, i.e., a normal distribution of the data in the population (Tabachnick/Fidell 2001, 72; Brosius 2006, 399). Although many statistical procedures are robust to violations of the assumption (Tabachnick/Fidell 2001, 72p., 588), a researcher should still test for normality to get an idea and feeling for the data and to anticipate possible challenges in the analyses. Moreover, even when the procedures do not require it, normality enhances the analysis and the results (Tabachnick/Fidell 2001, 72).

Normality of variables is usually assessed by both statistical and graphical methods. Two elements of normality are skewness and kurtosis. Skewness addresses the symmetry of the distribution, i.e., the mean is in the center of the distribution. Kurtosis describes the peakedness or flatness of a distribution compared with the normal distribution (Hair et al. 2006, 80). In a perfectly normal distribution values of both skewness and kurtosis are zero.

Frequency histograms with a superimposed normal distribution, expected normal probability plots as well as detrended expected normal probability plots are important graphical devices for assessing normality (Tabachnick/Fidell 2001, 75).

There are also statistical tests available to assess normality of variables. Among those, the Kolmogorov-Smirnov and the Shapiro-Wilks test are the most prominent ones. They test the null hypothesis that the variable is normally distributed in the population. One has to keep in mind that both statistical procedures test for a perfect normal distribution and will be likely to reject normality if the data does not have a perfectly normal distribution (as true for most cases).

The sample size of the data set also has quite an impact on the results of normality tests. While larger sample sizes (more than 100) reduce the detrimental effects of non-normality, deviations from normality can have a substantial impact in small sample sizes (Hair et al. 2006, 80pp.; Tabachnick/Fidell 2001, 74). Because in large samples, the statistical tests for normality (Kolmogorov-Smirnov and Shapiro-Wilks tests) are quite sensitive, a researcher should always use both graphical plots and any statistical test to assess the actual departure from normality (Hair et al. 2006, 82).

The 16 examined variables (q1401-q1416, see Table 5-2) were tested statistically and graphically for normal distribution. As to statistical measures, both the Kolmogorov-Smirnov and the Shapiro-Wilks test display an extremely high value of significance ($p < 0.0001$), which shows that the data does not have a perfectly normal distribution. However, graphical analyses of the histograms (with the superimposed normal distribution curve), the expected and detrended expected normal probability plot show that most variables are reasonably normally distributed. All values for skewness and kurtosis are close to zero. The few exceptions are the variables q1405, q1406, q1409, q1416 with an absolute value of skewness over 0.5 (but below 1.0), as well as the variables q1407, q1414, q1415 with a high value around -1.0. Looking at the histograms with the normal distribution, all variables except for q1409, q1415 and q1416 show a fairly normal bell distribution with values lined up closely along the diagonal in the expected normal probability plot.

One of the exceptions that will have to be investigated further is variable q1409 which shows a large value of skewness and also quite a few outliers.

Having examined the relevant variables with regard to missing values and normal distribution as two of the most prevailing procedures for testing the assumptions of multivariate analysis (Hair et al. 2006; Tabachnick/Fidell 2001; Brosius 2006), the next step is the actual investigation of patterns (factors and clusters) in the data.

5.4.2 Factor Analysis: Customer Expectations towards IS Outsourcing

The statistical and methodological details of factor analysis have been introduced in chapter 4.2.3 (p. 101ff.). This chapter will thus exclusively focus on the application of factor analysis for the purpose of this research.

As elaborated in chapter 3.4 (p. 39ff.), a variety of motivations for engaging in an outsourcing model exist ranging from cost-oriented motives to strategic issues of competitive advantages and innovative IT services. The questionnaire captured this variety and included 16 different motives and expectations towards outsourcing (see Table 5-2). In the previous chapter these variables were tested and analyzed for missing values and their distribution. But it has not been tested yet if there is any correlation between the motives for engaging in an outsourcing venture. Although several studies indicate that there is a trade-off between achieving efficiency and cost-oriented issues and strategic advantages, outsourcing motives might be rather multi-dimensional and should be considered cumulative, rather than mutually exclusive (Weill/Broadbent 1998; Kogut/Zander 1992; DiRomualdo/Gurbaxani 1998; McLellan/Marcolin/ Beamish 1995; Moran/Ghoshal 1999; Priem 2001; Miranda/Kavan 2005).

Variable ID	Variable name: outsourcing motive
q1401	Cost reduction
q1402	Flexibility of costs / cost transparency (rendering IT as a variable cost)
q1403	Quality improvements (lower error rate / shorter processing time)
q1404	Long-term use of systems, applications and data (stability, reliability, retention of status quo)
q1405	Improved service orientation

Variable ID	Variable name: outsourcing motive
q1406	Increased flexibility
q1407	Shift risk to service provider
q1408	Modernization of IT / replace legacy systems
q1409	Focus on core competencies
q1410	Enable and facilitate strategic competitive advantages
q1411	Access to highly skilled people
q1412	Access to better IT systems and new technology
q1413	Knowledge acquisition from service provider
q1414	Suggestions for new IT based products and services by your service provider (innovation, idea creation)
q1415	Shared development of IT based products and services together with your service provider (joint product and service development)
q1416	Business transformation

Table 5-2. Variety of IS outsourcing expectations included in the study

In order to handle this variety of motives and also assuming that some of these motives could be related, an exploratory factor analysis was conducted in order to see if and how many main factors of outsourcing motives exist. The primary goal of this step is to reduce data quantity and complexity and to get a selected number of manageable and interpretable factors. Moreover, cluster analysis – which is carried out following the factor analysis – is very sensitive to correlated variables because multicollinearity acts as a "weighting process" and is likely to cause biased results (Hair et al. 2006, 582; Ketchen/Shook 1996, 444). Thus, the preprocessing analysis of the variables with factor analysis is one way to eliminate the problems of multicollinearity (Hair et al. 2006, 582, 603; Ketchen/Shook 1996, 444; Punj/Stewart 1983).

5.4.2.1 Initial Factor Analysis with All Outsourcing Motives

The following procedures describe the original factor analysis that was conducted with all 16 expectation motives[16]. In the final factor solution, two variables had to be excluded and the factor analysis had to be re-run, which will be discussed in chapter 5.4.2.2 (p. 135ff.).

To identify first indices for a correlation among the variables, a correlation matrix is calculated. A poor result can be attributed to this first (correlation) analysis if all variables show a high or a low correlation overall. What is rather preferred in the light of a factor analysis is that some variable pairs have a strong correlation while others show a weak correlation. Such a result would account for some degree of collinearity among the variables, but not an extreme degree or singularity among the variables. This is a first indicator that some variables might have a superior factor that brings them together. The correlation matrix has strong correlations for a number of variable pairs (> 0.3 as recommended). For example, "cost reduction" and "cost variabilization" correlate highly with each other, but not with the rest of the

---

[16] The tables and figures for the initial (original) factor analysis with all 16 outsourcing motives are found in the appendix since the focus is laid on the actually used (improved) factor analysis and factor scores that are described in the next chapter.

variables. Also the variables "business transformation", "competitive advantages", "joint product-service development", "innovation", and "knowledge transfer from vendor" correlate highly with each other, but not with the rest of the variables. There is only one remarkable exception: Variable q1409 (focus on core competencies) shows very low correlation coefficients which might be an indicator for exclusion of the factor analysis (see Table 5-3 for the actually used calculation in the improved factor analysis).

After checking the extent of collinearity or common variance among the variables, KMO and Bartlett's test of squericity are calculated to determine factorability of the data. The KMO index is fairly high ("meritorious") and the Bartlett's test is highly significant[17] (appendix A 11). Overall, the factorability of the variables is deemed to be very good and thus if a factor analysis is conducted, the factors extracted will account for a good amount of variance (with the exception of variable q1409, which will be analyzed further) (see Table 5-4 for the actually used calculation in the improved factor analysis).

Finally, the measure of sampling adequacy (MSA) values for each variable are calculated. They are similar to the KMO measure (overall MSA), but correspond to single variables. They can be found in the anti-image-correlation matrix. The MSA evaluation shows good values, most of them ranging in Kaiser's "meritorious" evaluation, except for two items "cost reduction" and "cost variabilization". But since both are still above the minimum 0.5 level, they will not be dismissed from the factor analysis (see appendix A 9).

In the next step of the analysis, factors will be extracted from the variables and the number of meaningful factors will be determined. Appendices A 10 and A 13 show the initial as well as the extracted factor solution (see Table 5-5 for the actually used calculation in the improved factor analysis).

As an extraction method, principle components analysis (PCA) as one of the most commonly used methods is applied (Brosius 2006, 772)[18]. It shows that the cumulative % of variance explained by the first four factors is 56.51%, i.e., 56.51% of the common variance shared by the 16 variables can be accounted for by the four factors. For determining the number of factors, Eigen One Rule or Kaiser-Guttman was applied and factors with *eigenvalues* below 1 are discarded.

A scree plot to visually determine the number of useful factors to be extracted showed elbows for the 2-factor and the 4-factor solution. In accordance with the Kaiser-Guttman rule, the 4-factor solution will be adopted. Parallel Analysis was additionally used to determine the number of factors (appendix A 12), but showed only 3 factors to be extracted (for final results see Table 5-6, Table 5-7, Figure 5-6).

---

[17] The Bartlett test, however, does not allow to interpret the significance levels of each correlation coefficient between a variable pair (Brosius 2006, 769). The appendix thus additionally depicts the significance levels for each correlation coefficient, showing that – as preferred – some variable pairs have a highly significant value while others do not.

[18] Principal Axis Factoring (PAF) was also conducted to compare the two extraction methods. Some authors also recommend PAF instead of PCA. However, although PAF led to similar results and also produced 4 factors, the explained variance of these 4 factors were remarkably lower than with PCA and the factor correlation matrix also showed some fuzzy results, i.e., double-loaded items. Thus, PCA was the preferred choice.

The component matrix indicates the correlation of each variable with each factor (i.e., the factor loadings). To clarify the factor pattern in order to better interpret the nature of the factors, they will be rotated with an orthogonal rotation method (VARIMAX).

According to Thurstone's rules of eliminating or keeping items, two variables had to be removed. In contrast to all other items, variable q1409 (focus on core competencies) had a very low factor loading below 0.4 (0.368). The decision is also underpinned and in accordance with the finding in the correlation matrix where q1409 showed very low correlations to all other variables. Another item double-loaded on 2 other factors, i.e., q1411 (access to highly skilled people) and was thus dismissed from the final solution.

5.4.2.2 Final Improved Factor Solution

Because of the elimination of the two variables, factor analysis was conducted again without the two items. The new factor analysis showed similar, but much stronger results. Especially the values for the communalities (all above 0.4 and most above 0.5), the total variance explained (> 60%) and the factor loading matrix (no double or cross-loadings, all loadings above 0.5 and most above 0.6) show much stronger results compared to the original solution. Although parallel analysis came up with three factors, the scree test, Kaiser's eigenvalue criterion, as well as the logical interpretability of the factors suggested the 4-factor solution, which will be adopted and discussed.

While the results of the original factor analysis with 16 variables is depicted in detail in the appendices (0 to A 15), the results of the final, improved factor analysis that is used for further analyses are depicted here (they are referred to in the upper section).

		Cost reduction	Variabilization of costs / cost transparency	Quality improvements	Long-term use of systems, applications and data	Improved service orientation	Increased flexibility	Shift risk to service provider	Modernization of IT / replace legacy systems	Enable and facilitate strategic competitive advantages	Access to better IT systems and new technology	Knowledge acquisition from service provider	Suggestions for new IT based products and services	Joint product and service development	Business transformation
Correlation	Cost reduction	1.000	.460	.137	.015	.174	.077	-.011	.092	.184	.170	-.102	-.020	.084	.119
	Variabilization of costs / cost transparency	.460	1.000	.086	.075	.205	.193	.111	.176	.128	.116	-.026	.098	.027	.117
	Quality improvements	.137	.086	1.000	.337	.442	.289	.203	.314	.272	.349	.214	.332	.164	.133
	Long-term use of systems, applications and data	.015	.075	.337	1.000	.330	.120	.272	.378	.256	.294	.174	.142	.125	.240
	Improved service orientation	.174	.205	.442	.330	1.000	.443	.222	.290	.290	.295	.148	.246	.117	.277
	Increased flexibility	.077	.193	.289	.120	.443	1.000	.128	.249	.189	.188	.088	.133	.099	.141
	Shift risk to service provider	-.011	.111	.203	.272	.222	.128	1.000	.372	.164	.309	.177	.168	-.015	.168
	Modernization of IT / replace legacy systems	.092	.176	.314	.378	.290	.249	.372	1.000	.294	.522	.306	.420	.204	.279
	Enable and facilitate strategic competitive advantages	.184	.128	.272	.256	.290	.189	.164	.294	1.000	.336	.364	.451	.429	.472
	Access to better IT systems and new technology	.170	.116	.349	.294	.295	.188	.309	.522	.336	1.000	.366	.511	.242	.264

		Cost reduction	Variabilization of costs / cost transparency	Quality improvements	Long-term use of systems, applications and data	Improved service orientation	Increased flexibility	Shift risk to service provider	Modernization of IT / replace legacy systems	Enable and facilitate strategic competitive advantages	Access to better IT systems and new technology	Knowledge acquisition from service provider	Suggestions for new IT based products and services	Joint product and service development	Business transformation
	Knowledge acquisition from service provider	-.102	-.026	.214	.174	.148	.088	.177	.306	.364	.366	1.000	.622	.383	.338
	Suggestions for new IT based products and services (innovation, idea creation)	-.020	.098	.332	.142	.246	.133	.168	.420	.451	.511	.622	1.000	.515	.397
	Joint product and service development	.084	.027	.164	.125	.117	.099	-.015	.204	.429	.242	.383	.515	1.000	.484
	Business transformation	.119	.117	.133	.240	.277	.141	.168	.279	.472	.264	.338	.397	.484	1.000
Significance (one-sided)	Cost reduction		.000	.028	.420	.007	.143	.439	.100	.005	.009	.078	.392	.121	.049
	Variabilization of costs / cost transparency	.000		.114	.148	.002	.003	.060	.007	.037	.053	.357	.087	.356	.051
	Quality improvements	.028	.114		.000	.000	.000	.002	.000	.000	.000	.001	.000	.011	.031
	Long-term use of systems, applications and data	.420	.148	.000		.000	.047	.000	.000	.000	.000	.007	.023	.041	.000
	Improved service orientation	.007	.002	.000	.000		.000	.001	.000	.000	.000	.019	.000	.052	.000
	Increased flexibility	.143	.003	.000	.047	.000		.037	.000	.004	.004	.110	.031	.084	.024
	Shift risk to service provider	.439	.060	.002	.000	.001	.037		.000	.011	.000	.006	.009	.419	.009
	Modernization of IT / replace legacy systems	.100	.007	.000	.000	.000	.000	.000		.000	.000	.000	.000	.002	.000
	Enable and facilitate strategic competitive advantages	.005	.037	.000	.000	.000	.004	.011	.000		.000	.000	.000	.000	.000
	Access to better IT systems and new technology	.009	.053	.000	.000	.000	.004	.000	.000	.000		.000	.000	.000	.000
	Knowledge acquisition from service provider	.078	.357	.001	.007	.019	.110	.006	.000	.000	.000		.000	.000	.000
	Suggestions for new IT based products and services (innovation, idea creation)	.392	.087	.000	.023	.000	.031	.009	.000	.000	.000	.000		.000	.000
	Joint product and service development	.121	.356	.011	.041	.052	.084	.419	.002	.000	.000	.000	.000		.000
	Business transformation	.049	.051	.031	.000	.000	.024	.009	.000	.000	.000	.000	.000	.000	

Table 5-3. Correlation matrix of involved variables (final factor solution)

KMO and Bartlett's Test		
Kaiser-Meyer-Olkin Measure of Sampling Adequacy		.795
Bartlett's Test of Squericity	Approx. Chi-Square	763.124
	df	91
	Significance	.000

Table 5-4: KMO and Bartlett's test (final factor solution)

Variable	Initial	Extraction
Cost reduction	1.000	.745
Variabilization of costs / cost transparency	1.000	.673
Quality improvements	1.000	.514
Long-term use of systems, applications and data	1.000	.409
Improved service orientation	1.000	.683
Increased flexibility	1.000	.616
Shift risk to service provider	1.000	.577
Modernization of IT / replace legacy systems	1.000	.612
Enable and facilitate strategic competitive advantages	1.000	.537
Access to better IT systems and new technology	1.000	.574
Knowledge acquisition from service provider	1.000	.601
Suggestions for new IT based products and services (innovation, idea creation)	1.000	.695
Joint product and service development	1.000	.673
Business transformation	1.000	.508

Extraction Method: Principal Component Analysis

Table 5-5. Communalities of initial and extracted factor solution (final factor solution)

Component	Initial Eigenvalues			Extraction Sums of Squared Loadings			Rotation Sums of Squared Loadings		
	Total	% of Variance	Cumulative %	Total	% of Variance	Cumulative %	Total	% of Variance	Cumulative %
1	4.249	30.347	30.347	4.249	30.347	30.347	2.890	20.643	20.643
2	1.725	12.319	42.666	1.725	12.319	42.666	2.146	15.326	35.969
3	1.392	9.941	52.607	1.392	9.941	52.607	1.833	13.096	49.065
4	1.053	7.522	60.130	1.053	7.522	60.130	1.549	11.065	60.130
5	.901	6.435	66.565						
6	.816	5.827	72.391						
7	.645	4.608	76.999						
8	.618	4.417	81.416						
9	.534	3.813	85.229						
10	.528	3.775	89.004						
11	.453	3.232	92.237						
12	.428	3.056	95.293						
13	.400	2.855	98.147						
14	.259	1.853	100.000						

Extraction Method: Principal Component Analysis

Table 5-6. Extraction of factors and total variance explained (final factor solution)

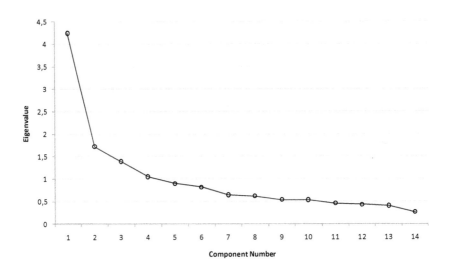

Figure 5-6. Visual solution using the Cattell's scree plot (final factor solution)

		Component			
		1	**2**	**3**	**4**
q1415	Joint product and service development	.812	-.098	.000	.035
q1414	Suggestions for new IT based products and services (innovation, idea creation)	.767	.311	.082	-.064
q1413	Knowledge acquisition from service provider	.677	.300	-.003	-.229
q1416	Business transformation	.676	.092	.140	.152
q1410	Enable strategic competitive advantages	.658	.139	.231	.177
q1407	Shift risk to service provider	-.034	.757	.047	.022
q1408	Modernization of IT / replace legacy systems	.276	.704	.169	.111
q1412	Access to better IT systems / new technology	.389	.626	.126	.123
q1404	Long-term use of systems, applications/data	.090	.542	.326	-.034
q1406	Increased flexibility	.063	.011	.779	.078
q1405	Improved service orientation	.139	.210	.774	.142
q1403	Quality improvements	.176	.324	.614	-.005
q1401	Cost reduction	.064	-.012	.068	.858
q1402	Variabilization of costs / cost transparency	.020	.132	.099	.803

Extraction Method: Principal Component Analysis. Rotation Method: Varimax with Kaiser Normalization

a. Rotation converged in 6 Iterations.

Table 5-7. Rotated component matrix (final factor solution)

		Cost reduction	Variabilization of costs / cost transparency	Quality improvements	Long-term use of systems, applications and data	Improved service orientation	Increased flexibility	Shift risk to service provider	Modernization of IT / replace legacy systems	Enable and facilitate strategic competitive advantages	Access to better IT systems and new technology	Knowledge acquisition from service provider	Suggestions for new IT based products and services (innovation, idea creation)	Joint product and service development	Business transformation
Reproduced correlation	Cost reduction	.745[a]	.696	.045	-.008	.181	.124	.011	.116	.208	.131	-.157	-.005	.087	.182
	Variabilization of costs / cost transparency	.696	.673[a]	.103	.078	.221	.143	.121	.204	.197	.202	-.131	.013	.038	.162
	Quality improvements	.045	.103	.514[a]	.392	.568	.492	.268	.380	.302	.348	.216	.286	.148	.234
	Long-term use of systems, applications and data	-.008	.078	.392	.409[a]	.374	.262	.422	.458	.203	.411	.230	.266	.038	.151
	Improved service orientation	.181	.221	.568	.374	.683[a]	.625	.194	.333	.325	.301	.123	.226	.144	.243
	Increased flexibility	.124	.143	.492	.262	.625	.616[a]	.044	.165	.237	.139	.025	.110	.099	.164
	Shift risk to service provider	.011	.121	.268	.422	.194	.044	.577[a]	.534	.097	.470	.198	.212	-.098	.056
	Modernization of IT / replace legacy systems	.116	.204	.380	.458	.333	.165	.534	.612[a]	.338	.583	.371	.437	.169	.292
	Enable and facilitate strategic competitive advantages	.208	.197	.302	.203	.325	.237	.097	.338	.537[a]	.393	.446	.555	.541	.517
	Access to better IT systems and new technology	.131	.202	.348	.411	.301	.139	.470	.583	.393	.574[a]	.422	.495	.266	.357
	Knowledge acquisition from service provider	-.157	-.131	.216	.230	.123	.025	.198	.371	.446	.422	.601[a]	.627	.512	.450
	Suggestions for new IT based products and services (innovation, idea creation)	-.005	.013	.286	.266	.226	.110	.212	.437	.555	.495	.627	.695[a]	.594	.549
	Joint product and service development	.087	.038	.148	.038	.144	.099	-.098	.169	.541	.266	.512	.594	.673[a]	.554
	Business transformation	.182	.162	.234	.151	.243	.164	.056	.292	.517	.357	.450	.549	.554	.508[a]
Residual[b]	Cost reduction		-.235	.092	.023	-.007	-.047	-.022	-.024	-.024	.038	.055	-.015	-.003	-.063
	Variabilization of costs / cost transparency	-.235		-.017	-.003	-.016	.051	-.010	-.028	-.069	-.086	.105	.085	-.011	-.045
	Quality improvements	.092	-.017		-.055	-.125	-.203	-.065	-.066	-.030	.001	-.002	.046	.016	-.101
	Long-term use of systems, applications and data	.023	-.003	-.055		-.044	-.142	-.150	-.080	.053	-.117	-.056	-.124	.087	.089
	Improved service orientation	-.007	-.016	-.125	-.044		-.182	.028	-.043	-.035	-.005	.025	.019	-.027	.033
	Increased flexibility	-.047	.051	-.203	-.142	-.182		.083	.083	-.048	.049	.063	.023	-.001	-.023
	Shift risk to service provider	-.022	-.010	-.065	-.150	.028	.083		-.162	.067	-.161	-.021	-.044	.083	.112
	Modernization of IT / replace legacy systems	-.024	-.028	-.066	-.080	-.043	.083	-.162		-.044	-.061	-.066	-.017	.035	-.012
	Enable and facilitate strategic competitive advantages	-.024	-.069	-.030	.053	-.035	-.048	.067	-.044		-.058	-.082	-.104	-.112	-.045
	Access to better IT systems and new technology	.038	-.086	.001	-.117	-.005	.049	-.161	-.061	-.058		-.057	.016	-.024	-.093
	Knowledge acquisition from service provider	.055	.105	-.002	-.056	.025	.063	-.021	-.066	-.082	-.057		-.005	-.130	-.112

	Cost reduction	Variabilization of costs / cost transparency	Quality improvements	Long-term use of systems, applications and data	Improved service orientation	Increased flexibility	Shift risk to service provider	Modernization of IT / replace legacy systems	Enable and facilitate strategic competitive advantages	Access to better IT systems and new technology	Knowledge acquisition from service provider	Suggestions for new IT based products and services (innovation, idea creation)	Joint product and service development	Business transformation
Suggestions for new IT based products and services (innovation, idea creation)	-.015	.085	.046	-.124	.019	.023	-.044	-.017	-.104	.016	-.005		-.079	-.151
Joint product and service development	-.003	-.011	.016	.087	-.027	-.001	.083	.035	-.112	-.024	-.130	-.079		-.069
Business transformation	-.063	-.045	-.101	.089	.033	-.023	.112	-.012	-.045	-.093	-.112	-.151	-.069	

Extraction Method: Principal Component Analysis
a. Reproduced communalities
b. Residuals are calculated between observed and reproduced correlations. There are 46 (50.0%) non-redundant residuals with absolute values above 0.05.

Table 5-8. Reproduced correlation matrix and residuals (final factor solution)

5.4.2.3   Reliability Analysis of the Final Factor Solution

After extracting 4 factors out of 14 variables, the reliability of the factor solution has to be evaluated. A measure for the reliability of the newly constructed scale, i.e., the variables that were condensed to one factor, is a reliability analysis for internal consistency. The reliability coefficient is measured using Cronbach's Alpha (Hair et al. 2006; Brosius 2006). Table 5-10 shows the Cronbach's alpha for all 4 factors with their respective items. The values are acceptable and show a value for Cronbach's alpha above 0.6. Although the generally agreed upon threshold is 0.7 (Nunnally 1978), in exploratory research, it may decrease to 0.6 (Robinson/Shaver/Wrightsman 1991). Furthermore, the lower values for factor 3 and 4 can be explained by the relation between the value for Cronbach's alpha and the number of items included in the scale. The more items are included, the higher Cronbach's alpha will be. Summing up, the scale can be regarded as reliable and used for further analysis, with two factors close to or exceeding the threshold of 0.7 and two factors fulfilling the minimum threshold of 0.6 for exploratory research (Hair et al. 2006; Robinson/Shaver/Wrightsman 1991).

Factor	Items included	Cronbach's Alpha	Cronbach's Alpha for standardized items
1	q1415	.800	.801
	q1414		
	q1413		
	q1416		
	q1410		
2	q1407	.688	.690
	q1408		
	q1412		
	q1404		
3	q1406	.657	.659
	q1405		
	q1403		
4	q1401	.622	.630
	q1402		

Table 5-9. Reliability / internal consistency of the factor scales

5.4.2.4   Interpretation of Factors

Out of the 14 expectation motives, 4 factors could be extracted that well explain dominant categories of outsourcing motives. Although interpreting these factors is subjective and lies in the eye of the researcher (Backhaus et al. 2006, 298), looking at the variables that define the factors, clear characteristics could be attributed to these factors. The first factor comprises all strategic and innovation-related motives that can be associated with an outsourcing decision: Knowledge acquisition from service provider, enable and facilitate strategic competitive advantages, business transformation, joint product and service development, and suggestions for new IT based products and services (innovation, idea creation). Strategic outsourcing ventures generally aim at achieving competitive advantage through greater intellectual depth and access, opportunity scanning, innovation, reliability, quality, or value-added solutions (Alexander/Young 1996; DiRomualdo/Gurbaxani 1998; Gottfredson/Puryear/Phillips 2005; King 1994; Quelin/Duhamel 2003; Quinn 1999; Quinn/Hilmer 1994). Clients with strategic outsourcing intents follow 'knowledge strategies' by concentrating their resources on a relatively few knowledge-based core competencies where they can develop best-in-world capabilities. These capabilities are leveraged with outside knowledge resources to achieve best-in world capabilities even with non-core activities.

The second factor aims at technological intents and IS improvement associated with the outsourcing decision. The underlying intent of IS improvement through outsourcing is to "do IS better" (DiRomualdo/Gurbaxani 1998, 70). Clients expect outside specialists such as an outsourcing vendor to better keep pace with new technologies and skills and thus to be better able to deliver up-to-date hardware, software, and services. But this technological aspect is not necessarily limited to modernization and transformation of IT. It also comprises keeping the status quo of the current IT and promises stability and reliability of the systems to the client. This also involves the client's demand to shift the risk (of unstable or outdated IT) to the service provider.

DiRomualdo and Gurbaxani (1998, 70) also mention cost reduction and service quality improvement as intents associated with the intent of IS improvement. The data in this thesis, however, shows that these two motives belong to other main factors and thus cannot be subsumed under one umbrella of outsourcing intent. This does not contradict the assumption that clients might expect more than one motive from their outsourcing vendor.

The third factor comprises items that clearly aim at what DiRomualdo and Gurbaxani (1998, 72) call "deploying IT to significantly improve critical aspects of business performance". This sort of expectation towards outsourcing is focused on delivering new skills and capabilities that link IT to business results, rather than those purely related to technology. Business impact can be achieved through, e.g., increased flexibility, improved service orientation, or quality improvements, i.e., items that define factor 3.

The last factor addresses the most prevailing outsourcing intents, i.e., cost-related outsourcing motives (Kern/Willcocks/van Heck 2002, 47). They comprise cost reduction as such, but also the variabilization of costs, i.e., rendering IT as a variable cost and thus handling IT as a more flexible resource.

Table 5-10 gives an overview of the factors, their characterization and included items.

No.	Factor Label	Constitutive keywords	Attributed items
1	Strategy / Innovation	Innovation, strategic advantages, joint product and service development	q1415
			q1414
			q1413
			q1416
			q1410
2	Technology improvement and reliability	IT, modernization, state-of-the-art technology, reliability, stability	q1407
			q1408
			q1412
			q1404
3	Business Support and Facilitator	Business impact, business support, service excellence, business flexibility, service orientation, quality improvement	q1406
			q1405
			q1403
4	Cost focus	Cost reduction, variabilization of costs, efficiency	q1401
			q1402

Table 5-10. Interpretation of identified factors

5.4.3   Cluster Analysis: Finding Configurations of Clients with Similar Outsourcing Expectations

The statistical and methodological details of cluster analysis have been introduced in chapter 4.2.1 (p. 86ff.). This chapter will thus exclusively focus on the application of cluster analysis for the purpose of this research to identify configurations of outsourcing clients with similar outsourcing expectations.

The cluster analysis is carried out with the condensed orthogonal factors as clustering variables (for a critical review of choosing the factor-cluster approach see introductory section of chapter 5.4, p. 126ff.). To balance the benefits and weaknesses of different clustering algorithms, the analysis is conducted in three steps as advocated by many researchers (cf.

Ketchen/Shook 1996, 446). It involves hierarchical clustering with single linkage to identify outliers, hierarchical clustering with ward to identify the number of clusters and the cluster centroids, followed by the iterative, partitioning approach of k-means to find an optimal cluster solution. Finally, the solution is validated with discriminant analysis.

5.4.3.1 Selecting and Preparing the Input Variables for the Cluster Analysis

As to the number of variables to include in the cluster analysis there is a balance between completeness and parsimony of the input variables (Homburg/Workman/Jensen 2002, 43). While some authors argue for an inclusion of as many variables as possible (McKelvey 1975), there is a general agreement that only necessary dimensions should be considered for the actual cluster analysis (Ketchen/Shook 1996; Homburg/Workman/Jensen 2002). Even more, "the presence of spurious dimensions has been shown to have detrimental effect on the performance of clustering methods" (Homburg/Workman/Jensen 2002, 43). To account for this issue, the study in this thesis distinguishes between two types of variables, following the suggestion and approach of Homburg et al. (2002) (see also chapter 3.8 for a more detailed argument, p. 71ff.). First, parsimonious sets of theory-based key constructs that serve as active input variables for the clustering algorithm are identified (as described in this chapter). Thereby, the expectation variables that were grouped into four constitutive, independent key factors of outsourcing motives served as input variables for the following cluster analysis. Second, several "passive", descriptive variables are used to give a rich and comprehensive picture of the different configurations. For these "passive" variables, theoretical, conceptual, and practical considerations were regarded as suggested by Hair et al. (2006, 569). This enhanced picture of the configurations will be laid out in the subsequent chapter 5.5 (p. 148ff.).

The basis for both the active clustering variables (focusing on the expectations and outsourcing motives) and the passive variables is the framework that was *conceptually* built and derived from theoretical considerations of TCE, social / relational exchange, expectation confirmation theory etc. (see chapter 3.8, p. 71ff.). Besides, the results of the qualitative expert interviews (see pre-study in chapter 5.1, p. 113ff.) contributed domain knowledge and thus helped to underpin practical considerations.

Scale conversion and standardization of the input variables was not an issue to be considered as the variables are factor scores that are already standardized and have the same level of measurement.

5.4.3.2 Identifying Outliers in the Data Set

Cluster analysis is not only sensitive to the inclusion of irrelevant variables, but also highly sensitive to outliers (i.e., objects different from all others), as they can severely distort and bias the results of the cluster analysis (Hair et al. 2006, 572).

Before conducting the actual cluster analysis, possible outliers were identified using the single linkage clustering algorithm. This algorithm tends to build snake-like chain and thus reveals outliers quite obviously (Backhaus et al. 2006, 529). From the heterogeneity measure in the agglomeration schedule as well as from the visual observation of the dendrogram it became obvious that six outliers pose a potential bias threat to distort the cluster solution. These six outliers were excluded from the following analysis. This reduced the data set to 190 data points.

5.4.3.3 Identifying the Number of Clusters and the Cluster Centroids

Ward's algorithm has been shown in many studies to be able to find very good partitions and also the "true cluster solution" (Backhaus et al. 2006, 528). It was thus used to identify the number of clusters and profile cluster centers that serve as initial cluster seeds in the non-hierarchical procedure.

Although no standard objective selection procedure exists to identify the number of clusters (Hair et al. 2006, 592, 626) and thus the ultimate decision how many clusters to consider lies with the subjective decision of the researcher, there are some best-practice rules of assistance. Three examination measures were used to identify the appropriate number of clusters.

For hierarchical methods, the most basic procedure is to visually inspect the dendogram. The dendrogram of the Ward algorithm (see appendix A 17) shows four or five dense branches and from a graphical observation both a *5 or 4 cluster solution* could be reasonable. But because this method heavily relies on interpretation, it should be used cautiously (Aldenderfer/Blashfield 1984). Another technique to evaluate the number of clusters from a graphical point of view is the *elbow criterion* which involves graphing the coefficient (y-axis) against the number of clusters (on an x-axis) (Ketchen/Shook 1996, 446; Hair et al. 2006, 594). Figure 5-7 shows that there is an elbow at the *four-cluster solution* with the heterogeneity increasing from 443.10 to 509.48.

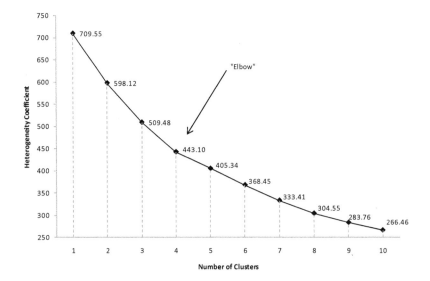

Figure 5-7. Estimating the number of clusters via the elbow criterion

A similar procedure involves examining the incremental changes in the coefficient by numbers, not visually. The percentage increase in the agglomeration coefficient can be calculated for each cluster solution. The solution should be chosen which has the largest percentage increase. Table 5-11 shows that there is a major leap between step 3 and step 4 when the clusters are to be merged from 4 to 3 clusters. There is a percentage increase of 15.0% which accounts for almost 6 (absolute) percentage points between the 4 and the 3 cluster solution causing a major jump in heterogeneity. As the number of clusters prior to the merger is deemed the most appropriate (Hair et al. 2006, 593), this calls for the *4-cluster solution.*

Step	Heterogeneity	Percentage Increase	Absolute Increase (in percentage points)
9	283.7630521	6.5%	-0.1%
8	304.5478657	7.3%	0.8%
7	333.4078276	9.5%	2.2%
6	368.4495792	10.5%	1.0%
5	405.3352897	10.0%	-0.5%
4	443.0973442	9.3%	-0.7%
3	509.4759368	*15.0%*	*5.7%*
2	598.1229345	17.4%	2.4%
1	709.5469955	18.6%	1.2%

Table 5-11. Changes in the heterogeneity coefficient of the Ward clustering algorithm

Despite the fact that no ultimately objective measure for determining the "true number of clusters" exists, both types of stopping rules have been shown to provide quite reliable decisions in empirical studies (Milligan/Cooper 1985).

Concluding, with the three measures of visual inspection of the dendrogram, visual inspection of the elbow criterion and statistical evaluation of the heterogeneity development, the four-cluster solution is deemed to be the appropriate and "good" solution (see appendices 0 and A 17 for detailed results).

In a next step, the mean values of the four clusters for each clustering variable are calculated. They will also serve as cluster centroids for the subsequent k-means clustering algorithm. Table 5-12 shows the means.

Cluster	Clustering variable	Factor In-novation	Factor Technology	Factor Business	Factor Cost
1	Mean	.0461107	-.8377512	.8665108	.2724379
	N	53	53	53	53
	Std. Dev.	.90994741	.71599518	.52911025	.94447665
2	Mean	-.6346792	-.1665055	-.6764279	.9589141
	N	29	29	29	29
	Std. Dev.	.53728581	.83133102	.57895739	.62889452
3	Mean	.6845172	.1117094	-.9274904	-.3903495
	N	47	47	47	47
	Std. Dev.	.95217216	.69388659	.68220916	.79139353
4	Mean	-.3433236	.7970057	.3819726	-.3706693
	N	61	61	61	61
	Std. Dev.	.88282233	.75982735	.64574236	.85685861
Total	Mean	-.0249067	.0244117	.0316681	.0067919
	N	190	190	190	190
	Std. Dev.	.97724346	.97595309	.95556126	.96624550

Table 5-12. Mean values of 4-cluster solution for clustering variables with Ward / initial cluster centroids

5.4.3.4   Optimizing the Cluster Solution with k-Means

While hierarchical clustering methods facilitate a comprehensive evaluation of a wide range of cluster solutions, they lack flexibility in such that observations cannot switch cluster membership. Therefore, the non-hierarchical clustering procedure of k-means is used to develop an optimal cluster solution and improve the results from the hierarchical procedure. As cluster centroids, the mean values in Table 5-12 were used as initial cluster seeds.

The results of the k-means algorithm such as the final cluster centers and the distances between the final cluster centers are shown in the appendices A 18 and A 19. Table 5-13 depicts the mean values of the final cluster solution as obtained from the k-means clustering algorithm.

Cluster	Clustering variable	Factor Innovation	Factor Technology	Factor Business	Factor Cost
1	Mean	.1471736	-.9842886	.9058009	.2005722
	N	44	44	44	44
	Std. Dev.	.86422090	.62257663	.52884209	.91493496
2	Mean	-.6870909	-.0865352	-.5274649	.7178529
	N	50	50	50	50
	Std. Dev.	.65103700	.81995792	.76546660	.80549826
3	Mean	.9341478	.2215094	-.6185698	-.3027022
	N	51	51	51	51
	Std. Dev.	.64579504	.70145965	.74219127	.84341234
4	Mean	-.5443310	.9105932	.5351558	-.6219899
	N	45	45	45	45
	Std. Dev.	.74592146	.72458846	.70827880	.73068434
Total	Mean	-.0249067	.0244117	.0316681	.0067919
	N	190	190	190	190
	Std. Dev.	.97724346	.97595309	.95556126	.96624550

Table 5-13. Mean values of final 4-cluster solution for clustering variables with k-means

5.4.3.5 Estimating and Validating the Cluster Solution with Discriminant Analysis

In order to validate the identified cluster solution a discriminant analysis is conducted. Discriminant analysis can to some extent substitute the missing confirmatory component of a cluster analysis (Wiedenbeck/Züll 2001) and is often used as a subsequent method to complement cluster analysis. As the dependent variable the grouping variable that shows the cluster affiliation of the cases as obtained from k-means clustering procedure is chosen. As predictors or independent variables, the four clustering variables are used.

Three discriminant functions are calculated (one less than the number of groups, which is 4). As validation measures to estimate the goodness of the solution, the *eigenvalues*, canonical correlation coefficient, Wilks' lambda as well as the classification ratio of objects are used. The results in appendix A 20 show that the canonical correlations for the three discriminant functions are fairly high, ranging between 0.695 and 0.780. The eigenvalue is also reasonably high with a value of 1.552 for the first, 1.246 for the second, and 0.935 for the third discriminant function. Wilks' lambda is highly significant ($p < 0.0001$). Regarding the group membership prediction accuracy, all cases (100%) were classified correctly which supports the goodness of the solution. For detailed results of the discriminant analysis, see appendices A 20 to A 27.

Overall, the goodness of the solution is deemed high and the discriminant analysis shows that the combinations of predictors (i.e., the discriminant functions) well explain the group differences and thus validate the cluster solution obtained in the two-step approach of combining hierarchical Ward clustering and non-hierarchical k-means clustering.

5.5   Interpretation of Statistical Analysis: Configurations of Different Outsourcing Client Groups

After having identified and validated the appropriate number of configurations of outsourcing clients with certain expectation profiles, this chapter is dedicated to describing and interpreting the results in more detail.

As mentioned above, for getting a rich and comprehensive picture of the four identified configurations of outsourcing clients, the approach of Homburg et al. (2002) is followed. First, the clusters are described along the four key factors that were used as active input variables for the clustering. Additionally, the clusters are portrayed along the 16 original expectation variables. Then, the clusters are illustrated along the key dimensions of the framework that was conceptually built to describe and distinguish different configurations of outsourcing clients.

The 4 clusters are contrasted using the univariate technique of ANOVA (one-way analysis of variance, mean value comparisons) to assess the statistical significance of differences between groups, i.e., to see which of the groups differ significantly with regard to the respective variables. Before conducting the following ANOVAs, the prerequisite of equality of variances is tested with a Levene test for each ANOVA. As the Levene test did not turn out to be significant, homogeneity or equality of the variances can be assumed and ANOVAs are conducted. The detailed results are found in the appendices A 28 to A 31 (for both the four factors and all 16 outsourcing expectation variables).

Figure 5-8 gives an overview of the 4 groups that are derived from the cluster analysis. The groups are of almost equal size, with cluster 3 a little larger and cluster 1 a little smaller. This might be a surprising result, but there is also and probably foremost a statistical answer to this finding: The Ward algorithm tends to group data points into clusters of similar size. Although this has to be mentioned as a limitation of this algorithm and as a caveat when interpreting the group sizes for representativeness in the population, the groups still fully meet the cluster characteristics of internally highly homogeneous and externally highly heterogeneous groups.

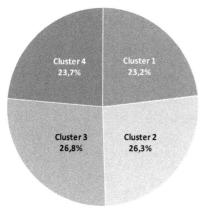

(n = 190)

Figure 5-8. Distribution and cluster size of the four configurations

5.5.1 Constitutive Elements of the Client Configurations: Major Outsourcing Expectations and Strategic Intents

Profiling the four groups against the original cluster variables (i.e., the four condensed factors of outsourcing expectations) is the first step to see how the groups differ with respect to their expectations towards outsourcing.

Thereby, the four expectation factors served as key anchor points to distinguish the groups along their basic underlying motivation of outsourcing. Figure 5-9 gives an overview of the 4 clusters with respect to differences among the four key factors. This figure is the graphical representation of Table 5-13 where the mean values of the four-cluster solution were depicted. The differences are all highly significant (ANOVA, $p < 0.0001$), but post-hoc tests will have to show which groups differ and how.

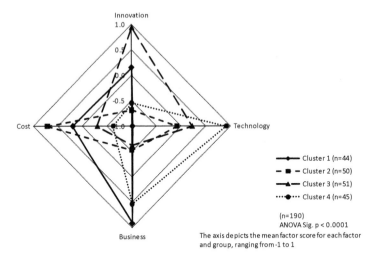

Figure 5-9. Overview of cluster profiles with regard to outsourcing expectations

Let's look at each of the expectation factors to see the characteristics of the clusters for each factor.

Figure 5-10 shows the mean factor values for the innovation and strategy factor among the 4 clusters (the whiskers in each column reflect the standard deviation). It becomes obvious that cluster 3 scores very high on the innovation expectation, while clusters 2 and 4 do not have any outsourcing expectations with regard to innovation and strategy. Accordingly, the post-hoc tests (S-N-K, Tukey-HSD, Scheffé; significance level alpha = 0.05) show that cluster 2 and 4 do not differ significantly from each other, while cluster 1 and 3 each differ from the others.

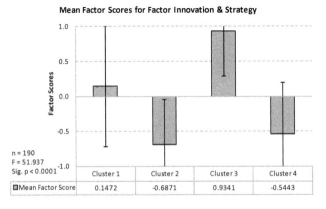

Figure 5-10. Mean factor scores for factor innovation and strategy expectations

Regarding the expectations towards IT-related issues (latest technology, technology excellence, IT stability and reliability), cluster 4 scores very high in this dimension, while cluster 1 and 2 do not have high expectations towards their vendor with regard to technology issues (see Figure 5-11). Cluster 3 shows a small, but positive technology expectation. All four clusters differ significantly and post-hoc tests (S-N-K, Tukey-HSD, Scheffé; significance level alpha = 0.05) show that each cluster significantly differs from each other, with cluster 2 and 3 being the closest in terms of their IT expectations.

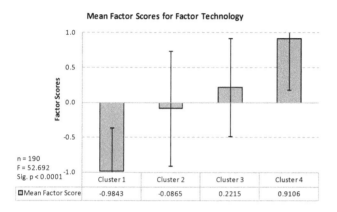

Figure 5-11. Mean factor scores for factor technology expectations

Business excellence, support and facilitation of business-related issues such as quality improvements, service orientation or flexibility are predominantly expected by cluster 1 as Figure 5-12 depicts. Cluster 4 also shows a fairly high value with regard to the business support and facilitation expectation, but cluster 2 and 3 both have very low expectations towards business-oriented goals. Accordingly, these two groups do not differ significantly from each other, but cluster 1 and 4 differ significantly as shown by the post-hoc tests (S-N-K, Tukey-HSD, Scheffé; significance level alpha = 0.05).

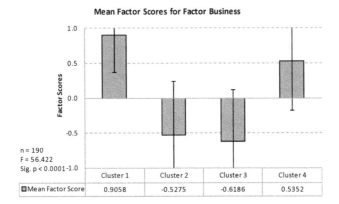

Figure 5-12. Mean factor scores for factor business expectations

With regard to the most prominent outsourcing expectation, i.e., cost-related issues, cluster 2 has the highest expectations (see Figure 5-13). Cluster 1 shows a low cost expectation, while cluster 3 and 4 do not have any cost expectations. Both clusters also do not differ significantly from each other as the post-hoc tests (S-N-K, Tukey-HSD, Scheffé; significance level alpha = 0.05) confirm. In contrast, post-hoc tests show that cluster 1 and 2 each differ significantly from all other clusters.

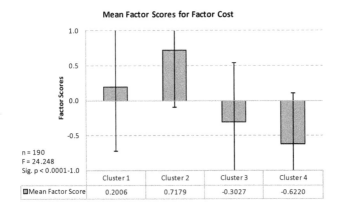

Figure 5-13. Mean factor scores for factor cost expectations

After having profiled the four client configurations along the key expectation factors and clustering variables, significant differences between the groups are identified according to the expectations. To get an even more detailed picture on these differences, the 16 original expectation variables are used to profile the four identified client configurations. In analogy to Figure 5-9, Figure 5-14 gives an overview of the four cluster profiles along the 16 detailed out-sourcing expectations variables (instead of the condensed factors).

Again, as expected, the four clusters differ significantly along all expectation variables (p < 0.0001). For example, for the first group, improved service orientation and increased flexibili-ty – both business-oriented factors – are among the most important motives associated with the outsourcing decision. Cost reduction and transparency are also central expectations for this group. In contrast, shifting the risk to the service provider, the reliability of the IT sys-tems, as well as the modernization of IT are among the low-priority goals with regard to out-sourcing. Group 2 has a very distinct profile, scoring only high with regard to the two cost motives. In all other categories, especially with regard to strategic motives such as "strategic competitive advantage", "joint product and service development", or "business transforma-tion", this group shows very low scores, indicating that these motives did not impact the out-sourcing decision in a considerable way. Group 3 shows high values for motives such as "knowledge acquisition from service provider", "suggestions for new IT-based products and services", or "joint product and service development" – all associated with a strategic compo-nent of outsourcing. Lastly, group 4 attributes major importance to the motives "quality im-provements", "long-term use of systems", "shift risk to service provider", and "improved ser-vice orientation", while de-prioritizing cost motives and strategic factors such as "joint prod-uct and service development" and "business transformation".

While the four clusters differ significantly along most expectation variables, there is one ex-ception: all 4 clusters heavily associate the expectation variable "focus on core competencies" (Var q1409) with the outsourcing decision. This can be well explained by the fact that one of the underlying prerequisites and core assumptions of any outsourcing decision is that re-sources that have become available by outsourcing can be dedicated to other (core) areas of the firm. Even when core areas of IT are outsourced, the free resources can still be used to invest in other core areas of the firm. Thus, "focus on core competencies" is one of the inhe-rent and meta expectations of any outsourcing venture and is therefore expected by almost all clients. This also explains the fact that this variable had to be excluded from the factor analy-sis because it could not be subsumed under any other factor as it stands alone as a meta expec-tation.

Besides analyzing the important motives for each group, one could also run post-hoc tests for each variable in order to show not only if, but how the groups differ from each other. There-by, it became obvious that in terms of "cost reduction", "cost transparency", "modernization of IT", "access to highly skilled people", and "access to better IT systems" groups 1 and 2 and also groups 3 and 4 have similar profiles and each group pair differs significantly from the other. With regard to "quality improvements", "service orientation", and "increased flexibili-ty", groups 1 and 4 as well as group 2 and 3 have similar expectation profiles. Lastly, there are also motives where one group distinguished itself from all other groups, e.g., regarding "long-term use of systems" and "shift risk to service provider", group 4 differs from all other groups. With regard to the strategic motives "joint product and service development" and "business transformation", group 1 and 3 each differs from group 2 and 4 that both show similar expectation profiles. For a detailed statistical analysis with post-hoc tests of the 16 expectation variables and their differences in the four clusters, see appendices A 31 and A 32.

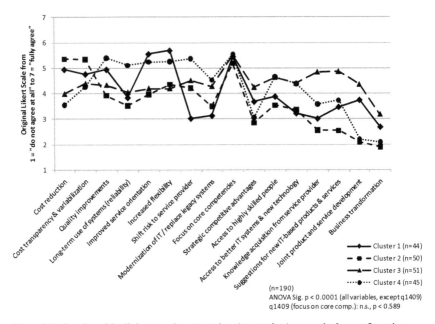

Figure 5-14. Overview of detailed outsourcing expectations (mean values) among the four configurations

Profiling the four configurations along the key factors (Figure 5-9 to Figure 5-13) as well as along the 16 detailed outsourcing expectations, it became obvious that the four client configurations differ significantly with respect to their outsourcing expectations. In the following, the clusters will be described along their 4 motivation factors and also along the 16 detailed outsourcing expectations depicted in Figure 5-14.

Cluster 1 (n=44) is very much focused on achieving business-related benefits with outsourcing. Major expectations of clients associated with this cluster comprise "improved service orientation", "increased flexibility", and "quality improvements". Besides expectations that facilitate or support the business, cost-oriented motives also play a decent role (especially in contrast to clusters 3 and 4). Selected innovation-focused aspects such as "joint product and service development" are also of importance for clients in this cluster. In contrast, IT-related factors that aim at IT improvement or reliability such as "modernization of IT / replace legacy systems", "shift risk to service provider", "access to better IT systems" as well as "knowledge acquisition" only play a minor role in the expectation profile of this group. Like all clusters, clients in this cluster also expect a focus on core competencies leveraged through the outsourcing venture. But as mentioned above, this is not a differentiating aspect of the cluster profiles. Summing up the characteristics of the outsourcing expectations, cluster 1 is labeled *"Business-efficiency clients"*.

In contrast, cluster 2 (n=50) exclusively expects cost benefits from the outsourcing venture. In this regard, clients in this cluster expect both cost reduction as well as cost transparency and rendering IT as a variable cost. In this respect, this cluster differentiates itself from all other clusters (with cluster 1 being the closest when it comes to cost expectations). Compared to the predominant cost motive, all other expectation categories are rather negligible, especially when it comes to strategy and innovation expectations such as "business transformation" or "joint product and service development". As clients that belong to the second group are very narrowly focused on this single benefit associated with outsourcing, cluster 2 is labeled *"Cost-conscious smart shoppers"*.

Cluster 3 (n=51) embraces outsourcing customers who focus on enhancing their (business and IT) innovation and strategy capabilities with outsourcing. This group clearly expects aspects such as "knowledge acquisition from service provider" or "suggestions for new IT-based products and services" from their outsourcing vendor. Cost motives as well as business-oriented motives play a moderate role for these clients. IT motives with regard to "resources", however, belong to the expectation portfolio, namely "access to highly skilled people" and "access to better IT systems". With regard to their IT expectations, clusters 3 and 4 share some of the IT motives. But since the predominant benefits clients associate with outsourcing in this group are strategic motives, cluster 3 is labeled *"Strategists and innovation seekers"*.

In contrast to all other clusters, members of cluster 4 (n=45) have *two* dominant motives. The first and prevailing one is the focus on IT-related expectations. Thereby, clients do not only expect IT development and improvement with regard to the latest state-of-the-art technology. They also look for IT reliability and stability of the systems, i.e., keeping the status quo and the maintenance of the current systems, not necessarily the replacement of legacy systems. The second motive is focused on business expectations. In the center of this aspect are expectations such as "quality improvements" where clients of cluster 4 have the highest expectation compared to the other clusters (even compared to the business cluster 1). But also "access to highly skilled people", "increased flexibility" and "improved service orientation" are benefits that clients of this group appreciate in an outsourcing venture. In line with the focus on (IT) reliability and stability described above, this group scores highest on the dimension "shift risk to service provider". Members of this cluster aim at a stable environment where risks are best transferred to the service provider who is then responsible for and should balance unforeseen events and situations. Because of the core focus on IT-related issues (both improvement and reliability matters), cluster 4 is labeled *"IT excellence and reliability-oriented clients"*.

What is astonishing about the cluster groups is that each group has only one dominant motive, while the last group, the IT excellence and reliability-oriented clients, expects benefits in two areas, i.e., business-oriented benefits as well as IT-focused benefits. Clear and focused expectations call for very informed clients knowledgeable about what to achieve with outsourcing and what not. The last group on the contrary has heterogeneous expectations, associating more than one clear objective with the outsourcing venture. The chapter on governance mechanisms will have to show whether clients with multi-mixed motives have different governance mechanisms in place and whether there are general differences compared to the three other groups.

Having described the distinctive features of the 4 client configurations with regard to their underlying outsourcing motives, Table 5-14 gives a summarizing overview of the clusters with their characteristics and 5 most distinguishing outsourcing motives (not only from an absolute point of view, but also in relation to the other clusters) associated with each group.

Cluster #	Label	Description / 5 most distinguishing outsourcing motives
1	Business-efficiency clients	• Service orientation • Flexibility • Quality improvements • Cost reduction • Joint product and service development + focus on core competencies
2	Cost-conscious smart shoppers	• Cost reduction • Cost transparency / variabilization • (no other characterizing outsourcing expectations) + focus on core competencies
3	Strategists and innovation seekers	• Suggestions for new IT-based products and services • Knowledge acquisition from service provider • Joint product and service development • Access to highly skilled people • Access to better IT systems and new technology + focus on core competencies
4	IT excellence and reliability-oriented clients	• Access to better IT systems and new technology • Modernization of IT / replace legacy systems • Quality improvements • Access to highly skilled people • Shift risk to service provider + focus on core competencies

Table 5-14. Constitutive outsourcing expectations of the four client configurations

Following the structure of the conceptual framework that was developed in chapter 3.8 (p. 71ff.), the subsequent chapters will describe the four clusters along the categories described in the framework, i.e., factors of the outsourcing context, the relational architecture of the venture, governance approaches, and interactions. Lastly, outsourcing success in the four client groups will be investigated.

5.5.2 Context Factors

5.5.2.1 Basic Company Characteristics

In order to get an understanding of the constitutive company features of the four client configurations, four basic attributes that characterize the context of the investigated firms are investigated: Industry, annual sales, firm size (number of employees), and IT budget.

Table 5-15 depicts the distribution of different industries overall and among the four client groups. The very last column on the right hand side of the table depicts the distribution overall (n=190). Banking/insurance/finance (11.6%), div. manufacturing (12.6%), and automotive (8.9%) are the most prominent industries represented in the data. When analyzing the distribution of the industries among the four client configurations, the chi-square test and other measures for nominal data (Phi, Cramer-V) show significant differences among the four groups. To better expose these differences, the residuals, i.e., the differences between the observed and the expected frequency values, are depicted. The expected cell counts provide a basis for comparison with the actual cell counts and allow for the calculation of a standardized measure of association (Hair et al. 2006, 666). Kromrey (2006, 480pp.) suggests this method in order to measure the association and the deviation of statistical independence. A positive residual means that more frequently than random, i.e., more systematically, companies/respondents are found in a certain category of a group. The amount of difference denotes the strength of the association and the sign represented in this value (Hair et al. 2006, 667). Those values are marked bold and italic.

Analyzing the four groups shows that the industries banking/insurance/finance and retail/wholesale are more prominently represented in the business-efficiency client group (cluster 1) than could be expected by chance. Consumer goods, electrical engineering, and IT services, in contrast, are heavily represented among the cost-conscious smart shoppers (cluster 2). The innovation- and strategy-focused clients (cluster 3) are most dominantly found in the automotive industry, engineering/machine construction, and in the public/governmental sector. Lastly, the manufacturing industry is heavily represented among the IT-focused clients (cluster 4).

Since the chi-square test shows that these findings and differences are significant at least on a moderate level, one can assume that the underlying outsourcing motivations of the four client groups are somehow related and associated with the industries of the respondents. For example, one could assume that in "engineering industries" such as automotive, engineering/machine construction, but surprisingly also in the public sector, the strategy and innovation demand and expectation is more distinct than in other industries.

Industry	Cluster 1	Cluster 2	Cluster 3	Cluster 4	Cluster 1	Cluster 2	Cluster 3	Cluster 4	Total
Automotive	0.1	-0.5	*2.4*	-2.0	9.1%	8.0%	13.7%	4.4%	8.9%
Chemicals and Pharma	1.0	0.6	-2.5	0.9	9.1%	8.0%	2.0%	8.9%	6.8%
Engineering / Machine Construction	-0.5	-1.9	*2.0*	0.4	6.8%	4.0%	11.8%	8.9%	7.9%
Electrical Engineering	-2.2	*2.3*	-0.8	0.7	2.3%	12.0%	5.9%	8.9%	7.4%
Consumer Goods	-0.6	*2.2*	-1.9	0.3	2.3%	8.0%	0.0%	4.4%	3.7%
Div. Manufacturing	-2.6	-0.3	-2.4	*5.3*	6.8%	12.0%	7.8%	24.4%	12.6%
Energy, Public Utilities	0.5	-0.9	0.0	0.4	6.8%	4.0%	5.9%	6.7%	5.8%
Banking, Insurance, Finance	*5.9*	0.2	-0.9	-5.2	25.0%	12.0%	9.8%	0.0%	11.6%
IT Services	-0.3	*2.4*	-1.7	-0.4	4.5%	10.0%	2.0%	4.4%	5.3%
Telecommunications	-0.7	0.2	1.2	-0.7	0.0%	2.0%	3.9%	0.0%	1.6%
Retail / Wholesale	*2.1*	-1.1	-0.1	-0.9	9.1%	2.0%	3.9%	2.2%	4.2%
Transport / Logistics	0.6	1.4	-0.6	-1.4	4.5%	6.0%	2.0%	0.0%	3.2%
Media	-1.4	0.4	-0.6	1.6	0.0%	4.0%	2.0%	6.7%	3.2%

Industry	Cluster 1	Cluster 2	Cluster 3	Cluster 4	Cluster 1	Cluster 2	Cluster 3	Cluster 4	Total
Medical Engineering	0.3	1.2	-0.8	-0.7	2.3%	4.0%	0.0%	0.0%	1.6%
Public Services, Government	-2.1	-1.4	*3.6*	-0.1	0.0%	2.0%	11.8%	4.4%	4.7%
Other	-0.1	-1.4	0.6	0.9	4.5%	2.0%	5.9%	6.7%	4.7%
Healthcare	0.3	-0.8	0.2	0.3	2.3%	0.0%	2.0%	2.2%	1.6%
Construction	-0.7	-0.8	1.2	0.3	0.0%	0.0%	3.9%	2.2%	1.6%
Tourism	0.3	-0.8	0.2	0.3	2.3%	0.0%	2.0%	2.2%	1.6%
Other Services	0.1	-1.1	0.9	0.1	2.3%	0.0%	3.9%	2.2%	2.1%
Total n					44	50	51	45	100%

Chi-Square = 71.741, p = 0.09; Phi = 0.614, p = 0.09; Cramer-V = 0.355, p = 0.09; n=190

Table 5-15. Relation between industry and client configurations (residuals between observed and expected frequencies; percentages of distribution)

Another measure to characterize the four client groups involves analyzing the annual sales of the company respondents (Table 5-16). The overall analysis of the distribution of annual sales among the respondents irrespective of group affiliation shows a rather homogeneous picture with few companies reporting annual sales below 50 mio. Euro. The largest represented group in the sample has annual sales between 1 and 5 billion Euro (20.2%).

Analyzing the groups with a chi-square test (p < 0.1) and Somers-d (p < 0.001) for ordinal data, however, shows significant differences. Again, as suggested by Kromrey (2006), the residuals are examined for great differences between observed and expected frequencies of each category in each group.

It becomes obvious that the business-efficiency-oriented clients (cluster 1) are most prominently found in very large companies (with more than 10 billion Euro annual sales). The cost-conscious smart shoppers are also rather established in larger companies (most prominently in companies with 1 to 5 billion Euro annual sales). Surprisingly, the innovation- and strategy-oriented clients seem to be over-represented in the non-profit sector and to some extent also to be found in medium-size companies (250+ - 500 mio. Euro annual sales). Lastly, clients that expect IT excellence and reliability are most often found in medium-size companies with annual sales between 50 and 500 million Euro.

Overall, as the chi-square test and also Somers-d reveal, there is a relation between firm size (measured in annual sales) and group affiliation.

Firm size (annual sales)	Cluster 1	Cluster 2	Cluster 3	Cluster 4	Cluster 1	Cluster 2	Cluster 3	Cluster 4	Total
below 10 mio. Euro	-0.9	0.9	-1.0	1.0	0.0%	4.1%	0.0%	4.7%	2.2%
10 - 50 mio. Euro	-1.5	1.0	1.2	-0.7	2.4%	8.2%	8.9%	4.7%	6.2%
50+ - 100 mio. Euro	-1.6	-1.5	-0.1	3.2	7.3%	8.2%	11.1%	18.6%	11.2%
100+ - 250 mio. Euro	0.4	-3.1	0.7	2.0	19.5%	12.2%	20.0%	23.3%	18.5%
250+ - 500 mio. Euro	-2.8	-2.8	1.7	3.9	4.9%	6.1%	15.6%	20.9%	11.8%
500+ mio. - 1 bill. Euro	1.9	1.0	-0.6	-2.3	14.6%	12.2%	8.9%	4.7%	10.1%
1+ - 5 bill. Euro	-0.3	2.1	-1.1	-0.7	19.5%	24.5%	17.8%	18.6%	20.2%
5+ - 10 bill. Euro	1.7	1.2	-1.5	-1.4	9.8%	8.2%	2.2%	2.3%	5.6%
more than 10 bill. Euro	4.2	1.2	-1.3	-4.1	22.0%	14.3%	8.9%	2.3%	11.8%
non-profit	-0.9	-0.1	2.0	-1.0	0.0%	2.0%	6.7%	0.0%	2.2%
Total n					41	49	45	43	100%

Chi-square = 36.810, p < 0.1; Somers-d = -0.198, p < 0.001; n=178

Table 5-16. Distribution of annual sales among the four client configurations (residuals and percentage of distribution)

Besides annual sales, firm size can also be measured by the number of employees (Table 5-17). First, looking at the overall distribution of the respondents in terms of firm size reveals a rather homogeneous picture with the distribution following a bell curve. There are some firms with very few employees (small sized companies with up to 250 employees) and some with a lot of employees (4.8% of all respondents have more than 50,000 employees). Medium-sized firms with 501 – 2000 employees are best represented in the data sample (34.6%) as well as lager firms with 5001 – 50,000 employees (21.8%).

While the chi-square test turned out to be significant at a 0.1 level, Somers-d, i.e., the association measure for ordinal scales, turned out to be extremely significant (p < 0.001). In order to examine these assumed group differences, again the residuals are analyzed. It becomes obvious that the business-efficiency-focused clients (cluster 1) are rather found in large companies with a lot of employees (more than 5000 employees). This is in accordance with the finding from analyzing the group affiliation with annual sales. Here likewise, the business-efficiency-oriented cluster can be found in large companies. The cost-conscious smart shoppers (cluster 2) are primarily located in medium-to-large size companies (2001 – 5000 employees), but also to some extent in very large companies with more than 50,000 employees. The strategy- and innovation-focused clients, in contrast, can predominantly be found in small-to-medium-size companies with 251 to 2000 employees, while the IT-focused clients (cluster 4) belong to smaller firms with 251-500 employees.

Firm size (employees)	Cluster 1	Cluster 2	Cluster 3	Cluster 4	Cluster 1	Cluster 2	Cluster 3	Cluster 4	Total
up to 250 employees	-0.4	-1.1	0.0	1.5	9.1%	8.0%	10.2%	13.3%	10.1%
251 to 500 employees	-3.4	-1.1	*2.0*	*2.5*	4.5%	10.0%	16.3%	17.8%	12.2%
501 to 2000 employees	-1.2	-4.3	*6.1*	-0.6	31.8%	26.0%	46.9%	33.3%	34.6%
2001 to 5000 employees	-1.3	*3.8*	-4.1	1.6	13.6%	24.0%	8.2%	20.0%	16.5%
5001 to 50,000 employees	*5.4*	1.1	-3.7	-2.8	34.1%	24.0%	14.3%	15.6%	21.8%
more than 50,000 employees	0.9	*1.6*	-0.3	-2.2	6.8%	8.0%	4.1%	.0%	4.8%
Total n					44	50	49	45	100%

Chi-square = 21.425, p < 0.1; Somers-d = -0.190, p < 0.001; n=188

Table 5-17. Distribution of company size (number of employees) among the four client configurations (residuals and percentage of distribution)

At last, the size of the IT budget of the companies was contrasted against the four client configurations (Table 5-18). In general, one can observe that almost half of all clients irrespective of group affiliation have an IT budget between 1 and 10 million Euro.

A chi-square test and Somers-d reveal very significant group differences. While the business-efficiency-focused clients (cluster 1) do not break ranks with regard to a certain over- or under-representation of allocated IT budget, the other client groups show surprising results. In contrast to the strategy- and innovation-focused clients and also in contrast to the IT-focused clients, the clients that focus on cost reduction, cost flexibility, and cost transparency are over-represented in companies that have a fairly high IT budget (between 100 and 500 million Euro). In contrast, clients that expect innovation and strategy or IT excellence / reliability from their outsourcing, rather have a quite low IT budget ranging not above 10 million Euro.

Obviously, the intention and underlying motivation to outsource IT as represented by the four client configurations is also somehow related to the amount of invested IT budget by the company.

Annual IT budget	Cluster 1	Cluster 2	Cluster 3	Cluster 4	Cluster 1	Cluster 2	Cluster 3	Cluster 4	Total
up to 1 mio. Euro	-2.6	-0.5	-0.5	3.5	5.3%	11.1%	11.1%	20.0%	12.1%
1+ - 10 mio. Euro	-2.6	-7.8	5.2	5.2	39.5%	28.9%	57.8%	57.8%	46.2%
10+ - 50 mio. Euro	1.6	2.8	-2.2	-2.2	28.9%	31.1%	20.0%	20.0%	24.9%
50+ - 100 mio. Euro	1.7	0.4	-1.6	-0.6	7.9%	4.4%	.0%	2.2%	3.5%
100+ - 500 mio. Euro	1.0	5.3	-1.7	-4.7	13.2%	22.2%	6.7%	0%	10.4%
more than 500 mio. Euro	0.9	-0.3	0.7	-1.3	5.3%	2.2%	4.4%	0%	2.9%
Total n					38	45	45	45	100%

Chi-square = 29.687, p < 0.01; Somers-d = -0.266, p < 0.001; n=173

Table 5-18. Distribution of IT budget among the four client configurations (residuals and percentage of distribution)

5.5.2.2   Role and Impact of IT for the Company

An unsolved issue both in research and practice is the question whether IT should be outsourced at all in companies where IT is regarded as a strategic and competitive asset or whether IT should only be outsourced if regarded as a commodity for the firm. For a long time companies only gave those parts of the IT to a third party provider that were non-business-critical and regarded as a non-strategic commodity. Since the Kodak case (Applegate/Montealegre 1991), not only the outsourcing of large portions of IT, but also the IT outsourcing in a company where IT is regarded as a business-critical and strategic asset, made all variations of strategic and non-strategic IT assets popular.

In order to see if the perceived importance of IT for the company in general differed among the client configurations an analysis of variance was conducted and significant differences were found (Sig. p = 0.073) (see Figure 5-15). While the first three groups did not differ a lot and all rated IT as relatively important for the company (the answer categories were from 1 = little importance to 7 = high importance), the client group that focused on achieving IT excellence / IT reliability stepped out of line as it rated IT as less important compared to the others as post-hoc tests could confirm (S-N-K, Tukey-HSD, Scheffé; significance level alpha = 0.1, see appendix A 33). This does not imply that this group does not regard IT as important at all because the group mean is still relatively high with a value of 4.89. But compared to the other groups, this finding allows the assumption that clients that strive for a streamlined IT (i.e., efficient, up-to-date, and stable) do not regard information technology (whether outsourced or not) as the ultimate strategic asset for their company. Instead, they use the outsourcing option to optimize their IT and thus to deliver a reliable and up-to-date technology that is streamlined and aligned for supporting the company's business.

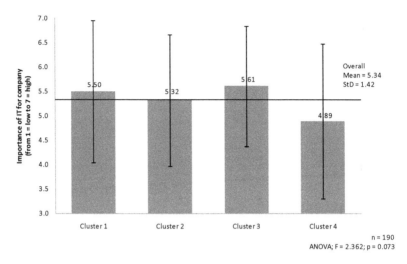

Figure 5-15. Group means for the average perceived importance of IT for the company among the four client configurations

In addition to assessing the perceived importance of IT for the company in general, one question aimed at estimating the impact of the outsourced systems on the firm's long-term business strategy in order to see if companies outsourced systems that are strategic to their business. While the overall impact was deemed relatively low (mean = 3.47, on a Likert scale from 1 = very low to 7 = very high), no significant differences could be found among the four client configurations.

5.5.3 Relational Architecture of the Outsourcing Ventures

After an initial characterization of the constitutive features of the four configurations with regard to their outsourcing expectations, this chapter will elaborate on the distinctive features of the four groups, thereby using passive, descriptive variables that were not included in the original clustering procedure. The group analyses will be conducted with the help of chi-square tests (for nominal and ordinal data), analyses of variance (ANOVA) and corresponding post-hoc tests for metric data in order to show how and which groups differ from each other (S-N-K, Tukey-HSD, Scheffé; significance level alpha = 0.05 or 0.1).

5.5.3.1 Experience with Outsourcing

As outsourcing as a general business practice has become more mature and diversified over the past decades, so have the outsourcing clients with respect to their outsourcing experience as well as with respect to their outsourcing motives and expectations (Dibbern et al. 2004; Lee et al. 2003). Thus, an appealing assumption and obvious guess could be that the four client groups which have been distinguished by their different outsourcing motives, also differ with respect to their outsourcing experience. One could, for example, assume that more mature outsourcing clients associate other outsourcing motives than young outsourcing clients. But as Table 5-19 shows no significant differences in terms of outsourcing experience could be found among the groups. The table shows that most client firms (regardless of the cluster affiliation) have between 6 and 10 years of outsourcing experience. In the business-efficiency group (cluster 1) almost 16% of the clients have more than 15 years of outsourcing experience. The innovation and strategy (cluster 3) as well as the IT-focused group (cluster 4) show the highest percentage of clients with low outsourcing experience (15.7% resp. 13.3%) compared to clusters 1 and 2 (4.5% resp. 4.0%), but these differences were not significant.

Experience of firm with IT/business process outsourcing	Cluster 1	Cluster 2	Cluster 3	Cluster 4	Total
0-2 years	4.5%	4.0%	15.7%	13.3%	9.5%
3-5 years	29.5%	34.0%	27.5%	26.7%	29.5%
6-10 years	40.9%	44.0%	31.4%	40.0%	38.9%
11-15 years	9.1%	12.0%	11.8%	11.1%	11.1%
More than 15 years	15.9%	6.0%	13.7%	8.9%	11.1%
Total	44	50	51	45	190

Chi-square = 10.000; df = 12; p = 0.616 (n.s.)

Table 5-19. Experience with outsourcing among the four client configurations

While Table 5-19 depicts the different outsourcing experience of the *client firm*, also the individual outsourcing experience of the *respondent* was examined. But again, no significant differences of individual outsourcing experience among the four groups could be identified (p = 0.409). Additionally, to confirm the findings above, the relation between outsourcing motives and outsourcing experiences was tested regardless of the four groups. It was examined if outsourcing motives differ among clients with a different amount of outsourcing experience. Outsourcing experience was used as an independent (grouping) variable and the 4 expectations factors as well as the 16 original expectation variables were used as dependent variables. The ANOVA results did not show any highly significant differences (p > 0.05 for all variables).

Summing up, the degree of outsourcing experience is not a differentiating aspect for clients with different expectation profiles.

5.5.3.2   Outsourcing Objects and Degree of Outsourced Functions

Outsourced functions can generally be distinguished into three areas: IT infrastructure, IT applications, and (IT-supported) business processes (Scardino/Young/Anderson 2007; Singh et al. 2007; Tramacere/Matlus 2007). But outsourcing functions differ with respect to their knowledge potential, knowledge intensity, and potential to create value. Willcocks et al. (2004), for example, emphasize that outsourcing whole business functions (BPO) can leverage knowledge potentials across organizations and create unique capabilities. These capabilities include, e.g., being more innovative, flexible, and integrated and enable outsourcers to provide their customers a unique set of services or products (Quinn 1999). In other words, the knowledge potential of outsourcing business processes is more promising in terms of leveraging knowledge gains compared to IT operations, since processes are seldom community processes and closer to the client's core business (Willcocks et al. 2004). Accordingly, one could assume that clients with a profile of innovation and strategy-focused expectations might be more likely to outsource whole business processes.

Examining the distribution of outsourced functions among the four clusters indeed shows some significant differences. Looking at the outsourcing degree of (IT-supported) business processes (see Table 5-20), it becomes apparent that clients throughout all four clusters have mostly outsourced their business processes partially to an outsourcing vendor. However, a closer look reveals that cluster 1 (business efficiency) and cluster 3 (innovation and strategy) obviously differ from the two other clusters: More than half of the business-efficiency-oriented clients (cluster 1) have selectively outsourced their business processes to an outsourcing vendor. This is quite a high percentage of clients compared to the other clusters. E.g. only 28.9% of the IT-focused clients (cluster 4) have selectively outsourced their business processes, while 31.1% in this group have not even considered business processes as possible candidates for outsourcing.

Surprisingly, albeit the fact that more than half of the business-efficiency-oriented clients (cluster 1) have selectively outsourced their business processes, none of them has outsourced business processes completely to an outsourcing vendor. For this cluster, business processes are regarded as a core competence and thus not be totally outsourced to a third-party provider.

In contrast, the strategy- and innovation-focused clients (cluster 3) do not only outsource their business processes selectively to an external provider, but also more than 10% of this group pursue a total outsourcing strategy with business processes. This large amount of total outsourcing of business processes (compared to the other clusters) can be explained by the inherent expectation profile of this group: members of this cluster aim at a shared development of products, services, and processes and thus share their business processes and the according knowledge with their outsourcing provider. Fully outsourcing whole business processes is part of the idea of sharing knowledge for innovative ideas.

(IT-supported) Business Processes	Cluster 1	Cluster 2	Cluster 3	Cluster 4	Total
Completely outsourced	0.0%	6.0%	11.8%	2.2%	5.3%
Selectively / partially outsourced	52.3%	36.0%	43.1%	28.9%	40.0%
Considered outsourcing option for this function	22.7%	26.0%	7.8%	22.2%	19.5%
Rejected outsourcing option for this function	11.4%	10.0%	17.6%	15.6%	13.7%
Function not considered for possible outsourcing	13.6%	22.0%	19.6%	31.1%	21.6%
Total	44	50	51	45	190

Chi-square = 20.322; df = 12; p = 0.06

Table 5-20. Outsourced functions among the four client configurations: business processes

In contrast to the different outsourcing strategies of the four groups with regard to outsourcing business processes, the strategy for outsourcing applications and infrastructure is quite similar among the four groups. The findings in Table 5-21 and Table 5-22 show that there are no significant differences among the four groups when it comes to outsourcing applications and infrastructure. All groups have mostly outsourced both applications and infrastructure partially to a third-party provider, while a fair amount of clients has also engaged in a total outsourcing of applications and infrastructure. This result is not surprising given the fact that compared to business processes the IT operation areas of applications and infrastructure are seldom seen a differentiator in terms of value creation or knowledge potential for the client business (Willcocks et al. 2004).

IT Applications (Planning, development, operation, support)	Cluster 1	Cluster 2	Cluster 3	Cluster 4	Total
Completely outsourced	6.8%	12.0%	13.7%	11.1%	11.1%
Selectively / partially outsourced	68.2%	62.0%	72.5%	60.0%	65.8%
Considered outsourcing option for this function	15.9%	10.0%	9.8%	13.3%	12.1%
Rejected outsourcing option for this function	2.3%	2.0%	3.9%	6.7%	3.7%
Function not considered for possible outsourcing	6.8%	14.0%	.0%	8.9%	7.4%
Total	44	50	51	45	190

Chi-square = 11.422; df = 12; p = 0.493 (n.s.)

Table 5-21. Outsourced functions among the four client configurations: IT applications

IT Infrastructure (Planning, development, operation, support)	Cluster 1	Cluster 2	Cluster 3	Cluster 4	Total
Completely outsourced	15.9%	16.0%	15.7%	8.9%	14.2%
Selectively / partially outsourced	70.5%	60.0%	64.7%	71.1%	66.3%
Considered outsourcing option for this function	9.1%	6.0%	9.8%	8.9%	8.4%
Rejected outsourcing option for this function	2.3%	6.0%	5.9%	4.4%	4.7%
Function not considered for possible outsourcing	2.3%	12.0%	3.9%	6.7%	6.3%
Total	44	50	51	45	190

Chi-square = 7.316; df = 12; p = 0.836 (n.s.)

Table 5-22. Outsourced functions among the four client configurations: IT infrastructure

5.5.3.3   Number of Involved Vendors: Single vs. Multi-Vendor Outsourcing

Many clients engage in multi vendor outsourcing arrangements in order to mitigate the risks associated with outsourcing (Currie 1998). By dedicating selective portions of IT to several suppliers, the risks of dependency on a single vendor or failure of delivery are mediated

(Lacity/Willcocks/Feeny 1996). But on the other hand, outsourcing deals where outsourcing client and vendor engage in a joint development of highly innovative IT products and services and thus share potential benefits and losses alike, are seldom established with several vendors. Those unique alliances require certain capabilities and a mutual basis for understanding, trust, and commitment and thus depend on mutual and equally balanced interdependencies between two parties (Willcocks/Choi 1995). It might thus be assumed that the underlying outsourcing intent of the client in some way determines the single- or multi-vendor strategy.

Analyzing the strategies that the four client configurations follow in terms of single or multi-vendor engagements shows some significant differences among the groups.

Number of vendors involved in client outsourcing	Cluster 1	Cluster 2	Cluster 3	Cluster 4	Total
One vendor (single vendor)	25.0%	22.4%	27.5%	26.7%	25.4%
2 – 3 vendors	31.8%	46.9%	51.0%	57.8%	47.1%
More than 3 vendors	43.2%	30.6%	21.6%	15.6%	27.5%
Total	44	49	51	45	189

Chi-square = 10.810, df = 6, p = 0.094; Somers-d = -.134, p = 0.034; Kendall-Tau-b = -0.135, p = 0.034;

Table 5-23. Number of outsourcing vendors among the four client configurations

Table 5-23 shows that most clients irrespective of their group affiliation engage in multi-vendor agreements with 2 or 3 vendors. However, a significantly higher amount of clients of the strategy and innovation group (cluster 3) engages in single-vendor arrangements in contrast to the other groups. This supports the assumption that unique alliances aiming at strategic issues and joint product or service development are seldom carried out with many vendors, but rather with one single vendor with whom an ongoing strategic partnership is established. In contrast, clients focused on business efficiency (cluster 1) mostly pursue a clear vendor-diversification strategy with almost half of the members of this group engaging in highly-multi-vendor outsourcing with more than 3 vendors.

5.5.3.4   Outsourcing Degree: Selective vs. Total Outsourcing

The granularity of outsourced IT portions is not only determined by the number of involved vendors, but also by estimating the outsourcing degree. The degree of external supply is usually distinguished in three categories: up to 20% of the IT budget is regarded as insourcing or very selective outsourcing, between 20% and 80% of the IT budget is regarded as selective outsourcing and if more than 80% of the IT budget is outsourced, a total outsourcing can be assumed (Lacity/Hirschheim 1995b, 4pp.).

Table 5-24 shows the degree of outsourcing among the client groups. Irrespective of group affiliation, most clients engaged in selective (47.8%) or highly selective (45.2%) outsourcing deals. The distribution of outsourcing degrees in cluster 4 (IT-focused cluster) steps a bit out of line as it is more focused towards the extreme points of the outsourcing degree scale compared to the other groups (almost 60% of the clients in this group engaged in highly selective, small-portioned outsourcing deals, while 11% engaged in total outsourcing deals). But these differences were not significant (Chi-square = 9.388, df = 6, p = 0.153).

Degree of outsourcing (compared to IT budget)	Cluster 1	Cluster 2	Cluster 3	Cluster 4	Total
0% - 20% of IT budget	42.9%	40.8%	40.0%	57.8%	45.2%
21% - 80% of IT budget	54.8%	55.1%	50.0%	31.1%	47.8%
More than 80% of IT budget	2.4%	4.1%	10.0%	11.1%	7.0%
Total	42	49	50	45	186

Chi-square = 9.388, df = 6, p = 0.153 (n.s.)

Table 5-24. Degree of outsourcing among the four client configurations

5.5.3.5   Length and Duration of Outsourcing Contracts

An assumption that can be derived from the findings above on the number of involved vendors is that the length of the contract also differs with respect to the different client groups. Clients with strategic and innovation intents might more likely engage in long-term outsourcing deals because the knowledge potential and added value can be best leveraged over time (Willcocks et al. 2004), while cost cutting and IT goals are more likely to be achieved within a shorter period of time (Willcocks/Choi 1995).

This assumption is not fully supported as Table 5-25 shows. Overall, the largest portion of clients engages neither in very short-term nor in extremely long-term outsourcing arrangements with 32.8% of the outsourcing contracts ranging between 3-4 years and another 29% of all contracts ranging between 5-7 years.

Two findings support the proposed assumption above: Compared to the mean of all clients members of the IT-focused cluster (cluster 4) rather engage in very short-term ventures (20.5% of the members of cluster 4 compared to 14% of all clients) aiming at quick wins and near-term results. This is surprising given the fact that this cluster does not only expect the latest technology implementations, but also stability and reliability of the systems over time. The short length of the contracts in this group could be explained by a continuous renewal of the contract in order to regularly adapt the contract to upcoming requirements and latest technology.

Another finding is that members of the strategy and innovation group (cluster 3) rather set ongoing contracts in place without a fixed contract length (27.5% of the members of cluster 3 compared to 19.9% of all clients). It seems that value creation and leveraging the knowledge potential which is expected by those clients is best achieved in ongoing outsourcing ventures without a fixed contract period.

However, these results did not turn out to be significant (Chi-square = 10.643; df = 12; p = 0.560 n.s.). Moreover, the question "since when is the current outsourcing contract in place? [please enter year of contract beginning]" did not turn out any significant differences among the groups, i.e., the groups do not differ significantly from the overall mean of 3.82 years (SD = 3.16) of all clients. This also supports the finding in chapter 5.5.3.1 (p. 162) which stated that overall outsourcing experience did not make a difference among the groups (even though this statement refers to overall experience while the question here refers to the establishment of the current contract).

Duration of the current outsourcing contract	Cluster 1	Cluster 2	Cluster 3	Cluster 4	Total
0 – 2 years	14.3%	12.2%	9.8%	20.5%	14.0%
3 – 4 years	33.3%	28.6%	31.4%	38.6%	32.8%
5 – 7 years	23.8%	34.7%	29.4%	27.3%	29.0%
More than 7 years	9.5%	4.1%	2.0%	2.3%	4.3%
Unlimited (but can be terminated)	19.0%	20.4%	27.5%	11.4%	19.9%
Total	42	49	51	44	186

Chi-square = 10.643; df = 12; p = 0.560 (n.s.)

Table 5-25. Duration of the current outsourcing contract among the four client configurations

5.5.3.6   Pricing Arrangements for Outsourced Services

Clients enter outsourcing contracts in several ways with regard to their pricing arrangements. Among these arrangements, cost-based (cost plus), fixed-price, time and material, transaction-based, and performance-based price models are the most popular ones (Currie 1996; Domberger/Fernandez/Fiebig 2000). Investigating the dominant pricing models, the most widespread arrangement is the fixed-price model which 38.4% of all clients have in place as their dominating pricing model (see Table 5-26). These results are in line with the findings of a study by Currie (1996) who found that both private and public sector organizations were looking to negotiate more fixed-term and fixed-price contracts, rather than flexible ones. She concluded that her findings were at odds with those of Clark et al. (1995) and McFarlan and Nolan (1995), who found that flexibility was a key outsourcing success factor. This may be partially explained by the fact that clients primarily engage in short-term contracts, which may provide a de facto element of flexibility through the frequency of renewal (Currie 1996). Furthermore, in this study, transaction-based pricing models (e.g., pay-per-use, pay-per-call, etc.) which allow for very flexible arrangements are also very popular among clients (with 28.4% of all clients using transaction-based models are their dominating price model). These findings support the assumptions of Clark et al. (1995) and McFarlan and Nolan (1995).

Overall, performance-based models with, e.g., risk-and-reward-sharing elements are almost not at all set in place.

As to group differences, fixed-price contracts are less popular among the strategy-oriented clients (cluster 3) compared to the other client groups. Compared to the other client groups (and the overall mean) the strategy and innovation clients rather focus on "looser", more flexible time-and-material based contracts (Currie 1996). Such flexible arrangements allow for adjustments over time and provide degrees of freedom, which is a necessary prerequisite in an environment where the outcome is focused on achieving strategic advantages and developing innovative products and services (Mahnke/Özcan 2006). In contrast, the cost-oriented clients (cluster 2) as well as the IT-focused clients (cluster 4) predominantly set up tight fixed-term contracts as these pricing models are more reasonable and easier to manage than flexible contracts. Frequencies in each group that are way higher or lower than the average are marked in gray.

But overall, the group differences did not turn out to be significant from a statistical point of view (Cramer-V = 0.180; Chi-square = 18.492; df = 15; p = 0.238).

Dominating pricing models for outsourced services	Cluster 1	Cluster 2	Cluster 3	Cluster 4	Total
Cost-based / Cost plus	13.6%	12.0%	15.7%	4.4%	11.6%
Time and material	9.1%	14.0%	27.5%	15.6%	16.8%
Transaction-based / use-based	31.8%	30.0%	23.5%	28.9%	28.4%
Fixed price	34.1%	42.0%	31.4%	46.7%	38.4%
Performance-based	2.3%	0.0%	2.0%	0.0%	1.1%
Other	9.1%	2.0%	0.0%	4.4%	3.7%
Total	44	50	51	45	190

Cramer-V = 0.180; Chi-square = 18.492; df = 15; p = 0.238 (n.s.)

Table 5-26. Dominant pricing arrangements among the four client configurations

5.5.3.7 Outsourcing Alliances

Although many outsourcing deals are labeled as "partnerships" in the outsourcing literature, this label is rather fallacious since most outsourcing deals are no partnerships, but rather simple transactions: a vendor providing a specified set of services for which it receives compensation from the client (Lacity/Hirschheim 1993a). Besides these classical outsourcing deals, recently real alliances and partnerships have emerged with equity holding deals or joint ventures where one partner takes some stake in the other (Dibbern et al. 2004).

Analyzing the results of this study, it becomes obvious that the classical outsourcing transaction is by far the dominating 'alliance' model with 80.5% of all clients engaging in this type of outsourcing cooperation. Much less, but at least another 13.7% of all clients have an internal service provider and use a shared-services model. Although Dibbern et al. (2004) lists some examples in practice, this study shows that joint ventures, where the vendor takes some stakes in the client and vice versa or both parties take the formation of a new entity, are scarcely used as an outsourcing model. A possible explanation could be that joint ventures are seldom seen or understood as such in the context of outsourcing. Outsourcing might rather be regarded as a hierarchical buyer-seller-relationship instead of a partnership with both parties equally devoting resources and taking risks and rewards alike.

Analyzing the four client configurations also reveals some highly significant differences. The most obvious deviation from the other client groups can be seen in the client group that is focused on IT excellence (cluster 4). Almost all clients of this group prefer a classical third-party-vendor outsourcing model – neither a joint venture nor an internal shared-services model. Obviously, clients that expect the latest state-of-the-art technology rather believe that technological excellence is best provided via the external market. Thereby, for each desired service the best-in-class providers can be engaged for premium service.

Another remarkable difference can be seen in the client group that is focused on strategy and innovation (cluster 3). In this group, almost a quarter of the clients (23.5%) sources the IT services from in-house or in-company (subsidiary) resources in a shared services model. One could explain this finding in such a way that strategy- and innovation-focused clients believe that innovation is best achieved with a close partner that already knows the business model and internal processes and thus shares a common basis with the client. This is predominantly true for in-house or in-company IT service providers.

Outsourcing alliance models					
	Cluster 1	Cluster 2	Cluster 3	Cluster 4	Total
Classical outsourcing (services provided for a client by a third-party vendor without one party taking some stake in the other)	68.2%	86.0%	70.6%	97.8%	80.5%
Shared services (internal, company-owned subsidiary)	18.2%	10.0%	23.5%	2.2%	13.7%
Joint Venture	4.5%	2.0%	3.9%	0.0%	2.6%
Other	9.1%	2.0%	2.0%	0.0%	3.2%
Total	44	50	51	45	190

Cramer-V = 0.194; Chi-square = 21.351; df = 9; p = 0.01

Table 5-27. Outsourcing alliance models among the four client configurations

5.5.3.8   Dependency on the Service Provider and Switching Costs

By engaging in selective outsourcing arrangements (i.e., the dominant strategy among the investigated client groups, see chapter 5.5.3.2 and 5.5.3.3, p. 163ff.) clients can alleviate the risk of dependencies, power imbalances, and lock-in effects (Kern 1997; Currie/Willcocks 1998; Willcocks/Lacity 1999; Willcocks/Lacity/Kern 1999). But nevertheless, in contrast to other business functions large switching costs are associated with IS sourcing decisions in case of an IT service provider change (Lacity/Willcocks 2001, 185). The threat of vendor opportunism due to the lock-in effect of the customer is extremely likely because the effort and switching costs to another vendor or to an in-house IT function are expensive. But the degree of dependency and switching costs might vary across the different client groups depending on the expectation basis of the outsourcing venture.

As can be inferred from Figure 5-16, the overall degree of dependency on the service provider irrespective of the group affiliation is relatively high (with an overall mean of 4.376 out of 7 indicating the highest degree of dependency). But there are differences among the groups.

The highest degree of dependency is attributed to the strategy and innovation focused clients (cluster 3). Obviously, this group is highly reliant on their service provider (with a group mean of 4.79). This is in line with the results above, which show that this client group is also narrowly focused on very few or even only one service provider and thus engages in very exclusive partnerships. But the trade-off becomes quite apparent: On the one hand, such an exclusive partnership that devotes mutual resources with associated risks and rewards for shared results (innovative products and services aimed at strategic advantages) might only be possible and reasonable with one carefully selected service provider (because of high monetary investments and also a great deal of trust and commitment between the partners). On the other hand, there is a great risk of dependency of the client on this single service provider and a potential threat of vendor opportunism associated with high switching costs.

The lock-in effect of the IT-focused clients (cluster 4) in contrast is fairly low compared to the other client groups. This is in line with the results above that the IT-focused client group outsources very selectively only small portions of IT to a wide range of different IT service providers. Thereby, clients try to minimize the risk and potential dependency on a single vendor. However, from a statistical point of view, these group differences are not significant (F = 1.568; p = 0.19).

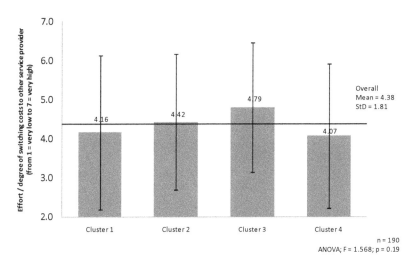

Figure 5-16. Group means for average effort / degree of switching costs to another service provider among the four client configurations

5.5.3.9   Goal Alignment between Outsourcing Parties

Potential outsourcing barriers might also arise because of conflicting interest factors between the stakeholders. As Lacity and Willcocks (2003, 122) state there is an inherent adversarial nature in outsourcing contracts "in that a dollar out of the customer's pocket is a dollar in the supplier's pocket". Some service providers are in the business of maximizing their profit at any cost, but this could run counter to a service receiver's interest.

Figure 5-17 and Figure 5-18 depict the degree of complementarity of the goals as well as the degree of conflicts of interests between the outsourcing parties. Overall, the goal alignment between the outsourcing parties is fairly high irrespective of group affiliation (with an overall mean of 4.96, measured on a scale from 1 = very low to 7 = very high) and accordingly, the degree of conflicts of interest is quite low (with an overall mean of 5.42, measured on a reverse scale from 1 = very high to 7 = very low). But despite this high level of accordance and satisfaction in terms of alignment, post-hoc tests of the group comparison show that there are some significant differences, especially between cluster 2 (the cost-conscious smart shoppers) and cluster 4 (the IT-focused clients). Both group 2 and 4 are significantly different from each other, while groups 1 and 3 are pretty close to both other groups (S-N-K, Tukey-HSD, Scheffé; significance level alpha = 0.1, see appendix A 34). The IT-focused client group scores very high on the goal alignment scale, i.e., the goals of receiving and delivering the latest best-in-class technology are quite congruent and well-aligned between client and provider. It seems that the client has carefully assessed its own requirements and level of service it seeks (i.e., latest, cutting-edge technology) and accordingly selected an appropriate vendor (i.e., best-in-class provider of specific piece of IT) that delivers the client's requirements best. According to Feeny et al. (2005) a careful self-due-diligence and self-assessment and a wary selection of the specific provider is the approach of savvy clients who attempt to gauge the supplier's relationship competency, i.e., the extent to which the supplier is willing and able to cultivate a "win-win" relationship that will align client and supplier goals and incentives over time.

Compared to cluster 4, the cost-conscious smart shoppers (cluster 2) do not perform that well with regard to goal alignment with a group mean of 4.64 on goal alignment. This might be to some extent due to the fact that for cost-oriented clients it is not as easy to select the best-in-class provider (i.e., the one with the least customer price and the most efficient cost structure). It is not easy to figure out which provider will leverage the best cost savings for the client. Even more, an explanation for the moderate goal alignment might also be the inherent adversarial nature of client and vendor as elaborated on by Lacity and Willcocks (2003, 122), because every saved cent for the client is less profit for the vendor and thus a complete goal alignment and no conflict of interest at all is not possible by definition.

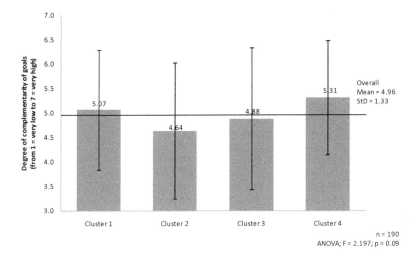

Figure 5-17. Degree of complementarity of goals among the four client configurations

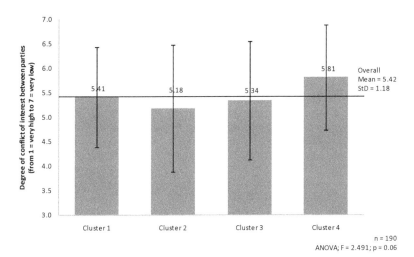

Figure 5-18. Degree of conflicts of interest among the four client configurations

5.5.4   Governance Approaches among the Different Client Groups

5.5.4.1   Outsourcing Governance: Role of the Contract

The outsourcing contract is generally seen as an essential part of every outsourcing arrangement and a powerful mechanism to manage an outsourcing venture (Saunders/Gebelt/Hu 1997). Although it has been acknowledged that in most cases a contract is not sufficient as the only approach to successfully govern an outsourcing venture (Klepper 1995, 1998; Goles/Chin 2005), it is still used as the primary vehicle of governance and is also established long before the actual relationship or partnership begins to grow.

Looking at the data, not surprisingly, the role and importance of the contract is acknowledged by all client groups irrespective of group affiliation and their underlying outsourcing motive (with an overall mean of 5.46, measured on a scale from 1 = very low to 7 = very high). Accordingly, the perceived importance of specified service level agreements and their degree of penetration in outsourcing contracts is also quite high (with an overall mean of 5.31, measured on a scale from 1 = very low to 7 = very high).

But when investigating in detail what a contract can or cannot provide, the groups differ a lot in their perception (although not statistically significant).

Figure 5-19 depicts the group means of the client groups with respect to their perception on the difficulty or easiness of task specification and governance via a contract. Irrespective of the group affiliation, the overall mean is not extraordinarily high, with a value of 4.58 (SD = 1.63). While both the IT-focused clients and the cost-conscious clients consider it relatively easy to primarily govern the outsourcing relationship with a contract, especially the innovation-focused clients see difficulties in specifying all tasks completely and exclusively with a contract. This is somewhat reasonable since in a complex strategic environment the outcome cannot easily be specified a priori and is rather vague and ambiguous for all involved parties. According to transaction cost economics theory, when the tasks are not well specified, a contract as a formal mechanism is not the (solely) appropriate approach for a successful outsourcing governance. This seems to be also true for clients that focus on business efficiency (cluster 1) because in an environment where the outsourcing vendor is expected to know the client's business well and contribute to the client's business value, a contract can hardly substitute for other governance measures. Chapter 6 (p. 215ff.) will pick up these governance mechanisms and show for each group which combination of governance approaches is best for a successful venture.

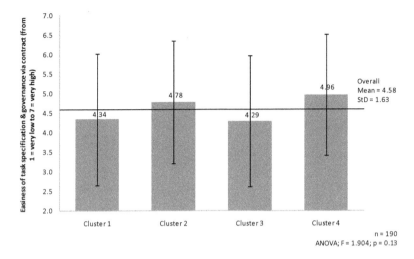

Figure 5-19. Easiness of task specification and governance via the contract among the four client configurations

The impression on the perception of the role of the contract for the outsourcing venture is even more expanded and substantiated by asking for the sufficiency of a contract for the outsourcing governance. Figure 5-20 depicts the overall findings and also shows significant group differences (F = 3.022, p < 0.05). Overall, one can conclude that the contract is seldom regarded as the solely adequate governance mechanism as the low value for the overall mean indicates (mean = 3.91, SD = 1.80). Post-hoc tests could reveal that significant differences can only be found between group 1 and 4 while groups 2 and 3 are relatively close to each other in their perception of the importance of the contract (S-N-K, Tukey-HSD, Scheffé; significance level alpha = 0.05, see appendix A 35).

In contrast to the other clients, the IT-focused clients deem the contract reasonably sufficient as a governance approach. But since the absolute value is not really high, there might also be other governance mechanisms that are appropriate for the IT-focused client group.

The group mean for the innovation-focused group (cluster 3) is also higher compared to the group means of cluster 1 and cluster 2. This can be explained by the fact that in high innovation-seeking settings, the delivered outcome is uncertain as it cannot be specified a priori. This results in a high perceived risk which could be mitigated by using contractual agreements. In this context, contractual agreements can at least set the basis for the cooperation environment. But as the overall low level of perceived sufficiency of the contract indicates (the group mean for the innovation-focused group is as low as 4.1), contracts alone seem to be not sufficient for a holistic outsourcing governance approach.

This view is also shared by customers that belong to the business-efficiency oriented group (cluster 1) and the cost-conscious group (cluster 2). The very low group means indicate that both groups expect or have other governance mechanisms in place in order to manage their venture successfully. Later chapters will show which other mechanisms are established.

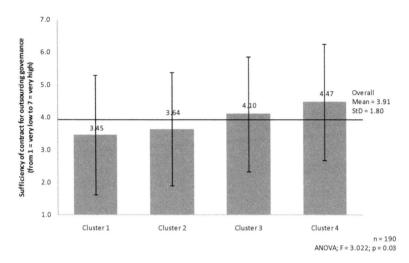

Figure 5-20. Sufficiency of contract for outsourcing governance among the four client configurations

5.5.4.2   Outsourcing Governance: Role of Processes

With the business practice of outsourcing being established for several decades now, one could assume that the degree of professionalism, institutionalism, and formalism with regard to management processes in outsourcing is quite high since the market with the involved clients and vendors has become so mature. Consequently, one could assume that processes are well established mechanisms to control both client and vendor.

The four main processes that were investigated to manage an outsourcing venture include 1) SLA and contract management processes (similar to the role of the contract in the previous chapter), 2) performance and service measurement processes, 3) strategy processes for both parties, and 4) benchmarking processes that evaluate services and prices of the vendor with the external market on a regular basis (Eckmüller 2006; Gottschalk/Solli-Sæther 2006b; Feeny/Lacity/Willcocks 2005; Lacity/Hirschheim 1995a; Reilly/Rouse/Seddon 2001; Goo/Kim/Cho 2006; Willcocks/Lacity/Fitzgerald 1995).

The following figures show how well the processes are established in the four client groups. From the relatively low overall means one can conclude that the overall maturity level with respect to established processes for managing and controlling the outsourcing venture is quite low. The strategy- and innovation-focused clients break ranks in this respect as they have established SLA and performance measurement processes even to a lesser degree than their colleagues in the other groups. This might be explained with the arguments already put forward above that innovation-focused outsourcing ventures are improperly managed with tight, formal processes such as precise service level agreements. An innovation-focused partnership rather requires a "loose" environment with degrees of freedom to deploy the innovation potential of both partners.

While SLA and performance measurement processes are reasonably widespread (with some differences among the client groups), strategy processes that align the goals, expectations and claims of both parties, are seldom set in place. Again, the strategy and innovation-focused clients break ranks here, but in the other direction. Compared to their peers in the other groups, the strategy clients obviously have some strategy processes (group mean of 4.04, measured on a scale from 1 = very low to 7 = very high) in place in order to align the goals, expectations, procedures etc. of both parties. Those strategy processes and the corresponding alignment are especially necessary for partnerships where the outcome is dependent on the commitment of both parties that share risks and rewards alike.

A process that is fairly neglected by all parties is benchmarking the vendor with current market prices and services. This finding is especially true for the strategy and innovation-focused clients. With a group mean of 2.99 (measured on a scale from 1 = very low to 7 = very high), this group has not established benchmarking processes. This is probably because pressure induced by continuous comparison with the market is not beneficial for establishing a trustful "sandbox-like" environment where innovation and value creation is the goal.

But despite interpretable differences between the groups regarding the establishment of various processes, from a statistical point of view, these differences were not statistically significant (p > 0.1).

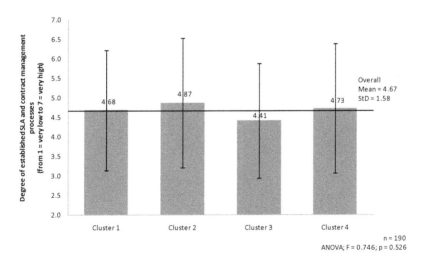

Figure 5-21. Degree of established SLA and contract management processes among the four client configurations

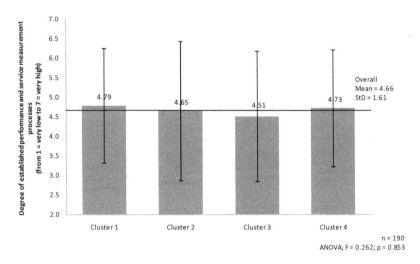

Figure 5-22. Degree of established performance and service measurement processes among the four client configurations

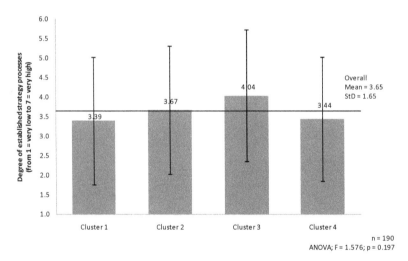

Figure 5-23. Degree of established strategy processes among the four client configurations

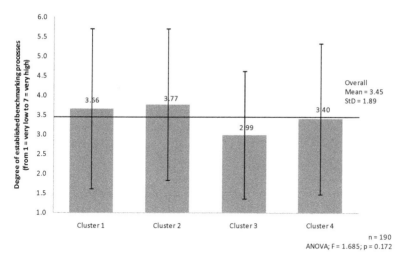

Figure 5-24. Degree of established benchmarking processes among the four client configurations

5.5.4.3   Outsourcing Governance: Role of Structures and Structural Liaison Devices

Besides classical means of contractual and relational governance or governance via established processes, outsourcing coordination and control can also be enhanced through defined roles and personnel structures. Liaison roles, task forces, and standing committees are among the well-documented examples of such formal structures (Mintzberg 1979, 1980) and are often established as interorganizational management structures in IS outsourcing ventures (see chapter 3.6.3.5 for details, p. 58ff.).

Investigating the role of steering committees, (operational) relationship or key account managers, and external consultants that manage the sourcing relationship for both parties, provides a rich, but diversified picture on the perceived importance (as measured by the degree of establishment of the role) of different management structures among the client configurations (see Figure 5-25 to Figure 5-27).

Overall, it becomes obvious that a relationship manager is seen as a pivotal element of a successful relationship and is thus set in place by most clients (overall mean = 5.55, measured on a scale from 1 = very low to 7 = very high, see Figure 5-26). Obviously, the contract itself is not seen as the one and only exclusive governance approach, but assigning a role that provides a relationship overview and balances possible difficulties between the parties seems to be crucial. Consequently, there are no significant differences among the four client groups as they all perceive establishing such a role as equally important.

In contrast to the role of an internal client relationship manager, an external consultant is hardly ever assigned with the role of managing the sourcing relationship for both parties irrespective of group affiliation (overall mean = 1.32, measured on a scale from 1 = very low to 7 = very high, see Figure 5-27). The strategy and innovation group (cluster 3), however, differs in some respect as clients in this group sometimes do appoint an external consultant, albeit not very often, as the overall low level of establishment shows (group mean = 1.63, measured on a scale from 1 = very low to 7 = very high). Post-hoc tests support this assumption, showing a significant difference between group 3 and all other groups (S-N-K, Tukey-HSD, Scheffé; significance level alpha = 0.05, see appendix A 36). Presumably, in partnerships where both parties are involved as equal partners and equally devote resources, man power, and intellectual capital, a neutral external source might balance potential difficulties between the parties by adopting a meta position.

The strategy and innovation clients also differ significantly (especially compared to the IT-focused cluster 4) with respect to their degree of establishing a management board such as a steering committee (see Figure 5-25). Post-hoc tests show that groups 3 and 4 differ significantly from each other, while groups 1 and 2 are close to each of the others (S-N-K, Tukey-HSD, Scheffé; significance level alpha = 0.1, see appendix A 36). This management structure is most widespread among the strategy-oriented clients, albeit not very often on an overall level (overall mean = 3.84; group mean for cluster 3 = 4.29, measured on a scale from 1 = very low to 7 = very high). For innovation- and strategy-focused clients, a steering committee with equal representation of both partners can represent, institutionalize, and substantiate the balanced partnership where both parties focus on mutual benefits and equally devote (intellectual and capital) resources for a joint value creation.

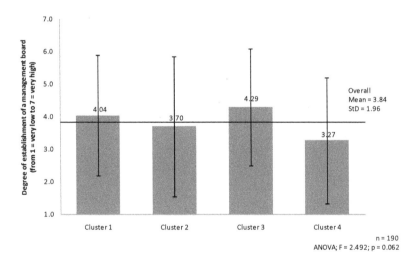

Figure 5-25. Establishment of a management board among the four client configurations

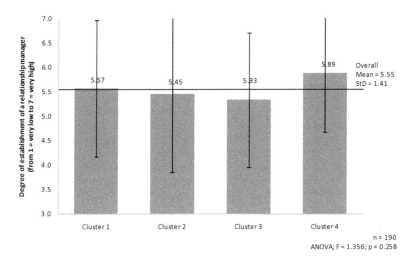

Figure 5-26. Establishment of a relationship manager among the four client configurations

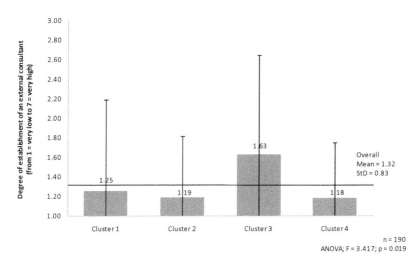

Figure 5-27. Establishment of an external consultant among the four client configurations

5.5.4.4   Outsourcing Governance: Informal Relationship

As elaborated in the previous chapters, the contract is the initial, but hardly a sufficient governance mechanism. In most cases, it is complemented by relational governance via informal factors. As will be seen in the next chapter, informal factors such as trust, communication, and commitment play a crucial role for every outsourcing venture irrespective of the underlying motive. Investigating the role of relationship management for the overall outsourcing venture, the groups differ only slightly in their perception.

Figure 5-29 and Figure 5-30 show that establishing informal governance is regarded as very important irrespective of group affiliation (overall mean of 5.01 resp. 5.53, measured on a scale from 1 = very low to 7 = very high). Consequently, the groups do not differ in a statistically significant way. One exception in the perception of the importance of relational issues is the rating of the importance of personal bonds for the daily working relationship between employees and teams on both sides (see Figure 5-28, statistically significant on a p < 0.1 level). Here, the cost-conscious smart shoppers (cluster 2) break ranks by rating the importance of personal bonds for the daily working relationship as fairly low (group mean of 3.32, measured on a scale from 1 = very low to 7 = very high). Post-hoc tests confirmed a significant difference between group 2 and all other groups (S-N-K, Tukey-HSD, Scheffé; significance level alpha = 0.1, see appendix A 37). This finding can be explained by the fact that this group is not necessarily focused on establishing a long-term trust-based partnership where personal bonds are essential for daily working routine. The group is rather focused on a streamlined cost-oriented management structure (best achieved via contracts, according service level agreements and performance measures).

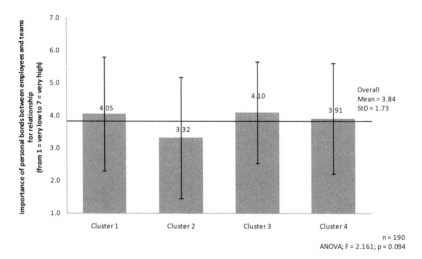

Figure 5-28. Degree / importance of personal bonds between employees and teams among the four client configurations

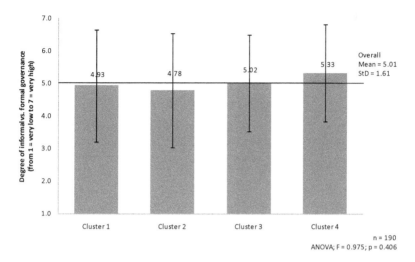

Figure 5-29. Degree of informal vs. formal relationship among the four client configurations

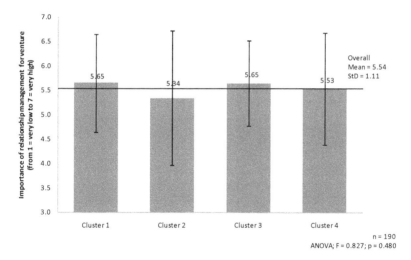

Figure 5-30. Importance of relationship management for outsourcing venture among the four client configurations

5.5.4.5 The Role of Staff Experience, Degrees of Freedom for the Vendor, and Risk-Reward Mechanisms as Governance Mechanisms

Beside the four common governance mechanisms contract, relationship, processes, and structures, there are three more issues that are related and have to be considered when designing a governance framework:

1. The experience of the involved staff on the client side with outsourcing projects as such and with the vendor

2. The degrees of freedom and decision rights the vendor has been attributed by the client

3. The establishment of risk-reward share and incentive models

These three issues do not belong to the classical and standard governance approaches, but they are closely related to them (e.g., establishing risk-reward-share models can be part of the contract). Thereby, they do not only set the stage for a governance framework as environmental factors, but also expand the standard governance approaches by, e.g., describing additional details such as risk-reward-mechanisms in a contract.

As to client staff experience with outsourcing and especially with the vendor, the degree of long-term client experience with the specific vendor is quite high irrespective of group affiliation, as Figure 5-31 shows (overall mean of 5.07, measured on a scale from 1 = very low to 7 = very high). From this it can be inferred that clients do not only have quite a bit of experience with outsourcing in general, but also with the specific outsourcing vendor. This could be either interpreted by the fact that the vendor market is not very diversified and can be focused on a few major players that provide outsourcing services, or that loyalty and good experience with that specific vendor tie client and vendor together so that the clients sticks with that vendor over time. Although the group differences are not statistically significant, it can still be seen in the figure that this loyalty or long-term experience with the vendor is somehow more distinct in the strategy- and innovation-focused group (cluster 3) where clients engage with one single trustful partner for a long-term partnership.

Figure 5-32 depicts a slightly different aspect of client experience, i.e., how the client rates its own know-how and experience to control the vendor. Here, the overall mean is again very high, indicating a self-confident client (overall mean = 5.14, measured on a scale from 1 = very low to 7 = very high). Despite not accounting for a statistically significant difference, the degree of perceived know-how and experience in controlling a vendor is higher in the group of cost-conscious smart shoppers (cluster 2). This indicates that cost-oriented outsourcing ventures might need very tight control mechanisms and experienced staff for the desired outcome to be achieved, which is in line with the findings and characteristics of this group above.

Despite no significant group differences could be found among the four client configurations, one cannot derive the impact of these mechanisms on the perceived outsourcing outcome (service quality, customer satisfaction), which is investigated in chapter 6 (p. 215ff.).

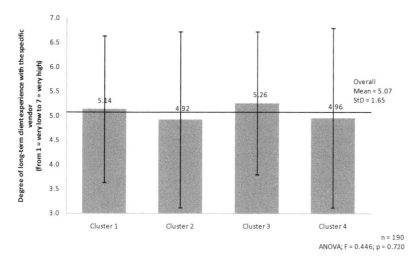

Figure 5-31. Degree of long-term client experience with the specific vendor among the four client configurations

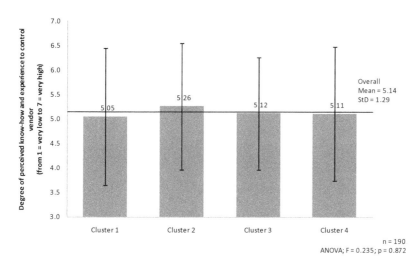

Figure 5-32. Degree of perceived know-how and experience of the client to control the vendor among the four client configurations

Regarding the degrees of freedom and decision rights that the client has attributed to the vendor, the overall level irrespective of group affiliation is quite low (see figures below, overall mean = 3.34 resp. 3.68, measured on a scale from 1 = very low to 7 = very high), indicating that the client keeps the management power and does not regard the vendor as a partner with according decision rights and involvement in management issues. Albeit not statistically significant, the strategy- and innovation-focused clients (cluster 3) again differentiate themselves from the other groups by exceeding the overall mean for attributed degrees of freedom and decision rights to the vendor. The strategy-oriented clients tend to attribute more management rights to the vendor compared to their colleagues (albeit on a low overall level) since this groups aims at achieving joint outcomes in a balanced partnership and thus should allocate rights and duties among the partners alike.

Figure 5-34 substantiates the distinct position of the innovation cluster, but also shows that the business-efficiency clients (cluster 1) also tend to involve the vendor in management issues to a higher extent compared to the cost-oriented (cluster 2) and IT-focused (cluster 4) clients. This finding is quite reasonable since business efficiency-oriented clients expect the vendor to understand their business and deliver service excellence. Consequently this group attributes more decision and management rights to the vendor in order to allow more insights to their business.

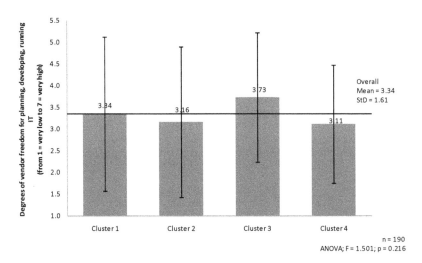

Figure 5-33. Degree of freedom attributed to the vendor for planning, developing, and running the client IT among the four client configurations

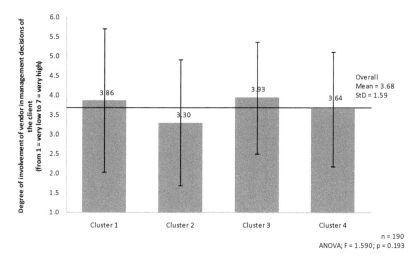

Figure 5-34. *Degree of involvement of the vendor in management issues of the client among the four client configurations*

Figure 5-35 depicts the degree to which client and vendor have agreed upon a model to share risks and rewards of the outsourcing venture alike. Three distinct and highly significant findings become obvious from interpreting Figure 5-35:

First, the overall level of establishing a risk-reward-share model is very low and tends to a negative acceptance (overall mean of 2.77, measured on a scale from 1 = very low to 7 = very high). This is not surprising, given the fact that sharing risks and rewards might be an essential element of strategic alliances as found by Lacity and Willcocks (1998), but not necessarily adequate for other types of outsourcing agreements.

Accordingly, among clients that focus on strategic goals and innovation (cluster 3) the level of establishment of risk-reward share mechanisms is significantly higher, albeit on a very low overall level (group mean of 3.38, measured on a scale from 1 = very low to 7 = very high). Post-hoc tests confirmed that group 3 differs significantly from all other groups, especially with regard to group 4 (S-N-K, Tukey-HSD, Scheffé; significance level alpha = 0.05, see appendix A 38). Among these clients – more than in any other group – the equal relationship among the outsourcing parties focused on mutual benefits and jointly developed results naturally requires to equally share potential benefits as well as potential risks associated with the outsourcing venture.

A third surprising result can be derived from analyzing the IT-focused clients (cluster 4). A post-hoc test showed that this group differed significantly especially from group 3 by having an extremely low, i.e., negative attitude towards risk-reward share approaches (group mean of 2.44, measured on a scale from 1 = very low to 7 = very high). This can be well explained by the underlying motive of this group. While on the one hand this group aims at getting access to the latest, cutting-edge technology, on the other hand it expects reliability and keeping the status quo of their IT. Consequently, clients in this group primarily contract an outsourcing provider for a stable and reliable provision of excellent IT services. Given this motivation, risk-reward-sharing structures are contra-productive and the opposite of what these clients expect from their sourcing approach.

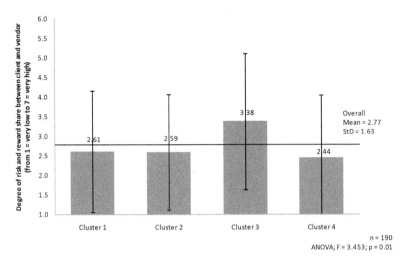

Figure 5-35. Degree of risk and reward share between client and vendor among the four client configurations

5.5.5   Interactions: Role of Specific Relationship Factors

Academia as well as practice have emphasized the pivotal role of relationship issues for a successful outsourcing venture (Kern/Willcocks 2000b; Hild 2008). Expanding the analysis of the role of relationship in general given in chapter 5.5.4.4 (p. 181ff.), this chapter aims at analyzing selected relationship factors and their impact among the client groups in greater detail. Due to questionnaire limitations, not all available relationship factors (for a literature overview on the vast variety of these factors, see chapter 3.6, p. 49ff.) could be assessed among the client CIOs. Instead, the most common and important factors according to Goles and Chin (2005) were investigated with respect to their potential differences among the four client groups.

Among the relationship processes and attributes, communication, conflict resolution, and cooperation have been emphasized as the most important processes, and commitment, cultural similarity, trust, flexibility, vendor proactivity have been selected as the most important attributes (Goles/Chin 2005; Lee/Kim 1999).

5.5.5.1   Communication

Communication as one of the key relationship factors for an outsourcing venture focuses on the proactive formal and informal sharing or exchange of meaningful and timely information between firms (Anderson/Narus 1990). It includes the permanent exchange of information between partners. Sharing information results in transparency and programmability of process characteristics and specificities. They provide more detailed agreements on quality levels and more precise rules of behavior (Goles/Chin 2005). Communication thereby comprises day-to-day exchanges of routine operational information in the ongoing working relationship, but also open exchanges of desires, needs, and resources to plan the future of the relationship (Heide/John 1990; Klepper 1995).

As found especially true for outsourcing relationships, communication is a means to realize contractual elements by enabling the continuous exchange on meeting requirements and achieving benefits between the parties, which will eventually lead to success and satisfaction with the overall outsourcing venture (Grover/Cheon/Teng 1996; Lee/Kim 1999).

In accordance with the literature, analyzing the findings of this study shows that the degree and role of communication is rated very high irrespective of group affiliation (overall mean = 5.604, SD = 1.26; measured on a scale from 1 = very low to 7 = very high). There are slight differences between the groups, i.e., the IT-excellence and reliability focused clients (cluster 4) seem to emphasize the role of communication a bit higher, but these group differences are not significant at all (see Figure 5-36).

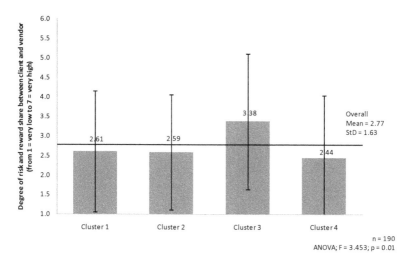

Figure 5-36. Degree of communication among the four client configurations

5.5.5.2   Conflict Resolution and Consensus

Conflict in a relationship is inevitable (Dwyer/Schurr/Oh 1987; Mohr/Spekman 1994). Conflict resolution aims at settling disagreements to produce mutual benefits (Dwyer/Schurr/Oh 1987) and can be understood as "the extent to which [...] disagreements are replaced by agreement and consensus" (Robey et al. 1989, 1174). From this definition it becomes obvious that conflict resolution and consensus are quite related and two sides of the same coin. Consensus is the extent of general agreement between the parties (Mejias et al. 1996). If performance levels are not met, partners are tempted to blame 'the other'. In these cases, the decision-makers of both parties have to sort out the problem and come to an agreement in order to avoid future recurrences. In an outsourcing arrangement conflict is especially problematic, given the complexity of technology, the level of detail in many contracts, and the sometimes disparate goals of the parties. The way conflicts are resolved has implications for the relationship success, not only in interorganizational relationships in general (Anderson/Narus 1990; Mohr/Spekman 1994; Monczka et al. 1998), but in outsourcing relationships in particular (Kern 1997; Lee/Kim 1999). This may be attributed to the benefits of constructive conflict resolution, which include more effective communication between the parties, an opportunity to learn from past actions, and the potential to improve productivity and efficiency (Anderson/Narus 1990; Dwyer/Schurr/Oh 1987; Fontenot/Wilson 1997).

Analyzing both the conflict resolution potential and the consensus between the outsourcing parties shows that both relationship factors are rated very high irrespective of group affiliation (overall mean = 5.61, SD = 0.99 for conflict resolution; overall mean = 5.50, SD = 0.96 for consensus, see figures below).

However, there are significant group differences when looking at the IT-focused clients (cluster 4). Post-hoc tests revealed a significant difference between group 4 and all other groups (S-N-K, Tukey-HSD, Scheffé; significance level alpha = 0.05, see appendix A 39). While all groups rate both relationship factors fairly high, the client group that focuses on IT excellence and reliability scores significantly higher ($p = 0.002$ resp. $p = 0.030$) with regard to the conflict resolution potential and the consensus between the outsourcing parties. Actually, this is a somewhat surprising result as the strategy and innovation-focused clients (cluster 3) would have been expected to deem these relationship factors as most important compared to the other client groups. But obviously, in outsourcing relationships that are primarily focused on achieving IT excellence and also IT reliability, both outsourcing parties have a clear vision and very congruent goals (i.e., providing and receiving best in class technology). Thus, to achieve these congruent goals, consensus and conflict resolution potential are important aspects of the day-to-day work relationship.

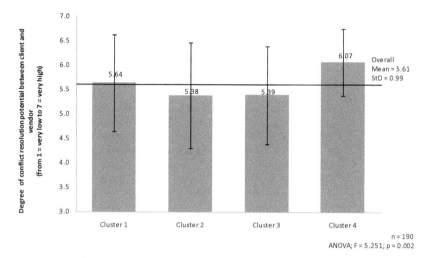

Figure 5-37. Degree of conflict resolution potential between client and vendor among the four client configurations

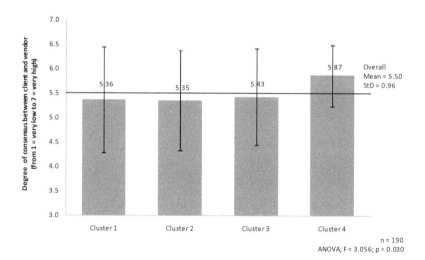

Figure 5-38. Degree of consensus between client and vendor among the four client configurations

5.5.5.3   Cooperation and Coordination

Cooperation can be understood as the "spirit of working together by firms on complementary activities with the objective of achieving mutual benefits" (Anderson/Narus 1990). The concept of cooperation has been analyzed by several researchers as the acknowledgement of and the agreement on planning and performance activities that are interdependent (Dwyer/Schurr/Oh 1987; Goles/Chin 2005). Such joint efforts are intended to set the rules and the way in which participants work together. The expected and achieved quality levels are discussed to find compromises between desires of the client and feasibilities of the vendor. Cooperation as well as coordination is especially important in the daily work relationship where client and vendor employees literally work together on the same project.

The data shows that all clients could establish a high level of both coordination and cooperation (overall mean = 5.00, SD = 1.26 for coordination; mean = 5.56, SD = 1.05 for cooperation). Significant group differences are seen for the IT-focused client group (cluster 4), as they show a significantly higher degree of coordination and cooperation (see Figure 5-39 and Figure 5-40). Post-hoc tests confirm a significant difference between group 4 and groups 1 and 2 with regard to coordination, while group 3 is close to all groups (S-N-K, Tukey-HSD, Scheffé; significance level alpha = 0.05, see appendix A 40). With regard to cooperation, post-hoc tests showed a significant difference between group 4 and all other groups (S-N-K, Tukey-HSD, Scheffé; significance level alpha = 0.05, see appendix A 40). From this finding one could interpret that client and vendor work closer together in the IT-focused cluster. But a more plausible explanation can be derived by assuming that goals that are easily specified between the two outsourcing parties, such as reaching and delivering IT excellence, coordination and consensus seem to be more easily reached because the common basis is clearly articulated and the goals are not conflicting. Even more, you get a good documentation to refer to in future situations. In settings where goals cannot be easily specified due to ambiguous outcomes (such as in the strategy and innovation group) or where goals might be adversarial in nature (such as in the cost-conscious smart shoppers group), coordination and cooperation might not be achieved to such a great extent. Nevertheless, the overall level of both relationship factors is still very high.

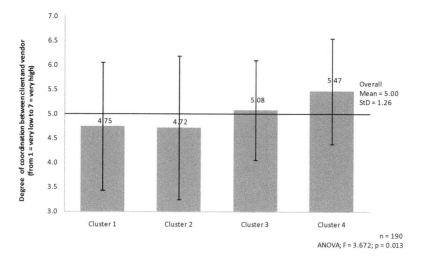

Figure 5-39. Degree of coordination between client and vendor among the four client configurations

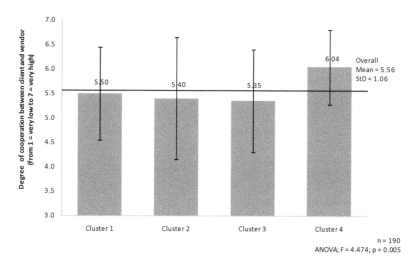

Figure 5-40. Degree of cooperation between client and vendor among the four client configurations

5.5.5.4   Commitment and Loyalty

Like many relationship factors, commitment and loyalty turn out to be key factors in success-ful relationships (Morgan/Hunt 1994). Commitment to a relationship is defined as an "endur-ing desire to maintain a valued relationship" (Moorman/Zaltman/Deshpande 1992, 316; Simpson/Mayo 1997, 211) and a "pledge of relationship continuity between exchange part-ners" (Dwyer/Schurr/Oh 1987, 19). It involves continuity, a long-term perspective, and future orientation by reflecting an underlying engagement to sustain the relationship over time (Mohr/Spekman 1994; Anderson/Weitz 1992). Consolidating various notions of commitment, overall it can be understood as the willingness of both outsourcing parties to exert effort and devote resources to keep an ongoing relationship.

The overall level of commitment and loyalty between the outsourcing parties is very high irrespective of client group affiliation (overall mean = 5.32, SD = 1.09; measured on a scale from 1 = very low to 7 = very high, see Figure 5-41). The IT-focused clients as well as the strategy and innovation clients differ significantly from the other two client groups, which score fairly lower with respect to their degree of loyalty and commitment (i.e., dedicating re-sources to the relationship). This finding is also confirmed by post-hoc tests that show that especially group 4 (but also group 3) shows significant differences from the other groups (S-N-K, Tukey-HSD, Scheffé; significance level alpha = 0.1, see appendix A 41).

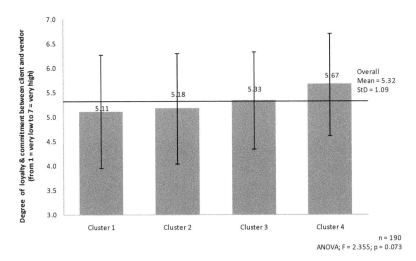

Figure 5-41. Degree of loyalty and commitment between client and vendor among the four client configura-tions

5.5.5.5   Cultural Similarity

Cultural similarity or better the compatibility of each outsourcing party's firm culture is the extent to which the parties can co-exist with each other's beliefs about what values, behaviors, and policies are appropriate, important or right (Goles/Chin 2005). Many studies consider cultural similarity as an important factor for interorganizational relationships in general (Kumar/Dissel 1996; Rai/Borah/Ramaprasad 1996) and outsourcing relationships in particular (Klepper 1998; Willcocks/Choi 1995; Willcocks/Kern 1998). They argue that minimizing cultural differences allows the client and vendor to make greater progress in achieving compatible goals (Kanter 1994). On the other hand, Lee and Kim (1999) could not find a relationship between cultural similarity and partnership quality. They assume that either the initial importance of cultural similarity fades over time, or the cultures of the two organizations evolve to become more tolerant or accepting of each other's culture.

The analysis of the four client groups shows no significant group differences, but shows two interesting findings (see figures below). While in line with the literature, the degree of understanding the culture of the other party is very high (overall mean = 4.98, SD = 1.10), the degree of cultural similarity of both parties is relatively low (overall mean = 3.75, SD = 1.65). This confirms the findings of Lee and Kim (1999) and allows the interpretation that the initial importance of cultural similarity fades over time. At the same time, the cultures of the two organizations evolve to become more tolerant or accepting of each other's culture (see Figure 5-42).

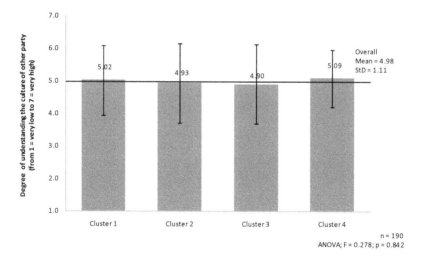

Figure 5-42. Degree of understanding the culture of the other party among the four client configurations

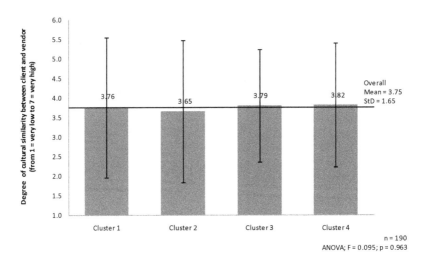

Figure 5-43. Degree of cultural similarity of both parties among the four client configurations

5.5.5.6   Trust

Among the various attributes generally ascribed to relationships, trust is the most important factor. It is the expectation that "a party will act predictably, will fulfill its obligations, and will behave fairly even when the possibility for opportunism is present" (Zaheer/McEvily/Perrone 1998, 143). Trust has been referred to as a meso-concept, integrating micro and macro facets and characteristics (Goles/Chin 2005). From a relationship perspective, trust has a long-term benefit since it allows a focus on long-term objectives, with less worry about day-to-day issues; it suppresses opportunism and enables risk-taking (Klepper 1995).

In many studies trust is typically treated as a uni-dimensional construct. The divergent motives for trust and the influence they can have on relationships are often neglected. In these studies, trust is treated equally with all other relationship factors, affecting, e.g., outsourcing success, satisfaction, risks etc. in the same way as other attributes (e.g., Goles 2001; Goles/Chin 2005; Lee/Kim 1999). However, a special issue of The Academy of Management Journal (Smith/Carroll/Ashford 1995) notes in its editorial that the role of trust in interfirm ties is of fundamental and outstanding importance. Thus, trust may be regarded as the predominant underlying characteristic of a successful outsourcing venture. Moreover, trust has to be regarded as a multidimensional relationship factor, not only affecting and shaping other relationship factors, but also being composed of and influenced by a variety of embedded notions (Corazzini 1977; Pressey/Mathews 2004).

In order to get a holistic understanding of this relationship construct, the clients were asked both the perceived importance of trust for an outsourcing relationship as well as the actually perceived degree of trust among the parties. Thereby, the actual status quo and the desired degree of trust (i.e., perceived importance) can be compared.

In terms of the importance of trust, no significant group differences could be found (see Figure 5-44, p > 0.1). Overall, all clients irrespective of their outsourcing motivation assign a pivotal role to trust for the overall relationship (overall mean = 6.04, SD = 0.95). This finding confirms the assumption in the literature that trust is a key feature of any outsourcing relationship regardless of the setup and strategic motivation of the venture.

Investigating the actual degree of trust between the outsourcing parties shows a slightly different picture, though. Here, the cost-conscious smart shoppers (cluster 2) break ranks with a significant lower degree of trust in their outsourcing relationship (group mean = 4.98, measure on a scale from 1 = very low to 7 = very high). Post-hocs tests corroborate this finding by revealing a significant difference between group 2 and all other groups, especially group 4 (S-N-K, Tukey-HSD, Scheffé; significance level alpha = 0.05, see appendix A 42). Obviously, in outsourcing relationships with cost cutting and variabilization of costs, trust is none of the constitutive features between the outsourcing parties.

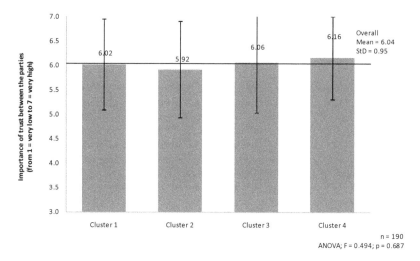

Figure 5-44. Importance of trust between the parties among the four client configurations

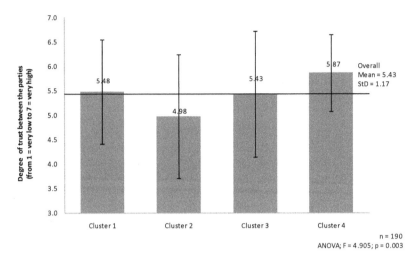

Figure 5-45. Degree of trust between the parties among the four client configurations

5.5.5.7   Vendor Flexibility

Given the length of an outsourcing relationship and the surrounding dynamic and unpredictable environment, flexibility is an important feature to allow for mutual adjustment of both parties (Macneil 1980) and also a basic mechanism for encouraging trust among the parties (Tan/Sia 2006). Flexibility as the ability to adapt to changes becomes an even more pressing issue if the outsourcing vendor becomes an integral part of business transformation at the level of the enterprise (Linder 2004). To manage a continuous and successful long-term partnership, the vendor has to be responsive to the basic conditions and development of the client, considering the client's changing business requirements, and thus gain the client's trust. The key to countering these challenges is thus a better analysis of flexibility requirements for outsourcing contracts implementing a sufficient degree of freedom to allow adaptation when business circumstances necessitate it. Many client demands to adapt contractual structures occur seemingly unpredictably although these demands could have been identified before. The ability to assess changes and necessary options may thus become an important part of relationship management competencies and, in particular, encourages trust in the vendor (Levina/Ross 2003). The positive impact of flexibility on trust has also been shown by several authors (see, e.g., Gietzmann 1996; Sabherwal 1999; Tan/Sia 2006).

Analyzing the degree of flexibility of the vendor shows a similar picture like the one for perceived trust (see chapter above). While the overall degree of flexibility is perceived as high among all clients irrespective of group affiliation (overall mean = 5.28, SD = 1.11, measured on a scale from 1 = very low to 7 = very high), the cost-conscious smart shoppers (cluster 2) show a significantly lower extent of trust among the outsourcing partners compared to all other groups as the post-hoc tests reveal (S-N-K, Tukey-HSD, Scheffé; significance level alpha = 0.1, see appendix A 43). Both the IT-focused clients and the business-efficiency-oriented clients score very high on this dimension. Obviously, for customers that source external IT to support and enhance their business and services and also for customers that source external IT to get the latest technology, flexibility is a crucial success factor. In contrast, among the cost-conscious smart shoppers flexibility is not established as the main relationship factor. This can be very well explained by the fact that planning and holding resources that allow for flexible adaptation requires cost-intense structures on the vendor side (Häberle/Jahner/Krcmar 2005). Such costs and expenditures are transferred to the client and make the outsourcing relationship more costly. Consequently, flexibility is not necessarily appreciated in a cost-oriented outsourcing venture.

Similarly, but with a different explanation, flexibility of the vendor is not necessarily one of the crucial requirements in an innovation-oriented outsourcing venture such as expected by the strategy- and innovation-focused client group (cluster 3). Here, the focus is on jointly developing strategic advantages and innovative services for mutual benefit with equally devoting resources rather than on one-sided vendor flexibility.

Overall, the degree of flexibility is on a quite high level among all clients.

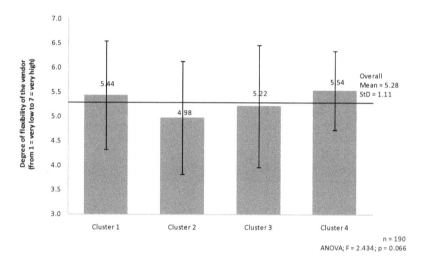

Figure 5-46. Degree of flexibility of the vendor among the four client configurations

5.5.5.8   Vendor Proactivity

Risk-reward sharing as well as promoting and suggesting innovations are two means to demonstrate action and enable value-added outsourcing (Kern/Willcocks 2001). Clients more and more seek some sort of co-sourcing model with performance-based contracts where the vendor is rewarded for improving the client's business performance, but also takes the risk of not achieving this (Lacity/Willcocks 2001). At the same time, Jahner et al. (2006a) found that many clients complain about the reactive behavior of the service provider and expect more transparency and active suggestions for process improvement over the contractual relation-ship, going as far as to demand proactive suggestions for innovation potential.

Examining the degree of vendor proactivity shows a diversified picture for the four client groups. Overall, the degree of vendor proactivity is medium / reasonably high (overall mean = 4.24, SD = 1.46, measured on a scale from 1 = very low to 7 = very high). But looking at the client groups in more detail reveals significant group differences. Post-hoc tests corroborate this finding by showing significant differences between groups 2 and 4 (S-N-K, Tukey-HSD, Scheffé; significance level alpha = 0.05, see appendix A 44).

While the business-efficiency clients (cluster 1) adopt a neutral position with regard to vendor proactivity, the cost-conscious smart shoppers (cluster 2) have a very low score of vendor proactivity. Similarly to flexibility (see chapter 5.5.5.7, p. 198ff.), for clients that focus on cost cutting, it is too expensive if the vendor plans for flexibility and proactive suggestions for improvements. Consequently, vendor proactivity is not expected in such cost-cutting-oriented outsourcing settings.

In contrast, innovation- and strategy-oriented clients report a high degree of vendor proactivi-ty in their outsourcing arrangements (group mean = 4.64, SD = 1.46, measured on a scale from 1 = very low to 7 = very high). Although client proactivity was not investigated, vendor proactivity seems to be a crucial element for partnership where joint efforts and mutual bene-fits are the main tie of the involved outsourcing partners.

Even a little higher is the degree of vendor proactivity for the IT-focused client group (cluster 4). Here, vendor proactivity involves anticipating latest technology leaps and a timely imple-mentation and provision of new IT services to the client. Consequently, in ventures where IT excellence is the main focus, vendor proactivity is highly appreciated and a building block for the outsourcing relationship.

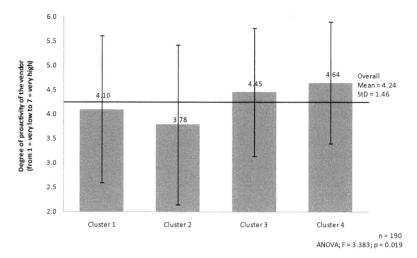

Figure 5-47. *Degree of proactivity and suggestions for innovation potential of the vendor among the four client configurations*

Summing up the described results of this chapter regarding the perceived importance and actual degree of the examined relationship factors among the client groups allows some noteworthy findings:

1. In general, relationship factors are considered important and necessary means to sustain a successful relationship by all clients irrespective of the underlying outsourcing motive. From a statistical point of view this is documented by the fact that for many relationship factors the group differences are not statistically significant (p > 0.1), and all clients are rather homogeneous with respect to their perception of the relationship factors.

2. The clients with a focus on IT excellence and technology reliability as their most prevailing underlying outsourcing motive (cluster 4) score surprisingly high on every relationship dimension, even higher than the strategy clients (cluster 3). Either this group is quite undifferentiated in its perception of different relationship factors or the clients have implemented a "hands-on" working relationship between client technology experts and vendor experts for achieving the IT goals and thus consider the relationship factors important for their daily collaboration.

3. Compared to the other client groups, three relationship factors, i.e., trust, flexibility, and vendor proactivity, receive significantly less attention among the cost-conscious smart shoppers (cluster 2). A plausible explanation for this finding is the fact that these relationship factors require pricey investments on the vendor side and make the whole outsourcing arrangement more expensive, a counter effect for the cost cutting motivation of the members of this group.

5.5.6 Outsourcing Success: Perceived Service Quality and Satisfaction

As elaborated in chapter 3.6.5 on outsourcing success (p. 66ff.), three categories of outsourcing outcomes exist according to Dibbern et al. (2004). These are satisfaction, expectation / realization of results, and performance. While Dibbern et al. (2004, 74) conclude that "satisfaction is a reasonable surrogate for a successful outcome because it allows the subjects to respond based on the criteria most relevant to them", many authors stress the role of perceived service quality (Susarla/Barua/Whinston 2003), which is not only one aspect of performance of an outsourcing venture (Grover/Cheon/Teng 1996), but also a strong determinant of outsourcing success (e.g., satisfaction according to Susarla/Barua/Whinston 2003). In this thesis, all three outcome categories of outsourcing success were examined.

First, the satisfaction with the overall outsourcing venture was investigated (Figure 5-48). The overall examination shows that all clients regardless of their group affiliation are very content with their outsourcing provider and the outsourcing venture in general, as the high overall mean indicates (overall mean = 5.44; SD = 1.21; measured on a scale from 1 = very low to 7 = very high). But a more detailed analysis of the groups shows that there are significant differences between the clients. While the cost-conscious smart shoppers (cluster 2) and the innovation and strategy-oriented clients (cluster 3) are fairly satisfied with their venture, both the business-efficiency-oriented clients (cluster 1) and especially the IT-focused clients (cluster 4) are extremely satisfied with their venture and break ranks towards the upper extreme. Post-hoc tests revealed that especially group 2 and 4 differ significantly from each other in their perception of satisfaction with the outsourcing venture (S-N-K, Tukey-HSD, Scheffé; significance level alpha = 0.1, see appendix A 45).

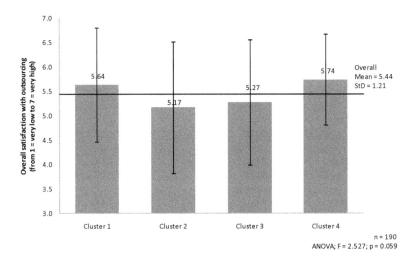

Figure 5-48. Overall satisfaction with outsourcing among the four client configurations

A similar picture can be observed when analyzing the performance category of outsourcing outcomes. Here, the perceived service quality of the outsourcing vendor was judged by the clients (see Figure 5-49). Overall, as with the satisfaction of the clients, the degree of perceived service quality of the outsourced services is very high among all clients irrespective of group affiliation (overall mean = 5.33; SD = 1.17; measured on a scale from 1 = very low to 7 = very high). But again, in accordance with satisfaction level of the client groups, significant group differences can be observed with both the business-efficiency-oriented clients (cluster 1) and the IT-focused clients (cluster 4) breaking ranks towards the upper extreme as the post-hoc tests also confirm (S-N-K, Tukey-HSD, Scheffé; significance level alpha = 0.05, see appendix A 46).

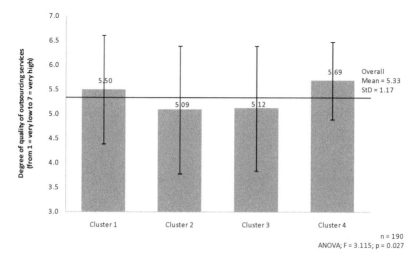

Figure 5-49. Degree of perceived service quality of the outsourced services among the four client configurations

The last category of outsourcing outcomes looks at the expected-achieved benefit ratio by contrasting the expected benefits vs. the achieved results of the outsourcing ventures. In order to do that, the respondents were asked 16 expectations towards the outsourcing venture (these were the same categories that were also used for the factor and cluster analysis afterwards). At the end of the questionnaire, the same 16 items were asked to what degree they were achieved. By subtracting the actually perceived results and the expectations in the beginnings, an index could be generated. Since both expectations and achieved results were measured on a 7-point-Likert scale, the maximum width of differences ranged from -6 to +6. A positive value indicates an over-achievement of the expected results, while a negative value indicates that the expected outcome was achieved to a lesser degree than expected. Figure 5-50 shows the calculated differences between the expected and the achieved results of the outsourcing ventures among the four client groups (the figure shows the mean values for each category and each cluster).

Overall, one can see that the differences between achieved and expected outsourcing results are very low (close to 0) which is a good result because it shows that the results were more or less achieved to the degree they were expected. Analyzing the groups, however, shows some significant differences. Post-hoc tests were conducted for all groups and all 16 variables to depict which groups differ from each other (S-N-K, Tukey-HSD, Scheffé; significance level alpha = 0.1). The detailed results of these post-hoc tests can be found in appendix A 47.

In accordance with the findings above (Figure 5-48 and Figure 5-49), it can be observed that the IT-focused clients (cluster 4) overall exceed their expectations. Especially regarding the items "cost reduction", "cost transparency / flexibility", "joint product and service develop-ment", the IT-focused clients exceeded their expectations by far. This is even more surprising, as these are categories that the IT-focused clients originally did not expect as their prevailing outsourcing motivation. Regarding their originally intended outsourcing motivations, i.e., long-term use of systems, modernization of IT, this group also scored high. The only excep-tion can be found when looking at the expectation "shift risk to service provider". This was one of the dominating intentions of this group, but the analysis of the differences shows that the originally expectations were not fully met (negative value). Overall, from regarding satis-faction, perceived service quality, and the expectation-realization ratio, this cluster has the best scores and has achieved more goals with outsourcing than originally intended.

Looking at the business-efficiency-oriented clients (cluster 1) the differences show that not all of the originally intended motivations could be successfully achieved (service orientation, better flexibility, and quality improvements). "Service orientation" and "better flexibility" show negative values indicating these clients expected more than they could realize with the outsourcing venture. To some extent this can be explained by the fact that when clients have a very straightforward and focused motive they tend to be more critical when not fully achiev-ing it (Oliver 1977).

A similar picture can be derived from analyzing the strategy and innovation-focused clients (cluster 3). Here, not all originally intended expectations (i.e., the strategy and innovation focus) could be fully reached. For example, suggestions for new products, knowledge acquisi-tion from the service provider, and joint product and service development show a negative value, indicating that expectations towards these items were higher than the actual result. Again, an explanation could be that clients that have a very straightforward and focused mo-tive tend to be more critical when not fully achieving it. The same explanation can be as-sumed for the cost-conscious smart shoppers (cluster 2) that did not quite reach their cost-oriented expectations.

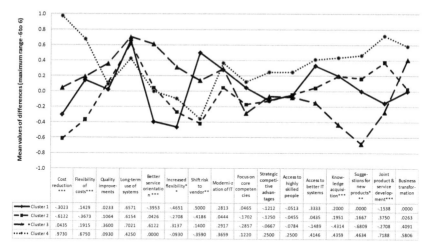

	Cost reduction ***	Flexibility of costs***	Quality improvements	Long-term use of systems	Better service orientation ***	Increased flexibility*	Shift risk to vendor**	Moderni-zation of IT	Focus on core competencies	Strategic competitive advantages	Access to highly skilled people	Access to better IT systems	Knowledge acquisition***	Suggestions for new products**	Joint product & service development***	Business transformation
Cluster 1	-.3023	.1429	.0233	.6571	-.3953	-.4651	.5000	.2813	.0465	-.1212	-.0513	.3333	.2000	.0000	-.1538	.0000
Cluster 2	-.6122	-.3673	.1064	.6154	.0426	-.2708	-.4186	.0444	-.1702	-.1250	-.0455	.0435	.1951	.1667	.3750	.0263
Cluster 3	.0435	.1915	.3600	.7021	.6122	.3137	.1400	.2917	-.2857	-.0667	-.0784	-.1489	-.4314	-.6809	-.2708	.4091
Cluster 4	.9730	.6750	.0930	.4250	.0000	-.0930	-.3590	.3659	.1220	.2500	.2500	.4146	.4359	.4634	.7188	.5806

Level of significant for group differences: * p < 0.1; ** p < 0.05; *** p < 0.01

Figure 5-50. Differences between expected and achieved benefits of outsourcing among the four client configurations

Overall, it can be observed that the level of satisfaction, perceived service quality, and also the expectation-realization is quite high, indicating overall content clients. Looking at the details, one can conclude that clients tend not to fully achieve their originally intended goals, but exceed other (non-main) expectations that were not in their original scope.

5.6 Summary and Consolidated Description of the Four Client Configurations

After analyzing the basic outsourcing motivations of the four outsourcing client groups as well as their characteristics with regard to different dimensions (context factors, relational architecture, governance approaches, interaction approaches), this chapter aims at consolidating the detailed findings of the previous chapter. Each outsourcing client type will be described in a summarized way to get an overall picture. The types will also be contrasted with the types identified in the qualitative pre-study.

The business-efficiency clients

Cluster 1 entails clients that engage in outsourcing ventures in order to support or enhance their business. IS outsourcing is thereby not necessarily seen as a means to support or improve the current information technology structure of the company. Nor is outsourcing regarded as a vehicle to cut costs by investing the saved money in other areas. Instead, goals and expectations associated with the outsourcing decision of this group comprise a better service orientation, more (business) flexibility, quality improvements, but also to some extent cost reduction and joint product and service development.

Looking at the context factors that shape the outsourcing environment reveals that clients of this group can predominantly be found in the banking/insurance/finance sector and also in the trade/wholesale industry. In terms of firm size measured by annual sales and also by the number of employees, clients with the motivation structure of business efficiency are mostly located in large companies (more than 10 bill. Euro annual sales, more than 5000 employees). Overall, the role of IT for the companies is regarded as important, although the investments in IT are not overwhelming with a medium IT budget (more than 10 mio. Euro).

With regard to the architecture of the outsourcing venture, the client companies in this group have a quite reasonable amount of outsourcing experience (most clients of this group have between 3 to 10 years of experience, but some also have more than 15 years). As to the outsourced services provided by a third-party-vendor, the clients engage in a selective outsourcing model and source not only IT applications and IT infrastructure components, but also whole IT-supported business processes. The emphasis on selectively sourcing IT-supported business processes is an important one, since in contrast to this group, other client groups do not engage in business process outsourcing so heavily. In order to spread the risk of lock-in effects and also in order to maximize the efficiency of providing high-quality services, the clients rather set up multi-vendor outsourcing deals with more than three vendors providing the IT services. These outsourcing deals are mostly established for a medium period of time with a contract length between 3-4 years. Most often, a fixed priced model, but sometimes also transaction-based pricing arrangements are agreed upon. In such outsourcing deals where business efficiency is the main motivation of the outsourcing clients, the goal alignment between the outsourcing parties is quite high, probably, because the outcome can be relatively easily specified, and the switching costs and degree of dependency on the outsourcing provider is at a medium level.

As to governance mechanisms of this client group, it becomes obvious that the contract plays a medium-to-high role for governing business-efficiency oriented ventures. Especially processes for SLA and contract management as well as performance and service management are well established. In contrast, strategy processes and benchmarking initiatives are seldom set up. While governance via structures such as a management board / steering committee or the role of a relationship manager is well established, external consultants are hardly ever asked to manage the client-vendor relationship. The role of informal relational governance, staff experience with outsourcing and the know-how to control the vendor are all regarded as important and well-established governance mechanisms. Interestingly, the motivation of business efficiency in this group goes along with a very tight management of the vendor who is hardly attributed any degrees of freedom or decision authority when planning, developing, and running the outsourced services. Also, risk-sharing models are not arranged among the outsourcing parties.

The detailed investigation of the perceived importance of selected relationship factors for this group revealed that in line with the other client groups, basic interorganizational factors such as communication, cooperation, commitment, trust, and flexibility are crucial and also well established between the outsourcing parties.

The cost-conscious smart shoppers

Cluster 2 groups clients that share a very clear and straightforward expectation towards out-sourcing and also one of the very basic and original motivations of outsourcing (Smith/Mitra/Narasimhan 1998; DiRomualdo/Gurbaxani 1998): the desire to cut costs, achieve more cost transparency, or render costs as a flexible resource (variabilization and transparency). While the other client groups have some other notions besides their main ex-pectations, this client group is exclusively focused on the cost-cutting aspect.

As to the environmental factors, dominating industries of this client group are the electro technology industry, consumer goods, as well as IT services. Clients are located in medium-to-large size companies with regard to annual sales and the number of employees. In contrast to the business-efficiency clients and also to the other two groups, the cost-conscious smart shoppers have the highest IT budget with more than 100 mio. Euro p.a. In line with the other groups, IT is attributed an important role for the company.

The building parameters of the outsourcing environment are somehow similar to the first client group. The companies' experience with outsourcing in general is fairly high (most clients of this group have between 3 to 10 years of experience, but some also have more than 15 years). As to the outsourced services provided by a third-party-vendor, the clients engage in a selective outsourcing model and most often source IT applications and IT infrastructure components. Some clients, but much less than in the business-efficiency group, engage in business process outsourcing. In order to spread the risk of lock-in effects and also in order to get the best prices for the outsourced services, the clients rather set up multi-vendor outsourc-ing deals with 2 to 3 vendors providing the IT services. Surprisingly, these outsourcing deals are mostly established for a medium-to-long-term period of time with a contract length be-tween 5-7 years. A fixed priced model is the dominating pricing arrangement. In such out-sourcing deals where cost cutting is the main motivation of the outsourcing clients, the goal alignment between the outsourcing parties is not too high. One of the reasons for the non-optimal goal alignment is the inherent adversarial nature in outsourcing contracts "in that a dollar out of the customer's pocket is a dollar in the supplier's pocket" as stated by Lacity and Willcocks (2003, 122). The switching costs and degree of dependency on the outsourcing provider is at a medium level.

The most prevailing governance mechanism established among these clients is the contract. Consequently, processes such as SLA and contract management, performance and service management play an important role for the cost-conscious clients. Benchmarking processes are established to some extent and play a higher role compared to the other client groups. In terms of structures for governing the outsourcing vendor, steering committees as well as a relationship manager are set in place. But just like the business-efficiency clients, engaging an external consultant for managing the client-vendor relationship is not an option. The role of an informal relationship and also staff experience is regarded as important, as is the role of know-how to control the vendor. What is especially noteworthy is the fact that the experience and know-how of the client to control the vendor is very distinct in this group and against the assumption that clients in this group are outsourcing newbies that look for quick and easy wins. As this client group is focused on a tight cost-oriented management of the outsourcing relationship, the vendor is rarely attributed with managerial control and decision making authority. Moreover, risk-sharing models are not agreed upon as this is somehow counterproductive to the original intention of the cost cutters and also too expensive to establish.

Regarding the role of relationship factors for the outsourcing relationships of these clients, the same finding as for the business efficiency clients can be reported. Against the general assumption that relationship issues are too expensive to be set in place, basic interorganizational factors such as communication, cooperation, commitment, trust, and flexibility are crucial and also well established between the outsourcing parties. One relationship factor breaks ranks, not only with regard to the other relationship factors in this group, but also with regard to the other groups: vendor proactivity is rated extremely low in this group. But again, the reasonable explanation here is that it is too expensive if the vendor plans for flexibility and proactive suggestions for improvements. Consequently, vendor proactivity is not expected in such cost-cutting oriented outsourcing settings.

The strategists and innovation seekers

The clients that belong to **cluster 3** have acknowledged "that outsourcing for short-term cost-cutting does not yield nearly as much as outsourcing for longer-term knowledge-based system or strategic benefit – like greater intellectual depth and access, opportunity scanning, innovation, reliability, quality, value-added solutions or worldwide outreach" (Quinn 1999, 10). Consequently, they engage in outsourcing ventures with certain strategic elements or a strategic intention. Those long-term strategic goals aim at generating innovation and thus enhance business value. Among others, they comprise suggestions for new IT-based products and services (innovation idea creation), knowledge acquisition from the service provider, a joint product and service development (joint innovation creation of new IT-based products and services), access to highly skilled people, and also to better IT systems and new technology. The focus of this group is on innovation excellence and thus creating business value by providing both cutting-edge technology and IT-based product and service innovations. The outsourcing vendor is regarded as an equal business partner rather than a simple provider of IT services.

Characterizing the environment of these clients, one can see that more often than in the other client groups, clients in the automotive and engineering/machine construction industry as well as client from the public sector/government are represented in this group. As to firm size, small-to-medium size companies (251-2000 employees) and also non-profit companies are predominantly found in this group. Overall, the role of IT for the companies is regarded as important, although the investments in IT are at a rather low level (up to 10 mio. Euro IT budget).

As to outsourcing experience this group does not differ from the three other peer groups, with a medium experience (mostly 3-10 years of company experience with outsourcing). While IT applications and IT infrastructure are the most commonly outsourced services (in most cases selectively), the percentage of clients that outsourced IT-supported business processes is highest in this group (compared to the three other client groups). Even more, the percentage of clients who *totally and fully* outsourced IT-supported business processes is also highest in this client group. Although multi-vendor outsourcing with 2-3 vendors is very popular among these clients (just like in all the other client groups), many clients of this group also engage in single-vendor ventures. This is in accordance and adequate to the primary motivation of this group, i.e., establishing a long-term strategic and value-oriented partnership with a focus on mutual benefits. Such a strategic partnership is seldom established and fostered with more than one outsourcing partner. Accordingly, the duration of the contract in such ventures is predominantly not fixed, i.e., unlimited, albeit the possibility of a termination. As pricing arrangements, fixed price and "time and material" are dominant models. This is a surprising finding since risk reward sharing price structures do not seem to be an established and attractive arrangement for the clients and vendors of this group. In line with the underlying expectation of shared innovation creation and strategic intentions, the dependency and switching costs between both parties is quite high, as is the goal alignment between both partners. Just like the business efficiency motive, the strategic intention and shared value and innovation creation motives seem to be congruent goals for both client and vendor and thus the goal alignment between both parties is quite high.

Governance mechanisms of this group comprise the arm's length approaches of contractual governance with established SLA and contract management processes as well as performance and service management processes. In contrast to the other groups, strategy processes between client and vendor are agreed upon and established. The role of a relationship manager is regarded as important, but benchmarking processes are not appreciated. Probably, benchmarking is regarded as counterproductive in an environment where long-term benefits instead of quick wins are expected. Also very low is the degree and use of an external consultant that could possibly balance between client and vendor interests. Although low on an overall level, the establishment of risk sharing models is higher in this group compared to the other client groups (this difference is significant on a $p < 0.01$ level).

Regarding the role of relationship factors for the outsourcing relationships of these clients, the findings do not differ significantly from the first two client groups. Basic interorganizational factors such as communication, cooperation, commitment, trust, and flexibility are crucial and also well established between the outsourcing parties. One relationship factor breaks ranks with regard to the other groups, i.e., the vendor proactivity. Vendor proactivity is rated medium to high in the strategy group. This finding is in accordance with the other constitutive elements of the group, as proactivity is a basic element in a partnership with mutual benefits and risks.

IT excellence and reliability-oriented clients

Cluster 4 groups IT managers that seek outsourcing for technological reasons. Outsourcing information systems is thereby seen as a way to either enhance the current client technology and deliver latest cutting-edge information technology or to provide long-term stable and reliable problem-free IT services. The service provider is chosen as an external source to gain a distinctive technical leadership (Kern/Willcocks/van Heck 2002, 65). Specific expectations of these customers comprise access to better IT systems and new technology and modernization of IT / replace legacy systems. But the client group also has another minor notion of expectations, i.e., business-oriented goals. Thus, quality improvements and access to highly skilled people are also among the outsourcing expectations of the IT-focused clients. Another motive dominates the outsourcing arrangement in this group and is also in line with the underlying notion of delivering problem-free, reliable IT, i.e., shifting the risk to the service provider. These clients have a very high risk aversion and assign the provision of up-to-date stable IT systems which support the business to a third party provider that acts like an "extended workbench".

The environment of the outsourcing arrangement reveals that manufacturing is the most dominantly represented industry of the IT-focused clients. Clients are primarily found in medium-size (50+ to 500 mio. Euro annual sales) as well as in small (251-500 employees) companies. The assigned IT budget is also rather low with up to 10 mio. Euro and the role of IT is regarded as medium. This perception of the medium role of IT is in contrast to all three other groups which regarded IT as important and in most cases assigned a medium or high IT budget. Possibly, because these clients only attribute a medium importance to IT, they rather tend to source external IT excellence, instead of investing IT capabilities and resources in the company.

The company experience with outsourcing did not significantly differ at all between the client groups and consequently, also the IT-focused customers (as well as the three other client groups) have a quite reasonable amount of outsourcing experience (between 3 to 10 years). While IT applications and IT infrastructure are selectively outsourced by most clients, business process outsourcing is hardly considered for possible outsourcing by many clients. Multi-vendor outsourcing with 2-3 vendors is most common in this group and in contrast to the other client groups, information technology is outsourced highly selective with a lot of very small portions of IT (less than 20% of the IT budget) spread among different providers. The duration of the outsourcing deals is also very short-term oriented (0-2 years) with some of the deals being entered for a medium period of time (3-4 years). Fixed price is the dominating pricing model and the dependency and switching costs of changing the service provider are medium. More than in any other client group, the goal alignment between the outsourcing parties is extremely high. A possible explanation could be derived from the easy specificity of the tasks provided by the third party vendor.

When analyzing the outsourcing governance mechanisms, it becomes obvious that the contract as well as SLA, contract management, performance and service management processes play a very important role. In contrast, other processes such as strategy processes or benchmarking play only a minor role as does the establishment of structures, such as a steering committee. Similar to the other groups, the role of an informal relationship governance is rated high by this group as is the role of staff experience with outsourcing and know-how to control the vendor. Risk sharing models are hardly ever set in place and the degrees of freedom attributed to the vendor are very limited.

The role of relationship factors for the outsourcing relationships of this client group is comparable to the findings in the other client groups. Basic interorganizational factors such as communication, cooperation, commitment, trust, and flexibility are crucial and also well established between the outsourcing parties. Just like for the strategy clients, vendor proactivity is rated medium to high for the IT-focused clients. While these clients seek to mitigate risks and transfer possible risks associated to their IT systems to the provider, they do appreciate proactive behavior of the outsourcing vendor to suggest continuous improvement ideas.

In contrast to the five relationship types identified in the qualitative pre-study, the quantitative study revealed only four outsourcing relationship types. The types, however, identified in both studies, are very similar. For example, what has been labeled "commodity supply relationship" in the pre-study was identified as the "cost-conscious smart shoppers" group in the survey. Here, the motives could be clearly ascribed to cost expectations instead of a vague focus of "commodity supply". In the pre-study, "technology excellence partnership" as well as "reliability-oriented clients" were identified as separate groups. The survey revealed that these motives merge in one large group labeled as "IT excellence and reliability-oriented clients". Also, the differentiation between long-term "strategy-oriented clients" and short-term "joint service development partnership" could not be sustained in the large study. Both types were merged in one group, named "strategists and innovation seekers". Lastly, the business motives did not form a discrete type in the pre-study, but the survey identified a group of "business-efficiency clients". A schematic overview of if and how the five types identified in the qualitative pre-study match to the types identified in the quantitative study is depicted in Figure 5-51.

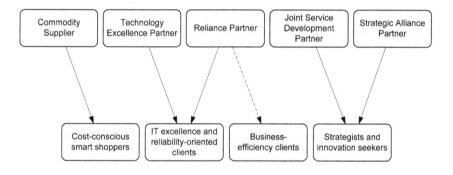

Figure 5-51. Schematic overview and comparison of five qualitatively derived and four quantitatively derived outsourcing client types

Overall, the quantitative study could show that the reality of outsourcing relationships is more complex and sophisticated and thus cannot be comprehensively described along only two dimensions as many classification approaches do. Extending the qualitative pre-study which was fruitful for getting a first glimpse on the idea of differentiating outsourcing clients along their expectations and characteristics, the results of the survey were much more profound, precise, and reliable. With the knowledge gained from this study, outsourcing clients, their motives, and characteristics can be comprehensively described and the anatomy of different outsourcing relationships is better understood.

Having described the four client configurations in their basic constitutive characteristics, Table 5-28 gives a summative overview of the four client groups and their characteristics by allocating them in the conceptually developed outsourcing governance framework. This table is to be interpreted regarding the distinct features of each client type. Each cell is to be interpreted in relation to and regarding the context of the other groups. For example, when interpreting the dominant industries, the business-efficiency clients (cluster 1) are proportionally more represented in the banking/insurance/finance sector and in the trade/wholesale industry compared to the other three groups. This does not necessarily indicate that these are absolute values.

Client Type / Category / Dimension	Cluster 1: Business-efficiency clients	Cluster 2: Cost-conscious smart shoppers	Cluster 3: Strategists and innovation seekers	Cluster 4: IT excellence and reliability-oriented clients	Group differences significant / significance measure
Strategic intent / expectation / motivation					
Dominant outsourcing motives / expectations	▪ Service orientation ▪ Flexibility ▪ Quality improvements ▪ Cost reduction ▪ Joint product and service development	▪ Cost reduction ▪ Cost transparency / variabilization / flexibility ▪ (no other characterizing outsourcing expectations)	▪ Suggestions for new IT-based products and services ▪ Knowledge acquisition from service provider ▪ Joint product and service development ▪ Access to highly skilled people ▪ Access to better IT systems and new technology	▪ Access to better IT systems and new technology ▪ Modernization of IT / replace legacy systems ▪ Quality improvements ▪ Access to highly skilled people ▪ Shift risk to service provider	p < 0.001 (ANOVA)
Context factors					
Dominant industries	Banking/insurance/finance, trade/wholesale	electrotechnology, consumer goods, IT services	automotive, engineering/machine construction, public/government	(other) manufacturing	p < 0.1 (Chi-square)
Firm size: annual sales	large (More than 10 bill. Euro)	medium-to-large-size (1+ - 5 bill. Euro)	non-profit / (medium-size)	medium (50+ - 500 mio. Euro)	p < 0.001 (Somers-d)
Firm size: number of employees	large companies (5001 to 50.000 employees)	medium-to-large-size companies (2001-5000 employees)	small-to-medium-size companies (251-2000 employees)	small companies (251-500 employees)	p < 0.001 (Somers-d)
IT budget	medium (more than 10 mio. Euro)	large (more than 100 mio. Euro)	small (up to 10 mio. Euro)	small (up to 10 mio. Euro)	p < 0.01 (Chi-square)
Role of IT for company	high	high	high	medium	p < 0.1 (ANOVA)
Relational architecture					
Company experience with outsourcing	medium (mostly 3 – 10 years)	medium (mostly 3 – 10 years)	medium (mostly 3 – 10 years)	medium (mostly 3 – 10 years)	n.s.
Outsourcing objects: IT-supported business processes	selectively outsourced by most clients	selectively outsourced by some clients	selectively outsourced by most clients in this group, percentage of clients who totally outsourced business processes highest in this group	business processes not considered for possible outsourcing by many clients	p < 0.1 (Chi-square)
Outsourcing objects: IT applications	selectively outsourced by most clients	selectively outsourced by most clients	selectively outsourced by most clients	selectively outsourced by most clients	n.s.
Outsourcing objects: IT infrastructure	selectively outsourced by most clients	selectively outsourced by most clients	selectively outsourced by most clients	selectively outsourced by most clients	n.s.

Category / Dimension ╲ Client Type	Cluster 1: Business-efficiency clients	Cluster 2: Cost-conscious smart shoppers	Cluster 3: Strategists and innovation seekers	Cluster 4: IT excellence and reliability-oriented clients	Group differences significant / significance measure
Number of involved vendors	more than 3 vendors	2-3 vendors	mostly 2-3 vendors, but many clients of this group also engage in single-vendor ventures	2-3 vendors	$p < 0.05$ (Somers-d)
Degree of outsourcing	selective (20-80% of IT budget)	selective (20-80% of IT budget)	selective (20-80% of IT budget)	highly selective (up to 20% of IT budget)	n.s.
Duration / length of outsourcing contract	medium (3-4 years)	medium to long-term (5-7 years)	unlimited (but option to terminate)	very short-term (0-2 years), also medium (3-4 years)	n.s.
Dominating pricing model	fixed price, transaction-based	fixed price	fixed price, time and material	fixed price	n.s.
Outsourcing alliance model	external third-party provider mostly	external third-party provider mostly	external third-party provider and shared services (internal subsidiary)	external third-party provider exclusively	$p < 0.01$ (Chi-square)
Dependency on service provider (degree of switching costs)	medium	medium	high	medium	n.s.
Goal alignment between outsourcing parties	high	medium	high	very high	$p < 0.1$ (ANOVA)
Governance mechanisms					
Role of contract	medium to high	high	medium to high	very high	n.s.
Role of processes: Established SLA and contract management processes	high	high	medium to high	high	n.s.
Role of processes: Established performance and service management	high	high	medium to high	high	n.s.
Role of processes: Established strategy processes	low	low	medium	low	n.s.
Role of processes: Established benchmarking processes	low	medium to low	very low	low	n.s.
Role of structures: Establishment of management board / steering committee	medium	medium to low	medium	low	$p < 0.1$ (ANOVA)
Role of structures: Establishment of relationship manager	high	high	high	high	n.s.
Role of structures: Establishment of external consultant	extremely low	extremely low	very low (but on a higher overall level compared to other groups)	extremely low	$p < 0.01$ (ANOVA)
Role of informal relationship	high	high	high	high	n.s.
Role of staff experience	high	high	(very) high	high	n.s.
Role of know-how to control vendor	high	very high	high	high	n.s.
Role of attributed degrees of freedom to vendor / Extent of vendor's managerial control and decision making authority	low	low	medium	low	n.s.
Role / establishment of risk sharing models	very low	very low	low	very low	$p < 0.01$ (ANOVA)
Interactions (relationship factors)					
Communication	high	high	high	(very) high	n.s.
Conflict resolution / consensus	high	high	high	very high	$p < 0.05$ (ANOVA)
Cooperation / coordination	high	high	high	very high	$p < 0.01$ (ANOVA)
Commitment / loyalty	high	high	high	very high	$p < 0.1$ (ANOVA)
Cultural similarity / understanding	medium	medium	medium	medium	n.s.
Importance of trust	very high	very high	very high	very high	n.s.
Degree of trust	high	medium to high	high	very high	$p < 0.01$ (ANOVA)

Client Type / Category / Dimension	Cluster 1: Business-efficiency clients	Cluster 2: Cost-conscious smart shoppers	Cluster 3: Strategists and innovation seekers	Cluster 4: IT excellence and reliability-oriented clients	Group differences significant / significance measure
Vendor flexibility	high	medium to high	high	high	$p < 0.1$ (ANOVA)
Vendor proactivity	medium	medium to low	medium to high	medium to high	$p < 0.05$ (ANOVA)

Table 5-28. Outsourcing relationship types framework: overview of four client groups and their characteristics

So far, this chapter described the characteristics of the four client groups and how strong the relationship between the groups and the respective characteristics is. It also depicted the role and establishment of different governance approaches among the clients. The anatomy of different clients has been characterized in detail, but it is yet unclear which of the different governance approaches are best suited to manage each client type. It has not been investigated yet how the described governance approaches are related to the outsourcing success in terms of outsourcing quality and satisfaction.

The following chapter will thus develop a model with different governance mechanisms to elaborate which governance approach is best suited (in terms of achieved quality and satisfaction) to manage each client group.

6 Governance of IS Outsourcing Relationship Types

Based on empirical evidence, the previous chapter identified four different outsourcing client types in practice. It laid out the main characteristics of these types in a descriptive way, for example, what is the main motivation of each type to engage in an outsourcing venture, how important is, e.g., the contract etc. However, while single governance mechanisms have been addressed and roughly described in the previous chapter, so far it remains still unclear how each client type is best, i.e., successfully, managed. Governance mechanisms have not yet been set in relation to any outcome measure (e.g., perceived service quality or satisfaction). This chapter is thus dedicated to introducing a model that investigates the impact of different governance mechanisms (introduced and described conceptually in chapter 3.6.3, p. 51ff.) on outsourcing outcome, thereby addressing research question 3: "What are appropriate governance approaches and mechanisms for the successful management of different outsourcing relationships?"

6.1 Research Design: Governance Model and Construct Development

The predominant aim of the research model is to test the impact of different governance mechanisms on outsourcing outcome and to analyze whether these governance mechanisms and their influence on success differ across the four identified outsourcing client types.

As chapter 3.6.3 (p. 51ff.) has laid out, the literature review and extant theories revealed six dominant governance mechanisms[19]:

1. Formal governance via a specified contract

2. Informal, relational governance

3. Governance via management processes

4. Governance via organizational management structures

5. Governance via staff experience with outsourcing

6. Governance via risk-reward sharing structures and incentives

These governance mechanisms were used as determinant constructs (independent variables) that impact on the dependent constructs of outcome measures. As to outcome measures, chapter 3.6.5 (p. 66ff.) has elaborated on three major categories of how to measure outsourcing outcomes: satisfaction, expectations and their realization, and performance. While the survey instrument measured items in all three categories, for this model, only two measures were considered:

---

[19] For a detailed description of the constructs, i.e., the governance mechanisms, please see chapter 3.6.3.

1. satisfaction

2. perceived service quality as a performance measure

Expectations and their realization were not considered for the model because a focus on only selected expectation criteria can cause a bias (see chapter 3.6.5, p. 66ff.). Since the four client groups were differentiated and clustered along different expectations, each group has to be measured against different expectation criteria and their realization. Thus, a comparability of different expectations might not be given and consequently, this outcome measure will be disregarded.

As to the relation of satisfaction and performance (i.e., service quality), there is a lack of definitional and methodological standardization as to whether satisfaction is a process or an outcome (Yi 1990). In this thesis, the view of Susarla et al. (2003) will be followed who understood satisfaction as an outcome measure and used performance as one determinant that impacts on satisfaction with IS outsourcing.

All indicators used to measure the constructs of the model described above are based upon intensive literature review (see chapter 3.6.3, p. 51ff., and chapter 3.6.5, p. 66ff.). The actual research model[20] is presented in Figure 6-1. Each construct consists of a number of items that measure the construct on an indicator and measurement model basis (for a detailed description on formative and reflective measurements see next chapter). The development of the constructs is shown in Table 6-1.

---

[20] The original research model does not include mediating effects between the determinant constructs. However, those mediating effects are likely to be realistic, see, e.g., the papers of (Miranda/Kavan 2005; Poppo/Zenger 2002). See chapter 6.3.5 for a test of mediating influences in the model.

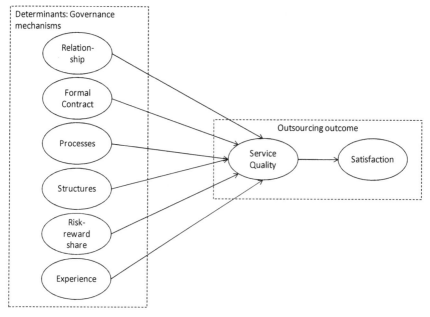

Figure 6-1. Governance research model

Construct	Item	Survey Question
Relational Go-vernance *reflective*	q3501	Trust is an important basis for our relationship.
	q3903	During the outsourcing project relationship management is very important.
	q3904	A cooperative collaboration with our service provider is important for our relationship.
Contractual Go-vernance *reflective*	q2301	The contractual agreement fully regulates all tasks and responsibilities for both partners.
	q2302	It is not a problem to cover and to control all tasks of the sourcing relationship in the contract.
	q2303	The contract itself is sufficient to cover and control all contingencies and events during the sourcing relationship.
	q2304	It is easy to specify the agreed tasks and expectations within the contract in detail.
Processes *formative*	q2501	We defined detailed processes for the SLA and contract management.
	q2502	We defined detailed performance and service level management processes that the service provider has to follow.
	q2503	We agreed on a detailed strategy process that controls and balances both partners' intentions.
	q2504	We agreed on a benchmarking process to compare our service providers' prices and performances with the market on a regular basis.

Construct	Item	Survey Question
Management Structures *formative*	q2601	An integral part of the governance is carried out by a committee that decides on decision-making powers, roles and activities within the sourcing relationship.
	q2602	An integral part of the controlling is carried out by a person in charge on our side who is the dedicated contact for our service provider (e.g., relationship manager).
	q2603	We control the relationship by an external consultant who takes care of all issues of the sourcing relationship.
Risk-reward share *reflective*	q3801	We agreed on a model of risk and benefit sharing with our service provider.
	q3802	Both our service provider and we take profit from the project, but we also both bear potential losses.
	q3803	We both share all opportunities and risks that are associated with the outsourcing equally.
Experience *reflective*	q2802	Our employees have experience with outsourcing projects.
	q2803	We have enough know-how to control the outsourcing project.
Service Quality *reflective*	q4401	The service delivery of the outsourcing provider is reliable.
	q4402	We are satisfied with our service provider's delivered quality.
	q4403	The overall quality of the sourcing relationship is high.
Satisfaction *reflective*	q4301	Overall, we are satisfied with the outsourcing project.
	q4302	We think that the outsourcing benefit is higher than the costs.
	q4303	From today's point of view sourcing is an attractive option that we would engage in again.
	q4304	From today's point of view we will renew the current outsourcing agreement.

Table 6-1. Construct measurement

6.2   Research Approach and Validation

In order to validate the causal model with its constructs and indicators elaborated in chapter 6.1 (p. 215ff.), the research model was operationalized and transferred into a structural equation model (SEM) to be analyzed with the Partial Least Squares (PLS) approach (Chin 1998; Wold 1985). In contrast to covariance-based approaches as, e.g., LISREL, AMOS, or EQS, PLS has minimal demands on measurement scales, sample size, and normal/residual distribution (Chin 1998). PLS is particularly suitable if a more explorative analysis close to the empirical data is appropriate and preferred (Chin 1998). It is also better suited for explaining complex relationships (Fornell/Bookstein 1982; Wold 1985, 589). A distinction can be made between the use of covariance structural approaching for theory versus predictive application (Fornell/Bookstein 1982; Chin/Marcolin/Newsted 2003). This distinction is important because it has fundamental implications for the choice of estimation method and development of the underlying predictive model. As there is no strong theoretical foundation on the impact of different governance mechanisms on outsourcing success among various outsourcing client types, an explorative, yet model-testing approach is most appropriate and promising for this research.

Each construct in the research model is represented by a set of indicators that were measured on a fully anchored 7-point Likert scale expressing attitudes ranging from "strongly disagree"

(1) to "strongly agree" (7). Whenever possible, the measures used in the model were derived from other studies and from existing scales and adapted to the specific research domain. The resulting draft questionnaire was discussed with academics from the field and pre-tested independently with several IT managers that were excluded from the final sample (see chapter 5.1, p. 113ff.). Based on the insights acquired in these pre-tests, the questionnaire was modified to be precise and understandable for the target audience before being sent out. As to further details on the questionnaire design and the data collection, the description is to be found in chapter 5.2 and 5.3 (p. 122ff.) since the model is based on the same data as the calculations in chapter 5.

The model was tested for all four outsourcing client configurations as well as for the overall data sample. By testing the model not only with the group samples, but also with the overall data sample, one is able to show if and to corroborate the assumption that a differentiated view on outsourcing relationships is necessary to derive sensible recommendations. The groups and their potential differences were statistically analyzed using PLS multi-group analysis (Chin 2000).

6.3   Model Validation and Results

All calculations for the following analysis of the measurement model were carried out with PLS-Graph Version 3.0. Settings were left to default, except the number of bootstrap samples, which was increased to 500. Compared to covariance-based structural equation modeling methods such as EQS, AMOS, and LISREL, PLS does not require a large sample size (Fornell/Bookstein 1982). According to a general rule established by Chin (1998, 311) the minimum number of data points is ten times the larger of the largest number of formative indicators constructing a latent variable (i.e., the largest measurement equation) or the largest number of independent constructs impacting a dependent construct (i.e., the largest structural equation). As another rule Chin et al. (1998) indicate that five data points for each path leading to the construct that has the most incoming paths is sufficient. The number of independent constructs in the model is six and the largest number of formative indicators is four, for the "processes" construct. Taking the larger number, the minimum sample size required is 60 data points. For the overall model this sample size requirement is satisfied. Since the overall data set is split up in four groups whereas the smallest group consists of 44 data points, the sample size requirement is still satisfied taking Chin's rule of the largest number of formative indicators. Overall, for all calculations reported in this thesis, this sample size requirement is satisfied.

6.3.1   Formative Measurement Model

In the model, the determinants of the formation of management processes and organizational management structures were operationalized in formative mode. In order to determine the relationship between the measures and the constructs applied in the research model (whether the constructs should be operationalized with a reflective or formative indicator measurement model) the four sets of questions suggested by Jarvis et al. (2003) were applied. Thereby, the relationship between the items and their constructs was examined by using conceptual and statistical criteria (Jarvis/MacKenzie/Podsakoff 2003) and also the semantic logic was assured with regard to the content (Rossiter 2002). In addition and in line with Rossiter (2002), opinions, expertise, and knowledge of experts were involved in pre-tests to develop items and constructs and used existing scales and constructs developed in extant research (see also the qualitative pre-study in chapter 5.1, p. 113ff.). Some of the constructs, i.e., processes and structures, could have been operationalized with both formative and reflective indicators. However, according to Huber et al. (2007), the constructs should be operationalized in a formative mode if manifest, measureable, and designable aspects of the construct are of interest. In this model, it was also of interest which items shape and constitute the determinants of the formation of outsourcing success with regard to different governance modes. Therefore, these constructs were operationalized in formative mode as they also meet the criteria put forward in Jarvis et al. (2003) for formative measurement models.

To evaluate the quality of the formative measurement model, the design of constructs (Diamantopoulos/Winklhofer 2001) as well as the relevance of indicators (Chin 1998) has to be analyzed.

According to the findings of Diamantopoulos and Winklhofer (2001) and Chin (1998) five critical issues to determine the quality of the measurement model have to be investigated: (1) content specification, (2) indicator specification, (3) indicator reliability, (4) indicator collinearity and (5) external validity.

Content specification consists of defining the scope of the latent constructs to be measured. This is of particular importance, as within formative models the indicators form the latent variable. "The breadth of definition is extremely important to causal indicators" (Nunnally/Bernstein 1994), because "failure to consider all facets of the construct will lead to an exclusion of relevant indicators" (Diamantopoulos/Winklhofer 2001). The research model included two latent constructs to be measured with formative indicators: management processes and organizational structures. These constructs were precisely defined and their domain intensively discussed, ensuring the proper specification of the applicable content of all the constructs deployed (see chapter 3.6, p. 49ff.).

Indicator specification comprises the identification and definition of indicators which constitute the latent constructs. As the aggregation of all formative indicators defines the scope of the formatively measured latent variable, indicator specification is particularly important for models using formative indicators (Diamantopoulos/Winklhofer 2001). The indicators used in this model were identified by intensive literature review and have been validated through a series of in-depth expert interviews with IT executives on the client side and also account managers on the vendor side who were knowledgeable about the topic of this research. Following their input, some initial indicators have been altered to become more precise and understandable for the target audience.

Indicator reliability analyzes the importance of each individual indicator that forms the relevant construct. Two quantitative arguments have to be accounted for: (1) the sign of the indicator needs to be correct as hypothesized and, (2) the weighting of the indicator should be at least 0.1 (Seltin/Keeves 1994) or 0.2 (Chin 1998). While in the overall data set, these criteria were mostly fulfilled (with few exceptions), the multi-group analysis revealed that some indicators did not fulfill the requirements in some of the four groups (i.e., sub data sets). Although eliminating indicators which do not fulfill the set criteria is in some cases recommended (Seltin/Keeves 1994), all indicators were kept in the model because the indicator itself fulfilled the requirements. The insufficiencies (e.g., negative signs or values below 0.1) only appeared in some of the four groups. In other groups the indicator fulfilled all requirements. In order to show which of the indicators have a significant effect in which group and which do not all indicators were left in the model. This is especially of interest to show differences in the four client groups.

Because formative measurement models are based on multiple regression and linear equation systems, substantial indicator collinearity would affect the stability of indicator coefficients (Diamantopoulos/Winklhofer 2001). In this study, multicollinearity among the indicators used did not pose a problem. The maximum variance inflation factor (VIF) was far below the common cut-off threshold of 10 (Cohen 2003) and even below the more conservative VIF threshold of 3.3 (except for two indicator values in group 2) (Diamantopoulos/Siguaw 2006). No further indicators needed to be rejected as no redundancy was identified. See appendix A 48 for VIF values of all four groups as well as for the overall sample.

External validity ensures the suitability of the deployed indicators and is of special importance for formative measurement models if indicators need to be eliminated. External validity shows the extent to which formative indicators actually capture the construct (Chin 1998). Following Diamantopoulos and Winklhofer (2001), external validity can be tested by using nomological aspects linking the formative construct with another construct to be expected as antecedent or consequence, i.e., by creating a phantom construct that is measured using reflective indicators. If the formatively measured construct strongly and significantly correlates with the reflectively measured construct, external validity is proven. The correlations of constructs within the tested model were all strong and significant at the 0.001 level. Thus, it was shown that the formative indicators used in this study actually form their respective constructs.

6.3.2 Reflective Measurement Model

Tests were conducted to show validity of the model constructs for all four client groups (sub samples). Before conducting the actual multi-group analysis comparison, it is necessary to ensure that the measures perform adequately for each group. The quality of the reflective measurement model is determined by (1) *convergent validity*, (2) *construct reliability*, and (3) *discriminant validity* (Bagozzi 1979; Churchill 1979; Peter 1981).

Convergent validity is analyzed by indicator reliability and construct reliability (Peter 1981). *Indicator reliability* can be examined by looking at the construct loadings. In the model tested, all loadings are significant at least at the 0.01 level (most of the indicators are significant at an extremely high level of 0.001) and above the recommended 0.7 parameter value (Carmines/Zeller 1979, 27), except for two indicators measuring the relational governance construct and two indicators measuring the contract construct in group 4, one indicator measuring the risk-reward share construct in group 1 and 2, and some values in the overall sample. However, as outlined by Hulland (1999, 198) new developed constructs may have relatively low indicator loadings and those low-reliability items must be interpreted with caution. Just like the formatively measure indicators were handled, also all reflectively measured indicators were kept in the model because the indicator itself fulfilled the requirements. The insufficiencies only appeared in some of the four groups. In other groups the indicator fulfilled all requirements. In order to show which of the indicators have a significant effect in which group and which do not all indicators were left in the model. This is especially of interest to show differences in the four client groups.

Construct reliability was tested using (1) the *composite reliability* (CR) and (2) the *average variance extracted* (AVE) (Fornell/Larcker 1981, 45). Estimated indices were above the recommended thresholds of 0.6 (Bagozzi/Yi 1988, 82) resp. 0.7 (Nunnally 1978, 245) for CR and 0.5 for AVE (Fornell/Larcker 1981, 46; Rodgers/Pavlou/Guiral 2003, 25), except for the relational governance and the contract constructs in group 4, as well as for the risk-reward share construct in group 1. Also the values of CR and AVE in the overall sample were below the threshold. For a detailed analysis of the indicator and construct reliability of all groups and the overall sample, see Table 6-2.

Discriminant validity of the construct items was assured by looking at the cross-loadings. They are obtained by correlating the component scores of each latent variable with both their respective block of indicators and all other items that are included in the model (Chin 1998, 321). As depicted in Table 6-3 to Table 6-7, all items load higher on their respective construct than on any other construct[21]. Furthermore, the square root of the AVE for each construct is higher than correlations between constructs. Therefore, discriminant validity for all four samples and also the overall sample is implied.

---

[21] There are only very few exceptions marked in light gray in Table 6-3 to Table 6-7, where an item loads higher on a "foreign" construct than the actual item that belongs to the construct.

Construct	Item	Group 1: Business-efficiency clients (n=44)				Group 2: Cost-conscious smart shoppers (n=50)				Group 3: Strategists and innovation seekers (n=51)				Group 4: IT excellence and reliability-oriented clients (n=45)				Overall data sample (n=196)			
		Load/Weight	Sign. Level	CR	AVE	Load/Weight	Sign. Level	CR	AVE	Load/Weight	Sign. Level	CR	AVE	Load/Weight	Sign. Level	CR	AVE	Load/Weight	Sign. Level	CR	AVE
Relational Governance *reflective*	q3501	0.7394	0.001			0.7887	0.001			0.7347	0.001			0.8607	0.007			0.7952	0.001		
	q3903	0.8771	0.001			0.7672	0.001			0.7102	0.001			-0.2159	*n.s.*			0.7733	0.001		
	q3904	0.9231	0.001	0.886	0.723	0.8688	0.001	0.85	0.655	0.8715	0.001	0.818	0.601	0.1302	*n.s.*	*0.4*	*0.27*	0.8943	0.001	0.862	0.677
Contractual Governance *reflective*	q2301	0.8056	0.001			0.6823	0.001			0.8761	0.001			0.9533	0.002			0.8071	0.001		
	q2302	0.9098	0.001			0.8863	0.001			0.8665	0.001			0.6187	0.02			0.8864	0.001		
	q2303	0.8884	0.001			0.9015	0.001			0.7206	0.001			0.2536	*n.s.*			0.8049	0.001		
	q2304	0.7814	0.001	0.911	0.719	0.9066	0.001	0.911	0.721	0.6433	0.01	0.862	0.613	0.2216	*n.s.*	*0.62*	*0.35*	0.7861	0.001	0.893	0.676
Processes *formative*	q2501	0.5092	*n.s.*			0.7724	*n.s.*			0.1398	*n.s.*			1.0825	*n.s.*			0.707	*n.s.*		
	q2502	0.0138	*n.s.*			-0.1386	*n.s.*			0.861	*n.s.*			-0.2239	*n.s.*			0.4326	*n.s.*		
	q2503	-0.423	*n.s.*			0.6637	*n.s.*			0.0128	*n.s.*			-0.7092	*n.s.*			-0.1867	*n.s.*		
	q2504	0.7762	0.04			-1.2314	0.04			0.0361	*n.s.*			0.2578	*n.s.*			-0.0141	*n.s.*		
Management Structures *formative*	q2601	-0.443	*n.s.*			0.4326	*n.s.*			0.5655	*n.s.*			0.3729	*n.s.*			-0.2204	*n.s.*		
	q2602	-0.235	*n.s.*			-0.7837	0.001			0.5303	*n.s.*			-0.2504	*n.s.*			0.829	0.001		
	q2603	0.8092	0.07			0.3795	*n.s.*			-0.494	*n.s.*			0.7882	0.01			-0.314	*n.s.*		
Risk-reward share *reflective*	q3801	0.3341	*n.s.*			0.4769	*n.s.*			0.8784	0.03			0.9002	0.001			-0.0969	*n.s.*		
	q3802	0.6976	0.001			0.9405	0.003			0.6068	0.04			0.945	0.001			0.6226	0.01		
	q3803	0.8472	0.001	*0.68*	*0.44*	0.9087	0.005	0.836	0.646	0.716	0.02	0.782	0.551	0.9332	0.001	0.948	0.858	0.6799	0.01	*0.48*	*0.27*
Experience *reflective*	q2802	0.7274	0.001			0.5425	0.02			0.7738	0.001			0.5601	0.09			0.6687	0.001		
	q2803	0.9647	0.02	0.841	0.73	0.9918	0.001	0.765	0.639	0.8956	0.001	0.823	0.7	0.9982	0.001	0.779	0.655	0.9729	0.001	0.816	0.697
Service Quality *reflective*	q4401	0.8307	0.001			0.9561	0.001			0.9577	0.001			0.8947	0.001			0.9288	0.001		
	q4402	0.9456	0.001			0.9275	0.001			0.9693	0.001			0.9569	0.001			0.9514	0.001		
	q4403	0.9203	0.001	0.927	0.81	0.9437	0.001	0.96	0.888	0.9557	0.001	0.973	0.923	0.9151	0.001	0.945	0.851	0.9433	0.001	0.959	0.886
Satisfaction *reflective*	q4301	0.8929	0.001			0.9068	0.001			0.8909	0.001			0.8965	0.001			0.8966	0.001		
	q4302	0.7781	0.001			0.7	0.001			0.6865	0.001			0.6099	0.001			0.7251	0.001		
	q4303	0.7604	0.001			0.8255	0.001			0.9104	0.001			0.7574	0.001			0.8317	0.001		
	q4304	0.8204	0.001	0.887	0.663	0.8429	0.001	0.892	0.676	0.5421	0.007	0.851	0.597	0.8627	0.001	0.866	0.623	0.7417	0.001	0.877	0.643

Insufficient or non-significant values are marked in italics.

Table 6-2. Indicator and construct reliability for group data samples and overall sample

	RelationalGov	Contract	Risk-reward	Experience	ServiceQuality	Satisfaction
q3501	0.739**	0.153	0.105	-0.082	0.273	0.232
q3903	0.877**	0.123	0.219	-0.072	0.326*	0.185
q3904	0.923**	0.002	0.333*	-0.106	0.384*	0.256
q2301	0.046	0.806**	-0.118	0.249	0.244	0.235
q2302	0.102	0.910**	-0.091	0.456**	0.283	0.208
q2303	0.116	0.888**	0.009	0.152	0.330*	0.222
q2304	0.046	0.781**	0.016	0.217	0.172	0.106
q3801	0.057	-0.125	0.334*	0.109	-0.075	-0.175
q3802	0.117	-0.177	0.698**	0.135	0.007	-0.145
q3803	0.213	-0.103	0.847**	0.09	0.125	-0.042
q2802	-0.122	0.300*	0.077	0.727**	0.132	0.171
q2803	-0.081	0.276	0.028	0.965**	0.345*	0.388**
q4401	0.285	0.218	0.242	0.194	0.831**	0.589**
q4402	0.360*	0.288	0.178	0.247	0.946**	0.711**
q4403	0.393**	0.331*	0.254	0.392**	0.920**	0.803**
q4301	0.331*	0.267	0.132	0.346*	0.751**	0.893**
q4302	0.116	0.267	0.038	0.305*	0.551**	0.778**
q4303	0.123	0.011	0.059	0.238	0.488**	0.761**
q4304	0.237	0.183	0.023	0.289	0.721**	0.820**

** correlation significant at a 0.01 level; * correlation significant at a 0.05 level

Table 6-3. PLS crossloadings of reflectively measured constructs for group sample 1

	RelationalGov	Contract	Risk-reward	Experience	ServiceQuality	Satisfaction
q3501	0.789**	0.11	-0.119	0.07	0.320*	0.208
q3903	0.767**	0.061	0.004	0.379**	0.195	0.201
q3904	0.869**	0.134	-0.005	0.362**	0.362**	0.362**
q2301	0.008	0.682**	0.351*	0.294*	0.19	0.252
q2302	0.09	0.886**	0.301*	0.314*	0.377**	0.369**
q2303	0.135	0.902**	0.313*	0.257	0.489**	0.342*
q2304	0.158	0.907**	0.412**	0.375**	0.515**	0.452**
q3801	0.124	0.168	0.477**	0.234	-0.046	-0.08
q3802	-0.042	0.386**	0.940**	0.2	0.138	0.114
q3803	0.007	0.334*	0.909**	0.19	0.097	0.085
q2802	0.029	0.104	0.288*	0.543**	0.091	0.153
q2803	0.337*	0.371**	0.15	0.992**	0.601**	0.530**
q4401	0.334*	0.490**	0.195	0.581**	0.956**	0.791**
q4402	0.304*	0.466**	0.129	0.553**	0.927**	0.710**
q4403	0.432**	0.451**	0.115	0.483**	0.944**	0.814**
q4301	0.355*	0.436**	0.119	0.535**	0.892**	0.907**
q4302	0.145	0.228	0.21	0.234	0.444**	0.700**
q4303	0.133	0.256	0.144	0.524**	0.562**	0.825**
q4304	0.378**	0.425**	0.035	0.346*	0.675**	0.843**

** correlation significant at a 0.01 level; * correlation significant at a 0.05 level

Table 6-4. PLS crossloadings of reflectively measured constructs for group sample 2

	RelationalGov	Contract	Risk-reward	Experience	ServiceQuality	Satisfaction
q3501	0.735**	0.271	-0.142	0.184	0.565**	0.558**
q3903	0.710**	0.098	0.038	0.279*	0.294*	0.248
q3904	0.871**	0.19	-0.15	0.317*	0.591**	0.656**
q2301	0.347*	0.876**	0.196	0.171	0.485**	0.432**
q2302	0.181	0.867**	0.127	0.217	0.339*	0.24
q2303	0.153	0.721**	0.181	-0.104	0.281*	0.1
q2304	0.003	0.643**	0.254	0.068	0.215	0.145
q3801	-0.176	0.359**	0.878**	-0.091	-0.064	-0.119
q3802	-0.08	0.1	0.607**	-0.036	0.029	-0.006
q3803	-0.038	-0.027	0.716**	-0.166	-0.058	-0.165
q2802	0.063	-0.027	-0.300*	0.774**	0.233	0.174
q2803	0.426**	0.212	-0.048	0.896**	0.332*	0.433**
q4401	0.692**	0.373**	-0.107	0.338*	0.958**	0.826**
q4402	0.634**	0.471**	-0.079	0.332*	0.969**	0.772**
q4403	0.584**	0.451**	-0.11	0.321*	0.956**	0.831**
q4301	0.650**	0.376**	-0.113	0.329*	0.844**	0.891**
q4302	0.352*	0.2	-0.169	0.204	0.485**	0.686**
q4303	0.539**	0.23	-0.244	0.338*	0.683**	0.910**
q4304	0.518**	0.164	-0.15	0.309*	0.506**	0.542**

** correlation significant at a 0.01 level; * correlation significant at a 0.05 level

Table 6-5. PLS crossloadings of reflectively measured constructs for group sample 3

	RelationalGov	Contract	Risk-reward	Experience	Service Quality	Satisfaction
q3501	0.861**	0.404**	0.273	0.274	0.19	0.179
q3903	-0.216	0.049	0.139	0.320*	-0.107	-0.032
q3904	0.13	0.099	0.131	0.385**	0.009	0.064
q2301	0.400**	0.953**	0.161	0.158	0.319*	0.443**
q2302	0.074	0.619**	0.111	0.259	0.125	0.364*
q2303	0.08	0.254	0.025	-0.026	-0.09	0.094
q2304	-0.042	0.222	0.223	0.078	-0.069	0.177
q3801	0.119	0.178	0.900**	0.072	-0.112	0.103
q3802	0.173	0.112	0.945**	0.006	-0.132	0.026
q3803	0.25	0.109	0.933**	-0.069	-0.167	-0.038
q2802	0.077	-0.06	-0.1	0.560**	-0.013	-0.025
q2803	0.115	0.218	-0.014	0.998**	0.174	0.259
q4401	0.245	0.448**	-0.073	0.195	0.895**	0.735**
q4402	0.232	0.334*	-0.175	0.103	0.957**	0.714**
q4403	0.223	0.256	-0.177	0.209	0.915**	0.650**
q4301	0.264	0.490**	0.048	0.24	0.720**	0.896**
q4302	-0.008	0.202	-0.144	0.183	0.421**	0.610**
q4303	0.067	0.316*	0.182	0.209	0.483**	0.757**
q4304	0.228	0.450**	-0.027	0.228	0.706**	0.863**

** correlation significant at a 0.01 level; * correlation significant at a 0.05 level

Table 6-6. PLS crossloadings of reflectively measured constructs for group sample 4

	RelationalGov	Contract	Risk-reward	Experience	Service Quality	Satisfaction
q3501	0.795**	0.179*	-0.001	0.086	0.411**	0.311**
q3903	0.773**	0.074	-0.042	0.218**	0.240**	0.181*
q3904	0.894**	0.154*	0.047	0.200**	0.451**	0.384**
q2301	0.172*	0.807**	-0.056	0.200**	0.333**	0.350**
q2302	0.140*	0.886**	-0.092	0.288**	0.294**	0.292**
q2303	0.136	0.805**	0.006	0.058	0.271**	0.184**
q2304	0.121	0.786**	0.051	0.168*	0.260**	0.229**
q3801	0.105	0.171*	-0.097	0.100	-0.039	-0.058
q3802	0.068	0.093	0.622**	0.080	0.031	0.006
q3803	0.101	0.103	0.680**	0.029	0.026	-0.021
q2802	0.076	0.079	0.068	0.669**	0.098	0.112
q2803	0.206**	0.237**	-0.043	0.973**	0.315**	0.385**
q4401	0.406**	0.333**	0.121	0.283**	0.929**	0.753**
q4402	0.430**	0.348**	0.052	0.258**	0.951**	0.727**
q4403	0.488**	0.323**	0.047	0.283**	0.943**	0.778**
q4301	0.415**	0.329**	0.106	0.323**	0.827**	0.897**
q4302	0.215**	0.207**	-0.016	0.230**	0.500**	0.725**
q4303	0.231**	0.217**	0.057	0.302**	0.579**	0.832**
q4304	0.299**	0.273**	-0.025	0.277**	0.595**	0.742**

** correlation significant at a 0.01 level; * correlation significant at a 0.05 level

Table 6-7. PLS crossloadings of reflectively measured constructs for overall sample

6.3.3 Structural Model

After having gained confidence that the item measures work appropriately for the four groups and the overall sample and after having identified possible insufficiencies and weaknesses where interpreting the results has to be cautious, the structural model is evaluated. The adequacy of constructs in the structural model not only allows to evaluate the explanatory power of the entire model, but also to estimate the predictive power of the independent variables for the four groups. Again, in order to show the advantage of analyzing the data sample in separate client groups, the model will be calculated for the overall sample as well.

The *explanatory power* is examined by looking at the squared multiple correlations (R^2) of the dependent variables. In all groups and in the overall sample, more than 30% of the variation of service quality is explained by the independent variables, i.e., the six governance mechanisms, which is sufficiently high. Particularly the R^2 value for group 2 and group 3 is astonishingly high, with R^2 values higher than 0.5. The R^2 value for group 4 is relatively low with a value of only 0.338 (see discussion section for an explanation). Also the R^2 values for the dependent variable outsourcing satisfaction are encouragingly high, with all values beyond 0.5 (see Figure 6-2 to Figure 6-6 for detailed results).

One cannot only look at the absolute R^2 values for each dependent latent variable provided by PLS for the structural model, but also at the change of R^2 in order to see whether the impact of a particular independent construct on a dependent construct has substantive impact (Chin

1998). This is calculated by the effect size (f^2). f^2 of .02, .15, and .35 can be viewed as a gauge for whether a predictor latent variable has a small, medium, or large effect at the structural level (Cohen 1988, 410pp.). Analysis of the overall effect size (f^2) of the antecedents of service quality as well as outsourcing satisfaction reveals that depending on the group, the effect size of the construct varies, indicating a smaller or higher impact of the specific governance mode on outsourcing success (see Table 6-8 for the detailed values; medium or high values are marked in gray).

Path	Group 1			Group 2			Group 3			Group 4			Overall Sample		
	R^2 incl.	R^2 excl.	f^2 value	R^2 incl.	R^2 incl.	R^2 excl.	f^2 value	R^2 excl.	f^2 value	R^2 incl.	R^2 excl.	f^2 value	R^2 incl.	R^2 excl.	f^2 value
Relationship - Service Quality	0.423	0.308	0.20	0.582	0.338	0.315	0.03	0.554	0.07	0.559	0.314	0.56	0.346	0.211	0.21
Contract - Service Quality	0.423	0.416	0.01	0.582	0.338	0.246	0.14	0.549	0.08	0.559	0.464	0.22	0.346	0.294	0.08
Processes - Service Quality	0.423	0.361	0.11	0.582	0.338	0.32	0.03	0.559	0.06	0.559	0.542	0.04	0.346	0.345	0.00
Structures - Service Quality	0.423	0.375	0.08	0.582	0.338	0.232	0.16	0.492	0.22	0.559	0.557	0.00	0.346	0.328	0.03
Risk-reward - Service Quality	0.423	0.415	0.01	0.582	0.338	0.335	0.00	0.581	0.00	0.559	0.558	0.00	0.346	0.338	0.01
Experience - Service Quality	0.423	0.377	0.08	0.582	0.338	0.335	0.00	0.481	0.24	0.559	0.536	0.05	0.346	0.323	0.04
Service Quality - Satisfaction	0.621	0	1.64	0.672	0.579	0	1.38	0	2.05	0.711	0	2.46	0.64	0	1.78

Table 6-8. f^2 effect size values for all four client groups

Predictive power is tested by examining the magnitude of the standardized parameter estimates between constructs together with the corresponding t-values that indicate the level of significance. It is recommended that the path coefficients exceed the 0.2 level (Chin 1998). As the aim of the multi-group approach was to identify which governance modes are most appropriate and mostly impact on outsourcing success, not every governance mechanism has a strong impact in every group. Figure 6-2 to Figure 6-6 show which mechanisms have a strong and highly significant impact on outsourcing success in the respective client group. For example, in group 1, relational governance as well as management processes have a strong influence on outsourcing success (path coefficient of 0.360 resp. 0.281) and are deemed to be appropriate governance modes for business-efficiency clients. Looking at the overall sample reveals that relational as well as formal governance have a significant and strong impact on service quality. But these governance mechanisms do not necessarily reflect appropriate approaches for specific clients (see discussion section for a detailed interpretation).

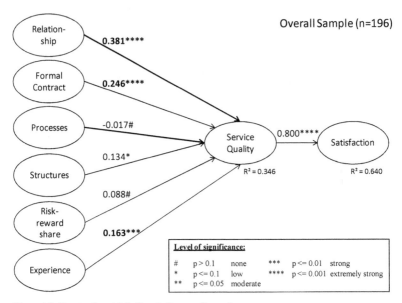

Figure 6-2. Structural model findings in the overall sample

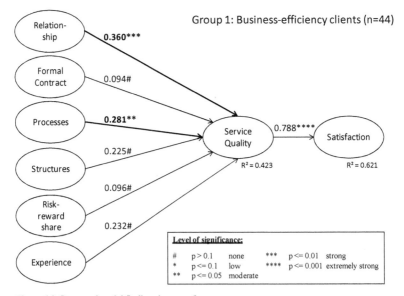

Figure 6-3. Structural model findings in group 1

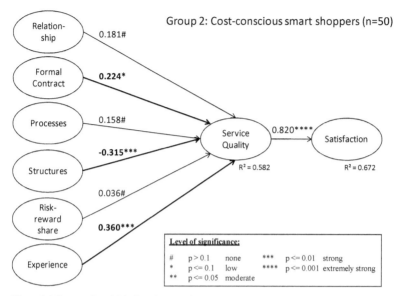

Figure 6-4. Structural model findings in group 2

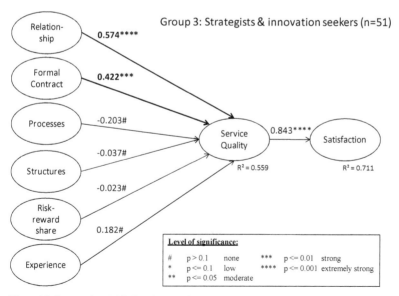

Figure 6-5. Structural model findings in group 3

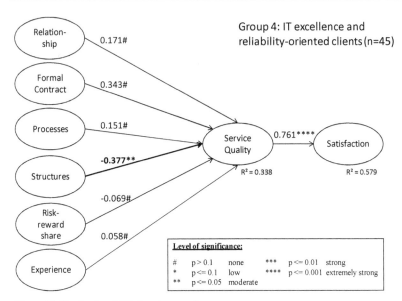

Figure 6-6. Structural model findings in group 4

6.3.4 Group Analysis: The Impact of Different Governance Mechanisms among the Four Client Groups

When analyzing the path coefficients of each of the four groups, one cannot only see that some governance mechanisms play an important role for a certain client group while others are not significant at all, but one can also see that the importance of certain governance mechanisms changes across the four groups. So after having analyzed the path coefficients of each group separately, it is of great interest to know whether the groups significantly differ from each other and if so, where and how.

The ideal approach for a multi-group comparison would be to do it non-parametrically and use a permutation approach which requires to randomly select cases from the combined multi-group set for each group and which is still under development in PLS Graph (Chin 2004). The other approach, which is the most expedient, is to treat the estimates of the re-sampling in a parametric sense via t-tests. Making a parametric assumption and taking the standard errors for the structural paths provided by PLS-Graph in the re-sampling output allows the research-er to hand calculate the t-test for the difference in paths between pairs of groups. The following formula was used in this thesis to calculate the t-values for the group differences of the path coefficients for a pair of groups (taken from Chin 2004):

$$t = \frac{Path_{sample\_1} - Path_{sample\_2}}{\left[\sqrt{\frac{(m-1)^2}{(m+n-2)} * S.E._{sample\_1}^2 + \frac{(n-1)^2}{(m+n-2)} * S.E._{sample\_2}^2}\right] * \left[\sqrt{\frac{1}{m} + \frac{1}{n}}\right]}$$

Table 6-9 shows the statistical results as well as the according levels of significance. From these results one can draw the conclusion that the impact of governance mechanisms on outsourcing success differs depending on the specific examined outsourcing intent resp. outsourcing client group (see discussion section for further interpretation of the results). It is important to notice that the t-test procedure suggested by Chin (2004) for multi-group comparison in PLS models only compares pairs of groups. Consequently, 6 pairs of groups had to be analyzed to investigate potential differences in the four groups.

Group (t-values) Path	Group 1 vs. Group 2	Group 1 vs. Group 3	Group 1 vs. Group 4	Group 2 vs. Group 3	Group 2 vs. Group 4	Group 3 vs. Group 4
Relational Governance → Service Quality	1.03	-1.09	0.84	-2.20**	0.05	1.81*
Formal Contract → Service Quality	-0.73	-1.62*	-0.94	-1.05	-0.48	0.30
Processes → Service Quality	0.58	2.13**	0.45	1.55	0.02	-1.19
Structures → Service Quality	2.8***	1.29	2.57***	-1.64*	0.31	1.63*
Risk-reward Share → Service Quality	0.28	0.57	0.75	0.31	0.52	0.24
Experience → Service Quality	-0.65	0.24	0.75	1.04	1.55	0.61
Service Quality → Satisfaction	-0.47	-0.83	0.25	-0.50	0.65	0.92

*** correlation significant at a 0.01 level; ** correlation significant at a 0.05 level; * correlation significant at a 0.1 level

Table 6-9. PLS multi-group comparison of structural model: t-values and level of significance for group differences between the four client groups

6.3.5 Mediating Effects in the Model

Structural equation models can become rather complex when trying to depict real-world phenomena. A literature review by Eggert et al. (2005) revealed that researchers struggle with two problems when applying structural equation models: first, many researchers assume mediating effects in their model, i.e., the effect of an exogenous variable on an endogenous variable is mediated by a third variable, but do not test for those effects. Second, moderating effects, i.e., effects on the relation between two variables, are rather neglected although literature explicitly emphasizes the importance of those effects (Chin/Marcolin/Newsted 2003). Moderating effects by, e.g., contingency variables such as industry, firm size etc. were not in the focus of this model. In its original version (see Figure 6-1) the model developed in this thesis did not account for mediating effects either. However, two mediating effects can be assumed based on the literature and should therefore be tested:

1. The interplay of contractual and relational governance has been a pervasive issue and research concern in the strategic management and also in the IS outsourcing literature (see also chapter 3.6.3.3, p. 56ff., for a detailed elaboration on the interplay). It is yet unclear whether these governance mechanisms work as substitutes or as complements. Many researchers argue for a complementary view, but even if one assumes a complementary relationship, how do both modes interact with each other. Rather than a parallel existence of the two governance devices, one could assume an indirect subsequent effect, with relational governance mediating the effect of formal contracts on outsourcing performance.

2. Risk-reward sharing mechanisms are usually seen as part of other formal governance modes, particularly the contract. Because of their outstanding and innovative character, these incentive mechanisms were tested as an independent construct in order to see their specific impact on outsourcing performance. However, one could yet assume that there is no direct effect, but rather an indirect effect of risk-reward sharing mechanisms on outsourcing performance via the contract.

According to Iacobucci and Duhachek (2003) a construct can be regarded as a mediator if (1) changes of the exogenous variable lead to significant effects of the mediating variable, (2) changes of the mediating variable lead to significant effects of the endogenous variable, and (3) the path coefficient between the exogenous and endogenous variable is significantly lower than the path coefficient in an alternative model without a mediating variable. This can be examined by looking at the z-value and the VAF (Variance accounted for) (Sobel 1982; Iacobucci/Duhachek 2003).

The two mediating effects, i.e., contractual via relational governance as well as risk-reward share mechanisms via contractual governance, were tested for all four groups. Surprisingly, only in group 3, i.e., the strategists and innovation seekers, a partial mediating effect of contractual through relational governance could be identified. The z-value was significant at the 0.07 level which supports the hypothesis that there is an indirect effect between contract and service quality via relational governance. The VAF depicts the degree of the mediating effect. The VAF value is 0.2661 which means that 26.61% of the effect of the exogenous variable (contract) on the endogenous variable (service quality) can be ascribed to the mediating variable (relational governance). As the path between the exogenous and endogenous variable is significantly different from zero, one can assume a partial mediation effect (Iacobucci/Duhachek 2003). In the other groups, no significant z-value could be found and also the VAF values were extremely low (see appendix A 49). Thus, one can reject a mediating effect for those groups.

A mediating effect of risk-reward share mechanisms via contractual governance could not be found in any of the four groups. Groups 2 and 4 show VAF values beyond 1, indicating a statistical suppressor effect. But no significant z-values could be found in any of the groups. Therefore, a mediating effect can be rejected for all four groups (see appendix A 49 for the mediating values in all groups).

6.4   Assessment of Common Method Bias

The influence of common methods variance (i.e., variance that is attributable to the measurement method rather than to the constructs the measures represent) has been a pervasively cited concern in behavioral organizational research (Podsakoff et al. 2003).

Method biases are a problem because they are one of the main sources of measurement error. Measurement error threatens the validity of the conclusions about the relationships between measures and is widely recognized to have both a random and a systematic component (see, e.g., Bagozzi/Yi/Phillips 1991; Nunnally 1978). Because common method biases can have potentially serious effects on research findings, it is important to understand their sources and when they are especially likely to become a problem. Podsakoff et al. (2003) summarize the most prominent potential sources of common method biases (see Table 6-10). They distinguish between four categories of potential CMB sources:

1. *Method effects produced by a common source or rater.* Here, the problem is caused by the fact that the respondent providing the measure of the predictor and criterion variable is the same person. This type of self-report bias might result from any artifactual covariance between the predictor and criterion variable produced by the fact that the respondent providing the measure of these variables is the same (Podsakoff et al. 2003, 881).

2. *Method effects produced by item characteristics.* Here, the bias may be produced by obtaining measures in which items are presented to respondents to produce artifactual covariance in the observed relationships. Then, the possibility that, in addition to its content, an item's form may also influence the scores obtained on a measure might be problematic (Podsakoff et al. 2003, 883).

3. *Method effects produced by item context.* Here, CMB might result from the context in which the items on a questionnaire are placed. Item context effects "refer to any influence or interpretation that a subject might ascribe to an item solely because of its relation to the other items making up an instrument" (Wainer/Kiely 1987, 187).

4. *Method effects produced by measurement context.* This last category of CMB sources refers to an artifactual covariation observed between constructs caused by the broader research context in which the measures are obtained. Major contextual influences are the time, location, and media used to measure the constructs.

Table 6-10 summarizes the most common potential sources of CMB by listing the four major categories and their corresponding sub-factors.

Potential cause	Definition
1. Common rater effects	Refer to any artifactual covariance between the predictor and criterion variable produced by the fact that the respondent providing the measure of these variables is the same.
Consistency motif	Refers to the propensity for respondents to try to maintain consistency in their responses to questions.
Implicit theories (and illusory correlations)	Refer to respondents' beliefs about the covariation among particular traits, behaviors, and/or outcomes.
Social desirability	Refers to the tendency of some people to respond to items more as a result of their social acceptability than their true feelings.
Leniency biases	Refer to the propensity for respondents to attribute socially desirable traits, attitudes, and/or behaviors to someone they know and like than to someone they dislike.
Acquiescence biases (yea-saying and nay-saying)	Refer to the propensity for respondents to agree (or disagree) with questionnaire items independent of their content.
Mood state (positive or negative affectivity; positive or negative emotionality)	Refers to the propensity of respondents to view themselves and the world around them in generally negative terms (negative affectivity) or the propensity of respondents to view themselves and the world around them in generally positive terms (positive affectivity).
Transient mood state	Refers to the impact of relatively recent mood-inducing events to influence the manner in which respondents view themselves and the world around them.
2. Item characteristic effects	Refer to any artifactual covariance that is caused by the influence or interpretation that a respondent might ascribe to an item solely because of specific properties or characteristics the item possesses.
Item social desirability	Refers to the fact that items may be written in such a way as to reflect more socially desirable attitudes, behaviors, or perceptions.
Item demand characteristics	Refer to the fact that items may convey hidden cues as to how to respond to them.
Item ambiguity	Refers to the fact that items that are ambiguous allow respondents to respond to them systematically using their own heuristic or respond to them randomly.
Common scale formats	Refer to artifactual covariation produced by the use of the same scale format (e.g., Likert scales, semantic differential scales, "faces" scales) on a questionnaire.
Common scale anchors	Refer to the repeated use of the same anchor points (e.g., extremely, always, never) on a questionnaire.
Positive and negative item wording	Refers to the fact that the use of positively (negatively) worded items may produce artifactual relationships on the questionnaire.
3. Item context effects	Refer to any influence or interpretation that a respondent might ascribe to an item solely because of its relation to the other items making up an instrument.
Item priming effects	Refer to the fact that the positioning of the predictor (or criterion) variable on the questionnaire can make that variable more salient to the respondent and imply a causal relationship with other variables.
Item embeddedness	Refers to the fact that neutral items embedded in the context of either positively or negatively worded items will take on the evaluative properties of those items.
Context-induced mood	Refers to when the first question (or set of questions) encountered on the questionnaire induces a mood for responding to the remainder of the questionnaire.
Scale length	Refers to the fact that if scales have fewer items, responses to previous items are more likely to be accessible in short-term memory and to be recalled when responding to other items.
Intermixing (or grouping) of items or constructs on the questionnaire	Refers to the fact that items from different constructs that are grouped together may decrease intraconstruct correlations and increase interconstruct correlations.
4. Measurement context effects	Refer to any artifactual covariation produced from the context in which the measures are obtained.
Predictor and criterion variables measured at the same point in time	Refers to the fact that measures of different constructs measured at the same point in time may produce artifactual covariance independent of the content of the constructs themselves.
Predictor and criterion variables measured in the same location	Refers to the fact that measures of different constructs measured in the same location may produce artifactual covariance independent of the content of the constructs themselves.
Predictor and criterion variables measured using the same medium	Refers to the fact that measures of different constructs measured with the same medium may produce artifactual covariance independent of the content of the constructs themselves.

Table 6-10. Summary of potential sources of common method biases
(Source: Podsakoff et al. 2003, 882)

Summarizing the table, common method biases can arise from having a common rater, a common measurement context, a common item context, or from the characteristics of the items themselves. Obviously and in many cases, in any given study, it is possible for several of these factors to be operative (Podsakoff et al. 2003). Although it is not always possible to avoid a CMB, it is important to carefully evaluate the conditions under which the data is obtained to assess the extent to which method biases might pose a problem.

Method biases are likely to be particularly powerful in studies in which the data for both the predictor and criterion variable are obtained from the same person in the same measurement context using the same item context and similar item characteristics (Podsakoff et al. 2003). These conditions are often present in behavioral research where many studies used some kind of self-report measure as either the primary or sole type of data gathered, as Sackett and Larson (1990) found.

But obviously, when designing a questionnaire and carrying out survey research, there is always a trade-off between practicability, standardization (e.g., by using established scale formats and anchors), and avoiding the trap of CMB.

The two primary ways to control for common methods biases are a) the design of the study's procedures (i.e., obtaining measures of the predictor and criterion variables from different sources, counterbalancing question order, or improving scale items), and b) statistical controls. While some design issues of the study in this thesis could not be prevented, e.g., the problem of single source measurement, statistical measures were used to control for a CMB threat. In order to evaluate a potential common method bias (CMB) of the study, the CMB was calculated based on a procedure recommended by Podsakoff et al. (2003, 887pp.). There are several statistical measures to control for the CMB (for an overview see Podsakoff et al. 2003). To ensure that common methods bias was not a significant problem in the data, the effects of an unmeasured latent method factor were controlled for, which is among the prominent approaches to control for a potential CMB. This method involves adding a first-order factor with all of the measures as indicators to the researcher's theoretical model and has been used in a number of studies (see e.g., Podsakoff et al. 2003). Thereby, each item is an indicator not only of its substantive trait, but also of an unmeasured latent method factor (Podsakoff et al. 2003). In short, besides theoretical constructs this procedure specifies an 'artificial' common method construct whose indicators consist of all used construct indicators. The variance explained by the common method constructs is then assessed relative to the variance explained by the substantive constructs. The significance of the structural parameters is examined both with and without the latent common method variance factor in the model.

One of the main advantages of this technique is that it does not require the researcher to identify and measure the specific factor responsible for the method effects. Also, no special scale needs to be administered and multiple types of method effects can be simultaneously modeled with the latent method factor. In addition, this technique models the effect of the method factor on the measures rather than on the latent constructs they represent and does not require the effects of the method factor on each measure to be equal. As with the explicitly modeled methods effect approach, this model controls for CMB via the factor loadings between the method factor and the indicators.

Among the disadvantages of this method is that although this technique controls for any systematic variance among the items that is independent of the covariance, it does not permit the researcher to identify the specific cause of the method bias (Podsakoff et al. 2003). Since it does not allow the researcher to identify the specific cause of the method variance, potential problems may be encountered with the identification of the model. Lastly, this technique assumes that the method factor does not interact with trait factors, i.e., the method factor does not interact with the predictor and criterion constructs.

Although this approach has some limitations, it is still attractive and widespread in use because it does not require the researcher to identify the potential source of the method variance in advance and delivers solid results.

The results of a potential common method bias measured for all four groups and also for the overall sample are depicted in appendix. As shown in appendices A 50 to A 54, the average variance explained by the substantive constructs is more than 66% in all groups as well as in the overall sample, while the average variance explained by the common method construct is less than 0.04. One can see that the third group has the worst CMB results, explaining "only" 66.9% of the variance by the substantive constructs, while 3.6% of the variance is explained by the CMB construct, but still these values are pretty fair (Podsakoff et al. 2003). This analysis sustains the conclusion that common methods bias did not impact the results of this study.

6.5   Discussion and Interpretation of Results

Analyzing the overall group and each of the four groups as well as the interrelation and differences among the groups reveals some astonishing findings.

In the overall sample as well as across all four groups, one dominant pattern could be identified, i.e., the perceived service quality with the outsourcing venture has a very strong and significant impact on outsourcing satisfaction.

This finding is in line with previous findings in the literature. Susarla et al. (2003) tested determinants of satisfaction with ASP and found that perceived provider performance (i.e., service quality in the case of this thesis) has a strong impact on satisfaction with ASP. Similarly, the data in this thesis shows that clients that perceive the quality of the service provided by the outsourcing vendor as high are satisfied with the outsourcing venture. Moreover, perceived service quality is a good predictor for outsourcing satisfaction, as can be interpreted from the high R^2 value. In all groups, the R^2 value is higher than 0.5 indicating that more than 50% of the variance of the satisfaction construct can be explained by the service quality construct.

In a next step, the determinants of service quality, i.e., the governance mechanisms, are analyzed in detail. The analysis of the overall sample reveals that relational as well as formal governance have a strong and significant impact on service quality. Also experience shows a significant path on service quality. These findings are in accordance with the literature that states that both formal and relational governance are important in an outsourcing relationship. However, as the detailed analysis of the different groups will show, this finding is not true for all clients. Consequently, as a next step, each of the groups will be analyzed and interpreted separately by its own before analyzing differences and similarities among the groups.

The first group is focused on business efficiency (see chapter 5.6, p. 205ff. for a detailed description of the group). Clients in this group have two governance mechanisms in place to manage their outsourcing venture successfully: Relational governance and governance via processes. Both path coefficients have a strong and significant impact on perceived service quality (0.360, p < 0.01; 0.281, p < 0.05) indicating that these two governance modes in contrast to the others (which show weak and not significant values) seem to impact the outsourcing success.

In order to understand and interpret the results, a closer look at this group might be helpful. As seen in chapter 5.6 (p. 205ff.), clients in this group are likely to be found in large companies. Moreover, these clients engage in multivendor outsourcing deals with more than 3 vendors and also engage (more than other clients) in business process outsourcing (BPO). Business process outsourcing is very knowledge-intense as it touches complex and sometimes even core processes of the client firm (Willcocks et al. 2004).

Given these characteristics of the business-efficiency group, governing via processes is a sensible management approach. When processes are formally laid out, both parties can more easily agree on how to work together and observe compliance (Mahoney/McNally 2004). Writing down business rules and procedures makes valuable business knowledge explicit and allows for more effective knowledge transfer between client and service provider. This is especially important in business process outsourcing deals with intense knowledge transfer and interaction.

When looking at the composition of the "governance via processes" construct in more detail, one can see that the item "benchmarking processes" holds a significant impact on the construct. Especially in extreme multi-vendor outsourcing arrangements with more than 3 vendors (as they are found predominantly in this group), benchmarking is an appropriate governance mechanism in order to ensure competitive market prices and best service quality (Reilly/Rouse/Seddon 2001).

Moreover, such a standardization of interactions and routines through processes leads to increased "embeddedness" (Uzzi 1997), which promotes the realization of mutual gains. Embeddedness is also promoted by a good relationship. Consequently, a governance approach with relational governance helps to promote such an embeddedness and a close interaction and relationship between client and vendor.

Surprisingly, other governance mechanisms, especially the contract, do not have any significant influence on the successful management (i.e., the perceived service quality) of the outsourcing venture. This might be explained by the fact that the contract is understood as a given (i.e., taken as granted) and is not mentioned as a special governance mechanism.

Group 2 comprises the cost-conscious smart shoppers. As predominant governance modes, the contract and staff experience could be identified which both have a highly significant (0.224, p < 0.1; 0.360, p < 0.01). A third governance mechanism shows a strong and highly significant, but negative impact, i.e., structural governance (-0.315, p < 0.01).

Recalling the description of this client group laid out in chapter 5.6 (p. 205ff.) shows that the cost-focused clients are a very down-to-earth, straightforward client group. They engage in medium-to-long term selective outsourcing arrangements with the traditional fixed price model. They are mostly found in medium-to-large size companies and have a large IT budget (to name only a few characteristics).

Since cost-cutting is one of the most obvious, basic, and oldest expectations and motivations to engage in an outsourcing arrangement, one could expect that this group entails inexperienced clients that are new to outsourcing and expect quick wins and heavy cost cuttings from sourcing parts of the information systems to a third-party provider (which is an unrealistic assumption, at least in the beginning of an outsourcing venture due to transaction costs etc., according to e.g., Kern/Willcocks/van Heck 2002; Willcocks/Lacity/Cullen 2006). On the other hand, one would expect that cost-focused clients strictly govern via the outsourcing contract and also via formalized structures, since formal governance mechanisms are rather easy to handle once they are set up (compared to more complex mechanisms such as relational governance) and also reasonable from a monetary perspective.

In line with this assumption, the formal contract is one of the main governance mechanisms that are applied by this client group. But more surprisingly, the analysis shows that the most prevailing governance mechanism is governance via staff experience[22]. Specifically, clients set managers and workers in place that have outsourcing experience from former outsourcing or client-vendor-relationship projects. They assign their experienced employees to work in an outsourcing relationship context and use staff experience rather than formalized or special informal relationship mechanisms to govern the outsourcing venture. Linking this finding with literature shows that the issue of managers' prior experience with outsourcing and its impact on the outsourcing management has been elaborated in quite a few studies (Benamati/Rajkumar 2002).

The findings here are also in line with Lacity and Willcocks (2003, 123) who found that clients that slowly and incrementally developed experience with outsourcing can feed back this experience into further outsourcing and thus govern the current outsourcing venture based on the experience collected from past experience with outsourcing. Furthermore, this finding revises the assumption that inexperienced customers strive for cost motives. Instead, customers that associate cost motives with their outsourcing decision are rather informed clients that have prior experience with outsourcing and also a realistic conception about what to achieve and what not to achieve with outsourcing. Consequently, they use the past experience of their staff to govern the cost-oriented outsourcing venture. Another argument for governance via staff experience is the degree of knowledge of the staff. A saying in another industry states that "retail is detail". This seems to be true also for IS outsourcing. When cost savings are the prevailing motives, efficiency is an issue of detail and detail is best achieved with experience. Consequently, one needs to set staff in place that knows the processes and parameters very well to identify options to save money. Hence, those employees are attributed with degrees of freedom regarding management decision rights.

---

[22] Staff experience is not to be mixed up with the overall experience of the company with outsourcing. Here, no differentiating results could be found (see chapter 5.5.3.1).

A last finding in this group is also counter-intuitive, i.e., the impact of management structures on the perceived service quality. Here, a strong and highly significant, but negative impact on service quality could be found. Rather than promoting the outsourcing venture, in the group of cost-oriented clients, structures such as a special relationship account manager or a steering committee seem to hinder a successful (i.e., cost-economic) outsourcing venture. Transaction cost theory provides a sensible explanation in this context in such that in market exchanges, the effort of exchanging information and getting an agreement on the service to be delivered is a significant part of transaction costs and leads to higher overall costs (Lacity/Hirschheim 1993a), which is counterproductive to the overall cost-saving goal of this group. An interme-diary (i.e., additional management structure) such as a relationship manager or a steering committee might increase those costs even more through the role itself and also due to coor-dination efforts.

Clients who strive for strategic advantages and innovation through outsourcing are comprised in group 3. Those clients primarily use the two "classic" governance mechanisms: the out-sourcing contract and relational governance. Both show a strong and highly significant impact on the perceived service quality (0.574, $p < 0.001$; 0.422, $p < 0.01$). Furthermore, in chapter 6.3.5 (p. 231ff.), a potential mediating effect between contract and relationship was tested and a partially mediating effect was found in such that the effect of contractual governance on service quality is partially mediated through relational governance.

The prevailing impact of relational governance on service quality can be explained by the inherent characteristics of this outsourcing relationship type. Strategy and innovation-focused outsourcing endeavors are characterized by uncertainty and reciprocal interdependence (Leimeister/Böhmann/Krcmar 2008). In such settings, the delivered outcome is uncertain as it cannot be specified a priori. This results in a high perceived risk which could be mitigated by using contractual agreements. But these circumstances do not permit the full specification of complete contracts and contracts alone are insufficient to govern the outsourcing venture (Gietzmann 1996). Instead, relational governance has to be set in place to balance uncertain-ties and risks inherent to innovation outsourcing. The close alignment of development activi-ties, the need to exchange technical knowledge and joint decision making thus require rela-tional governance through, e.g., constant communication. A study in the context of risk miti-gation in outsourcing through relational instruments showed that relational governance is mandatory in uncertain outsourcing situations (Wüllenweber/Jahner/Krcmar 2008).

Still, there is a considerable impact of contractual governance on service quality in this client group which is surprising given the limitations of this governance in situations with high un-certainty and reciprocal interdependence. Contracts, however, can facilitate innovation-seeking relationships in two ways. First, contracts can stipulate the right framework for rela-tional governance by defining institutions that facilitate ongoing communication, coordina-tion, and joint decision making. Contracts can define procedures for calculating uncertain activities, demand regular interaction between stakeholders on various levels, and finally de-fine procedures for contract change management. Secondly, contracts can also act as reposito-ries of interorganizational learning (Mayer/Argyres 2004). Firms may use contracts to docu-ment their evolving insight into the substance and the management of interorganizational rela-tionships. As long as uncertainty exists about the specific IT services needed for implementing a new service, contracts may not be able to define these services ex ante. This uncertainty may decrease over time when firms gain experience with the new service. Based on this knowledge, the outsourcing partners can amend their contract to reflect the learning about the services and their management.

Additionally, the mediating effect of contractual and relational governance in this setting can be explained by two arguments:

1. *Time and sequence of formal and relational governance*

   Instead of a parallel complementary relationship between formal contracts and relational governance, both governance devices should rather be seen in a sequence and time order as they are not developed contemporaneously. The nature of an outsourcing venture or relationship is not static, but changes and evolves over time (Argyres/Bercovitz/Mayer 2007, 6). Usually, the contract and an informal relationship between client and vendor do not grow at the same time. Rather, after the contract is set in place and the outsourcing venture is being carried out, the relationship between the parties will develop over time. In the initial negotiation, the parties frequently do not know each other and, so, begin by basing their relationship on the formal contract. During the negotiations and the subsequent implementation of the contract, the parties get to know each other and build the relational governance structure. One might speculate that a "good" contract would support a positive relational governance structure and a "poor" contract would support a negative one. Effectively, the emergent social structure is based on the formal contract. Consequently, the relationship part of the outsourcing venture starts to evolve after and as a consequence of the contract. A well-designed contract can thus shape a well-established outsourcing relationship (Poppo/Zenger 2002, 713), which will eventually lead to a successful venture.

   This is consistent with Homans' (1951) theory of group dynamics: Members of a group who have frequent task interaction "grow sentiments of liking" and develop friendly social interaction that leads to "further interactions, over and above the interactions of the external (task) system"(Homans 1951). In other words, task interactions among individuals precede their social interactions. Further, the latter evolve out of the task interaction. Drawing on Homans' work, Crouch and Yetton (1988) show that task interaction precedes and influences social interaction in pair-wise relationships in organizations.

2. *Co-evolution and learning of contracts through the client-vendor relationship*

   The subsequent order of the relation between formal and relational governance can also be explained by another argument: A well designed formal contract induces and sets a platform for a good following informal relationship. During the relationship learnings and experiences gathered in the ongoing liaison can reflect back in contractual structures (Argyres/Bercovitz/Mayer 2007; Mayer/Argyres 2004). Those evolutionary patterns in contract structures help to improve the formal contract over time which then again helps to evolve and promote a better informal relationship. Poppo and Zenger 2002 (p. 713) put forth a similar argument: "Relational governance may also promote the refinement (and hence increased complexity) of formal contracts. As a close relationship is developed and sustained, lessons from the prior period are reflected in revisions of the contract. Exchange experience, patterns of information sharing, and evolving performance measurement and monitoring may all enable greater specificity (and complexity) in contractual provisions. As a consequence, relational exchanges may gradually develop more complex formal contracts, as mutually agreed upon processes become formalized." Child (2001) also emphasizes that "the accumulation of mutual experience [...] might be used later in design and management [...] [of contractual structures]" (p. 664).

Consequently, formal contracts promote relational governance in exchange settings and relational governance enables the refinement of contracts and promotes stability in interorganizational exchanges. The contract thus partially indirectly affects outsourcing performance as could also be shown in the data with the mediating effect.

The last group (group 4) comprises outsourcing clients that strive for IT excellence on the one hand and service reliability in the provision of the outsourced services on the other hand. Recalling the descriptive details of this group (from chapter 5.6, p. 205ff.) reveals that compared to the other groups, this group attributes only a medium role to the IT of the company and assigns a low IT budget accordingly. Business processes are not considered for outsourcing by many clients in this group. Instead, infrastructure and applications are selectively outsourced by most clients. In contrast to all other groups, this group has more than one prevailing outsourcing motive, i.e., business efficiency and IT motives.

Interpreting the appropriate governance mechanisms that leads to successful outsourcing in this group leaves the reader a bit puzzled. Two governance mechanisms have a strong impact on the perceived service quality of the clients with the outsourcing venture, i.e., the formal contract (0.343, n.s.) and management structures (-0.377, $p < 0.05$). However, astonishingly, the impact of the contract is, although strong, not significant and even more, the impact of management structures on service quality is negative. All other governance modes have weak and non-significant loadings.

Analyzing the R^2 value of service quality shows that only 33.8% of the variance of perceived service quality can be explained by the six governance mechanisms that were tested altogether. This is quite a low value and one could assume that the clients are not satisfied with their outsourcing venture. But quite the contrary: Surprisingly, compared to the other groups, the clients in this group are very satisfied with their outsourcing venture (compare chapter 5.5.6, p. 202ff.).

Still, the low R^2 value indicates that none of the tested governance mechanism is fully appropriate for this client group or can explain the high perceived service quality and satisfaction with the outsourcing venture. Consequently, in search for a more appropriate governance mechanism or success determinant, an additional mechanism was tested for this group that is mentioned as important in the literature, i.e., vendor flexibility (Gietzmann 1996; Sabherwal 1999; Tan/Sia 2006). Vendor flexibility is especially important in volatile settings with, e.g., rapid technology changes (Häberle/Jahner/Krcmar 2005). The clients in this group expect (besides reliability of the systems) IT excellence, i.e., the latest up-to-date technology systems. Consequently, if the vendor can demonstrate its ability to adapt quickly to changes and has the latest technology in place, which is the prime goal of this group, the clients are satisfied with the venture.

Adding vendor flexibility as a reflectively measured construct increased the R^2 value from 0.338 in this group to 0.472. This reflects an f^2 value of 0.25 which accounts for a medium effect. The path coefficient between flexibility and service quality is strong and highly significant (0.395, $p < 0.01$).

Summing up, the six tested governance mechanism do not seem to be an appropriate approach to govern the group of IT-excellence and service reliability-oriented clients. The group seems to be too heterogeneous with respect to their expectations and consequently does not clearly reveal appropriate governance mechanisms that suit all clients in this group. Splitting up the group into clients that solely focus on IT motives and another group that focuses on business excellence (just like group 1) might reveal a better and clearer result of appropriate governance modes. Moreover, as tested, vendor flexibility seems to be a promising determinant for perceived service quality, but further analyses need to be conducted to find and examine appropriate governance mechanisms for this group.

7   Conclusion and Outlook on Future Research

This thesis was motivated by the need to improve the understanding why outsourcing outcomes and performance are so ambiguous among various client firms and why so many outsourcing projects fail while others are extraordinarily successful. The underlying assumption of this work to be examined was that different expectations and motivations towards an outsourcing venture form different outsourcing client types. These types need a specific portfolio and appropriate approaches of governance modes in order to achieve outsourcing success.

While previous literature has mainly focused on describing plain outsourcing characteristics, listing outsourcing motives and recently addressing relationship management issues of an outsourcing venture, this thesis adopted a more differentiated view, considering contingency factors and the context of an outsourcing venture to describe different outsourcing relationship types and their appropriate management comprehensively.

It was found that out of the variety of different outsourcing expectations, four main categories of outsourcing motives exist:

1. Strategy and innovation focus, involving motives such as strategic advantages or joint product and service development;

2. Technology improvement and reliability involving IT motives such as IT modernization, state-of-the-art technology, reliability, and stability;

3. Business support and facilitator involving motives such as business impact, business support, service excellence, business flexibility, service orientation, and quality improvement; and

4. Cost focus involving cost reduction, variabilization of costs, and efficiency motives.

Building upon these expectation motives, a cluster analysis could classify four different client types of IS outsourcing relationships:

1. Business-efficiency clients

2. Cost-conscious smart shoppers

3. Strategists and innovation seekers

4. IT excellence and reliability-oriented clients.

These types could be characterized not only along their essential underlying outsourcing motives, but also along a number of descriptive attributes that form the client type. It could be shown that a "one-size-fits-all" governance approach for all clients is not sensible. Analyzing the governance model with the whole data set does not reveal customer-specific mechanisms that are appropriate for different client groups.

Rather, each type has different governance modes in place that lead to the success of the outsourcing venture. The business efficiency clients have relational governance and governance via processes as their primary governance mechanisms. The cost-conscious smart shoppers have contractual governance and foremost the experience of their staff as the main governance approaches in place. The clients who strive for strategic advantages and innovation through outsourcing primarily use the two "classic" governance mechanisms: the outsourcing contract and relational governance. And finally, the results showed that for IT excellence and reliability-oriented clients, none of the six tested governance mechanisms were found to be an appropriate approach to govern the group. The group seems to be too heterogeneous to find governance modes that suit their expectations and characteristics. Instead, vendor flexibility seems to be a promising determinant for perceived service quality, but further analyses need to be conducted to find and examine appropriate governance mechanisms for this group.

These findings incorporate a number of insights and contributions that are valuable for both theory and practice and will thus be highlighted in the next chapters. Of course, this study also bears a number of shortcomings and limitations that will also be discussed in the following chapters before providing an outlook on and suggestions for future research directions.

7.1   Results and Contributions to Theory

In analogy to, e.g., Dibbern et al. (2008) or Gregor (2006), one can distinguish several kinds of theoretical contributions to Information Systems research depending on the goal and type of theory underlying this work. According to Gregor (2006, 619), theories can have several goals, i.e., analysis and description, explanation, prediction, and prescription. Similarly, Dibbern et al. (2008) distinguish (among others) between theory confirmation and theory extension. The following paragraphs will highlight the contribution of this work to selected categories of theory goals as put forward by Dibbern et al. (2008) and Gregor (2006).

Theory confirmation: Four dominant categories of outsourcing motives exist in practice

In accordance with the literature and with the theories underlying this thesis, i.e., mainly TCE, social exchange theory, and expectation confirmation theory, the empirical results gathered in this work could confirm four basic outsourcing motives. These findings help to condense and consolidate the myriad of outsourcing expectations in the literature to the core of outsourcing motives. It thus contributes to theory by clarifying the body of knowledge in the literature and helps to provide an informed decision which theories to apply in the context of the key outsourcing motives instead of focusing on derivates and variations of the actual underlying motive.

Theory analysis and description: Based on outsourcing expectations, four client types of outsourcing relationships could be distinguished and characterized

One of the main results of this work is having come up with a number of unique outsourcing client types with different characteristics. By combining and applying elements of transaction cost economics, social exchange theory, and expectation confirmation theory, the anatomy of these unique outsourcing client types could be described and characterized in a comprehensive, holistic, and broad way. Hence, the contribution here is that yet unknown insights on the phenomena of interest could be analyzed and described with the help of multiple theories.

Theories for explanation: Depending on the client type, different governance modes lead to outsourcing success

With the key outsourcing motives clarified and unique types of outsourcing clients analyzed and described, a third theoretical contribution arises with regard to the explanation potential of the results, relying on varying views of causality and methods for argumentation. Transaction cost economics (contract, structures, etc.), social exchange, and psychological contract theory (relational governance) provide a number of governance mechanisms that lead to perceived success of the outsourcing venture. But so far, it was unsolved and unclear, which mechanisms lead to success and which do not. Context factors such as the underlying outsourcing motive of the client have to be considered to determine which governance mode is most appropriate. Depending on the client type and its underlying key outsourcing motives, one can explain which governance mechanisms (each based on a specific theory) will lead to outsourcing success (i.e., perceived service quality and post-purchase satisfaction).

Theories for prediction: Based on the expectations towards outsourcing, one can assume a certain client profile and propose appropriate governance mechanisms

Similar to the previous theoretical contribution of explaining the phenomenon of interest in greater detail, the findings of this thesis also have a predictive character. By being able to describe outsourcing client types and by being able to tell which governance mode is applied by the clients in this study, one can infer on future outsourcing clients and predict which governance modes are likely to have an impact on the perceived and achieved success of the outsourcing venture. If certain preconditions hold, the findings can predict identified patterns in similar future situations.

Theory extension: TCE, social exchange, and psychological contract theory have to be considered in a context depending on the client type

The last theoretical contribution of this study lies in its differentiated analysis of the impact of certain governance modes on the perceived outsourcing success. So far, the theoretical discussion in IS outsourcing research has centered on whether contractual governance (as derived from TCE and assumed for decades) or relational governance (as one of the recent research topics) seems to be the panacea and universal remedy for successfully managing outsourcing ventures. In doing so, research has only listed different governance mechanisms out of context. This study could show that governance mechanisms have to be set in context and contingency factors have to be considered. Neither contractual governance nor relational governance (which was assumed in recent studies) are appropriate and the best choice in all settings. The approach of combining existing research on characteristics of outsourcing projects with contingency factors (expectations of clients) led to a more precise understanding and extended the body of knowledge by considering the context of an outsourcing venture.

Those various contributions to theory were promoted and endorsed by applying a method triangulation of literature review combined with various statistical techniques. Literature and theory application helped to provide a solid and profound basis for the upcoming empirical analyses, confirmed the empirical findings, and mirrored them with theoretical assumptions. A qualitative pre-study with expert interviews provided a sound understanding of the applicability of the research objective to be investigated in further detail. Factor analysis confirmed the findings on key outsourcing motives suggested in the literature. Cluster analysis (as well as discriminant analysis and ANOVA) helped to identify, explain, and analyze unique client types. Lastly, the structural equation model helped to explain, predict, and suggest design recommendations on how to design and manage a successful outsourcing relationship.

7.2   Results and Contributions to Practice

Although this thesis adopted an exclusive client focus on managing IS outsourcing relationships, practical implications arise for clients and vendors alike.

First of all, the findings reveal a number of insights for outsourcing clients. It has become obvious that self-assessment and self-due diligence of expectations towards the venture is essential: According to Feeny et al. (2005) a careful self-due-diligence and self-assessment and a wary selection of the specific provider is the approach of savvy clients who attempt to gauge the supplier's relationship competency, i.e., the extent to which the supplier is willing and able to cultivate a "win-win" relationship that will align client and supplier goals and incentives over time. Consequently, clients should focus on one single outsourcing goal, instead of a multi-motives approach. Streamlining expectations leads to better, i.e., easier and clearer governance approaches. It has become obvious that multi-expectation deals (see, e.g., client group 4) are harder to manage since the expectations are not clear and no easy appropriate governance concept can be designed for such situations. Very much to that point, Lacity and Willcocks stated that "conflicting stakeholders' expectations place IS managers in the precarious position of providing a Rolls Royce service at a Chevrolet price" (Lacity/Hirschheim 1995b, 158). This is not only true for the relation between the client and the vendor, but first and foremost for the client himself. He has to get a clear understanding of his own motivation why to outsource (parts of) the IT. With such a self-knowledge, the governance approaches described and analyzed in this work provide workable strategies for IT decision makers and support an optimal allocation of economic and human resources depending on the underlying outsourcing expectation.

As to the vendor side, this work provides valuable insights for IT service providers on the motivation structure of their clients. They do not only get to know which different motives the clients expect towards the vendor, but also get an idea of which client types expect which motives. With detailed insights into this motivation structure, the vendor can help the client to set up a mutually beneficial relationship by providing an assessment for the client. One of the complaints uttered in the expert interviews (see qualitative pre-study) was that the delivery model of the vendor does not fit to the outsourcing client, i.e., the vendor might expect other cost and gain leverages or the outsourcing client might be too small for a huge vendor (or vice versa). Consequently, knowing the client, its motives, and characteristics in a more profound way provides the vendor with the ability to tailor appropriate governance approaches for different clients. By tailoring a specific and customized governance concept for each client, the client feels understood, which increases the perceived post-purchase satisfaction. Consequently, as for the client, the insights of this study provide IT service providers with workable strategies and design recommendations on how to successfully manage outsourcing relationships with different clients. This eventually allows for a better allocation of economic and human resources while addressing and satisfying customers' needs appropriately.

7.3 Main Research Limitations

There are several limitations of this work to take into account. First and foremost, it should be recognized that the study findings are based on assessing data at only one point in time. The findings might be influenced to a certain extent by external and situational factors that could have been mitigated by a longitudinal study. Although the IT decision makers of the top 5000 companies were addressed and invited to participate in the survey, there is a self-selection of respondents who actually participated in the study. This fact bears all disadvantages of a convenient sample and thus might have led to a potential bias of the results. Not only with respect to data selection, but with respect to answering the questions a potential bias might have arisen among the respondents as the sample contains self-reported data only. This potential bias was countered by full anonymity of the questionnaire data, but still it is unclear whether the respondents had a common understanding of all questions. This challenge was met by extensive pre-tests of the questionnaire items with knowledgeable experts.

Another methodological limitation has to be addressed with regard to the chosen statistical technique of cluster analysis. Cluster analysis has some methodological limitations that have been extensively addressed in chapter 4.2.1.5 (p. 98ff.). One of the main problems is that the chosen Ward clustering algorithm tends to build equally large groups. Consequently, the identified group sizes do not necessarily reflect reality and thus have to be interpreted with caution. However, when interpreting the results, group size was not taken into account, but rather the focus was laid on the actual content of the group and its characteristics which differentiated well among the groups.

Apart from methodological issues, the design of the study bears some challenges. First of all, this study addressed only the client perspective. Although the respondents were asked to name the contact details of their counterpart on the vendor side and many respondents actually provided this data, due to time and budget restrictions, the vendor side could not be assessed in the context of this thesis. This is especially unfortunate since the phenomenon of interest in this thesis addresses IS outsourcing relationships which entails the idea of mutuality as a key aspect.

When designing the governance model, the six most widespread and well research governance approaches found in the literature were tested as determinants on outsourcing success. But as the last group (group 4, IT excellence and reliability-oriented clients) revealed, these governance approaches could not explain all phenomena of interest in this study. Consequently, the realm of governance approaches has to be extended.

7.4   Outlook on Future Research

The recommendations for future research directions can be deduced from the limitations laid out in the previous chapter. First of all, the research object of interorganizational relationships always involves a dynamic character. Thus, a long-term longitudinal study could reveal valuable insights on how the different client types evolve. Nam et al. (1996) tried to conceptually picture how different outsourcing relationships could develop from easy-to-set-up and loose arrangements to more complex, long-term oriented relationships.

Second, while all too many studies have the client in the center of the research, future approaches should focus much more on the vendor side of the outsourcing venture. An interesting question arises when asking why some vendors set up successful outsourcing arrangements that fit to the client and others do not. Is this a question of experience and professionalism of the vendor or is it the ability to tailor customized concepts for each client, thereby applying an internal modular concept of service delivery? Or does the vendor excel on the basis of personal key accounts? In order to research this question, different levels of relationship management have to be considered, i.e., on the CxO level, on the middle management, and on the actual operating level.

Third, other governance mechanisms than the ones tested in this work should be examined in greater detail. Thereby, consequences arise not only for confirmatory-oriented further research, but provide fruitful opportunities for future research in a design-oriented fashion. Researchers could help to develop effective instruments through which outsourcing partners can evaluate their current operating model and define targets for a future operating model of outsourced IS. This future operating model should amalgamate the proven services and practices of the existing relationship with the opportunities created by technology innovations. Innovative governance mechanisms that combine contractual and relational aspects provide a comprehensive basis for a successful management of different outsourcing clients.

Lastly, a promising extension of the current study design could be provided by conducting the study in a cross-national environment. As offshoring to Eastern Europe or India has become very popular in the last years, it is interesting to investigate whether the outsourcing client types vary in cross-cultural settings and whether the governance mechanisms suggested for the German sample also work for German clients that outsource to, e.g., an Indian IT service provider.

References

Aalders, R. (2002): IT Outsourcing. Making IT Work. http://whitepapers.zdnet.com/abstract.aspx?promo=50002&docid=79204, accessed March 20, 2006.

Adler, P. (2001): Market, hierarchy, and trust: the knowledge economy and the future of capitalism. In: Organization Science, Vol. 12, 2, pp. 214-234.

Alborz, S.; Seddon, P.; Scheepers, R. (2005): The Quality-of-Relationship Construct in IT Outsourcing. *9th Pacific Asia Conference on Information Systems.* Bangkok.

Alborz, S.; Seddon, P.B.; Scheepers, R. (2003): A Model for Studying IT Outsourcing Relationships. *7th Pacific Asia Conference on Information Systems PACIS* (pp. 1297-1313).

Alborz, S.; Seddon, P.B.; Scheepers, R. (2004): Impact of Configuration on IT Outsourcing Relationships. *Tenth Americas Conference on Information Systems* (pp. 3551-3560). New York.

Aldenderfer, M.S.; Blashfield, R.K. (1984): Cluster Analysis, Sage, Newbury Park, CA 1984.

Alexander, M.; Young, D. (1996): Strategic Outsourcing. In: Long Range Planning, Vol. 29, 1, pp. 116-119.

Allison, P.D. (2002): Missing data, Sage Publications, Thousand Oaks, CA 2002.

Alpar, P.; Saharia, A.N. (1995): Outsourcing Information Systems Functions: An Organizational Economics Perspective. In: Journal of Organizational Computing, Vol. 5, 3, pp. 197-217.

Alter, C.; Hage, J. (1993): Organizations Working Together, Sage Publications, London 1993.

Amason, A.C. (1996): Distinguishing the Effects of Functional and Dysfunctional Conflict on Strategic Decision Making: Resolving a Paradox for Top Management Teams. In: The Academy of Management Journal, Vol. 39, 1, pp. 123-148.

Anderson, E.; Lodish, L.M.; Weitz, B.A. (1987): Resource Allocation Behavior in Conventional Channels. In: Journal of Marketing Research, Vol. 24, 1, pp. 85-97.

Anderson, E.; Weitz, B. (1989): Determinants of Continuity in Conventional Industrial Channel Dyads. In: Marketing Science, Vol. 8, 4, pp. 310-323.

Anderson, E.; Weitz, B. (1992): The Use of Pledges to Build and Sustain Commitment in Distribution Channels. In: Journal of Marketing Research, Vol. 29, 1, pp. 18-34.

Anderson, J.; Narus, J. (1990): A Model of Distributor Firm and Manufacturer Firm Working Partnerships. In: Journal of Marketing, Vol. 54, 1, pp. 42-58.

Anderson, J.C.; Narus, J.A. (1984): A model of the distributor's perspective of distributor-manufacturer working relationships. In: Journal of Marketing, Vol. 48 4, pp. 62-74.

Ang, S.; Beath, C.M. (1993): Hierarchical Elements in Software contracts. In: Journal of Organizational Computing, Vol. 3, 3, pp. 329-361.

Ang, S.; Cummings, L.L. (1997): Strategic Response to Institutional Influences on Information Systems Outsourcing. In: Organization Science, Vol. 8, 3, pp. 235-256.

Ang, S.; Slaughter, S. (1998): Organizational Psychology and Performance in IS Employment Outsourcing and Insourcing. *31 International Conference on System Sciences* (pp. 635-643). Hawaii.

Applegate, L.M.; Montealegre, R. (1991): Eastman Kodak Co.: Managing Information Systems Through Strategic Alliances. In: Harvard Business School Cases, pp. 1-24.

Apte, U.; Winniford, M. (1991): Global outsourcing of information systems functions: opportunities and challenges. In: Managing Information Technology in a Global Society. Ed.: Khosrowpour, M. Idea Group Publishing, Harrisburg, PA 1991, pp. 58-59.

Apte, U.M. (1990): Global Outsourcing of Information Systems and Processing Services. In: The Information Society, Vol. 7, 4, pp. 287-303.

Apte, U.M.; Sobol, M.G.; Hanaoka, S.; Shimada, T.; Saarinen, T.; Salmela, T.; Vepsalainen, A.P.J. (1997): IS outsourcing practices in the USA, Japan and Finland: a comparative study. In: Journal of Information Technology, Vol. 12, pp. 289-304.

Arabie, P.; Hubert, L. (1994): Cluster Analysis in Marketing Research. In: Advanced Methods of Marketing Research. Ed.: Bagozzi, R.P. Blackwell, Cambridge, MA 1994, pp. 160-179.

Argyres, N.S.; Bercovitz, J.; Mayer, K.J. (2007): Complementarity and Evolution of Contractual Provisions: An Empirical Study of IT Services Contracts. In: Organization Science, Vol. 18, 1, pp. 3-19.

Arnett, K.P.; Jones, M.C. (1994): Firms that Choose Outsourcing: A Profile. In: Information & Management, Vol. 26, 4, pp. 179-188.

Assael, H. (1969): Constructive Role of Interorganizational Conflict. In: Administrative Science Quarterly, Vol. 14, 4, pp. 573-582.

Atteslander, P. (2008): Methoden der empirischen Sozialforschung. (12. Ed.), Erich Schmidt Verlag, Berlin 2008.

Aubert, B.A.; Dussault, S.; Patry, M.; Rivard, S. (1999): Managing the Risk of IT Outsourcing. *32nd Hawaii International Conference on System Sciences.*

Aubert, B.A.; Patry, M.; Rivard, S. (1998): Assessing the Risk of IT Outsourcing. *31st Hawaii International Conference on System Sciences.*

Aubert, B.A.; Patry, M.; Rivard, S. (2002): Managing IT Outsourcing Risk: Lessons Learned. In: Information Systems Outsourcing - Enduring Themes, Emergent Patterns and Future Directions. Ed.: Hirschheim, R.; Heinzl, A.; Dibbern, J. Springer, Berlin 2002, pp. 155-176.

Bacharach, S.B.; Lawler, E.J. (1981): Power and Politics in Organizations: The Social Psychology of Conflict, Coalitions, and Bargaining, Jossey-Bass Inc., San Francisco 1981.

Bacher, J. (1996): Clusteranalyse. Anwendungsorientierte Einführung, Oldenbourg, München, Wien 1996.

Backhaus, K.; Erichson, B.; Plinke, W.; Weiber, R. (2006): Multivariate Analysemethoden. Eine anwendungsorientierte Einführung. (11. Ed.), Springer, Berlin 2006.

Bagozzi, R.P. (1979): The Role of Measurement in Theory Construction and Hypothesis Testing: Toward a Holistic Model. In: Conceptual and Theoretical Developments in Marketing. Ed.: Ferrell, O.C.; Brown, S.W.; Lamb, C.W. American Marketing Association, Chicago 1979, pp. 15-32.

Bagozzi, R.P.; Yi, Y. (1988): On the Evaluation of Structural Equation Models. In: Journal of the Academy of Marketing Science, Vol. 16, pp. 74-94.

Bagozzi, R.P.; Yi, Y.J.; Phillips, L.W. (1991): Assessing Construct Validity in Organizational Research. In: Administrative Science Quarterly, Vol. 36, pp. 421-458.

Bailey, J.E.; Pearson, S.W. (1983): Development of a Tool for Measuring and Analyzing Computer User Satisfaction. In: Management Science, Vol. 29, 5, pp. 530-545.

Bailey, K.D. (1994): Typologies and taxonomies: an introduction to classification techniques, Sage, Thousand Oaks, CA 1994.

Balzert, H. (1998): Lehrbuch der Software-Technik. Software-Management, Software-Qualitätssicherung, Unternehmensmodellierung, Spektrum Akad. Verl., Heidelberg u. a. 1998.

Barney, J.; Lee, W. (2000): Multiple Considerations in Making Governance Choices: Implications of Transaction Cost Economics, Real Option Theory, and Knowledge Based Theories of the Firm, Oxford University Press, Oxford 2000.

Baskerville, R.; Myers, M. (2004): Special Issue on Action Research in Information Systems: Making IS Research Relevant to Practice-Foreword. In: MIS Quarterly, Vol. 28, 3, pp. 329-335.

Baskerville, R.; Wood-Harper, A.T. (1996): A Critical Perspective on Action Research as a Method for Information Systems Research. In: Journal of Information Technology, Vol. 11, pp. 235-246.

Bäumer, J. (1997): Weiterbildungsmanagement: eine empirische Analyse deutscher Unternehmen, Rainer Hampp Verlag, Mering 1997.

Beaumont, N. (2006): Service level agreements: An essential aspect of outsourcing. In: Service Industries Journal, Vol. 26, 4, pp. 381-395.

Beaumont, N.; Costa, C. (2003): Information technology outsourcing in Australia. In: Advanced topics in information resources management. Ed.: Khosrowpour, M. Idea Group Publishing, Hershey, PA, USA 2003, pp. 192-219.

Behrens, S. (2006): Governance and Information Systems Outsourcing Success: A Contingency Perspective. In Lehner, F.; Nösekabel, H.; Kleinschmidt, P. (Eds.), *Multikonferenz Wirtschaftsinformatik* (pp. 101-116). Passau.

Behrens, S. (2007): Information Systems Outsourcing - Five Essays on Governance and Success, Shaker Verlag, Aachen 2007.

Behrens, S.; Schmitz, C. (2005): Ein Bezugsrahmen für die Implementierung von IT-Outsourcing-Governance. In: HMD - Praxis der Wirtschaftsinformatik, Vol. 245, pp. 28-36.

Beimborn, D.; Franke, J.; Weitzel, T. (2005): The Role of Experience for Outsourcing Evaluation. In: Wirtschaftsinformatik, Vol. 47, 6, pp. 431-440.

Benamati, J.H.; Rajkumar, T.M. (2002): The Application Development Outsourcing Decision: An Application Of The Technology Acceptance Model. In: Journal of Computer Information Systems, Vol. 42, 4, pp. 35-43.

Benbasat, I.; Goldstein, D.K.; Mead, M. (1987): The Case Research Strategy in Studies of Information Systems. In: MIS Quarterly, pp. 369-386.

Benbasat, I.; Zmud, R.W. (1999): Empirical Research in IS: The Practice of Relevance. In: MIS Quarterly, Vol. 23, 1, pp. 3-16.

Benko, C. (1992): If Information System Outsourcing is the Solution, What is the Problem? In: Journal of Systems Management, Vol. 43, 11, pp. 32-35.

Bensaou, M.; Venkatraman, N. (1995): Configurations of Interorganizational Relationships: A Comparison between U.S. and Japanese Automakers. In: Management Science, Vol. 41, 9, pp. 1471-1492.

Berekoven, L.; Eckert, W.; Ellenrieder, P. (2006): Marktforschung - Methodische Grundlagen und praktische Anwendung. (11. Ed.), Gabler, Wiesbaden 2006.

Berkhin, P. (2002): Survey of Clustering Data Mining Techniques (Unpublished Manuscript). Accrue Software, 2002.

Bernstein, R.J. (1983): Beyond Objectivism and Relativism, University of Pennsylvania, Pennsylvania 1983.

Beulen, E. (2004): Governance in IT outsourcing partnerships. In: Strategies for Information Technology Governance. Ed.: Grembergen, W.V. Idea Group Publishing, Hershey, PA 2004.

Beulen, E.; Ribbers, P. (2002): Managing Complex IT Outsourcing-Partnerships. *35th Hawaii International Conference on System Sciences - 2002* (pp. 1-10). Hawaii.

Beulen, E.; Ribbers, P. (2003): IT Outsourcing Contracts: Practical Implications of the Incomplete Contract Theory. Paper presented at the 36th Hawaii International Conference on System Sciences, Hawaii, USA.

BITKOM (2009a): IT-Trends 2009: Kosten sparende Anwendungen haben Konjunktur. http://www.bitkom.org/57537_57520.aspx, accessed February 11, 2009.

BITKOM (2009b): Outsourcing wächst in der Krise. http://www.bitkom.org/ 57420_57416.aspx, accessed February 11, 2009.

Blau, P. (1964): Exchange and Power in Social Life, Wiley, New York 1964.

Böhmann, T. (2003): Modularisierung von IT-Dienstleistungen. Eine Methode für das Service Engineering. Dissertation, Universität Hohenheim 2003.

Boland, R.J. (1985): Phenomenology: A Preferred Approach to Research in Information Systems. In: Research Methods in Information Systems. Ed.: Mumford, E.; Hirschheim, R.A.; Fitzgerald, G.; Wood-Harper, A.T. North Holland, Amsterdam 1985, pp. 193-201.

Bongard, S. (1994): Outsourcing-Entscheidungen in der Informationsverarbeitung. Entwicklung eines computergestützten Portfolio-Instrumentariums, DUV, Wiesbaden 1994.

Bourgeois, L.J. (1980): Performance and Consensus. In: Strategic Management Journal, Vol. 1, 3, pp. 227-248.

Bräutigam, P.; Grabbe, H. (2004): Rechtliche Ausgangspunkte. In: IT-Outsourcing. Eine Darstellung aus rechtlicher, technischer, wirtschaftlicher und vertraglicher Sicht. Ed.: Bräutigam, P. Erich Schmidt Verlag, Berlin 2004, pp. 161-203.

Broadbent, M.; Weill, P. (1997): Management by Maxim: How Business and IT Managers Can Create IT Infrastructures. In: Sloan Management Review, Vol. 38, 3, pp. 77-92.

Brosius, F. (2006): SPSS 14. (1. Ed.), Mitp-Verlag, Heidelberg 2006.

Brown, J.R.; Frazier, G.L. (1978): The Application of Channel Power: Its Effects and Connotations. In: Research Frontiers in Marketing: Dialogues and Directions. Ed.: Jain, S.C. American Marketing, Chicago 1978, pp. 266-270.

Brussard, B.K. (1988): Information Resource Management in the Public Sector. In: Information & Management, Vol. 15, pp. 85-92.

Bryant, F.B.; Yarnold, P.R. (1995): Principal-components analysis and exploratory and confirmatory factor analysis. In: Reading and Understanding Multivariate Statistics. Ed.: Grimm, L.G.; Yarnold, P.R. American Psychological Association, Washington, DC 1995.

Buchowicz, B.S. (1991): A Process Model of Make vs. Buy Decision Making: The Case of Manufacturing Software. In: IEEE Transactions on Engineering Management, Vol. 38 1, pp. 24-32.

Buck-Lew, M. (1992): To Outsource or Not? In: International Journal of Information Management, Vol. 12 1, pp. 3-20.

Bühl, A. (2006): SPSS 14: Einführung in die moderne Datenanalyse. (10. Ed.), Pearson Studium, München 2006.

Bülow, R. (1996): Faktoren- und Clusteranalyse. Zwei multivariate statistische Analyseverfahren am Beispiel der Hauptkomponentenanalyse, des Clusterverfahrens nach Ward und der K-Means-Methode (Diskussionspapier 96-5). Ruhr-Universität Bochum, 1996.

Burns, T.; Stalker, G.M. (1961): The management of innovation, Tavistock Publications, London 1961.

Butters, I. (2005): IT-Outsourcing scheitert oft am Zwischenmenschlichen. CIO Magazin, http://www.cio.de/strategien/methoden/813614/index.html, accessed July 20, 2007.

Caldwell, B. (1994): Special Counsel – Outsourcing lawyers can help corporate clients avoid nasty pitfalls when signing billion-dollar deals. In: InformationWeek, Vol. 499, pp. 44-48.

Carmines, E.G.; Zeller, R.A. (1979): Reliability and Validity Assessment, Sage Publications, Beverly Hills, Ca 1979.

Carr, W.; Kemmis, S. (1986): Becoming Critical: Education, Knowledge and Action Research, Falmer Press, London 1986.

Cattell, R.B. (1966): The Scree Test for the Number of Factors. In: Multivariate Behavioral Research, Vol. 1, April, pp. 245-276.

Chalos, P. (1995): Costing, Control, and Strategic Analysis in Outsourcing Decisions. In: Cost Management, Winter, pp. 31-37.

Chandler, A.D. (1962): Strategy and Structure: Chapters in the History of the American Industrial Enterprise, The MIT Press, Cambridge, MA 1962.

Chang, M.K.; Cheung, W.; Lai, V.S. (2005): Literature derived reference models for the adoption of online shopping. In: Information & Management, Vol. 42, 4, pp. 543-559.

Chaudhury, A.; Nam, K.; Rao, H.R. (1995): Management of Information Systemy Outsourcing: A Bidding Perspective. In: Journal of Management Information Systems, Vol. 12, 2, pp. 131 -159.

Cheon, M.J.; Grover, V.; Teng, J.T.C. (1995): Theoretical perspectives on the outsourcing of information systems. In: Journal of Information Technology, Vol. 10, 4, pp. 209-219.

Child, J. (1987): Information Technology, Organization, and the Response to Strategic Challenges. In: California Management Review, Vol. 30 1, pp. 33-50.

Child, J. (2001): Learning through strategic alliances. In: Handbook of Organizational Learning and Knowledge. Ed.: Dierkes, M.; Antal, A.B.; Child, J.; Nonaka, I. Oxford University Press, New York 2001, pp. 657–680.

Chin, W.W. (1998): The Partial Least Squares Approach to Structural Equation Modeling. In: Modern Methods for Business Research. Ed.: Marcoulides, G.A. Lawrence Erlbaum Associates, Mahwah, NJ 1998, pp. 295-336.

Chin, W.W. (2000): Frequently Asked Questions – Partial Least Squares & PLS-Graph. http://disc-nt.cba.uh.edu/chin/plsfaq.htm, accessed October 25, 2005.

Chin, W.W. (2004): Multi-Group analysis with PLS. http://disc-nt.cba.uh.edu/ chin/plsfaq/multigroup.htm, accessed November 25, 2007.

Chin, W.W.; Marcolin, B.L.; Newsted, P.R. (2003): A partial least squares latent variable modeling approach for measuring interaction effects: Results from a monte carlo simulation study and an electronic mail emotion/adoption study. In: Information Systems Research, Vol. 14, pp. 189-217.

Churchill, G. (1979): A Paradigm for Developing Better Measures of Marketing Constructs. In: Journal of Marketing Research, Vol. 16, 1, pp. 64–73.

Churchill, G.; Suprenant, C. (1982): An Investigation into the determinants of customer satisfaction. In: Journal of Marketing Research, Vol. 19, pp. 491-504.

Clark, P.A. (1972): Action Research and Organizational Change, Harper and Row, London 1972.

Clark, T.D.; Zmud, R.W.; McCray, G.E. (1995): The outsourcing of information services: transforming the nature of business in the information industry. In: Journal of Information Technology, Vol. 10, 4, pp. 221-237.

Coase, R.H. (1937): The Nature of the Firm. In: Economica, Vol. 4, pp. 386-405.

Cohen, J. (1988): Statistical power analysis for the behavioral sciences. (2. Ed.), Lawrence Erlbaum Associates, Hillsdale 1988.

Cohen, J. (2003): Applied multiple regression/correlation analysis for the behavioral sciences, Lawrence Erlbaum Associates, London 2003.

Cohen, L.; Young, A. (2006): Multisourcing: Moving beyond outsourcing to achieve growth and agility, Harvard Business School Press, Boston, Mass., USA 2006.

Conklin, D.W. (2005): Risks and rewards in HR business process outsourcing. In: Long Range Planning, Vol. 38, pp. 579-598.

Cook, K.S. (1977): Exchange and Power in Networks of Interorganizational Relations. In: The Sociological Quarterly, Vol. 18, Winter, pp. 62-82.

Cook, K.S.; Emerson, R.M. (1978): Power, Equity and Commitment in Exchange Networks. In: American Sociological Review, Vol. 43, 5, pp. 721-739.

Corazzini, J.G. (1977): Trust as a complex multi-dimensional construct. In: Psychological Reports, Vol. 40, pp. 75-80.

Coughlin, M.A.; Knight, W. (2007): Exploratory Factor Analysis. SPSS, 2007.

Crouch, A.; Yetton, P. (1988): Manager-Subordinate Dyads: Relationships among Task and Social Contact, Manager Friendliness and Subordinate Performance in Management Groups. In: Organizational behaviour and human decision processes, Vol. 41, pp. 65-82.

Cullen, S.; Seddon, P.B.; Willcocks, L. (2005): IT outsourcing configuration: Research into defining and designing outsourcing arrangements. In: Journal of Strategic Information Systems, Vol. 14, pp. 357-387.

Currie, W.; Willcocks, L. (1998): Analysing four types of IT sourcing decisions in the context of scale, client/supplier interdependency and risk mitigation. In: Information Systems Journal, Vol. 8, pp. 119-143.

Currie, W.L. (1996): Outsourcing in the private and public sectors: An unpredictable IT strategy. In: European Journal of Information Systems, Vol. 4, 4, pp. 226-236.

Currie, W.L. (1998): Using multiple suppliers to mitigate the risk of IT outsourcing at ICI an Wessex Water. In: Journal of Information Technology, Vol. 13, pp. 169-180.

Dahl, R.A. (1957): The Concept of Power. In: Behavioral Science, Vol. 2, 3, pp. 201-215.

Das, T.K.; Teng, B.-S. (1998): Between trust and control: developing confidence in partner cooperation in alliances. In: Academy of Management Review, Vol. 23, 3, pp. 491–512.

Das, T.K.; Teng, B.-S. (2001): Trust, Control, and Risk in Strategic Alliances: An Integrated Framework. In: Organization Studies, pp. 251-283.

Das, T.K.; Teng, B.-S. (2002): Alliance constellations: A social exchange perspective. In: Academy of Management Review, Vol. 27, 3, pp. 445-456.

Davenport, T.H.; Hammer, M.; Metsisto, T.J. (1989): How executives can shape their company's information systems. In: Harvard Business Review Vol. 67, 2 (March-April), pp. 130-134.

Davenport, T.H.; Markus, L.M. (1999): Rigor vs. Relevance Revisited: Response to Benbasat and Zmud. In: MIS Quarterly, Vol. 23, 1, pp. 19-23.

Davis, K.J. (1996): IT Outsourcing Relationships: An Exploratory Study of Interorganizational Control Mechanism. Ph.D., Harvard University 1996.

de Looff, L.A. (1998): Information Systems Outsourcing: Theories, Case Evidence and a Decision Framework. In: Strategic Sourcing of Information Systems. Ed.: Willcocks, L.P.; Lacity, M.C. Wiley, Chichester 1998, pp. 249-282.

Decker, R.; Wagner, R.; Temme, T. (2000): Fehlende Werte in der Marktforschung. In: Marktforschung. Ed.: Herrmann, A.; Homburg, C., (2. Ed.). Gabler, Wiesbaden 2000, pp. 79-98.

Deichsel, G.; Trampisch, H.J. (1985): Clusteranalyse und Diskriminanzanalyse, Gustav Fischer Verlag 1985.

DeLone, W.H.; McLean, E.R. (1992): Information Systems Success: The Quest for the Dependent Variable. In: Information Systems Research, Vol. 3, 1, pp. 60-95.

DeSanctis, G.; Jackson, B. (1994): Coordination of Information Technology Management: Team-Based Structures and Computer-Based Communication Systems. In: Journal of Management Information Systems, Vol. 10, 4, pp. 85-110.

Deshpande, R.; Webster, F. (1989): Organizational Culture and Marketing: Defining the Research Agenda. In: Journal of Marketing, Vol. 53, 1, pp. 3-15.

Dess, G.G. (1987): Consensus on Strategy Formulation and Organizational Performance: Competitors in a Fragmented Industry. In: Strategic Management Journal, Vol. 8, 3, pp. 259-277.

Dess, G.G.; Origer, N.K. (1987): Environment, Structure, and Consensus in Strategy Formulation: A Conceptual Integration. In: The Academy of Management Review, Vol. 12, 2, pp. 313-330.

Diamantopoulos, A.; Siguaw, J.A. (2006): Formative Versus Reflective Indicators in Organizational Measure Development: A Comparison and Empirical Illustration. In: British Journal of Management, Vol. 17, 4, pp. 263-282.

Diamantopoulos, A.; Winklhofer, H.M. (2001): Index Construction with Formative Indicators: An Alternative to Scale Development. In: Journal of Marketing Research, Vol. 38, May, pp. 269–77.

Dibbern, J. (2004): The Sourcing of Application Software Services, Springer, Heidelberg et al 2004.

Dibbern, J.; Goles, T.; Hirschheim, R.; Jayatilaka, B. (2002): Multiple Perspectives on IS Outsourcing: An Integrative Model for Reviewing the Literature, 2002.

Dibbern, J.; Goles, T.; Hirschheim, R.; Jayatilaka, B. (2004): Information Systems Outsourcing: A Survey and Analysis of the Literature. In: The DATA BASE for Advances in Information Systems, Vol. 35, 4, pp. 6-102.

Dibbern, J.; Winkler, J.; Heinzl, A. (2008): Explaining Variations in Client Extra Costs Between Software Projects Offshored to India. In: MIS Quarterly Special Issue on Information Systems Offshoring, Vol. 32, 2, pp. 333-366.

Diekmann, A. (2008): Empirische Sozialforschung - Grundlagen, Methoden, Anwendungen, Rowohlt, Reinbek 2008.

DiRomualdo, A.; Gurbaxani, V. (1998): Strategic intent for IT outsourcing. In: Sloan Management Review, Vol. 39, 4, pp. 67-80.

Domberger, S.; Fernandez, P.; Fiebig, D.G. (2000): Modelling the price, performance and contract characteristics of IT outsourcing. In: Journal of Information Technology, Vol. 15, pp. 107-118.

Duda, R.O.; Hart, P.E.; Stork, D.G. (2001): Pattern Classification, John Wiley & Sons, Inc., New York 2001.

Due, R.T. (1992): The real costs of outsourcing. In: Information Systems Management, Vol. 9, 1, pp. 78-81.

Dwyer, F.R. (1980): Channel-Member Satisfaction: Laboratory Insights. In: Journal of Retailing, Vol. 56, 2, pp. 45-65.

Dwyer, F.R.; Schurr, P.H.; Oh, S. (1987): Developing Buyer-Seller Relationships. In: The Journal of Marketing, Vol. 51, 2, pp. 11-27.

Dyer, J.H.; Singh, H. (1998): The Relational View: Cooperative Strategy and Sources of Interorganizational Competitive Advantage. In: Academy of Management Review, Vol. 23, 4, pp. 660-679.

Earl, M.J. (1996): The Risks of Outsourcing IT. In: Sloan Management Review, Vol. 37, 3, pp. 26-32.

Easton, G. (1992): Industrial Networks. A Review. In: Industrial Networks: A New View of Reality. Ed.: Axelson, B.; Easton, G. Routledge, London 1992, pp. 1-34.

Eckey, H.-F.; Kosfeld, R.; Rengers, M. (2002): Multivariate Statistik. Grundlagen, Methoden, Beispiele, Gabler, Wiesbaden 2002.

Eckmüller, B. (2006): Benchmarking-Studie "Erfolgsmodelle im Outsourcing". Steria Mummert Consulting AG, 2006.

Eckstein, P.P. (2004): Angewandte Statistik mit SPSS. (4. Ed.) 2004.

Eggert, A.; Fassott, G.; Helm, S. (2005): Identifizierung und Quantifizierung mediierender und moderierender Effekte in komplexen Kausalstrukturen. In: Handbuch Pfadmodellierung: Methode, Anwendung, Praxisbeispiele. Ed.: Bliemel, F.; Eggert, A.; Fassott, G.; Henseler, J. Schäffer-Poeschel, Stuttgart 2005.

Eisenhardt, K.M. (1989): Building Theories from Case Study Research. In: Academy of Management Review, Vol. 14, 4, pp. 532-550.

El-Ansary, A.I. (1975): Determinants of Power-Dependence in the Distribution Channel. In: Journal of Retailing, Vol. 51, 2, pp. 59-94.

El-Ansary, A.I.; Stern, L.W. (1972): Power Measurement in the Distribution Channel. In: Journal of Marketing Research (JMR), Vol. 9, 1, pp. 47-52.

Elden, M.; Chisholm, R.F. (1993): Emerging Varieties of Action Research: Introduction to the Special Issue. In: Human Relations, Vol. 46, 2, pp. 121-142.

Elitzur, R.; Wensley, A. (1998): Can Game Theory help us to understand Information Service Outsourcing Contracts? In: Strategic Sourcing of Information Systems, Wiley, Chichester 1998. Ed.: Willcocks, L.P.; Lacity, M.C. Wiley, Chichester 1998, pp. 103-136.

Emerson, R. (1969): Operant Psychology and Exchange Theory. In: Behavioral Sociology. Ed.: Burgess, R.; Bushell, D. Columbia University Press, New York 1969, pp. 379-408.

Emerson, R. (1972): Exchange Theory, Part I: A Psychological Basis for Social Exchange and Exchange Theory, Part II: Exchange Relations and Network Structures. In: Sociological Theories in Progress. Ed.: Berger, J.; Zelditch, M.; Anderson, B. Houghton Mifflin, New York 1972.

Emerson, R.M. (1962): Power-Dependence Relations. In: American Sociological Review, Vol. 27, 1, pp. 31-41.

Etgar, M. (1976a): Channel Domination and Countervailing Power in Distributive Channels. In: Journal of Marketing Research (JMR), Vol. 13, 3, pp. 254-262.

Etgar, M. (1976b): Effects of Administrative Control on Efficiency of Vertical Marketing Systems. In: Journal of Marketing Research (JMR), Vol. 13, 1, pp. 12-24.

Etgar, M. (1977): Channel Environment and Channel Leadership. In: Journal of Marketing Research, Vol. 14 pp. 69-76.

Etgar, M. (1979): Sources and Types of Intrachannel Conflict. In: Journal of Retailing, Vol. 55, 1, pp. 61-78.

Etgar, M.; Cadotte, E.R.; Robinson, L.M. (1978): Selection of an Effective Channel Control Mix. In: Journal of Marketing Research, Vol. 42, 3, pp. 53-58.

Everitt, B.S.; Landau, S.; Leese, M. (2001): Cluster Analysis. (4. Ed.), Arnold, London 2001.

Featherman, M.S.; Pavlou, P.A. (2003): Predicting e-Services Adoption: A Perceived Risk Facets Perspective. In: International Journal of Human-Computer Studies, Vol. 59, 4, pp. 451-474.

Feeny, D.; Lacity, M.; Willcocks, L.P. (2005): Taking the Measure of Outsourcing Providers. In: MIT Sloan Management Review, Vol. 46, 3, pp. 41-48.

Feyerabend, P. (1975): Against Method - Outline of an anarchistic theory of knowledge, NLB, London 1975.

Fitzgerald, G.; Willcocks, L.P. (1994): Contracts and Partnerships in the Outsourcing of IT. In DeGross, J.I.; Huff, S.L.; Munro, M.C. (Eds.), *Fifteenth International Conference on Information Systems* (pp. 91-98). Vancouver, Canada.

Fontenot, R.; Wilson, E. (1997): Relational Exchange: A Review of Selected Models for a Prediction Matrix of Relationship Activities. In: Journal of Business Research, Vol. 39, 1, pp. 5-12.

Forgy, E.W. (1965): Cluster analysis of multivariate data: efficiency vs interpretability of classifications. In: Biometrics, Vol. 21, pp. 768-769.

Fornell, C.; Bookstein, F.L. (1982): Two structural equation models: LISREL and PLS applied to consumer exit-voice theory. In: Journal of Marketing Research, Vol. 19, 4, pp. 440-452.

Fornell, C.; Larcker, D.F. (1981): Evaluating Structural Equation Models with Unobservable Variables and Measurement Errors. In: Journal of Marketing Research, Vol. 18, pp. 39-50.

Foxman, N. (1994): Succeeding in Outsourcing: Cultivate the Outsourcing Relationship. In: Information Systems Management, Vol. 11, pp. 77-80.

Frank, U. (2003): Für Sie gelesen: IS Research Relevance Revisited: Subtle Accomplishment, Unfulfilled Promise, or Serial Hypocrisy? In: Wirtschaftsinformatik, Vol. 45, 3, pp. 354-357.

Frazier, G.L. (1983): Interorganizational Exchange Behavior in Marketing Channels: A Broadened Perspective. In: Journal of Marketing, Vol. 47, 4, pp. 68-78.

Friedrichs, J. (1990): Methoden empirischer Sozialforschung. (14. Ed.), Westdeutscher Verlag, Opladen 1990.

Frochot, I.; Morrison, A.M. (2000): Benefit Segmentation: A Review of it Application to Travel and Tourism Research. In: Journal of Travel and Tourism Marketing, Vol. 9, 4, pp. 21-45.

Gable, G. (1994): Integrating Case Study and Survey Research Methods: An Example in Information Systems. In: European Journal of Information Systems, Vol. 3, 2, pp. 112-126.

Ganesan, S. (1994): Determinants of Long-Term Orientation in Buyer-Seller Relationships. In: Journal of Marketing, Vol. 58, 2, pp. 1-19.

Garson, G.D. (2008a): Data Imputation for Missing Values. Statnotes: Topics in Multivariate Analysis, http://www2.chass.ncsu.edu/garson/pa765/statnote.htm, accessed June 16, 2008.

Garson, G.D. (2008b): Discriminant Function Analysis. Statnotes: Topics in Multivariate Analysis, http://www2.chass.ncsu.edu/garson/pa765/statnote.htm, accessed June 16, 2008.

Gaski, J.F. (1984): The Theory of Power and Conflict in Channels of Distribution. In: The Journal of Marketing, Vol. 48, 3, pp. 9-29.

Gellings, C. (2007): Outsourcing Relationships: The Contract as IT Governance Tool. *40th Hawaii International Conference on System Sciences*. Hawaii.

George, B.; Hirschheim, R.A.; Murungi, D. (2007): A Framework for IT Outsourcing Governance, 2007.

Gewald, H.; Helbig, K. (2006): A Governance Model for Managing Outsourcing Partnerships. *39th Hawaii International Conference on System Sciences - HICSS* (pp. 1-10).

Gewald, H.; Wüllenweber, K.; Weitzel, T. (2006): The Influence of Perceived Risks on Banking Managers' Intention to Outsource Business Processes - A Study of the German

Banking and Finance Industry. In: Journal of Electronic Commerce Research, Vol. 7, 2, pp. 78-96.

Ghoshal, S.; Moran, P. (1996): Bad for practice: a critique of the transaction cost theory. In: Academy of Management Review, Vol. 21, pp. 13-47.

Gietzmann, M.B. (1996): Incomplete contracts and the make or buy decision: Governance design and attainable flexibility. In: Accounting, Organizations and Society, Vol. 21, 6, pp. 611-626.

Glaser, B. (1992): Emergence vs. Forcing: Basics of Grounded Theory Analysis, Sociology Press, Mill Valley, CA 1992.

Glaser, B.; Strauss, A. (1967): The Discovery of Grounded Theory: Strategies for Qualitative Research, Aldine, Chicago, IL 1967.

Glass, R.L. (1996): The End of the Outsourcing Era. In: Information Systems Management, Vol. 13, 2, pp. 89-91.

Glossner, S. (2004): Datenschutz. In: IT-Outsourcing. Eine Darstellung aus rechtlicher, technischer, wirtschaftlicher und vertraglicher Sicht. Ed.: Bräutigam, P. Erich Schmidt Verlag, Berlin 2004, pp. 331-360.

Goldberg, V.P. (1976): Regulation and Administered Contracts. In: The Bell Journal of Economics, Vol. 7, 2, pp. 426-448.

Goles, T. (2001): The impact of the client-vendor relationship on information systems outsourcing success. Doctoral Thesis, University of Houston 2001.

Goles, T. (2003): Vendor Capabilities and Outsourcing Success: A Resource-based View. In: Wirtschaftsinformatik, Vol. 45, 2, pp. 199-206.

Goles, T.; Chin, W.W. (2002): Relational Exchange Theory and IS Outsourcing: Developing a Scale to Measure Relationship Factors. In: Information Systems Outsourcing: Enduring Themes, Emergent Patterns and Future Directions. Ed.: Hirschheim, R.; Heinzl, A.; Dibbern, J. Springer, Berlin, Heidelberg et al. 2002, pp. 221-250.

Goles, T.; Chin, W.W. (2005): Information systems outsourcing relationship factors: detailed conceptualization and initial evidence. In: SIGMIS Database, Vol. 36, 4, pp. 47-67.

Gonzalez, R.; Gasco, J.; Llopis, J. (2006): Information systems outsourcing: A literature analysis. In: Information & Management, Vol. 43, 7, pp. 821-834.

Goo, J.; Kim, D.J.; Cho, B. (2006): Structure of Service Level Agreements (SLA) in IT Outsourcing: The Construct and Its Measurement. *Twelfth Americas Conference on Information Systems* (pp. 3222-3232). Acapulco Mexico.

Goo, J.; Kishore, R.; Nam, K.; Rao, H.R.; Song, Y. (2003): Managing sourcing relationships using Service Level Agreements: a relational exchange approach. *Ninth Americas Conference on Information Systems*. Tampa, USA.

Goo, J.; Kishore, R.; Rao, H.R. (2004a): Management of Information Technology Outsourcing Relationships: The Role of Service Level Agreements. *25th International Conference on Information Systems* (pp. 325-338). Washington, D.C., USA.

Goo, J.; Kishore, R.; Rao, H.R. (2004b): Managing IT Outsourcing Relationships Using Service Level Agreements (SLAs): A Multi-Dimensional Fit Approach. *Tenth Americas Conference on Information Systems*. New York.

Gorsuch, R.L. (1983): Factor Analysis. (Orig. ed. 1974), Lawrence Erlbaum, Hillsdale, NJ 1983.

Göthlich, S.E. (2007): Zum Umgang mit fehlenden Daten in großzahligen empirischen Erhebungen. In: Methodik der empirischen Forschung. Ed.: Albers, S.; Klapper, D.; Konradt, U.; Walter, A.; Wolf, J. Gabler, Wiesbaden 2007, pp. 119-134.

Gottfredson, R.; Puryear, R.; Phillips, S. (2005): Strategic Sourcing from Periphery to the Core. In: Harvard Business Review, Vol. 83, 2, pp. 132-139.

Gottschalk, P.; Solli-Sæther, H. (2006a): Managing Successful IT Outsourcing Relationships, IRM Press, Hershey, London 2006a.

Gottschalk, P.; Solli-Sæther, H. (2006b): Maturity model for IT outsourcing relationships. In: Industrial Management & Data Systems, Vol. 106, 2, pp. 200-212.

Gregor, S. (2006): The Nature of Theory in Information Systems. In: Management Information Systems Quarterly, Vol. 30, 3, pp. 611-642.

Grover, V.; Cheon, M.; Teng, J.T.C. (1994a): An Evaluation of the Impact of Corporate Strategy and the Role of Information Technology on IS Functional Outsourcing. In: European Journal of Information Systems, Vol. 3, 3 (July), pp. 179-190.

Grover, V.; Cheon, M.J.; Teng, J.T.C. (1994b): A Descriptive Study on the Outsourcing of Information Systems Functions. In: Information & Management, Vol. 27, 1, pp. 33-44.

Grover, V.; Cheon, M.J.; Teng, J.T.C. (1996): The Effect of Service Quality and Partnership on the Outsourcing of Information Systems Functions. In: Journal of Management Information Systems, Vol. 12, 4, pp. 89-116.

Grzmik, B.; Glossner, S. (2004): Rechtliche Einordnung von IT-Outsourcing Leistungen. In: IT-Outsourcing. Eine Darstellung aus rechtlicher, technischer, wirtschaftlicher und vertraglicher Sicht. Ed.: Bräutigam, P. Erich Schmidt Verlag, Berlin 2004, pp. 203-267.

Guba, E.G.; Lincoln, Y.S. (1994): Competing Paradigms in Qualitative Research. In: Handbook of Qualitative Research. Ed.: Denzin, N.K.; Lincoln, Y.S. Sage Publications, Thousand Oaks, CA 1994, pp. 105-117.

Guiltinan, J.P.; Rejab, I.B.; Rodgers, W.C. (1980): Factors Influencing Coordination in a Franchise Channel. In: Journal of Retailing, Vol. 56, 3, pp. 41-58.

Gulati, R. (1995): Does Familiarity Breed Trust? The Implications of Repeated Ties for Contractual Choice in Alliances. In: The Academy of Management Journal, Vol. 38, 1, pp. 85-112.

Gulati, R.; Singh, H. (1998): The Architecture of Cooperation: Managing Coordination Costs and Appropriation Concerns in Strategic Alliances. In: Administrative Science Quarterly, Vol. 43, 4, pp. 781-814.

Gundlach, G.; Cadotte, E. (1994): Exchange Interdependence and Interfirm Interaction: Research in a Simulated Channel Setting. In: Journal of Marketing Research (JMR), Vol. 31, 4, pp. 516-532.

Gupta, B.; Iyer, L.S. (2003): A Theoretical Framework for Measuring the Success of Customer Relationship Management Outsourcing. In: Business strategies for information technology management. Ed. IRM Press; distributed by Independent Publishers Group, Chicago, Hershey, Pa.; London and Melbourne 2003, pp. 149-159.

Gupta, U.G.; Gupta, A. (1992): Outsourcing the IS function: Is It Necessary for Your Organization? In: Information Systems Management, Vol. 9, 3, pp. 44-50.

Guth, W.D.; MacMillan, I.C. (1986): Strategy Implementation Versus Middle Management Self-Interest. In: Strategic Management Journal, Vol. 7, 4, pp. 313-327.

Häberle, O.; Jahner, S.; Krcmar, H. (2005): Beyond the On Demand Hype: A Conceptual Framework for Flexibility in Outsourcing. Paper presented at the European Academy of Management Annual Conference (EURAM), Germany, May 4th - 7th 2005, TUM Business School Munich.

Habermas, J. (1995): Theorie des kommunikativen Handelns (Vol. Bd. 1, Handlungsrationalität und gesellschaftliche Rationalisierung). (1. Ed.), Suhrkamp, Frankfurt/Main 1995.

Hair, J.F.; Black, W.C.; Babin, B.J.; Anderson, R.E.; Tatham, R.L. (2006): Multivariate Data Analysis. (6. Ed.), Pearson, Prentice Hall, Upper Saddle River, NJ 2006.

Hall, R.H. (1972): Organizations: Structure and Process, Prentice-Hall, Englewood Cliffs, NJ 1972.

Hallén, L.; Johanson, J.; Seyed-Mohamed, N. (1991): Interfirm Adaptation in Business Relationships. In: Journal of Marketing, Vol. 55, 2, pp. 29-37.

Hancox, M.; Hackney, R. (1999): Information Technology Outsourcing: Conceptualizing Practice in the Public and Private Sector. *Proceedings of the Thirty-second Annual Hawaii International Conference on System Sciences-Volume 7 - Volume 7*: IEEE Computer Society.

Hart, O.D. (1998): Incomplete Contracts and the Theory of the Firm. In: Journal of Law, Economics and Organization, Vol. 4, 1, pp. 119-139.

Harvey, L.; MacDonald, M. (1996): Doing Sociology: A Practical Introduction (Contemporary Social Theory), Palgrave Macmillan, Basingstoke 1996.

Hatcher, L. (1994): A step-by-step approach to using the SAS system for factor analysis and structural equation modeling. SAS Institute, 1994.

Heckman, R.; King, W.R.; Beachboard, J. (1994): Behavioral Consequences of Customer Satisfaction with Outsourcing Services: Discretionary Collaboration, Relationship Commitment, and Conflict. *Fifteenth International Conference on Information Systems* (pp. 1-36). Vancouver.

Heide, J. (1994): Interorganizational Governance in Marketing Channels. In: Journal of Marketing, Vol. 58, 1, pp. 71-84.

Heide, J.; John, G. (1992): Do Norms Matter in Marketing Relationships? In: Journal of Marketing, Vol. 56, 2, pp. 32-44.

Heide, J.B.; John, G. (1990): Alliances in Industrial Purchasing: The Determinants of Joint Action in Buyer-Supplier Relationships. In: Journal of Marketing Research (JMR), Vol. 27, 1, pp. 24-36.

Held, D. (1980): Introduction to Critical Theory: Horkheimer to Habermas, University of California Press, Berkeley 1980.

Henderson, J.; Venkatram, N. (1992): Strategic Alignment: A Model for Organizational Transformation via Information Technology. In: Transforming Organizations. Ed.: Kochan, T.; Useem, M. Oxford University Press, New York 1992.

Henderson, J.C. (1990): Plugging into Strategic Partnerships: The Critical IS Connection. In: Sloan Management Review, Vol. 31, 3, pp. 7-18.

Hild, J. (2008): Eine Outsourcing-Beziehung ist nur so gut wie ihr Management. CIO Magazin, http://www.cio.de/markt/analysen/857109/, accessed July 2, 2008.

Hill, M. (1997): SPSS Missing Value Analysis 7.5, SPSS Inc, Chicago, IL 1997.

Hirschheim, R.; Lacity, M. (2000): The Myths and Realities of Information Technology Insourcing. In: Communications of the ACM, Vol. 43, 2, pp. 99-107.

Hirschheim, R.; Lacity, M.C. (1998): Reducing Information Systems Costs Through Insourcing: Experiences from the Field. *Proceedings of the 31st Annual Hawaii International Conference on System Sciences.* Hawaii, Hawaii.

Hirschheim, R.A. (1992): Information Sytems Epistemology: An Historical Perspective. In: Information Systems Research: Issues, Methods and Practical Guidelines. Ed.: Galliers, R. Blackwell Scientific Publications, Oxford, London 1992, pp. 28-60.

Hirschheim, R.A.; Klein, H. (1994): Realizing Emancipatory Principles in Information Systems Development: The Case for ETHICS. In: MIS Quarterly, Vol. 18, 1 (March), pp. 83-109.

Homans, G.C. (1951): The human group, Harcourt, Brace, New York 1951.

Homans, G.C. (1958): Social Behavior as Exchange. In: American Journal of Sociology, Vol. 63, 6, pp. 597-606.

Homans, G.C. (1961): Social Behavior. Its Elementary Forms, Harcourt Brace Jovanovich, New York 1961.

Homburg, C.; Workman, J.P.J.; Jensen, O. (2002): A Configurational Perspective on Key Account Management. In: Journal of Marketing, Vol. 66, pp. 38-60.

Horn, J.L. (1965): A rationale and test for the number of factors in factor analysis. In: Psychometrika, Vol. 30, pp. 179-185.

Hotho, A. (2004): Clustern mit Hintergrundwissen, Akademische Verlagsgesellschaft Aka GmbH, Berlin 2004.

Hu, Q.; Saunders, C.; Gebelt, M. (1997): Research Report: Diffusion of Information Systems Outsourcing: A Reevaluation of Influence Sources. In: Information Systems Research, Vol. 8, 3, pp. 288 - 301.

Huber, F.; Herrmann, A.; Meyer, F.; Vogel, J.; Vollhardt, K. (2007): Kausalmodellierung mit Partial Least Squares - Eine anwendungsorientierte Einführung, Gabler, Wiesbaden 2007.

Huff, S.L. (1991): Outsourcing of information services. In: Business Quarterly, Vol. 55, 4, pp. 62-65.

Hui, P.P.; Beath, C.M. (2002): The IT Sourcing Process: A Framework for Research. *Working paper, University of Texas at Austin.* Austin, TX.

Hulland, J. (1999): Use of Partial Least Squares (PLS) in Strategic Management Research: A Review of Four Recent Studies. In: Strategic Management Journal, Vol. 20, 2, pp. 195-204.

Hunger, J.D.; Stern, L.W. (1976): An Assessment of the Functionality of the Superordinate Goal in Reducing Conflict. In: Academy of Management Journal, Vol. 19, 4, pp. 591-605.

Hunt, S.D. (1991): Modern marketing theory: critical issues in the philosophy of marketing science, South-Western Publishing Co., Cincinnati, OH 1991.

Hunt, S.D.; Nevin, J.R. (1974): Power in a Channel of Distribution: Sources and Consequences. In: Journal of Marketing Research (JMR), Vol. 11, 2, pp. 186-193.

Huppertz, P. (2004): Urheberrechtliche Grundlagen und sonstige gewerbliche Schutzrechte. In: IT-Outsourcing. Eine Darstellung aus rechtlicher, technischer, wirtschaftlicher und vertraglicher Sicht. Ed.: Bräutigam, P. Erich Schmidt Verlag, Berlin 2004, pp. 267-330.

Hutcheson, D.G. (2005): Moore's Law: The History and Economics of an Observation that Changed the World. In: The Electrochemical Society INTERFACE, Vol. 14, 1 (Spring), pp. 17-21.

Hutcheson, G.; Sofroniou, N. (1999): The multivariate social scientist: Introductory statistics using generalized linear models, Sage Publications, Thousand Oaks, CA 1999.

Iacobucci, D.; Duhachek, A. (2003): Mediating Analysis - Round Table ACR 2003. Paper presented at the ACR 2003, Toronto.

ITGI (2003): Board Briefing on IT Governance. IT Governance Institute, 2003.

Ives, B.; Olson, M.H. (1984): User involvement and MIS success: a review of research. In: Management Science, Vol. 30, 5, pp. 586-603.

Jahner, S.; Böhmann, T.; Krcmar, H. (2006a): Anticipating and considering customers' flexibility demands in IS outsourcing relationships. *14th European Conference on Information Systems.* Göteborg, Sweden.

Jahner, S.; Böhmann, T.; Krcmar, H. (2006b): Relationship Archetypes in Information Systems Outsourcing Arrangements: An Exploratory Analysis. *Twelfth Americas Conference on Information Systems* (pp. 2133-3237). Acapulco, Mexico.

Jain, A.K.; Dubes, R.C. (1988): Algorithms for Clustering Data, Prentice Hall, Upper Saddle River, NJ 1988.

Jain, A.K.; Murty, M.N.; Flynn, P.J. (1999): Data Clustering: A Review. In: ACM Computing Surveys, Vol. 31, 3 (September), pp. 264-323.

Jarillo, J. (1988): On Strategic Networks. In: Strategic Management Journal, Vol. 9, 1, pp. 31-41.

Jarvis, C.B.; MacKenzie, S.B.; Podsakoff, P.M. (2003): A Critical Review of Construct Indicators and Measurement Model Misspecification in Marketing and Consumer Research. In: Journal of Consumer Research, Vol. 30, 2, pp. 199-218.

Jaworski, B.J. (1988): Toward a Theory of Marketing Control: Environmental Context, Control Types, and Consequences. In: Journal of Marketing, Vol. 52, 3 (July), pp. 23-39.

Jensen, M.C.; Meckling, W.H. (1976): Theory of the Firm. Managerial Behavior, Agency Costs and Ownership Structure. In: Journal of Financial Economics, Vol. 3, pp. 305-360.

John, G. (1984): An Empirical Investigation of Some Antecedents of Opportunism in a Marketing Channel In: Journal of Marketing Research, Vol. 21 3, pp. 278-289.

Johnson, W.J.; Bonoma, T.V. (1977): Reconceptualizing Industrial Buying Behavior: Toward Improved Research Approaches. In: Contemporary Marketing Thought. Ed.: Greenberg, B.A.; Bellenger, D.N. American Marketing Association, Chicago 1977, pp. 247-251.

Joshi, A.W.; Stump, R.L. (1999): Determinants of Commitment and Opportunism: Integrating and Extending Insights from Transaction Cost Analysis and Relational Exchange Theory. In: Canadian Journal of Administrative Sciences, Vol. 16, 4, pp. 334-352.

Judenberg, J. (1994): Applications maintenance outsourcing. In: Information Systems Management, Vol. 11, 4, pp. 34.

Jurison, J. (1995): The role of risk and return in information technology outsourcing decisions. In: Journal of Information Technology, Vol. 10, 4, pp. 239-247.

Jurison, J. (1998): A Risk-Return Model for Information Technology Outsourcing Decisions. In: Strategic Sourcing of Information Systems. Ed.: Willcocks, L.P.; Lacity, M.C. John Wiley & Sons Ltd., Chichester 1998, pp. 187-204.

Kaiser, H.F. (1974): An Index of Factorial Simplicity. In: Psychometrika, Vol. 39, 1, pp. 31-36.

Kanter, R.M. (1994): Collaborative Advantage. The Art of Alliances. In: Harvard Business Review, Vol. 72, 4, pp. 96-108.

Kaplan, B.; Duchon , D. (1988): Combining Qualitative and Quantitative Methods in Information Systems Research: A Case Study. In: MIS Quarterly, Vol. 12, 4, pp. 571-586.

Kaplan, B.; Maxwell, J.A. (1994): Qualitative Research Methods for Evaluating Computer Information Systems. In: Evaluating Health Care Information Systems. Ed.: Anderson, J., Thousand Oaks 1994, pp. 45-68.

Kaufman, L.; Roussseeuw, P.J. (1990): Finding groups in data: an introduction to cluster analysis, Wiley, New York 1990.

Kaufmann, T.; Schlitt, M. (2004): Effektives Management der Geschäftsbeziehung im IT-Outsourcing. In: HMD Praxis der Wirtschaftsinformatik, Vol. 237, Juni, pp. 43-53.

Kern, T. (1997): The *gestalt* of an information technology outsourcing relationship: an exploratory analysis. *Eighteenth International Conference on Information Systems* (pp. 37-58). Atlanta, GA.

Kern, T.; Blois, K. (2002): Norm Development in Outsourcing Relationships. In: Journal of Information Technology, Vol. 17, 1, pp. 33-42.

Kern, T.; Willcocks, L.P. (2000a): Contracts, Control and 'Presentation' in IT Outsourcing: Research in Thirteen UK Organisations. In: Journal of Global Information Management, Vol. 8, 4, pp. 15-28.

Kern, T.; Willcocks, L.P. (2000b): Exploring information technology outsourcing relationships: theory and practice. In: The Journal of Strategic Information Systems, Vol. 9, 4, pp. 321-350.

Kern, T.; Willcocks, L.P. (2001): The relationship advantage: Information technologies, sourcing, and management, Oxford University Press, Oxford 2001.

Kern, T.; Willcocks, L.P. (2002): Exploring relationships in information technology outsourcing: the interaction approach. In: European Journal of Information Systems, Vol. 11, 1, pp. 3-19.

Kern, T.; Willcocks, L.P.; van Heck, E. (2002): The Winner's Curse in IT Outsourcing: Strategies for avoiding relational trauma. In: California Management Review, Vol. 44, 2, pp. 47-69.

Ketchen, D.J.; Shook, C.L. (1996): The Application of Cluster Analysis in Strategic Management Research: An Analysis and Critique. In: Strategic Management Journal, Vol. 17, 6, pp. 441-458.

Kettler, K.; Walstrom, J. (1993): The Outsourcing Decision. In: International Journal of Information Management, Vol. 13, 6 (December), pp. 449-459.

Kim, J.-O.; Mueller, C.W. (1978): Factor Analysis: Statistical methods and practical issues, Sage Publications, Thousand Oaks, CA 1978.

Kim, S.; Chung, Y.-S. (2003): Critical success factors for IS outsourcing implementation from an organizational relationship perspective. In: Journal of Computer Information Systems, Vol. 43, 4, pp. 81-90.

King, W.R. (1994): Strategic Outsourcing Decisions. In: Information Systems Management, Vol. 11, 4, pp. 58-61.

Kishore, R.; Rao, H.; Nam, K.; Rajagopalan, S.; Chaudhury, A. (2003): A Relationship Perspective on IT Outsourcing. In: Communications of the ACM, Vol. 46, 12, pp. 87-92.

Klepper, R. (1994): A model of I/S partnering relationships. In: SIGCPR Comput. Pers., Vol. 15, 2, pp. 3-9.

Klepper, R. (1995): The management of partnering development in I/S outsourcing. In: Journal of Information Technology, Vol. 10, 4, pp. 249-258.

Klepper, R. (1998): The management of partnering development in IS outsourcing. In: Strategic Sourcing of Information Systems: Perspectives and Practices (Vol. 40). Ed.: Willcocks, L.P.; Lacity, M.C. John Wiley & Sons Ltd., Chichester 1998, pp. 305-325.

Klepper, R.; Jones, W. (1998): Outsourcing Information Technology, Systems and Services, Prentice Hall, Upper Saddle River, NJ 1998.

Kluge, S. (1999): Empirisch begründete Typenbildung - Zur Konstruktion von Typen und Typologien in der quantitativen Sozialforschung, Leske & Budrich, Opladen 1999.

Kock, N.; Gray, P.; Hoving, R.; Klein, H.; Myers, M.; Rockart, J.F. (2002): IS Research Relevance Revisited: Subtle Accomplishment, Unfulfilled Promise or Serial Hypocrisy? In: Communications of the Association for Information Systems, Vol. 8, 23, pp. 330-346.

Kogut, B.; Zander, U. (1992): Knowledge of the firm, combinative capabilities, and the replication of technology. In: Organization Science, Vol. 3, 3, pp. 383-397.

Koh, C.; Ang, S.; Straub, D.W. (2004): IT Outsourcing Success: A Psychological Contract Perspective. In: Information Systems Research, Vol. 15, 4, pp. 356-373.

Köhler-Frost, W. (2000): Outsourcing - Eine strategische Allianz besonderen Typs. Neue Erkenntnisse, Definitionen, Veränderungen. In: Outsourcing - Eine strategische Allianz besonderen Typs. Ed.: Köhler-Frost, W.; Bahrs, W., (4. Ed.). Erich Schmidt Verlag, Berlin 2000, pp. 12-24.

Konsynski, B.R.; McFarlan, E.W. (1990): Information partnerships - Shared data, shared scale. In: Harvard Business Review, Vol. 68, 5, pp. 115-120.

Korsgaard, M.A.; Schweiger, D.M.; Sapienza, H.J. (1995): Building Commitment, Attachment, and Trust in Strategic Decision-Making Teams: The Role of Procedural Justice. In: The Academy of Management Journal, Vol. 38, 1, pp. 60-84.

Krcmar, H. (1998): Einige Überlegungen zu Methoden der empirischen Forschung in der Wirtschaftsinformatik. *Arbeitstagung Wissenschaftstheorie in der Wirtschaftsinformatik.* Universität Münster.

Krcmar, H. (2005): Informationsmanagement. (4. Ed.), Springer, Berlin 2005.

Kreps, D.M.; Milgrom, P.; Roberts, J.; Wilson, R. (1982): Rational cooperation in the finitely repeated prisoners' dilemma. In: Journal of Economic Theory, Vol. 27, 2, pp. 245-252.

Krippendorff, K. (1980): Content Analysis: An Introduction to Its Methodology, Sage, Beverly Hills, CA USA 1980.

Kromrey, H. (2006): Empirische Sozialforschung. (11. Ed.), UTB für Wissenschaft, Opladen 2006.

Küchler, P. (2004): Technische und wirtschaftliche Grundlagen. In: IT-Outsourcing - Eine Darstellung aus rechtlicher, technischer, wirtschaftlicher und vertraglicher Sicht. Ed.: Bräutigam, P. Erich Schmidt Verlag, Berlin 2004, pp. 51-159.

Kuckartz, U. (1990): Computerunterstützte Suche nach Typologien in qualitativen Interviews. In: Fortschritte der Statistik-Software 2. SOFTSTAT '89. 5. Konferenz über die wissenschaftliche Analyse von Statistiksoftware. Ed.: Faulbaum, F.; Haux, R.; Jöckel, K.-H. Gustav Fischer, Heidelberg 1990.

Kuckartz, U. (1996): Information-Retrieval und Informationsanalyse in der qualitativen Sozialforschung: Methoden, Software, Trends. In: Herausforderungen an die Informationswissenschaft. Informationsverdichtung, Informationsbewertung und Datenvisualisierung. Ed.: Krause, J.; Herfurth, M.; Marx, J. Universitätsverlag Konstanz, Konstanz 1996, pp. 79-89.

Kumar, K.; Dissel, H.G.v. (1996): Sustainable Collaboration: Managing Conflict and Cooperation in Interorganizational Systems. In: MIS Quarterly, Vol. 20, 3, pp. 279-300.

Kumar, M.V. (2006): Information Technology Outsourcing at BBC. ICFAI, Center for Management Research, 2006.

Kuß, A. (2007): Marktforschung - Grundlagen der Datenerhebung und Datenanalyse. (2. Ed.), Gabler, Wiesbaden 2007.

Lacity, M.C.; Hirschheim, R.A. (1993a): Information Systems Outsourcing - Myths, Metaphors and Realities, John Wiley & Sons, Chichester, New York 1993a.

Lacity, M.C.; Hirschheim, R.A. (1993b): The Information Systems Outsourcing Bandwagon. In: MIT Sloan Management Review, Vol. 35, 1, pp. 73-86.

Lacity, M.C.; Hirschheim, R.A. (1994): Realizing Outsourcing Expectations: Incredible Expectations, Credible Outcomes. In: Information Systems Management, Vol. 11, 4, pp. 7-18.

Lacity, M.C.; Hirschheim, R.A. (1995a): Benchmarking as a Strategy for Managing Conflicting Stakeholder Perceptions of Information Systems. In: Journal of Strategic Information Systems, Vol. 4, 2, pp. 165-185.

Lacity, M.C.; Hirschheim, R.A. (1995b): Beyond the Information Systems Outsourcing Bandwagon: The Insourcing Response, John Wiley and Sons, New York, NY 1995b.

Lacity, M.C.; Janson, M.A. (1994): Understanding Qualitative Data: A Framework of Text Analysis Methods. In: Journal of Management Information Systems, Vol. 11, 2, pp. 137-155.

Lacity, M.C.; Willcocks, L.P. (1994): Information Systems Outsourcing: A Transaction Cost Interpretation of Empirical Evidence. OXIIM working paper, Templeton College, Oxford University, 1994.

Lacity, M.C.; Willcocks, L.P. (1995): Information Systems Outsourcing in Theory and Practice. In: Journal of Information Technology Vol. 10, 4, pp. 203-207.

Lacity, M.C.; Willcocks, L.P. (1998): An Empirical Investigation of Information Technology Sourcing Practices: Lessons from Experience. In: MIS Quarterly, Vol. 22, 3, pp. 363-408.

Lacity, M.C.; Willcocks, L.P. (2000a): Relationships in IT outsourcing: a stakeholder perspective (Research Paper). Oxford Institute of Information Management, 2000a.

Lacity, M.C.; Willcocks, L.P. (2000b): Survey of IT Outsourcing Experiences in US and UK Organizations. In: Journal of Global Information Management (JGIM), Vol. 8, 2, pp. 5-23.

Lacity, M.C.; Willcocks, L.P. (2001): Global Information Technology Outsourcing. In Search of Business Advantage, Wiley, Chichester, New York 2001.

Lacity, M.C.; Willcocks, L.P. (2003): IT Sourcing Reflections: Lessons for Customers and Suppliers. In: Wirtschaftsinformatik, Vol. 45, 2, pp. 115-125.

Lacity, M.C.; Willcocks, L.P.; Feeny, D.F. (1994): Information Systems Outsourcing: A Decision-making Framework. OXIIM working paper, Templeton College, Oxford University, 1994.

Lacity, M.C.; Willcocks, L.P.; Feeny, D.F. (1996): The Value of Selective IT Sourcing. In: Sloan Management Review, Vol. 37, 3, pp. 13-25.

Lambe, C.J.; Spekman, R.E.; Hunt, S.D. (2000): Interimistic Relational Exchange: Conceptualization and Propositional Development. In: Journal of the Academy of Marketing Science, Vol. 28, 2, pp. 212-225.

Lasher, D.; Ives, B.; Jarvenpaa, S. (1991): USAA-IBM Partnerships in Information Technology: Managing the Image Project. In: MIS Quarterly, Vol. 15, 4, pp. 551-566.

Lawley, D.N.; Maxwell, A.E. (1971): Factor analysis as a statistical method, Butterworth and Co., London 1971.

Lee, A.S. (1989): A Scientific Methodology for MIS Case Studies. In: MIS Quarterly, Vol. 13, 1, pp. 33-52.

Lee, A.S. (1991): Integrating positivist and interpretive approaches to organizational research. In: Organization Science, Vol. 2, 4, pp. 342-365.

Lee, A.S. (1999): Rigor and Relevance in MIS Research: Beyond the Approach of Positivism Alone. In: MIS Quarterly, Vol. 23, 1, pp. 29 - 34.

Lee, J.-N.; Huynh, M.Q.; Chi-wai, K.R.; Pi, S.-M. (2000): The Evolution of Outsourcing Research: What is the Next Issue? , *Proceedings of the 33rd Hawaii International Conference on System Sciences-Volume 7*: IEEE Computer Society.

Lee, J.-N.; Huynh, M.Q.; Kwok, R.C.-W.; Pi, S.-M. (2003): IT Outsourcing Evolution-- Past, Present, and Future. In: Communications of the ACM, Vol. 46, 5, pp. 84-89.

Lee, J.-N.; Kim, Y.-G. (1999): Effect of Partnership Quality on IS Outsourcing Success: Conceptual Framework and Empirical Validation. In: Journal of Management Information Systems, Vol. 15, 4, pp. 29-61.

Lee, J.-N.; Miranda, S.M.; Kim, Y.-M. (2004): IT Outsourcing Strategies: Universalistic, Contingency, and Configurational Explanations of Success. In: Information Systems Research, Vol. 15, 2, pp. 110-131.

Lee, J.N. (2001): The Impact of Knowledge Sharing, Organizational Capability and Partnership Quality on IS Outsourcing Success. In: Information & Management, Vol. 38, 5, pp. 323-335.

Leimeister, S.; Böhmann, T.; Krcmar, H. (2008): IS Outsourcing Governance in Innovation-Focused Relationships: An Empirical Investigation. Paper presented at the 16th European Conference on Information Systems, Galway, Ireland, p. CD-ROM.

Levina, N.; Ross, J.W. (2003): From the Vendor's Perspective: Exploring the Value Proposition in Information Technology Outsourcing. In: MIS Quarterly, Vol. 27, 3, pp. 331-364.

Levine, S.; White, P. (1961): Exchange as a Conceptual Framework for the Study of Interorganizational Relationships. In: Administrative Science Quarterly, Vol. 5, 4, pp. 583-601.

Levinson, H.; Price, C.R.; Munden, K.J.; Solley, C.M. (1962): Men, Management and Mental Health, Harvard University Press, Cambridge, MA 1962.

Lewis, J.D. (1990): Partnerships for Profit: Structuring and Managing Strategic Alliances, Free Press, New York 1990.

Linder, J.C. (2004): Transformational Outsourcing. In: MIT Sloan Management Review, Vol. 45, 2, pp. 52-58.

Lingnau, M.; Stauber, J. (2005): Erfolgreiches IT-Outtasking durch Kostensenkung, Qualitätsmangement und Innovationspartnerschaft. In: Outsourcing: Schlüsselfaktoren der Kundenzufriedenheit. Ed.: Köhler-Frost, W., (5., vollst. neu bearb. Ed.). Erich Schmidt Verlag, Berlin 2005, pp. 100-114.

Little, R.J.A.; Rubin, D.B. (1987): Statistical Analysis with Missing Data, John Wiley and Sons, New York 1987.

Little, R.J.A.; Rubin, D.B. (2002): Statistical Analysis with Missing Data. (2. Ed.), John Wiley & Sons, Inc., Hoboken, NJ 2002.

Lloyd, S.P. (1957, 1982): Least squares quantization in PCM. Technical Note. In: IEEE Transactions on Information Theory, Vol. 28, pp. 128-137.

Loh, L.; Venkatraman, N. (1991): 'Outsourcing' as a Mechanism of Information Technology Governance: A Test of Alternative Diffusion Models (Working Paper No. BPS 3271-91). MIT Sloan School of Management, 1991.

Loh, L.; Venkatraman, N. (1992a): Determinants of Information Technology Outsourcing: A Cross-Sectional Analysis. In: Journal of Management Information Systems, Vol. 9, 1, pp. 7-24.

Loh, L.; Venkatraman, N. (1992b): Diffusion of Information Technology Outsourcing: Influence Sources and the Kodak Effect. In: Information Systems Research, Vol. 3, 4, pp. 334-358.

Loh, L.; Venkatraman, N. (1995): An empirical study of information technology outsourcing: Benefits, risk and performance implications. *Sixteenth International Conference on Information Systems* (pp. 277-288). Amsterdam.

Lowell, M. (1992): Managing your Outsourcing Vendor in the Financail Services Industry. In: Journal of Systems Management, Vol. May, pp. 23-27.

Luftman, J.; Kempaiah, R.; Nash, E. (2006): Key Issues for IT Executives 2005. In: MIS Quarterly Executive, Vol. 5, 2, pp. 27-45.

Lusch, R.F. (1976a): Channel Conflict: Its Impact on Retailer Operating Performance. In: Journal of Retailing, Vol. 52, 2, pp. 3-90.

Lusch, R.F. (1976b): Sources of Power: Their Impact on Intrachannel Conflict. In: Journal of Marketing Research (JMR), Vol. 13, 4, pp. 382-390.

Lusch, R.F. (1977): Franchisee Satisfaction: Causes and Consequences. In: International Journal of Physical Distribution and Materials Management, Vol. 7, 3, pp. 128-140.

Lusch, R.F.; Brown, J.R. (1982): A Modified Model of Power in the Marketing Channel. In: Journal of Marketing Research, Vol. 19, 3, pp. 312-323.

Lyons, B.; Mehta, J. (1997): Contracts, opportunism and trust: self-interest and social orientation. In: Cambridge Journal of Economics, Vol. 21, 2, pp. 239-257.

Lyons, T.F.; Krachenberg, A.R.; Henke, J.W., Jr. (1990): Mixed Motive Marriages: What's Next for Buyer-Supplier Relations? In: Sloan Management Review, Vol. 31, 3, pp. 29-36.

Macaulay, S. (1963): Non-Contractual Relations in Business. In: American Sociological Review, Vol. 28, 1, pp. 55-67.

Macneil, I.R. (1974): The Many Futures of Contracts. In: Southern California Law Review, Vol. 47, 3, pp. 691-816.

Macneil, I.R. (1978): Contracts: Adjustment of Long-Term Economic Relations Under Classical, neoclassical, and Relational Contract Law. In: Northwestern University law Review, Vol. 72, 6, pp. 854-905.

Macneil, I.R. (1980): The New Social Contract: An Inquiry into Modern Contractual Relations, Yale University Press, New Haven 1980.

Mahnke, V.; Overby, M.L.; Vang, J. (2005): Strategic Outsourcing of IT Services: Theoretical Stocktaking and Empirical Challenges. In: Industry & Innovation, Vol. 12, 2, pp. 205-253.

Mahnke, V.; Özcan, S. (2006): Outsourcing Innovation and Relational Governance. In: Industry & Innovation, Vol. 13, 2, pp. 121-125.

Mahnke, V.; Özcan, S.; Overby, M.L. (2006): Outsourcing Innovative Capabilities for IT-Enabled Services. In: Industry and Innovation, Vol. 13, 2, pp. 189-207.

Mahoney, J.T.; McNally, R.C. (2004): Explaining and Predicting the Choice of Organizational Form: Integrating Performance Ambiguity and Asset Specificity Effects. College of Business, University of Illinois, 2004.

Malone, T.W.; Crowston, K. (1990): What is coordination theory and how can it help design cooperative work systems? , *Proceedings of the 1990 ACM conference on Computer-supported cooperative work*. Los Angeles, California, United States: ACM Press.

Malone, T.W.; Crowston, K. (1994): The Interdisciplinary Study of Coordination. In: ACM Computing Surveys (CSUR), Vol. 26, 1, pp. 87-119.

Malone, T.W.; Yates, J.; Benjamin, R.I. (1987): Electronic Markets and Electronic Hierarchies: Effects of Information Technology on Market Structure and Corporate Strategies. In: Communications of the ACM, Vol. 30, 6 (June), pp. 484-497.

Mani, D.; Barua, A.; Whinston, A.B. (2006): Successfully Governing Business Process Outsourcing Relationships. In: MIS Quarterly Executive, Vol. 5, 1, pp. 15-29.

Markus, M.L. (1983): Power, politics, and MIS implementation. In: Commun. ACM, Vol. 26, 6, pp. 430-444.

Martinez, J.I.; Jarillo, J.C. (1989): The Evoluation of Research on Coordination Mechanisms in Multinational Cooperations. In: Journal of International Business Studies, Vol. 20, 3 (Fall), pp. 489-514.

Martinsons, M.G. (1993): Outsourcing Information Systems: A Strategic Partnership with Risks. In: Long Range Planning, Vol. 26, 3, pp. 18-25.

Matiaske, W.; Mellewigt, T. (2002): Motive, Erfolge und Risiken des Outsourcings - Befunde und Defizite der empirischen Outsourcing-Forschung. (With English summary.). In: Zeitschrift fur Betriebswirtschaft, Vol. 72, 6, pp. 641-59.

Mayer, K.J.; Argyres, N.S. (2004): Learning to Contract: Evidence from the Personal Computer Industry. In: Organization Science, Vol. 15, 4, pp. 394-410.

Mayring, P. (2000): Qualitative Inhaltsanalyse. Grundlagen und Techniken. (7. Ed.), Deutscher Studien Verlag, Weinheim 2000.

McFarlan, F.W.; Nolan, R.L. (1995): How to Manage an IT Outsourcing Alliance. In: Sloan Management Review, pp. 9-23.

McKelvey, B. (1975): Guidelines for the Empirical Classification of Organizations. In: Administrative Science Quarterly, Vol. 20, 4, pp. 509-525.

McLellan, K.; Marcolin, B.L.; Beamish, P.W. (1995): Financial and strategic motivations behind IS outsourcing. In: Journal of Information Technology, Vol. 10, 4, pp. 299-321.

Mejias, R.; Shepard, M.; Vogel, D.; Lazaneo, L. (1996): Consensus and Perceived Satisfaction Levels: A Cross-cultural Comparison of GSS and non-GSS Outcomes within and between the United States and Mexico. In: Journal of Management Information Systems, Vol. 13, 3, pp. 137-161.

Meyer, A.D.; Tsui, A.S.; Hinings, C.R. (1993): Configurational Approaches to Organizational Analysis. In: Academy of Management Journal, Vol. 36, 6, pp. 1175-1195.

Meyer, N.D. (1994): A sensible approach to outsourcing: the economic fundamentals. In: Information Systems Management, Vol. 11, 4, pp. 22-27.

Michell, V.; Fitzgerald, G. (1997): The IT outsourcing marketplace: vendors and their selection. In: Journal of Information Technology, Vol. 12, 3, pp. 223-237.

Michie, D.A. (1978): Managerial Tactics: An Alternative Explanation of Warranty Satisfaction in a Channel of Distribution. In: Research Frontiers in Marketing: Dialogues and Directions. Ed.: Jain, S.C. American Marketing, Chicago 1978, pp. 260-265.

Miles, R.; Snow, C. (1978): Organizational Strategy, Structure and Process, McGraw-Hill, New York 1978.

Millar, V. (1994): Outsourcing Trends. Paper presented at the Outsourcing, Cosourcing and Insourcing Conference, University of California - Berkeley.

Miller, D. (1981): Toward a new contingency approach: The search for organizational gestalts. In: Journal of Management Studies, Vol. 18, 1, pp. 1–26.

Miller, D. (1996): Configuration revisited. In: Strategic Management Journal, Vol. 17, 7, pp. 505-512.

Miller, D.; Friesen, P.H. (1984): Organizations - A Quantum View, Prentice-Hall, Englewood Cliffs, NJ 1984.

Milligan, G.W. (1980): An Examination of the Effect of Six Types of Error Perturbation on Fifteen Clustering Algorithms. In: Psychometrika, Vol. 45, September, pp. 325-342.

Milligan, G.W. (1996): Clustering Validation: Results and Implications for Applied Analyses. In: Clustering and Classification. Ed.: Arabie, P.; Hubert, L.J.; De Soete, G. World Scientific, River Edge, NJ 1996, pp. 341-375.

Milligan, G.W.; Cooper, M.C. (1985): An Examination of Procedures for Determining the Number of Clusters in a Data Set. In: Psychometrika, Vol. 50, 2, pp. 159-179.

Mingers, J. (2001): Combining IS Research Methods: Towards a Pluralist Methodology. In: Information Systems Research, Vol. 12, 3, pp. 240-259.

Mintzberg, H. (1979): The Structuring of Organizations, Prentice-Hall, New York 1979.

Mintzberg, H. (1980): Structure in 5's: A Synthesis of the Research on Organization Design. In: Management Science, Vol. 26, 3 (March), pp. 322-341.

Mintzberg, H.; Raisinghani, D.; Theoret, A. (1976): The Structure of "Unstructured" Decision Processes. In: Administrative Science Quarterly, Vol. 21, 2, pp. 246-275.

Miranda, S.M.; Kavan, C.B. (2005): Moments of governance in IS outsourcing: conceptualizing effects of contracts on value capture and creation. In: Journal of Information Technology, Vol. 20, pp. 152-169.

Mirkin, B. (2005): Clustering for Data Mining. A Data Recovery Approach, Chapman & Hall, Taylor & Francis Group, Boca Raton, FL 2005.

Mohr, J.; Spekman, R. (1994): Characteristics of Partnership Success: Partnership Attributes, Communication Behavior, and Conflict Resolution Techniques. In: Strategic Management Journal, Vol. 15 2, pp. 135-152.

Moll, K.-R. (1994): Informatik-Management. Aufgabengebiete, Lösungswege und Controlling, Springer, Berlin u. a. 1994.

Monczka, R.M.; Petersen, K.J.; Handfield, R.B.; Ragatz, G.L. (1998): Success Factors in Strategic Supplier Alliances: The Buying Company Perspective. In: Decision Sciences, Vol. 29, 3, pp. 553-577.

Moorman, C.; Deshpandé, R.; Zaltman, G. (1993): Factors Affecting Trust in Market Research Relationships. In: Journal of Marketing, Vol. 57, 1, pp. 81-101.

Moorman, C.; Zaltman, G.; Deshpande, R. (1992): Relationships Between Providers and Users of Marketing Research: The Dynamics of Trust Within and Between Organizations. In: Journal of Marketing Research, Vol. 29, August, pp. 314-329.

Moran, P.; Ghoshal, S. (1999): Markets, Firms, and The Process of Economic Development. In: Academy of Management Review, Vol. 24, 3, pp. 390-412.

Morgan, R.M.; Hunt, S.D. (1994): The Commitment-Trust Theory of Relationship Marketing. In: Journal of Marketing, Vol. 59, 3, pp. 20-38.

Muller, N.J. (1999): Managing Service Level Agreements. In: International Journal of Network Management, Vol. 9, pp. 155-166.

Müller, P.P.; Schwarze, L. (2005): IT-Outsourcing – Erfahrungen, Status und zukünftige Herausforderungen. In: HMD - Praxis der Wirtschaftsinformatik, Vol. 245, pp. 6-17.

Myers, M.D. (1997): Qualitative Research in Information Systems. In: MIS Quarterly, Vol. 21, 2, pp. 241-242.

Myers, M.D. (1999): Investigating Information Systems with Ethnographic Research. In: Communications of the AIS, Vol. 2, 23, pp. 1-20.

Nagengast, J. (1997): Outsourcing von Dienstleistungen industrieller Unternehmen – eine theoretische und empirische Analyse. Hamburg.

Nahapiet, J.; Ghoshal, S. (1998): Social capital, intellectual capital, and the organizational advantage. In: Academy of Management Review, Vol. 23, 2, pp. 242-266.

Nam, K.; Rajagopalan, S.; Rao, H.R.; Chaudhury, A. (1996): A two-level investigation of information systems outsourcing. In: Communications of the ACM, Vol. 39, 7, pp. 36-44.

Narus, J.; Anderson, J. (1987): Distribution Contributions to Partnerships with Manufacturers. In: Business Horizons, Vol. 30, 5, pp. 34-42.

Norušis, M.J. (2005): SPSS 13.0 Statistical Procedures Companion, SPSS, Inc., Chicago 2005.

Nunnally, J.C. (1978): Psychometric Theory. (2. Ed.), McGraw-Hill Book Company, New York 1978.

Nunnally, J.C.; Bernstein, I.H. (1994): Psychometric Theory. (3. Ed.), McGraw-Hill, New York 1994.

OECD (2004): Principles of Corporate Governance: Organization for Economic Cooperation and Development, 2004.

Oliver, C. (1990): Determinants of Interorganizational Relationships: Integration and Future Directions. In: Academy of Management Review, Vol. 15, 2, pp. 241-265.

Oliver, R.L. (1977): Effect of Expectation and Disconfirmation on Postexposure Product Evaluations - an Alternative Interpretation. In: Journal of Applied Psychology, Vol. 62, 4, pp. 480.

Oliver, R.L. (1980): A Cognitive Model of the Antecedents and Consequences of Satisfaction Decisions. In: Journal of Marketing Research, Vol. 17, 4, pp. 460-469.

Oliver, R.L. (1996): Varieties of Value in the Consumption Satisfaction Response. In: Advances in Consumer Research, Vol. 23, pp. 143-147.

Orlikowski, W.J. (1991): Integrated Information Environment or Matrix of Control? The Contradictory Implications of Information Technology. In: Accounting, Management and Information Technologies, Vol. 1, 1, pp. 9-42.

Orlikowski, W.J. (1993): CASE Tools as Organizational Change: Investigating Incremental and Radical Changes in Systems Development. In: MIS Quarterly, Vol. 17, 3, pp. 309-340.

Orlikowski, W.J.; Baroudi, J.J. (1991): Studying Information Technology in Organizations: Research Approaches and Assumptions. In: Information Systems Research, Vol. 2, 1, pp. 1-28.

Ouchi, W.G.; Maguire, M.A. (1975): Organizational Control: Two Functions. In: Administrative Science Quarterly, Vol. 20, 4, pp. 559-569.

Overby, S. (2007): ABC: An Introduction to Outsourcing. http://cio.com/article/40380, accessed December 10, 2007.

Pallant, J. (2005): SPSS Survival Manual - a step by step guide to data analysis using SPSS version 12. (2. Ed.), Open University Press, Berkshire, UK 2005.

Palvia, P.C. (1995): A Dialectic View of Information Systems Outsourcing: Pros and Cons. In: Information & Management, Vol. 29, pp. 265-275.

Parasuraman, A.; Zeithaml, V.A.; Berry, L. (1988): SERVQUAL: a multiple-item scale for measuring consumer perceptions of service quality. In: Journal of Retailing, Vol. 64, 1, pp. 12-40.

Parasuraman, A.; Zeithaml, V.A.; Berry, L.L. (1985): A Conceptual Model of Service Quality and Its Implications for Future Research. In: Journal of Marketing, Vol. 49, 4, pp. 41-50.

Pearce, J.L. (1998): Review of 'Psychological contracts in organizations: understanding written and unwritten agreements'. In: Administrative Science Quarterly, Vol. 43, pp. 184-188.

Pearson, M.M. (1973): The Conflict-Performance Assumption. In: Journal of Purchasing, Vol. 9, 1, pp. 57-69.

Peled, A. (2001): Outsourcing and Political Power: Bureaucrats, Consultants, Vendors and Public Information Technology. In: Public Personnel Management, Vol. 30, 4, pp. 495-514.

Peter, J. (1981): Reliability: A Review of Psychometric Basics and Recent Marketing Practices. In: Journal of Marketing Research, Vol. 16, February, pp. 6-17.

Pfeffer, J. (1981): Power in Organizations, Pitman, Marshfield, Massachusetts 1981.

Pfeffer, J. (1982): Organizations and Organization Theory, Pitman, Boston 1982.

Pfeffer, J. (1992): Managing with Power: Politics and Influence in Organizations, Harvard Business School Press, Boston 1992.

Pfeffer, J.; Salancik, G.R. (1978): The External Control of Organizations: A Resource Dependence Perspective, Harper & Row, New York 1978.

Phillips, L.W. (1981): Assessing Measurement Error in Key Informant Reports: A Methodological Note on Organizational Analysis in Marketing. In: Journal of Marketing Research, Vol. 18, 4, pp. 395-415.

Piller, F.T. (2001): Mass Customization. Ein wettbewerbsstrategisches Konzept im Informationszeitalter. (2. Ed.), DUV, Wiesbaden 2001.

Podsakoff, P.M.; MacKenzie, S.B.; Lee, J.-Y.; Podsakoff, N.P. (2003): Common Method Biases in Behavioral Research: A Critical Review of the Literature and Recommended Remedies. In: Journal of Applied Psychology, Vol. 88, 5, pp. 879-903.

Poppo, L.; Zenger, T. (1998): Testing Alternative Theories of the Firm: Transaction Cost, Knowledge-based, and Measurement Explanation for Make-or-Buy Decisions in Information Services. In: Strategic Management Journal, Vol. 19, 9, pp. 853-877.

Poppo, L.; Zenger, T. (2002): Do Formal Contracts and Relational Governance Function as Substitutes or Complements? In: Strategic Management Journal, Vol. 23, 8, pp. 707-725.

Porter, M.E. (1974): Consumer Behavior, Retailer Power and Market Performance in Consumer Goods Industries. In: Review of Economics & Statistics, Vol. 56, 4, pp. 419-436.

Porter, M.E. (1985): Competitive Advantage: Creating and Sustaining Superior Performance, Free Press, New York, London 1985.

Porter, M.E.; Millar, V.E. (1985): How Information Gives You Competitive Advantage. In: Harvard Business Review, Vol. 63, 4, pp. 149-162.

Potter, K. (2007): Gartner on Outsourcing, 2007-2008. Gartner, 2007.

Pressey, A.D.; Mathews, B.P. (2004): Patterns of Trust in Buyer-Seller Relationships: Motives for Formation, Drivers, Outcomes and Temporal Relationships. In: Journal of Customer Behaviour, Vol. 3, 1, pp. 81-100.

Priem, R.L. (2001): The Business-level RBV: Great wall or Berlin wall. In: Academy of Management Review, Vol. 26, 4, pp. 499-501.

Pruitt, D.G. (1981): Negotiation Behavior, Academic Press, New York 1981.

Punj, G.; Stewart, D.W. (1983): Cluster analysis in marketing research: Review and suggestions for application. In: Journal of Marketing Research, Vol. 20, pp. 134-148.

Pütter, C. (2007): Von Green IT bis Business Technologie: IT-Trends 2008. CIO Magazin, http://www.cio.de/strategien/methoden/846817/index.html, accessed December 13, 2007.

Quelin, B.; Duhamel, F. (2003): Bringing Together Strategic Outsourcing and Corporate Strategy: Outsourcing Motives and Risks. In: European Management Journal, Vol. 21, 5, pp. 647-661.

Quinn, J.B. (1999): Strategic Outsourcing: Leveraging Knowledge Capabilites. In: Sloan Management Review, Vol. 40, 4, pp. 9-22.

Quinn, J.B. (2000): Outsourcing Innovation: The New Engine of Growth. In: Sloan Management Review, Vol. 41, 4, pp. 13-28.

Quinn, J.B.; Hilmer, F.G. (1994): Strategic Outsourcing. In: Sloan Management Review, Vol. 35, 4, pp. 43-55.

Rai, A.; Borah, S.; Ramaprasad, A. (1996): Critical Success Factors for Strategic Alliances in the Information Technology Industry: An Empirical Study. In: Decision Sciences, Vol. 27, 1, pp. 141-155.

Rapoport, R.N. (1970): Three Dilemmas in Action Research. In: Human Relations, Vol. 23, 4, pp. 499-513.

Reilly, C.T.; Rouse, A.C.; Seddon, P.B. (2001): Benchmarking and Information Technology Outsourcing Outcomes. *7th Americas Conference on Information Systems* (pp. 1873-1879). Boston, MA.

Rich, P. (1992): The organizational taxonomy: Definition and design. In: Academy of Management Review, Vol. 17, 4, pp. 758-781.

Richmond, W.; Seidmann, A. (1993): Software development outsourcing: contract structure and business value. In: Journal of Management Information Systems, Vol. 10, 1, pp. 57-72.

Richmond, W.B.; Seidmann, A.; Whinston, A.B. (1992): Incomplete contracting issues in information systems development outsourcing. In: Decision Support Systems, Vol. 8, 5, pp. 459-477.

Ring, P.S.; Van de Ven, A. (1994): Developmental Processes of cooperative interorganizational relationships. In: Academy of Management Review, Vol. 19, 1, pp. 90-118.

Robey, D.; Franz, C.; Franz, R.; Farrow, D.L.; Sabherwal, R. (1989): Group process and conflict in system development. The role of trust in outsourced IS development projects. In: Management Science, Vol. 35, 10, pp. 1172-1191.

Robicheaux, R.A.; El-Ansary, A.I. (1976): A General Model for Understanding Channel Member Behavior. In: Journal of Retailing, Vol. 52, 4, pp. 13-30, 93-94.

Robinson, J.P.; Shaver, P.R.; Wrightsman, L.S. (1991): Criteria for Scale Selection and Evaluation. In: Measures of Personality and Social Psychological Attitudes. Ed.: Robinson, J.P.; Shaver, P.R.; Wrightsman, L.S. Academic Press, San Diego, CA 1991.

Robinson, P. (2008): Why Settle For Less? Deloitte Consulting 2008 Outsourcing Report. Deloitte Consulting Outsourcing Advisory Services, 2008.

Robinson, S.L.; Kraatz, M.S.; Rousseau, D.M. (1994): Changing Obligations and the Psychological Contract: A Longitudinal Study. In: Academy of Management Journal, Vol. 37, 1, pp. 137-152.

Rodgers, W.; Pavlou, P.; Guiral, A. (2003): Developing a Predictive Model: A Comparative Study of the Partial Least Squares vs. Maximum Likelihood Techniques. Riverside, CA: Graduate School of Management, University of California.

Roehling, M. (1997): The origins and early development of the psychological contract construct. In: Journal of Management History, Vol. 3, 2, pp. 204-217.

Roering, K.J. (1977): Bargaining in Distribution Channels. In: Journal of Business Research, Vol. 5, 1, pp. 15-26.

Rosenberg, L.J.; Stern, L.W. (1971): Conflict Measurement in the Distribution Channel. In: Journal of Marketing Research (JMR), Vol. 8, 4, pp. 437-442.

Rossiter, J. (2002): The C-OAR-SE Procedure for Scale Development in Marketing. In: International Journal of Research in Marketing, Vol. 19, 4, pp. 305-335.

Rottman, J.W.; Lacity, M.C. (2004): Twenty Practices for Offshore Sourcing. In: MIS Quarterly Excecutive, Vol. 3, 3, pp. 117-130.

Rouse, A.C.; Corbitt, B.J.; Aubert, B.A. (2001): Perspectives on IT-Outsourcing Success: Covariance Structure Modelling of a Survey of Outsourcing in Australia. Paper presented at the Ninth European Conference on Information Systems, Bled, Slovenia.

Rousseau, D. (1995): Psychological Contracts in Organizations: Understanding Written and Unwritten Agreements, Sage Publications Inc., Thousand Oaks, CA 1995.

Rousseau, D.; Sitkin, S.; Burt, R.; Camerer, C. (1998): Not So Different after All: A Cross-Discipline View of Trust. In: Academy of Management Review, Vol. 23, 3, pp. 393-404.

Rousseau, D.M. (1989): Psychological and implied contracts in organizations. In: Employee Rights and Responsibilities Journal, Vol. 2, pp. 121-139.

Rousseau, D.M.; Tijoriwala, S.A. (1998): Assessing psychological contracts: Issues, alternatives and measures. In: Journal of Organizational Behavior, Vol. 19, pp. 679-695.

Sabherwal, R. (1999): The Role of Trust in Outsourced IS Development Projects. In: Communications of the ACM, Vol. 42, 2, pp. 80-86.

Sackett, P.R.; Larson, J.R., Jr. (1990): Research strategies and tactics in industrial and organizational psychology. In: Handbook of industrial and organizational psychology. Ed.: Dunnette, M.D.; Hough, L.M. Consulting Psychologists Press, Palo Alto, CA 1990, pp. 419-489.

Sambamurthy, V.; Zmud, R.W. (2000): Research Commentary: The Organizing Logic for an Enterprise's IT Activities in the Digital Era--A Prognosis of Practice and a Call for Research. In: Information Systems Research, Vol. 11, 2, pp. 105-114.

Sargent, A. (2006): Outsourcing relationship literature: an examination and implications for future research. Paper presented at the 2006 ACM SIGMIS CPR conference, Claremont, California, USA.

Saunders, C.; Gebelt, M.; Hu, Q. (1997): Achieving Success in Information Systems Outsourcing. In: California Management Review, Vol. 39, 2, pp. 63-79.

Scanzoni, J. (1983): Social Exchange and Behavioral Interdependence. In: Social Exchange in Developing Relationships. Ed.: Burgess, R.; Huston, T. Academic Press, New York 1983, pp. 61-98.

Scardino, L.; Young, A.; Anderson, D.S. (2007): Gartner on Outsourcing, 2007-2008: Application Outsourcing. Gartner, 2007.

Schaninger, C.M.; Bass, W.C. (1986): Removing Response-Style Effects in Attribute-Determinance Ratings to Identify Market Segments. In: Journal of Business Research, Vol. 14, pp. 237-252.

Schendel, D.; Hofer, C.W. (1979): Strategic Management. A New View of Business Policy and Planning, Little Brown & Company, Boston, Toronto 1979.

Schnell, R.; Hill, P.B.; Esser, E. (2005): Methoden der empirischen Sozialforschung. (7., völlig überarb. u. erw. Ed.), Oldenbourg, München, Wien 2005.

Seddon, P.B.; Cullen, S.; Willcocks, L. (2002): Does Domberger's theory of the contracting organization explain satisfaction with IT outsourcing? , *23rd International Conference on Information Systems 2002*.

Seltin, N.; Keeves, J.P. (1994): Path Analysis with Latent Variables. In: International Encyclopedia of Education. Ed.: Husen, T.; Postlethwaite, T.N. Pergamon Press, Oxford 1994, pp. 4352-4359.

Sethuraman, R.; Anderson, J.C.; Narus, J.A. (1988): Partnership advantage and its determinants in distributor and manufacturer working relationships. In: Journal of Business Research, Vol. 17, 4, pp. 327-347.

Sheppard, A.G. (1996): The Sequence of Factor Analysis and Cluster Analysis: Differences in Segmentation and Dimensionality through the Use of Raw and Factor Scores. In: Tourism Analysis, Vol. 1, pp. 49-57.

Silver, M.S.; Markus, M.L.; Beath, C.M. (1995): The Information Technology Interaction Model: A Foundation for the MBA Core Course. In: Management Information Systems Quarterly, Vol. 19, 3 (September), pp. 361-390.

Simon, H. (1953): Notes on the Observation and Measurement of Political Power. In: Journal of Politics, Vol. 15, pp. 500-516.

Simon, H. (1957): Models of Man: Social and Rational, Wiley, New York 1957.

Simpson, J.; Mayo, D. (1997): Relationship Management: A Call for Fewer Influence Attempts. In: Journal of Business Research, Vol. 39, 3, pp. 209-218.

Singh, T.; Brown, R.H.; Tornbohm, C.; Goldman, M.; Pring, B. (2007): Gartner on Outsourcing, 2007-2008: Business Process Outsourcing. Gartner, 2007.

Slaugther, S.; Ang, S. (1996): Employment Outsourcing in Information Systems. In: Communications of the ACM, Vol. 39, 7, pp. 47-54.

Smith, J.B. (1998): Buyer-Seller relationships: Similarity, relationship management, and quality. In: Psychology and Marketing, Vol. 15, 1, pp. 3-21.

Smith, K.G.; Carroll, S.J.; Ashford, S.J. (1995): Intra- and Interorganizational Cooperation: Toward a Research Agenda. In: Academy of Management Journal, Vol. 38, 1, pp. 7-23.

Smith, M.A.; Mitra, S.; Narasimhan, S. (1998): Information systems outsourcing: A study of pre-event firm Characteristics. In: Journal of Management Information Systems, Vol. 15, 2, pp. 60-92.

Smithson, S.; Hirschheim, R.A. (1998): Analysing information systems evaluation: Another look at an old problem. In: European Journal of Information Systems Research, Vol. 7, 3, pp. 158-174.

Sneath, P.H.A.; Sokal, R.R. (1973): Numerical Taxonomy, Freeman, San Francisco 1973.

Sobel, M.E. (1982): Asymptotic Confidence Intervals for Indirect Effects in Structural Equation Models. In: Sociological Methodology. Ed.: Leinhardt, S. Jossey-Bass, San Francisco 1982, pp. 290-312.

Sobol, M.G.; Apte, U. (1998): Outsourcing Practices and Views of America's Most Effective IS Users. In: Strategic Sourcing of Information Systems. Ed.: Willcocks, L.P.; Lacity, M.C. John Wiley & Sons Ltd., Chichester 1998, pp. 283-304.

Sparrow, E. (2003): Successful IT Outsourcing: From Choosing a Provider to Managing the Project, Springer-Verlag, London 2003.

Spekman, R.E.; Salmond, D.J.; Lambe, C.J. (1997): Consensus and Collaboration: Norm-regulated Behaviour in Industrial Marketing Relationships. In: European Journal of Marketing, Vol. 31, 11/12, pp. 835-856.

Spriggs, M.T. (1996): The New Social Contract: an Inquiry into Modern Contractual Relations. In: Journal of Public Policy and Marketing, Vol. 15, 1, pp. 157-159.

Stern, L.W.; El-Ansary, A. (1982): Marketing Channels. (2. Ed.), Prentice-Hall, Englewood Cliffs 1982.

Stern, L.W.; Sternthal, B.; Craig, C.S. (1973): Managing Conflict in Distribution Channels: A Laboratory Study. In: Journal of Marketing Research (JMR), Vol. 10, 2, pp. 169-179.

Straub, D.; Gefen, D.; Boudreau, M.-C. (2004): The IS World Quantitative, Positivist Research Methods Website. Galletta, D. In: http://www.dstraub.cis.gsu.edu:88/quant/, accessed December 5, 2007.

Strauss, A.; Corbin, J. (1994): Grounded Theory Methodology - An Overview. In: Handbook of Qualitative Research. Ed.: Denzin, N.K.; Lincoln, Y.S. Sage Publications, Thousand Oaks, London et al 1994, pp. 273-285.

Susarla, A.; Barua, A.; Whinston, A.B. (2003): Understanding the Service Component of Application Service Provision: An Empirical Analysis of Satisfaction with ASP Services. In: MIS Quarterly, Vol. 27, 1, pp. 91-123.

Tabachnick, B.G.; Fidell, L.S. (2001): Using Multivariate Statistics. (4. Ed.), Allyn and Bacon, Needham Heights, Boston 2001.

Tan, C.; Sia, S.K. (2006): Managing Flexibility in Outsourcing. In: Journal of the Association for Information Systems, Vol. 7, 4, pp. 179-206.

Tapscott, D.; Caston, A. (1993): Paradigm Shift: The New Promise of Information Technology, McGraw Hill, New York 1993.

Termenière, A. (2007): SITSI - Methodology and Segmentation. Pierre Audoin Consultants (PAC), 2007.

Thibaut, J.W.; Kelley, H.H. (1959): The Social Psychology of Groups, Wiley, New York 1959.

Thompson, J.D. (1967): Organizations in Action, McGraw-Hill, New York 1967.

Tramacere, G.; Matlus, R.T. (2007): Gartner on Outsourcing, 2007-2008: Infrastructure Outsourcing. Gartner, 2007.

Tryon, R.C. (1939): Cluster Analysis: Correlation Profile and Orthometric (Factor) Analysis for the Isolation of Unities in Mind and Personality, Edwards Brothers, Ann Arbor, MI 1939.

Tryon, R.C.; Bailey, D.E. (1970): Cluster Analysis, McGraw-Hill, New York 1970.

Tschamler, H. (1996): Wissenschaftstheorie: Eine Einführung für Pädagogen. (3. Ed.), Klinkhardt, Bad Heilbrunn 1996.

Tushman, M. (1977): A Political Approach to Organizations: A Review and Rationale. In: Academy of Management Review, Vol. 2, 2, pp. 206-216.

Uzzi, B. (1997): Social structure and competition in interfirm networks: The paradox of embeddedness. In: Administrative Science Quarterly, Vol. 42, 1, pp. 35-67.

van Bon, J. (2002): The Guide to IT Service Management, Vol. 1, Addison-Wesley 2002.

Van de Ven, A.H.; Delbecq, A.H.; Koenig, R. (1976): Determinants of Coordination Modes within Organizations. In: American Sociological Review, Vol. 41, 2, pp. 322-338.

van der Meer-Kooistra, J.; Vosselman, E.G.J. (2000): Management control of inter-firm transactional relationships: the case of industrial renovation and maintenance. In: Accounting, Organizations and Society, Vol. 25, 1, pp. 51-77.

van Grembergen, W. (2006): IT Governance and its Mechanisms - Introduction to Minitrack. *39th Hawaii International Conference on System Sciences HICSS.* Big Island, Hawaii.

Venkatesan, R. (1992): Strategic Sourcing: To Make or Not to Make. In: Harvard Business Review, Vol. 70, 6, pp. 98-107.

Venkatraman, N. (1989): The concept of fit in strategy research: toward verbal and statistical correspondence. In: Academy of Management Review, Vol. 14, 3, pp. 423-444.

Venkatraman, N.; Loh, L.; Koh, J. (1992): The Adoption of Corporate Governance Mechanisms: A Test of Competing Diffusion Models. Sloan School of Management, Massachusetts Institute of Technology, 1992.

von Jouanne-Diedrich, H. (2004): 15 Jahre Outsourcing-Forschung: Systematisierung und Lessons Learned. In: Informationsmanagement. Konzepte und Strategien für die Praxis. Ed.: Zarnekow, R.; Brenner, W.; Grohmann, H. dpunkt Verlag, Heidelberg 2004, pp. 125-133.

von Jouanne-Diedrich, H. (2007): Die IT-Sourcing-Map: Eine Orientierungshilfe im stetig wachsenden Dschungel der Outsourcing-Konzepte. http://www.ephorie.de/it-sourcing-map.htm, accessed January 3, 2009.

von Jouanne-Diedrich, H.; Zarnekow, R.; Brenner, W. (2005): Industrialisierung des IT-Sourcings. In: HMD - Praxis der Wirtschaftsinformatik, Vol. 245, pp. 18-27.

Wainer, H.; Kiely, G.L. (1987): Item clusters and computerized adaptive testing: A case for testlets. In: Journal of Educational Measurement, Vol. 24, pp. 185-201.

Walker, G. (1985): Strategic Sourcing, Vertical Integration and Transaction Costs. In: Interfaces, Vol. 18, 3, pp. 62-73.

Walker, G.; Weber, D. (1984): A Transaction Cost Approach to Make-or-Buy Decisions. In: Administrative Science Quarterly, Vol. 29, 3, pp. 373-391.

Walker, O.C. (1972): The Effects of Learning on Bargaining Behavior In: 1971 Combined Proceedings. Ed.: Allvine, F.C. American Marketing, Chicago 1972, pp. 194-199.

Walsham, G. (1993): Interpreting Information Systems in Organizations, John Wiley & Sons, Chichester 1993.

Walsham, G. (1995): Interpretive Case Studies in IS Research: Nature and Method. In: European Journal of Information Systems, Vol. 4, 2, pp. 74-81.

Wang, E.T.G. (2002): Transaction attributes and software outsourcing success: an empirical investigation of transaction cost theory. In: Information Systems Journal, Vol. 12, 2, pp. 153-181.

Webster, J.; Watson, R.T. (2002): Analyzing the Past to Prepare for the Future: Writing a Literature Review. In: MIS Quarterly, Vol. 26, 2, pp. 13-23.

Weill, P. (2002): Don't Just Lead, Govern: Implementing Effective IT Governance (CISR Working Paper 326), 2002.

Weill, P.; Broadbent, M. (1998): Leveraging the new infrastructure: how market leaders capitalize on information technology, Harvard Business School Press, Boston, Mass. 1998.

Weill, P.; Ross, J.W. (2004): IT Governance: How Top Performers Manage IT Decision Rights for Superior Results, Harvard Business School Press, Boston 2004.

Wibbelsman, D.; Maiero, T. (1994): Cosourcing. Paper presented at the Outsourcing, Cosourcing and Insourcing Conference, University of California, Berkeley.

Wiedenbeck, M.; Züll, C. (2001): Klassifikation mit Clusteranalyse: Grundlegende Techniken hierarchischer und k-means-Verfahren. ZUMA, 2001.

Wilder, C. (1989): Kodak hands processing over to IBM. In: Computerworld, Vol. July 31, pp. 1.

Wilder, C. (1990): DEC, IBM play ball in Kodak deal. In: Computerworld, Vol. January 15, pp. 8.

Wilkinson, I.; Kipnis, D. (1978): Interfirm Use of Power. In: Journal of Applied Psychology, Vol. 63, 3, pp. 315-320.

Wilkinson, I.F. (1974): Researching the Distribution Channels for Consumer and Industrial Goods: The Power Dimension. In: Journal of the Market Research Society, Vol. 16 1, pp. 12-32.

Wilkinson, I.F. (1979): Power and Satisfaction in Channels of Distribution. In: Journal of Retailing, Vol. 55, 2, pp. 79-94.

Wilkinson, I.F. (1981): Power, Conflict, and Satisfaction in Distribution Channels - An Empirical Study. In: International Journal of Physical Distribution and Materials Management, Vol. 11, 7, pp. 20-30.

Wilkinson, L.; Blank, G.; Gruber, C. (1996): Desktop Data Analysis with SYSTAT, Prentice-Hall, Upper Saddle River, NJ 1996.

Willcocks, L.; Fitzgerald, G. (1994): A Business Guide to Outsourcing Information Technology: A Study of European Best Practice in the Selection, Management and Use of External IT Services, Business Intelligence, London, UK 1994.

Willcocks, L.; Lacity, M. (1998a): The Sourcing and Outsourcing of IS: Shock of the New? In: Strategic Sourcing of Information Systems: Perspectives and Practices. Ed.: Willcocks, L.; Lacity, M. Wiley, Chichester 1998a, pp. 1-41.

Willcocks, L.; Lacity, M. (1998b): Strategic Sourcing of Information Systems: Perspectives and Practices, Wiley, Chichester 1998b.

Willcocks, L.; Lacity, M. (2000): Information Technology Outsourcing - Practices, Lessons and Prospects. http://www.templeton.ox.ac.uk/pdf/researchpapers/restricted/00-05.pdf, accessed May 17, 2006.

Willcocks, L.; Lacity, M.; Cullen, S. (2006): Information technology sourcing: Fifteen years of learning. *Working Paper Series* (pp. 1-41). London.

Willcocks, L.; Lacity, M.; Cullen, S. (2007): Information technology sourcing: Fifteen years of learning. In: The Oxford Handbook of Information and Communication Technologies. Ed.: Mansell, R.; Avgerou, C.; Quah, D. Oxford University Press, Oxford 2007, pp. 244-272.

Willcocks, L.; Lacity, M.; Fitzgerald, G. (1995): Information Technology Outsourcing in Europe and the USA: Assessment Issues. In: International Journal of Information Management, Vol. 15, 5, pp. 333-351.

Willcocks, L.P.; Choi, C.J. (1995): Co-operative partnership and 'total' IT outsourcing: From contractual obligation to strategic alliance? In: European Management Journal, Vol. 13, 1, pp. 67-78.

Willcocks, L.P.; Currie, W.L. (1997): Information Technology in Public Services: Towards the Contractual Organization? In: British Journal of Management, Vol. 8, 2, pp. 107-120.

Willcocks, L.P.; Fitzgerald, G.; Lacity, M.C. (1996): To Outsource IT or Not? Recent Research on Economics and Evaluation Practice. In: European Journal of Information Systems, Vol. 5, pp. 143-160.

Willcocks, L.P.; Hindle, J.; Feeny, D.F.; Lacity, M.C. (2004): IT and Business Process Outsourcing: The Knowledge Potential. In: Information Systems Management, Vol. 21, 3, pp. 7-15.

Willcocks, L.P.; Kern, T. (1998): IT outsourcing as strategic partnering: The case of the UK Inland Revenue. In: European Journal of Information Systems, Vol. 7, 1, pp. 29-45.

Willcocks, L.P.; Lacity, M.C. (1999): IT outsourcing in insurance services: risk, creative contracting and business advantage. In: Information Systems Journal, Vol. 9, 3, pp. 163-180.

Willcocks, L.P.; Lacity, M.C.; Fitzgerald, G. (1993): Market as Opportunity? Case Studies in Outsourcing Information Technology and Services. In: Journal of Strategic Information Systems, Vol. 2, 3, pp. 223-242.

Willcocks, L.P.; Lacity, M.C.; Kern, T. (1999): Risk mitigation in IT outsourcing strategy revisited: longitudinal case research at LISA. In: Journal of Strategic Information Systems, Vol. 8, 3, pp. 285-314.

Williamson, O.E. (1975): Markets and Hierarchies, Analysis and Antitrust Implications: A Study in the Economics of Internal Organization, The Free Press, New York 1975.

Williamson, O.E. (1979): Transaction-Cost Economics: The Governance of Contractual Relations. In: Journal of Law and Economics, Vol. 22, 2, pp. 233-261.

Williamson, O.E. (1981): The Economics of Organization: The Transaction Cost Approach. In: American Journal of Sociology, Vol. 87, 3, pp. 548-577.

Williamson, O.E. (1985): The Economic Institutions of Capitalism: Firms, Markets, and Relational Contracting, Free Press, Collier Macmillan, New York, London 1985.

Williamson, O.E. (1991a): Comparative Economic Organization: The Analysis of Discrete Structural Alternatives. In: Administrative Science Quarterly, Vol. 36, 2, pp. 269-296.

Williamson, O.E. (1991b): Strategizing, Economizing, and Economic Organization. In: Strategic Management Journal, Vol. 12, S2 (Winter), pp. 75-94.

Williamson, O.E. (1998): The Institutions of Governance. In: American Economic Review, Vol. 88, 2, pp. 75-79.

Wintergerst, A.; Welker, M. (2007): Die Rolle von Transaktionskosten bei Outsourcingentscheidungen. In: zfbf, Vol. 59, November 2007, pp. 938-954.

Wold, H. (1985): Partial Least Squares (Vol. 6), Wiley, New York 1985.

Womack, J.P.; Jones, D.T.; Roos, D. (1991): The Machine That Changed the World: The Story of Lean Production Harper Perennial, New York 1991.

Wooldridge, B.; Floyd, S.W. (1989): Strategic Process Effects on Consensus. In: Strategic Management Journal, Vol. 10, 3, pp. 295-302.

Wooldridge, B.; Floyd, S.W. (1990): The Strategy Process, Middle Management Involvement, and Organizational Performance. In: Strategic Management Journal, Vol. 11, 3, pp. 231-241.

Woolthuis, R.K.; Hillebrand, B.; Nooteboom, B. (2005): Trust, Contract and Relationship Development. In: Organization Studies, Vol. 26, 6, pp. 813-840.

Wüllenweber, K. (2007a): Evaluating and Managing Business Process Outsourcing Ventures in the German Banking Industry, Johann Wolfgang Goethe-Universität 2007a.

Wüllenweber, K. (2007b): The Role of Manager's Risk Attitude for Outsourcing Success. *15th European Conference on Information Systems* (pp. 430-441). St. Gallen, Switzerland.

Wüllenweber, K.; Gewald, H.; Franke, J.; Weitzel, T.; König, W. (2006): Business Process Outsourcing – Eine Nutzen- und Risikoanalyse in der deutschen Bankenbranche, Books on Demand, Norderstedt 2006.

Wüllenweber, K.; Jahner, S.; Krcmar, H. (2008): Relational Risk Mitigation: The Relationship Approach to Mitigating Risks in Business Process Outsourcing. *41th*

Hawaii International Conference on System Sciences (HICSS). Waikoloa, Big Island, Hawaii.

Yi, Y. (1990): A Critical Review of Consumer Satisfaction. In: Review of Marketing (Vol. 4). Ed.: Zeithaml, V. American Marketing Association, Chicago, IL 1990, pp. 68-123.

Yin, R.K. (2002): Case Study Research - Design and Methods. (3. Ed.), Sage Publications, Newbury Park 2002.

Yoshino, M.Y.; Rangan, U.S. (1995): Strategic Alliances: An Entrepreneurial Approach to Globalization, Harvard Business School Press, Boston 1995.

Zaheer, A.; McEvily, B.; Perrone, V. (1998): Does Trust Matter? Exploring the Effects of Interorganizational and Interpersonal Trust on Performance. In: Organization Science, Vol. 9, 2, pp. 141-159.

Zarnekow, R.; Brenner, W. (2004): Integriertes Informationsmanagement: Von Plan, Build, Run zum Source, Make, Deliver. In: Informationsmanagement. Konzepte und Strategien für die Praxis. Ed.: Zarnekow, R.; Brenner, W.; Grohmann, H. dpunkt Verlag, Heidelberg 2004, pp. 3-24.

Zubin, J.A. (1938): A technique for measuring likemindedness. In: Journal of Abnormal and Social Psychology, Vol. 33, 4, pp. 508-516.

Appendix

A 1.   Survey Instrument: German Version of Questionnaire

Institut für Informatik
Lehrstuhl für Wirtschaftsinformatik

Erfolgreiche IT-Sourcing-Governance

Prof. Dr. Helmut Krcmar
Technische Universität München

Technische Universität
München

Erfolgreiche IT-Sourcing-Governance

Sehr geehrte IT-Entscheiderin, sehr geehrter IT-Entscheider,

vielen Dank, dass Sie unsere Forschungsarbeit unterstützen und an unserer Befragung teilnehmen. Für die Beantwortung der Fragen bitten wir Sie um ca. 25 Minuten Ihrer Zeit.
Die Auswertung der Befragung erfolgt völlig anonym und lässt keine Rückschlüsse auf Ihre Person oder Ihr Unternehmen zu.

Begriffsverständnis IT-Sourcing:
Unter IT-Sourcing verstehen wir alle Formen der Auslagerung oder Fremdvergabe von Informationstechnologie oder IT-gestützten Geschäftsprozessen an Dritte. Darunter fallen in unserem Verständnis ebenfalls Unter- oder Mischformen wie Outtasking, selektives Outsourcing, Offshoring etc. IT-Sourcing beinhaltet dabei nicht notwendigerweise einen Personalübergang oder die Übertragung von Vermögungsgegenständen an den Dienstleister.

Wichtiger Hinweis:
Bedingt durch die Auswertungsmethode klingen Fragestellungen teilweise ähnlich. Dies ist beabsichtigt, um die Antworten statistisch validieren zu können. Bitte lassen Sie sich davon nicht irritieren.

Eine Teilnahme an unserer Studie ist nur möglich, wenn Ihr Unternehmen bereits Informationstechnologie oder Geschäftsprozesse ganz oder teilweise ausgelagert hat.

Pflichtfragen sind mit einem * gekennzeichnet.

Bei Rückfragen vor, während oder nach der Befragung wenden Sie sich bitte jederzeit an Frau Dipl. rer. com. Stefanie Leimeister (stefanie.leimeister@in.tum.de; jahner@in.tum.de, Tel. 089 / 289 19508).

Als Dankeschön für Ihre Teilnahme erhalten Sie auf Wunsch eine individuelle Auswertung der zentralen Umfrageergebnisse. Zusätzlich erhalten Sie die Chance, an der Verlosung eines **brandneuen Apple iPhone** teilzunehmen.

Herzliche Grüße,

Prof. Dr.
Helmut Krcmar

Dipl. rer. com.
Steffi Leimeister (Jahner)

1 / 13

Erfolgreiche IT-Sourcing-Governance

Prof. Dr. Helmut Krcmar
Technische Universität München

Institut für Informatik
Lehrstuhl für Wirtschaftsinformatik

Technische Universität
München

Allgemeine Rahmenbedingungen zur Auslagerung von IT oder IT-gestützten Geschäftsprozessen in Ihrem Unternehmen

Die nachfolgenden Fragen beziehen sich noch nicht auf ein bestimmtes Sourcingprojekt im Speziellen, sondern zunächst auf die allgemeine (Sourcing-) Situation in Ihrem Haus.

Frage 1: Wieviel Erfahrung hat Ihr Unternehmen bereits generell mit der Auslagerung von IT oder IT-gestützten Geschäftsprozessen?

Wir haben IT bzw. Geschäftsprozesse an einen Dienstleister vergeben seit...

☐ ... 0-2 Jahren   ☐ IT-Sourcing ist (noch) nicht konkret geplant

☐ ... 3-5 Jahren   ☐ IT-Sourcing ist aktuell erst in Planung

☐ ... 6-10 Jahren   ☐ Eine Auslagerung der IT oder von Geschäftsprozessen ist für uns nicht vorstellbar

☐ ... 11-15 Jahren

☐ ... mehr als 15 Jahren

Frage 2: Welche der folgenden Bereiche haben Sie insgesamt in Ihrem Unternehmen ausgelagert?

	Vollständig ausgelagert	Teilweise ausgelagert	Über Auslagerung nachgedacht	Auslagerung abgelehnt	Nicht in Sourcing-Überlegungen einbezogen
IT-gestützte Geschäftsprozesse	☐	☐	☐	☐	☐
Applikationen (Planung, Entwicklung, Betrieb, Support)	☐	☐	☐	☐	☐
Infrastruktur (Planung, Entwicklung, Betrieb, Support)	☐	☐	☐	☐	☐
Sonstige ____	☐	☐	☐	☐	☐

Frage 3: An wieviele unterschiedliche Dienstleister haben Sie Ihre IT ausgelagert?

☐ ein Dienstleister   ☐ 2-3 Dienstleister   ☐ mehr als 3 Dienstleister   ☐ weiß nicht

Frage 4: In welchem Umfang haben Sie ausgelagert (gemessen am IT-Budget)?

☐ 0%-20% des IT-Budgets   ☐ 21%-80% des IT-Budgets   ☐ mehr als 80% des IT-Budgets   ☐ weiß nicht

Frage 5: Wie schätzen Sie den Einfluss der ausgelagerten IT-Systeme und Dienstleistungen auf die langfristige Unternehmensstrategie ein?

sehr niedrig, kein strategischer Einfluss (IT als "Commodity")   ☐ ☐ ☐ ☐ ☐ ☐ ☐   sehr hoch, strategischer Einfluss (Auslagerung ermöglicht bspw. neue Geschäftsprozesse)

Frage 6: Welche Rolle spielt IT generell für Ihr Unternehmen?

keine strategische Rolle (Unterstützung)   ☐ ☐ ☐ ☐ ☐ ☐ ☐   strategische Rolle ("business enabler")

Frage 7: Wie beurteilen Sie die internen Rahmenbedingungen Ihres Unternehmens im Hinblick auf Veränderungsgeschwindigkeit und Dynamik?

(interne Rahmenbedingungen sind z.B. Umstrukturierungen, Veränderungen von Ausrichtung und Aufgabengebieten, Organisatorische Veränderungen etc.)

sehr stabil, vorhersehbar, wenig interne Veränderungen in der Organisation   ☐ ☐ ☐ ☐ ☐ ☐ ☐   sehr volatil, wenig vorhersehbar, schnelle interne Veränderungen in der Organisation

Erfolgreiche IT-Sourcing-Governance

Prof. Dr. Helmut Krcmar
Technische Universität München

Institut für Informatik
Lehrstuhl für Wirtschaftsinformatik

Technische Universität
München

Frage 8: Wie beurteilen Sie die **externen** Rahmenbedingungen Ihres Unternehmens im Hinblick auf Veränderungsgeschwindigkeit und Dynamik?

(externe Rahmenbedingungen sind z.B. Umfeld-, Markt- oder Branchenfaktoren, Wettbewerbs- und Konkurrenzsituation etc.)

sehr stabil, vorhersehbar, wenig Markt- oder Technologieveränderungen	☐ ☐ ☐ ☐ ☐ ☐ ☐ ☐	sehr volatil, wenig vorhersehbar, schnelle Markt- oder Technologieveränderungen

Wichtiger Hinweis:

Alle nachfolgenden Fragen beziehen sich nun nur noch auf **ein spezielles Sourcingprojekt**, das in Ihrem Verantwortungsbereich liegt.

Bitte beantworten Sie die Fragen nur mit Bezug auf **ein einziges** Projekt.
Wählen Sie hierfür das aus Ihrer Sicht **bedeutendste oder umfangreichste** Sourcingprojekt aus.

Frage 9: Welche Bereiche haben Sie im Rahmen des konkreten Sourcingprojektes ausgelagert?

Geschäftsprozesse (BPO)

☐ Gehaltsabrechnung	☐ Personalmanagement / Personalwesen	☐ Kundenservice / Call Center	☐ Sonstige ____

Applikationen

☐ Applikations- / Softwareentwicklung   ☐ Applikationshosting / Betrieb der Anwendungen

☐ Anwendungsintegration   ☐ Applikationswartung / -support (Software Maintenance)

☐ Sonstige ____

Infrastruktur

☐ Rechenzentrumsbetrieb (Mainframe & Server)	☐ Netzwerk (LAN / WAN)	☐ Desktop	☐ Disaster Recovery
☐ Infrastrukturintegration / Systemimplementierung	☐ Wartung und Support der Infrastruktur / Hardware	☐ Sonstige ____	

Management und Support

☐ Strategische IT-Planung	☐ Schulungen	☐ Help Desk	☐ Sonstige ____

Frage 10: Inwieweit verbinden Sie folgende Ziele und Erwartungen mit dem Auslagerungsprojekt?

	überhaupt nicht	kaum	eher wenig	teils / teils	eher stark	stark	sehr stark	weiß nicht
Kostensenkung	☐	☐	☐	☐	☐	☐	☐	☐
Variabilisierung von Kosten / Kostentransparenz	☐	☐	☐	☐	☐	☐	☐	☐
Erzielung von Qualitätsverbesserungen (geringe Fehlerrate / kürzere Durchlaufzeiten)	☐	☐	☐	☐	☐	☐	☐	☐
Langfristige Nutzbarkeit der Systeme, Anwendungen und Daten (Stabilität, Beibehaltung des Status Quo)	☐	☐	☐	☐	☐	☐	☐	☐
Verbesserung der Serviceorientierung	☐	☐	☐	☐	☐	☐	☐	☐
Erhöhung der Flexibilität	☐	☐	☐	☐	☐	☐	☐	☐
Risikoverlagerung auf den Dienstleister	☐	☐	☐	☐	☐	☐	☐	☐
Modernisierung der IT	☐	☐	☐	☐	☐	☐	☐	☐
Fokussierung auf Kernkompetenzen	☐	☐	☐	☐	☐	☐	☐	☐
Erzielung von strategischen Wettbewerbsvorteilen	☐	☐	☐	☐	☐	☐	☐	☐
Zugang zu hochqualifizierten Mitarbeitern	☐	☐	☐	☐	☐	☐	☐	☐
Zugriff auf bessere IT-Systeme und neueste Technologien	☐	☐	☐	☐	☐	☐	☐	☐
Wissenserwerb vom Anbieter	☐	☐	☐	☐	☐	☐	☐	☐

Erfolgreiche IT-Sourcing-Governance

Prof. Dr. Helmut Krcmar
Technische Universität München

Institut für Informatik
Lehrstuhl für Wirtschaftsinformatik

Technische Universität
München

Vorschläge für neue IT-basierte Produkte und Dienstleistungen durch den Anbieter (Innovations-Ideenentwicklung)	☐	☐	☐	☐	☐	☐	☐	☐
Gemeinsame Entwicklung von IT-basierten Produkten und Dienstleistungen zusammen mit dem Anbieter (gemeinsame Produkt- und Serviceentwicklung)	☐	☐	☐	☐	☐	☐	☐	☐
Geschäftstransformation	☐	☐	☐	☐	☐	☐	☐	☐

Frage 11: Wie lange läuft Ihr aktueller Auslagerungsvertrag insgesamt?

☐ 0 bis 2 Jahre   ☐ länger als 7 Jahre

☐ 3 bis 4 Jahre   ☐ unbegrenzt (kein Auslaufdatum, aber Möglichkeit der Beendigung)

☐ 5 bis 7 Jahre   ☐ keine Angabe

Frage 12: Seit wann läuft Ihr aktueller Auslagerungsvertrag?

seit _____ Jahren

Frage 13: Wie hoch ist das ungefähre Jahresvolumen des aktuellen Vertrages?

ca. _____ Tausend Euro pro Jahr

Frage 14: Welches der folgenden Preismodelle trifft am besten das mit Ihrem Anbieter vereinbarte Modell?

(Falls Sie mehrere Modelle im Einsatz haben, wählen Sie bitte das überwiegende Preismodell aus)

☐ Kostenbasiert (Kosten plus x% Aufschlag)

☐ Aufwandsabhängig (bspw. nach Personalaufwand oder Zeit)

☐ Transaktions- und nutzungsabhängig (z.B. x Euro pro Call; x Gigabyte Speicherkapazität)

☐ Festpreis (bspw. x Mio. Euro pro Jahr zum Betrieb des Callcenters)

☐ Erfolgsabhängige Vergütung (z.B. Risiko- /Gewinnteilung, "performance-based pricing")

☐ Anderes _____

Frage 15: Welches Modell der Zusammenarbeit wurde für das Sourcing gewählt? (Beteiligung am Partner)

☐ Fremdvergabe an externen Dienstleister (ohne Beteiligung am Dienstleister)

☐ Shared Services (internes Dienstleistungszentrum)

☐ Joint Venture

☐ Equity Holding (Beteiligung der Partner beim jeweils anderen, shared equity)

☐ Sonstige _____

Frage 16: Abhängigkeit, Wechselbarrieren, Lock-In Effekt

	stimme überhaupt nicht zu	stimme überwiegend nicht zu	stimme eher nicht zu	teils / teils	stimme eher zu	stimme überwiegend zu	stimme voll zu	weiß nicht
Wir sind in hohem Maße von unserem Service Provider abhängig.	☐	☐	☐	☐	☐	☐	☐	☐
Ein Wechsel zu einem Service Provider wäre für uns nur mit großem Aufwand möglich.	☐	☐	☐	☐	☐	☐	☐	☐
Unser Dienstleister hat einen Großteil der Systeme übernommen, von denen wir abhängig sind.	☐	☐	☐	☐	☐	☐	☐	☐
Ein Wechsel zu einem Service Provider wäre für uns mit hohen Kosten verbunden.	☐	☐	☐	☐	☐	☐	☐	☐

Erfolgreiche IT-Sourcing-Governance

Prof. Dr. Helmut Krcmar
Technische Universität München

Institut für Informatik
Lehrstuhl für Wirtschaftsinformatik

Technische Universität
München

Frage 17: Machtverhältnis / Ausgleich

	stimme überhaupt nicht zu	stimme überwiegend nicht zu	stimme eher nicht zu	teils / teils	stimme eher zu	stimme überwiegend zu	stimme voll zu	weiß nicht
Unser Dienstleister und wir sind gleichberechtigt „auf einer Augenhöhe".	☐	☐	☐	☐	☐	☐	☐	☐
Im Verhältnis zwischen uns und dem Dienstleister ist keiner dem anderen überlegen.	☐	☐	☐	☐	☐	☐	☐	☐
Unser Deliverymodell passt zueinander.	☐	☐	☐	☐	☐	☐	☐	☐

Frage 18: Gleichrichtung der Ziele und Erwartungen an die Auslagerung zwischen Kunde und Anbieter

	stimme überhaupt nicht zu	stimme überwiegend nicht zu	stimme eher nicht zu	teils / teils	stimme eher zu	stimme überwiegend zu	stimme voll zu	weiß nicht
Unser Dienstleister und wir verfolgen ähnliche Ziele mit der Auslagerung.	☐	☐	☐	☐	☐	☐	☐	☐
Unsere Ziele und die des Dienstleisters ergänzen sich gut und sind komplementär.	☐	☐	☐	☐	☐	☐	☐	☐
Die Erwartungen, die unser Dienstleister und wir mit der Auslagerung verbinden, stehen nicht in Konflikt zueinander.	☐	☐	☐	☐	☐	☐	☐	☐

Steuerungsmechanismen der Auslagerung

Bitte beurteilen Sie die folgenden Aussagen mit Bezug auf **ein** Sourcingprojekt.

Frage 19: Spezifikation und Steuerung über den Vertrag

	stimme überhaupt nicht zu	stimme überwiegend nicht zu	stimme eher nicht zu	teils / teils	stimme eher zu	stimme überwiegend zu	stimme voll zu	weiß nicht
Der Vertrag regelt vollständig die Aufgaben und Verantwortlichkeiten der Vertragspartner.	☐	☐	☐	☐	☐	☐	☐	☐
Es ist kein Problem, alle Vereinbarungen der Sourcingbeziehung im Vertrag festzulegen und darüber zu steuern.	☐	☐	☐	☐	☐	☐	☐	☐
Der Vertrag alleine reicht aus, um alle Eventualitäten und Ereignisse während der Sourcingbeziehung abzudecken und zu regeln.	☐	☐	☐	☐	☐	☐	☐	☐
Es ist einfach, die vereinbarten Leistungen und Erwartungen an die Zusammenarbeit im Vertrag genau zu spezifizieren.	☐	☐	☐	☐	☐	☐	☐	☐

Erfolgreiche IT-Sourcing-Governance

Prof. Dr. Helmut Krcmar
Technische Universität München

Institut für Informatik
Lehrstuhl für Wirtschaftsinformatik

Technische Universität
München

Frage 20: Steuerung über Service Level Agreements (SLAs)

	stimme überhaupt nicht zu	stimme überwiegend nicht zu	stimme eher nicht zu	teils / teils	stimme eher zu	stimme überwiegend zu	stimme voll zu	weiß nicht
Der Dienstleister hat durch die SLAs eindeutige Leistungsziele erhalten.	☐	☐	☐	☐	☐	☐	☐	☐
Mit Hilfe von Messkennzahlen und Leistungszielen (z. B. Verfügbarkeiten oder Reaktionszeiten) geben wir dem Dienstleister sehr detailliert und präzise vor, wie er die Leistung zu erbringen hat.	☐	☐	☐	☐	☐	☐	☐	☐
Insgesamt sind durch die SLAs die Leistungserwartungen sehr genau definiert und steuerbar.	☐	☐	☐	☐	☐	☐	☐	☐

Frage 21: Steuerung über Prozesse

	stimme überhaupt nicht zu	stimme überwiegend nicht zu	stimme eher nicht zu	teils / teils	stimme eher zu	stimme überwiegend zu	stimme voll zu	weiß nicht
Wir haben genaue Prozesse zum SLA- und Vertragsmanagement definiert.	☐	☐	☐	☐	☐	☐	☐	☐
Wir haben detaillierte Performance- und Servicelevelmanagement-Prozesse festgelegt, an denen sich der Dienstleister orientiert.	☐	☐	☐	☐	☐	☐	☐	☐
Wir haben einen detaillierten Strategieprozess vereinbart, der die Geschäftsabsichten beider Parteien regelt und abgleicht.	☐	☐	☐	☐	☐	☐	☐	☐
Wir haben einen Benchmarkingprozess vereinbart, um regelmäßig Preise und Leistungen des Anbieters mit dem Markt zu vergleichen.	☐	☐	☐	☐	☐	☐	☐	☐

Frage 22: Steuerung über Strukturen

	stimme überhaupt nicht zu	stimme überwiegend nicht zu	stimme eher nicht zu	teils / teils	stimme eher zu	stimme überwiegend zu	stimme voll zu	weiß nicht
Ein wesentlicher Teil der Steuerung erfolgt über ein Gremium (z.B. Lenkungsausschuss), das über Entscheidungsbefugnisse, Rollen und Aufgabenbereiche in der Sourcingbeziehung entscheidet.	☐	☐	☐	☐	☐	☐	☐	☐
Ein wesentlicher Teil der Steuerung erfolgt über einen Verantwortlichen auf unserer Seite, der dedizierter Ansprechpartner für den Service Provider ist (z.B. Relationship Manager).	☐	☐	☐	☐	☐	☐	☐	☐
Wir steuern die Beziehung über einen externen Berater, der sich um alle Belange der Sourcingbeziehung kümmert.	☐	☐	☐	☐	☐	☐	☐	☐

Erfolgreiche IT-Sourcing-Governance

Prof. Dr. Helmut Krcmar
Technische Universität München

Institut für Informatik
Lehrstuhl für Wirtschaftsinformatik

Technische Universität
München

Frage 23: Informelle Steuerungsmechanismen

	stimme überhaupt nicht zu	stimme überwiegend nicht zu	stimme eher nicht zu	teils / teils	stimme eher zu	stimme überwiegend zu	stimme voll zu	weiß nicht
Die Zusammenarbeit mit dem Dienstleister erfolgt durch implizite Regeln, die nicht unbedingt vertraglich festgelegt sind.	☐	☐	☐	☐	☐	☐	☐	☐
Die Sourcingbeziehung funktioniert auf Basis persönlicher Beziehungen zwischen einzelnen Mitarbeitern und Teams.	☐	☐	☐	☐	☐	☐	☐	☐
Wir steuern die Sourcingbeziehung vor allem über das gute Miteinander zwischen uns und dem Dienstleister.	☐	☐	☐	☐	☐	☐	☐	☐
In der laufenden Beziehung holen wir selten oder gar nicht den Vertrag hervor, sondern regeln die Zusammenarbeit über Diskussionen und Austausch.	☐	☐	☐	☐	☐	☐	☐	☐

Frage 24: Steuerung über Erfahrung / Mitarbeiter Know How

	stimme überhaupt nicht zu	stimme überwiegend nicht zu	stimme eher nicht zu	teils / teils	stimme eher zu	stimme überwiegend zu	stimme voll zu	weiß nicht
Wir können auf Erfahrung aus einer langjährigen Zusammenarbeit mit dem Dienstleister zurückgreifen.	☐	☐	☐	☐	☐	☐	☐	☐
Unsere Mitarbeiter haben Erfahrung mit Auslagerungsprojekten.	☐	☐	☐	☐	☐	☐	☐	☐
Wir haben ausreichend Know How zur Steuerung (Kontrolle und Überwachung) des Auslagerungsprojektes.	☐	☐	☐	☐	☐	☐	☐	☐

Frage 25: Einbindung und Entscheidungsautorität des Service Providers bei Planung und Management der ausgelagerten IT

	stimme überhaupt nicht zu	stimme überwiegend nicht zu	stimme eher nicht zu	teils / teils	stimme eher zu	stimme überwiegend zu	stimme voll zu	weiß nicht
Der Dienstleister hat umfangreiche Entscheidungsrechte und einen sehr hohen Freiheitsgrad bei Planung, Entwicklung und Betrieb unserer ausgelagerten IT.	☐	☐	☐	☐	☐	☐	☐	☐
Wir haben den Dienstleister stark in unsere Managemententscheidungen, die das Sourcingprojekt betreffen, eingebunden.	☐	☐	☐	☐	☐	☐	☐	☐
Wir geben dem Dienstleister nicht alles vor, sondern haben ihm umfangreiche Entscheidungsrechte, was die Steuerung des Sourcings angeht, eingeräumt.	☐	☐	☐	☐	☐	☐	☐	☐

Erfolgreiche IT-Sourcing-Governance

Prof. Dr. Helmut Krcmar
Technische Universität München

Institut für Informatik
Lehrstuhl für Wirtschaftsinformatik

Technische Universität
München

Interaktion und Verhalten in der Sourcingbeziehung

Frage 26: Kommunikation

	stimme überhaupt nicht zu	stimme überwiegend nicht zu	stimme eher nicht zu	teils / teils	stimme eher zu	stimme überwiegend zu	stimme voll zu	weiß nicht
Die Kommunikation zwischen unserem Dienstleister und uns ist gut.	☐	☐	☐	☐	☐	☐	☐	☐
Unser Dienstleister und wir kommunizieren regelmäßig über alle Belange im Sourcingprojekt.	☐	☐	☐	☐	☐	☐	☐	☐
Unser Dienstleister und wir reden viel über Aktivitäten im Sourcingprojekt.	☐	☐	☐	☐	☐	☐	☐	☐

Frage 27: Konsensfähigkeit und Konfliktlösungsbereitschaft

	stimme überhaupt nicht zu	stimme überwiegend nicht zu	stimme eher nicht zu	teils / teils	stimme eher zu	stimme überwiegend zu	stimme voll zu	weiß nicht
Meinungsverschiedenheiten lösen unser Dienstleister und wir meistens erfolgreich und in beiderseitigem Einvernehmen.	☐	☐	☐	☐	☐	☐	☐	☐
Unser Dienstleister und wir finden bei den meisten Themen Übereinstimmung.	☐	☐	☐	☐	☐	☐	☐	☐
Konflikte zwischen dem Anbieter und uns lassen sich zufriedenstellend beseitigen.	☐	☐	☐	☐	☐	☐	☐	☐

Frage 28: Kooperation und Koordination

	stimme überhaupt nicht zu	stimme überwiegend nicht zu	stimme eher nicht zu	teils / teils	stimme eher zu	stimme überwiegend zu	stimme voll zu	weiß nicht
Unser Dienstleister und wir stimmen unsere Aktivitäten immer aufeinander ab.	☐	☐	☐	☐	☐	☐	☐	☐
Unser Dienstleister und wir arbeiten gut zusammen.	☐	☐	☐	☐	☐	☐	☐	☐
Wir setzen uns regelmäßig mit dem Dienstleister zusammen, um Leistungserreichung und Leistungserwartung abzugleichen.	☐	☐	☐	☐	☐	☐	☐	☐

Frage 29: Loyalität und gegenseitige Bindung

	stimme überhaupt nicht zu	stimme überwiegend nicht zu	stimme eher nicht zu	teils / teils	stimme eher zu	stimme überwiegend zu	stimme voll zu	weiß nicht
Unser Dienstleister und wir fühlen uns beide einer guten Sourcingbeziehung verpflichtet.	☐	☐	☐	☐	☐	☐	☐	☐
Unser Dienstleister und wir setzen alle Ressourcen ein, um eine gute Sourcingbeziehung zu erhalten.	☐	☐	☐	☐	☐	☐	☐	☐
Unser Dienstleister und wir haben ein loyales Verhältnis.	☐	☐	☐	☐	☐	☐	☐	☐

Erfolgreiche IT-Sourcing-Governance

Prof. Dr. Helmut Krcmar
Technische Universität München

Institut für Informatik
Lehrstuhl für Wirtschaftsinformatik

Technische Universität
München

Frage 30: Ähnlichkeiten in der Unternehmenskultur

	stimme überhaupt nicht zu	stimme überwiegend nicht zu	stimme eher nicht zu	teils / teils	stimme eher zu	stimme überwiegend zu	stimme voll zu	weiß nicht
Unser Dienstleister und wir haben ähnliche Unternehmenskulturen.	☐	☐	☐	☐	☐	☐	☐	☐
Wir verstehen gegenseitig die Geschäftsregeln und Normen des anderen Unternehmens.	☐	☐	☐	☐	☐	☐	☐	☐
Die Firmenkultur unseres Anbieters passt zu unserer.	☐	☐	☐	☐	☐	☐	☐	☐

Frage 31: Vertrauen

	stimme überhaupt nicht zu	stimme überwiegend nicht zu	stimme eher nicht zu	teils / teils	stimme eher zu	stimme überwiegend zu	stimme voll zu	weiß nicht
Vertrauen ist eine wichtige Grundlage für unsere Geschäftsbeziehung.	☐	☐	☐	☐	☐	☐	☐	☐
Wir können unserem Dienstleister vertrauen, dass er uns fair behandelt.	☐	☐	☐	☐	☐	☐	☐	☐
Unser Dienstleister nutzt die Beziehung nicht zu seinem Vorteil aus.	☐	☐	☐	☐	☐	☐	☐	☐

Frage 32: Flexibilität des Dienstleisters

	stimme überhaupt nicht zu	stimme überwiegend nicht zu	stimme eher nicht zu	teils / teils	stimme eher zu	stimme überwiegend zu	stimme voll zu	weiß nicht
Unser Dienstleister ist flexibel, wenn sich Änderungen ergeben.	☐	☐	☐	☐	☐	☐	☐	☐
Der Dienstleister passt sich an, wenn sich die Bedingungen verändern.	☐	☐	☐	☐	☐	☐	☐	☐
Unser Dienstleister kann Änderungen schnell umsetzen.	☐	☐	☐	☐	☐	☐	☐	☐

Frage 33: Innovation und Weiterentwicklungsvorschläge durch den Anbieter

	stimme überhaupt nicht zu	stimme überwiegend nicht zu	stimme eher nicht zu	teils / teils	stimme eher zu	stimme überwiegend zu	stimme voll zu	weiß nicht
Unser Dienstleister befasst sich aktiv und eigenständig mit der Planung und Weiterentwicklung des Sourcingprojektes.	☐	☐	☐	☐	☐	☐	☐	☐
Unser Dienstleister macht uns eigenständig und aktiv Vorschläge zu Kosten- und Prozessverbesserungen.	☐	☐	☐	☐	☐	☐	☐	☐
Unser Dienstleister schlägt uns Innovationsmöglichkeiten im aktuellen Sourcingprojekt vor, wenn er Bedarf sieht.	☐	☐	☐	☐	☐	☐	☐	☐

Erfolgreiche IT-Sourcing-Governance

Prof. Dr. Helmut Krcmar
Technische Universität München

Institut für Informatik
Lehrstuhl für Wirtschaftsinformatik

Technische Universität
München

Frage 34: Nutzen- und Risikoteilung

	stimme überhaupt nicht zu	stimme überwiegend nicht zu	stimme eher nicht zu	teils / teils	stimme eher zu	stimme überwiegend zu	stimme voll zu	weiß nicht
Wir haben mit dem Dienstleister ein Modell zur Teilung von Risiken und Gewinnen vereinbart.	☐	☐	☐	☐	☐	☐	☐	☐
Unser Dienstleister und wir profitieren beide von möglichen Vorteilen des Projektes, tragen aber auch mögliche Verluste gleichermaßen.	☐	☐	☐	☐	☐	☐	☐	☐
Wir teilen gemeinschaftlich die mit der Auslagerung verbundenen Chancen und Risiken.	☐	☐	☐	☐	☐	☐	☐	☐

Frage 35: Gesamtbeurteilung der Beziehung

	stimme überhaupt nicht zu	stimme überwiegend nicht zu	stimme eher nicht zu	teils / teils	stimme eher zu	stimme überwiegend zu	stimme voll zu	weiß nicht
Wir haben eine gute und partnerschaftliche Beziehung zu unserem Dienstleister.	☐	☐	☐	☐	☐	☐	☐	☐
Die Beziehung zu unserem Dienstleister ist positiv und für beide Seiten vorteilhaft.	☐	☐	☐	☐	☐	☐	☐	☐
Im Umgang mit unserem Dienstleister ist Beziehungsmanagement sehr wichtig.	☐	☐	☐	☐	☐	☐	☐	☐
Für unsere Geschäftsbeziehung ist eine partnerschaftliche Zusammenarbeit wichtig.	☐	☐	☐	☐	☐	☐	☐	☐

Beurteilung ausgewählter Instrumente der Sourcingbeziehung

Innovation und Weiterentwicklung des Service Providers werden immer häufiger auf Kunden- wie auch auf Anbieterseite als wichtige Themen der Sourcingbeziehung addressiert.

Wir möchten daher nachfolgend ausgewählte Instrumente der Sourcingbeziehung untersuchen.

Frage 36: Bitte geben Sie an, wie häufig und mit welcher Beteiligung Sie die beiden nachfolgenden Instrumente nutzen.

	Unternehmens- leitung (CEO, CFO)	IT-Leitung (CIO)	Management der Fachbereiche	IT-Anwender	IT-Spezialisten	andere Lieferanten	wenigstens alle 6 Monate	wenigstens jedes Jahr	seltener	nie
Innovationsentwicklung: Workshops, bei denen der Anbieter zusammen mit Ihnen Ideen für neue IT-basierte Produkte und Dienstleistungen oder IT-Bedarfe entwickelt.	☐	☐	☐	☐	☐	☐	☐	☐	☐	☐
Lieferantenentwicklung: Workshops, bei denen Sie als Kunde dem Anbieter gezielt Vorschläge für die Weiterentwicklung der gelieferten Dienstleistungen und der Tätigkeitsfelder des Dienstleisters bei Ihnen machen.	☐	☐	☐	☐	☐	☐	☐	☐	☐	☐

Erfolgreiche IT-Sourcing-Governance

Prof. Dr. Helmut Krcmar
Technische Universität München

Technische Universität
München

Institut für Informatik
Lehrstuhl für Wirtschaftsinformatik

Frage 37: Bitte tragen Sie in das nachfolgende Feld ein, falls Sie Instrumente zur Steuerung der Sourcingbeziehung nutzen bzw. welche Instrumente in Ihrer Sourcingbeziehung zum Einsatz kommen.

(z.B. Teambuilding Events, Review Meetings, SLA-Monitoring etc.)

Gesamtbeurteilung des Sourcingerfolgs / Zufriedenheit mit der Auslagerung

Bitte beurteilen Sie folgende Aussagen mit Bezug auf ein Sourcingprojekt.

Frage 38: Inwiewelt wurden die erwarteten Ziele durch die Auslagerung erreicht?

	überhaupt nicht	kaum	eher wenig	teils / teils	eher überwiegend	überwiegend	voll und ganz	Nicht relevant
Kostensenkung	☐	☐	☐	☐	☐	☐	☐	☐
Variabilisierung von Kosten / Kostentransparenz	☐	☐	☐	☐	☐	☐	☐	☐
Erzielung von Qualitätsverbesserungen (geringe Fehlerrate / kürzere Durchlaufzeiten)	☐	☐	☐	☐	☐	☐	☐	☐
Langfristige Nutzbarkeit der Systeme, Anwendungen und Daten (Stabilität, Beibehaltung des Status Quo)	☐	☐	☐	☐	☐	☐	☐	☐
Verbesserung der Serviceorientierung	☐	☐	☐	☐	☐	☐	☐	☐
Erhöhung der Flexibilität	☐	☐	☐	☐	☐	☐	☐	☐
Risikoverlagerung auf den Dienstleister	☐	☐	☐	☐	☐	☐	☐	☐
Modernisierung der IT	☐	☐	☐	☐	☐	☐	☐	☐
Fokussierung auf Kernkompetenzen	☐	☐	☐	☐	☐	☐	☐	☐
Erzielung von strategischen Wettbewerbsvorteilen	☐	☐	☐	☐	☐	☐	☐	☐
Zugang zu hochqualifizierten Mitarbeitern	☐	☐	☐	☐	☐	☐	☐	☐
Zugriff auf bessere IT-Systeme und neueste Technologien	☐	☐	☐	☐	☐	☐	☐	☐
Wissenserwerb vom Anbieter	☐	☐	☐	☐	☐	☐	☐	☐
Vorschläge für neue IT-basierte Produkte und Dienstleistungen durch den Anbieter (Innovations-Ideenentwicklung)	☐	☐	☐	☐	☐	☐	☐	☐
Gemeinsame Entwicklung von IT-basierten Produkten und Dienstleistungen zusammen mit dem Anbieter (gemeinsame Produkt- und Serviceentwicklung)	☐	☐	☐	☐	☐	☐	☐	☐
Geschäftstransformation	☐	☐	☐	☐	☐	☐	☐	☐

Frage 39: Gesamtbeurteilung und Zufriedenheit mit der Auslagerung

	stimme überhaupt nicht zu	stimme überwiegend nicht zu	stimme eher nicht zu	teils / teils	stimme eher zu	stimme überwiegend zu	stimme voll zu	weiß nicht
Wir sind mit dem Auslagerungsprojekt insgesamt zufrieden.	☐	☐	☐	☐	☐	☐	☐	☐
Wir sind der Ansicht, dass der Nutzen der Auslagerung den Aufwand übersteigt.	☐	☐	☐	☐	☐	☐	☐	☐
Aus heutiger Sicht ist Sourcing für uns ein erfolgreiches Modell, das wir wieder durchführen würden.	☐	☐	☐	☐	☐	☐	☐	☐
Aus heutiger Sicht werden wir den aktuellen Auslagerungsvertrag verlängern.	☐	☐	☐	☐	☐	☐	☐	☐

Erfolgreiche IT-Sourcing-Governance

Prof. Dr. Helmut Krcmar
Technische Universität München

Institut für Informatik
Lehrstuhl für Wirtschaftsinformatik

Technische Universität
München

Frage 40: Beurteilung der Servicequalität

	stimme überhaupt nicht zu	stimme überwiegend nicht zu	stimme eher nicht zu	teils / teils	stimme eher zu	stimme überwiegend zu	stimme voll zu	weiß nicht
Der Serviceprovider ist verlässlich bei der Leistungserbringung.	☐	☐	☐	☐	☐	☐	☐	☐
Wir sind mit der Qualität der erbrachten Leistungen des Anbieters zufrieden.	☐	☐	☐	☐	☐	☐	☐	☐
Die Qualität der Sourcingbeziehung ist insgesamt hoch.	☐	☐	☐	☐	☐	☐	☐	☐

Angaben zum Unternehmen

Vielen Dank! Zum Abschluss erbitten wir noch einige Angaben zu Ihrem Unternehmen, die für Ihre individuelle und die allgemeine Auswertung wichtig sind.

Frage 41: Welcher Branche gehört Ihr Unternehmen (überwiegend) an?

Wir haben IT bzw. Geschäftsprozesse an einen Dienstleister vergeben seit...

☐ Automobilindustrie	☐ Chemie und Pharmaindustrie	☐ Maschinen- und Anlagenbau
☐ Elektro- und Informationstechnik	☐ Konsumgüterindustrie	☐ Sonst. Fertigungsindustrien (z.B. Metallverarbeitung, Möbel, Druck, Papier, Textil, Lebensmittel)
☐ Energie, Versorger und Entsorger	☐ Banken, Versicherungen, Finanzdienstleistungen	☐ IT-Dienstleistungen
☐ Telekommunikation	☐ Handel	☐ Transport / Logistik / Verkehr
☐ Medien	☐ Medizintechnik	☐ Öffentliche Verwaltung / Behörden / Stadtwerke
☐ Sonstige: _____		

Frage 42: Wie hoch war der Jahresumsatz Ihres Unternehmens im letzten Geschäftsjahr?

☐ unter 10 Mio. Euro	☐ 10 bis 50 Mio. Euro
☐ 50+ bis 100 Mio. Euro	☐ 100+ bis 250 Mio. Euro
☐ 250+ bis 500 Mio. Euro	☐ 500+ Mio. bis 1 Mrd. Euro
☐ 1+ Mrd. bis 5 Mrd. Euro	☐ 5+ Mrd. bis 10 Mrd. Euro
☐ Über 10 Mrd. Euro	☐ nicht zutreffend (Behörde, gemeinnützig, Bildungseinrichtung)
☐ keine Angabe	

Frage 43: Wie viele Mitarbeiter sind in Ihrem Unternehmen tätig?

☐ bis 250 Beschäftigte	☐ 251 bis 500 Beschäftige
☐ 501 bis 2000 Beschäftigte	☐ 2001 bis 5000 Beschäftigte
☐ 5001 bis 50.000 Beschäftigte	☐ mehr als 50.000 Beschäftigte
☐ keine Angabe	

Frage 44: Wie hoch war Ihr IT-Budget im letzten Geschäftsjahr?

☐ bis 1 Mio Euro	☐ 1+ bis 10 Mio Euro
☐ 10+ bis 50 Mio Euro	☐ 50+ bis 100 Mio Euro
☐ 100+ Mio bis 500 Mio Euro	☐ 500+ Mio Euro oder mehr
☐ keine Angabe	

12 / 13

Erfolgreiche IT-Sourcing-Governance

Prof. Dr. Helmut Krcmar
Technische Universität München

Institut für Informatik
Lehrstuhl für Wirtschaftsinformatik

Technische Universität
München

Angaben zum Befragten

Frage 45: Welche der folgenden Bezeichnungen trifft Ihren Tätigkeitsbereich am besten?

☐ Vorstand / CEO / Geschäftsführung ☐ Chief Information Officer (CIO)

☐ Chief Technology Officer (CTO) ☐ IT-Manager / IT-Leiter

☐ IT-Projektleiter ☐ DV-Berater / Consultant

☐ Sonstige:

Frage 46: Welche Erfahrung haben Sie persönlich mit Sourcing (in diesem oder in vorherigen Unternehmen)?

Ich habe bereits Erfahrung mit der Auslagerung von IT...

☐ ...seit 0-2 Jahren ☐ ...seit 3-5 Jahren

☐ ...seit 6-10 Jahren ☐ ...seit mehr als 10 Jahren

☐ Ich habe noch nie ein Auslagerungsprojekt betreut

Frage 47: Alter des Befragten

☐ unter 24 Jahre ☐ 25 - 34 Jahre

☐ 35 - 44 Jahre ☐ 45 - 54 Jahre

☐ 55 Jahre und älter ☐ keine Angabe

Frage 48: Seit wann sind Sie in diesem Unternehmen tätig?

seit ca.   Jahr(en)

Sie haben es geschafft!

Vielen Dank, dass Sie unsere Forschungsarbeit unterstützen.

Bitte wenden Sie sich bei Rückfragen jederzeit gerne an Frau Dipl. rer. com. Stefanie Leimeister (stefanie.leimeister@in.tum.de, jahner@in.tum.de), die diese Umfrage im Rahmen Ihres Dissertationsprojektes durchführt.

A 2.   Survey Instrument: English Version of Questionnaire (translated)

Department of Informatics
Information Systems

Successful IS Sourcing Governance

Prof. Dr. Helmut Krcmar
Technische Universität München

Technische Universität
München

Successful IS Sourcing Governance

Dear IT decision maker,

thank you very much for supporting our research and participating in this survey. You will need approximately 25 minutes to answer this questionnaire. We guarantee that your responses will be handled confidentially and anonymously.

Definition IS Sourcing:
In this study, IS sourcing is understood as if some or all of an organization's IS functions, where "functions" include one or more IT assets, activities, processes, or services to be provided over time." Sourcing in our understanding includes various forms such as offshoring, outsourcing, outtasking, selective outsourcing etc. It does not necessarily include the transfer of manpower or IT resources to the IT service provider.

Important notice:
Due to the analysis method some questions might sound similar. This is intended to validate the answers and provide high quality research. Please do not be distracted by this fact.

Please fill out this questionnaire only if your company has already outsourced information technology or business processes completely or partly.

In case of any questions, please do not hesitate to contact Mrs. Dipl. rer. com. Stefanie Leimeister (Jahner) (stefanie.leimeister@in.tum.de or jahner@in.tum.de). She conducts this survey in the context of her PhD thesis.

As a "thank you" for your participation you can get a management summary of the main results of this study. You can also win a brand new Apple iPhone.

Kind regards,

Prof. Dr.
Helmut Krcmar

Dipl. rer. com.
Steffi Leimeister (Jahner)

Successful IS Sourcing Governance

Prof. Dr. Helmut Kremar
Technische Universität München

Department of Informatics
Information Systems

Technische Universität
München

Basic conditions and environment of outsourcing information systems or IT supported business processes in your company
The following questions do not refer to a specific sourcing project, but to the general sourcing situation in your company.

Question 1: How much experience does your company have in outsourcing IT or IT supported business processes in general?

We have assigned IT or business processes to an outsourcing provider for...

☐ ... 0-2 years   ☐ IT sourcing is not (yet) planned

☐ ... 3-5 years   ☐ IT sourcing is in planning at the moment

☐ ... 6-10 years   ☐ Outsourcing IT or business processes is not an option for us

☐ ... 11-15 years

☐ ... more than 15 years

Question 2: Which of the following functions of your company have you outsourced so far?

	completely outsourced	partly outsourced	thought about outsourcing	outsourcing rejected	not involved in outsourcing consideration
IT supported business processes	☐	☐	☐	☐	☐
Applications (planning, development, operations, support)	☐	☐	☐	☐	☐
Infrastructure (planning, development, operations, support)	☐	☐	☐	☐	☐
Other _____	☐	☐	☐	☐	☐

Question 3: To how many different IT service providers have you outsourced your IT?

☐ one provider   ☐ 2-3 providers   ☐ more than 3 providers   ☐ I don't know

---

Question 4: To what extent have you outsourced your IT (in % of your IT budget)?

☐ 0%-20%   ☐ 21%-80%   ☐ more than 80%   ☐ I don't know

Question 5: How do you estimate the impact of the outsourced IT systems and services on your long-term company strategy?

very low, no strategic impact (IT is a commodity) ☐ ☐ ☐ ☐ ☐ ☐ ☐ very high, strategic impact (outsourcing enables new business processes)

Question 6: What role does IT play in your company in general?

no strategic role (support) ☐ ☐ ☐ ☐ ☐ ☐ ☐ strategic role (business enabler)

Question 7: How do you estimate the organizational situation **inside** your company with regard to speed of change and dynamics?

(internal organizational situation includes e.g. reorganizations, readjustment of activities, organizational changes etc.)

very stable, predictable, little change in internal organization ☐ ☐ ☐ ☐ ☐ ☐ ☐ very volatile, less predictable, fast internal change in organization

Successful IS Sourcing Governance

Prof. Dr. Helmut Krcmar
Technische Universität München

Department of Informatics
Information Systems

Technische Universität
München

Question 8: How do you estimate the **external** situation and conditions for your company with regard to speed of change and dynamics?

(external conditions include e.g. environmental, market or industry factors, competitive environment)

very stable, predictable, little market or technology change   ☐ ☐ ☐ ☐ ☐ ☐ ☐   very volatile, little predictable, fast market or technology changes

Important notice:

The following questions refer to **one specific sourcing project** that is in the area of your responsibility.

Please do answer the questions only with regard to **one single** project.
Please choose the **most important or comprehensive** sourcing project.

Question 9: Which of the following departments have you outsourced in a real sourcing project?

Business processes (BPO)

☐ Payroll accounting   ☐ Human resources   ☐ Customer service / Call Center   ☐ Other ____

Applications

☐ Application / software development   ☐ Application hosting / operations

☐ Application integration   ☐ Application maintenance / support

☐ Other ____

Infrastructure

☐ Data center operations (Mainframe & Server)   ☐ Network (LAN / WAN)   ☐ Desktop   ☐ Disaster recovery

☐ Infrastructure integration / System implementation   ☐ Infrastructure maintenance and support / hardware   ☐ Other ____

Management and support

☐ Strategic IT planning   ☐ Training   ☐ Help desk   ☐ Other ____

Question 10: To what extent do you associate the following goals and expectations with the sourcing project?

	not at all	barely	little	partly / neutral	somewhat strong	strongly	very strongly	I don't know
Cost reduction	☐	☐	☐	☐	☐	☐	☐	☐
Flexibility of costs / cost transparency	☐	☐	☐	☐	☐	☐	☐	☐
Realizing quality improvements (lower error rate / shorter processing time)	☐	☐	☐	☐	☐	☐	☐	☐
Long-term use of systems, applications and data (stability, retention of status quo)	☐	☐	☐	☐	☐	☐	☐	☐
Improved service orientation	☐	☐	☐	☐	☐	☐	☐	☐
Increased flexibility	☐	☐	☐	☐	☐	☐	☐	☐
Shift risk to service provider	☐	☐	☐	☐	☐	☐	☐	☐
Modernization of IT / replace lagacy systems	☐	☐	☐	☐	☐	☐	☐	☐
Focus on core competencies	☐	☐	☐	☐	☐	☐	☐	☐
Enable and facilitate strategic competetive advantages	☐	☐	☐	☐	☐	☐	☐	☐
Access to highly skilled people	☐	☐	☐	☐	☐	☐	☐	☐
Access to better IT systems and new technology	☐	☐	☐	☐	☐	☐	☐	☐
Knowledge acquisition from service provider	☐	☐	☐	☐	☐	☐	☐	☐

3 / 13

Successful IS Sourcing Governance

Prof. Dr. Helmut Krcmar
Technische Universität München

Department of Informatics
Information Systems

Technische Universität
München

Suggestions for new IT based products and services **by** your service provider (idea creation)	☐	☐	☐	☐	☐	☐	☐	☐
Shared development of IT based products and services **together with** your service provider (shared product and software development)	☐	☐	☐	☐	☐	☐	☐	☐
Business transformation	☐	☐	☐	☐	☐	☐	☐	☐

Question 11: How long does your outsourcing contract run all together?

☐ 0 - 2 years   ☐ more than 7 years

☐ 3 - 4 years   ☐ unlimited (no expiration date, but option to cancel)

☐ 5 - 7 years   ☐ not specified

Question 12: How long has your current outsourcing contract been running?

for _____ years

Question 13: How do you estimate the account size of the current contract per year?

approx. _____ thousand Euro per year

Question 14: Which of the following pricing models matches best with the model you agreed on with your service provider?

(If you use several pricing models, please choose the predominant one)

☐ Cost-based (cost plus x% premium)

☐ On a time and material basis (e.g. personnel or time expenses)

☐ Transaction and use-based (e.g. x Euro per call; x Gigabyte memory capacity)

☐ Fixed price (e.g. x mio. Euro per year for call center operations)

☐ Performance-based pricing (e.g. risk/profit sharing)

☐ Other _____

Question 15: Which model of cooperation did you choose for the sourcing project?

☐ Outsourcing to external service provider (without shareholding oder investments)

☐ Shared services (internal service provider within company)

☐ Joint venture

☐ Equity holding (shared equity)

☐ Other _____

Question 16: Dependency, switching costs, lock in effect

	Strongly disagree	Predominantly disagree	Rather disagree	Partly / neutral	Rather agree	Predominantly agree	Strongly agree	I don't know
We are highly dependent on our service provider.	☐	☐	☐	☐	☐	☐	☐	☐
Switching to another service provider would only be possible with great effort.	☐	☐	☐	☐	☐	☐	☐	☐
Our service provider is operating a majority of the systems on which we are dependent.	☐	☐	☐	☐	☐	☐	☐	☐
Switching to another service provider would only be possible at high costs.	☐	☐	☐	☐	☐	☐	☐	☐

Successful IS Sourcing Governance

Prof. Dr. Helmut Krcmar
Technische Universität München

Department of Informatics
Information Systems

Technische Universität
München

Question 17: Power structure / Balance

	Strongly disagree	Predominantly disagree	Rather disagree	Partly / neutral	Rather agree	Predominantly agree	Strongly agree	I don't know
We are at eye level with our service provider and equal in decision making.	☐	☐	☐	☐	☐	☐	☐	☐
In our relationship with the service provider no one is regarded to be superior.	☐	☐	☐	☐	☐	☐	☐	☐
Our delivery / business model fits the delivery model of the service provider.	☐	☐	☐	☐	☐	☐	☐	☐

Question 18: Goal and expectations alignment between customer and service provider

	Strongly disagree	Predominantly disagree	Rather disagree	Partly / neutral	Rather agree	Predominantly agree	Strongly agree	I don't know
Our service provider and we pursue similar goals with outsourcing.	☐	☐	☐	☐	☐	☐	☐	☐
Our service provider's goals and our goals are complementary.	☐	☐	☐	☐	☐	☐	☐	☐
Our service provider's expectations and our expectations towards the outsourcing project are not in conflict with each other.	☐	☐	☐	☐	☐	☐	☐	☐

Governance mechanisms for outsourcing

Please answer the following statements again with regard to **one** sourcing project.

Question 19: Assessment and specification of the outsourcing contract

	Strongly disagree	Predominantly disagree	Rather disagree	Partly / neutral	Rather agree	Predominantly agree	Strongly agree	I don't know
The contractual agreement fully regulates all tasks and responsibilities for both partners.	☐	☐	☐	☐	☐	☐	☐	☐
It is not a problem to cover and to control all tasks of the sourcing relationship within the contract.	☐	☐	☐	☐	☐	☐	☐	☐
The contract itself is sufficient to cover and control all contingencies and events during the sourcing relationship.	☐	☐	☐	☐	☐	☐	☐	☐
It is easy to specify the agreed tasks and expectations within the contract in detail.	☐	☐	☐	☐	☐	☐	☐	☐

Successful IS Sourcing Governance

Prof. Dr. Helmut Krcmar
Technische Universität München

Department of Informatics
Information Systems

Technische Universität
München

Question 20: Management via Service Level Agreements (SLAs)

	Strongly disagree	Predominantly disagree	Rather disagree	Partly / neutral	Rather agree	Predominantly agree	Strongly agree	I don't know
The service provider was given clear objectives and performance targets through SLAs.	☐	☐	☐	☐	☐	☐	☐	☐
We use performance indicators and objectives (e.g. availabilities or reaction times) to specify in detail how the service provider has to fulfill the given objectives.	☐	☐	☐	☐	☐	☐	☐	☐
Overall, we implemented very detailed and precisely defined SLAs.	☐	☐	☐	☐	☐	☐	☐	☐

Question 21: Management via processes

	Strongly disagree	Predominantly disagree	Rather disagree	Partly / neutral	Rather agree	Predominantly agree	Strongly agree	I don't know
We defined detailed processes for the SLA and contract management.	☐	☐	☐	☐	☐	☐	☐	☐
We defined detailed performance and service level management processes that the service provider has to follow.	☐	☐	☐	☐	☐	☐	☐	☐
We agreed on a detailed strategy process that controls and balances both partners' intentions.	☐	☐	☐	☐	☐	☐	☐	☐
We agreed on a benchmarking process to compare our service providers' prices and performances with the market on a regular basis.	☐	☐	☐	☐	☐	☐	☐	☐

Question 22: Management via structures

	Strongly disagree	Predominantly disagree	Rather disagree	Partly / neutral	Rather agree	Predominantly agree	Strongly agree	I don't know
An integral part of the governance is carried out by a committee that decides on decision-making powers, roles and activities within the sourcing relationship.	☐	☐	☐	☐	☐	☐	☐	☐
An integral part of the controlling is carried out by a person in charge on our side who is the dedicated contact for our service provider (e.g. relationship manager).	☐	☐	☐	☐	☐	☐	☐	☐
We control the relationship by an external consultant who takes care of all issues of the sourcing relationship.	☐	☐	☐	☐	☐	☐	☐	☐

6 / 13

Successful IS Sourcing Governance

Prof. Dr. Helmut Krcmar
Technische Universität München

Department of Informatics
Information Systems

Technische Universität
München

Question 23: Informal governance mechanisms

	Strongly disagree	Predominantly disagree	Rather disagree	Partly / neutral	Rather agree	Predominantly agree	Strongly agree	I don't know
The collaboration with our service provider takes place by implicit rules that are not necessarily written in the contract.	☐	☐	☐	☐	☐	☐	☐	☐
The sourcing relationship works on the basis of personal relationships between client and vendor employees and teams.	☐	☐	☐	☐	☐	☐	☐	☐
We manage the sourcing relationship through a good daily-work relationship between us and the service provider.	☐	☐	☐	☐	☐	☐	☐	☐
In the current relationship we do not or rarely insist on the contract, but arrange the collaboration by discussions or exchange.	☐	☐	☐	☐	☐	☐	☐	☐

Question 24: Management via experience / employees' know-how

	Strongly disagree	Predominantly disagree	Rather disagree	Partly / neutral	Rather agree	Predominantly agree	Strongly agree	I don't know
We can build upon experience from a longtime, established collaboration with our service provider.	☐	☐	☐	☐	☐	☐	☐	☐
Our employees have experience with outsourcing projects.	☐	☐	☐	☐	☐	☐	☐	☐
We have enough know-how to control the outsourcing project.	☐	☐	☐	☐	☐	☐	☐	☐

Question 25: Integration and decision making authority of the service provider for planning and managing the outsourced IT

	Strongly disagree	Predominantly disagree	Rather disagree	Partly / neutral	Rather agree	Predominantly agree	Strongly agree	I don't know
The service provider has substantial decision making authority and a very high degree of freedom in planning, developing and operating our outsourced IT.	☐	☐	☐	☐	☐	☐	☐	☐
We highly integrated our service provider in our management decisions that are relevant for the sourcing project.	☐	☐	☐	☐	☐	☐	☐	☐
We do not specify all our service providers' tasks in detail, but allow him substantial decision making powers with regard to control the sourcing.	☐	☐	☐	☐	☐	☐	☐	☐

Successful IS Sourcing Governance

Prof. Dr. Helmut Krcmar
Technische Universität München

Department of Informatics
Information Systems

Technische Universität
München

Interaction and behavior within the sourcing relationship

Question 26: Communication

	Strongly disagree	Predominantly disagree	Rather disagree	Partly / neutral	Rather agree	Predominantly agree	Strongly agree	I don't know
We have a good communication between us and our service provider.	☐	☐	☐	☐	☐	☐	☐	☐
We communicate with our service provider about all relevant issues on a regular basis.	☐	☐	☐	☐	☐	☐	☐	☐
We talk a lot about activities regarding the sourcing project.	☐	☐	☐	☐	☐	☐	☐	☐

Question 27: Consensus and conflict resolution

	Strongly disagree	Predominantly disagree	Rather disagree	Partly / neutral	Rather agree	Predominantly agree	Strongly agree	I don't know
Dissents between us and our service provider are solved successfully and consensually most times.	☐	☐	☐	☐	☐	☐	☐	☐
We agree with our service provider on most topics and issues.	☐	☐	☐	☐	☐	☐	☐	☐
Conflicts and disagreements between us and our service provider can be solved satisfactorily.	☐	☐	☐	☐	☐	☐	☐	☐

Question 28: Cooperation and coordination

	Strongly disagree	Predominantly disagree	Rather disagree	Partly / neutral	Rather agree	Predominantly agree	Strongly agree	I don't know
Our service provider and we coordinate activities well with each other.	☐	☐	☐	☐	☐	☐	☐	☐
The cooperation between us and our service provider is working well.	☐	☐	☐	☐	☐	☐	☐	☐
To align and synchronize expected and achieved service delivery we meet with our service provider on a regular basis.	☐	☐	☐	☐	☐	☐	☐	☐

Question 29: Loyalty and mutual commitment

	Strongly disagree	Predominantly disagree	Rather disagree	Partly / neutral	Rather agree	Predominantly agree	Strongly agree	I don't know
Our service provider and we both feel committed to a good sourcing relationship.	☐	☐	☐	☐	☐	☐	☐	☐
Our service provider and we dedicate all resources to achieve a good sourcing relationship.	☐	☐	☐	☐	☐	☐	☐	☐
Our service provider and we maintain a loyal relationship.	☐	☐	☐	☐	☐	☐	☐	☐

Successful IS Sourcing Governance

Prof. Dr. Helmut Krcmar
Technische Universität München

Department of Informatics
Information Systems

Technische Universität
München

Question 30: Cultural similarities

	Strongly disagree	Predominantly disagree	Rather disagree	Partly / neutral	Rather agree	Predominantly agree	Strongly agree	I don't know
Our service provider and we have similar corporate cultures.	☐	☐	☐	☐	☐	☐	☐	☐
We both understand the opposite side's rules and standards in the company.	☐	☐	☐	☐	☐	☐	☐	☐
Our service provider's company culture fits ours.	☐	☐	☐	☐	☐	☐	☐	☐

Question 31: Trust

	Strongly disagree	Predominantly disagree	Rather disagree	Partly / neutral	Rather agree	Predominantly agree	Strongly agree	I don't know
Trust is an important basis for our relationship.	☐	☐	☐	☐	☐	☐	☐	☐
We can trust our service provider to behave fairly.	☐	☐	☐	☐	☐	☐	☐	☐
Our service provider does not take advantage of the relationship to our disadvantage.	☐	☐	☐	☐	☐	☐	☐	☐

Question 32: Service provider's flexibility

	Strongly disagree	Predominantly disagree	Rather disagree	Partly / neutral	Rather agree	Predominantly agree	Strongly agree	I don't know
Our service provider is flexible circumstances change.	☐	☐	☐	☐	☐	☐	☐	☐
Our service provider adjusts quickly if the conditions change.	☐	☐	☐	☐	☐	☐	☐	☐
Our service provider can react on and implement changes very fast.	☐	☐	☐	☐	☐	☐	☐	☐

Question 33: Innovation through the service provider

	Strongly disagree	Predominantly disagree	Rather disagree	Partly / neutral	Rather agree	Predominantly agree	Strongly agree	I don't know
Our service provider actively and independently engages in planning and developing the sourcing project.	☐	☐	☐	☐	☐	☐	☐	☐
Our service provider actively and independently makes suggestions for cost and process improvements.	☐	☐	☐	☐	☐	☐	☐	☐
Our service provider will suggest potential innovations within the current sourcing project, if he sees the need for it.	☐	☐	☐	☐	☐	☐	☐	☐

Successful IS Sourcing Governance

Prof. Dr. Helmut Krcmar
Technische Universität München

Department of Informatics
Information Systems

Technische Universität
München

Question 34: Benefit and risk sharing

	Strongly disagree	Predominantly disagree	Rather disagree	Partly / neutral	Rather agree	Predominantly agree	Strongly agree	I don't know
We agreed on a model of risk and benefit sharing with our service provider.	☐	☐	☐	☐	☐	☐	☐	☐
Both our service provider and we take profit from the project, but we also both bear potential losses.	☐	☐	☐	☐	☐	☐	☐	☐
We both share all opportunities and risks that are associated with the outsourcing equally.	☐	☐	☐	☐	☐	☐	☐	☐

Question 35: Evaluation of the relationship

	Strongly disagree	Predominantly disagree	Rather disagree	Partly / neutral	Rather agree	Predominantly agree	Strongly agree	I don't know
We have a solid and cooperative relationship with our service provider.	☐	☐	☐	☐	☐	☐	☐	☐
The relationship with our service provider is positive and beneficial for both sides.	☐	☐	☐	☐	☐	☐	☐	☐
During the outsourcing project relationship management is very important.	☐	☐	☐	☐	☐	☐	☐	☐
A cooperative collaboration with our service provider is important for our relationship.	☐	☐	☐	☐	☐	☐	☐	☐

Evaluation of selected instruments of the sourcing relationship

Innovation and development of the service provider have recently been addressed as important topics of a sourcing relationship both on customer and on service provider side.

Therefore we would like to study selected instruments of a sourcing relationship.

Question 36: Please state how often and with what involvement you use the following instruments.

	Top management (CEO, CFO)	IT management (CIO)	Business unit	IT users	IT specialists	Other external suppliers	At least every 6 months	At least once a year	Less than once a year	never
Innovation development: Workshops where you work together with the service provider and jointly develop new ideas for new IT based products and services or IT needs	☐	☐	☐	☐	☐	☐	☐	☐	☐	☐
Supplier development: Workshops where you as a customer make suggestions for the further development of the delivered services and the activities of your service provider.	☐	☐	☐	☐	☐	☐	☐	☐	☐	☐

Successful IS Sourcing Governance

Prof. Dr. Helmut Krcmar
Technische Universität München

Department of Informatics
Information Systems

Technische Universität
München

Question 37: Please tell us what instruments you use to manage the sourcing relationship.
(e.g. teambuilding events, review meetings, SLA monitoring etc.)

Overall evaluation of the sourcing success / Satisfaction with the outsourcing

Please answer the following statements with regard to one single sourcing project.

Question 38: To what extent could you achieve the expected goals associated with the outsourcing project?

	not at all	barely	little	partly / neutral	somewhat strong	strongly	very strongly	not relevant
Cost reduction	☐	☐	☐	☐	☐	☐	☐	☐
Flexibility of costs / cost transparency	☐	☐	☐	☐	☐	☐	☐	☐
Realizing quality improvements (lower error rate / shorter processing time)	☐	☐	☐	☐	☐	☐	☐	☐
Long-term use of systems, applications and data (stability, retention of status quo)	☐	☐	☐	☐	☐	☐	☐	☐
Improved service orientation	☐	☐	☐	☐	☐	☐	☐	☐
Increased flexibility	☐	☐	☐	☐	☐	☐	☐	☐
Shift risk to service provider	☐	☐	☐	☐	☐	☐	☐	☐
Modernization of IT / replace legacy systems	☐	☐	☐	☐	☐	☐	☐	☐
Focus on core competencies	☐	☐	☐	☐	☐	☐	☐	☐
Enable and facilitate strategic competetive advantages	☐	☐	☐	☐	☐	☐	☐	☐
Access to highly skilled people	☐	☐	☐	☐	☐	☐	☐	☐
Access to better IT systems and new technology	☐	☐	☐	☐	☐	☐	☐	☐
Knowledge acquisition from service provider	☐	☐	☐	☐	☐	☐	☐	☐
Suggestions for new IT based products and services **by** your service provider (idea creation)	☐	☐	☐	☐	☐	☐	☐	☐
Shared development of IT based products and services **together with** your service provider (shared product and software development)	☐	☐	☐	☐	☐	☐	☐	☐
Business transformation	☐	☐	☐	☐	☐	☐	☐	☐

Question 39: Overall evaluation and satisfaction with the outsourcing

	Strongly disagree	Predominantly disagree	Rather disagree	Partly / neutral	Rather agree	Predominantly agree	Strongly agree	I don't know
Overall, we are satisfied with the outsourcing project.	☐	☐	☐	☐	☐	☐	☐	☐
We think that the outsourcing benefit is higher than the costs.	☐	☐	☐	☐	☐	☐	☐	☐
From today's point of view sourcing is an attractive option that we would do again.	☐	☐	☐	☐	☐	☐	☐	☐
From today's point of view we will renew the current outsourcing agreement.	☐	☐	☐	☐	☐	☐	☐	☐

Successful IS Sourcing Governance

Prof. Dr. Helmut Krcmar
Technische Universität München

Department of Informatics
Information Systems

Technische Universität
München

Question 40: Evaluation of service quality

	Strongly disagree	Predominantly disagree	Rather disagree	Partly / neutral	Rather agree	Predominantly agree	Strongly agree	I don't know
The service delivery of the outsourcing provider is reliable.	☐	☐	☐	☐	☐	☐	☐	☐
We are satisfied with our service provider's delivered quality.	☐	☐	☐	☐	☐	☐	☐	☐
The quality of the sourcing relationship is high.	☐	☐	☐	☐	☐	☐	☐	☐

Information about your company

Thank you very much! In the end, we would like to ask you some information about your company. This information helps us to evaluate your statements.

Question 41: What industry does your company (mainly) belong to?

☐ Automotive industry	☐ Chemical and pharmaceutical industry	☐ Machine and plant construction
☐ Electro and information technology	☐ Consumer goods industry	☐ Other Manufacturing industry (e.g. metal processing, furniture, print, paper, textile, groceries)
☐ Energy, suppliers and disposers	☐ Banking, insurances, financial services	☐ IT services and solutions
☐ Telecommunication	☐ Commerce	☐ Transportation / Logistics
☐ Media	☐ Medical engineering	☐ Public administration / Public services
☐ Other ____		

Question 42: What was the annual sale of your company in the last fiscal year?

☐ below 10 m Euro	☐ 10 to 50 m Euro
☐ 50+ to 100 m Euro	☐ 100+ to 250 m Euro
☐ 250+ to 500 m Euro	☐ 500+ m to 1 bn Euro
☐ 1+ bn to 5 bn Euro	☐ 5+ bn to 10 bn Euro
☐ more than 10 bn Euro	☐ not applicable (Public administration, nonprofit, education)
☐ I don't know	

Question 43: How many employees does your company have?

☐ up to 250 employees	☐ 251 to 500 employees
☐ 501 to 2000 employees	☐ 2001 to 5000 employees
☐ 5001 to 50.000 employees	☐ more than 50.000 employees
☐ I don't know	

Question 44: How much was your IT budget in the last fiscal year?

☐ up to 1 m Euro	☐ 1+ to 10 m Euro
☐ 10+ to 50 m Euro	☐ 50+ to 100 m Euro
☐ 100+ m to 500 m Euro	☐ 500+ m Euro or more
☐ I don't know	

Successful IS Sourcing Governance

Prof. Dr. Helmut Krcmar
Technische Universität München

Department of Informatics
Information Systems

Technische Universität
München

Information about the respondent

Question 45: Which of the following job titles describe your position best?

☐ Board of directors / CEO / Executive   ☐ Chief Information Officer (CIO)

☐ Chief Technology Officer (CTO)   ☐ IT Manager

☐ IT Project Manager   ☐ IT Consultant

☐ Other: _____

Question 46: Ho much experience do you personally have with sourcing (in your current or former companies)?

I have experience with IT sourcing for...

☐ ...0-2 years   ☐ ...3-5 years

☐ ...6-10 years   ☐ ...more than 10 years

☐ I have not managed a sourcing project so far

Question 47: Respondent's age

☐ under 24 years   ☐ 25 - 34 years

☐ 35 - 44 years   ☐ 45 - 54 years

☐ 55 years and older   ☐ not specified

Question 48: How long have you been working in this company?

for approx. _____ year(s)

You've completed the survey!

Thank you very much for supporting our research work. In case of any questions, please do not hesitate to contact Mrs.
Dipl. rer. com. Stefanie Leimeister (Jahner) (stefanie.leimeister@in.tum.de or jahner@in.tum.de). She conducts this
survey in the context of her PhD thesis.

A 3.   Extent of Missing Data: 16 Outsourcing Expectation Variables

Univariate Statistics

	N	Mean	Standard Deviation	Missing Number	Missing Percent	Number of extreme values[a] Low	Number of extreme values[a] High
q1401	196	4.46	1.650	0	.0	0	0
q1402	194	4.69	1.369	2	1.0	1	0
q1403	196	4.59	1.369	0	.0	3	0
q1404	189	4.08	1.521	7	3.6	0	0
q1405	195	4.66	1.395	1	.5	4	0
q1406	195	4.81	1.493	1	.5	6	0
q1407	195	4.27	1.650	1	.5	0	0
q1408	196	3.84	1.514	0	.0	0	0
q1409	194	5.40	1.451	2	1.0	23	0
q1410	195	3.45	1.660	1	.5	0	0
q1411	196	4.16	1.478	0	.0	0	0
q1412	196	3.83	1.516	0	.0	0	0
q1413	196	3.56	1.637	0	.0	0	0
q1414	194	3.67	1.680	2	1.0	0	0
q1415	193	3.13	1.696	3	1.5	0	0
q1416	187	2.50	1.373	9	4.6	0	0

a. Number of cases outside the range (Q1 − 1.5*IQR, Q3 + 1.5*IQR).

A 4.   Mean Differences between Missing and Non-Missing Values (13 Context Variables)

Dummy Variable Cases with missing values (group 1) Cases without missing values (group 2)		Company Experience with ITO / BPO	Number of outsourcing vendors	Extent of outsourcing (with regard to IT budget)	Company's Sales Volume	Firm size (employees)	IT budget	Extent of outsourcing: BPO	Extent of outsourcing: Applications	Extent of outsourcing: Infrastructure	Role of IT for company	Respondent Age	Working experience in this company	Respondent's experience with outsourcing
Cases with Missing Values	Mean	2.68	1.95	1.55	4.95	3.38	2.67	3.00	2.09	2.32	5.27	3.55	3.59	10.273
	N	22	21	22	21	21	18	22	22	22	22	22	22	22
	Standard Deviation	.780	.669	.671	2.109	1.396	1.455	1.309	.868	.995	1.638	1.011	1.098	8.0486
Complete Cases (without missing values)	Mean	2.89	2.02	1.63	5.66	3.42	2.63	3.06	2.33	2.22	5.34	3.55	3.75	12.705
	N	174	174	170	161	173	158	174	174	174	174	174	174	171
	Standard Deviation	1.147	.745	.614	2.277	1.364	1.228	1.268	.986	.967	1.400	.780	.940	8.8759
Total	Mean	2.86	2.02	1.62	5.58	3.42	2.64	3.06	2.30	2.23	5.33	3.55	3.73	12.427
	N	196	195	192	182	194	176	196	196	196	196	196	196	193
	Standard Deviation	1.112	.736	.619	2.265	1.364	1.248	1.270	.975	.968	1.424	.806	.957	8.8000

A 5. ANOVA Test of Significance Comparing Missing and Non-Missing Data Groups

			Square sum	df	Mean of squares	F	Significance
Company Experience with ITO / BPO	Between groups	(combined)	.807	1	.807	.651	.421
		Within groups	240.474	194	1.240		
		Total	241.281	195			
Number of outsourcing vendors	Between groups	(combined)	.093	1	.093	.172	.679
		Within groups	104.860	193	.543		
		Total	104.954	194			
Extent of outsourcing (with regard to IT budget)	Between groups	(combined)	.137	1	.137	.357	.551
		Within groups	73.107	190	.385		
		Total	73.245	191			
Company's sales volume	Between groups	(combined)	9.423	1	9.423	1.846	.176
		Within groups	918.841	180	5.105		
		Total	928.264	181			
Firm size (employees)	Between groups	(combined)	.031	1	.031	.017	.897
		Within groups	359.149	192	1.871		
		Total	359.180	193			
IT budget	Between groups	(combined)	.018	1	.018	.012	.914
		Within groups	272.709	174	1.567		
		Total	272.727	175			
Extent of outsourcing: BPO	Between groups	(combined)	.078	1	.078	.048	.826
		Within groups	314.305	194	1.620		
		Total	314.383	195			
Extent of outsourcing: Applications	Between groups	(combined)	1.094	1	1.094	1.153	.284
		Within groups	184.146	194	.949		
		Total	185.240	195			
Extent of outsourcing: Infrastructure	Between groups	(combined)	.194	1	.194	.207	.650
		Within groups	182.474	194	.941		
		Total	182.668	195			
Role of IT for company	Between groups	(combined)	.086	1	.086	.042	.837
		Within groups	395.358	194	2.038		
		Total	395.444	195			
Repondent Age	Between groups	(combined)	.000	1	.000	.000	.998
		Within groups	126.587	194	.653		
		Total	126.587	195			
Working experience in this company	Between groups	(combined)	115.285	1	115.285	1.493	.223
		Within groups	14753.200	191	77.242		
		Total	14868.484	192			
Respondent's experience with outsourcing	Between groups	(combined)	.477	1	.477	.519	.472
		Within groups	178.192	194	.919		
		Total	178.668	195			

A 6.   Statistical Tests for Normal Distribution of the 16 Outsourcing Expectation Variables: Komogorov-Smirnov and Shapiro-Wilk Test

	Kolmogorov-Smirnov[a]			Shapiro-Wilk		
	Statistics	df	Significance	Statistics	df	Significance
Cost reduction	.136	174	.000	.941	174	.000
Flexibility of costs / cost transparency	.189	174	.000	.930	174	.000
Quality improvements (lower error rate / shorter processing time)	.196	174	.000	.937	174	.000
Long-term use of systems, applications and data (stability, reliability, retention of status quo)	.143	174	.000	.946	174	.000
Improved service orientation	.190	174	.000	.922	174	.000
Increased flexibility	.192	174	.000	.909	174	.000
Shift risk to service provider	.148	174	.000	.937	174	.000
Modernization of IT / replace legacy systems	.137	174	.000	.951	174	.000
Focus on core competencies	.232	174	.000	.881	174	.000
Enable and facilitate strategic competitive advantages	.144	174	.000	.940	174	.000
Access to highly skilled people	.151	174	.000	.949	174	.000
Access to better IT systems and new technology	.134	174	.000	.951	174	.000
Knowledge acquisition from service provider	.127	174	.000	.944	174	.000
Suggestions for new IT based products and services by your service provider (innovation, idea creation)	.134	174	.000	.939	174	.000
Shared development of IT based products and services together with your service provider (joint product and service development)	.154	174	.000	.914	174	.000
Business transformation	.187	174	.000	.884	174	.000

a. Significance correction with Lilliefors

A 7.   Descriptive Measures of the Distribution of the 16 Outsourcing Expectation Variables

	Cost reduction	Flexibility of costs / cost transparency	Quality improvements	Long-term use of systems, applications and data	Improved service orientation	Increased flexibility	Shift risk to service provider	Modernization of IT / replace legacy systems	Focus on core competencies	Enable and facilitate strategic competitive advantages	Access to highly skilled people	Access to better IT systems and new technology	Knowledge acquisition from service provider	Suggestions for new IT based products and services by your service provider	Shared development of IT based products and services	Business transformation
Valid	196	194	196	189	195	195	195	196	194	195	196	196	196	194	193	187
Missing	0	2	0	7	1	1	1	0	2	1	0	0	0	2	3	9
Mean	4.46	4.69	4.59	4.08	4.66	4.81	4.27	3.84	5.40	3.45	4.16	3.83	3.56	3.67	3.13	2.50
Standard error of mean	.118	.098	.098	.111	.100	.107	.118	.108	.104	.119	.106	.108	.117	.121	.122	.100
Standard deviation	1.650	1.369	1.369	1.521	1.395	1.493	1.650	1.514	1.451	1.660	1.478	1.516	1.637	1.680	1.696	1.373
Variance	2.722	1.875	1.874	2.312	1.947	2.230	2.722	2.291	2.106	2.754	2.185	2.298	2.679	2.823	2.878	1.886
Skewness	-.141	-.395	-.358	-.135	-.562	-.694	-.170	-.033	-.924	.295	.003	.039	.130	.002	.324	.611
Standard error of skewness	.174	.175	.174	.177	.174	.174	.174	.174	.175	.174	.174	.174	.174	.175	.175	.178
Kurtosis	-.857	-.357	-.314	-.727	-.228	-.127	-1.004	-.490	.327	-.693	-.475	-.624	-.863	-.975	-1.032	-.312
Standard error of kurtosis	.346	.347	.346	.352	.346	.346	.346	.346	.347	.346	.346	.346	.346	.347	.348	.354

A 8. Initial Factor Analysis: Correlation Matrix of the 16 Outsourcing Expectation Variables

Column variables (left to right):
1. Cost reduction
2. Variabilization of costs / cost transparency
3. Quality improvements
4. Long-term use of systems, applications and data
5. Improved service orientation
6. Increased flexibility
7. Shift risk to service provider
8. Modernization of IT / replace legacy systems
9. Focus on core competencies
10. Enable and facilitate strategic competitive advantages
11. Access to highly skilled people
12. Access to better IT systems and new technology
13. Knowledge acquisition from service provider
14. Suggestions for new IT based products and services
15. Joint product and service development
16. Business transformation

Correlation

	1	2	3	4	5	6	7	8	9	10	11	12	13	14	15	16
Cost reduction	1.000	.460	.137	.015	.174	.077	-.011	.092	.131	.184	-.142	.170	-.102	-.020	.084	.119
Variabilization of costs / cost transparency	.460	1.000	.086	.075	.205	.193	.111	.176	.154	.128	-.064	.116	-.026	.098	.027	.117
Quality improvements	.137	.086	1.000	.337	.442	.289	.203	.314	.224	.272	.306	.349	.214	.332	.164	.133
Long-term use of systems, applications and data	.015	.075	.337	1.000	.330	.120	.272	.378	.135	.256	.185	.294	.174	.142	.125	.240
Improved service orientation	.174	.205	.442	.330	1.000	.443	.222	.290	.275	.290	.226	.295	.148	.246	.117	.277
Increased flexibility	.077	.193	.289	.120	.443	1.000	.128	.249	.232	.189	.161	.188	.088	.133	.099	.141
Shift risk to service provider	-.011	.111	.203	.272	.222	.128	1.000	.372	.248	.164	.211	.309	.177	.168	-.015	.168
Modernization of IT / replace legacy systems	.092	.176	.314	.378	.290	.249	.372	1.000	.261	.294	.310	.522	.306	.420	.204	.279
Focus on core competencies	.131	.154	.224	.135	.275	.232	.248	.261	1.000	.316	.187	.235	.106	.231	.121	.231
Enable and facilitate strategic competitive advantages	.184	.128	.272	.256	.290	.189	.164	.294	.316	1.000	.295	.336	.364	.451	.429	.472
Access to highly skilled people	-.142	-.064	.306	.185	.226	.161	.211	.310	.187	.295	1.000	.388	.542	.392	.159	.115
Access to better IT systems and new technology	.170	.116	.349	.294	.295	.188	.309	.522	.235	.336	.388	1.000	.366	.511	.242	.264
Knowledge acquisition from service provider	-.102	-.026	.214	.174	.148	.088	.177	.306	.106	.364	.542	.366	1.000	.622	.383	.338
Suggestions for new IT based products and services	-.020	.098	.332	.142	.246	.133	.168	.420	.231	.451	.392	.511	.622	1.000	.515	.397
Joint product and service development	.084	.027	.164	.125	.117	.099	-.015	.204	.121	.429	.159	.242	.383	.515	1.000	.484
Business transformation	.119	.117	.133	.240	.277	.141	.168	.279	.231	.472	.115	.264	.338	.397	.484	1.000

Significance (1-sided)

	1	2	3	4	5	6	7	8	9	10	11	12	13	14	15	16
Cost reduction		.000	.028	.420	.007	.143	.439	.100	.034	.005	.024	.009	.078	.392	.121	.049
Variabilization of costs / cost transparency	.000		.114	.148	.002	.003	.060	.007	.016	.037	.185	.053	.357	.087	.356	.051
Quality improvements	.028	.114		.000	.000	.000	.002	.000	.001	.000	.000	.000	.001	.000	.011	.031
Long-term use of systems, applications and data	.420	.148	.000		.000	.047	.000	.000	.030	.000	.005	.000	.007	.023	.041	.000
Improved service orientation	.007	.002	.000	.000		.000	.001	.000	.000	.000	.001	.000	.019	.000	.052	.000
Increased flexibility	.143	.003	.000	.047	.000		.037	.000	.001	.004	.012	.004	.110	.031	.084	.024
Shift risk to service provider	.439	.060	.002	.000	.001	.037		.000	.000	.011	.002	.000	.006	.009	.419	.009
Modernization of IT / replace legacy systems	.100	.007	.000	.000	.000	.000	.000		.000	.000	.000	.000	.000	.000	.002	.000
Focus on core competencies	.034	.016	.001	.030	.000	.001	.000	.000		.000	.004	.000	.070	.001	.045	.001
Enable and facilitate strategic competitive advantages	.005	.037	.000	.000	.000	.004	.011	.000	.000		.000	.000	.000	.000	.000	.000
Access to highly skilled people	.024	.185	.000	.005	.001	.012	.002	.000	.004	.000		.000	.000	.000	.013	.054
Access to better IT systems and new technology	.009	.053	.000	.000	.000	.004	.000	.000	.000	.000	.000		.000	.000	.000	.000
Knowledge acquisition from service provider	.078	.357	.001	.007	.019	.110	.006	.000	.070	.000	.000	.000		.000	.000	.000
Suggestions for new IT based products and services	.392	.087	.000	.023	.000	.031	.009	.000	.001	.000	.000	.000	.000		.000	.000
Joint product and service development	.121	.356	.011	.041	.052	.084	.419	.002	.045	.000	.013	.000	.000	.000		.000
Business transformation	.049	.051	.031	.000	.000	.024	.009	.000	.001	.000	.054	.000	.000	.000	.000	

A 9. Initial Factor Analysis: Anti-Image Covariance Matrix and Anti-Image Correlation Matrix of the 16 Outsourcing Expectation Variables

		Cost reduction	Variabilization of costs	Quality improvements	Long-term use of systems	Improved service orientation	Increased flexibility	Shift risk to service provider	Modernization of IT	Focus on core competencies	Enable and facilitate strategic competitive advantages	Access to highly skilled people	Access to better IT systems	Knowledge acquisition	Suggestions for new IT based products and services	Joint product and service development	Business transformation
Anti-Image-Covariance	Cost reduction	.661	-.302	-.088	.087	-.053	.069	.073	-.011	-.032	-.099	.100	-.132	.013	.104	-.054	-.013
	Variabilization of costs	-.302	.720	.057	-.029	-.034	-.099	-.056	-.048	-.023	.011	.033	.050	.023	-.075	.052	-.006
	Quality improvements	-.088	.057	.659	-.139	-.149	-.080	-.024	-.009	-.025	-.013	-.076	-.024	.029	-.085	-.011	.080
	Long-term use of systems	.087	-.029	-.139	.711	-.114	.081	-.066	-.143	.033	-.071	.019	-.061	-.032	.106	-.024	-.059
	Improved service orientation	-.053	-.034	-.149	-.114	.609	-.221	-.027	.020	-.043	-.016	-.044	-.009	.034	-.032	.055	-.093
	Increased flexibility	.069	-.099	-.080	.081	-.221	.745	.023	-.080	-.070	-.025	-.016	-.013	-.002	.055	-.039	.007
	Shift risk to service provider	.073	-.056	-.024	-.066	-.027	.023	.770	-.126	-.110	-.006	-.013	-.080	-.035	.032	.092	-.050
	Modernization of IT	-.011	-.048	-.009	-.143	.020	-.080	-.126	.585	-.037	.017	-.034	-.143	.006	-.073	.008	-.030
	Focus on core competencies	-.032	-.023	-.025	.033	-.043	-.070	-.110	-.037	.796	-.108	-.055	.001	.069	-.040	.026	-.052
	Enable and facilitate strategic competitive advantages	-.099	.011	-.013	-.071	-.016	-.025	-.006	.017	-.108	.597	-.074	.000	-.019	-.061	-.093	-.136
	Access to highly skilled people	.100	.033	-.076	.019	-.044	-.016	-.013	-.034	-.055	-.074	.584	-.097	-.215	.021	.027	.087
	Access to better IT systems	-.132	.050	-.024	-.061	-.009	-.013	-.080	-.143	.001	.000	-.097	.548	.011	-.131	.020	.000
	Knowledge acquisition	.013	.023	.029	-.032	.034	-.002	-.035	.006	.069	-.019	-.215	.011	.473	-.171	-.033	-.070
	Suggestions for new IT based products and services	.104	-.075	-.085	.106	-.032	.055	.032	-.073	-.040	-.061	.021	-.131	-.171	.388	-.143	-.019
	Joint product and service development	-.054	.052	-.011	-.024	.055	-.039	.092	.008	.026	-.093	.027	.020	-.033	-.143	.589	-.177
	Business transformation	-.013	-.006	.080	-.059	-.093	.007	-.050	-.030	-.052	-.136	.087	.000	-.070	-.019	-.177	.605
Anti-Image-Correlation	Cost reduction	.502[a]	-.437	-.134	.127	-.083	.098	.102	-.018	-.045	-.157	.161	-.220	.023	.205	-.086	-.020
	Variabilization of costs / cost transparency	-.437	.614[a]	.083	-.040	-.051	-.135	-.075	-.073	-.030	.017	.051	.079	.039	-.143	.081	-.009
	Quality improvements	-.134	.083	.845[a]	-.203	-.235	-.114	-.034	-.014	-.034	-.020	-.123	-.039	.052	-.169	-.018	.126
	Long-term use of systems	.127	-.040	-.203	.770[a]	-.173	.112	-.090	-.221	.044	-.109	.029	-.097	-.056	.201	-.037	-.090
	Improved service orientation	-.083	-.051	-.235	-.173	.821[a]	-.329	-.040	.034	-.062	-.026	-.074	-.016	.063	-.066	.092	-.153
	Increased flexibility	.098	-.135	-.114	.112	-.329	.755[a]	.030	-.121	-.091	-.037	-.024	-.021	-.003	.103	-.059	.011
	Shift risk to service provider	.102	-.075	-.034	-.090	-.040	.030	.834[a]	-.187	-.141	-.009	-.019	-.123	-.058	.059	.137	-.073
	Modernization of IT	-.018	-.073	-.014	-.221	.034	-.121	-.187	.879[a]	-.055	.028	-.059	-.253	.011	-.153	.013	-.050
	Focus on core competencies	-.045	-.030	-.034	.044	-.062	-.091	-.141	-.055	.877[a]	-.157	-.081	.001	.112	-.072	.038	-.076
	Enable and facilitate strategic competitive advantages	-.157	.017	-.020	-.109	-.026	-.037	-.009	.028	-.157	.894[a]	-.125	-.001	-.035	-.127	-.157	-.227
	Access to highly skilled people	.161	.051	-.123	.029	-.074	-.024	-.019	-.059	-.081	-.125	.790[a]	-.172	-.409	.043	.046	.147
	Access to better IT systems	-.220	.079	-.039	-.097	-.016	-.021	-.123	-.253	.001	-.001	-.172	.860[a]	.021	-.284	.035	-.001
	Knowledge acquisition	.023	.039	.052	-.056	.063	-.003	-.058	.011	.112	-.035	-.409	.021	.795[a]	-.398	-.063	-.130
	Suggestions for new IT based products and services	.205	-.143	-.169	.201	-.066	.103	.059	-.153	-.072	-.127	.043	-.284	-.398	.784[a]	-.299	-.040
	Joint product and service development	-.086	.081	-.018	-.037	.092	-.059	.137	.013	.038	-.157	.046	.035	-.063	-.299	.802[a]	-.297
	Business transformation	-.020	-.009	.126	-.090	-.153	.011	-.073	-.050	-.076	-.227	.147	-.001	-.130	-.040	-.297	.829[a]

a. Measure of Sampling Adequacy (MSA) for each variable

A 10. Initial Factor Analysis: Communalities (PCA) of the 16 Outsourcing Expectation Variables

	Initial	Extraction
Cost reduction	1.000	.660
Variabilization of costs / cost transparency	1.000	.584
Quality improvements	1.000	.501
Long-term use of systems, applications and data	1.000	.353
Improved service orientation	1.000	.661
Increased flexibility	1.000	.631
Shift risk to service provider	1.000	.564
Modernization of IT / replace legacy systems	1.000	.595
Focus on core competencies	1.000	.275
Enable and facilitate strategic competitive advantages	1.000	.547
Access to highly skilled people	1.000	.555
Access to better IT systems and new technology	1.000	.568
Knowledge acquisition from service provider	1.000	.653
Suggestions for new IT based products and services (innovation, idea creation)	1.000	.688
Joint product and service development	1.000	.677
Business transformation	1.000	.529

Extraction Method: Principal Component Analysis

A 11. Initial Factor Analysis: KMO and Bartlett's Test of the 16 Outsourcing Expectation Variables

Kaiser-Meyer-Olkin Measure of Sampling Adequacy		.805
Bartlett'sTest of Squericity	Approx. Chi-Square	903.904
	df	120
	Significance	.000

A 12. Initial Factor Analysis: Parallel Analysis (MonteCarlo PCA) of the 16 Outsourcing Expectation Variables

Component No.	Actual eigenvalue from PCA	Criterion value from parallel analysis	Decision
1	4.676	1.5232	accept
2	1.827	1.4108	accept
3	1.483	1.3262	accept
4	1.056	1.2537	reject

Calculated with MonteCarlo PCA for Parallel Analysis by Watkins, M.W. (2000)

A 13. Initial Factor Analysis: Extraction of Factors and Total Variance Explained of the 16 Outsourcing Expectation Variables

Component	Initial Eigenvalues			Extraction Sums of Squared Loadings			Rotation Sums of Squared Loadings		
	Total	% of Variance	Cumulative %	Total	% of Variance	Cumulative %	Total	% of Variance	Cumulative %
1	4.676	29.224	29.224	4.676	29.224	29.224	2.958	18.486	18.486
2	1.827	11.418	40.643	1.827	11.418	40.643	2.408	15.049	33.535
3	1.483	9.269	49.911	1.483	9.269	49.911	2.021	12.632	46.167
4	1.056	6.599	56.510	1.056	6.599	56.510	1.655	10.343	56.510
5	.979	6.118	62.628						
6	.912	5.700	68.328						
7	.767	4.792	73.120						
8	.679	4.246	77.366						
9	.606	3.788	81.153						
10	.574	3.587	84.740						
11	.523	3.271	88.011						
12	.456	2.853	90.864						
13	.431	2.695	93.559						
14	.404	2.523	96.082						
15	.388	2.424	98.506						
16	.239	1.494	100.000						

Extraction Method: Principal Component Analysis

A 14. Initial Factor Analysis: Scree Plot of the 16 Outsourcing Expectation Variables

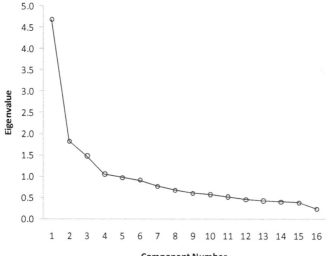

A 15. Initial Factor Analysis: Rotated Component Matrix of the 16 Expectation Variables

		Component			
		1	2	3	4
q1415	Joint product and service development	.815	-.090	.050	.047
q1414	Suggestions for new IT based products and services (innovation, idea creation)	.748	.318	.110	-.122
q1416	Business transformation	.680	.097	.121	.208
q1413	Knowledge acquisition from service provider	.658	.322	.024	-.340
q1410	Enable and facilitate strategic competitive advantages	.657	.167	.254	.151
q1407	Shift risk to service provider	-.055	.746	.055	.046
q1408	Modernization of IT / replace legacy systems	.258	.700	.172	.094
q1412	Access to better IT systems and new technology	.372	.636	.146	.053
q1404	Long-term use of systems, applications and data	.074	.528	.261	.019
q1406	Increased flexibility	.048	.002	.791	.046
q1405	Improved service orientation	.126	.208	.766	.121
q1403	Quality improvements	.155	.320	.610	-.050
q1409	Focus on core competencies	.184	.263	.368	.192
q1401	Cost reduction	.098	.029	.092	.801
q1402	Variabilization of costs / cost transparency	.047	.168	.130	.732
q1411	Access to highly skilled people	.325	.427	.243	-.456

Extraction Method: Principal Component Analysis. Rotation Method: Varimax with Kaiser Normalization

a. Rotation converged in 5 Iterations.

A 16. Cluster Analysis: Agglomeration Schedule of the Ward Algorithm

	Cluster Combined			Stage Cluster First Appears		
Stage	Cluster 1	Cluster 2	Coefficient	Cluster 1	Cluster 2	Next Stage
1	64	69	.008	0	0	31
2	42	71	.027	0	0	46
3	54	126	.051	0	0	81
4	131	186	.083	0	0	25
5	68	111	.115	0	0	37
6	56	134	.150	0	0	37
7	148	196	.186	0	0	128
8	90	155	.232	0	0	83
9	24	83	.284	0	0	24
10	41	153	.340	0	0	54
11	22	84	.402	0	0	135
12	82	132	.465	0	0	34
13	78	164	.530	0	0	57
14	74	145	.598	0	0	94
15	48	112	.667	0	0	79
16	127	184	.743	0	0	29
17	88	109	.820	0	0	40
18	39	118	.898	0	0	143

| | Cluster Combined | | | Stage Cluster First Appears | | |
Stage	Cluster 1	Cluster 2	Coefficient	Cluster 1	Cluster 2	Next Stage
19	62	177	.981	0	0	81
20	29	107	1.065	0	0	94
21	45	91	1.149	0	0	107
22	36	80	1.235	0	0	112
23	21	119	1.322	0	0	61
24	24	73	1.411	9	0	87
25	114	131	1.510	0	4	91
26	156	178	1.611	0	0	32
27	33	182	1.721	0	0	70
28	3	67	1.839	0	0	98
29	10	127	1.961	0	16	56
30	72	121	2.099	0	0	52
31	16	64	2.243	0	1	92
32	28	156	2.402	0	26	88
33	50	160	2.562	0	0	87
34	38	82	2.725	0	12	120
35	142	187	2.887	0	0	103
36	12	87	3.050	0	0	125
37	56	68	3.216	6	5	146
38	105	175	3.384	0	0	74
39	154	159	3.553	0	0	85
40	18	88	3.742	0	17	76
41	110	123	3.931	0	0	109
42	1	106	4.121	0	0	139
43	136	165	4.312	0	0	68
44	66	161	4.505	0	0	147
45	57	86	4.698	0	0	114
46	42	65	4.896	2	0	80
47	117	149	5.098	0	0	78
48	17	20	5.306	0	0	128
49	32	193	5.515	0	0	110
50	61	93	5.724	0	0	140
51	113	129	5.937	0	0	90
52	59	72	6.150	0	30	143
53	19	125	6.370	0	0	117
54	41	192	6.591	10	0	121
55	162	171	6.815	0	0	93
56	10	76	7.043	29	0	120
57	78	157	7.277	13	0	119
58	53	191	7.516	0	0	140
59	2	97	7.763	0	0	142
60	37	166	8.010	0	0	159
61	21	152	8.261	23	0	141
62	46	104	8.525	0	0	109
63	138	163	8.790	0	0	108
64	70	146	9.074	0	0	102
65	9	23	9.365	0	0	122
66	190	195	9.658	0	0	86
67	47	92	9.958	0	0	84
68	136	143	10.267	43	0	89
69	101	174	10.589	0	0	105
70	33	120	10.912	27	0	124

Stage	Cluster Combined		Coefficient	Stage Cluster First Appears		Next Stage
	Cluster 1	Cluster 2		Cluster 1	Cluster 2	
71	13	100	11.242	0	0	130
72	40	85	11.588	0	0	96
73	94	115	11.953	0	0	129
74	58	105	12.319	0	38	124
75	141	173	12.696	0	0	118
76	18	102	13.074	40	0	102
77	14	180	13.454	0	0	113
78	89	117	13.837	0	47	125
79	48	185	14.226	15	0	134
80	42	140	14.629	46	0	116
81	54	62	15.035	3	19	144
82	63	103	15.454	0	0	133
83	90	167	15.875	8	0	129
84	47	81	16.319	67	0	158
85	79	154	16.767	0	39	132
86	35	190	17.223	0	66	151
87	24	50	17.686	24	33	113
88	28	133	18.154	32	0	111
89	136	147	18.627	68	0	154
90	27	113	19.114	0	51	142
91	114	150	19.604	25	0	137
92	16	96	20.098	31	0	119
93	98	162	20.595	0	55	156
94	29	74	21.107	20	14	103
95	176	179	21.628	0	0	130
96	40	122	22.157	72	0	137
97	60	158	22.691	0	0	166
98	3	181	23.239	28	0	114
99	128	144	23.803	0	0	126
100	168	189	24.375	0	0	121
101	34	172	24.953	0	0	136
102	18	70	25.538	76	64	149
103	29	142	26.134	94	35	153
104	151	169	26.732	0	0	151
105	101	108	27.347	69	0	112
106	4	139	27.988	0	0	138
107	45	170	28.661	21	0	160
108	95	138	29.340	0	63	147
109	46	110	30.028	62	41	153
110	32	49	30.718	49	0	117
111	28	43	31.429	88	0	144
112	36	101	32.165	22	105	157
113	14	24	32.911	77	87	139
114	3	57	33.719	98	45	133
115	6	55	34.533	0	0	145
116	11	42	35.355	0	80	152
117	19	32	36.198	53	110	168
118	15	141	37.041	0	75	134
119	16	78	37.891	92	57	162
120	10	38	38.770	56	34	162
121	41	168	39.687	54	100	141
122	9	116	40.626	65	0	150

Stage	Cluster Combined Cluster 1	Cluster 2	Coefficient	Stage Cluster First Appears Cluster 1	Cluster 2	Next Stage
123	77	124	41.573	0	0	171
124	33	58	42.607	70	74	163
125	12	89	43.689	36	78	154
126	5	128	44.795	0	99	170
127	52	137	45.907	0	0	159
128	17	148	47.112	48	7	148
129	90	94	48.335	83	73	160
130	13	176	49.599	71	95	135
131	99	194	50.897	0	0	161
132	7	79	52.212	0	85	172
133	3	63	53.569	114	82	164
134	15	48	54.927	118	79	146
135	13	22	56.389	130	11	168
136	31	34	57.884	0	101	158
137	40	114	59.397	96	91	167
138	4	25	60.928	106	0	163
139	1	14	62.461	42	113	164
140	53	61	64.233	58	50	149
141	21	41	66.102	61	121	165
142	2	27	68.072	59	90	161
143	39	59	70.089	18	52	157
144	28	54	72.169	111	81	167
145	6	130	74.292	115	0	176
146	15	56	76.420	134	37	178
147	66	95	78.572	44	108	155
148	17	44	80.887	128	0	170
149	18	53	83.220	102	140	177
150	9	51	85.623	122	0	155
151	35	151	88.076	86	104	156
152	11	188	90.530	116	0	177
153	29	46	93.227	103	109	173
154	12	136	95.938	125	89	166
155	9	66	98.881	150	147	171
156	35	98	101.865	151	93	181
157	36	39	104.911	112	143	165
158	31	47	107.999	136	84	169
159	37	52	111.149	60	127	172
160	45	90	114.383	107	129	169
161	2	99	117.729	142	131	174
162	10	16	121.665	120	119	174
163	4	33	126.054	138	124	175
164	1	3	130.662	139	133	175
165	21	36	135.577	141	157	178
166	12	60	140.622	154	97	176
167	28	40	145.940	144	137	173
168	13	19	151.368	135	117	183
169	31	45	156.976	158	160	182
170	5	17	163.763	126	148	179
171	9	77	170.566	155	123	179
172	7	37	177.647	132	159	180
173	28	29	184.937	167	153	180
174	2	10	193.202	161	162	181

Stage	Cluster Combined		Coefficient	Stage Cluster First Appears		Next Stage
	Cluster 1	Cluster 2		Cluster 1	Cluster 2	
175	1	4	202.829	164	163	186
176	6	12	213.498	145	166	182
177	11	18	224.268	152	149	183
178	15	21	235.603	146	165	185
179	5	9	250.078	170	171	185
180	7	28	266.458	172	173	184
181	2	35	283.763	174	156	187
182	6	31	304.548	176	169	186
183	11	13	333.408	177	168	184
184	7	11	368.450	180	183	188
185	5	15	405.335	179	178	187
186	1	6	443.097	175	182	189
187	2	5	509.476	181	185	188
188	2	7	598.123	187	184	189
189	1	2	709.547	186	188	0

A 17. Cluster Analysis: Dendrogram using the Ward Algorithm

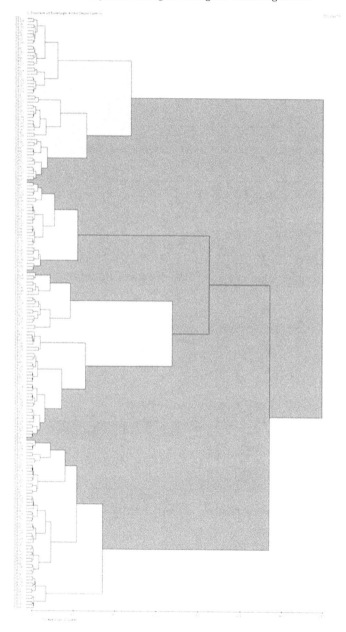

A 18. Cluster Analysis: Cluster Centers of the Final Solution (k-means)

	Cluster			
	1	2	3	4
Factor Innovation	.14717	-.68709	.93415	-.54433
Factor Technology	-.98429	-.08654	.22151	.91059
Factor Business	.90580	-.52746	-.61857	.53516
Factor Cost	.20057	.71785	-.30270	-.62199

A 19. Cluster Analysis: Distances between Cluster Centers of the Final Solution (k-means)

Cluster	1	2	3	4
1		1.955	2.156	2.210
2	1.955		1.942	1.985
3	2.156	1.942		2.023
4	2.210	1.985	2.023	

A 20. Discriminant Analysis: Eigenvalues and Canonical Correlations for Discriminant Functions

Function	Eigenvalue	% of Variance	Cumulated %	Canonical corre-lation
1	1.552[a]	41.6	41.6	.780
2	1.246[a]	33.4	75.0	.745
3	.935[a]	25.0	100.0	.695

a. The first 3 canonical discriminant functions are used in this analysis.

A 21. Discriminant Analysis: Test of Equality of Group Means

	Wilks' Lambda	F	df1	df2	Significance
Factor Innovation	.544	51.937	3	186	.000
Factor IT	.541	52.692	3	186	.000
Factor Business	.524	56.422	3	186	.000
Factor Cost	.719	24.248	3	186	.000

A 22. Discriminant Analysis: Wilks' Lambda of Discriminant Functions

Test of Functions	Wilk's-Lambda*	Chi-Quadrat	df	Significance
1 to 3	.090	445.090	12	.000
2 to 3	.230	271.780	6	.000
3	.517	122.085	2	.000

* Small values for Wilks' lambda show that the groups can be discriminated well.

A 23. Discriminant Analysis: Summary of Classification Results

Classification Results[b,c]

			Predicted group membership				
			1	2	3	4	Total
Original	#	1	44	0	0	0	44
		2	0	50	0	0	50
		3	0	0	51	0	51
		4	0	0	0	45	45
	%	1	100.0	.0	.0	.0	100.0
		2	.0	100.0	.0	.0	100.0
		3	.0	.0	100.0	.0	100.0
		4	.0	.0	.0	100.0	100.0
Cross-Validated[a]	#	1	43	1	0	0	44
		2	1	48	0	1	50
		3	0	0	51	0	51
		4	0	0	0	45	45
	%	1	97.7	2.3	.0	.0	100.0
		2	2.0	96.0	.0	2.0	100.0
		3	.0	.0	100.0	.0	100.0
		4	.0	.0	.0	100.0	100.0

a. Cross-Validation is only done for cases in this analysis. Leave-one-out classification is available as a form of cross-validation of the classification table. Under this option, each case is classified using a discriminant function based on all cases except the given case. This is thought to give a better estimate of what classificiation results would be in the population.

b. 100.0% of grouped cases were classified correctly.

c. 98.4% of the cross-validated grouped cases were classified correctly.

A 24. Discriminant Analysis: Structure Matrix

	Function		
	1	2	3
Factor Technology	.623[*]	.423	-.165
Factor Innovation	.245	-.561	.614[*]
Factor Business	-.432	.509	.565[*]
Factor Cost	-.321	-.231	-.420[*]

Shared correlations within the groups between the discriminant variables and standardized canonical discriminant functions. Structure coefficients, also called structure correlations or discriminant loadings, are the correlations between a given independent variable and the discriminant scores associated with a given discriminant function. They are used to tell how closely a variable is related to each function in discriminant analysis. Looking at all the structure coefficients for a function allows the researcher to assign a label to the dimension it measures, much like factor loadings in factor analysis. The structure coefficients are whole (not partial) coefficients, similar to correlation coefficients, and reflect the uncontrolled association of the discriminating variables with the criterion variable, whereas the discriminant coefficients are partial coefficients reflecting the unique, controlled association of the discriminating variables with the criterion variable, controlling for other variables in the equation (Garson 2008b).

*. Largest absolute correlation between each variable and a given discriminant function.

A 25. Discriminant Analysis: Standardized Canonical Discriminant Functions Coefficients

	Function		
	1	2	3
Factor Innovation	.350	-.681	.643
Factor IT	.820	.516	-.166
Factor Business	-.538	.624	.574
Factor Cost	-.534	-.358	-.604

The standardized discriminant function coefficients indicate the semi-partial contribution (the unique, controlled association) of each variable to the discriminant function(s), controlling the independent but not the dependent for other independents entered in the equation (just as regression coefficients are semi-partial coefficients). In contrast, structure coefficients are whole (not partial) coefficients, similar to correlation coefficients, and reflect the uncontrolled association of the discriminant scores with the criterion variable. That is, the structure coefficients indicate the simple correlations between the variables and the discriminant function or functions. The structure coefficients should be used to assign meaningful labels to the discriminant functions. The standardized discriminant function coefficients should be used to assess the importance of each independent variable's unique contribution to the discriminant function (Garson 2008b).

A 26. Discriminant Analysis: Functions for Group Centroids

	Function		
Cluster	1	2	3
1	-1.861	-.182	.962
2	-.473	-.267	-1.541
3	1.387	-1.206	.494
4	.773	1.842	.211

Non-standardized canonical discriminant functions that are evaluated with regard to group mean.
Functions at group centroids are the mean discriminant scores for each of the dependent variable categories for each of the discriminant functions in MDA. Two-group discriminant analysis has two centroids, one for each group. We want the means to be well apart to show the discriminant function is clearly discriminating. The closer the means, the more errors of classification there likely will be (Garson 2008b).

A 27. Discriminant Analysis: Casewise Diagnostics

			Highest group				2nd highest group			Discriminant scores		
			P(D>d | G=g)			Squared			Squared			
Case #	Actual Group	Predicted group	p	df	P(G=g | D=d)	Mahalanobis distance to centroid	Group	P(G=g | D=d)	Mahalanobis distance to centroid	F1	F2	F3
1	1	1	.334	3	.997	3.401	2	.003	14.894	-3.544	-.892	.711
2	2	2	.312	3	.681	3.572	1	.315	5.112	-2.274	.212	-1.226
3	1	1	.836	3	.787	.857	2	.171	3.910	-1.231	-.240	.285
4	1	1	.761	3	.999	1.169	2	.001	15.311	-2.511	-.403	1.797
5	2	2	.793	3	.748	1.032	3	.202	3.651	.270	-.593	-.930
6	1	1	.875	3	.858	.693	2	.081	5.401	-1.086	-.044	.690
7	4	4	.092	3	1.000	6.432	2	.000	26.662	1.724	4.174	-.087
9	3	3	.547	3	.681	2.125	2	.205	4.526	-.002	-1.477	.145
10	2	2	.927	3	.936	.463	4	.041	6.705	-.458	.413	-1.563
11	4	4	.605	3	.696	1.846	3	.266	3.772	1.048	.674	.849
12	1	1	.318	3	.641	3.521	3	.242	5.472	-.188	-.079	1.806
13	4	4	.617	3	.757	1.791	2	.227	4.196	.531	1.448	-1.045
14	1	1	.566	3	.868	2.033	2	.125	5.909	-2.035	-1.255	.038
15	3	3	.145	3	1.000	5.391	4	.000	21.397	2.678	-1.803	2.329

Case #	Actual Group	Predicted group	P(D>d | G=g) p	df	P(G=g | D=d)	Squared Mahalanobis distance to centroid	Group	P(G=g | D=d)	Squared Mahalanobis distance to centroid	F1	F2	F3
			Highest group				**2nd highest group**			**Discriminant scores**		
16	2	2	.567	3	.822	2.025	3	.163	5.259	.859	-.745	-1.689
17	4	4	.133	3	.869	5.593	3	.105	9.812	2.714	1.216	-.985
18	4	4	.877	3	.862	.685	2	.073	5.616	.879	1.114	-.170
19	4	4	.145	3	.846	5.402	2	.143	8.963	1.790	1.664	-1.871
20	4	4	.396	3	.920	2.972	2	.047	8.926	1.917	1.447	-1.017
21	3	3	.588	3	.998	1.925	2	.001	15.253	1.606	-2.521	.878
22	4	4	.456	3	.980	2.610	2	.019	10.491	.100	2.847	-.860
23	3	3	.624	3	.707	1.758	1	.167	4.645	.242	-.641	.851
24	1	1	.915	3	.919	.516	2	.076	5.500	-1.972	-.303	.263
25	1	1	.056	3	.974	7.561	3	.021	15.206	-1.999	-2.884	1.455
27	2	2	.981	3	.968	.178	1	.016	8.405	-.620	-.655	-1.615
28	4	4	.956	3	.975	.324	1	.011	9.299	.301	1.922	.518
29	2	2	.508	3	.455	2.322	3	.221	3.766	-.200	-.227	-.042
31	1	1	.168	3	.961	5.054	2	.039	11.461	-3.656	-.194	-.391
32	4	4	.017	3	.767	10.167	2	.232	12.558	1.625	2.281	-2.830
33	1	1	.885	3	.960	.648	3	.021	8.297	-1.241	-.451	1.399
34	1	1	.466	3	.977	2.552	4	.015	10.936	-2.421	1.312	.886
35	2	2	.725	3	.996	1.317	4	.001	14.448	-.641	-.190	-2.673
36	3	3	.659	3	.778	1.601	2	.212	4.201	1.033	-1.380	-.708
37	4	4	.173	3	.999	4.987	3	.001	18.645	1.886	2.861	1.857
38	2	2	.874	3	.919	.696	3	.068	5.893	.063	-.907	-1.518
39	3	3	.060	3	.621	7.391	2	.346	8.559	-.270	-3.042	-.635
40	3	3	.333	3	.693	3.406	4	.220	5.703	.798	.013	1.748
41	3	3	.678	3	.924	1.518	2	.045	7.542	.397	-1.937	.459
42	3	3	.960	3	.928	.300	2	.033	6.971	.950	-.892	.594
43	4	4	.214	3	.666	4.486	1	.327	5.907	-.724	1.832	1.709
44	2	2	.001	3	.771	16.020	4	.124	19.680	3.041	.424	-3.328
45	1	1	.666	3	.990	1.570	2	.006	11.673	-2.594	.833	.902
46	4	4	.774	3	.846	1.114	3	.127	4.906	1.050	.970	.738
47	1	1	.343	3	.921	3.332	2	.079	8.255	-2.895	-1.094	-.235
48	3	3	.244	3	.990	4.168	4	.010	13.342	2.595	-.723	2.068
49	4	4	.015	3	.977	10.473	2	.022	18.045	2.272	2.836	-2.479
50	1	1	.674	3	.622	1.535	2	.350	2.684	-1.382	-.266	-.178
51	3	3	.363	3	.996	3.193	1	.003	14.721	1.361	-1.901	2.140
52	4	4	.140	3	1.000	5.485	3	.000	21.556	2.231	3.279	1.348
53	4	4	.522	3	.816	2.253	2	.159	5.522	1.175	1.362	-1.153
54	4	4	.564	3	.648	2.040	1	.233	4.083	-.477	1.172	.385
55	1	1	.411	3	.963	2.876	4	.034	9.545	-1.948	1.386	1.602
56	3	3	.968	3	.951	.255	2	.019	8.037	1.041	-.949	.757
57	2	2	.614	3	.750	1.803	1	.232	4.147	-1.391	-.969	-.857
58	1	1	.428	3	.630	2.772	3	.301	4.247	-.303	-.513	1.448
59	2	2	.660	3	.674	1.597	3	.222	3.821	-.255	-1.020	-.549
60	1	1	.093	3	.875	6.421	3	.101	10.748	-.416	-.207	3.043
61	4	4	.821	3	.998	.918	2	.001	15.056	.966	2.757	.419
62	4	4	.464	3	.551	2.564	1	.303	3.757	-.150	.727	.896
63	2	2	.480	3	.687	2.474	4	.222	4.732	-.891	1.152	-1.008
64	2	2	.748	3	.970	1.222	3	.024	8.658	.380	-.538	-2.189
65	3	3	.604	3	.599	1.850	4	.227	3.790	.618	-.085	.450
66	3	3	.679	3	.782	1.514	4	.195	4.288	1.659	-.006	.513
67	1	1	.849	3	.818	.803	2	.124	4.582	-1.176	.086	.450

Case #	Actual Group	Highest group Pre-dicted group	P(D>d | G=g) p	df	P(G=g | D=d)	Squared Mahalanobis distance to centroid	2nd highest group Group	P(G=g | D=d)	Squared Mahalanobis distance to centroid	F1	F2	F3
68	3	3	.936	3	.985	.419	4	.008	9.950	1.510	-1.088	1.118
69	2	2	.688	3	.958	1.473	3	.036	8.014	.501	-.672	-2.141
70	4	4	.894	3	.865	.609	3	.067	5.732	.805	1.076	.062
71	3	3	.927	3	.888	.461	2	.063	5.739	.803	-.875	.394
72	3	3	.688	3	.693	1.473	2	.280	3.284	.601	-1.215	-.430
73	1	1	.899	3	.881	.591	2	.108	4.795	-1.682	-.473	.273
74	2	2	.551	3	.520	2.102	3	.273	3.392	.649	.018	-.667
76	2	2	.941	3	.860	.399	1	.071	5.376	-.503	-.321	-.912
77	3	3	.003	3	1.000	14.008	2	.000	29.757	3.022	-4.365	-.671
78	3	3	.574	3	.577	1.993	2	.351	2.987	1.001	-.509	-.671
79	4	4	.512	3	.999	2.300	2	.000	18.634	.851	3.341	.424
80	3	3	.732	3	.910	1.289	2	.086	6.017	1.024	-1.828	-.383
81	1	1	.560	3	.824	2.061	2	.172	5.192	-2.380	.097	-.347
82	2	2	.652	3	.833	1.634	3	.128	5.386	.804	-.324	-1.572
83	1	1	.974	3	.971	.219	2	.026	7.428	-2.124	-.375	.625
84	4	4	.271	3	.979	3.910	2	.020	11.661	-.119	3.091	-1.034
85	4	4	.168	3	.831	5.049	3	.135	8.681	.978	1.075	2.314
86	2	2	.717	3	.656	1.350	1	.302	2.901	-1.085	-.232	-.553
87	1	1	.663	3	.852	1.582	4	.093	6.011	-.805	.365	1.370
88	4	4	.943	3	.957	.387	3	.027	7.556	.824	1.476	.712
89	1	1	.991	3	.978	.110	2	.012	8.841	-1.628	-.161	1.197
90	1	1	.229	3	.923	4.318	2	.064	9.645	-2.757	1.320	-.159
91	1	1	.451	3	.989	2.636	2	.008	12.346	-2.860	1.063	.668
92	2	2	.138	3	.593	5.506	1	.406	6.265	-2.714	-.911	-1.276
93	4	4	.754	3	.992	1.194	2	.007	11.125	.586	2.698	-.441
94	2	2	.232	3	.852	4.286	1	.105	8.470	-1.843	1.285	-1.551
95	3	3	.607	3	.996	1.838	4	.004	13.011	2.352	-1.157	1.446
96	2	2	.469	3	.744	2.536	4	.184	5.335	.599	.427	-1.605
97	2	2	.128	3	.873	5.683	1	.126	9.550	-2.807	-.055	-1.977
98	2	2	.146	3	.893	5.383	3	.081	10.190	-.786	-2.562	-1.410
99	2	2	.100	3	.999	6.261	4	.001	19.706	-.849	.780	-3.782
100	2	2	.351	3	.761	3.278	4	.234	5.632	.179	1.348	-2.033
101	3	3	.816	3	.986	.938	2	.012	9.833	1.988	-1.617	-.144
102	3	3	.495	3	.509	2.391	4	.437	2.696	1.396	.323	.263
103	1	1	.532	3	.475	2.202	2	.411	2.492	-.947	.247	-.125
104	4	4	.990	3	.971	.115	3	.012	8.858	.677	1.685	.496
105	3	3	.371	3	.563	3.140	4	.281	4.531	.539	.076	1.377
106	1	1	.721	3	.987	1.336	2	.012	10.166	-2.619	-1.013	.696
107	2	2	.703	3	.632	1.409	1	.256	3.213	-.689	-.072	-.390
108	3	3	.155	3	.849	5.245	2	.151	8.700	1.351	-2.576	-1.340
109	4	4	.891	3	.878	.621	3	.064	5.873	.627	1.094	.415
110	4	4	.724	3	.718	1.321	3	.120	4.903	.390	.761	.291
111	3	3	.954	3	.969	.331	4	.015	8.732	1.194	-.979	.986
112	3	3	.278	3	.962	3.849	4	.038	10.310	2.628	-.303	1.718
113	2	2	.811	3	.841	.961	1	.141	4.526	-1.303	-.014	-1.084
114	4	4	.375	3	.460	3.108	3	.360	3.598	.428	.332	1.054
115	2	2	.069	3	.513	7.090	1	.462	7.301	-2.544	1.360	-1.149
116	3	3	.789	3	.882	1.049	2	.093	5.557	.528	-1.614	.115
117	1	1	.907	3	.996	.553	2	.002	12.952	-2.148	-.075	1.639
118	3	3	.065	3	.751	7.216	2	.172	10.163	-.413	-3.109	-.098

Case #	Actual Group	Pre-dicted group	Highest group P(D>d | G=g) p	df	P(G=g | D=d)	Squared Mahalanobis distance to centroid	2nd highest group Group	P(G=g | D=d)	Squared Mahalanobis distance to centroid	Discriminant scores F1	F2	F3
119	3	3	.402	3	1.000	2.936	2	.000	19.666	2.186	-2.566	1.163
120	1	1	.317	3	.852	3.530	4	.075	8.392	-.516	.196	2.217
121	2	2	.485	3	.514	2.445	3	.418	2.856	-.002	-1.298	-.463
122	3	3	.176	3	.575	4.938	4	.411	5.609	1.478	.440	1.985
123	4	4	.754	3	.740	1.196	2	.211	3.705	.359	1.125	-.503
124	3	3	.206	3	.990	4.571	2	.010	13.692	2.254	-2.660	-.812
125	4	4	.051	3	.974	7.754	2	.018	15.707	2.749	2.032	-1.742
126	4	4	.578	3	.645	1.975	1	.233	4.012	-.355	1.050	.489
127	2	2	.992	3	.963	.100	1	.021	7.737	-.746	-.114	-1.586
128	2	2	.354	3	.792	3.258	3	.115	7.110	1.273	.081	-1.839
129	2	2	.937	3	.980	.414	1	.012	9.253	-.892	.051	-1.912
130	4	4	.036	3	.795	8.529	1	.203	11.256	-1.606	3.147	1.291
131	3	3	.409	3	.444	2.890	4	.270	3.884	.256	.029	.788
132	2	2	.850	3	.891	.799	3	.085	5.491	.390	-.495	-1.504
133	4	4	.293	3	.991	3.726	1	.008	13.245	-.285	3.086	1.240
134	3	3	.905	3	.932	.564	4	.041	6.801	1.149	-.639	.925
136	1	1	.396	3	.813	2.973	3	.169	6.113	-.862	-1.489	1.480
137	4	4	.230	3	.988	4.313	1	.011	13.267	.225	2.591	2.069
138	3	3	.668	3	.985	1.563	2	.010	10.832	2.400	-1.209	-.240
139	1	1	.240	3	.980	4.210	3	.019	12.115	-1.395	-1.355	2.580
140	2	2	.584	3	.508	1.944	3	.375	2.554	.435	-.380	-.489
141	3	3	.457	3	.995	2.601	4	.005	13.329	2.914	-1.015	.977
142	2	2	.939	3	.858	.408	3	.054	5.932	-.205	-.105	-.984
143	1	1	.642	3	.936	1.676	2	.032	8.419	-1.482	-1.420	.924
144	2	2	.345	3	.963	3.319	3	.035	9.943	.754	-1.107	-2.593
145	2	2	.589	3	.540	1.918	4	.268	3.322	.404	.254	-.604
146	4	4	.456	3	.526	2.606	3	.449	2.923	1.369	.472	.823
147	1	1	.625	3	.868	1.755	3	.091	6.277	-1.055	-1.230	1.050
148	3	3	.277	3	.650	3.856	2	.279	5.544	1.858	-.402	-1.235
149	1	1	.834	3	.993	.864	3	.004	12.012	-1.801	-.678	1.746
150	3	3	.787	3	.852	1.060	4	.125	4.901	1.488	-.199	.686
151	2	2	.185	3	.973	4.822	3	.014	13.303	-1.118	-2.335	-1.904
152	3	3	.597	3	.998	1.885	2	.002	14.359	1.697	-2.541	.576
153	3	3	.901	3	.955	.579	2	.034	7.253	.834	-1.701	.327
154	4	4	.867	3	.997	.725	3	.001	13.816	1.314	2.499	.196
155	1	1	.189	3	.846	4.779	2	.123	8.632	-2.535	1.443	-.335
156	4	4	.701	3	.984	1.418	1	.011	10.414	.382	2.112	1.303
157	2	2	.579	3	.676	1.966	3	.296	3.618	.830	-.697	-1.252
158	1	1	.007	3	.964	12.117	3	.030	19.051	-.655	-.232	4.227
159	4	4	.779	3	.991	1.092	3	.006	11.273	1.771	2.099	.039
160	1	1	.710	3	.670	1.380	2	.236	3.467	-.915	-.243	.268
161	3	3	.327	3	.671	3.450	4	.325	4.902	2.322	.371	.796
162	2	2	.340	3	.748	3.355	1	.236	5.659	-1.603	-1.581	-.945
163	3	3	.974	3	.984	.219	2	.009	9.709	1.832	-1.179	.348
164	2	2	.521	3	.519	2.255	3	.422	2.671	.858	-.529	-.896
165	1	1	.338	3	.973	3.374	3	.023	10.893	-1.626	-1.860	1.672
166	4	4	.068	3	.999	7.128	3	.001	21.174	1.398	2.894	2.584
167	1	1	.039	3	.926	8.349	4	.059	13.853	-2.901	2.431	.302
168	1	1	.309	3	.927	3.592	1	.069	8.783	.277	-2.071	1.763
169	2	2	.018	3	.984	10.074	1	.016	18.372	-2.556	-2.392	-2.645

Case #	Actual Group	Pre-dicted group	Highest group P(D>d | G=g) p	df	P(G=g | D=d)	Squared Mahalanobis distance to centroid	2nd highest group Group	P(G=g | D=d)	Squared Mahalanobis distance to centroid	Discriminant scores F1	F2	F3
170	1	1	.100	3	1.000	6.261	2	.000	23.805	-3.999	.947	1.606
171	2	2	.493	3	.851	2.402	1	.135	6.079	-1.444	-1.406	-1.138
172	1	1	.271	3	1.000	3.916	2	.000	19.417	-3.697	.426	1.383
173	3	3	.639	3	.998	1.692	4	.001	15.527	2.612	-1.616	.652
174	3	3	.382	3	.823	3.060	2	.170	6.216	1.795	-1.247	-1.207
175	4	4	.319	3	.488	3.516	1	.271	4.695	.158	.495	1.362
176	4	4	.307	3	.901	3.607	2	.098	8.050	.279	2.468	-1.512
177	4	4	.421	3	.490	2.818	1	.300	3.799	-.055	.547	.887
178	4	4	.669	3	.935	1.558	1	.054	7.243	-.176	1.915	1.019
179	2	2	.071	3	.562	7.043	4	.404	7.706	-1.310	2.251	-1.577
180	1	1	.441	3	.771	2.695	2	.224	5.169	-2.108	-1.224	-.283
181	1	1	.589	3	.890	1.920	2	.105	6.194	-2.427	.409	-.156
182	1	1	.785	3	.980	1.065	4	.010	10.333	-1.363	.067	1.831
184	2	2	.967	3	.915	.265	4	.045	6.301	.157	-1.323	
185	3	3	.845	3	.988	.820	4	.008	10.337	1.739	-1.022	1.308
186	3	3	.351	3	.362	3.277	4	.301	3.640	.159	.106	.714
187	2	2	.672	3	.675	1.547	4	.170	4.305	-.640	.601	-.666
188	3	3	.154	3	.948	5.261	4	.050	11.158	3.410	-.204	.086
189	3	3	.619	3	.992	1.782	2	.004	12.835	1.003	-2.411	.921
190	2	2	.482	3	.994	2.460	1	.005	13.179	-1.297	-1.225	-2.469
191	4	4	.734	3	.725	1.278	2	.228	3.588	.351	1.123	-.553
192	3	3	.971	3	.952	.242	2	.033	6.988	.933	-1.373	.406
193	2	2	.039	3	.509	8.356	4	.490	8.434	.915	1.995	-2.685
194	2	2	.053	3	.998	7.673	1	.002	20.430	-2.397	-.080	-3.525
195	2	2	.405	3	.997	2.917	3	.002	15.629	-.875	-1.414	-2.741
196	3	3	.317	3	.686	3.530	2	.190	6.093	1.933	-.198	-.995

A 28. Levene Test for Equality / Homogeneity of Variances of the 4 Factors

	Levene Statistic	df1	df2	Significance
Factor Innovation	1.648	3	186	.180
Factor IT	1.408	3	186	.242
Factor Business	1.369	3	186	.254
Factor Cost	.459	3	186	.711

Levene's test is used to test if k samples have equal variances. Equal variances across samples is called homogeneity of variance. Some statistical tests, for example, the analysis of variance, assume that variances are equal across groups or samples. Levene's test is often used before a comparison of means. The Levene test can be used to verify that assumption and test the null hypothesis that the group variances are equal. If the resulting p-value of Levene's test is less than some critical value (typically .05), the obtained differences in sample variances are unlikely to have occurred based on random sampling. Thus, the null hypothesis of equal variances is rejected and it is concluded that there is a difference between the variances in the population. When Levene's test is not significant, homogeneity of variance can be assumed and ANOVAs and t-tests can be conducted.

A 29. Analysis of Variance of the 4 Factors (ANOVA)

		Sum of Squares	df	Mean Square	F	Significance
Factor Innovation	Between Groups	82.277	3	27.426	51.937	.000
	Within Groups	98.218	186	.528		
	Total	180.496	189			
Factor IT	Between Groups	82.705	3	27.568	52.692	.000
	Within Groups	97.315	186	.523		
	Total	180.020	189			
Factor Business	Between Groups	82.223	3	27.408	56.422	.000
	Within Groups	90.352	186	.486		
	Total	172.575	189			
Factor Cost	Between Groups	49.609	3	16.536	24.248	.000
	Within Groups	126.847	186	.682		
	Total	176.456	189			

A 30. Levene Test for Equality / Homogeneity of Variances of the 16 Outsourcing Expectation Variables

	Levene Statistic	df1	df2	Significance
Cost reduction	.970	3	186	.408
Flexibility of costs / cost transparency (rendering IT as a variable cost)	.333	3	186	.801
Quality improvements (lower error rate / shorter processing time)	.199	3	186	.897
Long-term use of systems, applications and data (stability, reliability, retention of status quo)	.747	3	186	.525
Improved service orientation	1.818	3	186	.145
Increased flexibility	4.964	3	186	.002
Shift risk to service provider	1.251	3	186	.293
Modernization of IT / replace legacy systems	.733	3	186	.533
Focus on core competencies	.311	3	186	.817
Enable and facilitate strategic competitive advantages	1.247	3	186	.294
Access to highly skilled people	.356	3	186	.785
Access to better IT systems and new technology	.853	3	186	.467
Knowledge acquisition from service provider	4.413	3	186	.005
Suggestions for new IT based products and services by your service provider (innovation, idea creation)	2.093	3	186	.103
Shared development of IT based products and services together with your service provider (joint product and service development)	3.292	3	186	.022
Business transformation	2.348	3	186	.074

A 31. Analysis of Variance of the 16 Outsourcing Expectation Variables

		Sum of Squares	df	Mean Square	F	Significance
Cost reduction	Between Groups	99.790	3	33.263	15.486	.000
	Within Groups	399.521	186	2.148		
	Total	499.311	189			
Flexibility of costs / cost transparency (rendering IT as a variable cost)	Between Groups	34.473	3	11.491	6.920	.000
	Within Groups	308.847	186	1.660		
	Total	343.320	189			
Quality improvements (lower error rate / shorter processing time)	Between Groups	60.993	3	20.331	13.519	.000
	Within Groups	279.722	186	1.504		
	Total	340.716	189			
Long-term use of systems, applications and data (stability, reliability, retention of status quo)	Between Groups	65.747	3	21.916	12.101	.000
	Within Groups	336.850	186	1.811		
	Total	402.596	189			
Improved service orientation	Between Groups	86.249	3	28.750	21.089	.000
	Within Groups	253.562	186	1.363		
	Total	339.811	189			
Increased flexibility	Between Groups	73.409	3	24.470	14.411	.000
	Within Groups	315.830	186	1.698		
	Total	389.239	189			
Shift risk to service provider	Between Groups	125.937	3	41.979	21.019	.000
	Within Groups	371.471	186	1.997		
	Total	497.408	189			
Modernization of IT / replace legacy systems	Between Groups	58.672	3	19.557	10.304	.000
	Within Groups	353.039	186	1.898		
	Total	411.711	189			
Focus on core competencies	Between Groups	3.828	3	1.276	.641	.589
	Within Groups	369.976	186	1.989		
	Total	373.804	189			
Enable and facilitate strategic competitive advantages	Between Groups	59.255	3	19.752	8.355	.000
	Within Groups	439.697	186	2.364		
	Total	498.952	189			
Access to highly skilled people	Between Groups	45.142	3	15.047	8.025	.000
	Within Groups	348.773	186	1.875		
	Total	393.916	189			
Access to better IT systems and new technology	Between Groups	56.592	3	18.864	9.587	.000
	Within Groups	365.982	186	1.968		
	Total	422.574	189			
Knowledge acquisition from service provider	Between Groups	146.396	3	48.799	27.255	.000
	Within Groups	333.020	186	1.790		
	Total	479.416	189			
Suggestions for new IT based	Between Groups	137.443	3	45.814	22.758	.000

		Sum of Squares	df	Mean Square	F	Significance
products and services by your service provider (innovation, idea creation)	Within Groups	374.445	186	2.013		
	Total	511.888	189			
Shared development of IT based products and services together with your service provider (joint product and service develop-ment)	Between Groups	186.322	3	62.107	35.485	.000
	Within Groups	325.541	186	1.750		
	Total	511.863	189			
Business transformation	Between Groups	50.428	3	16.809	11.994	.000
	Within Groups	260.665	186	1.401		
	Total	311.092	189			

A 32. Post-hoc Tests for the 16 Outsourcing Expectation Variables

The mean values for the homogenous subgroups are shown; a. Uses a harmonic mean for sample size = 47.305.

Cost reduction

		N	Subgroup for Alpha = 0.05.	
			1	2
Student-Newman-Keuls-Procedure[a]	4	45	3.556	
	3	51	3.980	
	1	44		4.955
	2	50		5.360
	Significance		.160	.180
Tukey-HSD[a]	4	45	3.556	
	3	51	3.980	
	1	44		4.955
	2	50		5.360
	Significance		.495	.535
Scheffé-Procedure[a]	4	45	3.556	
	3	51	3.980	
	1	44		4.955
	2	50		5.360
	Significance		.576	.614

The mean values for the homogenous subgroups are shown.
a. Uses a harmonic mean for sample size = 47.305.

Flexibility of costs

		N	Subgroup for Alpha = 0.05.	
			1	2
Student-Newman-Keuls-Procedure[a]	4	45	4.267	
	3	51	4.392	
	1	44	4.773	
	2	50		5.347
	Significance		.139	1.000
Tukey-HSD[a]	4	45	4.267	
	3	51	4.392	
	1	44	4.773	4.773
	2	50		5.347
	Significance		.227	.136
Scheffé-Procedure[a]	4	45	4.267	
	3	51	4.392	
	1	44	4.773	4.773
	2	50		5.347
	Significance		.305	.199

The mean values for the homogenous subgroups are shown.
a. Uses a harmonic mean for sample size = 47.305.

Quality improvements

		N	Subgroup for Alpha = 0.05.		
			1	2	3
Student-Newman-Keuls-Procedure[a]	2	50	3.920		
	3	51	4.333		
	1	44		4.955	
	4	45		5.400	
	Significance		.103	.079	
Tukey-HSD[a]	2	50	3.920		
	3	51	4.333	4.333	
	1	44		4.955	4.955
	4	45			5.400
	Significance		.359	.069	.293
Scheffé-Procedure[a]	2	50	3.920		
	3	51	4.333	4.333	
	1	44		4.955	4.955
	4	45			5.400
	Significance		.445	.112	.376

The mean values for the homogenous subgroups are shown.
a. Uses a harmonic mean for sample size = 47.305.

Long-term use of systems

		N	Subgroup for Alpha = 0.05.	
			1	2
Student-Newman-Keuls-Procedure[a]	2	50	3.525	
	1	44	3.843	
	3	51	4.043	
	4	45		5.113
	Significance		.150	1.000
Tukey-HSD[a]	2	50	3.525	
	1	44	3.843	
	3	51	4.043	
	4	45		5.113
	Significance		.245	1.000
Scheffé-Procedure[a]	2	50	3.525	
	1	44	3.843	
	3	51	4.043	
	4	45		5.113
	Significance		.324	1.000

The mean values for the homogenous subgroups are shown.
a. Uses a harmonic mean for sample size = 47.305.

Improved service orientation

		N	Subgroup for Alpha = 0.05.	
			1	2
Student-Newman-Keuls-Procedure[a]	2	50	3.960	
	3	51	4.196	
	4	45		5.244
	1	44		5.560
	Significance		.327	.190
Tukey-HSD[a]	2	50	3.960	
	3	51	4.196	
	4	45		5.244
	1	44		5.560
	Significance		.759	.554
Scheffé-Procedure[a]	2	50	3.960	
	3	51	4.196	
	4	45		5.244
	1	44		5.560
	Significance		.809	.630

The mean values for the homogenous subgroups are shown.
a. Uses a harmonic mean for sample size = 47.305.

Increased flexibility

		N	Subgroup for Alpha = 0.05.	
			1	2
Student-Newman-Keuls-Procedure[a]	3	51	4.196	
	2	50	4.360	
	4	45		5.267
	1	44		5.700
	Significance		.541	.107
Tukey-HSD[a]	3	51	4.196	
	2	50	4.360	
	4	45		5.267
	1	44		5.700
	Significance		.928	.371
Scheffé-Procedure[a]	3	51	4.196	
	2	50	4.360	
	4	45		5.267
	1	44		5.700
	Significance		.945	.456

The mean values for the homogenous subgroups are shown.
a. Uses a harmonic mean for sample size = 47.305.

Shift risk to service provider

		N	Subgroup for Alpha = 0.05.		
			1	2	3
Student-Newman-Keuls-Procedure[a]	1	44	3.029		
	2	50		4.220	
	3	51		4.510	
	4	45			5.378
	Significance		1.000	.320	1.000
Tukey-HSD[a]	1	44	3.029		
	2	50		4.220	
	3	51		4.510	
	4	45			5.378
	Significance		1.000	.751	1.000
Scheffé-Procedure[a]	1	44	3.029		
	2	50		4.220	
	3	51		4.510	
	4	45			5.378
	Significance		1.000	.803	1.000

The mean values for the homogenous subgroups are shown.
a. Uses a harmonic mean for sample size = 47.305.

Modernization of IT

		N	Subgroup for Alpha = 0.05.		
			1	2	3
Student-Newman-Keuls-Procedure[a]	1	44	3.136		
	2	50	3.500		
	3	51		4.275	
	4	45		4.533	
	Significance		.201	.362	
Tukey-HSD[a]	1	44	3.136		
	2	50	3.500		
	3	51		4.275	
	4	45		4.533	
	Significance		.574	.798	
Scheffé-Procedure[a]	1	44	3.136		
	2	50	3.500	3.500	
	3	51		4.275	4.275
	4	45			4.533
	Significance		.649	.062	.841

Focus on core competencies

		N	Subgroup for Alpha = 0.05.
			1
Student-Newman-Keuls-Procedure[a]	2	50	5.188
	1	44	5.455
	3	51	5.510
	4	45	5.542
	Significance		.614
Tukey-HSD[a]	2	50	5.188
	1	44	5.455
	3	51	5.510
	4	45	5.542
	Significance		.614
Scheffé-Procedure[a]	2	50	5.188
	1	44	5.455
	3	51	5.510
	4	45	5.542
	Significance		.685

The mean values for the homogenous subgroups are shown.
a. Uses a harmonic mean for sample size = 47.305.

Strategic competitive advantages

		N	Subgroup for Alpha = 0.05.		
			1	2	3
Student-Newman-Keuls-Procedure[a]	2	50	2.849		
	4	45	3.044		
	1	44		3.682	
	3	51		4.235	
	Significance		.537	.082	
Tukey-HSD[a]	2	50	2.849		
	4	45	3.044	3.044	
	1	44		3.682	3.682
	3	51			4.235
	Significance		.926	.186	.301
Scheffé-Procedure[a]	2	50	2.849		
	4	45	3.044		
	1	44	3.682	3.682	
	3	51		4.235	
	Significance		.077	.384	

The mean values for the homogenous subgroups are shown.
a. Uses a harmonic mean for sample size = 47.305.

Access to highly skilled people

		N	Subgroup for Alpha = 0.05.	
			1	2
Student-Newman-Keuls-Procedure[a]	2	50	3.540	
	1	44	3.886	
	3	51		4.627
	4	45		4.667
	Significance		.220	.889
Tukey-HSD[a]	2	50	3.540	
	1	44	3.886	
	3	51		4.627
	4	45		4.667
	Significance		.609	.999
Scheffé-Procedure[a]	2	50	3.540	
	1	44	3.886	3.886
	3	51		4.627
	4	45		4.667
	Significance		.680	.056

The mean values for the homogenous subgroups are shown.
a. Uses a harmonic mean for sample size = 47.305.

Access to better IT systems

		N	Subgroup for Alpha = 0.05.	
			1	2
Student-Newman-Keuls-Procedure[a]	1	44	3.227	
	2	50	3.360	
	4	45		4.378
	3	51		4.392
	Significance		.646	.960
Tukey-HSD[a]	1	44	3.227	
	2	50	3.360	
	4	45		4.378
	3	51		4.392
	Significance		.968	1.000
Scheffé-Procedure[a]	1	44	3.227	
	2	50	3.360	
	4	45		4.378
	3	51		4.392
	Significance		.976	1.000

The mean values for the homogenous subgroups are shown.
a. Uses a harmonic mean for sample size = 47.305.

Knowledge acquisition

| | | N | Subgroup for Alpha = 0.05. | | |
			1	2	3
Student-Newman-Keuls-Procedure[a]	2	50	2.560		
	1	44	3.023		
	4	45		3.578	
	3	51			4.843
	Significance		.094	1.000	1.000
Tukey-HSD[a]	2	50	2.560		
	1	44	3.023	3.023	
	4	45		3.578	
	3	51			4.843
	Significance		.336	.185	1.000
Scheffé-Procedure[a]	2	50	2.560		
	1	44	3.023	3.023	
	4	45		3.578	
	3	51			4.843
	Significance		.421	.258	1.000

The mean values for the homogenous subgroups are shown.
a. Uses a harmonic mean for sample size = 47.305.

Suggestions for innovation

| | | N | Subgroup for Alpha = 0.05. | | |
			1	2	3
Student-Newman-Keuls-Procedure[a]	2	50	2.547		
	1	44		3.477	
	4	45		3.733	
	3	51			4.863
	Significance		1.000	.381	1.000
Tukey-HSD[a]	2	50	2.547		
	1	44		3.477	
	4	45		3.733	
	3	51			4.863
	Significance		1.000	.816	1.000
Scheffé-Procedure[a]	2	50	2.547		
	1	44		3.477	
	4	45		3.733	
	3	51			4.863
	Significance		1.000	.856	1.000

The mean values for the homogenous subgroups are shown.
a. Uses a harmonic mean for sample size = 47.305.

Joint product and service development

| | | N | Subgroup for Alpha = 0.05. | | |
			1	2	3
Student-Newman-Keuls-Procedure[a]	2	50	2.085		
	4	45	2.203		
	1	44		3.750	
	3	51			4.353
	Significance		.666	1.000	1.000
Tukey-HSD[a]	2	50	2.085		
	4	45	2.203		
	1	44		3.750	
	3	51		4.353	
	Significance		.973	.123	
Scheffé-Procedure[a]	2	50	2.085		
	4	45	2.203		
	1	44		3.750	
	3	51		4.353	
	Significance		.980	.182	

The mean values for the homogenous subgroups are shown.
a. Uses a harmonic mean for sample size = 47.305.

Business transformation

| | | N | Subgroup for Alpha = 0.05. | | |
			1	2	3
Student-Newman-Keuls-Procedure[a]	2	50	1.900		
	4	45	2.089		
	1	44		2.693	
	3	51			3.177
	Significance		.439	1.000	1.000
Tukey-HSD[a]	2	50	1.900		
	4	45	2.089	2.089	
	1	44		2.693	2.693
	3	51			3.177
	Significance		.865	.066	.197
Scheffé-Procedure[a]	2	50	1.900		
	4	45	2.089	2.089	
	1	44		2.693	2.693
	3	51			3.177
	Significance		.896	.108	.271

The mean values for the homogenous subgroups are shown.
a. Uses a harmonic mean for sample size = 47.305.

A 33. Post-hoc Test for Role and Impact of IT for the Company

Role and Impact of IT for the company

		N	Subgroup for Alpha = 0.1. 1	2
Student-Newman-Keuls-Procedure[a]	4	45	4.89	
	2	50	5.32	5.32
	1	44		5.50
	3	51		5.61
	Significance		.137	.579
Tukey-HSD[a]	4	45	4.89	
	2	50	5.32	5.32
	1	44	5.50	5.50
	3	51		5.61
	Significance		.151	.751
Scheffé-Procedure[a]	4	45	4.89	
	2	50	5.32	
	1	44	5.50	
	3	51	5.61	
	Significance		.106	

The mean values for the homogenous subgroups are shown.
a. Uses a harmonic mean for sample size = 47.305.

A 34. Post-hoc Test for the Degree of Complementarity of Goals and Conflicts of Interest

Degree of complementarity

		N	Subgroup for Alpha = 0.1. 1	2
Student-Newman-Keuls-Procedure[a]	2	50	4.637	
	3	51	4.882	4.882
	1	44	5.068	5.068
	4	45		5.310
	Significance		.255	.260
Tukey-HSD[a]	2	50	4.637	
	3	51	4.882	4.882
	1	44	5.068	5.068
	4	45		5.310
	Significance		.390	.397
Scheffé-Procedure[a]	2	50	4.637	
	3	51	4.882	
	1	44	5.068	
	4	45	5.310	
	Significance		.110	

The mean values for the homogenous subgroups are shown.
a. Uses a harmonic mean for sample size = 47.305.

Degree of conflicts of interest

		N	Subgroup for Alpha = 0.1. 1	2
Student-Newman-Keuls-Procedure[a]	2	50	5.176	
	3	51	5.341	5.341
	1	44	5.409	5.409
	4	45		5.809
	Significance		.595	.126
Tukey-HSD[a]	2	50	5.176	
	3	51	5.341	5.341
	1	44	5.409	5.409
	4	45		5.809
	Significance		.765	.208
Scheffé-Procedure[a]	2	50	5.176	
	3	51	5.341	5.341
	1	44	5.409	5.409
	4	45		5.809
	Significance		.814	.284

The mean values for the homogenous subgroups are shown.
a. Uses a harmonic mean for sample size = 47.305.

A 35. Post-hoc Test for the Sufficiency of the Contract

Sufficiency of contract for outsourcing governance

		N	Subgroup for Alpha = 0.05.	
			1	2
Student-Newman-Keuls-Procedure[a]	1	44	3.455	
	2	50	3.638	3.638
	3	51	4.098	4.098
	4	45		4.467
	Significance		.185	.063
Tukey-HSD[a]	1	44	3.455	
	2	50	3.638	3.638
	3	51	4.098	4.098
	4	45		4.467
	Significance		.295	.109
Scheffé-Procedure[a]	1	44	3.455	
	2	50	3.638	
	3	51	4.098	
	4	45	4.467	
	Significance		.056	

The mean values for the homogenous subgroups are shown.
a. Uses a harmonic mean for sample size = 47.305.

A 36. Post-hoc Tests for Governance via an External Consultant and a Management Board

Governance via external consultant

		N	Subgroup for Alpha = 0.05.	
			1	2
Student-Newman-Keuls-Procedure[a]	4	45	1.178	
	2	50	1.186	
	1	44	1.250	
	3	51		1.627
	Significance		.903	1.000
Tukey-HSD[a]	4	45	1.178	
	2	50	1.186	
	1	44	1.250	1.250
	3	51		1.627
	Significance		.973	.115
Scheffé-Procedure[a]	4	45	1.178	
	2	50	1.186	
	1	44	1.250	
	3	51	1.627	
	Significance		.07	

The mean values for the homogenous subgroups are shown.
a. Uses a harmonic mean for sample size = 47.305.

Governance via management board

		N	Subgroup for Alpha = 0.1.	
			1	2
Student-Newman-Keuls-Procedure[a]	4	45	3.267	
	2	50	3.697	3.697
	1	44	4.042	4.042
	3	51		4.294
	Significance		.130	.294
Tukey-HSD[a]	4	45	3.267	
	2	50	3.697	3.697
	1	44	4.042	4.042
	3	51		4.294
	Significance		.214	.441
Scheffé-Procedure[a]	4	45	3.267	
	2	50	3.697	3.697
	1	44	4.042	4.042
	3	51		4.294
	Significance		.290	.525

The mean values for the homogenous subgroups are shown.
a. Uses a harmonic mean for sample size = 47.305.

A 37. Post-hoc Test for Governance via Personal Bonds

Governance via personal bonds.

		N	Subgroup for Alpha = 0.1.	
			1	2
Student-Newman-Keuls-Procedure[a]	2	50	3.317	
	4	45		3.911
	1	44		4.045
	3	51		4.098
	Significance		1.000	.857
Tukey-HSD[a]	2	50	3.317	
	4	45	3.911	3.911
	1	44	4.045	4.045
	3	51		4.098
	Significance		.170	.952
Scheffé-Procedure[a]	2	50	3.317	
	4	45	3.911	
	1	44	4.045	
	3	51	4.098	
	Significance		.184	

The mean values for the homogenous subgroups are shown.
a. Uses a harmonic mean for sample size = 47.305.

A 38. Post-hoc Test for Degree of Risk and Reward Share

Degree of risk and reward share

		N	Subgroup for Alpha = 0.05.	
			1	2
Student-Newman-Keuls-Procedure[a]	4	45	2.444	
	2	50	2.586	
	1	44	2.609	
	3	51		3.378
	Significance		.871	1.000
Tukey-HSD[a]	4	45	2.444	
	2	50	2.586	2.586
	1	44	2.609	2.609
	3	51		3.378
	Significance		.959	.078
Scheffé-Procedure[a]	4	45	2.444	
	2	50	2.586	2.586
	1	44	2.609	2.609
	3	51		3.378
	Significance		.969	.125

The mean values for the homogenous subgroups are shown.
a. Uses a harmonic mean for sample size = 47.305.

A 39. Post-hoc Tests for Degree of Conflict Resolution and Consensus

Conflict resolution.

		N	Subgroup for Alpha = 0.05. 1	2
Student-Newman-Keuls-Procedure[a]	2	50	5.380	
	3	51	5.392	
	1	44	5.636	
	4	45		6.067
	Significance		.397	1.000
Tukey-HSD[a]	2	50	5.380	
	3	51	5.392	
	1	44	5.636	5.636
	4	45		6.067
	Significance		.564	.132
Scheffé-Procedure[a]	2	50	5.380	
	3	51	5.392	
	1	44	5.636	5.636
	4	45		6.067
	Significance		.639	.194

The mean values for the homogenous subgroups are shown.
a. Uses a harmonic mean for sample size = 47.305.

Consensus

		N	Subgroup for Alpha = 0.05. 1	2
Student-Newman-Keuls-Procedure[a]	2	50	5.350	
	1	44	5.364	
	3	51	5.431	
	4	45		5.867
	Significance		.908	1.000
Tukey-HSD[a]	2	50	5.350	
	1	44	5.364	5.364
	3	51	5.431	5.431
	4	45		5.867
	Significance		.975	.051
Scheffé-Procedure[a]	2	50	5.350	
	1	44	5.364	
	3	51	5.431	
	4	45		5.867
	Significance		.074	

The mean values for the homogenous subgroups are shown.
a. Uses a harmonic mean for sample size = 47.305.

A 40. Post-hoc Test for Degree of Coordination and Cooperation

Degree of coordination

		N	Subgroup for Alpha = 0.05. 1	2
Student-Newman-Keuls-Procedure[a]	2	50	4.720	
	1	44	4.750	
	3	51	5.078	5.078
	4	45		5.467
	Significance		.337	.128
Tukey-HSD[a]	2	50	4.720	
	1	44	4.750	
	3	51	5.078	5.078
	4	45		5.467
	Significance		.494	.422
Scheffé-Procedure[a]	2	50	4.720	
	1	44	4.750	
	3	51	5.078	5.078
	4	45		5.467
	Significance		.575	.506

The mean values for the homogenous subgroups are shown.
a. Uses a harmonic mean for sample size = 47.305.

Degree of cooperation

		N	Subgroup for Alpha = 0.05. 1	2
Student-Newman-Keuls-Procedure[a]	3	51	5.353	
	2	50	5.400	
	1	44	5.500	
	4	45		6.044
	Significance		.766	1.000
Tukey-HSD[a]	3	51	5.353	
	2	50	5.400	
	1	44	5.500	5.500
	4	45		6.044
	Significance		.899	.052
Scheffé-Procedure[a]	3	51	5.353	
	2	50	5.400	
	1	44	5.500	5.500
	4	45		6.044
	Significance		.922	.088

The mean values for the homogenous subgroups are shown.
a. Uses a harmonic mean for sample size = 47.305.

A 41. Post-hoc Test for Degree of Loyalty and Commitment

Degree of loyalty and commitment

| | | N | Subgroup for Alpha = 0.1. | |
			1	2
Student-Newman-Keuls-Procedure[a]	1	44	5.114	
	2	50	5.178	
	3	51	5.333	5.333
	4	45		5.667
	Significance		.587	.136
Tukey-HSD[a]	1	44	5.114	
	2	50	5.178	5.178
	3	51	5.333	5.333
	4	45		5.667
	Significance		.758	.129
Scheffé-Procedure[a]	1	44	5.114	
	2	50	5.178	
	3	51	5.333	
	4	45	5.667	
	Significance		.108	

The mean values for the homogenous subgroups are shown.
a. Uses a harmonic mean for sample size = 47.305.

A 42. Post-hoc Test for Degree of Trust

Degree of trust

| | | N | Subgroup for Alpha = 0.05. | |
			1	2
Student-Newman-Keuls-Procedure[a]	2	50	4.980	
	3	51	5.431	5.431
	1	44	5.477	5.477
	4	45		5.867
	Significance		.085	.149
Tukey-HSD[a]	2	50	4.980	
	3	51	5.431	5.431
	1	44	5.477	5.477
	4	45		5.867
	Significance		.145	.243
Scheffé-Procedure[a]	2	50	4.980	
	3	51	5.431	5.431
	1	44	5.477	5.477
	4	45		5.867
	Significance		.209	.323

The mean values for the homogenous subgroups are shown.
a. Uses a harmonic mean for sample size = 47.305.

A 43. Post-hoc Test for Degree of Flexibility of Vendor

Degree of flexibility of vendor

		N	Subgroup for Alpha = 0.1.	
			1	2
Student-Newman-Keuls-Procedure[a]	2	50	4.980	
	3	51	5.216	5.216
	1	44	5.438	5.438
	4	45		5.540
	Significance		.109	.327
Tukey-HSD[a]	2	50	4.980	
	3	51	5.216	5.216
	1	44	5.438	5.438
	4	45		5.540
	Significance		.183	.482
Scheffé-Procedure[a]	2	50	4.980	
	3	51	5.216	
	1	44	5.438	
	4	45	5.540	
	Significance		.110	

The mean values for the homogenous subgroups are shown.

a. Uses a harmonic mean for sample size = 47.305.

A 44. Post-hoc Test for Degree of Proactivity and Suggestions for Innovation Potential of the Vendor

Degree of proactivity and suggestions for innovation potential of the vendor.

		N	Subgroup for Alpha = 0.05.	
			1	2
Student-Newman-Keuls-Procedure[a]	2	50	3.785	
	1	44	4.096	4.096
	3	51	4.451	4.451
	4	45		4.644
	Significance		.064	.154
Tukey-HSD[a]	2	50	3.785	
	1	44	4.096	4.096
	3	51	4.451	4.451
	4	45		4.644
	Significance		.112	.250
Scheffé-Procedure[a]	2	50	3.785	
	1	44	4.096	4.096
	3	51	4.451	4.451
	4	45		4.644
	Significance		.169	.330

The mean values for the homogenous subgroups are shown.

a. Uses a harmonic mean for sample size = 47.305.

A 45. Post-hoc Test for Satisfaction with Outsourcing Venture

Degree of satisfaction with outsourcing venture.

		N	Subgroup for Alpha = 0.1.	
			1	2
Student-Newman-Keuls-Procedure[a]	2	50	5.168	
	3	51	5.275	5.275
	1	44	5.636	5.636
	4	45		5.742
	Significance		.142	.142
Tukey-HSD[a]	2	50	5.168	
	3	51	5.275	5.275
	1	44	5.636	5.636
	4	45		5.742
	Significance		.232	.233
Scheffé-Procedure[a]	2	50	5.168	
	3	51	5.275	
	1	44	5.636	
	4	45	5.742	
	Significance		.147	

The mean values for the homogenous subgroups are shown.
a. Uses a harmonic mean for sample size = 47.305.

A 46. Post-hoc Test for Degree of Service Quality

Degree of perceived service quality

		N	Subgroup for Alpha = 0.1.	
			1	2
Student-Newman-Keuls-Procedure[a]	2	50	5.086	
	3	51	5.118	
	1	44	5.500	5.500
	4	45		5.689
	Significance		.189	.425
Tukey-HSD[a]	2	50	5.086	
	3	51	5.118	
	1	44	5.500	5.500
	4	45		5.689
	Significance		.300	.855
Scheffé-Procedure[a]	2	50	5.086	
	3	51	5.118	5.118
	1	44	5.500	5.500
	4	45		5.689
	Significance		.383	.123

The mean values for the homogenous subgroups are shown.
a. Uses a harmonic mean for sample size = 47.305.

A 47. Post-hoc Tests for Differences between Expected and Achieved Benefits

Cost reduction: difference between expected and achieved values

	N	Subgroup for Alpha = 0.1.	
		1	2
Student-Newman-Keuls-Procedure[a] 2	49	-.6122	
1	43	-.3023	
3	46	.0435	
4	37		.9730
Significance		.156	1.000
Tukey-HSD[a] 2	49	-.6122	
1	43	-.3023	
3	46	.0435	
4	37		.9730
Significance		.253	1.000
Scheffé-Procedure[a] 2	49	-.6122	
1	43	-.3023	
3	46	.0435	
4	37		.9730
Significance		.333	1.000

The mean values for the homogenous subgroups are shown.
a. Uses a harmonic mean for sample size = 43.276.

Flexibility of costs: difference between expected and achieved values

	N	Subgroup for Alpha = 0.1.	
		1	2
Student-Newman-Keuls-Procedure[a] 2	49	-.3673	
1	42	.1429	.1429
3	47	.1915	.1915
4	40		.6750
Significance		.182	.213
Tukey-HSD[a] 2	49	-.3673	
1	42	.1429	.1429
3	47	.1915	.1915
4	40		.6750
Significance		.290	.334
Scheffé-Procedure[a] 2	49	-.3673	
1	42	.1429	.1429
3	47	.1915	.1915
4	40		.6750
Significance		.373	.418

The mean values for the homogenous subgroups are shown.
a. Uses a harmonic mean for sample size = 44.202.

Quality improvements: difference between expected and achieved values

	N	Subgroup for Alpha = 0.1. 1
Student-Newman-Keuls-Procedure[a] 1	43	.0233
4	43	.0930
2	47	.1064
3	50	.3600
Significance		.634
Tukey-HSD[a] 1	43	.0233
4	43	.0930
2	47	.1064
3	50	.3600
Significance		.634
Scheffé-Procedure[a] 1	43	.0233
4	43	.0930
2	47	.1064
3	50	.3600
Significance		.702

The mean values for the homogenous subgroups are shown.
a. Uses a harmonic mean for sample size = 45.564.

Long-term use of systems: difference between expected and achieved values

	N	Subgroup for Alpha = 0.1. 1
Student-Newman-Keuls-Procedure[a] 4	40	.4250
2	39	.6154
1	35	.6571
3	47	.7021
Significance		.843
Tukey-HSD[a] 4	40	.4250
2	39	.6154
1	35	.6571
3	47	.7021
Significance		.843
Scheffé-Procedure[a] 4	40	.4250
2	39	.6154
1	35	.6571
3	47	.7021
Significance		.878

The mean values for the homogenous subgroups are shown.
a. Uses a harmonic mean for sample size = 39.805.

Improved service orientation: difference between expected and achieved values

		N	Subgroup for Alpha = 0.1. 1	2
Student-Newman-Keuls-Procedure[a]	1	43	-.3953	
	4	41	.0000	
	2	47	.0426	
	3	49		.6122
	Significance		.267	1.000
Tukey-HSD[a]	1	43	-.3953	
	4	41	.0000	.0000
	2	47	.0426	.0426
	3	49		.6122
	Significance		.406	.134
Scheffé-Procedure[a]	1	43	-.3953	
	4	41	.0000	.0000
	2	47	.0426	.0426
	3	49		.6122
	Significance		.491	.196

The mean values for the homogenous subgroups are shown.
a. Uses a harmonic mean for sample size = 44.777.

Increased flexibility: difference between expected and achieved values

		N	Subgroup for Alpha = 0.1. 1	2
Student-Newman-Keuls-Procedure[a]	1	43	-.4651	
	2	48	-.2708	-.2708
	4	43	-.0930	-.0930
	3	51		.3137
	Significance		.419	.120
Tukey-HSD[a]	1	43	-.4651	
	2	48	-.2708	-.2708
	4	43	-.0930	-.0930
	3	51		.3137
	Significance		.589	.199
Scheffé-Procedure[a]	1	43	-.4651	
	2	48	-.2708	-.2708
	4	43	-.0930	-.0930
	3	51		.3137
	Significance		.663	.274

The mean values for the homogenous subgroups are shown.
a. Uses a harmonic mean for sample size = 46.002.

Shift risk to service provider: difference between expected and achieved values

		N	Subgroup for Alpha = 0.1. 1	2
Student-Newman-Keuls-Procedure[a]	2	43	-.4186	
	4	39	-.3590	
	3	50	.1400	.1400
	1	30		.5000
	Significance		.258	.310
Tukey-HSD[a]	2	43	-.4186	
	4	39	-.3590	
	3	50	.1400	.1400
	1	30		.5000
	Significance		.394	.739
Scheffé-Procedure[a]	2	43	-.4186	
	4	39	-.3590	-.3590
	3	50	.1400	.1400
	1	30		.5000
	Significance		.479	.122

The mean values for the homogenous subgroups are shown.
a. Uses a harmonic mean for sample size = 39.127.

Modernization of IT: difference between expected and achieved values

		N	Subgroup for Alpha = 0.1. 1
Student-Newman-Keuls-Procedure[a]	2	45	.0444
	1	32	.2812
	3	48	.2917
	4	41	.3659
	Significance		.703
Tukey-HSD[a]	2	45	.0444
	1	32	.2812
	3	48	.2917
	4	41	.3659
	Significance		.703
Scheffé-Procedure[a]	2	45	.0444
	1	32	.2812
	3	48	.2917
	4	41	.3659
	Significance		.762

The mean values for the homogenous subgroups are shown.
a. Uses a harmonic mean for sample size = 40.529.

Focus on core competencies: difference between expected and achieved values

		N	Subgroup for Alpha = 0.1. 1
Student-Newman-Keuls-Procedure[a]	3	49	-.2857
	2	47	-.1702
	1	43	.0465
	4	41	.1220
	Significance		.312
Tukey-HSD[a]	3	49	-.2857
	2	47	-.1702
	1	43	.0465
	4	41	.1220
	Significance		.312
Scheffé-Procedure[a]	3	49	-.2857
	2	47	-.1702
	1	43	.0465
	4	41	.1220
	Significance		.396

The mean values for the homogenous subgroups are shown.
a. Uses a harmonic mean for sample size = 44.777.

Strategic competitive advantages: difference between expected and achieved values

		N	Subgroup for Alpha = 0.1. 1
Student-Newman-Keuls-Procedure[a]	2	40	-.1250
	1	33	-.1212
	3	45	-.0667
	4	36	.2500
	Significance		.629
Tukey-HSD[a]	2	40	-.1250
	1	33	-.1212
	3	45	-.0667
	4	36	.2500
	Significance		.629
Scheffé-Procedure[a]	2	40	-.1250
	1	33	-.1212
	3	45	-.0667
	4	36	.2500
	Significance		.698

The mean values for the homogenous subgroups are shown.
a. Uses a harmonic mean for sample size = 37.986.

Access to highly skilled people: difference between expected and achieved values

		N	Subgroup for Alpha = 0.1. 1
Student-Newman-Keuls-Procedure[a]	3	51	-.0784
	1	39	-.0513
	2	44	-.0455
	4	40	.2500
	Significance		.553
Tukey-HSD[a]	3	51	-.0784
	1	39	-.0513
	2	44	-.0455
	4	40	.2500
	Significance		.553
Scheffé-Procedure[a]	3	51	-.0784
	1	39	-.0513
	2	44	-.0455
	4	40	.2500
	Significance		.629

The mean values for the homogenous subgroups are shown.
a. Uses a harmonic mean for sample size = 43.022.

Access to better IT systems: difference between expected and achieved values

		N	Subgroup for Alpha = 0.1. 1
Student-Newman-Keuls-Procedure[a]	3	47	-.1489
	2	46	.0435
	1	36	.3333
	4	41	.4146
	Significance		.257
Tukey-HSD[a]	3	47	-.1489
	2	46	.0435
	1	36	.3333
	4	41	.4146
	Significance		.257
Scheffé-Procedure[a]	3	47	-.1489
	2	46	.0435
	1	36	.3333
	4	41	.4146
	Significance		.337

The mean values for the homogenous subgroups are shown.
a. Uses a harmonic mean for sample size = 42.024.

Knowledge acquisition: difference between expected and achieved values

		N	Subgroup for Alpha = 0.1.	
			1	2
Student-Newman-Keuls-Procedure[a]	3	51	-.4314	
	2	41		.1951
	1	35		.2000
	4	39		.4359
	Significance		1.000	.650
Tukey-HSD[a]	3	51	-.4314	
	2	41	.1951	.1951
	1	35		.2000
	4	39		.4359
	Significance		.102	.813
Scheffé-Procedure[a]	3	51	-.4314	
	2	41	.1951	.1951
	1	35	.2000	.2000
	4	39		.4359
	Significance		.150	.853

The mean values for the homogenous subgroups are shown.
a. Uses a harmonic mean for sample size = 40.729.

Suggestions for innovation: difference between expected and achieved values

		N	Subgroup for Alpha = 0.1.	
			1	2
Student-Newman-Keuls-Procedure[a]	3	47	-.6809	
	1	36		.0000
	2	42		.1667
	4	41		.4634
	Significance		1.000	.332
Tukey-HSD[a]	3	47	-.6809	
	1	36	.0000	.0000
	2	42		.1667
	4	41		.4634
	Significance		.161	.488
Scheffé-Procedure[a]	3	47	-.6809	
	1	36	.0000	.0000
	2	42		.1667
	4	41		.4634
	Significance		.229	.570

The mean values for the homogenous subgroups are shown.
a. Uses a harmonic mean for sample size = 41.129.

Joint product and service development: difference between expected and achieved values

		N	Subgroup for Alpha = 0.1.	
			1	2
Student-Newman-Keuls-Procedure[a]	3	48	-.2708	
	1	39	-.1538	
	2	40	.3750	.3750
	4	32		.7188
	Significance		.125	.298
Tukey-HSD[a]	3	48	-.2708	
	1	39	-.1538	
	2	40	.3750	.3750
	4	32		.7188
	Significance		.206	.723
Scheffé-Procedure[a]	3	48	-.2708	
	1	39	-.1538	
	2	40	.3750	.3750
	4	32		.7188
	Significance		.281	.779

The mean values for the homogenous subgroups are shown.
a. Uses a harmonic mean for sample size = 38.939.

Business transformation: difference between expected and achieved values

		N	Subgroup for Alpha = 0.1.
			1
Student-Newman-Keuls-Procedure[a]	1	28	.0000
	2	38	.0263
	3	44	.4091
	4	31	.5806
	Significance		.245
Tukey-HSD[a]	1	28	.0000
	2	38	.0263
	3	44	.4091
	4	31	.5806
	Significance		.245
Scheffé-Procedure[a]	1	28	.0000
	2	38	.0263
	3	44	.4091
	4	31	.5806
	Significance		.324

The mean values for the homogenous subgroups are shown.
a. Uses a harmonic mean for sample size = 34.184.

A 48. Variance Inflation Factor (VIF) of Formative Constructs

Group1	Item	R²	VIF
Processes	q2501	0.587	2.421
	q2502	0.649	2.849
	q2503	0.260	1.351
	q2504	0.339	1.513
Structures	q2601	0.122	1.139
	q2602	0.199	1.248
	q2603	0.118	1.134

Group2	Item	R²	VIF
Processes	q2501	0.744	3.906
	q2502	0.830	5.882
	q2503	0.475	1.905
	q2504	0.500	2.000
Structures	q2601	0.005	1.005
	q2602	0.024	1.025
	q2603	0.022	1.022

Group3	Item	R²	VIF
Processes	q2501	0.657	2.915
	q2502	0.674	3.067
	q2503	0.413	1.704
	q2504	0.238	1.312
Structures	q2601	0.002	1.002
	q2602	0.071	1.076
	q2603	0.072	1.078

Group4	Item	R²	VIF
Processes	q2501	0.596	2.475
	q2502	0.560	2.273
	q2503	0.167	1.200
	q2504	0.191	1.236
Structures	q2601	0.186	1.229
	q2602	0.152	1.179
	q2603	0.053	1.056

Overall	Item	R²	VIF
Processes	q2501	0,643	2,801
	q2502	0,668	3,012
	q2503	0,288	1,404
	q2504	0,305	1,439
Structures	q2601	0,022	1,022
	q2602	0,065	1,070
	q2603	0,046	1,048

A 49. Mediating Effects of Contractual via Relational Governance on Service Quality in the Four Client Groups

Sample group 1			
Mediator effect Contract -> Relationship -> Service Quality			
a=	0,101	s(a)=	0,2223
b=	0,397	s(b)=	0,1522
c=	0,059		
z=	0,4476		
VAF=	0,4046		

Sample group 2			
Mediator effect Contract -> Relationship -> Service Quality			
a=	0,128	s(a)=	0,1396
b=	0,179	s(b)=	0,1145
c=	0,235		
z=	0,7909		
VAF=	0,0888		

Sample group 3			
Mediator effect Contract -> Relationship -> Service Quality			
a=	0,259	s(a)=	0,1296
b=	0,588	s(b)=	0,1452
c=	0,42		
z=	1,7921	p = 0,07	
VAF=	0,2661		

Sample group 4			
Mediator effect Contract -> Relationship -> Service Quality			
a=	0,3	s(a)=	0,3425
b=	0,06	s(b)=	0,2435
c=	0,232		
z=	0,2372		
VAF=	0,0720		

A 50. Assessment of Common Method Bias (CMB) for Group 1

Variable	Item	construct	(construct)^2	CMB	(CMB)^2
Relational Governance	q3501	0,735	0,540	0,052	0,003
	q3903	0,879	0,773	-0,003	0,000
	q3904	0,926	0,857	-0,040	0,002
Contractual Gover-	q2301	0,746	0,557	0,067	0,004
nance	q2302	0,856	0,733	0,078	0,006
	q2303	0,853	0,728	0,022	0,000
	q2304	0,944	0,891	-0,176	0,031
Processes	q2501	0,732	0,536	0,166	0,028
	q2502	0,900	0,810	-0,010	0,000
	q2503	0,763	0,582	-0,123	0,015
	q2504	0,798	0,637	-0,061	0,004
Management Struc-	q2601	0,575	0,331	-0,122	0,015
tures	q2602	0,865	0,748	-0,016	0,000
	q2603	0,570	0,325	0,151	0,023
Risk-reward share	q3801	0,912	0,832	-0,058	0,003
	q3802	0,963	0,927	-0,025	0,001
	q3803	0,957	0,916	0,081	0,007
Experience	q2802	0,930	0,865	-0,119	0,014
	q2803	0,814	0,663	0,119	0,014
Service Quality	q4401	1,055	1,113	-0,255	0,065
	q4402	0,941	0,885	0,005	0,000
	q4403	0,715	0,511	0,236	0,056
Satisfaction	q4301	0,700	0,490	0,239	0,057
	q4302	0,785	0,616	0,021	0,000
	q4303	1,063	1,130	-0,358	0,128
	q4304	0,732	0,536	0,074	0,005
Average			**0,713**		**0,019**

A 51. Assessment of Common Method Bias (CMB) for Group 2

Variable	Item	construct	(construct)²	CMB	(CMB)²
Relational Governance	q3501	0,768	0,590	-0,043	0,002
	q3903	0,861	0,741	-0,043	0,002
	q3904	0,812	0,659	0,081	0,007
Contractual Gover-nance	q2301	0,874	0,764	-0,158	0,025
	q2302	0,972	0,945	-0,087	0,008
	q2303	0,836	0,699	0,047	0,002
	q2304	0,740	0,548	0,184	0,034
Processes	q2501	0,843	0,711	0,037	0,001
	q2502	0,943	0,889	-0,005	0,000
	q2503	0,761	0,579	0,102	0,010
	q2504	0,849	0,721	-0,130	0,017
Management Struc-tures	q2601	0,182	0,033	-0,018	0,000
	q2602	0,728	0,530	0,103	0,011
	q2603	-0,767	0,588	0,106	0,011
Risk-reward share	q3801	0,846	0,716	-0,092	0,008
	q3802	0,899	0,808	0,057	0,003
	q3803	0,882	0,778	0,025	0,001
Experience	q2802	1,039	1,080	-0,324	0,105
	q2803	0,653	0,426	0,324	0,105
Service Quality	q4401	0,883	0,780	0,083	0,007
	q4402	1,023	1,047	-0,107	0,011
	q4403	0,925	0,856	0,021	0,000
Satisfaction	q4301	0,597	0,356	0,338	0,114
	q4302	0,981	0,962	-0,291	0,085
	q4303	1,000	1,000	-0,192	0,037
	q4304	0,752	0,566	0,097	0,009
Average			**0,707**		**0,024**

A 52. Assessment of Common Method Bias (CMB) for Group 3

Variable	Item	construct	(construct)²	CMB	(CMB)²
Relational Governance	q3501	0,299	0,089	0,405	0,164
	q3903	1,073	1,151	-0,334	0,112
	q3904	0,866	0,750	0,055	0,003
Contractual Gover-	q2301	0,600	0,360	0,311	0,097
nance	q2302	0,825	0,681	0,012	0,000
	q2303	0,889	0,790	-0,163	0,027
	q2304	0,849	0,721	-0,180	0,032
Processes	q2501	0,882	0,778	-0,010	0,000
	q2502	0,795	0,632	0,139	0,019
	q2503	0,824	0,679	-0,032	0,001
	q2504	0,745	0,555	-0,133	0,018
Management Struc-	q2601	0,026	0,001	0,232	0,054
tures	q2602	0,777	0,604	0,049	0,002
	q2603	-0,817	0,667	0,074	0,005
Risk-reward share	q3801	0,672	0,452	0,094	0,009
	q3802	0,931	0,867	0,025	0,001
	q3803	0,892	0,796	-0,098	0,010
Experience	q2802	0,925	0,856	-0,195	0,038
	q2803	0,755	0,570	0,195	0,038
Service Quality	q4401	0,949	0,901	0,009	0,000
	q4402	1,004	1,008	-0,040	0,002
	q4403	0,929	0,863	0,031	0,001
Satisfaction	q4301	0,616	0,379	0,306	0,094
	q4302	0,983	0,966	-0,293	0,086
	q4303	1,096	1,201	-0,207	0,043
	q4304	0,256	0,066	0,284	0,081
Average			**0,669**		**0,036**

A 53. Assessment of Common Method Bias (CMB) for Group 4

Variable	Item	construct	(construct)²	CMB	(CMB)²
Relational Governance	q3501	0,594	0,353	0,211	0,045
	q3903	0,910	0,828	-0,117	0,014
	q3904	0,953	0,908	-0,048	0,002
Contractual Gover-	q2301	0,542	0,294	0,325	0,106
nance	q2302	0,829	0,687	0,110	0,012
	q2303	0,959	0,920	-0,317	0,100
	q2304	0,863	0,745	-0,103	0,011
Processes	q2501	0,802	0,643	0,109	0,012
	q2502	0,860	0,740	-0,024	0,001
	q2503	0,634	0,402	-0,074	0,005
	q2504	0,694	0,482	-0,051	0,003
Management Struc-	q2601	0,824	0,679	0,116	0,013
tures	q2602	0,783	0,613	-0,151	0,023
	q2603	0,353	0,125	0,038	0,001
Risk-reward share	q3801	0,862	0,743	0,134	0,018
	q3802	0,969	0,939	-0,043	0,002
	q3803	0,951	0,904	-0,091	0,008
Experience	q2802	0,959	0,920	-0,201	0,040
	q2803	0,835	0,697	0,201	0,040
Service Quality	q4401	0,818	0,669	0,115	0,013
	q4402	0,988	0,976	-0,049	0,002
	q4403	0,957	0,916	-0,059	0,003
Satisfaction	q4301	0,878	0,771	0,003	0,000
	q4302	0,881	0,776	-0,316	0,100
	q4303	0,664	0,441	0,156	0,024
	q4304	0,770	0,593	0,090	0,008
Average			**0,683**		**0,023**

A 54. Assessment of Common Method Bias (CMB) for Overall Sample

Variable	Item	construct	(construct)²	CMB	(CMB)²
Relational Governance	q3501	0,644	0,415	0,109	0,012
	q3903	0,911	0,830	-0,128	0,016
	q3904	0,867	0,752	0,036	0,001
Contractual Gover-nance	q2301	0,684	0,468	0,140	0,020
	q2302	0,867	0,752	0,031	0,001
	q2303	0,879	0,773	-0,091	0,008
	q2304	0,855	0,731	-0,075	0,006
Processes	q2501	0,818	0,669	0,085	0,007
	q2502	0,871	0,759	0,046	0,002
	q2503	0,729	0,531	-0,048	0,002
	q2504	0,784	0,615	-0,110	0,012
Management Struc-tures	q2601	0,543	0,295	0,174	0,030
	q2602	-0,740	0,548	0,134	0,018
	q2603	0,664	0,441	0,021	0,000
Risk-reward share	q3801	0,829	0,687	0,026	0,001
	q3802	0,936	0,876	-0,004	0,000
	q3803	0,911	0,830	-0,019	0,000
Experience	q2802	0,954	0,910	-0,203	0,041
	q2803	0,771	0,594	0,203	0,041
Service Quality	q4401	0,926	0,857	0,000	0,000
	q4402	0,999	0,998	-0,050	0,003
	q4403	0,887	0,787	0,059	0,003
Satisfaction	q4301	0,644	0,415	0,275	0,076
	q4302	0,919	0,845	-0,220	0,048
	q4303	0,992	0,984	-0,184	0,034
	q4304	0,664	0,441	0,105	0,011
Average			**0,685**		**0,015**

A 55. Empirical Foundation of Authors and Studies of Relationship Factors

Authors	Empirical Foundation	
	Method / Approach	N / Number of Cases
(Aalders 2002)	None (Whitepaper)	N/A
(Amason 1996)	Quantitative (Survey)	45+21
(Anderson/Narus 1984)	Quantitative (Survey)	153
(Anderson/Lodish/Weitz 1987)	Quantitative (Survey)	71(492)
(Anderson/Weitz 1989)	Exploratory (Expert interviews)	690
(Anderson/Narus 1990)	Quantitative (Survey)	1365
(Anderson/Weitz 1992)	Quantitative (Survey)	378
(Applegate/Montealegre 1991)	Exploratory (Case Study)	1
(Assael 1969)	Exploratory (Expert interviews)	90
(Bailey/Pearson 1983)	Quantitative (Survey)	29
(Balzert 1998)	None (Teaching book)	N/A
(Bensaou/Venkatraman 1995)	Quantitative (Survey)	447
(Böhmann 2003)	Exploratory (Expert interviews)	17
(Bongard 1994)	None (Literature based)	N/A
(Bourgeois 1980)	Quantitative (Survey)	67 (12)
(Bräutigam/Grabbe 2004)	None (Literature based)	N/A
(Brown/Frazier 1978)	Exploratory (Expert interviews)	28
(Cook/Emerson 1978)	Lab experiment	112
(Dahl 1957)	None (Literature based)	N/A
(DeSanctis/Jackson 1994)	Exploratory (Case Study)	1
(Deshpande/Webster 1989)	None (Literature based)	N/A
(Dess 1987)	Quantitative (Survey)	74
(Dess/Origer 1987)	None (Literature based)	N/A
(Dibbern et al. 2002)	None (Literature based)	81
(Dwyer 1980)	Lab experiment	80
(Dwyer/Schurr/Oh 1987)	None (Literature based)	N/A
(El-Ansary/Stern 1972)	Quantitative (Survey)	27
(El-Ansary 1975)	Quantitative (Survey)	27
(Emerson 1962)	None (Literature based)	N/A
(Etgar 1976b)	Quantitative (Survey)	116
(Etgar 1976a)	Quantitative (Survey)	113
(Etgar 1977)	Quantitative (Survey)	99
(Etgar/Cadotte/Robinson 1978)	Quantitative (Survey)	99
(Etgar 1979)	Quantitative (Survey)	138
(Fitzgerald/Willcocks 1994)	Quantitative (Survey)	162
(Fontenot/Wilson 1997)	None (Literature based)	N/A
(Ganesan 1994)	Quantitative (Survey)	176
(Gaski 1984)	None (Literature based)	N/A
(Glossner 2004)	None (Literature based)	N/A
(Goldberg 1976)	None (Literature based)	N/A
(Goles 2001)	Quantitative (Survey)	366
(Goles/Chin 2005)	Quantitative (Survey)	175
(Grover/Cheon/Teng 1996)	Quantitative (Survey)	188
(Grzmik/Glossner 2004)	None (Literature based)	N/A
(Guiltinan/Rejab/Rodgers 1980)	Quantitative (Survey)	154
(Gulati 1995)	Analysis of secondary data (Literature based)	2400+
(Gundlach/Cadotte 1994)	Quantitative (Survey)	179
(Gupta/Iyer 2003)	None (Literature based)	N/A
(Guth/MacMillan 1986)	Exploratory (Expert interviews)	90
(Heide/John 1990)	Quantitative (Survey)	155
(Heide/John 1992)	Quantitative (Survey)	235
(Heide 1994)	Quantitative (Survey)	215
(Henderson 1990)	Exploratory (Expert interviews) / Focus Group	28 / 2
(Hunger/Stern 1976)	Lab experiment	108
(Hunt/Nevin 1974)	Quantitative (Survey)	815
(Huppertz 2004)	None (Literature based)	N/A
(John 1984)	Quantitative (Survey)	147
(von Jouanne-Diedrich 2004)	None (Literature based)	N/A
(Judenberg 1994)	None	N/A
(Kanter 1994)	Exploratory (Expert interviews)	>500
(Kern 1997)	Exploratory (Case Studies)	11
(Kern/Willcocks 2000a)	Exploratory (Expert interviews)	13
(Kern/Willcocks/van Heck 2002)	None (Literature based)	N/A
(Klepper 1994)	None (Literature based)	N/A
(Klepper 1995)	Exploratory (Case Studies)	2
(Köhler-Frost 2000)	None (Literature based)	N/A

Authors	Empirical Foundation	
	Method / Approach	N / Number of Cases
(Konsynski/McFarlan 1990)	None (Literature based)	N/A
(Korsgaard/Schweiger/Sapienza 1995)	Experiment	109
(Küchler 2004)	None (Literature based)	N/A
(Lacity/Hirschheim 1993b)	Exploratory (Case Study)	14
(Lacity/Hirschheim 1993a)	Exploratory (Case Studies)	13
(Lacity/Hirschheim 1995b)	Exploratory(Case Studies)	5-15
(Lacity/Willcocks 1995)	Exploratory	61
(Lacity/Willcocks/Feeny 1996)	Exploratory (Expert interviews)	145
(Lacity/Willcocks 1998)	Exploratory (Expert interviews)	145
(Lacity/Willcocks 2000a)	Exploratory (Expert interviews)	271
(Lacity/Willcocks 2003)	Exploratory (Expert interviews)	543
(Lasher/Ives/Jarvenpaa 1991)	None (Literature based)	N/A
(Lee/Kim 1999)	Exploratory (Expert interviews)	148
(Lewis 1990)	None (Literature based)	N/A
(Lusch 1976a) / (Lusch 1976b)	Quantitative (Survey) – National Survey	162 / 567
(Lusch 1977)	Quantitative (Survey) – National Survey	567
(Lusch/Brown 1982)	Quantitative (Survey) – National Survey	567
(Macaulay 1963)	Exploratory (Expert interviews)	68 (89)
(Malone/Crowston 1990)	None (Literature based)	N/A
(Malone/Crowston 1994)	None (Literature based)	N/A
(Mejias et al. 1996)	Quantitative (Survey)	469
(Michie 1978)	Quantitative (Survey)	161
(Mintzberg/Raisinghani/Theoret 1976)	Exploratory (Case Studies)	200+ (25)
(Mohr/Spekman 1994)	Quantitative (Survey)	124
(Monczka et al. 1998)	Quantitative (Survey)	77
(Moorman/Deshpandé/Zaltman 1993)	Quantitative (Survey)	779
(Morgan/Hunt 1994)	Quantitative (Survey)	204
(Müller/Schwarze 2005)	Quantitative (Survey) - Deloitte	25
(Narus/Anderson 1987)	None (Literature based)	N/A
(Pearson 1973)	Quantitative (Survey)	55
(Pfeffer/Salancik 1978)	None (Literature based)	N/A
(Phillips 1981)	Quantitative (Survey)	1531 (506)
(Piller 2001)	Exploratory (Case Study)	118
(Porter 1974)	Analysis of secondary data	N/A
(Pruitt 1981)	None (Literature based)	N/A
(Rai/Borah/Ramaprasad 1996)	Quantitative (Survey)	70
(Ring/Van de Ven 1994)	None (Literature based)	N/A
(Robey et al. 1989)	Exploratory (Expert interviews)	62
(Robicheaux/El-Ansary 1976)	None (Literature based)	N/A
(Roering 1977)	Lab experiment	160
(Rosenberg/Stern 1971)	Quantitative (Survey)	110
(Rousseau et al. 1998)	None (Literature based)	N/A
(Sargent 2006)	None (Literature based)	N/A
(Scanzoni 1983)	None (Literature based)	N/A
(Sethuraman/Anderson/Narus 1988)	Quantitative (Survey)	361
(Siakas and Siakas 2008)	None (Literature based)	N/A
(Simpson/Mayo 1997)	Quantitative (Survey)	331
(Spekman/Salmond/Lambe 1997)	Exploratory (Expert interviews)	46
(Stern/Sternthal/Craig 1973)	Lab experiment	282
(Stern/El-Ansary 1982)	None (Literature based)	N/A
(Thompson 1967)	None (Literature based)	N/A
(Van de Ven/Delbecq/Koenig 1976)	Quantitative (Survey)	197
(Walker 1972)	Lab experiment	72
(Wilkinson 1974)	Exploratory (Expert interviews)	50
(Wilkinson/Kipnis 1978)	Exploratory (Expert interviews)	67
(Wilkinson 1979)	Exploratory (Expert interviews)	50
(Wilkinson 1981)	Exploratory (Expert interviews)	60 (75)
(Willcocks/Choi 1995)	Exploratory (Case Study)	3
(Willcocks/Currie 1997)	Exploratory (Longitudinal Case Study)	2
(Willcocks/Kern 1998)	Exploratory (Panel)	8
(Willcocks/Lacity 1998b)	Triangulation of multiple methods	N/A
(Willcocks/Lacity 1999)	Exploratory (Expert interviews)	45
(Willcocks/Lacity 2000)	Quantitative (Survey)	116
(Willcocks et al. 2004)	None (Literature based)	N/A
(Wooldridge/Floyd 1989)	None (Literature based)	N/A
(Wooldridge/Floyd 1990)	Quantitative (Survey)	157
(Yoshino/Rangan 1995)	None (Literature based)	N/A
(Zaheer/McEvily/Perrone 1998)	Exploratory (Expert interviews)	153
	Quantitative (Survey)	205

GPSR Compliance
The European Union's (EU) General Product Safety Regulation (GPSR) is a set
of rules that requires consumer products to be safe and our obligations to
ensure this.

If you have any concerns about our products, you can contact us on

ProductSafety@springernature.com

In case Publisher is established outside the EU, the EU authorized
representative is:

Springer Nature Customer Service Center GmbH
Europaplatz 3
69115 Heidelberg, Germany